AUTOBIOGRAPHY AND PI

OF MAJOR-

[signature: Benj. F. Butler]

BUTLER'S BOOK.

BY

BENJ. F. BUTLER.

A REVIEW OF HIS LEGAL, POLITICAL, AND MILITARY CAREER.

ILLUSTRATED WITH 125 ENGRAVINGS, MAPS, PHOTOGRAVURES, ETC.

TO BE ISSUED IN FRENCH AND GERMAN LANGUAGES.

This book is published as a subscription book, and to be sold only as such. Each copy is registered. Any person, or persons, buying or selling the same for purpose of re-sale or other than through subscription will be prosecuted.

ALL RIGHTS RESERVED.

A. M. THAYER & CO.

PRINTERS, BINDERS,

Book Publishers,

BOSTON.

1892.

Printing Statement:

Due to the very old age and scarcity of this book,
many of the pages may be hard to read due to the
blurring of the original text, possible missing pages,
missing text and other issues beyond our control.

Because this is such an important and rare work, we
believe it is best to reproduce this book regardless of
its original condition.

Thank you for your understanding.

Part 2

CHAPTER XIII.

OCCUPATIONS IN 1863; EXCHANGE OF PRISONERS.

T is superfluous to say that on my journey home I was received with the greatest regard and affection by every good and loyal man ; and was abused in the most violent and calumnious language, and with the falsest of charges, by every Copperhead newspaper.

At Philadelphia I was received with most enthusiastic attention, and had the pleasure of meeting there especially the Hon. S. M. Felton, president of the Philadelphia & Wilmington Railroad, by whose patriotic exertions my regiment was enabled to get through Baltimore, the first reinforcement to the capital.

On my arrival at the city of New York, I was the recipient of every possible courtesy. One hundred of the leading men and merchants of New York were appointed a committee to invite me to a public dinner, in accordance with the resolutions of a public meeting, containing names and sentiments which make it the proudest memento that any man in this country can show. It will ever be kept most gratefully as a vindication of every act of mine then done in the service of my country, and I shall leave it as the richest heirloom to those who come after me. A fac-simile of these resolutions is herein most gratefully produced.

I felt obliged to decline this most flattering attention, saying in reply : —

I too well know the revulsion of feeling with which the soldier in the field, occupying the trenches, pacing the sentinel's weary path in the blazing heat, or watching from his cold bivouac the stars shut out by the drenching cloud, hears of feasting and merry-making at home by those who ought to bear his hardships with him, and the bitterness with which he speaks of those who, thus engaged, are wearing his uniform. Upon the scorching sand, and under the brain-trying sun of the Gulf coast, I have too much shared that feeling to add one pang, however slight, to the discomfort which my fellow-soldiers suffer, doing the duties of the camp and field, by my own act, while separated momentarily from them by the exigencies of the public service.

I promised, at the committee's request, that as soon as might be after I had visited my family and made some necessary arrangements in my private affairs, I would make an address to the good people of New York. This I did, on the 2d of April, 1863, at the Academy of Music. The occasion was thus described in the New York *Tribune* : —

The magnificent assemblage of the choicest of the city, which gathered last evening in the Academy of Music to greet the hero of the Gulf, has seldom been paralleled in the history of this continent. The house was completely filled in every part long before the hour of commencement. . . .

At 7.30 o'clock precisely, Senator Morgan, accompanied by several gentlemen, conducted General Butler upon the stage. Immediately there began a cry of enthusiasm and a scene of excitement which very few people in this city have witnessed. With the thunders of applause, shouts of admiration, waving of hats, bouquets, and handkerchiefs, the whole interior of the Academy, except the roof, was alive and in motion. For several minutes this continued. At last when it had partially subsided, Senator Morgan presented General Butler to the mayor. The presentation was but a pantomime, for the cheering was yet so great that the Senator's words could not be heard.

The mayor then welcomed General Butler, in an exceedingly pertinent and happy address, which was enthusiastically received, the general, who was in citizen's dress, standing the while.

I shall venture to give some extracts from the speech made then and there, to show that my views then of the Rebellion afterwards became the policy of the government, even to reconstruction. I have found no occasion since to change them materially : —

When the mayor had concluded, General Butler advanced, and after the tumultuous applause with which he was again greeted had subsided, he said : —

"Mr. Mayor, with the profoundest gratitude for the too-flattering commendation of my administration of the various trusts committed to me by the government, which, in behalf of your associates, you have been pleased to tender me, I ask you to receive my most heartfelt thanks. To the citizens of New York here assembled in kind appreciation of my services supposed to have been rendered to the country, I tender the deepest acknowledgments. [Applause.] I accept it all; not for myself but for my brave comrades of the Army of the Gulf. [Renewed applause.]

. . . .

" Upon the same theory upon which I felt myself bound to put down insurrection in Maryland, while it remained loyal, whether that insurrection consisted of blacks or whites, by the same loyalty to the Constitution and laws, I felt bound to confiscate slave property in the rebellious State of Virginia. [Applause.] Pardon me, sir, if right here I say that I am a little sensitive upon this subject. I am an old-fashioned Andrew Jackson Democrat of twenty years' standing. [Applause. A voice: " The second hero of New Orleans." Renewed applause culminating in three cheers.] And, so far as I know, I have never swerved, so help me God, from one of his teachings. [Applause.] . . .

" And now, my friends, if you will allow me to pass on for a moment in this line of thought, as we come up to the point of time when those men laid down their constitutional obligations. What were my rights, and what were theirs? At that hour they repudiated the Constitution of the United States, by solemn vote in solemn convention; and not only that, but they took arms in their hands, and undertook by force to rend from the government what seemed to them the fairest portion of the heritage which my fathers had given to me as a rich legacy to my children. When they did that, they abrogated, abnegated, and forfeited every constitutional right, and released me from every constitutional obligation. [Loud cheers.] And when I was thus called upon to say what should be my action with regard to slavery, I was left to the natural instincts of my heart, as prompted by a Christian education in New England, and I dealt with it accordingly, as I was no longer bound. [Immense applause.]

RECONSTRUCTION.

" I am not for the Union as it was. [Great cheering. " Good! Good!"] I have the honor to say as a Democrat, and an Andrew Jackson Democrat, I am not for the Union to be again as it was. Understand me, I was for the Union as it was, because I saw, or thought I saw, the troubles in the future which have burst upon us; but having undergone those troubles, having spent all this blood and this treasure, I do not mean to go back again and be cheek by jowl, as I was before, with

South Carolina, if I can help it. [Cheers. "You're right."] Mark me now ; let no man misunderstand me ; and I repeat, lest I may be misunderstood (for there are none so difficult to understand as those that don't want to) — mark me again, I say, I do not mean to give up a single inch of the soil of South Carolina. If I had been living at that time, and had the position, the will, and the ability, I would have dealt with South Carolina as Jackson did, and kept her in the Union at all hazards ; but now she has gone out, I will take care that when she comes in again she will come in better behaved; that she shall no longer be the firebrand of the Union, ay, that she shall enjoy what her people never yet enjoyed, the blessings of a republican form of government. [Applause.] And, therefore, in that view I am not for the reconstruction of the Union as it was. I have spent treasure and blood enough upon it, in conjunction with my fellow-citizens, to make it a little better [cheers], and I think we can have a better Union. It was good enough if it had been let alone. The old house was good enough for me, but the South pulled the " L " down, and I propose, when we build it up, to build it up with all the modern improvements. [Prolonged laughter and applause.] Another one of the logical sequences, it seems to me, that follow inexorably, and not to be shunned, from the proposition that we are dealing with alien enemies, is, What is our duty with regard to the confiscation of their property? And that would seem to me to be very easy of settlement under the Constitution, and without any discussion, if my first proposition is right. Hasn't it been held from the beginning of the world down to this day? From the time the Israelites took possession of the land of Canaan, which they got from alien enemies, hasn't it been held that the whole of the property of those alien enemies belongs to the conqueror, and that it has been at his mercy and his clemency what should be done with it? And for one, I would take it and give it to the loyal man, who was loyal from the heart, at the South, enough to make him as well as he was before, and I would take the balance of it and distribute it among the volunteer soldiers who have gone forth in the service of their country ; and so far as I know them, if we should settle South Carolina with them, in the course of a few years I should be quite willing to receive her back into the Union. [Renewed applause.]

NO DANGER FROM THE ARMY.

"There never has been any division of sentiment in the army itself. They have always been for the Union unconditionally, for the government and the laws at any and all times. And who are this army? Are they men different from us? Not at all. I see some here that have come back from the army, and are now waiting to recover their health to go back and join that army. Are they to be any different on the banks of the Potomac or in the marshes of Louisiana, or struggling with the turbid current of the Mississippi than they are here? Are our sons, our brothers, to have different thoughts and different feelings from us, simply because to-day they wear blue and to-morrow they wear black, or to-day they wear black and to-morrow they wear blue? Not at all. They are from us, they are of us, they are with us. The same love of liberty, ay, and you will pardon me for saying it, a little more love for the Union, have caused them to go out than have actuated those who have stayed behind. The same desire to see the Constitution restored has sent them out that animates us; the same love of good government, the same faith in this great experiment of freedom and free government that actuates us actuates them, and there need be no trouble, it seems to me, in the mind of any man upon the question of what is the army to do? There need be no fears. I have seen men, too, good, virtuous, candid, upright, patriotic men, who seem to feel this great increase of the army to be somewhat dangerous to our liberties. Is the army to take away their own liberties? is the army to destroy their own country? is the army to do anything that patriotic men won't do? Oh, no; they answer with universal accord upon that subject. Then where is the danger men see? Why, in the olden time, at the head of large armies, some ambitious man, some ambitious military leader, gets the control of the army and destroys the liberty of the country; but the difficulty is, the examples of nations in the old world are by no means analogies for this. No general of the old world ever commanded such an army; no general of the old world ever had such a country; no general of the old world ever had such a government to fight for, to fight with, to fight under, or will have ever and forever; and no general of the old world, no general thus far on the face of the earth, ever was in a country, where, by elevating his country first, last, and all the time, he might more surely elevate himself. But we do not depend upon either the patriotism, or the ability, or the prudence, or the courage of any one man; we depend upon the courage, the patriotism, and the intelligence of this half million of men in the army who know that the place to regulate government affairs is in the ballot-box, and who, as long as they can get matters regulated, and can have fair-play through the ballot-box, will go home and be much more ready to use the ballot-box than the cartridge-box.

"Therefore, I say to you, sir, let no man have fear on this subject. There are no better friends of free institutions, there are no more intelligent, no truer men and citizens at home and in peace, than in the army of the United States."

I received similar receptions in Harrisburg, Philadelphia, Portland, and other cities.

At a meeting in my honor at Boston in Faneuil Hall, after a lengthened speech, I remained several hours to receive a hand-shake of three thousand persons. I was invited to a public dinner in the evening and had the most distinguished consideration. A poem was read by New England's most distinguished author, her most charming and cherished poet, Dr. Oliver Wendell Holmes, two lines of which I take leave here to quote from memory :

> " The mower mows on, though the adder may writhe,
> And the copperhead curl round the blade of the scythe."

In the course of my address at Boston I spoke as follows concerning the war debt : —

A question has been a thousand times asked me since I arrived home, how is this great war debt to be paid? That speaks to the material interests. How can we ever be able to pay this war debt? Who can pay it? Who shall pay it? Shall we tax the coming generations? Shall we overtax ourselves? For one — and I speak as a citizen to citizens — I think I can see clearly a way in which this great expense can be paid by those who ought to pay it, and be borne by those who ought to bear it. Let us bring the South into subjection to the Union. We have offered them equality. If they choose it, let them have it. But, at all events, they must come under the power of the Union. And when once this war is closed by that subjugation, if you please, if necessary, then the increased productions of the great staples of the South, cotton and tobacco — with which we ought, and can, and shall supply the world — this increased production, by the immigration of white men into the South, where labor shall be honorable as it is here, will pay the debt. With the millions of hogsheads of the one, and the millions of bales of the other, and with a proper internal tax, which shall be paid by England and France, who have largely caused this mischief, this debt will be paid. Without stopping to be didactic or to discuss principles here, let us examine this matter for a moment. They are willing to pay fifty and sixty cents a pound for cotton; the past has demonstrated that even by the uneconomical use of slave labor, it can be profitably raised — ay, profitably beyond all conception of agricultural profit here — at ten cents a pound. A simple impost of ten cents a pound, which will increase it to twenty cents only, will pay the interest of a war debt double what it is to-day. And that cotton can be more profitably raised under free labor than under slave labor, no man who has examined the subject doubts. By the imposition of this tax those men who fitted out the Alabama and sent her forth to prey upon our commerce, will be compelled by the laws of trade and the laws of nations to pay for the mischief they have done. So that when we look around in this country, which has just begun to put forth her strength, because no country has ever come to her full strength until her institutions have proved themselves strong enough to govern the country against the will, even the voluntary will of the people — when this government, which has now demonstrated itself to be the strongest government in the world, puts forth her strength as to men, and when this country of ours, richer and more abundant in its harvests and in its productions than any other country on earth, puts forth her riches, we have a strength in men, we have an amount in money, to battle the world for liberty, and for the freedom to do, in the borders of the United States and on the continent of America, that which God, when He sent us forth as a missionary nation, intended we should do. So allow me to return your words of congratulation and your words of welcome, with words of good cheer. Be of good cheer ! God gave us this continent to civilize and to free, as an example to the nations of the earth; and if He has struck us in His wrath, because we have halted in our work, let us begin again and go on, not doubting that we shall have His blessing to the end. Be, therefore, I say, of good cheer; there can be no doubt of this issue. We feel the struggle ; we feel what it costs to carry on this war. Go with me to Louisiana — go with me to the South, and you shall see what it costs our enemies to carry on this war; and you will have no doubt, as I have none, of the result of this unhappy strife, out of which the nation shall come stronger, better, purified, North and South — better than ever before.

The glory and high honors of my reception by the Northern people cannot be more fully described than it was set forth in an extract from the Richmond (Va.) *Examiner* of even date therewith : —

After inflicting innumerable tortures upon an innocent and unarmed people; after outraging the sensibilities of civilized humanity by his brutal treatment of women and children; after placing bayonets in the hands of slaves; after peculation the most prodigious, and lies the most infamous, he returns, reeking with crime, to his own people, and they receive him with acclamations of joy in a manner that befits him and becomes themselves. Nothing is out of keeping; his whole career and its rewards are strictly artistic in conception and in execution. He was a thief. A sword that he had stolen from a woman — the niece of the brave Twiggs — was presented to him as a reward of valor.[1] He had violated the laws of God and man. The law makers of the United States voted him thanks, and the preachers of the Yankee gospel of blood came to him and worshipped him. He had broken into the safes and strong boxes of merchants. The New York Chamber of Commerce gave him a dinner. He had insulted women. Things in female attire lavished harlot smiles upon him. He was a murderer, and a nation of assassins have deified him. He is at this time the representative man of a people lost to all shame, to all humanity, all honor, all virtue, all manhood. Cowards by nature, thieves upon principle, and assassins at heart, it would be marvelous, indeed, if the people of the North refused to render homage to Benjamin Butler — the beastliest, bloodiest poltroon and pickpocket the world ever saw.

I was called to Washington, and the question of my taking command on the Mississippi River was again discussed between the President and myself. He wished me to go on to the Mississippi River from St. Louis down, and examine what, if anything, was being done in the way of civil administration of the several departments, and also to advise him upon the military situation. I heard him fully and told him that I would take that proposition into consideration. When I saw him afterwards he produced an authorization and pass, written wholly by his own hand, dated February 11, 1863, a fac-simile of which is herewith published, and presenting it said: " Now, Butler, if you go down there, and find anything that wants to be set right, report to me and I will put you in command, in the hope that you will also carry out what I indicated to you about enrolling the slaves."

I replied: " And there comes the difficulty, Mr. President. This rather adds to my embarrassment, because if I should be put in command under such circumstances the cry would be that I told tales in order to get for myself a command." [2]

I had learned from Senator Sumner that the President had said he hoped to return me to New Orleans very soon. That was the only

---

[1] Twiggs' sword, being deposited in the treasury by me, after the war was returned to his daughter, although his reputed mistress, from whose possession it was taken, brought suit against me in New York for it, which I successfully defended.

[2] At that time I did not know, as I now do from the correspondence between McClellan and Halleck, that theretofore there had been fault found with General Grant, so that upon Halleck's grave accusations, McClellan had ordered the removal of Grant from command, and his arrest by Halleck.

Executive Mansion
Washington, February 11, 1863

Whom it may concern.

Major General Butler, bearer of this, visits the Mississippi River, and localities thereon, at my request, for observation. The Military and Naval Commanders, whom he may meet, will please facilitate his passage from point to point, and make him as comfortable as possible during his stay with them respectively. I will thank them also to impart to him such information as they may possess, and to may reasonably not inconsistent with the military service,

A. Lincoln

thing I desired, and I was almost encouraged to think it might happen. Therefore I said to the President : —

"I will go down and serve you on the Mississippi as well as I can in making observations, and will faithfully report everything there as well as I know how, if it shall be understood between us, Mr. President, that when I get through that I shall be sent back to New Orleans."

" I cannot promise you that," said he.

" Very well," said I, "then my service in this behalf would be only in the character of a chief detective."

I now know, but did not know then, why he could not send me back. Seward had already tried to break up his Cabinet by tendering his resignation, and Lincoln had been obliged to ask his return.

Had I fully known how the President's hands were tied, I should have yielded to his wishes and performed the services indicated, however distasteful to me. As it was, the President allowed me to return home, and wait until called upon for other service. This I was glad to be permitted to do, for I had no desire in any way to take service in the field amid the wrangling, the conspiracies, the jealousies, and the enmities of the commanding generals of the army. I knew I was not wanted by McClellan, because he was aware that as a volunteer officer I would under no conceivable circumstances take part with him in aid of a belief and expectation which he had entertained for months, that the army, if successful, would sustain him in his hope of becoming dictator.

I have stated that General McClellan aspired to be " dictator." To have become one on any pretext would simply have been treason of the deepest dye. There was no power in the Constitution, in Congress, or in the President to establish a dictatorship. It could only have been done by an over-turn of our whole system of government. I would not dare to make such an accusation as a matter of history, although very fully credited assertions of such design were rife during his command of the army, did I not have the evidence from his own pen, in " McClellan's Own Story," in confidential letters written to his wife, who, he says, shared his inmost thoughts, and in other statements of his own view of public affairs therein contained. Incredible as it is, " 'tis true and pity 'tis, 'tis true."

A dictatorship could have been established only by subduing the people of the country by the armies of the United States.

At the time McClellan was summoned to take charge of our greatest army, his only military achievement had been in a short campaign with a few regiments, a battery, two companies of cavalry and three detached companies.[1] His first action was on the 10th of July, 1861, and was fought without the loss of an officer on his side. His second battle was fought on the 13th of July and resulted in the surrender of the enemy, consisting of one brigade officer, two colonels, twenty-five officers, and five hundred and sixty men. The entire results of the campaign he himself sums up in these words : "Nine guns taken, twelve colors, lots of prisoners, and all this was done with so little loss on our side, ten killed, thirty-five wounded."[2]

Bull Run was fought between the Confederate army with about thirty-five thousand men, of whom three hundred and eighty-seven were killed and eighteen hundred and fifty-two wounded, and the Union army of about thirty thousand men, of whom four hundred and eighty-one were killed, and a thousand and upward wounded.

McDowell was not censured for any action of his in the loss of that battle. He had been in command of his army three months. McClellan had been in command of his brigade twenty days. Contrast the experience of the two generals.

McClellan, the second day afterwards, was sent for from Washington, and on the sixth day after that was put in command of all the forces which could be brought to defend the capital. Let McClellan from his own book tell his own story of how he was received : —

. . . I find myself in a new and strange position here : President, Cabinet, General Scott, and all deferring to me. By some strange operation of magic I seem to have become *the power* of the whole land.[3]

They give me my way in everything, full swing and unbounded confidence. All tell me that I am held responsible for the fate of the nation, and that all its resources shall be placed at my disposal. It is an immense task that I have on my hands, but I believe I can accomplish it. . . . Who would have thought, when we were married, that I should so soon be called upon to save my country?[4]

---

[1] McClellan's letter, July 2. "His Story," page 59.
[2] McClellan's letter, July 21. "His Story," page 62.
[3] McClellan's letter, July 27, 1861. "His Story," page 82.
[4] McClellan's letter, July 30, 1861. "His Story," page 83.

He had been in Washington four days. "Upon what meat doth this our Cæsar feed that he is grown so great?"

Came back and had a long interview with Seward about my "pronunciamento" against General Scott's policy. . . . But the old general always comes in the way. He understands nothing, appreciates nothing.[1]

. . . General Scott is the greatest obstacle. I have to fight my way against him. To-morrow the question will probably be decided by giving me absolute control independently of him. I suppose it will result in an enmity on his part against me, but I have no choice; the people call upon me to save the country. I must save it and cannot respect anything that is in the way.

I receive letter after letter, have conversation after conversation, calling on me to save the nation, alluding to the presidency, dictatorship, etc. As I hope one day to be united with you in heaven, I have no such aspiration. I would cheerfully take the dictatorship and agree to lay down my life when the country is saved. [Become dictator and save the country from what? From a republican form of government; from freedom and liberty, — for what? To retain slavery and reduce the white people to subjection to a despotism, — from whom? From Lincoln and the advocates of freedom for all men?] I am not spoiled by my unexpected new position. I feel sure that God will give me the strength and wisdom *to preserve this great nation ;* but I tell you, who share all my thoughts, that I have no selfish feeling in this matter. I feel that God has placed a great work in my hands. I have not sought it. I know how weak I am, but I know that I mean to do right, and I believe that God will help me and give me the wisdom I do not possess. Pray for me, that I may be able to accomplish my task, the greatest, perhaps, that any poor, weak mortal ever had to do. God grant that I may bring this war to an end and be permitted to spend the rest of my days quietly with you.[2]

General Scott is the most dangerous antagonist I have. Our ideas are so widely different that it is impossible for us to work together much longer — *tant pour cela.*[3]

I am weary of all this. I have no ambition in the present affairs; I only wish to save my country, and find the *incapables* around me will not permit it.[4]

McClellan had then been only twenty days in Washington. His opinion of himself seems to have risen very rapidly, although in all

[1] McClellan's letter, Aug. 8, 1861. "His Story," page 84.
[2] McClellan's letter, Aug. 9, 1861. "His Story," page 85.
[3] McClellan's letter, Aug. 15, 1861. "His Story," page 87.
[4] McClellan's letter, Aug. 16, 1861. "His Story," page 87.

things else he was constitutionally tardy in all his movements. Was there ever such dog-day madness?

As he [Scott] threw down the glove and I took it up, I presume war is declared. Be it so. I have one strong point, that I do not care one iota for my *present* position.[1]

I enclose a card just received from A. Lincoln. It shows too much deference to be seen outside.[2]

At one time during the autumn of 1861, Secretary Cameron made quite an abolition speech to some newly arrived regiment. Next day Mr. Stanton *urged* me to arrest him for inciting insubordination. He often advocated the propriety of my seizing the government and taking affairs into my own hands.[3]

Mr. Stanton's card came up, and as soon as possible I went down to see him.

He told me that he had been appointed Secretary of War, and that his name had been sent to the Senate for confirmation, and that he had called to confer with me as to his acceptance. . . . If I wished him to accept he would do so, but only on my account; that he had come to know my wishes and determine accordingly. I told him that I hoped he would accept the position.

.   .   .   .

Soon after Mr. Stanton became Secretary of War it became clear that, without any reason known to me, our relations had completely changed.

Instead of using his new position to assist me he threw every obstacle in my way, and did all in his power to create difficulty and distrust between the President and myself. I soon found it impossible to gain access to him.[4]

I am becoming daily more disgusted with this administration — perfectly sick of it.[5]

I was obliged to attend a meeting of the Cabinet at 8 P. M., and was bored and annoyed. There are some of the greatest geese in the Cabinet I have ever seen — enough to tax the patience of Job.[6]

I presume the Scott war will culminate this week. Whatever it may be I will try to do my duty to the army and to the country with God's help, and a single eye to the right. I hope that I may succeed. I appreciate all the difficulties in my path; the impatience of the people, the venality and bad faith of the politicians, the gross neglect that has occurred

---

[1] McClellan's letter, Sept. 27, 1861. "His Story," page 91.
[2] McClellan's letter, September, 1861. "His Story," page 91.
[3] McClellan's letter. "His Story," page 152.
[4] McClellan's letter. "His Story," page 153.
[5] McClellan's letter, Oct. 2, 1861. "His Story," page 168.
[6] McClellan's letter, Oct. 10, 1861. "His Story," page 169.

in obtaining arms, clothing, etc., and above all I feel in my inmost soul how small is my ability in comparison with the gigantic dimensions of the task, and that even if I had the greatest intellect that was ever given to man, the result remains in the hands of God.[1] I do not feel that I am an instrument worthy of this great task, but I do feel that I did not seek it, — it was thrust upon me; I was called to it. My previous life seems to have been unwittingly directed to this great end, and I know that God can accomplish the greatest results with the weakest instruments. "Therein lies my hope."

It is sickening in the extreme, and makes me feel heavy at heart, when I see the weakness and unfitness of the poor beings who control the destinies of the great country. How I wish that God had permitted me to live quietly and unknown with you. But His will be done.[2]

I have not been home for some three hours, but am concealed at Stanton's to dodge all enemies in the shape of "browsing presidents." I have a set of men to deal with unscrupulous and false. If possible, they will throw whatever blame there is on *my* shoulders, and I do not intend to be sacrificed by such people. I shall trust that the all-wise Creator does not intend our destruction, and that in His own good time He will free the nation from men who curse it, and will restore us to His favor. . . . The people think me all-powerful. Never was there a greater mistake. I am thwarted and deceived by these incapables at every turn.[3] I have one great comfort in all this, — that is, that I did not seek this position, as you well know; and I still trust that God will support me and bear me out. "*He could not have placed me here for nothing.*"

In a memorandum which he sent to the President in August, 1861, he says : —

For the main army of operations [his own] I urge the following composition :

250 Regiments of Infantry, say	225,000 men.
100 Field Batteries, 600 Guns, ...	15,000 ,,
28 Regiments of Cavalry, ...	25,500 ,,
5 Regiments Engineer Troops, ...	7,500 ,,
Total	273,000 men.

I therefore feel that the interests of the nation demand that the ablest soldiers in the service should be on duty with the Army of the Potomac, and that contenting ourselves with remaining on the defensive for the

---

[1] McClellan's letter, Oct. 31, 1861. "His Story," page 172.
[2] McClellan's letter, Nov. 17, 1861. "His Story," page 175.
[3] McClellan's letter, November, 1861. "His Story," page 176.

present at all other points, this army should be reinforced at once by all the disposable troops that the East, and West, and North can furnish. . . .

I would also urgently recommend that the whole of the regular army, old and new, be at once ordered to report here, excepting the mounted batteries actually serving in other departments and the minimum numbers of companies of artillery actually necessary to form the nucleus of the garrisons of our most important permanent works. There should be no delay in carrying out this measure.[1]

The regular troops of all countries are always relied upon by those who seek to become dictators and tyrants to enslave the people.

It is incredible that McClellan could have published his treasonable utterances. Although they are private letters, his family has made them the property of the historian.

What a spectacle! A young man not only receiving many letters — that he could not help — but having a great many conversations with those who were urging him to commit the direst wrong that man could contemplate, and he not ninety days from a peaceful home, and, is there any doubt, using his best influence to get a Secretary of War appointed who is advising him to this treason, and who would be by his energy and strength best fitted to make it successful.

Was he in earnest? He says: "I would cheerfully take the dictatorship and agree to lay down my life when the country is saved." Yet he says in the same letter, with naïve simplicity: "I am not spoiled by my unexpected new position." And this on the 9th day of August, within less than ninety days after he quit the employment of building bridges over railroads, and within fifteen days after he got to Washington, and before he had done a thing or struck a stroke except to get old General Scott out of his way, and in which he succeeded, as we have seen. Not spoiled by his position? A young general who is himself contemplating committing the direst act of treason not spoiled, whose position tempted him to be willing to commit treason when called upon to put down a treasonable rebellion which had then scarcely made head? Not spoiled? Then he must have began as a very bad egg indeed.

He admits that after Stanton became Secretary of War that "instead of using his new position to assist me he threw every obstacle in my way, and did all in his power to create difficulty and distrust

---

[1] McClellan's letter, Sept. 8, 1861. "His Story," page .

between the President and myself. I soon found it impossible to gain access to him."

" McClellan claims that Stanton got his influence to get into the Cabinet in order to thwart him, but that Stanton was wholly loyal to the country and desirous of having the Rebellion put down and slavery with it." I agree with the general in both propositions. Stanton was thoroughly loyal, and he saw that this aspiring young man was trying to get the army in his possession by getting the appointment of all the officers, and that he had got rid of General Scott. He saw also that McClellan had determined, as he admits, not to prosecute the war if the abolition of slavery were to be accomplished. Seeing these things, Stanton did try to get into the Cabinet to put down the Rebellion and to put down the dictators, too.

There was a crop of dictators about that time, there being several parties which wanted a dictator. One was composed of McClellan's political friends, the Copperheads, who thought there was danger that Mr. Cameron and President Lincoln would carry on the war so as to obliterate both the Rebellion and slavery. Their candidate for dictator, who should take the government, was McClellan. The other party were the over-zealous abolitionists who thought that Lincoln was going too slow in the endeavor of abolishing slavery and who declared that the Constitution was " a league with death and a covenant with hell." Their candidate for dictator was Fremont, as was well known at the time. When he was in command in Missouri, he was flattered into making a proclamation abolishing slavery within the bounds of his command. This attempt President Lincoln dealt with by abolishing that proclamation on the ground that it was one " which could be good only by a dictorial and not by a legal act," as he puts it in his letter to Fremont. Lincoln ever afterwards took care that Fremont should be, if anywhere, in a position where he could do no possible mischief in that direction ; and with a genius for administration, he put McClellan, when he thought it safe to so do, in the same category by removing him from command.

A third was the property men of the country, who thought that the expenses of the war were so enormous that it should be immediately ended by negotiation ; and the New York *Times*, in an elaborate editorial, proposed that George Law, an extensive manufacturer of New York, should be made dictator for such purpose.

To show how thoroughly McClellan had been corrupted, or corrupted himself, and that he was utterly unfit to serve under the President and his constitutional advisers in putting down the Rebellion, let us see how he spoke of the government and of his relations with it. On the 10th of October he says : " I was obliged to attend a meeting of the Cabinet at 8 P. M., and was bored and annoyed. There are some of the greatest geese in the cabinet I have ever seen — enough to tax the patience of Job." And yet he says : " I will try again to write a few lines before I go to Stanton's to ascertain what the law of nations is on this Slidell and Mason seizure."

I preferred to be foot-loose, and free to take command of volunteers, and stand by Lincoln and constitutional government in the event of an attempted dictator's trip.

Before I had my second consultation with the President I had been examined by the Committee on the Conduct of the War as to the operations in the Department of the Gulf. I gave a report of them generally from memory and substantially as I have already given it here, save that there were some points to which I gave more elaboration, but I believe no substantial difference will be found. I was especially examined upon the question of the capabilities of negroes for soldiers and fighting, and gave the opinion that I have already given here and that I entertain to-day. I believe it was in consequence of those opinions upon that subject so fully expressed to the committee that I was again called in consultation with the President.

In the spring of 1863, I had another conversation with President Lincoln upon the subject of the employment of negroes. The question was, whether all the negro troops then enlisted and organized should be collected together and made a part of the Army of the Potomac and thus reinforce it. He remarked that the States were beginning to organize negro troops, and that I could soon have a large corps, and he wanted me in the Army of the Potomac. I then said to him : —

"Frankly, Mr. President, I do not want to go into the Army of the Potomac. I have never given cause for any prejudice against me by the officers from West Point. Now McClellan has put almost all the brigades in charge of lieutenants, captains, and majors of the regular army, and they all think they are very much my superior in the knowledge of everything pertaining to the art of war. Even members of my staff, good men and true, have occasionally intruded upon me such belief. When I went to New Orleans, you will remember, I told you when you said something of my taking some place in the Army of the Potomac, that the jealousies, feuds, and embroilments of the various officers were such that I did not believe I could do much good there, and that for that reason I did not want to take any part in the campaigns at Washington, although it

BREVET MAJ.-GEN. J. B. KINSMAN.

certainly appeared the most likely to redound in glory to those who should carry them on, and I still remain of that mind."

We then talked of a favorite project he had of getting rid of the negroes by colonization, and he asked me what I thought of it. I told him that it was simply impossible; that the negroes would not go away, for they loved their homes as much as the rest of us, and all efforts at colonization would not make a substantial impression upon the number of negroes in the country.

Reverting to the subject of arming the negroes, I said to him that I thought it might be possible to start with a sufficient army of white troops, and, avoiding a march which might deplete their ranks by death and sickness, to take them in ships and land them somewhere on the Southern coast. These troops could then come up through the Confederacy, gathering up negroes, who could be armed at first with arms that they could handle, so as to defend themselves and aid the rest of the army in case of rebel charges upon it. In this way we could establish ourselves down there with an army that would be a terror to the whole South.

He asked me what I would arm them with. I told him John Brown had intended, if he got loose in the mountains of Virginia, to arm his negroes with spears and revolvers; and there was a great deal in that. Negroes would know how to use those arms, and the Southern troops would not know how to meet their use of them, and they could be easily transported in large numbers and would require no great expense or trouble in supplying ammunition.

"That is a new idea, General," said he.

"No, Mr. President," I answered, "it is a very old one. The fathers of these negroes, and some of the negroes themselves, fought their battles in Africa with no other weapon, save a club. Although we have substituted the bayonet for the spear, yet as long as the soldier can shoot he is not inclined to use the bayonet. In fact, bayonets are of no use; they are only for show. But probably the time has not come for dropping them."

I ventured to call the attention of the President to the fact that several months had now elapsed since I was relieved from the command of a few troops in the Department of the Gulf, and had up to that time eminent success; but nothing worthy of mention had been done since, although some fifty thousand troops, more or less, had been sent down there.

Our conversation then turned upon another subject which had been frequently a source of discussion between us, and that was the effect of his clemency in not having deserters speedily and universally punished by death. I called his attention to the fact that the great bounties then being offered were such a temptation for a man to desert in order to get home and enlist in another corps where he would be safe from punishment, that the army was being continually depleted at the front even if replenished at the rear.   He answered with a very sorrowful face, which always came over him when he discussed this topic: "But I can't do that, General."

"Well, then," I replied, "I would throw the responsibility upon the general-in-chief and relieve myself of it personally."

With a still deeper shade of sorrow he answered: "The responsibility would be mine, all the same."

I returned home and remained there substantially during the rest of the year, settling up my somewhat extended law business, which I had deserted at a moment's notice, and to which, up to that time, I had paid little attention.

Soon after my return home Hon. Stephen M. Allen, of Massachusetts, called upon me bringing a letter of introduction from the Chairman of the House Committee on the Conduct of the War, the Hon. John Covode, a truer, better, and more patriotic man than whom never lived.   We had been, and were to the day of his death, the warmest personal friends.   It was he who left his seat at the Capitol and went over to the Treasury and subscribed and paid for the first $50,000 worth of United States bonds that were issued, and when reproached for it by one of his friends, who said: "You will never get anything back, Covode," he answered: "Well, I can live without it."

I said to Mr. Allen: "You need no letter of introduction to me. You and I have been long known to each other, and I recognize you as President of the First Republican Convention of Massachusetts."

He then said that he was sent to me by the Committee on the Conduct of the War to consult with me about the manner in which the war was being conducted, and to see whether I would take part in it and in any event what I would advise to be done about it.

I told him that it was a delicate matter upon which to advise, but that I would express my opinion to him frankly and confidentially, and if the matters which I should propose could be carried out that I would again take part in the war.   I said that it seemed to me that the management of the war had got entirely mixed up with politics.   Most of the officers of the army were not in accord with the administration.   I doubted whether the administration was in accord with itself; there were divisions in it which paralyzed its efforts. A large majority of the officers of the army were of Democratic inclination, or, to speak more accurately, were in favor of the Union as it was; that is to say, believed in states' rights, including the restoration of the negroes to slavery. Certain it was that the almost universal feeling of the army was against the employing of negroes as soldiers, and that volunteering had so far stopped that unless we were able to conquer the Rebellion with what troops we had it would be very difficult to get many more. I doubted whether the people would be willing to sustain the emancipation proclamation unless the negroes could be so far employed as to show that they were willing to fight for their freedom, a thing which no considerable portion had yet been permitted to do. Great reliance had been placed upon their aid by the people of the North, in the beginning of the war. But instead of aiding us they had quietly stayed at home, taking care of the families of their masters, and raising crops for the support of the Rebellion. The rebel congress had taken advantage of this by exempting from enrolment all slaveholders owning twenty-one slaves or upwards.

I suggested that the war was being carried on in a way which certainly up to that time had not been successful and did not seem to promise many elements of success. The most strenuous effort so far had been an endeavor to capture Richmond by marching troops through the swamps and thick morasses of Virginia, of which we knew nothing, only to be repulsed by the rebels on unknown ground behind fortifications, and to be destroyed by the malarial diseases of the climate and location. There were parts of the Southern States, especially the mountains of North Carolina and Tennessee, the plains and highlands of Georgia and Alabama, which were as healthy for Northern men as they were for Southern men, and our operations therein seemed so far to be rather for local than general conquest. We had had no actually successful result thus far, certainly none adequate to our great superiority of numbers. A course of operations might be pursued by the Confederates with a view of making a Northern invasion, to which they would be induced by the reply of foreign nations when asked for the recognition of the Confederacy, that "it has shown no power as yet save to act on the defensive, and that before it can be recognized it must show capability and means not only to sustain its own territory substantially but to attack the loyal portions of the United States." If yielding to that, after the paralysis of our operations against Richmond, they should attack the Northern States by marching into Pennsylvania and Ohio, and be successful or show prospect of success, then the North would arouse and probably either volunteer in sufficient numbers, or submit to a draft, which last would be a delicate and somewhat dangerous recourse.

It occurred to me, I said, that instead of expending the greater part of our means substantially to capture an unimportant city, the better way with us would be to throw an army directly into the centre of the Confederacy, or at least, into the eastern part of it, to take, overcome, and hold territory to the utmost extent, leaving troops enough in the North at least to defend itself against the incursion of the enemy. Then, if attacked in the North, we should be acting upon the defensive, and have the advantage against the Confederacy of fighting at home where we knew the ground and where we had our resources. As it was, we had been continually fighting them in one particular part of the Confederacy, where we destroyed nothing of their resources, and did not diminish their capabilities of defending themselves.

I stated that such a plan of operations could be carried on well enough, because Washington was then entrenched and fortified so sufficiently that if defended with half of the Army of the Potomac it could be held against any army that could be brought against it, especially as I thought there might be sufficient drain upon the Confederacy so that they could by no means duplicate their armies, as they certainly could not their resources.

"Therefore," I said, "say to the Committee on the Conduct of the War, that I think that an army of sixty thousand men should be raised, properly armed, equipped, and supplied. Not to be marched through the unhealthy swamps and districts that lie immediately around the southern line of the loyal States, so that before it gets to the proper place, and before it has fired a shot, it will need reinforcements; but land it in North Carolina, or, if thought best, at Mobile, in the centre of Alabama, and move it up, letting it supply itself ruthlessly from the country wherever a smoke-house or corn-barn permits, taking all the negroes that can be collected, giving every inducement for them to accompany the army, letting them supply themselves as far as possible; and, having swept through Alabama, Georgia, and South Carolina, denuding that territory as far as possible of its black population, let it spend the winter in the pine lands of North Carolina in organizing those negroes into troops with which to go to Richmond the other way. For to take away all the producers, to stop the production of the country and everything else contributing to the power of the Confederacy, and to capture every white man capable of carrying arms, not leaving them there to be conscripted or to join the rebel service, will be such a movement as will determine our strength and the weakness of the Confederacy, for it is but a shell. Assuming the worst, before that army, if properly led, can be captured, there will have to be a very much larger army of the rebels brought upon it, and then our army can be sent down to help us as soon as Washington is relieved, and the fears of the administration for its safety quieted.

"This plan of operations," said I, "is more or less faultless; but if something like this can be done, and I can have permission to get such a force together, and can be allowed to take advantage of the sea, of which up to the present we have made no special use for the purpose of conveying our armaments and our armies, I will take hold and do what I can; and although I am outlawed by the proclamation of Davis, I will venture my own life there, and I will administer to him and his friends some of the law of the outlaw, which is very much needed to be done, as I understand matters. You may report my views substantially to our friends of the committee, and if they want to see me to have any further explanations, I will go to Washington."

I did go to Washington, but at the time I was there, Lee had made a movement into Maryland and Pennsylvania, and fear had seemed to have taken possession of everybody, especially the general-in-chief. Indeed, I was told by one major-general that I had better get out of Washington as he thought it would be in the hands of the enemy in three days. I waited three days, but it was not, and as it was none of my business I came away.

I discussed the propositions above set forth with two or three of the committee, but it was evident nothing could be done.

During the first days of July was fought that most indecisive of all conflicts, the Battle of Gettysburg, of which I may speak hereafter as an illustration of the fact that in none of our battles, even the most successful, did we obtain what is known to military history as a victory, which I understand to be a conflict between two armies in which one is overcome, and its efficiency as an army substantially destroyed. The army in this case was only repulsed, and allowed quietly to retreat across the Potomac in a condition not to be further molested by our army.

There is one episode in my life of the greatest possible interest and importance, not only to myself personally but to the whole country. It caused the deepest feeling and the most acrimonious discussion, and as the true history of it is necessary to be stated at some length, it may as well be done here as elsewhere, as it wholly disconnects itself from any subsequent phase of my history.

Fortress Monroe was the point from which all exchange of prisoners, east of the Alleghanies, had been made during the disagreement between the commissioners of exchange on the part of the United States, and the rebel commissioner, Mr. Ould. This disagreement was substantially as to the number which had been determined and credited on either side, and in consequence of it all exchange of prisoners had ceased. The rebels were confessedly in debt to us in a balance of some eighteen thousand prisoners for whom they had given us no equivalent.

Major-Generals Grant and Banks had paroled large numbers of prisoners at Port Hudson and Vicksburg. If they had been held as prisoners they could not have been put again into the Confederate service without a corresponding number being given us in exchange. The fact that these men were soon afterwards re-enlisted was claimed by us to be a breach of the cartel on the part of the Confederates. Meanwhile our prisoners, to the number of some thirteen thousand, were suffering and dying by cold and starvation in Richmond and elsewhere, while we held in our prisons some twenty-six thousand of the rebel officers and men well cared for, properly clothed, and well fed.

I had been appointed to the command of the Department of Virginia and North Carolina Nov. 2, 1863, and subsequently commissioner for the exchange of prisoners.

Upon assuming command my attention was called to the suffering of the prisoners at Belle Isle and Libby Prison, at Richmond. In consultation with the Secretary of War, I proposed retaliation by placing the rebel officers held by us in a condition identical, as nearly as possible, as to shelter, clothing, fuel, and food, with that of our soldiers at Richmond, with notice to the Confederate authorities that any alleviation of the condition of our men, duly certified to us, would at once be followed by a corresponding difference in favor of their prisoners in our hands. The Secretary of War, feeling deeply the hardships of our captured soldiers, approved of the suggestion, and gave me permission to carry the plan into execution. This I proposed to do by placing Confederate officers to the number of some three thousand, either upon Hatteras Bank or at Sewall's Point near Fortress Munroe, both of which were nearly isothermal with Richmond in climate, and there treating them with scrupulous exactness to the same shelter, clothing, and fare which our men received, furnishing them while thus faring, with plenty of pens and paper, and every facility for communicating with the Confederacy. The effect could not be doubted. While I was engaged in preparing a proper encampment, the subject was referred by the Secretary of War to the general-in-chief of the army, Halleck, and my plan was abandoned.[1]

GEN. J. W. SHAFFER.

Learning unofficially that the Confederates were anxious to exchange the prisoners actually held in custody by us, and were willing to give man for man and officer for officer so held, except colored soldiers, I proposed to the Secretary of War the plan of so exchanging until we had exhausted all our prisoners held by the rebels, and as we should then have a surplus of some ten thousand, to hold these as hostages for our colored troops, of whom the rebels held only hundreds, and to retaliate upon this surplus such wrongs

---

[1] See Appendix No. 1.

as the rebels might perpetrate upon our soldiers. This was set out in a letter to the Secretary of War.[1]

About the 16th of December the business of exchange was confided to me. In pursuance of my plan I sent Major Mulford, assistant agent of exchange (to whose faithfulness to his duties, and unvarying kindness to the unfortunates under his charge of both armies, I bear most cheerful witness), with some five hundred Confederates up to City Point with a proposal to deliver them for a like number of our men. It seemed to me quite certain that the Confederate authorities could never withstand the pressure of the friends of these prisoners, who, after being brought in sight of their homes and liberty, should be sent back to a prison because their government would not give an equivalent for them. I was still more certain that when a black soldier, or, as they regarded him, a piece of property, was to be the only equivalent to be given for their own sons and brothers, and those not held by us in equal numbers but in a ratio of twenty to one, the Confederate general could not control his troops if the exchange was not acceded to.

The event justified the experiment. More than an equivalent for those sent up were sent down by the rebels. Debates were held in the rebel cabinet on the subject, with a decided division of opinion. It was finally decided that the United States Government should be notified that as General Butler had been outlawed by Mr. Davis' proclamation, in company with all officers who should command negro troops, they would not treat with him as agent of exchange. In this way it was supposed the issue presented by the United States commissioner might be avoided. A letter to this effect was forwarded by Mr. Ould under date of December 27. This letter was promptly returned, with the information that the government did not recognize the right of the rebel authorities to outlaw its officers, and that neither General Butler nor his officers could be intimidated from the performance of their duties by any such threats, and that the government knew how to protect itself and retaliate outrages upon their persons.

The Virginia legislature, as I was informed, passed a resolution asking Mr. Davis to reverse the outlawry and recognize General

---

See Appendix No. 2.

Butler. After some delay another boatload of prisoners was sent up and exchanged.

Learning that the Union prisoners in the South were suffering from the small-pox, I took the responsibility of forwarding to the rebel commissioner for their use, vaccine matter sufficient for six thousand vaccinations, with information that as much more as was required would be furnished. No more was ever asked for. My action in this regard was approved by the War Department.[1]

Finding the expedient of refusing to recognize the United States commissioner ineffectual, they renewed negotiations, and after some delay the exchange of sick and wounded officers and soldiers went on. During this delay the Confederate prisoners at Point Lookout were informed of the action of their authorities, and at my request, by the direction of the President, each one of them was called upon to answer and sign his name to these questions : —

First, Whether he desired to be sent South for exchange.

Second, Whether he desired to take the oath of amnesty prescribed by the President's proclamation, and be allowed to return to his home in our lines.

Or, *Third*, whether he desired to enlist in the military or naval service of the United States.

Of the ten thousand prisoners at Point Lookout, two regiments of infantry were enlisted, and many recruits went into the navy upon the solemn engagement that they should not be sent South to fight their rebel brethren. These regiments were afterwards sent to General Pope to fight the Indians, and did good service during the war. Thus, more than two thousand men and two millions of dollars in expense of recruitment and bounties were saved to the loyal States.

This work was done by a young officer from Salem, Massachusetts, Col. Charles A. R. Dimon. He went out with me with the three months men, and I later promoted him to be a colonel. He took command of this enlisted regiment, which did most efficient service.

On the 29th of March I received this letter from Mr. Ould, agent of exchange : —

---

[1] See Appendix No. 3.

C. S. Steamer Roanoke,

Mouth of James River, March 29, '64.

Maj.-Gen. B. F. Butler, U. S. Agent of Exchange:

Sir: — I am here for the purpose of having a conference with you in relation to matters connected with the delivery and exchange of prisoners.

Respectfully, yr. obt. svt.,

Ro. Ould,

C. S. Agent of Exchange.

Deeming this a full abnegation of the refusal to treat with me, and a virtual withdrawal of the proclamation of outlawry, I invited Mr. Ould to meet me at Fortress Monroe. Here a full and free conference and discussion was had upon all questions in relation to exchange. The discussion convinced me that although Mr. Ould made the non-delivery of slaves a *sine qua non*, yet, after the other exchanges had been made, a slight experiment of retaliation of the treatment received by the colored soldiers would release them. The result of this negotiation was communicated to the War Department by the following letter : —

Headquarters Department of Virginia and North Carolina,

Fortress Monroe, April 9, 1864.

Hon. E. M. Stanton, Secretary of War:

Sir: — Upon the last flag of truce boat which carried up Confederate prisoners in our hands, I sent up from Point Lookout some four hundred and odd prisoners, being the wounded and sick Confederates who were sufficiently convalescent to bear the voyage.

Upon the return of the boat, I was informed by Major Mulford, that the Confederate agent of exchange would meet me on the James River on Wednesday, the 29th day of March. Accordingly I received notice from Admiral Lee, late in the evening of that day, that a flag of truce boat was seeking communication at the outer picket line of the blockading fleet at the mouth of the James River.

The same messenger brought a communication from Robert Ould, Esq., agent of exchange of the authorities of the belligerents at Richmond, directed to Major-General Butler, agent for the exchange of prisoners on behalf of the United States, signed with the official signature of "Robert Ould, Agent of Exchange, Confederate States," informing me that he was then on board of the Confederate States steamer Roanoke and desired an interview upon the subject of exchange.

Deeming this to be an official recognition of the commissioner of exchange of the United States, on behalf of the belligerent authorities at Richmond, and an abnegation of the letter to General Hitchcock, commissioner of exchange, of the date of Dec. 27, 1863, refusing to treat with myself as commissioner of exchange on the part of the United States, I sent Major Mulford with a steamer, to officially inform Mr. Ould that I would confer with him as proposed, and suggested as a matter of comfort to both parties that he should meet me with his assistant at Fortress Monroe. Owing to the darkness and storminess of the weather, he was not able to come down the river until the following day.

Upon meeting, Mr. Ould informed me that most of the soldiers of the United States, in the hands of his authorities, had been sent to Americus, Ga., for the convenience of furnishing them with food, and for the purpose of relieving us from the temptation of continual movements upon Richmond for the purpose of their liberation, and that in further exchange, he would desire to have these prisoners delivered to us at Fort Pulaski in Savannah River, and urged as a reason that it was more desirable to have them come by sea than to suffer the discomfort of a ride of many hundred miles by railroad. From motives of tenderness to the prisoners, and to prevent their being broken down by the journey, I assented that in case the exchange went forward, our government would receive those prisoners at that point, although the expenditure would be much heavier than at City Point; but leaving that question, as well as the one whether the prisoners held by us in the West might not be delivered somewhere on the Mississippi River, and thus save an expensive land transportation, to be adjusted by future conference, after other questions of more moment were settled.

We then proceeded to discuss the points of difference which had arisen in the matter of exchange, and the points reduced themselves to a few, which for more convenience for reference were put on a memorandum. I confess, that excepting the first point, as to persons of color, which I beg leave to discuss last, I can see no reason why an agreement upon all points of difference cannot be arrived at, upon just and equitable terms.

In regard to the paroles, the Confederate commissioner claims nothing, so far as I can see, which he is not willing to concede to us, acting under the cartel, and our general orders, with the exception that I believe on both sides it should be yielded that as well before as subsequently to Order No. 207 of July 3, 1863, paroles should not be accepted by either belligerent, of officers or soldiers, who were not so far in the power of the captor as to be taken to a place of safety, and I believe this proposition will be agreed to by the Confederate commissioner, although for paroles given prior to July 3d, I was at a loss to answer the fact claimed, which I suppose to be the fact, that paroles of prisoners taken on raids had been insisted upon on behalf of the United States, as in the case of Kilpatrick's first expedition to Richmond, and had been allowed and counted by the Confederate authorities.

All other points of difference were substantially agreed upon so that the exchange might go on readily and smoothly, man for man and officer for officer, of equal rank, and officers for their equivalents in privates as settled by the cartel. The first point of difference between the parties may be succinctly stated thus : —

The Confederates had asserted by and through the proclamation of their President and an act of their congress that all officers commanding colored troops, instead of being paroled for exchange as prisoners, should be delivered over to the governors of the States to be tried and convicted by their State tribunals of aiding the servile insurrection ; and that the colored soldiers serving in the armies of the United States, when captured, should be treated as slaves and turned over to their masters or confiscated to the government as property. This, the United States claimed, was a breach of the cartel by which it was agreed that all the officers and soldiers of either government should be exchanged man for man and officer for officer.

It will be remembered that by the declaration and proclamation of Jefferson Davis, of Dec. 23, 1862, all officers commanding colored troops were to be delivered over to the governors of States to be punished under their laws for inciting negro insurrections, which is a paraphrase for punishment by ignominious death, and that the colored soldiers so commanded were not to be treated as prisoners of war, but were to be turned over to their masters to hard labor as slaves, and that this was substantially the recommendation of Mr. Davis' message to the Confederate congress, and that an act was passed substantially in accordance with this recommendation. Now, while it may be conceded as a usage of civilized warfare, that prisoners of war necessarily supported by the capturing government may be employed by that government to labor upon public work, yet it has never been among nations making professions of Christianity, held that captives of war, either by land or sea, could be made slaves. And it will also be remembered, that the United States Government went to war with Tripoli and other Barbary powers in 1804, to force them at the cannon's mouth to repudiate this doctrine. It will be seen that the Confederate commissioner, however, has so far modified his claim, that officers in command of colored troops and free negroes, although both may be serving in company with slaves as soldiers in the army of the United States, are to be treated as prisoners of war, so that the question of difference between us now is not one of color, because it is admitted now that free black men of the loyal States are to be treated as prisoners of war. But the claim is that every person of color who ever was a slave in any of the eleven Confederate States, shall not be treated as prisoners of war, but when captured are to be deemed to be slaves, and may be turned over to their masters as such, by the Confederate government.

Now, as the United States Government has by the proclamation of the President, and by the law of Congress, emancipated all slaves that have sought refuge within the lines of the Union army, declared that they shall never be returned to their masters, and as men heretofore slaves, when duly enrolled in the United States army must be deemed and taken to be within the Union lines, therefore, we have no slaves in our army, and the question is whether we shall permit the belligerents opposed to us to make slaves of the free men that they capture in our uniform, simply because of their color ; because upon no ground of national law, so far as I am advised, can it be claimed for a moment that to any slave from any State when found within our lines, any right of property can attach in behalf of his former master, because treating the slave as property, only his captured by us from a belligerent would give the captor the right of property, the *jus disponendi*, and we have exercised that right of disposition by making him free.

But suppose we had not done so, recapture on land by the Confederate forces, treating them as representatives of a government, would make the slave as an article of property, the property of the government that captured him, and would by no means revest the title in the former owner.

To use an illustration which has occurred to my mind, suppose on land we captured from the rebels a horse belonging to " A " ; that horse is disposed of by our government taking it into its own service, and it is afterwards recaptured by the Confederate forces ; would there be any doubt that the property in the animal would have been divested from the original owner A, by the first capture, and come to the United States, and then been taken from the United States and given to the Confederate government by the recapture ?

Further, to permit this would be a violation of the laws of some of these very Confederate States. Virginia has emancipated her slaves by provisions which no one can doubt must be held according to any usage to be operative within the lines of the United States army. Many slaves are thus made free who are now in our army, and we cannot, of course, suffer them to be enslaved by the fact of capture by the rebels.

I understand this right to thus dispose of black soldiers in arms to be made a *sine qua non* by the Confederates, and therefore I take leave to suggest that I may be instructed to settle with the Confederate commissioner, upon further conference with him, all points of difference except this, and to declare exchanged, numbers equal on either side, heretofore delivered and paroled, so that this point may be left standing out sharply alone, and in regard to it, to insist that the cartel applies, as it does apply, to these colored prisoners of war, and that no further exchange can go on by the delivery of prisoners captured, until this point is yielded, with the purpose, but not with the threat, of exact retaliation, in exact kind and measure, upon their men, of the treatment received by ours.

Awaiting instructions, I have the honor to be,

Very respectfully, your obedient servant,

Benj. F. Butler,

Maj.-Gen. and Commr. of Exchange.

Mr. Ould left on the 31st of March with the understanding that I would get authority and information from my government by which all disputed points raised could be adjusted, and would then confer with him further, meeting him either at City Point or elsewhere for that purpose. In the meantime the exchange of sick and wounded and special exchanges were to go on.

Lieutenant-General Grant visited Fortress Monroe on the 1st of April. This was the first time I ever met him. To him the state of the negotiations as to exchange was communicated, and most emphatic verbal directions were received from the lieutenant-general not to take any steps by which another able-bodied man should be exchanged until further orders from him.

He then explained to me his views upon these matters. He said that I would agree with him that by the exchange of prisoners we got no men fit to go into our army, and every soldier we gave the Confederates went immediately into theirs, so that the exchange was virtually so much aid to them and none to us. For we gave them well men who went directly into their ranks, — and we had but few others, as the returns showed. Yet we received none from them substantially but disabled men, and by our laws and regulations they were to be allowed at once three months' furlough and were taken to camps and allowed to go home to recuperate, which few of them did, and fewer still came back to our armies. Now, the coming campaign was to be decided by the strength of the opposing forces, for the contest would all centre upon the Army of the Potomac and its immediate adjuncts. His proposition was to make an aggressive -fight upon Lee, trusting to the superiority of numbers and to the practical impossibility of Lee getting any considerable reinforcements to keep up his army. We had twenty-six thousand Confederate prisoners, and if they were exchanged it would give the Confederates a corps, larger than any in Lee's army, of disciplined veterans better able to stand the hardships of a campaign and more

GEN. U. S. GRANT.
From a Photograph taken in Field.

capable than any other. To continue exchanging upon parole the prisoners captured on one side and the other, especially if we captured more prisoners than they did, would at least add from thirty to perhaps fifty per cent. to Lee's capability for resistance.

Or, if the Confederates chose to turn them against Sherman they would bring his force to such inferiority in numbers as to determine his campaign. While the great sufferings of our prisoners remaining in their hands was much to be regretted, yet, being held, it gave us their equivalent and many more, because in their desperation the rebels would have no hesitation in putting, as they had done, their paroled prisoners before exchange was declared, directly into their armies, which we had never done; and this ought to be taken into consideration as to the question of exchange. He was further inclined to think that if exchanges were to cease that fact would take away the great temptation to that class of our soldiers who were not Americans, or if Americans who had not enlisted voluntarily into our armies or were induced by great bounties to do so, to surrender themselves prisoners so as to escape the perils of the campaign and be exchanged and go home. If these men came back at all, it was only upon the temptation of still larger bounties. Therefore one of our prisoners detained in custody in rebel hands was equivalent to at least three soldiers in the rebel line. He concluded by saying that at all hazards exchanges were to be stopped.

I told him that I had no doubt, as I had expressed it in a letter to the Secretary of War, that all the points of difference between us would be yielded by the rebels, except the question of the exchange of our colored soldiers captured by them. I said I doubted whether, if we stopped exchanging man for man, simply on the ground that our soldiers were more useful to us in rebel prisons than they would be in our lines, however true that might be, or speciously stated to the country, the proposition could not be sustained against the clamor that would at once arise against the administration. For such a course would be thought to be a sanction and permission by the government to the rebels to continue the alleged starvations, hardships, and slow torture. I doubted whether the government could or would stand the pressure of our people, intensified, as it would be, by the letters, communications, and complaints of all our prisoner soldiers; and I suggested that the effect of this course was well worth considering because of the use the Copperhead party would make of it in the coming presidential election which was to be debated while we were carrying on the coming political campaign.

I said to him further that as commissioner of exchange I was subject to a great deal of animadversion and it was alleged that on account of my proposition prisoners had not been exchanged, and I called his attention to certain newspaper articles in that direction, which he knew were unjust. These attacks had been made because I had tried by retaliation to enforce good treatment of the prisoners, and had opened the exchange (which, when I came to Fortress Monroe, had been closed for some months), by exchanging soldier for soldier and officer for officer, not pressing upon the rebels the question of the exchange of colored soldiers. I then suggested to him that that exchange could not be made without a repeal of the act of the Confederate congress which had adopted the provisions of outlawry of Davis' proclamation against all officers who should serve with colored troops, who were to be turned over for condign punishment. Besides the question would probably have a great influence upon the planters, who were exempt from conscription if they owned twenty or more slaves. These men dreaded exceedingly the effect of our proclamation of emancipation and the enrolment of their slaves in our army, because it induced their slaves to desert, and so brought the planters within the Confederate law of conscription and enrolment. Therefore I felt sure that the treatment of their captured slaves enrolled in our army as prisoners of war, and the recognition of equality with other officers of those commanding colored troops, would be the last requirements for exchange to which the rebels would surrender.

I further said that we could not enforce a new draft during the presidential campaign, however much our armies might be disabled, and therefore we could not abandon to death, or treatment worse than death, our colored soldiers, and as soon as it would be understood we had done so, the enlistment of colored soldiers would substantially cease. It was hard enough now, to get the proper class of officers to take command of colored troops, and it would be still more difficult if they were to be exposed to the threatened action of the Confederacy against them. Therefore, we could not give up the colored troops question in matters of exchange, and we must insist on protecting them and their officers, in the strongest and most effective terms and requirements, enforcing retaliation to the last degree in case the rebels insisted upon carrying out their act of congress upon the proclamation of Davis.

I said further that I had no doubt that if we put this stoppage of exchange upon this proposition, keeping that to the front, the patriotism, heartiness, and conceptions of justice of every right-minded man would sustain us in that very vital and dignified position which became us as a nation; so that if the rebels stopped the exchange upon such grounds and no other, the question properly stated to the country would assist the administration politically, rather than do it harm; and that therefore I would put forward this view of the question in a communication to the Secretary of War with all the strength of which I was master.

I suggested to him that perhaps meanwhile a limited exchange of the sick and wounded might go on, and that I would take care that the Confederates should have all their men who were not in condition to go into service in exchange for such men as they sent us who were in like condition.

He approved of my suggestions as to the course to be taken, and said he would confer with the secretary upon that subject upon receipt of my communication.

Before we parted he told me not to make any more exchanges of prisoners until the terms and questions were determined at Washington.

On the 14th day of April I received notice by telegraph that my letter of the 9th with the accompanying papers had been referred to General Grant for his orders,[1] and on the 20th of April I received a letter of instructions from General Grant.[2]

These instructions in the then state of negotiations rendered any further exchange impossible and retaliation useless. Being anxious that this unfortunate state of the question should not affect the sick and wounded, I telegraphed as follows : —

FORTRESS MONROE, April 20, 1864.

Lieutenant-General Grant's instructions shall be implicitly obeyed. I assume that you do not mean to stop the special exchange of the sick and wounded now going on.

BENJ. F. BUTLER,

Major-General and Commissioner of Exchange.

And to that telegram I received the following reply : —

---

[1] See Appendix No. 4. [2] See Appendix No. 5.

WASHINGTON, April 20, 1864, 9.30 P. M.

To MAJ.-GEN. B. F. BUTLER:

Receive all the sick and wounded the Confederate authorities will send you, but send no more in exchange.

U. S. GRANT,
Lieutenant-General.

To obtain the delivery of even sick and wounded prisoners without any return would be a somewhat difficult operation, save that the enemy by giving us our wounded and sick in their hands, we retaining all the rebel sick and wounded in ours, burdened us with the care and cost of all the sick and wounded of both sides, an operation of which it is difficult to see the strategic value, and is only to be defended because of its humanity in rescuing our wounded from the destitution and suffering permitted to them by the Confederates.

Nothing further was done with the exchange save to receive from Richmond such sick and wounded as they delivered to us, till the 15th of August, when I received a note from Major Mulford, assistant agent of exchange, from which the following is extracted: —

The Confederate authorities will exchange prisoners on the basis heretofore proposed by our government, that is, *man for man.* This proposition was *proposed* formally to *me* after I saw you. Shall I come to you before I arrange to go up river again for wounded? I intend to leave there Wednesday morning unless you direct otherwise. . . .

To this I telegraphed the following reply: —

HEADQUARTERS DEPARTMENT OF VIRGINIA AND NORTH CAROLINA,
IN THE FIELD, Aug. 16, 1864, 8.15 A. M.

MAJOR MULFORD, AGENT OF EXCHANGE, FORTRESS MONROE:

Bring up with you General Walker to be exchanged for General Bartlett, and what wounded Confederate officers there are at the hospitals at Fortress Monroe.

Also send for Captain Woolford. I do not want any women for this trip from Norfolk or Fortress Monroe.[1] Come up as soon as you can with the New York.

BENJ. F. BUTLER,
Major-General Commanding.

[1] Many Southern women, claiming to be from the North, made application to be sent South by flag of truce boat, and in some instances passage had been given; but it was ascertained that most of them were female Southern spies, who conveyed information to the enemy.

The flag of truce steamer New York appeared off City Point on the 18th of August, causing the following telegraphic correspondence, which testifies as well to the anxiety of the commissioner of exchange to protect, so far as he could, our imprisoned soldiers from suffering and the retaliatory measures of the rebels, as to the fear of the lieutenant-general lest any further exchange of prisoners should be effected : —

CITY POINT, Aug. 18, 1864.

GENERAL BUTLER :

I see the steamer New York has arrived. Is she going to Aiken's Landing or elsewhere under flag of truce?

U. S. GRANT,
Lieutenant- General.

[*Telegram.*]

HEADQUARTERS DEPARTMENT OF VIRGINIA AND NORTH CAROLINA,
IN THE FIELD, Aug. 18, 1864.

LIEUTENANT-GENERAL GRANT, CITY POINT :

Steamer New York is to go to Aiken's Landing under flag of truce, at which place she is to receive certain communications and special exchanges, among whom is General Bartlett, and to arrange a meeting between Commissioner Ould and myself for a conference in regard to the treatment of our prisoners and some cases of retaliation.

BENJ. F. BUTLER,
Major- General Commanding.

Finding how fearfully sensitive the lieutenant-general was lest Sherman's defeat should be insured and our safety compromised, and not then knowing what information the lieutenant-general had of the force of the enemy in Sherman's front, and having but to obey the orders of my superior, the following telegram was sent to assure him that I should take no steps in opposition to his wishes : —

Aug. 18, 1864, 4 P. M.

LIEUTENANT-GENERAL GRANT :

Telegram received. No exchange has been or will be made by me which will give the enemy any advantage. . . . I have exchanged nobody but wounded men since the first of May except surgeons, non-combatants, and a few cases of special exchange. . . .

BENJ. F. BUTLER,
Major- General and Commissioner of Exchange.

Accident prevented my meeting the rebel commissioner, so that nothing was done. But after conversation with General Grant I wrote an argument showing our right to our colored soldiers in reply to the proposition of Mr. Ould to exchange all prisoners of war either side held, man for man, officer for officer. This argument set forth our claims in the most offensive form possible yet consistent with ordinary courtesy of language, for the purpose of carrying out the wishes of the lieutenant-general that no prisoners of war should be exchanged, and was published, so as to bring a public pressure by the owners of slaves upon the rebel government to forbid their exchange. Here is the letter : —

ROB. OULD, ESQ., C. S. AGENT OF EXCHANGE:

In May last I forwarded to you a note, desiring to know whether the Confederate authorities intended to treat colored soldiers of the United States army as prisoners of war. To that inquiry no answer has yet been made. To avoid all possible misapprehension or mistake hereafter as to your offer now, will you now say whether you mean by " prisoners held in captivity," colored men, duly enrolled and mustered into the service of the United States, who have been captured by the Confederate forces; and if your authorities are willing to exchange *all* soldiers so mustered into the United States army, whether colored or otherwise, and the officers commanding them, man for man, officer for officer ?

At an interview which was held between yourself and the agent of exchange on the part of the United States at Fortress Monroe in March last, you will do me the favor to remember the principal discussion turned upon this very point; you, on behalf of the Confederate government, claiming the right to hold all negroes who had heretofore been slaves and not emancipated by their masters, enrolled and mustered into the service of the United States when captured by your forces, not as prisoners of war, but upon capture to be turned over to their supposed masters or claimants, whoever they might be, to be held by them as slaves.

By the advertisements in your newspapers calling upon masters to come forward and claim these men so captured, I suppose that your authorities still adhere to that claim. That is to say, that whenever a colored soldier of the United States is captured by you, upon whom any claim can be made by any person residing within the States now in insurrection, such soldier is not to be treated as a prisoner of war, but is to be turned over to his supposed owner or claimant, and put at such labor or service as that owner or claimant may choose, and the officers in command of such soldiers, in the language of a supposed act of the Confederate States, are to be turned over to the governors of States, upon requisitions, for the purpose of being punished by the laws of such States for acts done in war in the armies of the United States.

You must be aware that there is still a proclamation by Jefferson Davis, claiming to be chief executive of the Confederate States, declaring in substance that all officers or colored troops mustered into the service of the United States were not to be treated as prisoners of war, but were to be turned over for punishment to the governors of States.

I am citing these public acts from memory, and will be pardoned for not giving the exact words, although I believe I do not vary the substance and effect.

These declarations on the part of those whom you represent yet remain unrepealed, unannulled, unrevoked, and must, therefore, be still supposed to be authoritative. By your acceptance of our proposition, is the Government of the United States to understand that these several claims, enactments, and proclaimed declarations are to be given up, set aside, revoked and held for naught by the Confederate authorities, and that you are ready and willing to exchange, man for man, those colored soldiers of the United States duly mustered and enrolled as such who have heretofore been claimed as slaves by the Confederate States, as well as white soldiers?

If this be so, and you are so willing to exchange these colored men claimed as slaves, and you will so officially inform the Government of the United States, then, as I am instructed, a principal difficulty in effecting exchanges will be removed.

As I informed you personally, in my judgment, it is neither consistent with the policy, dignity, nor honor of the United States, upon any consideration to allow those who by our laws, solemnly enacted, are made soldiers of the Union, and who have been duly enlisted, enrolled, and mustered as such soldiers, who have borne arms in behalf of their country, and who have been captured while fighting in vindication of the rights of that country, not to be treated as prisoners of war, and remain unexchanged, and in the service of those who claim them as masters; and I cannot believe that the Government of the United States will ever be found to consent to so gross a wrong.

Pardon me if I misunderstood you, in supposing that your acceptance of our proposition does not in good faith mean to include all the soldiers of the Union, and that you still intend, if your acceptance is agreed to, to hold the colored soldiers of the Union unexchanged, and at labor or service, because I am informed that very lately, almost contemporaneously with this offer on your part to exchange prisoners, and which seems to include *all* prisoners of war, the Confederate authorities have made a declaration that the negroes heretofore held to service by owners in the States of Delaware, Maryland, and Missouri are to be treated as prisoners of war when captured in arms in the service of the United States. Such declaration that a part of the colored soldiers of the United States were to be treated as prisoners of war would seem most strongly to imply that others were not to be so treated, or, in other words, that colored men from the insurrectionary States are to be held to labor and returned to their masters, if captured by the Confederate forces while duly enrolled and mustered into, and actually in, the armies of the United States.

In the view which the Government of the United States takes of the claim made by you to the persons and services of these negroes, it is not to be supported upon any principle of national or municipal law.

Looking upon these men only as property, upon your theory of property in them, we do not see how this claim can be made, certainly not how it can be yielded. It is believed to be a well-settled rule of public international law, and a custom and part of the laws of war, that the capture of movable property vests the title to that property in the captor, and therefore when one belligerent gets into his full possession property belonging to the subjects or citizens of the other belligerent, the owners of that property are at once divested of their title, which vests in the belligerent government capturing and holding such possession. Upon this rule of international law all civilized nations have acted, and by it, both belligerents have dealt with all property, save slaves, taken from each other during the present war.

If the Confederate forces capture a number of horses from the United States, the animals immediately are claimed to be, and, as we understand it, become the property of the Confederate authorities.

If the United States forces capture any movable property belonging to persons in the Rebellion, by our regulations and laws, in conformity with international law and the laws of war, such property is to be held by our government as its property. Therefore, if we obtain possession of that species of property, known to the laws of the insurrectionary States as slaves, why should there be any doubt that the title to that property, like any other, vests in the United States?

If the property in the slave does so vest, then the "*jus disponendi*," the right of disposing of that property, rests in he United States.

Now, the United States have disposed of the property which they have acquired by capture in slaves taken by them, by giving that right of property to the man himself, to the slave; i. e., by emancipating him and declaring him free forever, so that if we have not mistaken the principles of international law and the laws of war, we have no slaves in the armies of the United States. All are free men, being made so in such manner as we have chosen to dispose of our rights in them, which we acquired by capture.

Slaves being captured by us, and the right of property in them thereby vested in us, that right of property has been disposed of by us by manumitting them, as has always been the acknowledged right of the owner to do to his slave. The manner in which we dispose of our property while it is in our possession, certainly cannot be questioned by you.

Nor is the case altered if the property is not actually captured in battle, but comes either voluntarily or involuntarily from the belligerent owner into the possession of the other belligerent. I take it no one would doubt the right of the United States to a drove of Confederate mules or a herd of Confederate cattle, which should wander or rush across the Confederate lines into the lines of the United States army. So, it seems to me, treating the negro as property merely, if that piece of property passes the Confederate lines and comes into the lines of the United States, that property is as much lost to its owner in the Confederate States, as would be the mule or ox, the property of the resident of the Confederate States which should so come into our possession.

If, therefore, the principles of international law and the laws of war used in this discussion are correctly stated, then it would seem that the deduction logically flows therefrom, in natural sequence, that the Confederate States can have no claim upon the negro soldiers captured by them from the armies of the United States, because of the former ownership of them by their citizens or subjects, and only claim such as result, under the laws of war, from their captor merely.

Do the Confederate authorities claim the right to reduce to a state of slavery freemen, prisoners of war captured by them? This claim our fathers fought against under Bainbridge and Decatur, when set up by the Barbary powers on the northern shore of Africa about the year 1800, and in 1864 their children will hardly yield it upon their own soil!

This point I will not pursue further, because I understood you to repudiate the idea that you will reduce free men to slaves because of capture in war, and that you base the claim of the Confederate authorities to re-enslave our negro soldiers, when captured by you, upon the "*jus post limini*," or that principle of the law of nations which rehabilitates the former owner with his property taken by an enemy, when such property is recovered by the forces of his own country. Or, in other words, you claim that by the laws of nations and of war, when property of the subjects of one belliger-ent power captured by the forces of the other belligerent, is recaptured by the armies of the former owner, then the property is to be restored to its prior possessor as if it had never been captured; and, therefore, under this principle, your authorities propose to restore to their masters the slaves which heretofore belonged to them which you may capture from us.

But this postliminary right, under which you claim to act, as under-stood and defined by all writers on national law, is applicable simply to *immovable property*, and that, too, only after the complete resubjugation of that portion of the country in which the property is situated, upon which

LIBBY PRISON.

this right fastens itself. By the laws and customs of war, this right has never been applied to *movable* property.

True it is, I believe, that the Romans attempted to apply it to the case of slaves; but for two thousand years no other nation has attempted to set up this right as ground for treating slaves differently from other property.

But the Romans ever refused to enslave men captured from opposing belligerents in a civil war, such as ours unhappily is.

Consistently, then, with any principle of the law of nations, treating slaves as property merely, it would seem to be impossible for the Government of the United States to permit the negroes in their ranks to be re-en-slaved when captured, or treated otherwise than as prisoners of war.

I have forborne, sir, in this discussion, to argue the question upon any other or different grounds of right than those adopted by your authorities, in claiming the negroes as property, because I understand that your fabric of opposition to the Government of the United States has the right of property in man as its corner-stone. Of course, it would not be profitable in settling a question of exchange of prisoners of war, to attempt to argue the question of abandonment of the very corner-stone of their attempted political edifice. Therefore I have omitted all the considerations which should apply to the negro soldier as a man, and dealt with him upon the Confederate theory of property only.

I unite with you most cordially, sir, in desiring a speedy settlement of all these questions, in view of the great suffering endured by our pris-oners in the hands of your authorities, of which you so feelingly speak. But let me ask, in view of that suffering, why you have delayed eight months to answer a proposition which by now accepting you admit to be right, just, and humane, allowing that suffering to continue so long? One cannot help thinking, even at the risk of being deemed uncharitable, that the benevolent sympathies of the Confederate authorities have been lately stirred by the depleted condition of their armies, and a desire to get into the field, to affect the present campaign, the hale, hearty, and well-fed prisoners held by the United States, in exchange for the half-starved, sick, emaciated, and unserviceable soldiers of the United States now languish-ing in your prisons. The events of this war, if we did not know it before, have taught us that it is not the northern portion of the American people alone who know how to drive sharp bargains.

The wrongs, indignities, and privations suffered by our soldiers would move me to consent to anything to procure their exchange, except to barter away the honor and faith of the Government of the United States, which has been so solemnly pledged to the colored soldiers in its ranks.

Consistently with national faith and justice we cannot relinquish this position. With your authorities it is a question of property merely. It seems to address itself to you in this form. Will you suffer your soldier, captured in fighting your battles, to be in confinement for months rather than release him by giving for him that which you call a piece of property, and which we are willing to accept as a man?

You certainly appear to place less value upon your soldier than you do upon your negro. I assure you, much as we of the North are accused of loving property, our citizens would have no difficulty in yielding up any piece of property they have in exchange for one of their brothers or sons languishing in your prisons. Certainly, there could be no doubt that they would do so were that piece of property less in value than five thousand dollars in Confederate money, which is believed to be the price of an able-bodied negro in the insurrectionary States.

Trusting that I may receive such a reply to the questions propounded in this note as will lead to a speedy resumption of the negotiations for a full exchange of all prisoners, and a delivery of them to their respective authorities,

I have the honor to be, very respectfully, your obedient servant,

BENJ. F. BUTLER,

Major-General and Commissioner of Exchange.

In case the Confederate authorities should take the same view as General Grant, believing that the exchange of prisoners would "defeat Sherman and imperil the safety of the Armies of the Potomac" and the James "here," and therefore should yield to the argument and formally notify me that their slaves captured in our uniform would be exchanged as other soldiers were, and that they were ready to return to us all our prisoners at Andersonville and elsewhere in exchange for theirs, I had determined, with the consent of the lieutenant-general, as a last resort, in order to prevent exchange, to demand that the outlawry against me should be formally reversed and apologized for before I would further negotiate the exchange of prisoners.

My propositions were approved by Lieutenant-General Grant.[1]

But the argument was enough and the Confederates never offered to me afterwards to exchange the colored soldiers who had been slaves, held in prison by them.

It may be remarked here that the rebels were ready enough to exchange prisoners at this time, man for man, where we would permit it to be done; because another exchange of a part of the prisoners captured from our navy, held by the Confederates, was arranged with the Secretary of the Navy, who made the agreement outside of our commission by means of our flag of truce boat at Aiken's landing. As will be seen by a telegram,[2] General Grant readily consented to this particular exchange, as it would not "defeat Sherman" or "imperil our safety here."

---

[1] See Appendix No. 6.   [2] See Appendix No. 7.

Against this exchange of sailors when I heard of it, as well as against the partial exchange of able-bodied soldiers going on in several military departments through their commanders, I protested as vigorously as I was able, because it tended to breed discontent in our armies and was grossly unjust,— as will be seen by the following despatch to the Secretary of War:—

HEADQUARTERS ARMY OF THE JAMES,
NEAR JUNCTION OF VARINA AND NEW MARKET ROADS,
Oct. 3, 1864, 7.45 P. M.

HON. E. M. STANTON, SECRETARY OF WAR:—

. . . .

I have received a letter from Captain Smith of the navy proposing to Ould an exchange of naval prisoners "independently of our commissioner." There have been many negroes captured from the navy who are thus abandoned to their fate. Is it not possible for the government to have a policy? If Sherman exchanges at Atlanta, if Foster at Charleston, if Canby at New Orleans, and Rosecrans in Missouri, then I do not see why we should not exchange here. Our soldiers will not be too well pleased to hear that sailors can and soldiers cannot be exchanged.

BENJ. F. BUTLER,
Major-General Commanding.

It will be observed that the rebels had exchanged all the naval colored prisoners, so that the negro question no longer impeded exchange of prisoners in fact, nor would have even if we had demanded the exchange of all, man for man, officer for officer. It was now settled that no general exchange of prisoners would be allowed by the commanding general to take place, and as I felt deeply the sufferings and privations of our soldiers in Andersonville and Salisbury, and other rebel prisons, I negotiated the special exchange of the sick and wounded, and for the exchange of naval prisoners, black and white, and also arranged that our government should be allowed to provide for the soldiers in the hands of the rebels. The condition of these exchanges and negotiations fully appear in the letter of instructions under which Lieutenant-Colonel Mulford sailed for Savannah carrying down the rebel sick, to bring back ours. This exchange covered about twelve hundred of our men.

In an attack on Fort Gilmer on the 29th of September about one hundred and fifty of the negro soldiers of the Army of the James were captured. On the 12th of October I was credibly informed that these prisoners of war had been set at work in the trenches under fire in front of our lines. I immediately notified Mr. Ould, the agent of exchange, of this outrage, and failing to get an answer at 12 o'clock on the 13th of October, I determined to try the virtue of retaliation for wrong, and issued an order which will explain itself : —

HEADQUARTERS DEPARTMENT OF VIRGINIA AND NORTH CAROLINA,
ARMY OF THE JAMES.
IN THE FIELD, Oct. 13, 1864.

General Order No. 126.

It being testified to the commanding general by a number of refugees and deserters from the enemy, that from one hundred to one hundred and fifty soldiers of the United States, captured in arms by the Confederates on the lines near Chapin's Bluff, have been taken from Libby Prison and otherwheres, and placed to labor on the intrenchments of the enemy's lines in front of their troops, the commanding general on the 13th day of October notified the Confederate agent of exchange, Robert Ould, of the outrage being perpetrated upon his soldiers, and informed him that unless the practice was stopped, retaliation in kind would be adopted by the Government of the United States.

Being assured by General Ewell, commanding Confederate forces on the north side of the James, that an answer to this communication, if any, would be sent by 11 o'clock A. M., to-day and it being now past 12 (noon) and no answer having been received,

It is ordered : That an equal number of prisoners of war, preferably members of the Virginia reserves, by and under whose charge this outrage is being carried on, be set to work in the excavation at Dutch Gap, and elsewhere along the trenches, as may hereafter seem best, in retaliation for this unjust treatment of the soldiers of the United States so kept at labor and service by the Confederate authorities.

It being also testified to by the same witnesses, that the rations served to the soldiers of the United States so at labor is one pound of flour and one third of a pound of bacon daily, it is ordered that the same ration precisely be served to these Confederate prisoners so kept at work, daily, and no other or different.

It being further testified to, that the time of labor of the soldiers of the United States so at work under the Confederates is ten hours each day, these Confederate prisoners so kept at work will be made to work, and work faithfully, daily during the same period of time.

This order will be read to the prisoners set to work, the first time they are mustered for labor, in order that they may know why it is that they do not receive that kind and courteous treatment they have heretofore from the United States, as prisoners of war.

Upon any attempt to escape by any of these prisoners so kept at work, they will be instantly shot.

By command of

MAJOR-GENERAL BUTLER.

[*Official.*]

ED. W. SMITH, *Assistant Adjutant-General.*

The succeeding day the order was exactly executed. The experiment was a success. October 20 General Lee officially notified General Grant that the negro prisoners had been withdrawn from the trenches and would be treated as prisoners of war, and thereupon an order [1] was issued and they were released.

This experiment was a success in another point of view, showing how readily the rebels under pressure can be converted to loyalty, as nearly, if not quite, all of them, being citizens of Richmond, offered to take the oath of allegiance if they could be released.

Colonel Mulford was much delayed in carrying out his instructions because of the interference with his steamers devoted to this purpose. They were taken for the transportation of troops, to make up the complement by orders from some of the bureaus at Washington, the remainder of his transports being filled with prisoners who were not sick. While I was in command at New York he wrote me that his vessel had been taken away from him by some sub-official in Washington, to transport troops. [2]

Having before that procured the assent of the Secretary of War to the lease of the steamers Atlantic and Baltic for this humane enterprise, I answered in the most imperative manner that he should not yield to subordinate interference at Washington, — a thing of which I had seen something too much, — and that he should hold his transportation at all hazards. [3]

In compliance with the order Colonel Mulford got off, and arrived in Savannah River about the 15th of November and reported his

---

[1] See Appendix No. 8.   [2] See Appendix No. 9.   [3] See Appendix No. 10.

success in arranging for the delivery of all the sick and wounded.[1] He was also enabled to effect an arrangement for feeding and clothing our prisoners, whom he found in a most filthy and destitute condition.

The further exchange had to be transferred to Charleston because of the operations of General Sherman, but Colonel Mulford succeeded in getting about twelve thousand men. In pursuance of the negotiations concluded by Colonel Mulford, an order[2] was issued,

CONVALESCENT COLORED UNION SOLDIERS AT AIKEN'S LANDING.

and with this order all action on my part as commissioner of exchange practically ceased.

I have felt it my duty to give with this particular carefulness an account of my participation in the business of exchange of prisoners, the orders under which I acted, and the negotiations attempted, which comprise a faithful narration, in order that all that was done may become a matter of history. The great importance of the questions; the fearful responsibility for the many thousands of lives which, by the refusal to exchange, were lost by the most cruel forms of deaths

---

[1] See Appendix No. 11.　　　　　　　　　　[2] See Appendix No. 12.

from cold, starvation, and pestilence in the prison pens of Raleigh, Salisbury, and Andersonville, — many more in number than all the *British* soldiers ever had by Great Britain on any field of battle with Napoleon ;[1] the anxiety of fathers, brothers, sisters, mothers, wives, to know the exigency which caused this terrible, and perhaps as it may have seemed to them useless and unnecessary, destruction of those dear to them by horrible deaths, — each and all have compelled me to this exposition, so that it might be seen that these lives were spent as a part of the system of attack upon the Rebellion, devised by the wisdom of the general-in-chief of the armies to destroy it by depletion, depending upon our superior number to win the victory at last. The loyal mourners will doubtless derive solace from this fact and appreciate all the more highly the genius which conceived the plan and the success won at so great a cost.

Before closing this exposition of the exchange of prisoners, I deem it my duty to call attention to two or three correlative matters of complaint which have been very much magnified on the part of the Confederates and the people of the North.

While I do not mean to apologize for or palliate the manner in which our prisoners were treated, which was inexcusable, I feel bound to say that from careful examinations of the subject I do not believe that either the people or the higher authorities of the Confederacy were in so great degree responsible as they have been accused. In the matter of starvation the fact is incontestable that a soldier of our army would have quite easily starved on the rations which in the latter days of the war were served out to the Confederate soldiers before Petersburg. I examined the haversacks of many Confederate soldiers captured on picket during the summer of 1864 and found therein, as their rations for three days, scarcely more than a pint of kernels of corn, none of which were broken but only parched to blackness by the fire, and a piece of meat, most frequently raw bacon, some three inches long by an inch and a half wide and less than a half an inch thick. Now, no Northern soldier could have lived three days upon that, and the lank, emaciated condition of the prisoner fully testified to the meagreness of his means of sustenance. I have been informed by a major-general commanding one of the larger corps of

---

[1] The effective strength of the British troops (English, Irish, and Scotch) in the allied army at the commencement of the battle of Waterloo was 25,389. (See Maxwell's "Life of Wellington," Vol. III., Appendix, page 564. Appendix No. 13, page 593.)

Lee's army[1] that in the winter of 1864–5 himself and General Lee examined a return of rations issued to the corps under Lee's command, and found that the amount of meat divided by the number of men present would make the allowance a little more than one sixth of an ounce per soldier per day, and this was a regulation issue. But his corps was not in that condition because he used his wagons to supply a little more when it could be found in the almost devastated country in his rear.[2]

With regard to clothing, it was simply impossible for the Confederates at that time and for many months preceding to have any sufficient clothing upon the bodies of their soldiers, and many passed the winters barefoot. Necessity, therefore, would seem to have compelled the condition of food and clothing given by them to the Federal prisoners, for it was not possible for the authorities to supply it without taking the clothing from their soldiers in the field.

There are two other complaints as to the condition of the prisoners. One was that sufficient water was not supplied at Andersonville. That I do not charge to the authorities, but to the brutality of the officers of subordinate rank and of brutal disposition, who were put in charge of them. I cannot believe the higher officers of the Confederacy were aware of the facts. Because all the higher officers of the Confederate army and of the government were so exceedingly pressed with rapidly recurring duties and transpiring events, they neglected to make proper inspections, and undoubtedly the strong hatred felt on the part of those who had no high motive to control them may account for such neglect.

I find more difficulty, however, in regard to the other complaint, the failure to supply fuel for fire during that winter for our prisoners. The winters of North Carolina and a part of Georgia are sufficiently severe. Indeed, the only time any of my troops had their feet frozen was when a regiment of them bivouacked in North Carolina after a hard march, and a sudden cold wave was so severe that their feet were considerably frozen before morning Their camp hardly seemed to me to be an excuse for that want of wood, except for the negligence or incompetency of the under officers having the prisoners in charge, which quite possibly may never have come to the knowledge of their

---

[1] General J. B. Gordon. [2] See Appendix No. 13.

superiors. Andersonville, for example, was in a wooded country with wood in plenty close at hand, which could be procured with a little energy and thoughtfulness, and no expense.

Indeed, the prisoners could, without escaping or attempting to escape, have procured the wood for themselves, except for the grossest inefficiency and want of sense of those having them in charge in refusing to permit them to so do.

I have no personal knowledge of the condition of the rebel prisoners of war except at Point Lookout, where I had from twelve to fifteen thousand under my immediate charge from December, 1863, when I first inspected them, to April, 1864, when I last inspected them, except through the medium of gentlemen of my staff.

In December, 1863, I made two personal inspections at Point Lookout of the condition of the rebel prisoners of war. I went into their camp, which covered some acres, and was well laid out. There were tents to accommodate all of them, placed upon a perfectly proper camping ground laid out in streets. At the corners many of the prisoners assembled around me, and I asked them to state to me any complaints they had to make as to the clothing, food, or anything else. They all said they had no complaint to make except that, as the weather was cold, they wanted more firewood than our army regulations allowed.

I then subjected several of them to personal inspection with their leave, examining even the condition of their gums, — because in looking over the ration I had come to the conclusion that it was possible that not sufficient fresh vegetables had been given them, and that I might find, as I did, slight indications of the scurvy by the condition of their gums, their complaints of stiffness of their joints, and from the fact of their growing too fat from being without exercise.

I then said to them: "Upon your pledge that you will take no improper advantage of the concession, I will permit you to furnish yourselves with as much firewood as you choose to burn, the fire to be raked out after taps. I will direct that a number not exceeding one hundred of you, whom your officers will detail, — for I suppose you have some organization, — may go out and cut from a neighboring forest which belongs to a secession friend of yours, as much wood as you like, and four mule teams with a wagon to haul it in will be furnished. And this may be done every pleasant day. But this must be upon your solemn pledge that none of you will attempt to escape when allowed beyond the camp fence for this purpose. If any man forgets the pledge it will result unfavorably to you, because I shall direct that no more shall be allowed to go out, and you will be left with only the regulation amount of wood for your use."

This they all agreed to with great alacrity, and they treated me with the utmost respect and grateful kindness. General Marston was in command of their camp, but I had not taken him with me because I wanted them to feel at full liberty to make any complaints without his knowing who it was that complained.

On returning to the office I detailed my visit to General Marston, expressed my thanks to him for the fine condition of his command, and suggested to him that I thought he ought to make fresh vegetables a part of his rations ; that it did not appear that any increase in the amount of food was necessary but rather a decrease. He replied that he had no authority to issue such rations. I answered that he might do so and I would see that the proper measures were taken to have his account allowed. I then said to him: "I have some knowledge derived from my experience concerning sailors, especially whalemen, of the necessity for some preventive for the scurvy, and therefore you had better send North for a schooner load of onions for their rations, and they had better be served raw, cider vinegar to be given with them, and I know of no better anti-scorbutic than these, save, perhaps, lemon-juice, which would be too expensive." I also informed him that he might draw upon my " provost fund " for the expenses.

No better hearted man lived than Marston, and he joyfully undertook to carry out the orders. From that hour I never had a complaint of the treatment of the prisoners at Point Lookout, although many hundreds passed through Fortress Monroe on their way to be exchanged, and I sometimes saw them on the flag of truce boat.

I heard of but two disturbances in the camp. One was when unfortunately one man did not return with the chopping party. There was great excitement and some inspection of the guards, until the reason of the absence was ascertained. The poor fellow had lost his way. He came into camp a couple of hours later, and was joyfully hailed by his comrades. The other was when it became necessary to change the regiment guarding them for one of colored troops. A number of ill-advised men made public declarations that they would not be guarded by negroes, and one night when they should have retired at taps a noisy demonstration was made. That was officially stopped in the most effective manner.

I had twenty-five hundred Confederate officers, more or less. They occupied the buildings erected for hospitals, as we had very few sick prisoners, and very large provisions had been made for hospital purposes. I never received any complaint from them. Many of them, I trust, are alive and well. With them there was never any disturbance but this once. The colored sergeant in charge directed an officer to retire to his quarters after taps, according to the regulations, and that respectful order was greeted with " Get out, you d—d nigger; why do you speak to a gentleman?" and the officer jumped upon the sergeant, who at once used his revolver very effectively. That being reported to me, I ordered an investigation by a commission composed of five officers, two of whom were prisoners, and upon their unanimous report I sustained the sergeant and ordered any other to shoot under like circumstances.

I can give no further personal testimony as to the treatment of the prisoners of war held by us.

Very much complaint and very strong animadversion has been made, and to the unthinking with apparent reason, against our medical officers that they treated the sick and wounded prisoners of war less carefully than they treated our own wounded and sick men, and the official returns of the number of men who died from operations because of the same class of wounds and of sickness from the same diseases, show that the mortality of the rebel prisoners exceeded, in very considerable number, that of our own troops having the same class of afflictions. They were all treated in the same hospitals, when possible, which gives a seeming ground for this complaint.

Indeed, Mr. Davis makes it quite savagely. It ought to be supported by very substantial and conclusive evidence, before being believed by any just, right-minded man, for it is the gravest possible charge that our medical officers, a body of men who had no superiors in any country, deliberately neglected the sick and wounded men in their official charge, so as to leave them to die. And there should be every desire to examine closely and see if there cannot be full and just reason for this admitted difference in the number of deaths.

I think the explanation is to be found in the difference of the physical condition of the patients. I appeal to the right-minded and just men who were the medical officers of the Confederacy, and also to the commanders of their troops, to agree to the fact that the very great deprivation of proper and substantial food supplied to the Confederates in the field brought their men to such a condition of constitutional health that they could not bear up under the sufferings and loss of blood resulting from wounds and operations, rendering them more susceptible to attacks of gangrene which were incurable. And the same want of proper food left them to become so weak in bodily strength and of so low vitality as to render them more susceptible to attacks of the diseases for which they were treated and with less recuperative power, so that much larger percentages of death resulted than would have been the case if they had been in full fed health and strength as were our prisoners when captured.

Would not a scratch from a minie ball upon the body of a Confederate, which would hardly be noticed on one of our soldiers, very frequently be followed by death? I feel very certain that this condition of the Confederates is the whole cause of the difference in the results of wounds and diseases of prisoners captured from their armies. Indeed, I believe I can say from my actual knowledge on the subject that the Confederate soldiers in the field could and did live on less good and solid food than our army wasted.

I do not desire, on my part, to accuse of deliberate cruelty and wrong any considerable portion of my countrymen who were my enemies, or to have my countrymen who served with me so accused by others. As a general fact, I do not believe it existed on either side.

Mr. Davis makes one assertion of fact which is very possibly true. It is based upon the statistical report of General Barnes, Surgeon-General of the United States Army, which I always believed to be erroneous, and which is now held so to be. In this report Barnes places the whole number of prisoners on the Union side at 270,000, and I believe that he is approximately correct, and that of the rebel prisoners at 260,000, instead of 220,000, as Davis puts it on the strength of General Barnes' estimate. Then Mr. Davis says that 26,000 of the rebel prisoners died in our hands, and only 20,000 of ours died in the hands of the Confederates, making an aggrégate death of twelve per cent. more of rebel prisoners than Union prisoners.

I have an authority for the statement of the number of Confederate prisoners held by us which would relieve substantially the imputation, but it is hardly necessary to go into such examination to do so. Can anybody doubt upon the statement of Davis even, considering the condition of his men in the field, especially of those wounded, that there would not be twelve per cent. more of them die than there would be of our prisoners? He places his imputation only upon the fact of death in general and not death of wounded.[1]

---

[1] Owing to the very great difficulty in getting at the exact number of our prisoners and the exact number of the Confederate prisoners, and especially the number of our men who died within the rebel prisons, as no reliable data or regular official reports of those facts have yet been discovered, — if they were ever made, — the "Board of Publication," acting under the direction of the Secretary of War, engaged in publishing all the data of the operations of war that can be obtained, have not yet been able to publish the official reports of the facts in this regard which I have just been discussing. At the time of my writing I have been unable to pursue the subject with the minuteness and exactness that I would desire. I have asked for such data, and if they can be got, I know through the kindness of the Board they will be furnished me as soon as collected; and if they are received before my work is finished they will be inserted in the Appendix.

CHAPTER XIV.

IN COMMAND OF THE ARMY OF THE JAMES.

O N the second day of November, 1863, without solicitation, I was detailed to the command of the Department of Virginia and North Carolina, with headquarters at Fortress Monroe. The Union forces were then in occupation of the peninsula between the York and James Rivers, up to the line of Williamsburg, the cities of Norfolk and Portsmouth, and a line extending towards Suffolk, about seven miles from Norfolk, on the line of the Dismal Swamp Canal in Virginia, and by the aid of the gunboats, the Currituck, Albemarle, and Pamlico Sounds, Roanoke Island, Hatteras Bank, Morehead City, Beaufort, the line of railroad from New Berne, and the cities of New Berne, Plymouth, and Washington, and as much land as was fairly within the pickets of the garrison of those cities in North Carolina.

Upon inspection of these several posts it appeared to me that holding Washington and Plymouth was useless, because, while Washington was distant from New Berne only about twenty miles, and Plymouth perhaps a less distance from Washington by land, the enemy held the intervening territory, and the only communication between these places was by water by travelling a distance of from 120 to 170 miles. This opinion was reported to the War Department, but no action was taken, and I did not feel at liberty to order the evacuation of either place.

November 16, an expedition under Colonel Quinn, with 450 men of the One Hundred and Forty-Eighth New York Volunteers, captured a rebel marine brigade organized to prey upon the commerce of Chesapeake Bay, and a dangerous nest of pirates was broken up.

November 27, Colonel Draper, with the Sixth U. S. Colored Troops, made a successful raid into the counties lying on the sounds in Virginia and North Carolina, capturing and dispersing organized guerillas.

December 4, Brigadier-General Wilde, at the head of two regiments of colored troops, overran all the counties as far as Chowan River, releasing some two thousand slaves and inflicting much damage upon the enemy.

December 13, Brigadier-General Wistar sent a force from Williamsburg to Charles City Court-House and captured two companies of rebel cavalry, being the outposts of Richmond. The force was gallantly led by Col. Robert West.

The army being much in need of recruits, and Eastern Virginia claiming to be a fully organized loyal State, by permission of the President an enrolment of all the able-bodied loyal citizens of Virginia within my command was ordered for the purposes of a draft, when one should be called for in the other loyal States. This order was vigorously protested against by Governor Pierpont, and this was all the assistance the United States ever received from the loyal government of Virginia in defending the State. My predecessors in command had endeavored to recruit a regiment of loyal Virginians, but after many months of energetic trial, both by them and by myself, the attempt was abandoned. A company and a half was all the recruits that State would furnish to the Union, and these were employed in defending the lighthouses and protecting the loyal inhabitants from the outrages of their immediate neighbors.

January 25, 1864, the roads being impassable, Brigadier-General Graham, with some armed transports, went up the James River to Lower Brandon and destroyed a large quantity of provisions and forage stored there, and captured some smuggling vessels.

Major-General Pickett, of the Confederate forces, made an attack upon New Berne and our lines at Beaufort, N. C., on the 1st of February, but was cleverly repulsed with loss, Brigadier-General Palmer commanding the district.

By a surprise of an outpost, fifty-three of the Second North Carolina (loyal) Regiment were captured by General Pickett. By his order they were tried by court martial and twenty-two of them were hanged. Their supposed offence was that they, being enrolled in the Confederate army, had enlisted in the Union army. Upon remonstrance by General Peck, commanding in North Carolina, Pickett replied, that being deserters they were executed by his orders, and if retaliation was attempted he would execute ten United States soldiers for every one upon whom we retaliated, unless, indeed, the Confederates were deserters from our army, in which case hanging them would be proper. As Pickett himself deserted our army to take up arms in the Rebellion, the exception was quite suggestive of the duty of our government towards such men as he.

The correspondence in relation to this affair is illustrative of the mode of warfare which we endured.[1]

I referred the whole correspondence to General Grant with recommendation that stringent measures be taken for the protection of loyal Southern men in our armies, but nothing was done.

I have been often asked why our war was so protracted. Was not the pusillanimity and want of executive force of the government as exhibited in this transaction, one sufficient answer? Why was not Pickett hanged for these twenty-two deliberate murders when he was captured by us?

It is needless to say that recruiting for our forces in North Carolina ceased.

Information was received from my correspondents at Richmond that while the troops usually around Richmond were away operating in North Carolina, the enemy, relying upon the almost impassable condition of the roads, had left but a small guard at Bottom's Bridge, over the Chickahominy, eleven miles from Richmond. Believing that a rapid march and a surprise would carry the intrenchments around the city if the bridge could be seized, Brigadier-General Wistar, whose suggestion it was, was permitted to make the attempt with about three thousand men from Williamsburg.[2] His march was a brilliant one, his dispositions admirable, but success was snatched from him, because of the escape, from his guard at Williamsburg, the night before the expedition started, of a *prisoner who had been ordered to be executed for the wilful murder of an officer, and who had been reprieved by the President.* The man fled to the enemy and gave information, so that when our men reached Bottom's Bridge, we found it held by a strong force.[3]

A few words are needed to explain fully the objects of this expe-

---

[1] See Appendix No. 14. [2] See Appendix No. 15. [3] See Appendix No. 16.

dition, which did not succeed because it failed to be a surprise.   Had it not been for the escape of the condemned murderer who gave information that the expedition was in progress, and had it not been for the unwise clemency of the President, of which I have spoken before, in interfering with his execution, the surprise would doubtless have been complete.

I tried to get that murderer sent to me in exchange for any Confederate the rebels desired me to give, but they, knowing his service to them, always took care of him, and smuggled him to New York to vote the Democratic ticket for them.   As the man's pardon was in the direct line of my argument with Mr. Lincoln upon the uselessness of his pardons, I addressed confidentially a note to him explaining all that he had lost by his clemency to this wretch.

GEN. GODFREY WEITZEL.

Upon looking into the reports of Brig.-Gen. Eppa Hunton, who commanded the Confederate forces in Richmond, I find that he was thoroughly puzzled to learn what we were up there for, and why if we intended to assault the city we did not do it with more vigor than by a mere reconnoissance of cavalry.   We had learned that there was but half a company of artillerymen at Bottom's Bridge, and that there were no forces between Bottom's Bridge and Capitol Square in Richmond, for in less than a week previous trusty men had traversed that road.

It will be observed that General Wistar speaks of ulterior and "specific" objects.   He was well instructed in them.   The first and most important was to release the large number of prisoners there, who would have made a very great addition to our force; and the second was to capture the Confederate Cabinet and Mr. Jefferson Davis.

We had for one of our guides when the city was reached, his gardener, who had deserted to us, and if we could have laid our hands upon Davis in the early morning he would certainly have taken a ride to Fortress Monroe to greet an old friend of his who would have taken special care to keep him there, certainly as long as the telegraph wires would not work between there and Washington so that the President's pardon could not reach him. If the city could have been reached, and the Union prisoners there added to our force, Wistar was instructed to hold on if possible, and I was ready to march with all my available command into Richmond, and once there I doubt if anybody would have desired to have the rebel capital there any longer.

In view of the possibility of my march upon Richmond with my whole force, in case it was found as unprepared for attack as it had been reported, I desired that Lee might be detained from sending any part of his army to Richmond, and asked that the Army of the Potomac lying in front of Lee might make a movement upon him as a feint. General Meade being sick, General Sedgwick, who was in command, was ordered to co-operate with me. But after considerable correspondence he telegraphed that he could not get ready in time.

On the 4th of March I received notice that General Kilpatrick had started, with a cavalry force, on a raid to Richmond from the Army of the Potomac, and was directed to make dispositions to aid him, or cover with infantry his march to Fortress Monroe. Accordingly I marched a column to New Kent Court-House, and there met General Kilpatrick on his return.

On the 9th of March the Confederates made a demonstration upon our lines at Suffolk. Not knowing the force of the enemy, and Kilpatrick's men being recruiting from their march at Yorktown, I asked his aid to meet this advance, which was promptly and kindly given, and the movement of the enemy handsomely met and repulsed.

When I had reported for duty to Mr. Stanton in obedience to his order to take command, he informed me of the probable importance of my department in the campaign of the coming spring and summer, in which would be a movement upon Richmond. Whereupon in all my spare moments I examined particularly the topography of Virginia and North Carolina and that, too, in connection with the campaigns of McClellan around Richmond and his final retreat to Harrison's Landing.

I was a good deal impressed with the peculiar topographical formation of the country below Richmond on the south side of the James down as far as its junction with the Appomattox. In their windings the rivers approach each other within two miles and a half, at a point on the James about eight miles in direct line from Richmond, and on the Appomattox about the same distance from Petersburg. A glance at the map will show these two places, the "Point of Rocks" near Port Walthall five miles up the Appomattox, and "Osborn" nineteen miles down the James River from Richmond. The banks of both rivers are, at these points, bluffs some 120 feet high. A line drawn across from point to point includes within the rivers a peninsula of more than thirty square miles. The neck of this peninsula by this line across it is cut by deep, wide, and quite impassable ravines for about a quarter of the distance up from the James and nearly half way up from the Appomattox, leaving considerably less than a mile of hard, dry land between the heads of the two ravines, to be fortified and intrenched. The water of both rivers around the whole peninsula and opposite the ravines was deep enough to float our largest draught monitors.

I took special pains to have this position thoroughly examined and reported upon by a very competent man who made a good map of it. It was evident that if this neck of land could be seized, as it might well be with the aid of the navy, and a properly intrenched line from river to river put across at that point, there would be more than thirty square miles of land, large enough for a base of supplies and encampment of an army of any probable size, easily defensible by five thousand men against any possible attack on the land side, the navy holding the waters. With a battery which would protect a naval depot at City Point, a bluff at the junction of the two rivers, water transportation could be covered, within eight miles of Richmond, and less from Petersburg, and an intrenched camp could be made of Bermuda Hundred more impregnable than Fortress Monroe. I thought this should be the basis of operations by the Army of the Potomac against Richmond. Troops could be brought from Washington and the North by water transportation in three days to the amount of a hundred thousand men without the loss of

BANQUET AT FIFTH AVENUE HOTEL, NEW YORK, NOVEMBER 15, 1864. TO GENERAL BUTLER FOR PRESERVING THE PEACE AT THE NEW YORK ELECTIONS.
REV. HENRY WARD BEECHER NOMINATING HIM FOR PRESIDENT.

a single man by straggling, desertion, or sickness. The location was a healthy one. Supplies could always come up the river from the North by water, and the enormous cost of supplying the army through the sixty odd miles of march by land from Washington to Richmond would be saved.

On the 1st day of April, General Grant came down to Fortress Monroe to consult with me as to the campaign against the rebel capital. It was the first time I ever met him. I showed him my maps of the department and also of the lay of the land around Richmond. I showed him also that Richmond was by no means as strongly fortified on the south side as it had been on the north, and that the country surrounding it on the south side was high, healthy land suitable for campaigning. But whether it was determined to make the attack on the north side of the James or on the south, Bermuda and City Point should be used as a base of operations. City Point on the opposite side of the peninsula, which was known as Bermuda Hundred, needed to be fortified and held as a depot for the navy and for the water transportation of the army. At Wilson's Wharf, afterwards Fort Pocahontas, on the north side of the James River, and at Fort Powhatan, shortly above, on the south side, were the only two points where batteries could be erected by the rebels to hinder the passage of transports on the river. These points were to be seized and strongly fortified so as to be surely held. This was afterwards done.

Grant was very much struck with my views thus given and the information thus imparted. After a full consideration, he said he thought such a plan should be adopted, and he approved of it. "But," said he, "bringing my troops to the James by water will uncover Washington, and Lee may attack there."

To that I answered: "Lee cannot march troops enough to attack Washington in eight days after he gets in motion. Keeping our transportation here ready, we can send sufficient men to Washington in three days to meet him, without losing a man, because it is all inland navigation." [1]

It also happened that I was proven right, for in the summer

---

[1] In the re-transfer of McClellan's army in 1862, Halleck reports that "On the *first* of August I ordered General Burnside to immediately embark his troops at Newport News [on the James River], transfer them to Acquia Creek [near Washington], and take position opposite Fredericksburg. This officer moved with great promptness, and reached Acquia Creek on the night of the *third*."

Lee did send Early to make an attack on Washington with his corps, it being known that quite all the veteran troops had been drawn to the Army of the Potomac, and substantially all others. Early began his attack upon Washington, and Wright with his Sixth Corps was sent from City Point by water, and I sent a portion of the Nineteenth Corps, and although the transportation was by no means conducted with all the celerity possible, yet our troops got to Washington in time to repulse Early's attack.

Grant seemed very doubtful whether the march could be made as quickly as I claimed. He appeared to have no idea of the capabilities of transportation by vessels in smooth water. I endeavored to convince him that the transportation could be thus speedily effected, but he called my attention to the fact that it took McClellan three months to move less than thirty thousand troops from Washington to Fortress Monroe, and the whole country was ransacked for boats, and all knew of the expedition during that time.

He said he was quite sure that the government at Washington would not permit him thus to uncover it. He said he thought the campaign could be best conducted in this way: The Army of the Potomac should attack Lee's army and drive it back to Richmond. An army under my command, if, as I said, it could be done, should be put around Richmond on the south side of the James, marching by the left flank. The two armies should join above Richmond and thus scoop it out of the Confederacy, cutting off all the sources of supply for Lee's army unless he could break through our lines when we were acting together on the defensive.

Grant asked me if I supposed it possible to surprise City Point and this peninsula of Bermuda Hundred and so hold it as to get around Richmond with my troops with my left resting on the James, ready to join with him in ten days after the Army of the Potomac crossed the Rapidan.

I told him there was not the slightest trouble about that. I would undertake to transport thirty thousand men up to Bermuda Hundred and City Point with all their ammunition and supplies in twenty-four hours after I was notified of the march of his army across the Rapidan. By besieging West Point, at the head of York River, and beginning to fortify it, erecting store-houses, as if I was making a base of supplies for my army when it landed to meet the army of the enemy,

I could so far hoodwink Lee and his officers that they would believe I was there fifty miles away from Richmond for the purpose of joining Grant's army. I could gather the water craft to transport my army from Yorktown, Gloucester, and Fortress Monroe in twenty-four hours, so as to be up the James River at City Point and Bermuda before the enemy knew that I was moving in that direction. I explained to him in great detail every step that I proposed to take to do this, and thus showed him every one by which I afterwards did that very thing.

He at first said it was impossible, but I so far convinced him that he agreed that the enterprise should be undertaken, and that he him- self would move upon the quartermaster-general to allow me to procure my own transportation so that I might make the expedition secretly. He pressed upon me over and over again that my objective point must be Richmond, and that I must be there on the south side within ten days after his march began, as he would be there on the north side of the James to join me.

General Grant further informed me that General Banks was moving up Red River, and had been ordered to get through within a limited time, so that if I needed additional force, a part of his army would be ordered to reinforce me instead of moving against Mobile.

He said that it was particularly desirable that I should have the Weldon Railroad cut at Hicksford, as that would prevent reinforce- ments coming from the South and supplies from reaching Richmond, so that we should be able the more easily to starve Lee out.

He remained some three days examining into the details of the proposed campaign, studying with care the topography of the country around Richmond, with which he seemed to have no acquaintance, and discussing matters of the exchange of prisoners.

One thing he impressed upon me: that I must be sure to hold City Point in any event, and make Bermuda impregnable; so that if he failed in turning the left flank of General Lee and driving him back into Richmond, he could march with his own army by the left flank across the James and join me at City Point.

I insert his orders. Let them tell the story of that planned cam- paign, which was carried out in every point by the Army of the James, and in no single particular by the Army of the Potomac, save that they came down to take advantage of the refuge we had prepared for them.

[*Confidential.*]

FORTRESS MONROE, VA., April 2, 1864.

General: — In the spring campaign, which it is desirable shall commence at as early a day as practicable, it is proposed to have co-operative action of all the armies in the field, as far as this object can be accomplished. It will not be possible to unite our armies into two or three large ones, to act as so many units, owing to the absolute necessity of holding on to the territory already taken from the enemy. But, generally speaking, concentration can be practically effected by armies moving to the interior of the enemy's country from the territory they have to guard. By such movement they interpose themselves between the enemy and the country to be guarded, thereby reducing the numbers necessary to guard important points, or at least occupy the attention of a part of the enemy's force, if no greater object is gained. Lee's army and Richmond being the greater objects towards which our attention must be directed in the next campaign, it is desirable to unite all the force we can against them. The necessity of covering Washington with the Army of the Potomac, and of covering your department with your army, makes it impossible to unite these forces at the beginning of any move. I propose, therefore, what comes nearest this of anything that seems practicable. The Army of the Potomac will act from its present base, Lee's army being the objective point. You will collect all the forces from your command that can be spared from garrison duty,— I should say not less than twenty thousand men — to operate on the south side of James River, Richmond being your objective point. To the force you already have will be added about ten thousand men from South Carolina, under Major-General Gillmore, who will command them in person. Maj.-Gen. W. F. Smith is ordered to report to you, to command the troops sent into the field from your own department.

General Gillmore will be ordered to report to you at Fortress Monroe, with all the troops on transports, by the 18th instant, or as soon thereafter as practicable. Should you not receive notice by that time to move, you will make such disposition of them and your other forces as you may deem best calculated to deceive the enemy as to the real move to be made.

When you are notified to move, take City Point with as much force as possible. Fortify, or, rather, intrench at once, and concentrate all your troops for the field there as rapidly as you can. From City Point directions cannot be given at this time for your further movements.

The fact that has already been stated — that is, that Richmond is to be your objective point, and that there is to be co-operation between your force and the Army of the Potomac — must be your guide. This indicates the necessity of your holding close to the south bank of the James River as you advance. Then, should the enemy be forced into his intrenchments in Richmond, the Army of the Potomac would follow, and by means of transports the two armies would become a unit.

All the minor details of your advance are left entirely to your direction. If, however, you think it practicable to use your cavalry south of you so as to cut the railroad about Hicksford about the time of the general advance, it would be of immense advantage. You will please forward for my information, at the earliest practicable day, all orders, details, and instructions you may give for the execution of this order.

U. S. GRANT,
Lieutenant-General.

To MAJ.-GEN. B. F. BUTLER.

It was specially enjoined upon me to regulate my movements by those of the Army of the Potomac, so as to co-operate with it, and that both should move at the same moment, "rain or shine."

Early in the spring of 1864 the political campaign for the presidency was in progress. Indeed, the hopes of the most far-seeing rebel statesmen, and of General Lee especially, and the conduct of the military campaign by the enemy, were to a great extent regulated by the endeavor to hold on with such success in the war as to tire out the people of the North. This was done with the expectation that the Democrats and the Peace Party, as it was called, would be able to elect a President, who it was foreshadowed would be McClellan. This idea expressed itself in the Chicago Democratic Convention by the resolution that the war was a failure. Indeed, I have always believed that Lee's only hopes were to prolong the war with such success as might be gained until the presidential election should take place. I have blamed him because, when Lincoln was elected, which determined the fate of the Confederacy, the decision was not gracefully acceded to. It doubtless would have been except for the obstinacy of President Davis, who insisted upon the revocation of the proclamation of emancipation as one of the terms of peace.

Secretary Chase was making a very strenuous endeavor to be the candidate of the Republican party, using, as he well might, all the great power of his office as Secretary of the Treasury for that purpose.

In the early spring I was visited by one of his most confidential officials, who held his place directly from the Secretary and without the intervention of the President or Senate, and who at the time controlled the means of enabling men to make fortunes greater in number and larger in amount than any other treasury official has ever held to my knowledge. This control was in connection with the administration of the captured and abandoned property act, and also with the admitting of cotton into our lines. This power alone could furnish plenty of funds for a political campaign. His official duties brought him in not unfrequent contact with myself.

In the early spring he called upon me at Fortress Monroe, ostensibly upon some official business. After that was finished the actual object of his visit was disclosed.

" There has been some criticism, General," said he, " based upon the assertion that Mr. Chase is using the powers of his office to aid his presidential aspirations. What do you think of Mr. Chase's action, assuming that he does so ? "

" I see no objection," I answered, " to his using his office to advance his presidential aspirations by every honorable means, providing President Lincoln will let him do it. It is none of my business, but I have for some time thought that Lincoln was more patient than I should have been, but if he doesn't object, nobody else has either the right or the power so to do."

· " Then, General, you approve of Mr. Chase's course in this regard ? "

" Yes ; he has a right to use in a proper manner every means he has to further a laudable ambition."

" As Chase is a Western man," he continued, " had not the Vice-President better come from the East ? Who, General, do you think would make a good candidate with Mr. Chase ? "

" There are plenty of good men," I answered, " but as Chase is a very pronounced anti-slavery man and Free-Soiler, Gen. John A. Dix, of New York, would bring to his banner and at the polls the War Democrats, of whom Dix claims to be a fair representative."

" You are a War Democrat, General," said he ; " would you take that position with Chase, yourself ? "

" Are you authorized by Mr. Chase to put this question to me and report my answer to him for his consideration ? "

" You may rest assured," was the reply ; " I am fully empowered by Mr. Chase to put the question, and he hopes the answer will be favorable."

"Say, then," I answered, " that I have no desire to be Vice-President. I am forty-five years old ; I am in command of a fine army ; the closing campaign of the war is about beginning, and I hope to be able to do some further service for the country, and I should not, at my time of life, wish to be Vice-President, even if I had no other position. Assure him that my determination in this matter has no connection with himself personally. I will not be a candidate for any elective office whatever until the war is over."

SIMON CAMERON.

"I will report your determination to Mr. Chase," said he, " and I can assure you, for I know his feelings, that he will hear it with regret."

We shook hands and parted.

Within three weeks afterwards, the Hon. Simon Cameron, who stood very high in Mr. Lincoln's confidence, came to me at Fortress Monroe. This was after a high position in the coming military campaign had been allotted me by General Grant, in the results of which I had the highest hope, and for which I had been laboring. Cameron and myself had from the beginning of the war been in warm friendly relations and I owed much to him which I can never repay save with gratitude. Therefore, he spoke with directness.

"The President, as you know," said he, " intends to be a candidate for re-election, and as his friends indicate that Mr. Hamlin should no longer be a candidate for Vice-President, and as he is from New England, the President thinks his place should be filled by someone from that section.   Besides reasons of personal friendship which would make it pleasant to have you with him, he believes that as you were the first prominent Democrat who volunteered for the war, your candidature would add strength to the ticket, especially with the War Democrats, and he hopes that you will allow your friends to co-operate with his to place you in that position."

"Please say to Mr. Lincoln," I replied, "that while I appreciate with the fullest sensibilities his act of friendship and the high compliment he pays me, yet I must decline.   Tell him that I said laughingly that with the prospects of a campaign before me I would not quit the field to be Vice-President even with himself as President, unless he would give me bond in sureties in the full sum of his four years' salary that within three months after his inauguration he will die unresigned.   Ask him what he thinks I have done to deserve to be punished at forty-six years of age by being made to sit as presiding officer of the Senate and listen for four years to debates more or less stupid in which I could take no part or say a word, or even be allowed to vote upon any subject which might concern the welfare of the country, except when my enemies might think my vote would injure me in the estimation of the people, and therefore by some parliamentary trick make a tie upon such questions so that I might be compelled to vote.   And then at the end of four years, as nowadays no Vice-President is ever elected President, because of the dignity of the position I have held, I should not be permitted to go on with my profession, and therefore there would be nothing open for me to do, save to ornament my lot in the cemetery tastefully and get into it gracefully and respectfully as a Vice-President should do.   No, no, my friend.   To be serious, tell the President I will do everything I can to aid his election if he is nominated, and that I hope he will be, as until this war is finished there should be no change of administration."

"I am sorry you won't go on with us," replied my friend, "but I think you are sound in your judgment." [1]

---

[1] The following is a statement of the matter made by Mr. Cameron during his lifetime: —

"I had been summoned from Harrisburg by the President to consult with him in relation to the approaching campaign.   He was holding a reception when I arrived, but after it was over we had a long and earnest conversation.   Mr. Lincoln had been much distressed at the intrigues in and out of his Cabinet to defeat his renomination; but that was now assured, and the question of

"Is Mr. Chase making any headway in his candidature?" I asked.

"Yes, some; and he is using the whole power of the treasury to help himself."

"Well," said I, "that is the right thing for him to do."

"Do you think so?" said he.

"Yes. Why ought not he to do that if Lincoln lets him?"

"How can Lincoln help letting him?"

"By tipping him out. If I were Lincoln I should say to the Secretary of the Treasury: 'You know I am a candidate for re-election, as I suppose it is proper for me to be. Now, every one of my equals has a right to be a candidate against me, and every citizen of the United States is my equal who is not my subordinate. Now, if you desire to be a candidate I will give you the present opportunity to be one by making you my equal and not my subordinate, and I will do that in any way which will be the most pleasant to you, but things cannot go on as they are.' You see I think it is Lincoln's fault and not Chase's that he is using the treasury against Lincoln."

"Right again," said Cameron; "I will tell Mr. Lincoln every word you have said."

What happened after that is history.

Preparations were pushed with vigor for the opening campaign. During the early days of April despatches came from General Peck that the enemy were preparing to attack Plymouth.

General Wessels, in command there, however, whose gallant defence of the place is applauded, gave me his belief that the post could be held, if the navy could hold the river. Commander Flusser (who was a Farragut, wanting thirty years' experience, and no higher praise can be given) was sure that he could meet the rebel iron-clad ram, and laughed to scorn the idea of her driving out his gun-

---

a man for the second place on the ticket was freely and earnestly discussed. *Mr. Lincoln thought and so did I that Mr. Hamlin's position during the four years of his administration made it advisable to have a new name substituted.* Several men were freely talked of, but without conclusion as to any particular person. Not long after that I was requested to come to the White House again. I went and the subject was again brought up by the President, and the result of our conversation was *that Mr. Lincoln asked me to go to Fortress Monroe and ask General Butler if he would be willing to run, and, if not, to confer with him upon the subject.*

"General Butler positively declined to consider the subject, saying that he preferred to remain in the military service, and he thought a man could not justify himself in leaving the army in the time of war to run for a political office. The general and myself then talked the matter over freely, and it is my opinion at this distance from the event that he suggested that a Southern man should be given the place. After completing the duty assigned by the President, I returned to Washington and reported the result to Mr. Lincoln. *He seemed to regret General Butler's decision, and afterwards the name of Andrew Johnson was suggested and accepted.* In my judgment Mr. Hamlin never had a serious chance to become the vice-presidential candidate after Mr. Lincoln's renomination was assured."

boats. An attack was made in the night of the 19th of April, by the rebel ram. Flusser was killed by the recoil of a shell from a gun fired by his own hands; the Southfield was sunk; the Miami partially disabled and the rest of our fleet driven out of the Roanoke; the rebel gunboats commanded the town, and Plymouth, after a brave defence, was captured with some sixteen hundred men and considerable provisions.

By direction of the lieutenant-general, I ordered Washington, N. C., to be evacuated, and the troops sent to join the force preparing for the campaign. It will thus be seen that my opinion, given to the War Department upon taking command of this department, that Plymouth and Washington were worse than useless to us, was unhappily verified.

On the 9th of April, General Grant wrote to General Meade a letter [1] in which he set out his whole plan of campaign, which shows how fully at that time the plan of my operations became a fixed fact, and further, how fully it was determined that General Grant should strike the left flank of Lee and turn that so as to drive him into Richmond, which he afterwards did. But Grant was repulsed at the Battle of the Wilderness, so that it became necessary for him to march by his left flank and come down to co-operate with me against Lee, as he afterwards did, at City Point, Bermuda Hundred, and Petersburg.

In consultation with Gen. Wm. F. Smith, as to the movements of the enemy in North Carolina, the subject of my proposed army co-operation with the Army of the Potomac, by moving it to that State, was discussed with General Grant at his visit. Smith very much favored it, saying our army should be called the " Army of Cape Fear River." I learned afterwards from General Smith that General Grant had considerably favored such co-operative movement before he came to Fortress Monroe, and that Smith himself was quite impressed with it, as, among other things, it would be a means of relieving our forces in North Carolina from their impending danger. Meanwhile, orders came to the quartermaster to prepare transportation for two and a half millions of rations to North Carolina. With this fact in view, knowing that General Smith had strongly advised a movement into North Carolina instead of up the James, and fearing lest the lieu-

---

[1] See Appendix No. 17.

tenant-general, in his kindness of heart and delicacy toward me, a stranger, had, partly from these motives, yielded to my plan of movement up the James, when his own unbiassed judgment would have dictated a different course, and thinking perhaps, also, that he might have desired to give General Smith a separate command, if it would not interfere with mine, I sent General Smith, at his own request, to General Grant, bearing a letter in which I took leave to say that if a movement upon the enemy in North Carolina was intended, as I was inclined to believe was the case because of the fact that the quartermaster had been called upon to furnish transportation for two and a half millions of rations to that State, any disposition of the troops under my command which he might think best in the interests of the service, would be most agreeable to me, and that I should be happy to co-operate with him in any such movement.[1]

I received from General Grant a generous and considerate reply to my letter, in which he assured me that no operations in North Carolina were intended, and that it was his wish that with all the forces of the Army of the James that could be spared from other duty, and such additional troops as had been ordered to report to me at Fortress Monroe, I should seize upon City Point and act directly in concert with the Army of the Potomac, with Richmond as the objective point.[2]

On the 21st of April, Lieutenant-Colonel Dent, of General Grant's staff, came to Fortress Monroe as bearer of a letter and memorandum of instructions.[3] Before his arrival Plymouth, which General Grant desired should be held at all hazards, had fallen; but everything else for which they provided had already been done.

From my conversation with Grant and from his reiterated instructions that I was to "intrench and fortify at City Point and Bermuda Hundred;" that "our new base was to be established there;" that "I was to obtain a footing as *far up the south side of the James as I could, in co-operation with the navy;*" that "if I could reach the James above Richmond, with my left resting on the south bank, he would join me there," i. e., on the north bank of the James, thus scooping Richmond out of the Confederacy; that "that might be advisable, anyhow;" that I should "make an attack on the city only in case" I heard of his advance on that side, "or the enemy

---

[1] See Appendix No. 18. [2] See Appendix No. 19. [3] See Appendix No. 20.

looking for danger on that side ; " and because it was impossible for the fleet to go above Osborn, which is just below Trent's Reach, I drew and sent to Admiral Lee, in obedience to the lieutenant-general's letter, after full verbal conference with the admiral and at his request, a plan of the operations to be made, a copy of which was sent to General Grant, and submitted to the President, and never dissented from in any quarter.[1]

It appears, both from the instructions and the plan, that while Richmond was my " objective point," yet it was never contemplated by them or by me, that any attack or assault should be made upon Richmond, except in co-operation with the Army of the Potomac, or any movement made further up the river than the navy could aid me.   General Grant had told me, in conversation, if I could hold the Petersburg and Richmond Railroad cut *for ten days*, and secure our proposed base at Bermuda and City Point, that by that time he would join me there, or on the James above Richmond, having either whipped Lee's army or forced it into the intrenchments around Richmond, when the combined armies of the Potomac and my command would invest Richmond, the navy holding the James as we approached.

It further appeared from the reply of Admiral Lee [2] that it was considered by him impossible for the navy to go above Trent's Reach or Osborn, on the right of the proposed intrenched lines of Bermuda Hundred, which was the highest point ever reached by the navy until after the surrender of Richmond.   The admiral also doubted whether it was possible to make the movement a surprise, and argued strenuously against an attempt by the joint expedition to go above City Point,— Osborn, the point proposed by me, being almost twenty miles beyond by the river.

To divert the enemy's attention, all the white troops were concentrated at Yorktown and Gloucester Point, and all the colored infantry and artillery at Hampton, the colored cavalry at Williamsburg, and all the white cavalry at the line beyond Norfolk in the direction of Suffolk.

About the 1st of May West Point, at the head of York River, was seized, preparations were made for building wharves and landings, and fortifications were begun, as if with the intention of making this the base of operations for a junction with Grant's army.

---

[1] See Appendix No. 21.   [2] See Appendix No. 22.

General Meigs, quartermaster-general, was of opinion that it would be nearly, if not quite impossible to gather sufficient transportation to move at one time thirty thousand men more than a hundred and thirty miles, or move with their artillery and supplies, at least without attracting the attention of the enemy, because when General McClellan tried to move the Army of the Potomac from Washington to Fortress Monroe, scarcely twenty-five thousand men were able to be got afloat at one time, after months of preparations known to the whole country.

But, notwithstanding his opinion, General Meigs most earnestly and zealously aided our enterprise, and allowed me to procure in my own way all the transportation I deemed necessary to move the army and its supplies. But it was impossible to obtain sufficient transportation to take with us all the supply trains of the army, and it was some days before our whole trains got up, although every exertion was made by Colonel Biggs, chief quartermaster of the department, and Col. J. Wilson Shaffer, my chief of staff, to whose powers of business organization the country is largely indebted for a movement of troops which, for numbers, celerity, distance, and secrecy, was never before equalled, in any particular, in the history of war.

On the 30th of April I received from General Grant my final orders,[1] to start my forces on the night of the 4th of May so as to get up James River as far as possible by daylight the next morning, and to push on with the greatest energy from that time for the accomplishment of the object designated in the plan of campaign.

General Gillmore did not arrive from Charleston until the 3d of May, so that I was deprived of the full opportunity of organizing the Tenth Corps, and did not have so much consultation with him upon the plans of the movement as was desirable. His reasons for the delay were substantially set forth in a letter which I addressed to General Grant on the 20th of April.[2]

The iron-clads had not come up, and both these causes of delay were sources of great anxiety as well to the lieutenant-general as to the general commanding the department.[3]

On the 4th of May the embarkation began at Yorktown,[4] of the Tenth and Eighteenth Army Corps, under the command of Generals W. F. Smith and Q. A. Gillmore, amounting to about twenty-five

---

[1] See Appendix No. 23.   [2] See Appendix No. 24.
[3] See Appendix No. 25.   [4] See Appendix No. 26.

thousand men. The colored troops (part of the Eighteenth Corps), about fifty-five hundred men, under command of Brig.-Gen. E. W. Hincks, embarked at Fortress Monroe. At sunrise of the 5th, General Kautz, with three thousand cavalry, moved from Suffolk to cut the Weldon Railroad at Hicksford, and thence to join us at City Point. Col. Robert West, with eighteen hundred colored cavalry, moved at the same time from Williamsburg to meet us at Turkey Bend, opposite City Point.

The armed transports, under the command of Brig.-Gen. Charles K. Graham, moved at night on the 4th up James River, destroyed the enemy's signal stations, and arrived at City Point at 11 A. M., of the 5th, finding no torpedoes. This service was most gallantly and skilfully performed.

At daylight of the 5th the whole transport fleet was assembled at Newport News, and ascended the river, led by the iron-clads and the vessels of the fleet, under Acting Rear-Admiral Lee. Wilson's Wharf was seized and occupied by two regiments of colored troops. Fort Powhatan, seven miles above, was also occupied by a regiment of the same troops, all under the immediate command of Brig.-Gen. E. A. Wilde, who had remained in the service although he lost an arm at the battle of Gettysburg.

General Hincks, with the remainder of his division, seized City Point and began fortifying it, while the white troops of the two corps pushed on to Bermuda Hundred, and by eight o'clock ten thousand men, with their artillery, were landed. The colored troops thus took the first possession of the James, and were intrusted with the duty of keeping open the water communications of the army, which duty was ever after fully done by them, although they were several times attacked by the enemy.

We arrived about five o'clock in the evening. As soon as my boat had come to anchor one of my confidential scouts came off to it. He had been at Richmond some weeks, and he brought me a letter from my correspondent there, Miss Van Lieu. He stated that quite all the troops had gone from Richmond to Lee's army, relying upon that city being garrisoned by troops which had shortly before been sent down to North Carolina from there, and were expected back. But they had not yet returned, and if I would send up at once before it was known that I was there, Richmond could be taken without any difficulty. The Southern troops were expected very soon, so that the attack must be made at once.

I placed the most implicit reliance upon this statement and was very much tempted to march myself with what troops I had landed and seize Drury's Bluff at least. It was a march of but a little rising fourteen miles. My map showed that there was a stage road direct up to the Richmond turnpike, and then, of course, directly into Richmond.

I called on my generals, Smith and Gillmore, and explained this plan. I said to them that our troops were perfectly fresh, and that

CONFEDERATE CAPITOL AT RICHMOND.

indeed they would be better for a march, having been twenty-four hours on the transports. I showed them by the map that there was a direct road up there. The night was a fair one and not dark, and I suggested to them that they march as soon as the men had got their coffee and supper. The men all had two days' rations in their haversacks and I would send up plenty of supplies by the wagons in the morning, and they could easily get there by daylight. They both very strongly objected to the expedition. One of them intimated that he should feel it his duty to refuse it even if it were ordered. I said I should not order it for I could have no hopes of an expedition made against the will of the commander.

I was tempted to go myself, but I had Kautz out before the enemy, and West with his negro cavalry out making a demonstration on the Chickahominy. I had all the details of the movement of the army only under the personal supervision and knowledge of my staff, and I thought it was my duty not to go. I sent, however, for Weitzel, but then it had got quite well along in the night. Weitzel said to me: "General, I shall go if you order me to, as you know, and do the very best I can, but it is exceedingly hazardous, and if it should fail after your two corps commanders, Smith and Gillmore, have so strenuously advised that it should not be undertaken, it would entirely ruin you, although to take charge of it under your orders would not harm me. They have been to me and told me what you want done, and supposing you would send for me have advised very strongly against it. And as your strongest friend, I myself must advise against it, especially because I think they will throw every obstacle in the way of our having an early march." At this I gave it up.

The only delay experienced in the movement up James River came from General Gillmore, who did not effect his embarkation with the celerity which his orders and place in line required, and I telegraphed him that having waited for his corps from Port Royal, I was not a little surprised at the necessity for waiting for him at Fortress Monroe, and instructed him to push forward.[1]

During the 6th the remainder of the troops were landed. A march of about seven miles brought us to the proposed line, which was at once occupied, and intrenching begun. It was discovered that on the opposite side of the Appomattox, at Springhill, the ground overlooked the Bermuda side. We occupied this point by General Hincks with his colored troops, and a very strong redoubt was constructed, effectually holding the right bank of that river, and covering the left flank of our line.

On the same day General Smith made a reconnoissance toward the railroad between Petersburg and Richmond, but did not strike the road.

On the evening of the 5th of May our operations were communicated by telegraph to the lieutenant-general.[2]

In pursuance of my instructions from General Grant that I should cut the railroad leading into Richmond so as to stop the enemy's

---

supplies, as fast and as early as possible, without waiting for the report of Kautz's cavalry which were to cut the railroad south of Petersburg, I determined at once to make a demonstration in my front to destroy the railroad as far as possible between Petersburg and Richmond, especially at Chester Junction, where there was a branch road which came around Petersburg and led to it and Richmond.

Accordingly, on the morning of the 7th, I ordered Gillmore to move to his front and demonstrate against the railroad for that purpose. He reported to me that he "did not make the movement for reasons which appeared to him perfectly satisfactory."

On the same morning I received a telegram from Mr. Stanton, giving such information as the department possessed in regard to the operations of General Grant, a copy of which I at once sent to my two corps commanders, Generals Gillmore and Smith, accompanied by despatches urging upon them the necessity for diligence in putting their lines in posture of defence.[1]

Meanwhile I determined to cut the railroad by a movement which should not fail, and putting it under the command of General Smith, I issued an order to General Gillmore to cause one brigade of each division of his command to report, for the purpose, to General Smith at eight o'clock on the 7th. I informed General Smith of this order, and also directed him to make a like detail from his command for the purposes of this movement.[2]

Although my order to Gillmore was explicit, yet he claimed that his troops which I had ordered should report to General Smith, were still under his own command; and because of his unofficer-like interference it became necessary that I should issue a general order placing General Smith in command of the detached forces of the Tenth and Eighteenth Army Corps, which had been ordered to operate toward Petersburg and Richmond on the railroad.[3]

By this movement we succeeded in destroying a portion of the railroad between Richmond and Petersburg, so as to break off communication between these points and interrupt the forwarding of troops and supplies from the South to Lee's army.

On the evening of the same day a report of operations was telegraphed to the Secretary of War.[4]

---

[1] See Appendix No. 29.   [2] See Appendix No. 30.
[3] See Appendix No. 31.   [4] See Appendix No. 32.

In my report 'to the Secretary of War I made a request for a portion of the reserves which General Grant had assured me were to be collected in Washington, to be sent to the "weak points," with the idea that if we had them we could demonstrate toward Petersburg with one portion of our force, and toward Richmond with the other, each column strong enough to sustain itself, after leaving enough to complete the intrenchment of our lines, which was deemed of the first importance. Besides, as the Army of the Potomac was to join us in a few days "anyhow," the reserves would be with us ready for service. But, I suppose, we were not the "weak point," as with the exception of a single regiment of heavy artillery for the trenches, no substantial reinforcements ever came to us until after we were joined by the Army of the Potomac; but, on the contrary, as will be seen hereafter, we sent seventeen thousand men to the rescue of Grant's army at Cold Harbor.

GEN. CHARLES A. HECKMAN.

Finding it impossible to get on with Major-General Gillmore's tardiness of movement, and knowing that he was before the Senate for confirmation to the grade which he filled, I wrote a note to the Chairman of the Military Committee of the Senate, asking that he bring his name before the Senate at once and have it rejected by that body, giving my reasons for making the request.[1]

I prefer to give from the documents and contemporaneous action, such criticism or laudation of the acts of officers under my command as occurred from day to day, when the mind could view them impartially by light of results, and omissions, or blunders in action or conduct, unprejudiced by subsequent events or malign influences, rivalries, or ambitions. I never gave an officer my confidence whom I did not think worthy, and if any blame or praise was due to him it came at the time. It was never an afterthought arising from

---

[1] See Appendix No. 33.

his subsequent acts toward me, censuring either my military or political conduct.

On the 7th General Smith struck the railroad near Port Walthall Junction, and began its destruction. Generals Brooks and Heckman of his corps had severe fighting, with some loss, but with more damage to the enemy.

Colonel West, of the colored cavalry, had most successfully performed his march, having driven the enemy from the fords of the Chickahominy after a lively skirmish, and crossing and joining us opposite City Point, as ordered.

During the day of the 8th no movement was made, but the troops were given rest, dispositions being made to move our whole force to the railroad and destroy as much of it as possible. General Smith was to endeavor to reach the railroad bridge over Swift Creek, supported by General Gillmore on the left toward Chester Station.

It was found quite impossible to discover any ford to cross the creek, and the railroad bridge was strongly held by the enemy with intrenched artillery. General Gillmore's command destroyed a large portion of the road, and in the afternoon the troops were got in position to force the enemy back on the next day. That evening I had a consultation with my corps commanders, and it was determined that we should make a vigorous movement on the morrow to pass Swift creek, to reach the Appomattox, and destroy the bridges across it. Co-operating with this, General Hincks was to move on the south side of the Appomattox upon Petersburg itself, and at least create a diversion, if he did not carry the city, while the enemy were defending the line of the creek. Orders were prepared and sent to General Hincks for that purpose. At the close of the consultation he was advised by a despatch that it was thought best he should not advance beyond his picket-line before 7 A. M., so as to give an opportunity for all the rebel forces to be drawn to the front of General Smith, from whom Hincks should have word before engaging the enemy.[1]

Upon my return to my headquarters that evening I found several despatches from the Secretary of War, giving information of the movements of General Grant.

The first stated that on Friday night Lee's army was in "full retreat" for Richmond, Grant pursuing; that Hancock had passed

---

[1] See Appendix No. 34.

Spottsylvania Court-House, on the morning of the 8th; and that Fredericksburg was occupied by Federal forces.[1]

This was followed by the information that another despatch from Grant had just been received at the War Department; that he was marching with his whole army to make a junction with me, but had not determined his route.[2]

A despatch of a still later hour brought from the War Department the intelligence that advices from the front gave ground for the belief that Grant's operations would prove a success and complete victory, and that the enemy's only hope was in heavy reinforcements from Beauregard.[3]

To this news, which I fully credited, save as to the reinforcements, as I had Beauregard at Petersburg, I made reply, detailing the operations under my command, and stating that Beauregard, with a large portion of his force, was, by the cutting of the railroads by Kautz's cavalry, left south of Petersburg, while the portion of his forces under the command of Hill which reached that city had been whipped by us that day, after a severe fight, so that General Grant would not be troubled with further reinforcements to Lee from Beauregard's army.[4]

If " Lee's army was in full retreat toward Richmond," " Grant pursuing with his army on Friday night" (the 6th) (not true), if " Hancock had passed Spottsylvania Court-House on Sunday morning, the 8th " (not true), if " Grant, on that day, was on the march to join me, but had not determined the route " (not true), if " General Grant's operations had proved a great success and a complete victory " (not true), and " the only hope of Lee was in heavy reinforcements from Beauregard " (which I knew was futile), then it was plain that I should carry out my instructions, secure my base at Bermuda Hundred, and move as far up the James as possible, to co-operate with the Army of the Potomac in its investment of Richmond.[5]   No

---

[1] See Appendix No. 35.   [2] See Appendix No. 36.
[3] See Appendix No. 37.   [4] See Appendix No. 38.

[5] Lieutenant-General Grant, in his report to the country, made fifteen months afterwards, gives a different account of the "victories," "full retreats," and "rapid pursuit," of the days from the 6th to the 9th of May. It is not true that he had not determined his route on the 8th, assuming his now report to be true; for he says that on the 7th, "I determined to push on, and put my whole force between him and Richmond; and orders were at once issued for a movement by his (the enemy's) *right* flank." This would bring General Grant to the James, below Richmond.

Extract from General Grant's Official Report, pp. 6, 7.

" The Battle of the Wilderness was renewed by us at 5 o'clock on the morning of the 6th, and continued with unabated fury until darkness set in, each army holding substantially the same

time was to be lost in attacking Petersburg upon either side of the Appomattox, but Richmond was to be invested on the south side of the James in ten days from the 4th of May, to hold all the troops there from marching to the aid of Lee, and I was to throw my force between Beauregard and Lee, and prevent a possible junction of their forces. General Grant's victorious army was pressing the broken troops of Lee within three days' march of Richmond at the moment, and while I was securing the line of the Appomattox, Lee might be upon my rear and line of communications. At the same time I received a despatch which showed that the enemy had withdrawn from North Carolina, and might be concentrating upon Richmond to form a junction with Lee.[1]

The enemy had already withdrawn all their troops from South Carolina. While meditating upon all this information, the correctness of which I could not doubt, for it had been sent from General Grant for my guidance, I was roused by a communication from both of my corps commanders, in the handwriting of General Gillmore, suggesting, as the result of a conference between them, whether it would not be better to withdraw our forces to our lines, destroying all that part of the road north of Chester Station, and then cross the Appomattox on a pontoon bridge and cut all the roads, entering Petersburg on that side.[2]

To that letter I at once replied that, while regretting the infirmity of purpose which did not permit them to state to me while personally present the suggestion contained in their note, but allowed me to go to my headquarters under the impression that a far different purpose was advised by them, I should not yield to their written suggestions which implied a change of plan within thirty minutes after I left

---

position that they had on the evening of the 5th. After dark, the enemy made a feeble attempt to turn our right flank, capturing several hundred prisoners and creating considerable confusion. But the promptness of General Sedgwick, who was personally present and commanded that part of our line, soon re-formed it and restored order. On the morning of the 7th, reconnoissances showed that the enemy nad fallen behind his intrenched lines, with pickets to the front, covering a part of the battle-field. From this it was evident to my mind that the two days' fighting had satisfied him of his inability to further maintain the contest on the open field, notwithstanding his advantage of position, and that he would wait an attack behind his works. I therefore determined to push on, and put my whole force between him and Richmond, and orders were at once issued for a movement by his right flank. On the night of the 7th, the march was commenced towards Spottsylvania Court-House, the Fifth Corps moving on the most direct road. But the enemy, having become apprised of our movement, and having the shorter line, was enabled to reach there first. On the 8th, General Warren met a force of the enemy which had been sent out to oppose and delay his advance, to gain time to fortify the line taken up at Spottsylvania. This force was steadily driven back on the main force, within the recently constructed works, after considerable fighting, resulting in severe loss to both sides. On the morning of the 9th, General Sheridan started on a raid against the enemy's lines of communication with Richmond. The 9th, 10th, and 11th were spent in manœuvring and fighting without decisive results.

[1] See Appendix No. 39.   [2] See Appendix No. 40.

them. I also stated to them that the advices received from the Army of the Potomac convinced me that our movement should be toward Richmond, and gave orders for the disposition of their troops, having in view an early demonstration up James River from the right of our position. And with this letter I sent the proper orders to my corps commanders to carry out the movement indicated in it.[1]

General Gillmore having stated in reply to my letter that he did not know what I intended to do, I directed that he should meet with me for consultation. He did so, and after the fullest explanation of my plan of operations made no objection.

After he retired, I sent a despatch to General Hincks informing him that the news received from the Army of the Potomac would involve a change of plan, and gave him orders not to move on Petersburg as was intended, but to devote his energies to perfecting the defences at City Point and Fort Powhatan.[2]

It will be observed that one movement to take Petersburg was thus frustrated by information from headquarters through Washington which was in every substantial particular *misleading and untrue.*

There was severe fighting on the night of the 9th, the enemy making an attack in force upon Generals Brooks and Heckman, but were handsomely repulsed.

On the 10th the plan of withdrawal of the troops from Swift Creek was carried out without loss, and the railroad wholly destroyed for seven miles, under my personal supervision, there being no such agreement between my corps commanders as would lead them to do any other thing in unison save to protest against the plans of the commanding general.[3]

Generals Smith and Gillmore made separate replies to my letter. These replies did not agree with each other, and, what was of more consequence, they had no effect upon my plans under the instructions and recent information I had received from Lieutenant-General Grant. Another letter of General Smith[4] shows the state of co-operative feeling between my two corps commanders upon other subjects of joint action. They would not now be published save that justice requires that their answers to my implied censure should be made public. This is but fair-play.

[1] See Appendix No. 41.   [2] See Appendix No. 42.
          [3] See Appendix No. 43.   [4] See Appendix No. 44.

Those letters plainly demonstrate that which had become painfully evident before — that my two corps commanders agreed upon but one thing and that was, how they could thwart and interfere with me. Smith's letter shows that Gillmore would do nothing in the world to aid Smith. I did not then think Smith was quite in that frame of mind towards Gillmore, but other evidence has shown me that he was. Indeed, as will appear, it was impossible even to get them to join their intrenchments on our line. One insisted on building on one line, and the other insisted on building on another. This required me to detail General Weitzel from the command of his division to be chief engineer of the department, in order to get these intrenched fortifications, on which our whole safety depended, put in order so that they could be capable of being defended by a small force while we demonstrated towards Richmond.

About twelve o'clock, while the movement of the 9th was going on, the enemy, advancing from Richmond upon our rear, attacked the covering force of the Tenth Corps under Colonel Voorhis of the Sixty-Seventh Ohio, and for a moment forced him back, although he gallantly held his position. General Terry, with the reserve of that corps, advanced from Port Walthall Junction. Two pieces of artillery that had been lost were re-captured by a gallant achievement of the Seventh Connecticut Volunteers, under Lieutenant-Colonel Roman, who drove the enemy back with loss to them of three hundred killed. The woods from which the enemy had been driven took fire under a high wind and their dead and severely wounded were burned. General Terry held his position till night and then withdrew to his place in line. As Brigadier-General Turner's division was retiring, General Hagood, by authority of General Bushrod Johnson of the Confederate forces, sent a flag of truce asking permission to bury their dead and to bring off their wounded, which was granted.

On the morning of the 10th I received advices by signal from General Kautz announcing his return with his entire command. He had failed to reach Hicksford, but had burned the Stony Creek bridge, the Nottoway Bridge, and Jarratt's Station, and captured about one hundred and thirty prisoners, with a loss to his command of about thirty, killed and wounded.[1]

Wishing to have the assistance of General Kautz's cavalry in the

---

[1] See Appendix No. 45.

contemplated movement I gave them rest, and to put the lines in the best possible order to be held with a small force, I rested on the 11th, making ready to move by daylight on the 12th. On the 11th the following orders were issued to the corps commanders and preparations were made to carry them out :—

HEADQUARTERS IN THE FIELD,
May 11, 1864, 9.30 P. M.

MAJOR-GENERAL GILLMORE, COMMANDING TENTH ARMY CORPS :

A movement will be made to-morrow morning at daybreak of the troops in the manner following : General Smith will take all of his corps that can be spared from his line with safety, and will demonstrate against the enemy up the turnpike, extending his line of advance to the left, with his right resting, at the beginning of the movement, on the river at or near Howlett's house, pressing the enemy into their intrenchments with the endeavor to turn them on the left, if not too hotly opposed. General Gillmore will order one division of his corps to report to General Smith with two days' rations ready to march at any time at or after daylight, at General Smith's order. General Gillmore will make such dispositions with the remainder of his corps as to hold the enemy in check if any movement is made upon the rear of General Smith or upon our lines from the direction of Petersburg, holding such troops as may not be necessary to be thrown forward by him upon the turnpike, in reserve, ready to reinforce any point that may be attacked.

Of course, General Smith's demonstration will cover the right of General Gillmore's line of works, unless he [General Smith] is forced back. General Kautz has orders to proceed as soon as the demonstration of General Smith's troops has masked his movements from, at, or near Chester Station, to make demonstrations upon the Danville railroad for the purpose of cutting it. It is intended to develop [by this movement] the entire strength of the enemy in the direction of Richmond, and, if possible, either to force them within their intrenchments or turn them, as the case may be. If successful, it is supposed that the troops will occupy, during the night, the line of advance secured. General Hincks has orders to seize and hold a point [on the Appomattox] opposite General Smith's headquarters pending this movement. The commanding general fails to make further orders in detail because of personal explanation given to each corps commander of the movement intended.

Respectfully,

BENJ. F. BUTLER,
Major-General Commanding.

For good and sufficient reasons, although it called me to abandon my base temporarily, I came to the conclusion to take command in person of this movement so that nothing should be lost because of any disagreement between my corps commanders, neither of whom really desired that the other should succeed.

At daybreak on the 12th, all the movements were made in conformity with these orders. Brigadier-General Ames' brigade was posted near Port Walthall Junction to cover our rear from the enemy's forces arriving at Petersburg from the South. The enemy met us at Proctor or Mill Creek, and after several severe engagements were forced back into their first line of works around Drury's Bluff. As soon as the roads by Chesterfield Court-House were opened by our advance, in obedience to the instructions of the lieutenant-general, General Kautz was sent with his cavalry by those roads to cut the Danville Railroad and the James River Canal. He was not able to strike the canal, but cut the road near Appomattox Station, and thence marched along the line of the road destroying it at several points, but did not succeed in destroying the Nottoway Bridge. Thence, he struck across to the Weldon Railroad again destroying it at Jarratt's Station, and thence by a detour came to City Point.

On the 13th, the enemy making a stand at their line of works, General Gillmore was sent to endeavor to turn their right while Smith attacked the front. Both movements were gallantly accomplished after severe fighting. Meantime, I endeavored to have the navy advance so as to cover our right, which rested near the river, from the fire of the enemy's fleet. But from the correspondence that ensued, it was obvious that we could have no assistance from the navy above Trent's Reach.[1]

On the 14th, General Smith drove the enemy from the first line of works, which we occupied. In the morning of that day I received a telegram from the Secretary of War stating that a despatch just received reported a general attack by Grant, in which great success was achieved; that Hancock had captured Maj.-Gen. Edward Johnson's division, and taken him and Early, and forty cannon, and that the prisoners were counted by thousands.[2]

Twelve hours later the Secretary of War sent me a second tele-

---

[1] See Appendix No. 46.   [2] See Appendix No. 47.

gram confirmatory of the first, in which I was informed that Lee had abandoned his works, and that Grant was pursuing.[1]

These telegrams strengthened me still further in the view that it was necessary to invest Richmond as closely as possible, and prepare to meet General Grant around the intrenchments above the city, to which point I supposed he was marching.

Oh, that the news contained in those despatches had been true! [2]

Believing the information to be true I sent a despatch at 7 P. M. to General Ames, who was watching the enemy at Petersburg,

GENERAL BUTLER'S HORSE.

enclosing "glorious news from Grant," and asking him to guard against surprise and night attack, and to report to me frequently.[3]

Having sent away General Kautz with his cavalry, in obedience to "instructions," I was much crippled in my movements for want of a sufficient cavalry force to cover my left flank, which was "in the air."

---

[1] See Appendix No. 48.

[2] General Grant, in his report (page 7), gives a very different account of the operations of "yesterday" (the 12th), as will be seen by the following : —

"The 9th, 10th, and 11th were spent in manœuvring and fighting, without decisive results. . . . Early on the morning of the 2th a general attack was made on the enemy in position. The Second Corps, Major-General Hancock commanding, carried a salient of his line, capturing most of Johnson's division of Elwell's Corps and twenty pieces of artillery. But the resistance was so obstinate that the advantage gained did not prove decisive. The *13th, 14th, 15th, 16th, 17th,* and *18th* were consumed in manœuvring and *awaiting* the arrival of reinforcements from Washington."

[3] See Appendix No. 49.

To observe the enemy in my rear so as to release the large force which I was obliged to leave there for the purpose of covering my rear, I endeavored to supply this deficiency as below set forth.

At evening of the 14th General Sheridan was reported by Lieutenant-Colonel Fuller, chief quartermaster, as having arrived at Haxalls, or Turkey Bend, on the opposite side of the river, some fourteen miles below, where he asked to be supplied with rations and forage. I telegraphed to Colonel Fuller to give General Sheridan all the forage and rations he needed.[1]

Later in the day I sent a despatch to General Sheridan requesting that he join me with his command, and suggesting that I wished he might be able to capture Chaffin's farm on his side of the river, where there were about two hundred men.[2] But in any event I desired that he send up a force along the north bank of the James to search for torpedoes, and the wires and batteries by which they may be discharged, with instructions to burn any house in which such machines were found, and send to me any persons captured having anything to do with them. I also asked for a personal interview at the earliest moment.

On the 15th General Sheridan called on me at the front, and in conference with him I learned that he thought it would take seven or eight days to refit the horses and men of his command to make his return march. Trusting that General Grant would be with me before that time, and deeming that if General Sheridan's command, numbering four thousand effective men, were encamped on the right of my lines near Howlett's house, where there was an admirable place for a cavalry encampment, that it would be so much in effect addition to my force, holding the position which I desired should be held by the navy, I gave him orders to bring his command at once across the river to Bermuda landing, and encamp it between Howlett's house and the railroad, and informed him that the quartermaster would supply him with the necessary transportation and forage.[3]

At the same time I instructed him to turn over all his disabled and unserviceable horses to the quartermaster at Bermuda, to be turned out to graze.[4]

---

[1] See Appendix No. 50.   [2] See Appendix No. 51.
          [3] See Appendix No. 52.   [4] See Appendix No. 53.

General Sheridan on the next day sent me a copy of his instructions from the Army of the Potomac, but declined to make the movement ordered, although I believe by the Articles of War, having come within the territorial command of a superior officer, he was bound to obey his orders. On the 17th, however, finding that his horses were recruited sooner than he expected, he left us and began his return march. He found out very soon that his horses could be recruited in two days instead of *eight*, when he was called upon to do something for his country.[1]

---

[1] This statement implies a censure on General Sheridan. It seemed to me, when I wrote it, to be just, as it did at the time of the occurrence, and so I choose to let it stand; but since then I have seen publications in which it appears that after General Sheridan called on me and received my orders, — which he disobeyed, — he had a consultation upon the situation with Maj.-Gen. Wm. F. Smith, and got advice from him as to what he should do, which seems to have determined his conduct. So that censure, and very much more, belongs to Smith.

CHAPTER XV.

OPERATIONS OF THE ARMY OF THE JAMES AROUND RICHMOND AND PETERSBURG.

ON the morning of May 16, shortly before five o'clock, I was awakened by a very sharp musketry fire. I at once mounted my horse and rode to the field. I ascertained that the demonstration on the right was too vigorous to be a feint. I immediately issued an order to Gillmore to attack the enemy with rapidity,[1] supposing that they had massed their troops on the right and that Gillmore would be able to go through their line if he attacked with promptness and resolution. But the enemy had made a feint on his line by some artillery fire, and by the exhibition of hardly more than a skirmish line.

I got a reply[2] from him some hours afterwards in which he stated that the enemy had made two attacks upon his front and were handsomely repulsed, but he made no explanation why, with my order in his hands, he did not, having repulsed the enemy, follow up the repulse and make his attack while the repulsed troops were retreating.

I did not appreciate then, as I do now, that it was not the practice in our war where the enemy's attacks were repulsed, that the advantage gained should at once be followed up. A very notable instance of this was at the battle of Gettysburg, where, if the repulse of Lee's army had been followed up, all know now it would inevitably have been destroyed, and every officer ought to have known it then. On the other hand, an example of what can be done by following up a repulse is seen in the result of the action of General Thomas at Nashville, by which he substantially destroyed Hood's army.

From an interview with Sheridan, I learned what Lee and Grant had done in the march from the Rapidan. The position of

---

[1] See Appendix No. 54.   [2] See Appendix No. 55.

Grant's army and its distance from Richmond, contradicted all the despatches I had received from Washington, and I judged that it was impossible for him to do otherwise than to take the alternative in the plan agreed upon between us, in case he failed to turn Lee's left and drive him back into Richmond, where I was to meet him in ten days. Evidently Grant was not coming to Richmond but had marched by his left flank to join me at City Point, intending to continue his operations on the south side. I had performed my part by being around Richmond, holding its outer defences on the south side of James River, and now that Richmond had been so largely reinforced, and as the army of Beauregard was continually receiving troops from the South in my rear, I concluded that I would not continue to hold my position more than a day or two longer —long enough to hold a road open for Kautz to find his way back to join us if he had met with disaster. The fortifications of our intrenched camp at Bermuda were by no means in such condition as they needed to be, to be thoroughly impregnable to the attack of the whole of Lee's army, he having the interior or shorter line. He might attempt to carry them and thus force Grant, whom he had learned was to make this his new base, into the position in which McClellan was at Harrison's landing. Accordingly it was imperative that I should no longer peril the safety of Grant's new base, and also probably the safety of his army.

In other words, I must carry out the other branch of the plan agreed upon between Grant and myself, namely, to make him an impregnable base to which to bring his army in case of repulse, and whence he might commence his operations against Richmond, — where, in my belief, they ought to have been begun at first.

Impressed with these considerations I had determined, — in case of failure in getting possession of Drury's Bluff, which, once obtained, could be held by us as an almost impregnable camp for any length of time, as it could be reached by our boats on the James, — to retire and finish the intrenchments at Bermuda Neck.

I had done up to this time what I had agreed with General Grant to do: I had seized City Point and Bermuda by a surprise; I had brought my army, against all opposition and without any considerable loss, to the intrenchments of Richmond, and was there victoriously awaiting him; and I had kept more than thirty thousand rebel troops more than ten days, busy defending Richmond, so that they might not join Lee's army. I had also cut the Weldon Railroad two successive times by my cavalry. I had cut the Petersburg Railroad and prevented the sending forward of troops and supplies, and I had cut in many places the Danville Railroad, the other supply road of Lee. This statement needs no corroboration now, but if it did, the despatches of Beauregard to the rebel war authorities would be sufficient. They would show the danger to which I was exposed, as the Confederates believed, if they should get between me and my intrenched camp, — a danger wholly frustrated by the conclusion to which I came. They also bear witness to the enhanced value and the great importance to our forces of the strategic movement, admittedly devised by myself, of seizing and holding City Point and Bermuda Hundred.

To determine advisedly any course of action at once save the one directed to Gillmore, it was necessary to wait until the very thick fog, which had enveloped everything, could be cleared away by the sun. When that had been done, I learned that the Confederates had massed by far the largest portion of their troops in the breastworks opposite my right flank, which was held by the Eighteenth Corps, with the intention of turning it and then seizing the shortest and best road to my intrenchments, the river road, getting their forces there by a break through the weak line I had left, and seizing Bermuda Hundred with all its advantages, thus accomplishing results of the greatest moment.[1]

During the day before the battle of Drury's Bluff, May 16, the line covering Smith's corps had been intrenched. The line of Gillmore's corps was defended by the outer line of the enemy's intrenchments which we had taken and were using substantially in reverse.

Breast-high intrenchments had been made in front of the line held by the Eighteenth Corps, and in a substantially clear field almost within cannon shot of the intrenchments of the enemy. These works had been extended as far as the line could be covered, leaving only a short space, say a quarter of a mile, between the James River and the right of the line, which was held by the cavalry pickets only.

---

[1] See Appendix No. 56.

To prevent a night surprise, a farmhouse about one hundred yards beyond the right of my line had been seized, and I had ordered it to be held by a picket of some sixty sharp-shooters. This would prevent a noiseless turning of our flank in the night-time. The enemy, appreciating this, had twice during the day attempted its capture, but it was held.

At the suggestion of General Weitzel, General Smith had ordered the front of his corps to be protected by telegraph wires taken from the poles of the line along the railroad — of which we had nine miles uninterrupted possession — and wound around the stumps of trees in front of his line and around posts driven into the ground. This wire was strung at such a height that the enemy making a charge in the night would assuredly stumble over it and be thrown down in masses within some fifty yards of the muzzles of our guns.

That order was carefully and properly executed by Weitzel and Brooks in the front. They commanded the left and centre divisions of the Eighteenth Corps line. Heckman's brigade and Weitzel's division held the extreme right. For some reason, never yet satisfactorily explained, the putting up of that wire, which events proved would have been of the greatest security, was neglected in front of Heckman's brigade, the extreme and exposed right of the line. As that brigade was "in the air," that is, substantially without support on its right, there was almost a necessity for a double line of wire in its front. But there was none whatever there. The order to put it there, his division commander reports, was given to Heckman. I have seen in one of the many publications of Smith on this subject that he says it was because there was not enough wire with which to do it. How that can be I do not understand, for there was nine miles of that wire to be had for the taking, and the time in which to do it was more than ample.

In one of his later publications Smith says that no wire was ordered to be put in front of Heckman's brigade, and Heckman in his report speaks of no order to put the wire in his front. If there was no order given to have it done, it is very clear the order should have been given, as Heckman's brigade was on the right, in a position which most needed such protection.

It would have been better to have extended the wire a considerable distance to the right of Heckman's brigade.

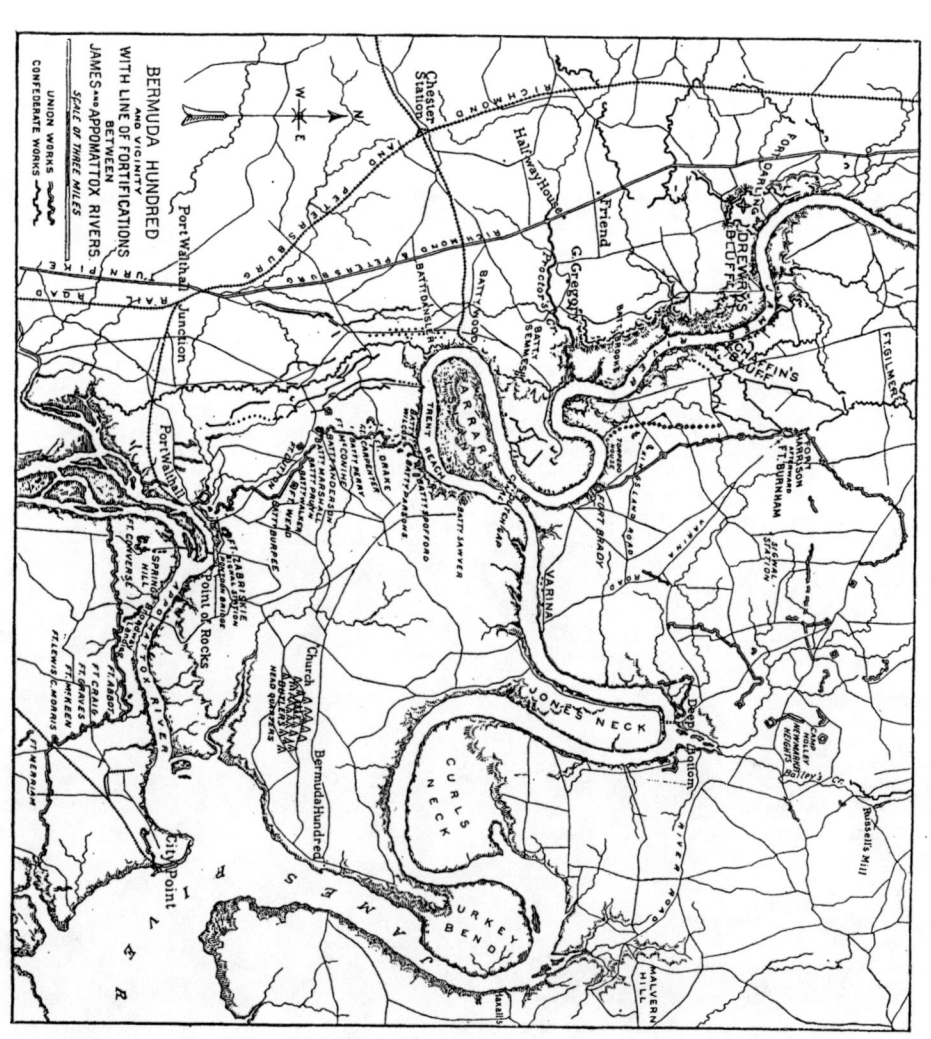

BERMUDA HUNDRED
AND VICINITY
WITH LINE OF FORTIFICATIONS
BETWEEN
JAMES AND APPOMATTOX RIVERS.
SCALE OF THREE MILES

UNION WORKS
CONFEDERATE WORKS

Before dark there were two regiments in reserve near the centre of Smith's line, one of which would have covered the assumed gap on Heckman's right.

I give Heckman's account of the attack: —

In the afternoon General Smith visited my line and everything having been explained to him he seemed to realize our peril, as no military man could help doing, and exclaimed: "Heckman, this is fearful!"

Belger's battery and a section of twenty-inch rifles were sent me later in the afternoon, and subsequently withdrawn to the centre for safety, where they were captured the next day. Afterwards a breastwork of such material as could be hastily gathered, was thrown up so that the position so essential to the safety of the army could be defended to the last. At midnight the rebels moved out from their works, massing strongly on my assumed right held by the Ninth New Jersey, and just at daylight, having obtained position, rushed with great impetuosity on my pickets, but after a desperate struggle were forced back by Captain Lawrence. Shortly after this a dense fog suddenly enveloped us and completely concealed the enemy from our view, and five picketed brigades in column debouched from their works and rapidly advanced on a run to our main line. When only five paces intervened between our inflexible line and the rebel bayonets, a simultaneous scorching volley swept into the faces of the exulting foe, smiting hundreds to the earth and hurling the whole column backward in confusion. Five times encouraged and rallied by their officers, that magnificent rebel infantry advanced to the attack, but only to be met and driven back by those relentless volleys of musketry. Finding it impossible to succeed by a direct attack, they advanced on my flank, in column by brigade and for the first time during the war we were compelled to fall back and take up a new position. In the dense fog I soon after found myself in front of an Alabama brigade, commanded by Archie Gracie, formerly of New Jersey, who recognized me and said he was glad to see me, and was proud to say he had been fighting Jerseymen, but that he had only a skirmish line left.

I never at any other time experienced such a musketry fire as on that day. It was one incessant volley and its terrible fatality may be judged from the fact that the enemy acknowledged a loss of 4,500 men — more than the Star Brigade [Heckman's] numbered — on my front alone; and I lost nearly all my field and line officers.

The ultimate results will be sadder when it is remembered that it was all caused by the incompetent handling of the Army of the James.

General Grant laid the onus of the failure on General Butler in a caustic paragraph of his official report. The press and the histories of the war blame Butler with the severest language, and even now the nation at large call him " Bottled-up-Butler." But the opinions of intelligent officers who fought in the campaign, and who judged it impartially from a military point of view as well as the facts, will rather lay the fault at the door of his corps commanders, Generals Gillmore and Smith. They did not seem to comprehend what was to be done, and then failed to co-operate in what attempts they did make.

General Heckman also makes some very severe strictures upon the fact that General Butler and his command were around Richmond instead of being around Petersburg.

These are the result of his want of information. I was where I was, in direct obedience to the plan of campaign to which I was confined by the orders of General Grant. After General Heckman was captured and saw the numbers and condition of the rebel troops in front of us, he declared that if Gillmore had made the attack on the left at the time of the rebel attack on the right of our line, he could have gone in and captured the enemy's works.

The rest of the Eighteenth Corps, having been aided by the wire which threw down the enemy as they attempted to rush upon its lines, maintained a steady fire, inflicting upon the enemy a very terrible loss. Meanwhile, having left to General Gillmore's discretion, after several hours' delay, whether he should make an attack, and he having informed me that he was falling back, and for other reasons that I have in part stated, I came to the conclusion that it was my duty, Grant not having met me " in ten days " from the time of his crossing the Rapidan, to proceed to carry out the rest of his instructions by ordering a withdrawal of my force from the enemy's front. This was done leisurely, and without any attack or interference by the enemy.

As soon as we reached our line of intrenchments the most laborious and pressing endeavors were made to strengthen them, and particularly to close up the gap a little north of the centre of our line, where the intrenchments had not been joined on account of the disagreement of Smith and Gillmore as to where the line should be. For that purpose, by a general order, I made General Weitzel chief engineer of my army, putting the whole work under his immediate order and command as representing myself.[1]

[1] See Appendix No. 57.

With all our diligence we were not soon enough to be ready for the enemy. They commenced demonstrations on the 18th, on the right of my line, which were repulsed. These were followed up, on the 19th, by further demonstrations, which were apparently reconnoissances.

On the morning of the 20th, Beauregard, with a large force, made a very vigorous attempt to force our lines, striking, as he naturally would, at the weakest point. This point was where the work of constructing and arming the redoubt to flank any movement upon the main line had not been fully completed. Between nine and ten o'clock in the morning the enemy set fire to the brush and dry wood that extended out a very considerable distance before our line, and the wind being favorable, the fire was driven in upon us. Before the smoke had cleared, the enemy came rushing on. They were met by the troops of the Tenth Corps, who steadily held their position and repulsed each attempt to dislodge them.

The enemy's attacks were made with great impetuosity, and I was under the impression that it was possible that the left of the Tenth Corps might be obliged to give way. I knew the right of that corps was being demonstrated against further north. There was no movement against the line on Smith's front, although to be prepared for it his troops stood in line of battle, and could have met it well. Having observed all the conditions from a little eminence just inside our lines, where the enemy chose to do me honor by opening with some light artillery upon myself, staff, and orderlies there assembled, I sent one of my aides to General Smith with direction to have his right division under General Brooks march by his right flank to the rear of Gillmore's left division, which was bearing the brunt of the attack, as a reserve in case they showed symptoms of breaking. The distance which Brooks' division would have to move was but little more than half a mile. Just before my staff officer started with the order, a very daring charge upon our line was made under the leadership of Brigadier-General Walker. Whether it might have been a success, partial or other, it is impossible to determine, because he fell with desperate wounds from which he soon afterwards died.[1]

---

[1] On General Walker's body was found a photographic map of all that part of Virginia between Richmond and Petersburg, in which we were operating. This was exceedingly valuable, as in our army we had no map which gave us any correct information of the topography of the country or the position of the enemy's works.

In a few minutes my staff officer saluted me and said: "General, I have delivered your order."

"What was General Smith's answer?"

"General Smith replied: 'Damn Gillmore! He has got himself into a scrape; let him get out of it the best way he can.'"

I said to my aid, "Ride with me," and we rode to Brooks' line, and fortunately found him at the head of his division. I then repeated my order to him and told him that he must execute it without waiting for it to come from General Smith, for there was necessity that he should, and that I would go and see General Smith.

I then immediately rode on to General Smith's headquarters, which were at the centre of his line, and said to him: "General, I sent you an order. My staff officer has reported to me your answer to it. Captain, state in the presence of General Smith his reply."

My staff officer repeated the reply as he had at first stated it to me. Smith then said: "By what I said I meant no disrespect to yourself."

"It is not such an answer as should have been made to one of my staff officers," said I. "But now is not the time to deal with that question. I have directed General Brooks to make the movement, and I now direct you personally to see that it is promptly done. You will report upon this subject to my headquarters this evening, provided the battle is over by that time." I rode rapidly back to my point of observation. Shortly afterwards Brooks' division crossed the crown of the knoll behind where I stood, and came in sight of the enemy. From that time their efforts weakened, and after a while ceased, and they withdrew and left us to go on diligently putting our line of defences in perfect order.

On the 19th of May, Beauregard had twenty-five thousand men, not reckoning those in Petersburg or Richmond.[1]

On the morning of the 21st he attacked our lines and we held them against him.[2]

At that time I had not more than twenty thousand effective men at Bermuda Hundred.

In the meantime General Meigs and General Barnard had been sent down by Halleck to inspect my department to ascertain how

---

[1] See Appendix No. 58.　　　　　[2] See Appendix No. 59.

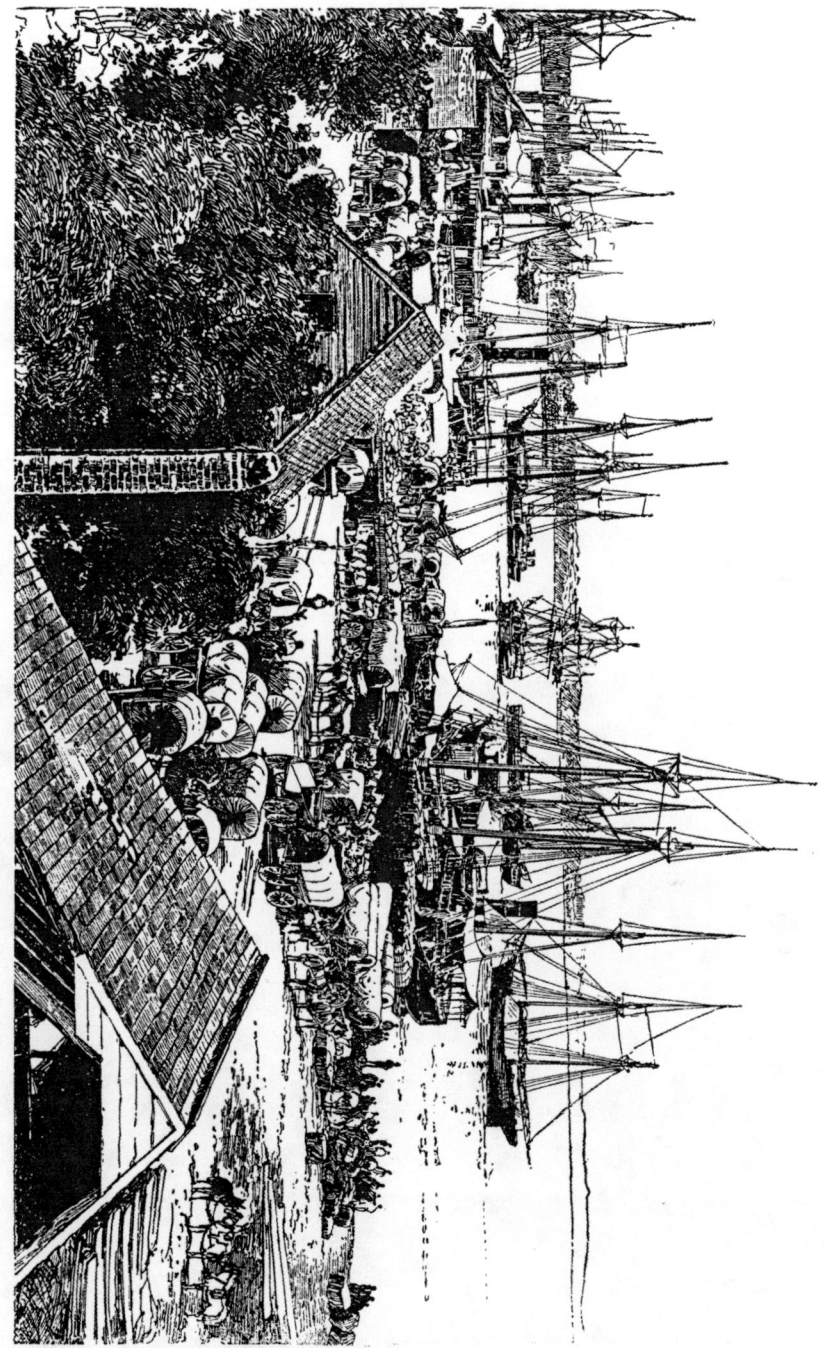

HEADQUARTERS OF GENERAL GRANT AT CITY POINT, VA. From a Photograph.

many men could be sent to the aid of Grant.   Owing to the disputes between Gillmore and Smith as to the line of fortification, it was in no condition to be safely held by fifteen thousand men.

The rebel troops being driven away, Beauregard came to the conclusion to make no further attack upon my lines.   About nine thousand of his men were sent to Lee by the way of Richmond,[1] and Colquitt's brigade of fourteen hundred men was sent to Chaffin's Bluff.   Those which were ordered to Lee could not have joined him, under the condition their railroad transportation and supplies were in, before the 3d of June.   Between that time and the battle of Cold Harbor there were no considerable losses, and, as Grant reports, the contests during that time were in his favor; so that he was not impeded at all by the want of troops from the Army of the James. He got sixteen thousand of them on the 28th of May before the next great battle at Cold Harbor was fought, and they included the best men I had.

Whoever, therefore, reported to Grant that I was not holding ten thousand men from Lee's army, simply told what was not the fact, probably to break up my army.   I believe it to have been Halleck. It may have been Sheridan, as he made a raid upon Richmond at that time expecting to capture it, because, as he supposed, the troops had been drawn from there to Lee's army, and they would fear no attack from me, my troops being withdrawn from Bermuda Hundred.

Those sixteen thousand men under Smith were of no earthly advantage to Grant.   It would have been very much more to his advantage if he had not had them, as without them he probably would not have made the fight at Cold Harbor.   That fight was simply an indiscriminate slaughter of our men to the number of eighteen thousand, and more than three thousand were of the troops I had sent, — and better officers and soldiers never stood in line.

On the 22d of May, Fitzhugh Lee was sent to capture Wilson's Wharf, Fort Pocahontas.   As has been already stated, the place was seized when we went up the river, so that our transports should not be stopped.

Fitzhugh Lee thought that with his cavalry, infantry, and artillerymen, amounting to some twenty-five hundred men, he could easily

[1] See Appendix No. 60.

capture that place, which was held only by two regiments of negroes under General Wilde.   Accordingly, before he began, he sent a summons to surrender, informing the commanding officer that if he surrendered, the officers and negro troops should be treated as prisoners of war, but if they did not, and he captured the place, he would not be answerable for their treatment.   That treatment was stated in Davis's proclamation to be that the negroes should be returned to their masters, and the officers sent to the governors of the States, to be there tried for inciting negro insurrection.

The noble answer of General Wilde to those propositions was: "We will try that."   Thereupon Fitzhugh Lee did his best.   The negroes held firmly, and Lee retired beaten in disgrace, leaving his dead on the field.

It will be observed from the instructions which I gave General Hinks,[1] who commanded the troops holding Fort Powhatan, that I was exceedingly anxious for the safety of that point, because that was the weak point of my whole position.   For, although it was some twelve miles below City Point on the James, yet if it were once in possession of the enemy, it would be impossible to get any troops or supplies up the river, as the channel ran close under it. My experience with Vicksburg, which was on a bluff high above the possible range of the guns of the fleet, which were not mortars, told me that if Fort Powhatan were once captured by the rebels, it could be easily held against the naval vessels.   I was anxious lest it should be taken by surprise, and therefore, from day to day almost, I persisted in cautioning Major-General Hinks, who was in command.   He was a very excellent and able officer, with but a single drawback, and that was very infirm health, arising from wounds received in the army of McClellan before Richmond.

It may be asked why, if it was of so much importance, I entrusted its defences to a garrison of negro troops.   I knew that they would fight more desperately than any white troops, in order to prevent capture, because they knew — for at that time no measures had been taken to protect them — that if captured they would be returned into slavery, under Davis's proclamation, and the officers commanding them might be murdered.   So there was no danger of a surrender.   Wilde's answer to Fitzhugh Lee, and the gallant fight of

---

[1] See Appendix No. 61.

his negroes at Fort Pocahontas, Wilson's Wharf, when threatened that this should be done to the negroes if they did not surrender, made me certain that nothing but a surprise would get that position; and nobody ever did get it.

The experiment of Fitzhugh Lee at Wilson's Wharf taught the rebels a lesson as to the conduct of negro troops. Negro troops were never captured in a fort entrusted to their defence.

I at length learned that General Grant would now certainly come and join me at City Point, and that he was waiting for events to determine whether he would call to his assistance the Eighteenth Corps.[1] Having also learned that there was in Petersburg a possible aggregation, including reserves, militia, and convalescents, of some two thousand men, of which not more than two thirds would be substantially effective, I organized an expedition of eleven thousand men under General Smith, and put them in column at Bermuda Hundred to attack Petersburg on the 29th of May. They were ready to march the very next morning, but on the evening of the 28th the transportation to take them away arrived with positive orders that they should at once go to Grant.

Much as I desired the capture of Petersburg, which was as certain as any future event could be, I felt it my duty, knowing in what straits General Grant believed himself to be, to give, although reluctantly, the order for their embarkation.

The Eighteenth Corps, as then reorganized, contained some sixteen thousand effective men, and their removal left me actually at Bermuda, — reckoning the cavalry, a part of whom were armed only with pistols, and possible convalescents in the hospitals, — less than eight thousand effective troops,[2] leaving only small garrisons at Spring Hill on the enemy's side of the Appomatox, City Point, Fort Powhatan, and Fort Pocahontas.

The capture of Fort Powhatan or Fort Pocahontas, or both, by the rebels would render it impossible for Grant to cross his army over the James, because the boats could not get up near enough to allow him to continue his line of march by the Chickahominy route across the James River.

I should have felt little alarm for the safety of Bermuda had my fortifications been completed in Gillmore's front. Although twice

---

[1] See Appendix No. 62.   [2] See Appendix No. 63.

as much time had been wasted as was necessary to complete them, General Weitzel, my chief engineer, reported to me that not half the work which I supposed had been completed, had been done.

Still the capture of Petersburg lay near my heart. It will be seen that the removal of Smith's corps on the 29th of May, when they were ready to march to capture Petersburg, had frustrated that capture for the second time, as the false reports from Washington had done the first time. I caused the most accurate reports possible of the strength of my forces to be made to me, and I also caused the most accurate investigations to be made into the question whether some portions of the enemy's troops had not been withdrawn from Petersburg after the removal of Smith's corps had become known to the rebels, upon the supposition on their part that I would afterwards undertake no offensive operations.

In all movements my corps commanders put little or no reliance upon the efficiency of my negro troops. There was a stupid, unreasoning, and quite vengeful prejudice against them among the regular officers of our army with the exception of General Weitzel, who had seen their performances in conjunction with his expedition in the Department of the Gulf.

There was a belief among the rebels that we were evacuating Bermuda Hundred, and they tested it by several reconnoissances, and by one quite determined attack upon the right of the line. This attack was easily repulsed by General Terry, but with very considerable loss.

After conferring with General Hinks as to the number of negro troops that he could furnish — and he, not being a regular officer, relied upon them, — I planned an expedition against Petersburg, and summoned him to a conference upon that subject.

While we were conferring, General Gillmore, who had been called upon to report what number of troops could possibly be spared from his intrenchments for a movement, visited headquarters and was admitted to the conference. When the condition of things at Petersburg was disclosed to him, and when he learned that I proposed to send General Hinks in command of the expedition, he became very strongly impressed with the great probability of its success, and insisted that he ought to command it, being senior officer. He volunteered to go, and claimed it as his right and as a matter of

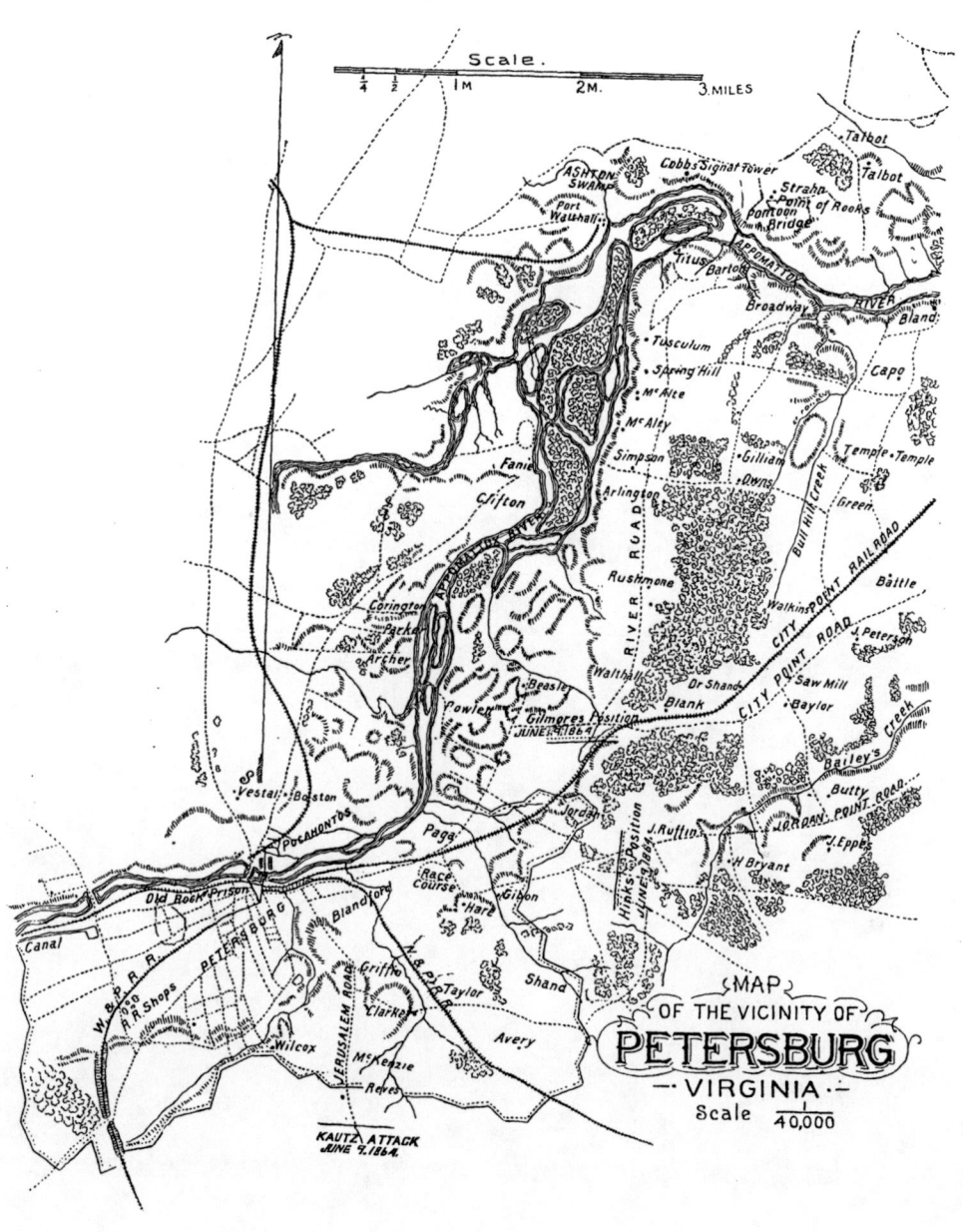

Scale.

¼ ½ 1M 2M. 3.MILES

MAP
OF THE VICINITY OF
PETERSBURG
VIRGINIA
Scale 1/40,000

military courtesy, and I was fool enough to yield to him. I did not then think him a coward, although Grant declined to employ him because he had shown "timidity."[1] I believed that the glory he expected from the success of the expedition would incite him to do all he could. Besides, a large portion of his command would be colored troops under General Hinks, on whom I relied to go forward, if necessary. I gave orders that the white troops should start from my pontoon bridge at daylight, and as it was a march of but some six or seven miles to the outer line of defences of Petersburg, I supposed the attack would be made quite early in the morning. It was also arranged that Kautz's cavalry, starting at the same time, should make a diversion by a feint on Petersburg along the Jerusalem Road, getting there earlier than Gillmore's and Hinks' commands would do, so that the attention of the enemy would be drawn towards Kautz.

The expedition started in time, because I stood behind them and hurried them off. Gillmore had some sixty-five hundred men under his command, besides nearly two thousand of Kautz's cavalry.

The first telegram I received after the expedition started was a complaint and grumble from Gillmore, in which he said: "My command has just crossed the river; some of it has been delayed by losing the road. I have no doubt that the enemy are fully apprised of my movement by the noise of the bridge. It is not muffled at all, and the crossing of the cavalry can be heard for miles."

But why was not the bridge muffled, General Gillmore? You had the command of the expedition in all its parts, and it was your duty to see it properly conducted; why didn't you muffle the bridge? Was it the duty of the commanding general to lug straw and other materials with which pontoon bridges are usually muffled? Further, I have never supposed that the tramp of horses on a bridge could be heard seven miles. And why were your troops not instructed in the road across their own camps so that there should not have been delay in getting there?

From the hour of getting that despatch, heartsick I doubted the result of the expedition.

Kautz went on to the Jerusalem Road, and at ten o'clock Gillmore had approached within "twenty minutes' march" of the intrench-

---

[1] See Appendix No. 64.

ments at the point where he was to make the attack. Then he halted his troops and went to a "secesh" lady's house to get his dinner. While there, as he afterwards averred, he was informed by her that Petersburg was full of troops. He also halted Hinks' division so far off as not to be in supporting distance of him, he says, but only the same distance from the enemy's lines. Both columns rested there and went no further. The position of affairs will explain itself to one looking at the very accurate map showing their relative positions.

Gillmore got his dinner, picked his teeth, waited until half past three o'clock on a still fair day, with a three quarter moon at night, and then turned about and marched home, encountering the same opposition that he met in marching out, leaving Kautz and his cavalry to take care of themselves.

Kautz had charged up the Jerusalem plank road, driven the force opposing him away, captured a piece of artillery and forty prisoners, and ridden into the town as far up as Jordan's, and then, not hearing anything from Gillmore, although he was within the sound of musketry, he came leisurely back, and without being interfered with.

Gillmore reported to me on his return that the expedition had not succeeded, and that he had not heard of Kautz.

I had the sorrowful pleasure of answering that I had heard of Kautz, as Kautz had been into Petersburg and waited for him as long as he could, and had reported to my headquarters, and brought in his prisoners.

Upon the examination of some of the prisoners captured, I found there was almost no effective force at that time in Petersburg.

I think I cannot better state the condition of the troops of the city of Petersburg than by quoting from the very extraordinary congratulatory order of Brigadier-General Wise, to his command: —

On approaching with nine regiments of infantry and cavalry, and at least four pieces of artillery, they searched our lines from battery Number 1 to battery Number 29, a distance of nearly six miles.

How true that is will be seen, as nobody but Kautz was in sight of the fortifications that day, and Kautz made his entry into Petersburg. General Kautz reported that near City Point he separated himself from the infantry and marched down Jerusalem plank road

parallel with the line of defences of Petersburg, and met no resistance except from some pickets, until he reached a point on that road
some four miles distant from the enemy's intrenchments.

General Wise was evidently very much misinformed. He further
said in his congratulatory order that he had Hood's and Batte's battalions of Virginia militia, about two hundred men each; the Forty-
Seventh Regiment of Virginia Volunteers numbering about three
hundred men ; one company of Woods' Twenty-Third South Carolina
with some fifty men; Sturdivant's Battery and Taliaferro's Cavalry,
with which he kept our forces at bay and punished them severely
until they reached the Jerusalem plank road.

General Kautz reports again that he captured all there were of
Taliaferro's cavalry outside of the intrenchments.

Wise further adds that he had the following additional forces :
Major Archer's corps of reserves, second-class militia, and one
howitzer under the command of Brigadier-General Colston, which
forces he puts at less than one hundred and fifty; one company of
convalescents of say a hundred men more, with say one hundred men
for the two batteries of artillery, Graham's and Young's, and say one
hundred and twenty men more for a company of convalescents, and a
company of *penitents.*[1] These, then, constituted the entire number
of men south of the Appomattox under General Wise's command,
being, all told, not more than fifteen hundred effective men.

General Kautz reports that he passed the entire line of the
intrenchments, being opposed only by a small body of infantry and
artillery which did him no damage, and hearing nothing from Gillmore, and not hearing his guns, he burned the camp of the enemy,
destroyed their stores and ammunition, and came quietly home.

I felt that Gillmore's conduct was wholly inexcusable and cowardly, and I took measures to have him relieved from his command.
He desired a court of inquiry, and was ordered to Washington for that
purpose. For reasons unexplained to me that court never assembled,
as it certainly did not report. General Gillmore's active service with
the armies of the United States during the remainder of the war was
desultory in character, and migratory in detail and assignment.

---

[1] Penitents are soldiers who have been tried by court-martial and committed to prison for their
crimes. In some emergencies at Richmond and Petersburg they were released and formed into
companies to fight in defence of their prison. How much they would fight after they got a chance
to run away need not be discussed.

Prior to the 9th of June, I had erected a lookout in the neighbor-hood of two hundred feet high. It was composed of trestle work, and the illustration will save a further description. It stood on Cobb's Hill just at the left and near the Appomatox end of my fortifications. It was a great annoyance to the enemy and of exceed-ing usefulness to me. There was a nine-foot square space on the top to

LOOKOUT AND SIGNAL STATION, COBB'S HILL, BUTLER'S FRONT, ARMY
OF THE JAMES.

which two observers could be drawn up in a large basket by means of a windlass. Once at the top of this lookout, a large portion of the peninsula, with all the works of the enemy, and my own lines of pickets and fortifications, for the space of more than three miles, lay like a map under my eyes. Thus the enemy could move no force on the Petersburg turnpike or railroad to or from Richmond without its being reported to me, a relay of signal officers being always stationed there to make observations through their telescopes, and by means of signal flags communication could be had with all the other points along my lines.

The very deep ravine of which I have spoken, lay between the lookout and the enemy's lines. On the farther side of this ravine was a very high wooded bluff, the elevation of which from the bottom of the ravine to the top was quite equal to the height of the observatory, from which I could communicate by signals to City Point.

On the 9th of June General Beauregard sent the following despatch: —

DONLOP'S HOUSE, June 9, 1864, ʾ2 M.

GENERAL BRAXTON BRAGG:

Enemy has erected an observatory at Cobb's which overlooks surrounding country. The twelve pounder Whitworth at arsenal is absolutely required to destroy it. Please send it by express forthwith, with ammunition complete.

G. T. BEAUREGARD.

A day or two after that I observed from the lookout a small force of men in some activity on the side of the bluff opposite. With our glasses we could observe closely enough to distinguish an officer there. I had been accustomed to be drawn up to the top of the lookout, and to occupy the position there an hour or more almost daily between the hours of ten and twelve, when the atmosphere was clear, examining the condition of my picket line and camps, and the rebel works.

Some days after this I went up to make my observations, as was my custom, and after spending an hour or more I was about to come down when I heard the report of a Whitworth gun, and the terrific shriek of its projectile, which was some two feet long and in shape a four-sided bolt, and, revolving on its axis, made a great noise. Turning my glass as the smoke cleared away, I saw that a small lunette battery had been erected on the bluff, and that from this battery the gun had been discharged. I knew then that the enemy proposed to knock me off my perch. The noise of the first explosion attracted my soldiers. They came running down from their tents behind the breastworks, and gathering at the foot of the tower, many of them kindly called out to me: "Come down, General, come down."

I was considerably frightened, because if one of the projectiles should hit either of the corner posts of the tower, it would have undoubtedly come down, and myself with it, faster than would have been agreeable. But this was no time for the general to show the white feather either to the enemy, who knew I was up there, or to my own men. I ordered my signal officer to signal for two batteries of artillery of six ten-pounders each to come into battery at the breastwork to the right of my tower. The order was obeyed with great celerity.

It takes some time to load a Whitworth gun, but before my battery came up it threw another projectile at me, which went too high. Before they could load again, my guns were put in position, and I signaled them to commence firing slowly by number from left to right, and that I would communicate the faults of their aim, for I could see where their shells struck.

I called out, and my signal officer signalled: "Fire slowly by order." The left gun was then fired. Waiting for the shell to strike I saw the aim was too low.

"Number one fires too low by fifty feet," I called out. "Number two fire."

"Number two fires to the left by some yards."

"Number three, to the right by some yards."

"Number four, good line shot, but too high."

"Number five, a good line shot, but too low. Adjust your aim."

"Number six, good shot, just under the battery."

"Number seven," — and so on with the whole twelve.

Meantime the enemy had sent us another shot but that was much too high, the range of the Whitworth gun being some three miles.

"Now, number one."

"Good shot."

"Number two, too high."

"Number three, too low," — and so on through.

The next shot of the enemy was a little to the left, and not very far off. But our men had got their aim. The order went down: "Carefully, take aim, and fire now as fast as you can along the whole line."

In five seconds the twelve guns were fired, and twelve ten-pound shells struck all about and in that battery. The order went down "Fire away," and another volley went, the aim being got with exactness. Another volley went, and I saw the men running out of the battery down into a depression in the bluff, and I saw, also, that one or more shells had struck the gun, and that it was overturned. "One more volley; then cease firing," was the order.

I then signalled to my four stout orderlies, who manned the winch that raised and lowered the basket, to take hold, and myself and signal officer were lowered to the ground.

The high appreciation manifested by my men quite paid for the risk.

I never heard from that Whitworth gun afterwards.

I built another observatory, but not so high, at the opposite end of our line on the high bank of the James River, and by means of signals we were in possession of everything material done beyond the James River.

Meanwhile I learned from Grant that he desired a pontoon bridge across the James, at what I thought to be the most proper place, and he sent Colonel Comstock of his staff to confer with me upon the matter.

The pontoon equipment had been sent to Fortress Monroe under the command of General Benham. But when instructed by Colonel Comstock to bring his pontoon train up to City Point, Benham refused to obey, upon the ground that having been ordered there by General Meade, he could not leave there without an order from him. So Benham remained there until he got a direct order from Grant.

While this was going on we had determined, on account of the openness of the country and the roads leading towards Petersburg, that the troops should land at Fort Powhatan. On the north side of the river, however, was a marsh nearly a mile long, over which we decided to make a corduroy road for the passage of the troops and began the construction of a good bridge-head.

Although the pressure of time was very great, I had heard nothing of the pontoon train, and after waiting for it nearly two whole days I went down the river in my headquarters boat, the Greyhound. About twelve miles below Fort Powhatan I found the tugs, which had the pontoon train in tow. They were at anchor. I saw the officer in command and asked why he was anchored there. He said he thought it was getting near night — it was five o'clock — and that he concluded to stop for the night. I peremptorily ordered the tugs to proceed, whoever said anything to the contrary; and they did proceed.

I examined the pontoon train as it went up the river to ascertain the provisions for anchoring the bridge. The tidal current opposite the fort where the bridge was to be built, was very strong both ways. The engineer officer had nothing to hold the boats but ordinary grapnels of a few pounds in weight, and inch warps, about sixty feet long, to each boat. I saw that those, the moment the boats were pressed down, with the current running, would not hold, and

DESPATCH BOAT GREYHOUND.

that the bridge would give way, and the troops, and especially the artillery crossing it, would be lost.

Here was a dilemma and what to do I did not know. But remembering there were quite a number of large sized sutler schooners anchored at City Point, I turned my boat to Bermuda Hundred, called for the provost guard, and seized as many schooners as were necessary. I had them tugged down and anchored stem and stern across the river in two rows, leaving an interval between them wide enough for the bridge, and also leaving an opening for a draw in the bridge to allow vessels to pass up and down when it was not occupied. All of them had strong chains and heavy anchors by which they were securely fastened so as not to swing with the tide. The sterns of the vessels were to be placed on opposite sides of the bridge facing each other. That is, all the vessels on the upper side of the bridge were anchored with their sterns down river. All below the bridge were anchored with their sterns up river. Then by fastening the warps of the pontoons, head and stern, to the schooners the bridge could be laid and held with safety. The bridge train men worked under my personal direction until late at night, and in the morning the bridge was ready for passage. The engineer had provided himself with no material with which to cover the planks, and they would have been worn out before one third of the troops with their supplies and wagons could have crossed; but, fortunately, I had six saw-mills sawing out planks from the timber of the vicinity for use in building hospitals, and from these mills we were enabled to renew those planks three times, as was necessary, before the bridge ceased to be used. But they would not have so lasted had not great pains been taken to cover the roadway over the bridge as thickly as possible with hay and straw. This was imperative, because when the wheels of a heavy gun rested upon one portion of a pontoon it would be sunk down, and that would turn up the edge of the plank nearest the gun, and it would be almost inevitably splintered and ground off. I received the personal thanks of General Grant for my endeavors in putting the bridge in order with so little delay.

At my suggestion the remainder of the Eighteenth Corps was marched to the White House on York River and placed upon transports and landed at my pontoon bridge at Bermuda Hundred, arriving there on the night of the 14th of June.

General Grant had instructed me that if I thought Petersburg could be captured I should send that corps under command of Smith the next morning with such force as I thought I could spare to make the attack. I knew that but a few more troops had been added to Wise's command in Petersburg, and that all the troops with arms, second class militia, reserves, penitents, and convalescents, did not exceed two thousand effective men. The only anxiety General Grant had about such an attack was lest Lee, knowing

Grant had crossed the James, and having the shorter line and the railroad from Richmond to Petersburg, should move directly to Petersburg, and that when Smith got there, he should find the city occupied by Lee's veterans. Grant was at that time at Charles City Court-House near Wilson's Landing, Fort Pocahontas. He asked me to send two regiments down to that landing to aid Sheridan in defending himself from the attacks of the Confederate troops who were close upon his rear. I sent the troops but advised that Sheridan should fall back the space of three or four miles from where he was to Fort Pocahontas where he would receive from Wilde's troops all the aid and protection he wanted. That suggestion I believe was adopted, but of the details of that I have no recollection, as Sheridan got across safely.

I had advised very strongly that the Second Corps, commanded by General Hancock, which was leading, and Burnside's corps, which was following, both arriving at the river on the 14th, should be hurried with the utmost celerity to occupy the intrenchments around Petersburg. I was sorry, however, to receive an order to send Hancock sixty thousand rations at Windmill Point, which was quite out of the direction for the purpose of a rapid march on Petersburg. Hancock had rations enough to last him three days, and I received an order to send the rations to City Point and thence up the Appomattox to be landed within four or five miles of the rear of Hancock's corps.

I did not share Grant's apprehensions that Lee had undertaken to outmarch him via Richmond to Petersburg. I supposed that Lee would have seen the rear of Grant's forces while they were being passed over the river, always the most dangerous movement for a withdrawing army, and if Lee had marched for the purpose of getting ahead of him he would have been far ahead, for the delays in getting across the river were to me at the time unexplainable.

I knew also that up to that time no troops could have passed through Richmond or below to Petersburg. My lookouts commanded that matter by their eyes and ears day and night. If so much of the defences of Petersburg could be taken as would enable our force to reach the bridges at Swift Creek so as to get that creek and the Appomattox between us and Lee, then by holding that line of communication and demonstrating toward Richmond so as to cut the

Danville road thoroughly and the canal, Lee would be immediately forced South and Richmond would be ours.   After consultation I directed General Smith to make his attack upon the upper batteries of the line around Petersburg, although I had learned that the fortifications were stronger there, — that is, they were more pronounced works than those lower works over which Kautz had trotted on the 9th of June.   This Smith did.

Smith had with him some eighteen thousand effective men.   There were in Petersburg, as I have said, but twenty-two hundred, or one man to every four and one half feet of intrenchments around that city.[1] Of all that Smith had been so thoroughly informed that he knew it. He knew the situation of that part of the fortifications of Petersburg, because up to the time of his attack there had been no substantial change in them for months.   My proposition to him was, as to Gillmore, to go in by an attack and "rush," and I represented to him strongly that Gillmore on his expedition had only rushed at his dinner.

Now I think Smith was an efficient soldier in many respects,— although it would seem that I have every cause to dislike the man in every relation of life.   But he had one inevitable regular army failing — the vice Assistant Secretary Dana wrote to the War Department[2] Wright and Warren were accused of : "interminable reconnoissances " — waiting and waiting, not going at a thing when he was told, but looking all around to see if he could not do something else than what he was told to do, or do it in a different way from what he was told.

Fearing lest he might believe, as an excuse for reconnoitring, that Lee's troops had gone into Petersburg or could get there before him, I telegraphed him that since he marched, not a body of troops had passed through Richmond on the Petersburg road, the only way they could get to Petersburg.[3]   This information I also gave to Grant.

It was impossible for any considerable body of troops to pass into Petersburg through Swift Creek or across the Mattoax Bridge without its being known at my signal stations.   In the clear, warm, dry weather that we had, the cloud of dust itself would announce the passage of a squadron of cavalry, and if they came by rail, such passage would be detected at night by the noise of the train, and in the daytime by seeing the cars.

---

[1] Article of General Beauregard in *North American Review*, Vol. 145, page 372.
[2] See Appendix No. 65.   [3] See Appendix No. 66.

Any considerable artillery fire at the works where Smith was to attack could instantly be seen from our observatory, and there I spent the earlier part of the 15th, the morning of his march, in watching for his demonstration.   Hour after hour passed and nothing was seen or heard.   But the observatory gave me an opportunity of examining the line of rebel intrenchments opposite to my line across the James, and the neck between, also the lines of the enemy. I fully convinced myself that the enemy's lines had been abandoned on the night before, and I ordered a demonstration to be made by the few men I had left for the purpose of ascertaining that fact and found that it was true.   I could not get that reconnoissance made in force because General Terry was impressed with the idea, which all had, that Lee's troops would be coming down by the thousands within three miles of that line upon the railroad in such force as to be able quite to sweep away the small force with which I held my line, having withdrawn all I could to go with Smith.   Now I knew that Lee had not come to Richmond.

I communicated that fact to General Grant and asked him to order one of his corps — and it was unfortunately Wright's corps which he did order — to land at Bermuda and in conjunction with my forces seize and destroy the Petersburg railroad.   I did not suppose that we could successfully hold it against Lee's whole army, when it advanced, but I knew that we could delay his advance for hours so as to give Smith time to take Petersburg and allow Hancock's corps, as well as other corps of Grant's army, to get up into that city and hold Swift Creek and Mattoax Bridge over the Appomattox, which, if done, would be substantially an end of the war.   Therefore I sent order after order by my staff officers to Smith to attack and so get the Appomattox between himself and Lee.   While I thought I could detect some slight skirmishing where Smith's forces should be by the smoke of musketry, and now and then a piece of artillery, yet no movement was being made which deserved the name.

About seven o'clock I observed a semblance only, so far as the smoke of the fighting was concerned, of an attack, and a little later on I got a despatch from Smith saying that he had captured a wide line of intrenchments from Battery Five to Battery Nine of the line, which he had occupied, and I knew this was the capture of the single line of the Petersburg defences.

Hearing nothing from General Smith, early in the afternoon I despatched Lieutenant Davenport of my staff to General Smith to ascertain and report to me why he had not attacked the works in front of Petersburg, and with directions to give to General Smith in person my order for an immediate attack.

Davenport reported to me about 7 P. M. that he had found General Smith on his picket line and had delivered to him in person my orders for an immediate attack, and that General Smith had replied that he had been employed in reconnoitring the enemy's position and had just satisfied himself in that regard and would at once make the attack as ordered. Davenport also reported that in the neighborhood of half past five, he had passed a division of Hancock's corps (Birney's) some four miles from Smith and on the march.

About 8.30 P. M., General Smith's aid reported to me that at 7.25 P. M. General Smith had carried the line of defences near Jordan's and was pushing forward toward the river.

Shortly after General Smith's aid had gone I became anxious lest Smith should cease his movement, and therefore, about 9 P. M. I sent Lieutenant Davenport back to see General Smith and to say to that officer that I desired there should be no question as to his continuing his movement upon the enemy and his attack upon his works.

Lieutenant Davenport reported to me between eleven and twelve that night that he found nothing being done; that General Hancock was up with two of his divisions; that he found General Smith at General Hancock's headquarters; that he delivered to General Smith my orders and received from him the reply that he had determined to make no further attack that night; that General Smith, while not saying that General Hancock,— who was his senior in rank but my junior, and who had been ordered by me, by General Grant's directions, to support General Smith,— claimed to be the ranking officer, did say to him (Davenport) for the evident purpose of creating the impression that such claim was made by Hancock, that Hancock's arrival had left him (Smith) the junior officer; that he had, however, before leaving to return to me, ascertained the fact that Hancock had made no claim to command the movement by reason of his greater rank, but on the contrary had waived his rank and was relieving Smith's troops in the line with his own men.

Upon Davenport's report that Smith refused to obey my orders to renew the attack and purposed losing the advantages the presence of the Second Corps gave him as well as the prestige of success he had gained, with a night as bright and clear as a nearly full moon could make it, I sent Davenport back for the third time with directions to find Smith personally and say to him that I peremptorily ordered an immediate night attack to be made with all his force. This order Davenport was unable to deliver until between four and five o'clock in the morning of the 16th, owing to the fact that General Smith could not be found. His staff officers declared that he had gone to General Hancock's headquarters during the night of the 15th and had not returned to his headquarters camp. As a matter of fact, Smith had hidden himself in a tent pitched among the bushes in the rear of his own camp, among his orderlies and servants, and was there found by Davenport about sunrise.[1]

I can hardly believe that the fact was, as I know it to have been, that from that time Smith made no movement whatever but concluded to wait, and not make any attack until the morning. At that hour there was no other line of intrenchments before him to attack that could have interrupted for a moment his march to hold the bridge over the Appomattox. Smith says that from his knowledge of the topography he held the key to Petersburg. True, he did; but what is the use of holding the key when you have not the courage to turn it in the lock? Smith's curse was that he had graduated as a topographical engineer,— that is, a picture drawer or map maker,— and he was continually making maps before he made his assaults.

I sent him word again to go in with Hancock and he had the mendacity to send me the following despatch: —

> COBB'S HILL SIGNAL STATION, 12 P. M.
> June 15, 1864.
>
> GENERAL BUTLER:
>
> It is impossible for me to go further to-night, but unless I misapprehend the topography, I hold the key to Petersburg.
>
> *General Hancock not yet up;* General Ames not here; General Brooks has three batteries; General Martindale one, and General Hinks ten light guns.
>
> W. F. SMITH,
> *Major-General.*

---

[1] See Appendix No. 67.

But my staff officer had seen Smith and Hancock talking together. Smith got Hancock at nine o'clock at night to relieve his own men from their position in the fortifications on the ground that they were tired and hadn't ammunition. That they were tired in one sense is most true, not because they had marched some seven or eight miles in the morning, but only because they had stood around doing nothing all the rest of the day. As to his being out of ammunition there was no excuse for that because his men hadn't fired five shots apiece all day and why was not Smith's ammunition there? If he had sent to me, there was time enough in three hours for me to have supplied them with ammunition from Bermuda Hundred, or with anything else they needed. And yet, if they were out of ammunition, he never asked me for a cartridge.

I can imagine the reason why Smith withdrew his troops from the line and got them in a movable column, and had Hancock hold the lines with his men. If Smith had moved at daylight on the 16th, as I rather think he meant to do, then Smith's troops would lead the column and he would get the glory of having captured Petersburg.

Here it is opportune to state a fact that is hardly conceivable save that the evidence of it is overwhelming. *Lee was caught napping.*[1] Although a large portion of Grant's army had crossed the James River on the 15th, and substantially all of it by noon of the 16th, Lee had no knowledge of that fact. Indeed, he had lost Grant's army entirely, and did not know where it was. This fact Beauregard learned at Petersburg on the 16th by a despatch from Lee in which he asks whether he has heard of Grant crossing the James River.[2]

Lee himself did not reach Petersburg until the 18th of June, at 11.20, not until then being convinced that Grant's army had passed the James. This explains fully why none of his troops passed our lines on the 14th, 15th, or 16th, and not until late in the afternoon or evening of the 17th of June.

If General D. H. Hill, of the Confederate Army, is correct, Lee had been caught napping many times.[3]

It is established by incontestable evidence that when Smith made his attack upon Petersburg with more than sixteen thousand men, the negroes under his command captured the redoubts on the line Nos. 5 to 9 inclusive, and broke throught the line from Nos. 3 to

[1] See Appendix No. 68. [2] See Appendix No. 69. [3] See Appendix No 70.

11, inclusive.   The line of redoubts around Petersburg was a single line which extended seven and one half miles.[1]

Smith had that force with which to make the attack.   Beauregard had but twenty-two hundred effective men all told, which would give one man to every four and one half yards of the defended line; and from Butterworth's Bridge to the Appomattox, a distance of four and one half miles, the line was wholly undefended.   And yet before that line so defended, Smith spent from nine o'clock in the morning of a clear bright day until 7.30 o'clock in the afternoon reconnoitring; and he does not say in his report that he saw a single infantry soldier of the enemy during that reconnoissance.

He left the negroes to do all the work, and they did it; and from General Hinks' statement it appears they would have done a great deal more if Smith would have let them.   But Hinks further says that with the concurrence of Smith and Hancock his troops were taken out of the line before ten o'clock and encamped seventy-five to one hundred yards in the rear, and Hancock's men put in to hold the lines which had been captured by the negroes.[2]

In view of these facts, and in view of the statements of my staff officer Lieutenant Davenport, as to where he met the Second Corps marching in the direction of Smith's forces, am I not justified in using the hard word I have used as to the despatch sent me by Smith, *"General Hancock not yet up "*?

I have another fact which determines the reason why this falsehood was sent me: —

Immediately upon the return of my staff officer, I sent him back, after receiving the information that a part of Hancock's corps was with Smith, with a message to the latter to "renew the attack and push on," and that was received by Smith between ten and eleven o'clock at night, and he returned the answer that he could not make an attack that night.   I again sent Lieutenant Davenport back with the most positive orders that he should make an immediate attack.

Smith knew that Hancock had been ordered by Grant to move up his corps in connection with Smith to make an attack, and Hancock, gallant soldier as he was, had waived all questions of rank and put the whole affair into the hands of Smith.

[1] General Beauregard in *North American Review*, Vol. 145, p. 374.
[2] See Appendix No. 71.

My last positive commands did not reach Smith until five o'clock in the morning because he had hidden himself away, as will be seen by the statement of Lieutenant Davenport.

This ended all proper interference of mine with the attack on Petersburg, because, on the morning of the 16th, Petersburg was invested by the army of General Grant under his own command.

Notwithstanding the evidence I had before me of General Smith's wilful disobedience of orders, entire insubordination and mendacity,

AIKENS' MANSION ON JAMES RIVER.

I was still unwilling to report him, as I ought to have done, to be relieved by the lieutenant-general; and so I attempted to remain, as I had been, on friendly terms with him. Although, in order to get rid of my orders to make the attack on Petersburg, he had misrepresented a fact to me, I concluded to overlook it.

We went on, nothing coming up to cause any disagreement until a demonstration was ordered by General Grant to be made from Bermuda Hundred across the James to seize and hold Deep Bottom. This was to be done by a surprise early in the morning, and I ordered that the movement should be made by the several divisions of the Tenth and Eighteenth Corps at daybreak.

Colonel Foster of the Tenth Corps got there with his troops in time, and the movement was successful. Late that morning I saw General Martindale's brigade pass my headquarters, having to march a large seven miles before he could reach with his command the point at which he was to take part in the movement. If Smith, his immediate commander, had sent Martindale his orders as they were given to him, then here was a very gross dereliction of duty in not moving when ordered. Whereupon I sat down and wrote a letter to General Smith stating the fact,[1] asking him to have the matter brought to the attention of General Martindale in a proper manner. The letter is published to be open to criticism.

Smith telegraphed me back a reply in which he insisted that I had threatened him with relief from command.[2] I had not intended to do any such thing, and the letter does not bear that construction. He was seeking a quarrel, and proceeded to write me that he had moved troops longer than I had, and that he was my superior in that.

As Smith had reported to me at Fortress Monroe in 1861 as a lieutenant of topographical engineers who had never commanded a man in his life except his servant, when I was a major-general in command of several thousand men, and had been moving large bodies of troops from Boston to Annapolis, from Annapolis to Washington, from the capital to the Relay House, and from the Relay House to Baltimore; and had afterwards moved troops from Boston to Ship Island, and from Ship Island to New Orleans, and from New Orleans all over the State of Louisiana, it seemed to me that I had had much more experience in moving troops than he had; and as a topographical engineer is not the highest grade at West Point, I did not think I should be insulted by a second grade West Pointer. I overlooked all that, however, and wrote him an unofficial letter explaining my first letter, asking him if he did not regret sending me such a reply.[3]

By the regulations of the service all communications in regard to military matters are to be forwarded to the superior officer through the officer in the next highest grade, and if this is not done it may be inquired into by a court-martial. Yet Smith sent my letter and

---

[1] See Appendix No. 72. [2] See Appendix No. 73. [3] See Appendix No. 74.

his reply, but not my unofficial letter explaining it, to General Rawlings, chief of staff of the lieutenant-general, with a note asking that he might be relieved from his command in the department of Virginia and North Carolina.[1]

Of this General Grant took no notice of which there is any official evidence, and Smith went to Washington without the leave of his commanding general, and there saw Senator Foote, of Vermont, and used influence and what statements I know not with the War Department to get an order from the President giving him command of the Eighteenth Corps, which he then had, having taken it out, in fact, from under my command. All this was done through Major-General Halleck, chief of staff, without any notice to me or explanation sought. The order No. 225 was sent to me directly from Washington, and paragraph I. reads as follows: —

The troops of the Department of North Carolina and Virginia serving with the Army of the Potomac in the field under Major-General Smith will constitute the Eighteenth Army Corps, and Maj.-Gen. William F. Smith is assigned by the President to the command of the Corps. Maj.-Gen. B. F. Butler will command the remainder of the troops in the Department, having his headquarters at Fortress Monroe.

Upon receiving the order I called upon General Grant with it, showed it to him, and asked him if this was his act and his desire, and if so would he kindly tell me what act or fault of mine had caused such action on his part. He replied: "But I don't want this."[2]

Meanwhile, before the order reached General Grant, Smith had asked leave of absence to go to New York. That application, which was *not* sent through me, as it should have been, was granted.[3]

I narrated to General Grant exactly what had taken place with Smith, and said that if I might be permitted to advise, Smith should not be put in charge of the Eighteenth Corps, whatever might happen to me. I said that his conduct in disobeying my order and that of General Grant to make the attack on Petersburg was not

---

[1] See Appendix No. 75.

[2] It will be observed that the despatch from General Grant to Halleck was before any complaint had been made by me to Grant of Smith, and Grant asked Halleck to appoint a committee to report the facts and condition of my command.

[3] See Appendix No. 76.

only sufficient to cause his removal, but had caused a very great disaster to the country; yet, while he was a brave enough soldier when left to his separate command, he always employed his time in making reconnoissances and not in making movements when ordered. I said to him: "You know his obstinacy and insubordination, and you know that he is not satisfied with anything that anybody else suggests, and he has not." [1] And I appealed to his justice whether such an act could be done against me upon the representations of such a man. He said this was not what he wanted at all, and that he would remedy it. I bowed and left him. Soon after he issued an order [2] revoking the order referred to, and a little later he relieved Smith from command, and sent him after his friend McClellan into retirement, of whom in New York Smith immediately became a very violent political supporter. Grant then ordered the Nineteenth Corps to my command. [3]

I am thus careful in giving exactly what was said between General Grant and myself for a reason which will presently appear.

Within ten days after the receipt by Smith of the lieutenant-general's order relieving him from command, he wrote a letter [4] to Senator Foote, his coadjutor, in the attempt to get me relieved, who put it in such condition that it has been published. It is such a letter as no honorable, decent, well-disposed man could have written under any possible temptation. It contains calumnies upon myself as well as upon General Grant. · Fortunately I am alive to contradict them.

Smith says in this letter that the last of June or the first of July, 1864, General Grant, accompanied by myself, came to his (Smith's) headquarters, and that the lieutenant-general, after having been there a while said to me: "General, that drink of whiskey I took has done me good," and then asked Smith to give him another, — intending it to be inferred that I gave Grant the whiskey. And knowing, as he says, that Grant drank too much, and not thinking that it would be polite to refuse him in my presence, he had a bottle opened for him, and gave him a glass of whiskey, without asking me to a glass or taking one himself. After Grant had taken a drink the bottle was corked up again and put away, — not the usual manner in which

---

[1] See Appendix No. 77.   [2] See Appendix No. 78.
[3] See Appendix No. 79.   [4] See Appendix No. 80.

hosts deal with liquor which their guests ask for. Smith goes on to say that after the lapse of an hour or less Grant asked for another drink which he took; that soon after he left, and Smith says he went out to see him upon his horse,— he doesn't say he helped him to mount. But he does say that as he returned to his tent he said to a staff officer of his: "General Grant has gone away drunk; General Butler has seen it, and will never fail to use the weapon which has been put into his hands."

Let us examine this story a little: The commanding general of the armies of the United States, and a particular personal friend of his subordinate general, calls upon the latter with his commander upon a visit of ceremony. This subordinate general, being asked for a drink when he claims to know that that is not good for his friend, gives it to him. When his friend calls for another he gets that and starts for home. Then his subordinate officer calls the attention of his aid to the fact that his superior officer is drunk, — although if Grant was drunk, there was no occasion to call attention to the fact, for it would be plainly visible, — and says that General Butler will use it as a weapon which has been put into his hands.

General Smith, who put it there? When was it heard before that a general in the army takes pains to disclose the condition of drunkenness to which he has brought the commanding general of the armies? If there was no relation but that of host and guest between them, how could an honorable man do that? A man judges another by himself, and Smith must have judged me by himself when he stated to his staff officer that I would use, as a weapon against his friend, the drunkenness which *he* had caused. That declaration shows that Smith had it in his mind that that was a potent weapon, which might be used. Again, Smith's relations and mine, as we have seen, were more than strained. He was endeavoring to get out from under my command, after having insulted me. Why put a weapon in my hands to be used against him to prevent the accomplishment of his project? He explains our relations by saying that the next time he saw me with General Grant, a few days afterwards, he did not speak to me.

I have no reason as a man of sobriety to quarrel with the story of Smith as against my character in that regard. He doesn't offer me a drink, but corks up the bottle and puts it away so that I shall not get one, and he doesn't offer me any the second time the bottle is brought out, thereby paying tribute to my temperance.

Now I know, and solemnly aver, that no such thing ever did happen or could have happened between the three of us. First, I was under no such relations at that time as to have been visiting Smith at his headquarters. I don't usually visit, until apology is made, any man, general or other, who has insulted me. I did meet him at Grant's headquarters about that time. The inference which Smith seeks to have drawn is that Grant got that first glass of whiskey, which he said did him good, from me or at my head-quarters. But Smith knew, and all of the other officers under my command knew, that I drank no spirituous liquors in the field nor had any at my headquarters. Smith, reckless as he is, does not dare to say what he cowardly insinuates.

Again, he does not give any word or act of Grant that shows that he was drunk, but only says that his voice showed plainly that the liquor had affected him. That I can deny, because there never was any such happening as Smith relates. I never saw General Grant drink a glass of spirituous liquor in my life. I had heard of such slanders against him in his younger days, and I observed his con-duct in that regard narrowly. I had seen him drink wine at the dinner table but nowhere else, and upon the question of his drinking or not drinking, or having drank or not having drank, no word ever passed between Grant and myself. I should never have dreamed of insulting General Grant by such an accusation. If I could have so far demeaned myself, I should have expected Grant to dismiss me from the service at once, as he ought to have done, and as I would have done to him under the same circumstances. Smith's letter shows that he is dastard enough to use such weapons.

The official orders and correspondence which I publish will show the state of facts. I had not suggested that he be relieved from the army for his misconduct, even after the insulting and garbled correspondence which he sent to Grant in an unmilitary manner. On the 21st of June he had asked that he be relieved from under my command. Grant had taken no official action in regard to this application. On the 2d of July Smith had asked for a leave of absence, pleading ill-health. That was granted for a period of ten days.

General Order No. 225 of the 7th of July relieved Smith from under my command, but the Tenth Corps and Kautz's cavalry division and the rest of the troops remained under my command. The headquarters of the department were continued, as they had always been, at Fortress Monroe. The effect of this was to relieve Smith and the troops under his command from being under my command. Therefore, at General Grant's suggestion, the President had taken him out of my command.

I was more than willing that Smith should go out from under my command. I would have given up a corps to get rid of him. As

HEADQUARTERS OF GEN. GODFREY WEITZEL BEFORE RICHMOND.

soon as this order was promulgated, as I have stated, and I received it, I called on General Grant on the 10th day of July, and I have already stated what passed between us, at which interview he said it did not suit him at all.

Smith says he called upon Grant on Sunday the 10th of July, and found me there but did not speak to me, and that after I had left he had a long confidential conversation with General Grant, after which he went to New York on leave of absence.

The record shows that at thirty minutes past one o'clock P. M. on that Sunday after Smith had gone, Grant suspended the operation of the order of July 7, and directed that the Eighteenth Army Corps should remain under my command, and that another army corps, the Nineteenth, should be added to my department.

I heard nothing more of Smith and thought nothing more about him or his purposes, and did not again see General Grant on this subject.

Again Smith, in his letter, says: —

On my return from a short leave of absence on the 19th of July, General Grant sent for me to report to him, and then told me that he "could not relieve General Butler," and that as I had so severely criticised General Meade he had determined to relieve me from the command of the Eighteenth Corps and order me to New York City to await orders. The next morning the General gave some other reason, such as an article in the *Tribune* reflecting on General Hancock, which I had nothing in the world to do with.

The *Tribune* article stated that Hancock did not come up until midnight after the negro troops had captured the works around Petersburg, and that after his arrival he refused the use of his troops to co-operate with Smith, — thus throwing the blame for not taking that city upon Hancock.

Smith says that he knew nothing about the article in which Hancock was slandered in the New York *Tribune*, but he doesn't say that he told Grant so, because he says that General Grant assigned his connection with that letter as a reason for his removal. And why? Before the 2d of July a complaint was made by General Hancock of this article, asking that the author, who was a reporter at the headquarters of the Eighteenth Corps, might be dealt with. On the 2d of July Grant sent me the following order: —

CITY POINT, July 2, 1864, 11 o'clock A. M.

MAJOR-GENERAL BUTLER:

A correspondent, Mr. ——, understood to be with your command, has published in the N. Y. *Tribune* of 27th an article false and slanderous upon a portion of the army now in the field. You will please direct his arrest and have him sent here.

U. S. GRANT.

General Grant obtained an interview with Mr. ——, and upon an examination sent him from the army, being satisfied that he wrote the article with the knowledge of Smith, and knowing that when Hancock came up he made the generous offer to surrender his command to Smith for that part of the work, because Smith knew the ground upon which the operations were to be performed.

Now, if anything has been proven it is that Hancock arrived early in the evening and offered to co-operate with Smith in every way, even to giving up the command of the movement of his corps to Smith. Smith knew that he had knowledge of the article, and knew that Grant had ascertained that fact, and yet he denied it, and he knew that Grant relieved him, not for his insubordination, or any other thing done during his absence on leave, but for having participated in publishing a libel upon his brother superior officer, before that, and for denying the truth about it. No one, upon reading the article, which comprises nearly seven columns of closely printed matter in the *Tribune*, can doubt that Grant was right.

To remove from the memory of General Grant all obloquies in the letter of Smith, I ought in justice to say a few more words before I dismiss him, I trust, forever.

Because of the very decided contradiction of Smith's statements I have above given, it is due that I show by facts that his official statements, even, in any matter, are not reliable. I have already touched upon the mendacity of his report to me at midnight of the 15th of June that "General Hancock had not then come up," and called attention to the statements of Lieutenant Davenport, my staff officer, directly and fully contradicting him.

I also call attention to the letter of General Hinks which likewise . contradicts him in that point: —

The Second Corps was on the march towards Petersburg on the 15th, arriving within a mile of that portion of the works already captured by my division at about sunset, and about ten o'clock at night moved into these works, *General Smith being then upon the ground; and by his orders* my division was withdrawn to the rear some seventy-five or one hundred yards.

Again I call attention to what has passed into history relative to the hour of Smith's attack and Hancock's arrival.

Capt. Gordon McCabe, at the head of Pegram's Battery, of the Army of Northern Virginia, in an address delivered before the Association of the Army of Northern Virginia,[1] says: —

---

[1] Vol. II., Southern Historical Society Papers, Nov. 1, 1876, p. 257.

Smith's attack was made at 7.30 P. M. and scarcely had the assault ended when Hancock came up.

Gen. Francis A. Walker, chief of staff of General Hancock, says : —[1]

The head of General Hancock's column was now, say 6.30 P. M., at the Bryant House, about a mile in the rear of Hinks' position (see map) and left instructions for Birney and Gibbon to move forward as soon as they could ascertain where they were needed. General Hancock rode to General Smith, and informed him that two of his divisions were close at hand ready for any movement which in his judgment should be made, General Smith informing him that the enemy had been reinforced during the evening, and requesting him to relieve his troops (Smith's) in the front line of the captured works. This relief was completed by 11 o'clock.

Horace Greeley says,[2] after stating the fact of the attack by Smith, and his success : —

Fatalities multiplied. Hancock, with two divisions forming the van of the Army of the Potomac, came up just after nightfall, and, waiving his seniority, tendered his force to Smith to put part of it into the captured works relieving his own troops, but made no further use of it.

Smith in his official report,[3] says : —

. . . We had thus broken through the strong line of rebel works, but heavy darkness was upon us,[4] and as I heard some hours before that Lee's army was rapidly crossing at Drury's Bluff,[5] I deemed it was wiser to hold what we had than by attempting to reach the bridges to lose what we had gained, and have the troops meet with a disaster. I knew also that some portion of the Army of the Potomac was coming to aid

---

[1] History of the Second Army Corps, p. 531.

[2] The American Conflict, p. 585.

[3] Dated August 9, 1864.

[4] This must have been at about quarter of eight o'clock, for the reason that Smith in his report of the 16th of June, states that he made his attack at seven, and that in about twenty minutes the works at Jordan's House and on its left were carried by the divisions of Generals Brooks and Hinks; that he then ordered the colored troops to carry some heavy profile works in the rear of the line captured, which was gallantly done, and at the same time General Martindale had advanced and carried the enemy's works toward Jordan's House and the Appomattox,—where as a matter of fact, as General Beauregard says, that part of the enemy's lines was undefended.

[5] Troops at Drury's Bluff, the railroad being cut, could not have got to where Smith was in twenty-six hours. Who could have told him that Lee's army was crossing at Drury's Bluff? The truth was that none of Lee's army got to Petersburg until the morning of the 18th of June.

Vide Military Operations of General Beauregard, Vol. II., p. 236.

us, and therefore the troops were placed so as to occupy the commanding positions and wait for daylight.[1] The Second Corps began to come in after midnight and relieved my extended lines, and our gallant men rested after a toilsome day.

If Lee was coming, the sooner Smith could get the Appomattox between himself and Lee the better. Why wait? In fact, the troops of Lee did not get into Petersburg until the morning of the 18th. Kershaw's division of Anderson's Corps, the first of General Lee's force that arrived at Petersburg, only reached that place on the morning of the 18th of June, as is established by the following telegram: —

HEADQUARTERS, PETERSBURG, June 18, 1864, 11.30 A. M.

GEN. BRAXTON BRAGG, RICHMOND, VA.:

Occupied last night my new lines without impediment. Kershaw's division arrived about 7.30 and Field's at about 9.30 o'clock. They are being placed in position. All apparently quiet this morning. General Lee has just arrived.

G. T. BEAUREGARD,

Major-General.[2]

Mr. Greeley further says: —

And now, though the night was clear and the moon nearly full, Smith rested until morning, after the old but not good fashion of 1861–1862.

Quoting further from Captain McCabe: —[3]

The prize was now within his [Smith's] grasp, had he boldly advanced, and the moon, shining brightly, favored such enterprise. But Smith, it would seem, although possessed of considerable professional skill, was not endowed with that intuitive sagacity which swiftly discerned the chances of the moment, and thus halting at that threshold of decisive victory contented himself with partial success, and having relieved his division in the captured works with Hancock's troops, waited for the morning.

Frank Wilkeson, of the Eleventh New York Battery (Hancock's), says: —[4]

That night was made to fight on. A bright and almost full moon shone above us.

---

[1] The sun rose at 4.28 the next morning; daylight would have come to Smith at four certainly.

[2] Military Operations of General Beauregard, Vol. II., p. 236

[3] Southern Historical Society Pape s, Vol. II., No 6, p 268.

[4] Recollections of a Private Soldier in the Army of the Potomac, p 161

General Grant says in his official report of the operations of his army : —[1]

With a part of his men only he made an assault and carried the lines northeast of Petersburg from the Appomattox River, for a distance of over two and one half miles, captured fifteen pieces of artillery and three hundred prisoners. This was about 7 P. M. *Between the line thus captured and Petersburg, there were no other works, and there was no evidence that the enemy had reinforced Petersburg with a single brigade* from any source. The night was clear, the moon shining brightly, and favorable to further operations.

Hancock, with two divisions of the Second Corps, reached General Smith *just after dark*, and offered the services of his troops as he (Smith) might wish, waiving rank to the commander whom he actually supposed, having passed the position of the enemy's force, knew what to do with the troops. But instead of taking these troops and pushing at once into Petersburg, he requested General Hancock to relieve a part of his line in the captured works, which was done before midnight.

When was the heavy darkness that Smith says in his report prevented his going on?

At the time of Smith's arrival Beauregard had under his command at Petersburg twenty-two hundred effective men. The line was seven and one half miles long, and these troops occupied three miles of it, leaving four and one half miles undefended. On the Bermuda Hundred front was Jackson's division less Ransom's and Gracie's brigades, giving him thirty-two hundred men there, or a total force of fifty-four hundred on that front and in Petersburg. Hoke's division was ordered to him at 11.30 A.M., on the 15th, and Hagood's brigade thereof reached Petersburg just after Smith's fight at seven o'clock and the capture of the batteries. They were followed by two other brigades within a few hours. At 10.20 P. M. of the 15th, General Beauregard ordered the abandonment of the Bermuda Hundred lines, and the removal of that portion of Johnson's division to Petersburg. Johnson evacuated the Bermuda Hundred line at dawn on the 16th, and arrived in Petersburg at 10 A. M. Thus reinforced, Beauregard had an effective force in Petersburg of ten thousand men. On the 16th and on the 17th after dusk Gracie's brigade arrived, twelve hundred strong.[2]

---

[1] War Records, Vol. 36, Part I., p. 25.
[2] Military Operations of General Beauregard, pp. 229-232.

In planning Smith's movement, the fact that the troops in our front might be sent to reinforce Petersburg was taken into account, as, if they all got there, we should still be four to one of the enemy. And when Beauregard had ten thousand men there on the 17th and 18th, Grant's corps of fifty-five thousand men were attacking the new line built during Smith's delay, and they failed to carry the new works even with the great superiority of numbers.

A great misfortune and fault of the Army of the Potomac which enabled the rebels to defend themselves successfully was that the men of the Army of the Potomac were put in to attack intrenched lines, and that they substantially would not do. They had been for six weeks led to abortive attacks accompanied with great slaughter and no success,[1] and their great desire was to have Lee attack them when they were behind defensive works, as they would have been if Lee's men had been stopped, by holding the enemy's line of works at the Appomattox bridges as Smith had been ordered to do.

Of this opinion was General Hancock. By the order of General Meade he attacked the enemy's new line at 6.30 P. M. on the 16th and fought all night (so that it seems the moonlight was sufficient for him to fight), and reported to General Meade the reason of his repulse as follows: —

I do not think the loss heavy but in officers. I do not think the men attacked with persistence; they appeared to be wearied.

General Meade, in a despatch to General Grant at 6 A. M. of the 17th, describing the attack of the 16th, says: —

Advantage was taken of the fine moonlight to press the enemy all night. A rough return would make our loss two thousand killed and wounded. I regret to say that many officers are among the numbers. Our men are tired and the attack could not be made with the vigor and force which characterized our fighting in the Wilderness. If they had not been, I think they might have been more successful.

The men were tired and weary of assaulting works, of being led to assault intrenchments; not tired and weary in the sense of physical fatigue. Most of them had rested quietly during the night of the 15th, and the day of the 16th before they were led to the attack

---

[1] Appendix No. 81.

without having any distance to march. What the weariness of the tired men was, and of what they were tired, and their joy in knowing that they were marching to have some works to defend, cannot be better stated than by one of their number, then a private soldier, Frank Wilkeson of the Eleventh New York Battery, who for his gallantry and good conduct was soon after appointed a lieutenant in the regular artillery. He says : —[1]

On the night of June 14, 1864, the battery to which I belonged went into park close to the James River, but not within sight of it.

.　　.　　.　　.　　.　　.　　.　　.　　.　　.　　.　　.

On the morning of June 15th we moved close to the James River and parked. I was lying under a tree near an old abandoned house. Below me and a little to my left, a pontoon bridge stretched across the muddy waters of the river James. A few steamboats were paddling to and fro, some ferrying troops across the river, others apparently doing nothing. The Second Corps troops were rapidly marching across the pontoon bridge, which swayed up and down under their heavy tread. On the other side was a village of tents and great piles of boxes. Many men were swimming in the river. . . .

Infantry hurried past us; batteries of artillery rolled by. We recognized some of the latter, and said : " There goes K of the Fourth United States Artillery ; " and we waved our hands to the men whom we knew. There was a gap in the column of hurrying troops. Our captain swung himself into his saddle and commanded : " By piece from the right front into column, march ! " and we were off for Petersburg. We crossed on the pontoon bridge, which had a peculiar earthquaky motion, and entered the village of tents. Thousand of boxes of hard bread and barrels of pork were there, but instead of being open and we helping ourselves as we marched, the troops were halted, and jammed, and irritated, by having to stand around with open haversacks, while a comparatively few commissary employees slowly dealt out the precious provisions to us. Hours were worth millions of dollars each on this flank movement. They were really priceless, and we dawdled away three of them in getting a little food into our haversacks. This was Potomac Army economy. The Second Corps, if the boxes of hard bread, and barrels of pork, and coffee, and sugar had lined the road, and we enlisted men had helped ourselves, might have carried off twenty thousand dollars worth of extra provisions; but we would have saved three hours, and they, if properly used, would have been worth one hundred million dollars each, and would have saved

---

[1] Recollections of a Private Soldier, p. 153.

thousands of men's lives also. But we fooled away the time; we stood and chaffed one another; and the cannon in our front roared and the musketry rolled. Then we marched. We were in high spirits. We marched free. Every enlisted man in the Second Corps knew that we had outmarched the Confederates. We knew that some of our troops were assaulting the Confederate works at Petersburg. The booming of the cannon cheered us. We were tired, hungry, worn with six weeks of continuous and bloody fighting and severe marching; but now that we, the enlisted men of the Second Corps, knew that at last a flank movement had been successful, we wanted to push on and get into the fight and capture Petersburg. We knew that we had outmarched Lee's veterans, and that our reward was at hand. The Second Corps was in fine mettle. On all sides I heard men assert that Petersburg and Richmond were ours; that the war would virtually be ended in less than twenty-four hours.

Night came. The almost full moon arose above the woods, and gold-flecked the dust column which rose above us. We had heard heavy firing about sundown, and judged that we should be drawing near the battle-line. We entered a pine woods, and there we met a mob of black troops, who were hauling some brass guns. They had attached long ropes to the limbers, and, with many shouts, were dragging them down the road. Some of them bore flaming torches of pine knots in their hands. They sang, they shouted, they danced weirdly, as though they were again in Congo villages making medicine. They were happy, dirty, savagely excited, but they were not soldiers. As we, the Second Corps, met these victorious troops, the eager infantrymen asked: " Where did you get those guns?" They replied: " We 'uns captured them from the rebels to-day." "Bah!" an infantry sergeant, who was marching by my side, exclaimed; "you negroes captured nothing from Lee's men. The city is ours. There is not a brigade of the Army of Northern Virginia ahead of us." And we all exclaimed: " The city is ours! We have outmarched them!" And we strode on through the dense dust clouds, with parched throats, foot-sore and weary. Not a grumble did I hear. But with set jaws we toiled on, intent on capturing Petersburg before the Army of Northern Virginia got behind the works. It was: " March, march, march! No straggling now. It is far better to march to-night than to assault earthworks defended by Lee's men to-morrow. Hurry along! hurry, hurry, hurry!" And we marched our best. We passed a group of soldiers who wore the distinctive badge of the Second Corps, cooking by the roadside, their muskets stacked by their fire. We asked how far it was to the battle-line. " Only a few hundred yards," they replied. Then we asked what Confederate troops were ahead of us. They answered, with a scornful laugh:

"Petersburg militia." We asked what Union troops were engaged, and they replied : "Some of Butler's men." With the dislike all soldiers have for unknown troops, we said heartily : "Damn Butler's men! We do not know them. We wish the Fifth or Sixth Corps were here instead of them." Many soldiers anxiously inquired: "Will Butler's men fight?" Then some private, who was better informed than the most of us, told us that Butler's men had been lying at Bermuda Hundred, and that there were many negro troops among them. The noses of the Second Corps men were cocked sharply in the air at this information.

Word was passed among us that the negro troops had had famous success that day; that they had wrested a heavy line of earthworks from the Confederates, and had captured eighteen guns. The soldiers halted for an instant. They examined their rifles, and shifted their cartridge-boxes to a position where they could get at them easily, and they drank deeply from their canteens. Then belts were tightened, blanket rolls shifted, the last bits of hardtack the men had been chewing were swallowed, and their mouths again filled with water and rinsed out, and then, throughout the ranks, murmurs arose of : "Now for it;" "Put us into it, Hancock, my boy; we will end this damned Rebellion to-night!" and we laughed lowly, and our hearts beat high. Soon we heard commands given to the infantry, and they marched off. My battery moved forward, twisted obliquely in and out among the stumps, and then the guns swung into battery on a cleared space.

And then — and then — we went to cooking. That night was made to fight on. A bright and almost full moon shone above us. The Confederate earthworks were in plain view before us, earthworks which we knew were bare of soldiers. There was a noisy fire from the Confederate pickets in front of us. So unnerved and frightened were they that their bullets sang high above us. We cooked and ate, and fooled the time away. This when every intelligent enlisted man in the Second Corps knew that not many miles away the columns of the Army of Northern Virginia were marching furiously to save Petersburg and Richmond and the Confederacy. We could almost see those veteran troops, lean, squalid, hungry, and battle-torn, with set jaws and anxious-looking eyes, striding rapidly through the dust, pouring over bridges, crowding through the streets of villages, and ever hurrying on to face us. And we knew that once they got behind the earthworks in our front, we could not drive them out. They did not surrender cannon and intrenchments to disorderly gangs of armed negroes. They did not understand how troops could lose earthworks when assailed by equal numbers of soldiers. Still we cooked and ate, and sat idly looking into one another's eyes, questioningly at first, then impatiently and then angrily. Gradually the fact that we were not to fight that night impressed itself on us. I walked over to the limber of my gun, opened my knapsack, and took out a campaign map and a pair of compasses. Returning to the fire the map was spread on the ground. As I measured the distances a group of excited soldiers gathered around and watched the work. We had the less distance to march, about nine hours the start, and allowing for the time lost at the crossing of the James River we were at 11 P. M. four or five hours ahead of the Army of Northern Virginia. "Will they be in the works by morning, men?" I asked; and all answered, "By God, they will!" Discouraged, I put away the map, loaded a pipe, lighted it, and strolled off down the line, stopping at almost every fire I came to to talk to the infantry soldiers. The rage of the intelligent enlisted men was devlish. The most blood-curdling blasphemy I ever listened to I heard that night, uttered by the men who knew they were to be sacrificed on the morrow. The whole corps was furiously excited. I returned to my battery a little after midnight. Seated on the ground I rested my back against one of the ponderous wheels of my gun. Resting there I slept.

CAMP OF COLORED VOLUNTEERS BEFORE RICHMOND.

At early dawn I was awake and tried to examine the Confederate line. I noticed that the noisy, wasteful picket-firing of the night before had ceased; that the main line of earthworks, indistinctly seen in the gray light, was silent. Some of our infantry came into our slight earthwork, and we stood gazing into the indistinctness before us. All of us were greatly depressed.

It grew lighter and lighter, and there before us, fully revealed, was a long, high line of intrenchments, with heavy redoubts, where cannon were massed at the angles, silent, grim. No wasteful fire shot forth from that line. Now and then a man rose up out of the Confederate rifle-pits, and a rifle-ball flew close above us, no longer singing high in the air. Sadly we looked at one another. We knew that the men who had fought us in the Wilderness, at Spottsylvania, North Anna, and Cold Harbor were in the works, sleeping, gaining strength to repulse our assault, while their pickets watched for them.

At intervals tiny columns of smoke rose from behind their line. . . . It was broad daylight. I had eaten my breakfast and was looking over the field of yesterday's fighting. Some dead men lay on the ground; but the scarcity of those in gray plainly showed that they had no stomach for fighting, that they were raw, undisciplined militia, who had abandoned their powerful line of earthworks when attacked by a few black troops. At sixty feet in front of the captured works I saw pine trees which had been struck with Confederate bullets thirty feet from the ground. This told, better than words, the nervous condition of the men who pretended to defend the line.

Wandering toward the rear, I came on the line of rifle-pits which had been used by the Confederate pickets, and saw two dead men lying close together. I walked over to them. One was a burly negro sergeant, as black as coal, in blue; the other was a Confederate line sergeant, in gray. Their bayoneted rifles lay beside them. Curious at the nearness of the bodies, I turned them over and looked carefully at them. They had met with unloaded rifles and had fought a duel with their bayonets, each stabbing the other to death.

The battery bugler blew "Boots and Saddles!" and I hastened back to my gun, to hear that the other corps of the Potomac Army had arrived and that the infantry would make a general assault that day, probably in the afternoon. We limbered up, then marched to the left and took a new position on a bit of level land which gradually sloped toward a creek which flowed between us and the silent Confederate line. The preliminary artillery practice began, so as to announce in thunder tones that we were getting ready to make an assault. I worked listlessly to and fro from the muzzle of my three-inch gun, carelessly looking ahead to see if the fire produced any result. It did not. The gunners of the Confederate batteries were evidently husbanding their ammunition. They treated us with silent contempt. But, unable to withstand our steady hammering, they at last coldly responded to our attentions. Shot skipped by us, shell exploded among us; but, with very unusual luck, we lost but few men. . . .

The afternoon passed quickly away. One of the caissons, which belonged to a battery that was in action alongside of us, struck by a shell, blew up, and two men were blown up with it. A long bolt made by our English brothers did this work, and it added to my dislike of all things English. As the sun sank the infantry prepared to deliver the assault that we had been announcing as to be made. A staff officer rode up; we ceased firing. The smoke drifted off of the field. Utterly exhausted, I threw myself on the hot ground and watched the doomed men who were to try to carry the Confederate line. The charging cheer rang out loudly, the line of blue-clad soldiers rushed forward, the Confederate pickets emptied their rifles, jumped from their rifle-pits, and ran for their main line, which was still silent excepting the artillery. This was served rapidly but not very effectively. The line of blue swept on in good order, cheering loudly and continuously. They drew near to the Confederate earthworks. Canister cut gaps in the ranks. Then the heads of Lee's infantry rose above their intrenchments. I saw the glint of the sun on their polished rifle barrels. A cloud of smoke curled along the works. Our men began to tumble in large numbers; some fell forward, others backward, others staggered a few steps and then sank down as though to rest. Still I did not hear the roll of the musketry. Suddenly it burst on me, mingled with the fierce Confederate battle-cry. The field grew hazy with smoke. Rifles were tossed high in the air. Battle-flags went down with a sweep to again appear and plunge into the smoke. Wounded men straggled out of the battle. Fresh troops hurried by the battery and disappeared in the hazy smoke. Away off to our right I heard the charging cheer of our soldiers and the thunderous roll of musketry; to the left more musketry and exultant howls, as though we had met with success. In our front the fire grew steadily fiercer and fiercer. The wounded men, who drifted through the battery, told us that the works were very strong, and that beyond them there was another and still stronger line, and that our troops were fighting in the open before the front line and were not meeting with any success. Night settled down, and the fight still went on; but it fagged. The musketry was no longer a steady roar, and we could see the flashes of the rifles, and the Confederate parapet glowing redly. At points the musketry fire broke out fiercely, then died down. In our front the fight was over. My battery moved forward under the direction of a staff officer, and we threw up an earthwork.

That night the news gatherers walked the battle lines. They told us that the assault had been bloodily repulsed, excepting at one or two unimportant points. And they also brought an exceedingly interesting bit of news or gossip, or a camp rumor. They said: "We have heard from some of Butler's men that in the breast pocket of the coat of a Confederate officer, who was killed in front of their lines at Bermuda Hundred, on June 15, was found the 'morning report' of the Confederate army which was defending Petersburg on that day, and that this report showed that Beauregard did not have over ten thousand men, most of whom were militia, with which to defend Petersburg, and that Butler had laid this report before Baldy Smith and Hancock, and had urged them to make the assault and capture Petersburg before the Army of Northern Virginia came up; but that they, Smith and Hancock, had hesitated and dawdled the night away." . . .

About seventy thousand of the good men we had crossed the Rapidan with lay dead behind us, or were in hospitals, or languished in Confederate military prisons. So I, one morning, claimed my discharge, which had been ordered by Secretary of War Stanton while we were fighting in front of Cold Harbor. Getting it, I went to Washington, where a commission in the Fourth United States Artillery awaited me.

The reader will now see why the whole Army of the Potomac was repulsed on the nights of the 17th and 18th of June, with plenty of moonlight to fight in, with a loss of prisoners captured, and two thousand killed and wounded. This was the last attempt of the Army of the Potomac to capture Petersburg for many months, save by a mine and a siege, both of which were ineffectual to that end.

Having exhibited General Smith's entire untruthfulness in his statements that I have brought to the reader's attention, I turn to the further statements contained in the letter to Senator Foote which has already been referred to, that I had threatened Grant, as he had been informed, with opposing the election of Lincoln: —

I also learned that General Butler had threatened to make public something that would prevent the President's re-election.

Smith did not know that I had been offered by the President the second place on his ticket, and had declined it with my promise to give him my fullest support, which I ever after did do.

He also says: —

General Butler had made some threat, with reference to the Chicago Convention, which he (Butler) said he had in his breeches pocket.

That is simply a falsifier's rank nonsense. Lincoln had been nominated almost by acclamation more than a month before. What could I do with the Chicago Convention where the southern majority of delegates and their Copperhead allies hated me with more virulence and vigor than they did any other man in the United States, and where I should have expected to be murdered had I appeared. That convention was held on the 29th of the following August.

Smith also says: —

Since I have been in New York I have heard from two different sources (one being from General Grant's headquarters, and one from a staff-officer of a general on intimate official relations with General Butler) that General Butler went to General Grant and threatened to expose his intoxication if the order was not revoked.

Let him produce his informants, or let him stand only upon his own uncontradicted word. I challenge the result in either case.

I also call attention to the most wonderfully revengeful postscript of this letter: —

I have not referred to the state of things existing at headquarters when I left, and to the fact that General Grant was then in the habit of getting liquor *in a surreptitious manner*, because it was not relevant to my case, but if you think that at any time the matter may be of importance to the country, I will give it to you.

Got liquor surreptitiously? The lieutenant-general could have commanded all the whiskey of the United States to his army if he thought proper, and it would have come. If he had let it be known that he would use it, his admiring friends all over the North and West would have sent him the choicest brands in the most boundless profusion. A man that would write such a postscript as that, it is hard to describe.

Let us examine a moment to see what kind of a creature this Smith is. Appointed a brigadier and promoted a major-general by the influence of his intimate friend, McClellan, *when, as we have seen, he was seeking to be dictator,* "for some service unexpressed, yet by its wages only to be guessed," he was rejected by the Senate. In 1863, for his conduct in battle, he was relieved from his command by General Burnside, then in command of the Army of the Potomac, and went to the Southern army. He ingratiated himself with Grant by his topographical performances in matters which resulted

HEADQUARTERS OF GEN. ALFRED TERRY BEFORE RICHMOND.

in the difficulty between Generals Thomas and Grant, which lasted until after the battle of Nashville, in September, 1864. Grant, in September, 1863, again recommended Smith's promotion to the President, but his name was not sent in till March, 1864. After Grant was put in command as general-in-chief in the spring of 1864, he once more took him up and had him again appointed major-general. The Senate delayed confirming his appointment, but Grant, by his great influence, procured his confirmation. He detailed him in command of a corps under myself, and sustained

Smith in all his insubordinations, taking him with his corps of more than twenty-thousand men to Cold Harbor where Smith lost nearly a quarter of the troops, for which he criticised Grant, as he confesses. This detail Grant afterwards over and over regretted.[1]

Then in the latter part of June he says Grant called at his headquarters. Knowing Grant's infirmity, he claims he gave him liquor sufficient to make him "drunk," and then went "out to see him on his horse," but called the attention of his staff officer as a witness to the condition of the general-in-chief of the army, saying of his confiding and ever-supporting friend that he would take it as a weapon to use against him, and which Smith himself afterwards did use. Then he got leave of absence, meantime writing to Washington to his coadjutor, Senator Foote, to have himself put in command of the Eighteenth Corps, independent of me, by his influence through his friend Senator Foote with Halleck.[2]

Before the 2d of July Grant learned that Smith had, in addition to his abuse of Meade, whose command of the Army of the Potomac he sought from Grant, induced a *Tribune* correspondent to publish a libel upon Hancock. Grant gave me an order to arrest the correspondent, and send him to him. Thereupon Grant caused the order in favor of Smith to be suspended, and had a confidential conversation with him on his return from his leave on the 18th, and then told him he could not relieve me, and sent Smith to New York, virtually dismissing him from the army. Being so dismissed, in ten days he wrote this most infamous and astounding letter, in which he recites to Foote his own base betrayal of his friend and commander, and his misconduct toward him as his guest, and offers to furnish Foote with further evidence by which to defame and vilify Grant, the commander of the whole armies of the United States, on whose skill and conduct the safety of the country depended, — showing that he could be true to no friend. After his friend McClellan, — the only other one we hear that Smith ever had, — was sent forever to private

---

[1] In the February number (1886) of the *Century Magazine*, page 576, is a paper written by General Grant, in which he says : —

" General W. F. Smith, who had been promoted to the rank of major-general shortly after the battle of Chattanooga, on my recommendation, had not yet been confirmed. I found a decided prejudice against his confirmation by a majority of the Senate, but I insisted that his services had been such that he should be rewarded. My wishes were now reluctantly complied with, and I assigned him to the command of one of the corps under General Butler. I was not long in finding out that the objections to Smith's promotion were well founded."

[2] See Appendix No. 82.

life by Lincoln in November, 1864, Smith turned upon him. In
December he wrote a letter to this same Foote to be shown to Lincoln, as was done, and the letter left with him disclosing to him
the fact that McClellan had written a protest against the President's
Proclamation of Emancipation, and had consulted with Smith on
the question of its publication, thus betraying both his friends, —
violating every duty in every relation with every general commanding, defaming, and attacking his best friends who supported him, —
violating every instinct of a gentleman or a man of honor by disclosing acts which he, as a host, calls his guests to commit, calling his
staff officer as a witness to the weapon he has obtained against
Grant, — and in the postscript of his letter offering to procure for
Foote other evidence to destroy the character and influence of Grant,
and to disclose their confidential secrets. He devotes his after life
to telling these tales of his own disgraceful perfidy in the magazines
of his country published after Grant's death.

Does not Smith show himself to be, though of human form,
only an animal of the lowest class, found nowhere but in America,
the generic name of the whole species being "MEPHITIS AMERI-
CANA"?

CHAPTER XVI.

CAPTURE OF FORTIFICATIONS AROUND RICHMOND, NEWMARKET HEIGHTS, DUTCH GAP CANAL, ELECTIONS IN NEW YORK AND GOLD CONSPIRACY.

IN August we had a small holding on the north side of the James River at a point known as Deep Bottom. General Grant wanted to get north of the James still further up so that if it became convenient or necessary the united armies of the Potomac and the James,— leaving enough men in the trenches before Petersburg to hold our position there, and in our front, to hold the position of the Army of the James at Bermuda Hundred,— could be thrown across the river by pontoon bridges, and make a full attack upon the city of Richmond. To be able to get there before Lee, he relied upon the fact that we had much the shorter line, as will be seen by the map. Although Lee had a railroad, yet it was in such meagre equipment and repair that only a few troops could be transported over it rapidly to the south side of Richmond, Drury's bluff; and Grant proposed that his movement should be made on the north side of Richmond against the fortifications at Chaffin's farm.

To extend his lines on the north side he detailed, on the 13th of August, Hancock with the Second Corps, to be transported from City Point by the river to Deep Bottom. At the same time I ordered General Birney to go with the Tenth Corps across from Bermuda Hundred and join Hancock in an attack upon the enemy in that quarter. The plan was that they should carry the enemy's fortifications,— the left of which, substantially, was Fort Wilkinson,— at a point known as Newmarket Heights, where there was a strong redoubt enclosed by a double line of abatis, and defended with artillery.[1]

---

[1] See Appendix No. 83.

That attack was to be made at daybreak by both corps. Grant put Hancock's corps on board transportation to go around by river, because he supposed that by marching to the river from City Point and embarking, their destination would be concealed and the surprise be more effectual.

The expedition was very well planned, but for a reason that was inherent in the movements of the Army of the Potomac, it was not well executed in point of time. I had Birney's corps ready to cross the pontoon bridge at Deep Bottom at midnight, and as he held the right of my line, and any movement of his troops upon our side of the river would be very likely to attract attention, he waited for the Second Corps. As I was to have nothing to do with the matter except to give orders to Birney to move, I remained quietly at my headquarters.

The first of the vessels containing Hancock's troops, as I was informed, reached Deep Bottom between nine and ten o'clock in the morning. Imagine my surprise at about eleven o'clock when General Hancock with his staff, — who preferred to ride from the lines before Petersburg across my pontoon bridge at Point of Rocks, and then passing over the peninsula of Bermuda Hundred, cross at Deep Bottom on the pontoon bridge there, — rode up to my headquarters. I greeted him with great cordiality, which was the state of our intercourse until the day of his death, and as we were chatting, and he seemed in no hurry, I invited him to take an early lunch with me, which, after New England fashion, was at twelve o'clock. He did so, and between twelve and one left for a ride of about seven miles to the bridge at Deep Bottom.

The attack was made quite late in the day, and was not successful. It was renewed the next day, and was in part successful, a minor fortification and four guns being captured. Then, deeming the position of the enemy to be too strong to be taken, Hancock withdrew his troops back to the lines at Petersburg, and Birney came home.[1]

The enemy having repulsed the two corps of our army, I supposed would become careless, not thinking the attack would be renewed.

[2] About the 25th of July General Grant had made a formal demonstration with Hancock's Second Corps and Birney's Corps from Bermuda Hundred across the James River by the pontoon bridge at Deep Bottom, which, for reasons that need not be discussed, was not successful, and he renewed the attempt on the 13th of August, as has been hereinbefore described.

GEN. BIRNEY, COMMANDING TENTH CORPS, ARMY OF THE JAMES, AND STAFF. (From a Photograph.)

With a view of finding out exactly how matters stood with them in that part of their lines, I caused my scouts and secret service men to make a most thorough investigation. As I have stated, I had an exceedingly accurate map, drawn by the rebels themselves, of all their fortifications, and I instructed my secret service men to find out exactly how many men were holding each fortification, including the works at Chaffin's farm and Fort Harrison, and the connecting lines of forts between them. I got such reports that upon reinvestigation I was satisfied they were correct. This took some time, but about the 20th of September I went to General Grant and explained to him my preparation, and asked his leave to make an attack in that quarter with such men as I could spare from the Army of the James. I felt satisfied that I could leave comparatively few men in my intrenchments, for while I was attacking Richmond on one side of the James I was quite sure the enemy would not find itself sufficiently at leisure to make an attack upon my lines on the other side of the river.

I drew out my plan carefully in the shape of a general order with explanations, and read it to General Grant. He was pleased to compliment the order in high terms, and yielded his assent. I told him that I hoped to do two things which had not been done before — to surprise the enemy and at least gain and hold the outer line of their fortifications, and perhaps, if I had good luck, take Chaffin's farm and get into Richmond.

I further told him that I had another thing in view. The affair of the mine at Petersburg, which had been discussed between us, had convinced me that in the Army of the Potomac negro troops were thought of no value, and with the exception of an attack under Smith on the 15th of June, where they were prevented from entering Petersburg by the sloth, inaction, or I believe worse, of Smith, the negro troops had had no chance to show their valor or staying qualities in action. I told him that I meant to take a large part of my negro force, and under my personal command make an attack upon Newmarket Heights, the redoubt to the extreme left of the enemy's line. If I could take that and turn it, then I was certain that I could gain the first line of the enemy's intrenchments around Richmond. I said: "I want to convince myself whether, when under my own eye, the negro troops will fight; and if I can take with the negroes, a redoubt that turned Hancock's corps on a former occasion, that will settle the question." ·I proposed to try this in a manner that I had not before seen attempted, either in the Army of the Potomac or elsewhere, — that is, by a regular "dash," such as I had read of in the history of the wars of Europe.

What I intended to do, and how I intended to do it, is better set forth in the order that I read to General Grant, and which I here reproduce from my order book. I give it as it was then written, because William F. Smith has stated in a magazine article that I was a "child, and incapable of giving an order in the field." That is true or false, and to substantiate its falsity I propose to submit to military critics everywhere whether I was either "a child or incapable of giving an order in the field," and allow my reputation as a commanding general to stand or fall with it.

[Confidential.]

HEADQUARTERS DEPARTMENT VIRGINIA AND NORTH CAROLINA.
IN THE FIELD, Sept. 28, 1864.

To MAJOR-GENERAL ORD, COMMANDING EIGHTEENTH CORPS;
  MAJOR-GENERAL BIRNEY, COMMANDING TENTH CORPS;
  BRIGADIER-GENERAL KAUTZ, COMMANDING DIVISION OF CAVALRY.

Pursuant to the verbal directions and written instructions of the lieutenant-general commanding, the Army of the James is about to make a movement on the north side of the James River.

ITS OBJECT

is to surprise the Confederate forces in our front here and, passing them, to get possession of the city of Richmond. Failing that, to make such serious and determined demonstration to that end as shall draw reinforcements from the right of the enemy's line in sufficient numbers so as to enable the Army of the Potomac to move upon the enemy's communication near Petersburg. The forces appropriated to this purpose are so much of the Army of the James as can be spared from the lines at Bermuda Hundred and the garrisoned posts on the river — the strength of which forces you know.

THE MANNER IN WHICH THE MOVEMENT IS TO BE MADE.

The acting chief of engineers will have caused by twelve (12) o'clock midnight of the 28th inst., a sufficient pontoon bridge, well covered to prevent noise, to be laid from the road on the south side of the James to a point near Varina or Aikens' Landing.

The Eighteenth Army Corps, with the exception of the colored division at Deep Bottom, will move across that bridge and make an attack upon the enemy's line in the manner hereinafter to be detailed.

At the same time the Tenth Corps will cross the pontoon bridge at Deep Bottom and make in like manner, and at the same time, demonstration in connection with the third (3d) division of the Eighteenth Corps from that point.

THE POSITION AND NUMBERS OF THE ENEMY.

As near as can be ascertained, the enemy hold a line of earthworks starting at a point at or near Cox's Ferry, at a station called by them "Signal Hill," running thence easterly in the rear of Cox's overseer's house, from thence to a point in the rear of J. Aikens' house, to the hill in rear of the point marked "Newmarket" on the map, across the Varina road, partially along the Kingsland road, which line, it is believed, terminates substantially as a continuous intrenched line at that point. Most of the line has abatis but no ditch.

The troops holding that line, from all the information gathered, are Bushrod Johnson's (Tennessee) brigade, about four hundred and fifty (450) men for duty, with its pickets advanced beyond Cox's overseer's house toward Dutch Gap, holding the line nearly three quarters of a mile beyond that point to a point near the Varina road, at a point about three hundred (300) yards to the west of which the line of breastworks terminates — to be resumed on the other side of road.

The Twenty-Fifth Virginia (City Battalion), numbering not to exceed two hundred (200) men for duty, are extended along the line toward Buffin's house in front of our position at Deep Bottom.

They are there joined by Bennings' (old) Georgia Brigade, commanded by Colonel Dubow, numbering about four hundred (400) men, who are extended along the line past Buffin's house — the picket line being near the house of J. Aikens.

They are there joined by Griggs' Texas Brigade, numbering about four hundred (400) men for duty, who extend along the line to a place called "Newmarket," where the enemy have a pretty strong work on a height commanding the Newmarket road.

These are all the infantry forces, except a battalion of militia reserves, numbering about one hundred and seventy-five (175) men for duty, who are in camp some distance to the rear, who form a connecting line between Johnson's Brigade and the City Battalion. These reserves are composed of soldiers below the age of eighteen (18), and above the age of forty-five (45), but they, with the City Battalion, have never been under fire.

At the place marked on the map " Drill Room," is stationed a regiment believed to be about four hundred (400) men, the Seventh South Carolina Cavalry.

At the place marked "Sweeny's Pottery," Wade Hampton's Legion, numbering about four hundred (400) men, are stationed on the easterly side of Four-Mile Creek and Bailey's Run, apparently to guard the road by which General Hancock advanced over Strawberry Plains from below Four-Mile Creek, and picketing out toward Malvern Hill. In the rear, at the intersection of the roads near the point marked " W. Throgmorton," is a regiment, the Twenty-Fourth Virginia Cavalry, numbering about four hundred (400) men.

In Chaffin's farm there is no garrison, except about one hundred (100) heavy artillerists holding that place as an intrenched camp. It is also a camp for the sick and convalescents of the Virginia battalion.

There are then no other troops between the troops herein enumerated and Richmond, except an artillery company in each of the detached works of that class numbered twenty-three (23) on the map, and the one at Toll Gate and the Race Course. The continuous line of works shown on the map are wholly unoccupied.

It will be seen, therefore, that these bodies of which we have knowledge, if the information is correct, should be two thousand eight hundred and seventy-five (2,875) men, and it may be safely predicted that there are not three thousand (3,000) effective men outside of the limits of the city of Richmond on the north side of the river.

It is upon this information, which is fully credited, that the movement is largely based.

THE MEANS OF REINFORCEMENT BY THE ENEMY.

There are between the Appomattox and the James less than thirty-five hundred (3,500) men holding a line nearly ten (10) miles in extent, and the nearest considerable body of Confederate troops are massed some seven (7) miles still further off below Petersburg.

Most of the force between the Appomattox and the James is directly in the front of our lines and cannot be much depleted.

Their means of crossing the river are by the pontoon bridge, one between the fortifications of Drury's Bluff on the west, and Chaffin's farm on the east of the James. These fortifications are about a mile apart, and have two or three barbette guns bearing on the bridge-heads. There is no other *tete du pont.* This is a pontoon bridge and is above fortifications at Chaffin's on the one side, and below Drury's on the other. These fortifications are about a mile apart. Next a trestle-work bridge with schooners for a draw at a point opposite the place of William Throgmorton at the mouth of Falling Creek landing on the westerly side of the river at the southerly side of the mouth of the creek; again a trestle bridge at a point opposite Colonel Knight's house; another trestle bridge nearly opposite the battery marked twenty-three (23) on plan. These three last have no *tetes du ponts* on the north side.

THE MANNER OF ATTACK.

A large element of the complete success of this movement depends upon the celerity and the co-operation in point of time of the several commands in the attack. It is proposed that Major-General Ord shall dispose one of the divisions of his corps in such positions as to mass them near Varina on the north bank during the night silently, so as not to be observed by the enemy, and from thence just before daybreak, which is assumed to be thirty (30) minutes past four (4) o'clock A. M., and that will govern in point of time, to make a sudden sharp attack in column upon the enemy's lines nearly opposite his position upon the Varina road. At the same time, General Birney, having massed such divisions as he chooses, or using the third division of the Eighteenth Corps at Deep Bottom for that purpose, for which it will temporarily report to him, will make a like attack substantially at the point where he attacked before in the late essay across the James, and endeavor to carry Newmarket road and the heights adjacent if he cannot turn them to the left without too great loss.

If successful, and the way can be opened, General Kautz's cavalry, having been massed near the pontoon bridge at Deep Bottom and crossing while the attack is going on, will immediately push out, attempt to cross the Newmarket road, turning the enemy's forces and left flank if possible, avoiding a fight as a preference, and attempt to reach the central, or, as it is called in the country there, Darbytown road. If successful in striking that road, General Kautz is to make the utmost diligence and celerity of marching up that road toward Richmond, or, if he finds himself opposed in such manner as to render it advisable, he will still further flank to the right and strike the Charles City road, as both roads lead into the city within a mile of each other.

If General Ord is successful in passing the enemy's line in his front he is to move right on up the Varina road, and endeavor to reach the intrenched camp at Chaffin's farm, and if possible to take it, and secure and destroy the pontoon crossing just above.

Perhaps General Ord will find the better way to take the works at Chaffin's farm is to pass them by the Varina road, or turn them near the house of J. Aikens and pass to the rear, as the demoralization of their defenders, if any get there from Johnson's command, will be greater when they find themselves cut off from Richmond.

General Ord will observe that the Varina road runs within two miles of the river, and he may be annoyed by the enemy's gunboats, but they would seem to amount to an annoyance only at that distance, yet an attempt to take the work would seem the most feasible from the northwest side of the salient extending in that direction, as there he will be entirely protected by the high bluff from the fire of the enemy's gunboats.

But much of this detail, of course, must be left to his discretion on the ground, which he is enjoined to use largely as to modes and places and of attack. General Ord is expressly cautioned, however, to lose no time in attempting to envelop Chaffin's farm, but rather if he can take the line of works extending across his path to place what in his judgment may be a sufficient force, with orders to intrench so as to hold the bridge, and with the rest of his forces to push up toward the Newmarket road at the junction of which with the Varina road he will probably be met with some force, that being near the station of the cavalry.

If Chaffin's farm can be taken, a force should be detached to hold it, although it becomes of minor importance, except as a possible bridge-head for a new pontoon bridge to be thrown, brought from the Appomattox ; but that is a question of time. Leaving sufficient force to protect his rear from the enemy crossing after striking the Newmarket junction, at which point it is hoped he will be joined by General Birney, who will have proceeded up the Newmarket road, General Ord will move to the left and attempt to strike the Richmond and Osborne old turnpike, and also to detach a force, and destroy or hold the bridge next above, and proceed onwards up that road until the junction with the Newmarket road, at which point the only other force of the enemy is supposed to be found on the garrisons of the detached works.

Again, an attempt should be made to destroy the bridge opposite battery twenty-three (23).

If these bridges can be destroyed with reasonable celerity there can be but little doubt of the complete success of the movement.

Meanwhile General Birney will have moved by the Newmarket road up to the point of intersection, where it may be necessary to turn the works by a flank movement to the left in the direction marked on the map " Cox," but that, like the other method of attack, must be left largely to the discretion of General Birney.

As soon as possible after the advance has been made from Deep Bottom, whether the attack is made by the third (3d) division of the Eighteenth Corps, or a division of the Tenth Corps, the third (3d) division under General Paine will have position upon the left of General Birney's column of march, so that when the junction is formed with General Ord that division may report to him, relieved from its temporary assignment to duty with the Tenth Corps.

The commanding general of the army will endeavor to keep himself in communication with the corps commanders so as to afford any direction, advice, or assistance that may be in his power, and by being kept advised of the movements of the one and the other of the corps commanders, as well as the command of General Kautz, he may be thus enabled to secure more perfect co-operation than would otherwise be possible.

If the movement is made with celerity ; if the march is held uninterruptedly as much as possible, and if in the first attack the element of unity of time is observed, which has been greatly neglected in some of the movements of the army, we shall gain over the enemy, so far as any considerable reinforcements are concerned, some eight (8) to twelve (12) hours, and perhaps more of valuable time which ought not to be lost, and which should bring us far on our journey in the twelve (12) miles which we are to go.

As the force of the enemy is so small, there will need to be none of those delays for deployments, which generally take so much time in movements on the army.

If we are not mistaken in the force opposed to us, and if we are we shall learn it very early, that force or any other that may be got on that side of the river for six (6) hours need give us no alarm or trouble, nor indeed when the two corps have joined, need we fear any force which the enemy by possibility can detach from the army without abandoning his position on his right altogether, in which case we shall be likely to get reinforcements nearly as early as he will. Upon approaching the detached works at Richmond, if we are fortunate enough to succeed so far, as they will be found to be some three quarters of a mile apart, and not connected with rifle-pits, and as they are all open in the rear, a quick movement of a small column of troops between them will put them into the hands of the attacking party.

Of course, receiving the fire of the heavy guns in position, which are manned by inexperienced artillerists, and are therefore far less destructive than light guns in the same position.

Getting between two of their works so as to get into the rear would open the gates of Richmond.

WHAT IS TO BE DONE IN RICHMOND.

Whatever division or other body of troops shall get into Richmond, it will be their duty immediately, without waiting for parley or doing anything else, to proceed at once to the bridges across the James River, seizing upon inhabitants to guide them for that purpose, if necessary, and destroy them. Fire is the readiest way of destroying bridges, such as these are, of wooden spans. As soon as that destruction has been accomplished, then unless both columns and the cavalry column have reached the city, as large a body as can possibly be spared will be sent to open the way upon the road by which such tardy column is supposed to be advancing, by a sharp attack upon any enemy opposing in the rear.

No large body of troops, it is believed, will be needed for this purpose, as the enemy under such circumstances would make no stand.

In case a portion of the troops reach Richmond, and the troops holding either bridge-head below Richmond are attacked, they are to hold the ground as long as possible, having, the moment that they strike the point which they intend to hold, strengthened themselves by intrenchment as much as possible, for which reason the battalion of engineers has been ordered to report to Major-General Ord, and will be well at the front, furnished with their intrenching implements.

In case the troops guarding the bridges are forced back they will retire upon the position held by our army, not allowing the enemy to get between them and the main body.

In case any portion of the troops have reached Richmond, and those outside are attacked by a force of the enemy which they are unable to resist, they will retire towards Richmond and not from it.

It being intended if the town is once reached to hold it at all risks and at all hazards, all commanders of divisions, and others in advance, are especially cautioned not to recognize or regard flags of truce if any are sent, but immediately receiving the bearer to press on. It will be time enough to deal with flags of truce after the object of the expedition is accomplished.

DETAILS OF THE MARCH AND OF THE EQUIPMENT OF THE TROOPS.

As so much depends upon the celerity of movement, and the distance over which we are to move is so short, the troops will leave everything except a single blanket rolled over their shoulders, and haversack with three (3) days' cooked rations and sixty (60) rounds of cartridge in their cartridge boxes and on their persons. All tents, camp equipage, and cooking utensils are to be left behind. No wagon will be allowed to cross the river without orders from these headquarters. The wagon trains, however, will be supplied with six (6) days' rations and half forage for the same time and forty (40) rounds of extra ammunition per man, ready to start as soon as ordered.

As this movement will necessarily be a failure as it degenerates into an artillery duel, there is no necessity for any artillery to cross until after the attempt to carry the first line of works, and then only such batteries as have been designated in the conversations between the commanding general and his corps commanders.

The two battalions of horse artillery, reporting to General Kautz, will cross and travel with him.

Ambulances will be parked near the southern head of each pontoon bridge, ready to be used when occasion requires.

Hospital boats will be at Deep Bottom for the purpose of receiving any wounded. General Kautz will take with him three (3) days' cooked rations per man, and what forage he can conveniently carry. Assuming that he is better mounted than the enemy's cavalry, and fresh, he will have no difficulty in case it should be necessary to cut loose from the infantry column, and circle the city as far as may be necessary, remembering always that celerity of movement in cavalry in a far greater degree than infantry, is the principal means of success.

The commanding general cannot refrain in closing these instructions, from pressing one or two points upon the attention of corps commanders.

First, the necessity of being ready to move, and moving at the moment designated.

Secondly, the fact that the commanding general is under no substantial mistake in regard to the force to be at first encountered, and, therefore, there is no necessity of time spent in reconnoitring or taking special care of the flanks of the moving columns.

The commanding general would also recommend to the corps commanders, as soon as it may be done with safety from discovering the movement, to impress upon each of the division commanders with directions for them to transmit the information through their subordinates, even to the privates, of the number and kind of troops we are required to meet, so there may be no panic from supposed flanking movements of the enemy or attacks in the rear — always a source of demoralization where the troops do not understand the force of the enemy. Let us assure and instruct our men that we are able to fight anything we will find either in front, or flank, or rear, wherever they may happen to be.

Lastly, the commanding general will recommend for promotion to the next higher grade the brigadier-general commanding division, colonel commanding brigade, and so down to all officers and soldiers of the leading division, brigade, or regiment which first enters Richmond, and he doubts not that his recommendation will be approved by the lieutenant-general, and acted upon by the President, and if Richmond is taken he will pledge to the division, brigade, or regiment first entering the city to each officer and man six (6) months' extra pay.

While making this offer so general to officers and men the commanding general desires to say that he has not included the major-generals commanding corps, because he knows of no incentive which could cause them to do their duty with more promptness and efficiency than they will do it.

Very respectfully,

BENJ. F. BUTLER,
Major-General Commanding.

Unfortunately at the date fixed for the execution of that order, the 29th of September, General Birney was sick. The command of his corps was about to devolve upon Gen. A. H. Terry, who would have very well executed his part, but General Birney returned.

Just before sunset on the 28th of September I rode along the James River on the south side from a point opposite Aikens' Landing down to Deep Bottom. There was no more appearance of the proposed movement than if there had not been a soldier within fifty miles of the place — not the slightest appearance of any preparation for throwing a pontoon or other bridge across the river, and no pontoons in the river or in sight.

When darkness fell the work began, and at half past eleven I was again there. A thoroughly serviceable pontoon bridge had been thrown across the river to convey infantry and artillery, and it was entirely muffled.

At five minutes of midnight the head of Ord's column struck the bridge, and with a quiet that was wonderful the march across was performed.

I had sent an aid to Deep Bottom, and he met me half way coming back to say that at precisely twelve o'clock Birney's column silently began crossing the bridge, and that General Birney had said that after he had bivouacked three divisions of colored troops as well as his own, he should remain quiet and move exactly at daybreak; and that he expected that I would take personal command of the colored troops at that time.

I rode quickly to my headquarters and snatched a few minutes' sleep. At three o'clock I took my coffee, and at four I was crossing the Deep Bottom Bridge.

At half past four o'clock I found the colored division, rising three thousand men, occupying a plain which shelved towards the river, so that they were not observed by the enemy at Newmarket Heights. They were formed in close column of division right in front. I rode through the division, addressed a few words of encouragement and confidence to the troops. I told them that this was an attack where I expected them to go over and take a work which would be before them after they got over the hill, and that they must take it at all hazards, and that when they went over the parapet into it their war cry should be, "Remember Fort Pillow."

The caps were taken from the nipples of their guns so that no shot should be fired by them, for whenever a charging column stops to fire, that charge may as well be considered ended. As there was to be no halt after they turned the brow of the hill, no skirmishers were to be deployed.

We waited a few minutes, and the day fairly shining, the order was given to go forward, and the troops marched up to the top of the hill as regularly and quietly as if on parade.

Then the scene that lay before us was this: There dipped from the brow of the hill quite a declivity down through some meadow land. At its foot ran a brook of water only a few inches deep, a part of the bottom, as I knew, being gravelly and firm. The brook drained a marsh which was quite deep and muddy, a little to the left of the direct line. The column of division unfortunately did not oblique to the right far enough to avoid that marsh wholly. Then rose steadily, at an angle of thirty to thirty-five degrees, plain, hard ground to within one hundred and fifty yards of the redoubt. At this point there was a very strong line of abatis.[1]

A hundred yards above that, the hill rising a little faster, was another line of abatis. Fifty yards beyond was a square redoubt mounting some guns *en barbette*, that is, on top of the embankment, and held by not exceeding one thousand of the enemy. I rode with my staff to the top of the first hill, whence everything was in sight, and watched the movement of the negroes. The column marched down the declivity as steadily as if on parade. At once when it came

---

[1] If practicable in war a line of abatis is composed of heavy trees laid down or felled around a fort, the tops or upper portions of which are cut off, and the branches sharpened and so interlaced that men cannot crawl through them, certainly not in a body.

in sight the enemy opened upon it, but at that distance there was not much effect.

Crossing the brook their lines broke in little disorder, the left of the divisions having plunged into the morass, but the men struggling through, held their guns above their heads to keep them dry. The

ARRIVAL OF FIRST CONFEDERATE CANNON CAPTURED BY GEN. BUTLER'S COLORED TROOPS.

From a Drawing.

enemy directed its fire upon them; but, as in all cases of firing downwards from a fort, the fire was too high. The leading battalion broke, but its colonel maintained his position at its head. Words of command were useless, as in the melee they could not be heard; but calling his bugler to him the rally rang out, and at its call his men formed around him. The division was at once re-formed, and then at double quick they dashed up to the first line of abatis. The axemen laid to, vigorously chopping out the obstructions. Many of them went down. Others seized the axes. The enemy concentrated their fire upon the head of the column. It looked at one moment as if it might melt away. The colors of the first battalion went down, but instantly they were up again but with new color bearers. Wonderfully they managed to brush aside the abatis, and then at double quick the re-formed column charged the second line of abatis. Fortunately they were able to remove that in a few minutes, but it seemed a long time to the lookers on. Then, with a cheer and a yell that I can almost hear now, they dashed upon the fort. But before they reached even the ditch, which was not a formidable thing, the enemy ran away and did not stop until they had run four miles, I believe. They were only fired at as they ran away, and did not lose a man.

As I rode across the brook and up towards the fort along this line of charge, some eighty feet wide and three or four hundred yards long, there lay in my path five hundred and forty-three dead and wounded of my colored comrades. And, as I guided my horse this way and that way that his hoof might not profane their dead bodies, I swore to myself an oath, which I hope and believe I have kept sacredly, that they and their race should be cared for and protected by me to the extent of my power so long as I lived.

When I reached the scene of their exploit their ranks broke, but it was to gather around their general. They almost dragged my horse up alongside the cannon they had captured, and I felt in my inmost heart that the capacity of the negro race for soldiers had then and there been fully settled forever.

Meanwhile the white troops under Birney had advanced up the Newmarket road in the direction indicated by his orders without meeting any force except a few skirmishers and pickets who fled before him, and occupied the abandoned line of the enemy's intrenchments, which had been carried by the colored division.

Not long after I joined Birney, neither of us having heard anything from the operations of Ord, Captain DeKay, my aid who had accompanied General Ord so that he might communicate to me when desirable, rode up with haste and informed me that General Ord had been very eminently successful; that with his troops of the Eighteenth

Corps he had, with great gallantry, stormed Fort Harrison, a very strong work near James River, being the salient point of their line, and captured it without very considerable loss, the enemy retreating up the river line of fortifications.   All the redoubts, as far as could be seen, had been abandoned largely because they could all be taken in the rear.   But General Ord, desiring to reconnoitre the position, mounted upon the top of the highest point of Fort Harrison, and stood looking at the country, and while so doing, unfortunately received a very serious wound in his ankle from a single shot of a rebel sharp-shooter, which entirely disabled him, and from which he suffered great pain.   As will be remembered, for the purpose of having a surprise the orders for the movement were intrusted only to the commanders of corps.   Ord's staff, in their anxiety for the condition of their chief, immediately got him into an ambulance and took him to Deep Bottom, some miles down the river, where he could have proper facilities for surgical care, but very unfortunately, he not being in condition to remember about it himself, carried away in his pocket his orders, so that General Heckman who succeeded him in command knew not what to do.

Meanwhile General Grant, in natural concern as to the success of the expedition, rode over from City Point, arriving after a delay of some hours, and found my troops occupying Fort Harrison.

DeKay had ridden to find me and given me information of the condition of affairs.   I asked him by what road he came.   He said: "By the Varina road," and I said to him: "That is covered by the enemy's line of fortifications."   He said: "They had all been abandoned, General, I saw as I came by them."   Thereupon I called a couple of orderlies and said: "DeKay, ride with me to Fort Harrison by the shortest route."   We rode out until we got on the Varina road, and there I could see plainly at a distance of some three or four hundred yards the line of redoubts and their connecting intrenchments apparently abandoned.   We had ridden but a short distance when I was saluted by the discharge of a shell which passed over my head.   Supposing this line of redoubts was occupied by our troops, as they ought to have been, and would have been I doubt not except for the accident to Ord, I said: "Well, DeKay, it is not usual to salute the commanding general with a shell."   He raised his glass and said: "But, General, that redoubt is occupied by the rebels." I said: "You told me it was evacuated when you came by." He said: "So it was, but they have reoccupied it." The word was scarcely out of his mouth when an artillery shot came over, and we found ourselves in this dilemma: We must either return,— and we had got so far down that that was a pretty hazardous operation,— or we must ride on. We could not abandon our horses because the turnpike was laid over a morass, and the rebels would have only to send out a party to pick us up. So I said: "My boy, we must ride for it," and we did. Then they opened upon us with musketry by battalion, and the singing of the minie balls as they passed over our heads was inspiriting but not pleasant music. I confess that I put my horse to his quickest pace; and under it all, I could not help smiling to see DeKay, who rode a fine hunter, trying to manage, as she was going at her best gait, to keep his thread-paper body between me and the fire, which continued during our ride, quite three quarters of a mile.

When we got in sight of Fort Harrison the firing ceased. No damage had been done except that a horse of one of the orderlies got a pretty sharp wound, and when I got to the fort I found the crupper strap of my saddle cut off, by what means I know not. I found also that a tuft of cotton under my shoulder strap, which the tailor had been kind enough to put there, was torn out. As I had not been that day where anything of the kind could have happened before, I attributed both to the shots of the enemy.

At Fort Harrison I found General Grant. He had made a hasty examination of the premises, and found that the gorge of the fort was open towards the river and the enemy's gunboats had opened upon that gorge, and, not knowing the great success we had had on the right, he had come to the conclusion that the line of fortifications extending into the country from the river could not be held, and had better be abandoned as soon as the fort could be dismantled. He had already sent off two very heavy guns across the bridge at Varina. In a few minutes' consultation I assured him that, in my judgment, a line could certainly be held against any force that was now on the north side of the James, the numbers of which I knew. It would take quite twelve hours for Lee to get any sufficient number of his troops from Petersburg there to attempt to dislodge us. In the meantime we could so far protect ourselves by filling up the

gorge that the fire of the rebel gunboats would be of no consequence, and at their distance the gunboats could not aid Lee in the
attack upon us. By turning the line of intrenchments I felt sure
that with my force I could hold that most important line of the outer
fortifications of Richmond. Grant laughingly said: "Well, General,
if you say so, and as this is your expedition, I do not think I
ought to interfere. You can take the responsibilities of your own
command. I am sorry I sent off those two guns."

"Well," I said, "they would be of very little consequence here;
they are siege guns and our light guns will be all that we need.
But I am afraid the men that were sent off with the guns will never
know how to get them across the pontoon bridge without tipping
them over into the river and losing them," — which, unfortunately,
happened. Grant went home, after giving us his congratulations
upon what had been done and saying it was worth all we should lose
unless we were driven from the works with great loss. General
Weitzel immediately commenced preparations for the reception of
Lee if he sent over his men. The greatest diligence was used to put
ourselves in posture of defence. The activity and enthusiasm of the
negro troops in the later afternoon and night were wonderful.

The outside line of the fortification we made the inside line by
occupying the ditch. This sheltered us more than if we had not
turned the line, and was of the greatest service, especially as it was
a dry ditch.

Birney, acting on the information that the enemy's line of redoubts
in his front next the river had been abandoned in whole or in part,
made a strenuous attack with his colored division upon the principal
redoubt, known to us as Fort Gilmour. That was the salient point in
the line, and its occupation would have caused the evacuation of the
whole line.

The men rushed up to the breastworks in spite of a heavy fire.
They found that the works were very high and the ditch very deep,
from the bottom of the ditch to the parapet being about fifteen feet.
The colored soldiers, not daunted, attempted to assault the parapet,
and climbed upon each other's shoulders for the purpose of getting at
the enemy. But after a prolonged struggle and the capture of some
one hundred and forty of them who got over the parapet, they were
obliged to retire to the line of intrenchments they had occupied.

But the manner of their attack more than compensated for their loss, for it was another demonstration that the negro would fight.

Lee appreciated the great importance of recovering his line, and on the following morning, with two of his best divisions, as we were informed, he made a very energetic attempt to carry our position. His troops were formed between us and the river so that his advance was over a substantially open field.

Fort Harrison and the intrenchments nearest it, captured by the gallant officers and men of the Eighteenth Corps the day before, were most bravely and inflexibly held by them. Our loss was very considerable, and especially in officers, who I suspect were too proud and courageous to shelter themselves, as they did their men, behind the reversed intrenchments. We lost there the very efficient General Burnham, in memory of whose gallantry Fort Harrison was afterwards named Fort Burnham. We lost many others of our higher field officers, so that before the battle was ended majors were in command of brigades, and captains of regiments. Every man was a hero on that day.

Three times our line was charged by the rebel North Carolina troops with the most persevering energy.

GEN. HIRAM BURNHAM.

But our troops held their intrenchments and in comparative shelter swept the field. The North Carolina division was substantially destroyed. Nineteen battle-flags and several hundred prisoners were captured. The day was a very rainy one, but the rebels kept up the attack until nearly night, when they withdrew. No attack was ever afterwards made on that line, but we occupied it from that time until our negro troops marched from it to take possession of Richmond.

Further up to our right about a mile from our line I bivouacked with my staff and some dozen orderlies in a grove of stunted pines. My headquarters guard had not come from Bermuda with me, and I saw no necessity for detailing from the line any of my tired troops to make a guard. The night was an exceedingly dark one.

About nine o'clock General Weitzel's provost marshal came up to headquarters, where he naturally supposed there would be a sufficient guard, and turned over to my headquarters provost marshal some three hundred prisoners, took his receipt and rode back to his own camp, some three miles to the left, and I found myself in this singular situation — with fifteen or twenty of my staff and orderlies, having in charge that large number of prisoners on a very dark night.

I directed my orderlies, from a quantity of wood that had fortunately been cut and left there, to instruct the prisoners to build fires to dry themselves, and as our supply wagon was very well filled, the prisoners were seated upon the ground and served with rations, which in the warmth of the fire they very gratefully appreciated. The orderlies, changing their clothes, appeared amongst them quite often and they never guessed that the general and staff of their captors were wholly within their power. How it would be when daylight came was another question, so I sent a staff officer up to General Birney's headquarters and asked for a couple of companies to report as soon as possible. They got there between eleven and twelve o'clock, and were posted with a proper line of sentries, and in the morning the prisoners were marched under guard to Deep Bottom. I sent for my headquarters guard, however, and my belongings at my headquarters at Bermuda Hundred, and took possession of a beautiful grove in which the house of a planter named Cox was situated. This house and its outbuildings I turned over to my guards and attendants. I had headquarters built of logs for the occupation of myself and staff, because I would rather have a fresh log house for that purpose than a planter's deserted house, which, from my experience, I found sometimes too thickly populated to be comfortable. Those headquarters were never abandoned until Richmond was taken.

Except for the unfortunate accident of General Ord's disability, this whole movement was most successful, but not all we had hoped for, and it was characterized by General Grant as one of the best things of the kind done in the war.

In a book published by Maj.-Gen. A. A. Humphreys, General Meade's chief of staff, purporting to be a history of the movements

HEADQUARTERS OF GEN. BUTLER ON NORTH BANK OF THE JAMES, EIGHT MILES FROM RICHMOND.

1. Office and Room of Gen. Butler. 2. Kitchen. 3. Servants' Lodgings.

from the Rapidan, this movement is narrated, and although it was carried on in obedience to my express orders and under my own personal superintendence and command, he forgets to mention that I was there at all or had anything to do with it, simply because he was, and I was not, a captain in the regular army. I hope what I say may not give too great a sale to his book, which can be bought anywhere for a dollar.

In the attack on Newmarket Heights by my column of colored troops I violated for the first time a rule of my own military action. I admit that as generals go I was not fit to be a general, in that I never did, nay, never could, order a movement of troops to be made without carefully stopping to count the loss I was likely to make of men in doing it, however successful it might prove. Nor did I ever forget the still more important fact, whether the thing to be done by a given movement would be worth its cost. And I trust I was never overweighed as to those results by the consideration that if successful the movement would result in my military renown. In other words, for my own glory I never incurred large "butcher's bills."

Unfortunately if I erred, it was because I deemed the lives of my men too valuable. Sitting in my tent at night, pondering with pen in hand, and making memoranda for a military movement in the morning, I could hear in the mess-tent near me many of the officers of my command gathered together enjoying themselves with music, and genial, hilarious laughter, and I could not help the thought from intruding upon me: How many of those young men am I condemning to death or mutilation on the following day by the order I am considering, to say nothing of the gallant soldiers to be condemned with them. Leaving out any sentiment in the matter, every man I have in my command has cost the government on the average more than three thousand dollars in his preparation to serve the Union. If I gain what I am to undertake, shall I not lose to the country more than its worth toward the termination of the war? And as these sounds greeted my ears, more than once the pen has dropped from my hand and with deep agitation I have paced my tent, painfully reflecting upon these topics. This shows I was no Napoleon, for he told his men at Saragossa, when they were falling around him, says the historian, " Never mind, boys; a single night in Paris will make this all up." I confess that if such sentiment is necessary to fit a man for a general, I am not so fitted.

But in the attack on Newmarket Heights I did deliberately expose my men to the loss of greater numbers than I really believed the capture of the redoubt was worth; for if the enemy's lines at Fort Harrison were captured, as they were, then Newmarket Heights would have been evacuated without loss, for I do not know that they were ever reoccupied by either side afterwards during the war. Now comes the inquiry in the minds of reflecting men: "Why make the attack?" Because it was to be done with my negro troops. "Are we to understand that you would sacrifice your negro troops where you would not your white troops?" No; except for a great purpose in behalf of their race and in behalf of the Union. If I have tried to make anything apparent up to this time in what I have written, it is that from prejudice and ignorance of their good qualities it was not really believed in and out of the army by military men, with a very few exceptions, that the negroes would fight. My white regiments were always nervous when standing in line flanked by colored troops, lest the colored regiments should give way and they (the white) be flanked. This fear was a deep-seated one and spread far and wide, and the negro had had no sufficient opportunity to demonstrate his valor and his staying qualities as a soldier. And the further cry was that the negroes never struck a good blow for their own freedom. Therefore, I determined to put them in position, to demonstrate the fact of the value of the negro as a soldier, *coûte qui coûte*, and that the experiment should be one of which no man should doubt, if it attained success. Hence the attack by the negro column on Newmarket Heights.

After that in the Army of the James a negro regiment was looked upon as the safest flanking regiment that could be put in line.

I had the fullest reports made to me of the acts of individual bravery of colored men on that occasion, and I had done for the negro soldiers, by my own order, what the government has never done for its white soldiers — I had a medal struck of like size, weight, quality, fabrication and intrinsic value with those which Queen Victoria gave with her own hand to her distinguished private soldiers of the Crimea.

I have caused an engraving of that medal to be printed in this book in honor of the colored soldiers and of myself.

The obverse of the medal shows a bastion fort charged upon by negro soldiers, and bears the inscription, " Ferro iis libertas perveniet." The reverse bears the words, " Campaign before Richmond," encircling the words, " Distinguished for Courage," while there was plainly engraved upon the rim, before its presentation, the name of the soldier, his company and his regiment. The medal was suspended by a ribbon of red, white, and blue, attached to the clothing by a strong pin, having in front an oak-leaf with the inscription in plain letters, " Army of the James." These I gave with my own hand, save where the recipient was in a distant hospital wounded, and by the commander of the colored corps after it was removed from my command, and I record with pride that in that single action there were so many deserving that it called for a presentation of nearly two hundred. Since the war

I have been fully rewarded by seeing the beaming eye of many a colored comrade as he drew his medal from the innermost recesses of its concealment to show me.

Although we had now obtained a position some ways up the James

River towards Richmond, the enemy had four iron-clads on the river. But it was supposed they could not come below Trent's Reach because that had been partially obstructed by the navy. As the draft of water in one place at an ordinary low tide was not more than eight feet, and as the land was low on the north bank of the river, it was evident that we could make no further advance upon the enemy's works upon that side of the river while they were protected by the enfilading fire of their gunboats.

I went with Captain Melancthon Smith of the navy,— who assured me that it was impossible for the monitors and larger vessels of his fleet — they drawing sixteen feet of water and over — to get up the river further than Trent's Reach, — to make a reconnoissance with him and devise a plan, if possible, by which he might ascend the James with his vessels, which were then lying below at the point called " Dutch Gap," to the defences of Richmond.

Here is a peculiar formation : The river running up by Trent's Reach bends very sharply to the right and returns again, in an elongated horseshoe form, so directly that while it has passed over a distance of more than seven miles, the waters of the river, at a depth of twenty-five feet, approach so nearly that there is only about four hundred and twenty-five feet from the water on the upper side across the neck at Dutch Gap to twenty-five feet of water on the lower side. So a canal wide and deep enough for our gunboats to get through it, would require a cut less than five hundred feet long, sixteen feet deep, and sixty feet wide on the bottom and ninety at the top. Any engineer will understand that this was a cut that our troops could make easily and without any very considerable delay or expense.

After having made a reconnoissance of this position with Commodore Smith, who then commanded the naval forces of James River, I went down to City Point and asked General Grant and Chief Engineer Barnard to come up with us and examine the premises. This they did, and made a very careful exploration of the point. It was known as Dutch Gap for the reason that some enterprising German had cut down quite a gap in undertaking to build a waterway through there many years before. We came to the conclusion that to dig the canal was a very desirable thing to do, and General Grant directed me to undertake it.

The peninsula of land around which the river winds is at this point some sixty feet high. This made the excavation of the canal, from the lower side, very safe, as it was protected from the direct fire of the enemy, either from their gunboats or from batteries erected on either side, until it had been cut through.

An exploration of the nature of the ground showed it to be of a very hard lime-stone gravel. In it was imbedded a great deal of

DUTCH GAP CANAL, ON JAMES RIVER, BELOW RICHMOND. COMMENCEMENT OF OPERATIONS. From Photograph.

petrified wood, whole trees being found which had been transformed into a very friable, easily broken stone, which still preserved the grain of the wood and the knots and branches of the trees. Thus a substantially straight cut could be made in it without any danger of a slide of the earth on the sides of the excavation.

General Grant asked me how long it would take to cut the canal through. I said, "After we get at it, sixty days, — possibly more, — depending somewhat upon the interruptions made by the enemy." I said I thought the best way would be, and in that General Barnard agreed with me, to commence by placing a coffer-dam at the lower end of the canal, and then to cut the excavation wide and deep enough up to within twenty-five or thirty feet of the river on the other side, and let the bank at the upper cut stand as a shield against the enemy's direct fire.

The work proceeded according to this plan, under the direction of my skilled engineer, Maj. Peter S. Michie, now one of the board of instructors of West Point Military Academy, than whom I know of no better or more efficient engineer. It was pursued with great diligence and success. Once it was finished we could hold the James River up to Fort Darling with our fleet, if the naval forces of the United States were able to compete with the enemy's fleet above, which we assumed they were able to do. And when at Fort Darling we should be in condition to make an attack upon Richmond itself, which would lie almost under our guns, for we would be inside of the interior defences of that city.

The enemy, appreciating the importance of this strategic undertaking, and finding that we could not be reached by direct fire of their artillery from any point, because of our "shield," erected some mortar batteries on the other side of the James and undertook to stop our work by a continuous and frequent fire of mortar shells, dropping them into our excavation. After a little time they dropped them there with considerable frequency, but did very little damage, and scarcely any harm to the workmen. At a mile and a half distance it is not easy to drop a shell with any certainty into a space three hundred feet long and ninety feet wide. The soil, as I have said before, was very hard on the sides, so that along the banks we could dig caves, or, as they were called, bomb-proofs, in which the workmen could take refuge whenever there was any danger of a shell

falling where the explosion would be injurious to them. The line
which a shell describes on being thrown for the purpose indicated, is
a parabola of about two miles.   I was familiar with this matter, for I had
watched the bombardment of Fort Jackson, on the Mississippi, during
the considerable part of a week, and thus made its acquaintance.

The first thing to do was to station a couple of well-instructed
men at points from which every shell could be watched during its
whole flight.   These observers could tell after a little practice almost
precisely where the missile would land, that is, whether it would

BOMB-PROOF QUARTERS AT DUTCH GAP CANAL.

come in our excavation so as to do harm or not. While the men
were at work these men were on watch, and a shell being seen coming, if it was likely to fall in our way, the watchmen would call out
" Holes! " whereupon the workmen would at once protect themselves by rushing into their adjacent and convenient bomb-proofs,
to come out and resume their work again as soon as the shell had
struck and exploded without harm.

If the shell was not to strike within the excavation or near to it, the
watchers allowed it to take its course and the men were not alarmed.

So that substantially all the damage we suffered was to our single mule tipcarts, which were used for removing the earth. A number of mules were killed or wounded, and some of the carts were stove up, but under the circumstances the work was successfully prosecuted.

VIEW OF DUTCH GAP CANAL, ON JAMES RIVER, BELOW RICHMOND. COMPLETION OF OPERATIONS BEFORE EXPLODING OF MINE.

From Photograph.

When we got within twenty-five feet of the water on the upper side we put a mine under that portion, leaving an arch over it which was sufficient to sustain the weight of the superincumbent earth, and loaded that mine with some tons of gunpowder. Our shield of earth above the mine which was twenty-five feet thick at the bottom was gradually sloped until at the top it was scarcely more than twelve inches thick.

Commodore Smith was very enthusiastic about the canal and kept continually urging me to complete the work. When we were ready we were to blow up this mine and the earth over it would, of course, be thrown up into the air and fall back into our excavation. A goodly portion of it would be in such state as to be at once easily removed with a dredger, and then the canal completed.

We got all ready in the latter part of December to explode our mine. General Grant telegraphed me, that he had made some arrange-

VIEW OF DUTCH GAP CANAL, ON JAMES RIVER, BELOW RICHMOND.

BLOWING OUT BULKHEAD.

From a Drawing.

ments to utilize the canal by a movement toward Richmond in co-operation with the navy, and that I had better blow out the head of the canal. Meanwhile I had procured a dredger, and in twenty-four hours, or two nights' work, when the enemy could not annoy us with their shells, the canal could be made navigable. On Christmas day the mine was discharged. A tall mass of hard dirt was elevated into the air and came down in fragments into the canal, low enough to allow the waters of the James River to flow over it about three feet deep before it was dredged.

But in the meantime a very untoward occurrence had happened. Commodore Smith was wanted elsewhere by the Navy Department ; and without giving any notice whatever to us or inquiring into his value where he was, — for he was both an intrepid and an enterprising officer,— he was relieved and sent elsewhere, and in his place a naval commander, one Parker, was sent. He had been a witness of the explosion and had examined the canal, and the first thing that I heard from him was by his letter to my commandant of the work, Major B.

C. Ludlow, begging him not to open Dutch Gap Canal because, this done, Parker was afraid that the enemy's fleet would come down, and he did not know that he could sustain himself against their attack.

Here was a situation ; I had been trying to make an opening by which the dog could get at the fox and destroy him, and the dog begged of me that I would not, lest the fox should eat him up. And so I never did a stroke more work on the canal, and the country rang with " another of Butler's failures " at Dutch Gap Canal. I could not publish that letter in my justification to show that the canal was not a failure, because I should have to disclose to our enemy, as well as to our people, the fact that our navy did not consider itself capable of meeting the rebel navy on James River. As a patriot I must keep that fact quiet, and I have so done.

I may as well finish the story of this matter now by saying that I was relieved from my command of the Army of the James on the 8th of January, 1865, perhaps ten or twelve days later, and possibly this " failure " of mine was one of the grounds in the mind of 'the President for my being allowed to be removed, or which caused the removal, and so I suffered.

But within less than thirty days afterwards Farragut was summoned to City Point to look into the naval matters on James River. The enemy, taking courage, had come down through Trent's Reach, with three of their light-draught, iron-clad gunboats during the high water to attack our monitors lying near the lower mouth of Dutch Gap Canal. Parker ordered his vessels to up anchor, and he ran away with them so fast down the river that he could not stop to have the draw in the pontoon bridge opened to let him through, which might have taken five minutes, and so broke through the bridge and never stopped running until he got down to City Point. He would not have stopped then had he not found that from some cause, he knew not what, he was not pursued. What prevented the rebels from following Parker and capturing City Point, destroying all Grant's transports and shipping, was that one of the rebel ironclads got aground in Trent's Reach, and the others went back to help it off. This took so long that the night passed, and in daylight when they got the vessel off, the forts opened upon them, and they ran back up river and never came down afterwards.

A court-martial was held on Parker, presided over by Admiral Farragut, which found him guilty of cowardice, and he was sentenced to be dismissed from service. This sentence was changed to a lighter punishment by Gideon Welles, who thought cowardice excusable.

Dutch Gap has since been dredged out, and is the main channel of commerce between Richmond and the outer world. The waters of James River being diverted by the canal no longer flow around at any depth through Trent's Reach, and that which was the former channel of the river will soon, if it has not already, become marsh land.

Dutch Gap Canal is the only military construction of all that were done by the army which remains of use to the country in time of peace, a monument to its projector and constructor, one of "Butler's failures."

In October 28, 1864, all was quiet on the James, and as I desired to examine some statute law and some books on international law in order to deal with the argument of Mr. Ould, the Confederate Commissioner of Exchange, that international law governed the right of the capturing party to return prisoners of war into slavery, I started for Fortress Monroe on my headquarters boat, with a couple of my staff officers, and boat's crew, and orderlies. I stopped at City Point and called on General Grant. He welcomed me cordially.

"Are you going to do anything for a day or two?" I said.

"Not that I know of," said he.

"I want to go down to Fortress Monroe," said I, "and consult some books, and I am on my way there with your permission."

"Why, General," said he, "that is in your department, and you have a right to go anywhere in your department with or without my permission."

"But not without your knowledge, General."

I went down the river, and within three hours was at the fort. I spent some days there, in the routine business of the department, and in other duties. Late in the day of November 1st the telegraph operator came in and handed me a cipher despatch which he had just received, saying: "This message was directed to your headquarters in the field, but knowing that you were here I brought it to you without forwarding it to City Point." To reach my headquarters in the field such despatches were retransmitted at General Grant's headquarters. I read these words. —

Report at once in person to the Secretary of War.

EDWIN M. STANTON.

I ordered my vessel to be coaled as soon as possible for two days' sailing. I reflected upon the despatch. What could it mean? Was I to be summarily dismissed? Was I to be promoted? What had happened? As in duty bound I at once telegraphed the despatch to General Grant for his orders and received Grant's answer.[1] I reached my boat with my officers before the coaling was completed, and ordered the captain to stand out to Cape Henry until he received further orders. When fully out of sight of the fort I directed him to steam slowly until dark, and then to proceed with all speed to Washington.

We arrived the next morning. As soon as a landing could be effected I mounted my horse and rode to the War Department, where I arrived just before nine o'clock. Throwing my reins to an orderly I went to the office of the Secretary of War, where I was instantly admitted. Even at that early hour he had three visitors.

"I am here, Mr. Secretary, by your orders," said I. "What am I to do?"

"Step into my private office and wait until I can come to you."

I did so, and in a few minutes he came in bringing a thick bundle of papers.

"Read these papers, General. They contain very important information from New York. Before you get through I will be with you."

I carefully read the papers. They were the reports of his confidential agents and detectives, and of prominent loyal men in the city and State as to the condition of affairs there. They contained matter sufficiently alarming, but, as is always the case, exaggerated.

In substance they stated that there was an organization of troops which was to be placed under command of Fitz John Porter; that there was to be inaugurated in New York a far more widely extended and far better organized riot than the draft riot in July, 1863; that

---

[1] See Appendix No. 84.

the whole vote of the city of New York was to be deposited for McClellan at the election to be held just one week from that date; that the Republicans were to be driven from the polls; that there were several thousand rebels in New York who were to aid in the movement; and that Brig.-Gen. John A. Green, who was known to be the confidential friend of the governor, was to be present, bringing some forces from the interior of the State to take part in the movement.

The fact of such an organization was testified to over and over again. The number of troops on Governor's Island under General Dix, who commanded the Department of the East, was shown to be very small, indeed, and was counted on as unreliable, as they were a garrison of the regular army.

The secretary came in just after I had finished reading the papers.

"What do you think of that, General?" he asked.

"Do you believe all this?" I said.

"The information is perfectly reliable," he replied, "and I must act upon it."

"What do you want me to do?"

"I want you to go there and take command of the Department of the East, relieving General Dix, and I will have sent you from the front a sufficient force to put down any insurrection."

"I don't want to take command of the Department of the East and lose my command in the front," said I. "And then I think it would not be good politics to relieve General Dix, a New Yorker, from his command, just on the eve of election. Let me suggest that if I am to go I might be sent there with troops enough to take care of the city, and let me report to General Dix, leaving him in command."

"But," said Stanton, "Dix won't do anything. Although brave enough, he is a very timid man about such matters, as he wants to be governor of New York himself one of these days."

"Well," I said, "then send me with directions to report to him to command the troops that are to preserve the peace in the city of New York.[1] But I want to go only upon the understanding that if we come to a row I shall have a confidential order from the President by which I can relieve General Dix at once, and take supreme

---

[1] See Appendix 85.

command of the fight, if there is one. I will coddle the general and be his obedient servant until it becomes necessary to be something else, and of that you must leave me to judge."

"Very well, but keep the peace with Dix if you can." He then asked what troops I wanted, and I said:—

"A couple of batteries of artillery, say twelve pieces, and about three thousand men will be enough, but a larger show of force may be better for overawing an outbreak."

"I suppose you will want your Massachusetts troops sent."

"Oh," said I, "not Massachusetts men to shoot down New Yorkers; that won't do. I have as faithful, loyal, good soldiers in my New York regiments as there are in the world, and I can fully rely on them. Perhaps I will take a Connecticut regiment or two and select the batteries."

"Do you think there are enough?"

"Plenty, with the addition of my headquarters guard of Pennsylvanians, who have already voted in the field."

"Make out your list of troops," said he, "and I will have them sent." [1]

"Well," I said, "you cannot get them there under a few days at best, and, Mr. Secretary, see; I have just come from the field in a flannel blouse with my staff in the same condition. We have not a white shirt with us."

"Never mind that, General; there are plenty of tailors in New York."

"Very well, Mr. Secretary, I want a new uniform, and if you order me off in this condition of rig I shall put it in the bill. When do you want me to go?"

"By the next train."

"As the troops cannot get there for three days, you will permit me to have my headquarters guard sent to Fortress Monroe to meet my own very fast boat, and come up and bring some of my staff to me?"

"Oh, yes; order anything you like."

"All right, I am gone;" and I left Washington for New York that night.

Our appearance there in Washington was such that it did not draw any attention to us, so that it was not publicly known that I

---

[1] See Appendix 86.

was in Washington, and no notice of my being there got into the New York papers.

I arrived in Jersey City the next morning and was met there by a prominent loyal man of New York, one of Stanton's correspondents, who greeted me and desired me to make his house — a very fine one on Fifth Avenue — my headquarters while I remained in the city.

I said to him : —

"You know not what you ask. I will come down and dine with you, but to come into your house with my staff and orderlies, and the hundreds of people who may be brought there or visit me would drive you from your home. Besides, I must have very much more extensive accommodations."

I had telegraphed to Assistant Quartermaster-General Van Vliet to meet me there, and he told me that he had looked about for headquarters for me. He said that the Hoffman House, in the rear part of which General Scott had rooms, had not yet been opened, and that he had taken the whole of the building for my use.

Early in the morning of the 4th of November I occupied my headquarters. As the first incident I learned that one Judge Henry Clay Dean, in utter ignorance that I was at that time in New York, had made a speech the night before in which, according to a newspaper report, he stated that if I should attempt to march up Broadway I would be hanged to a lamp-post, or words to that effect. Although I had no troops in New York then except my orderlies and aids, I sent my compliments to Judge Dean with the information that I would like to see him at my headquarters at the Hoffman House. He reported at once, and I received him. He seemed to be in a great fright. I greeted him and told him that such a speech had been brought to my attention, and as I was sure that a gentleman of his position never could have made it in the words reported, I desired to ascertain the facts from him.

He said he had been wholly misrepresented.

"Well," I said, "I supposed so, and I rely upon you to correct that matter by having the report withdrawn, or, if that cannot be done, by making some explanatory statement." He said he certainly would, and there the matter ended.

I then reported to the commander of the Department of the East, General Dix, and he issued an order that I was in command of the troops sent to preserve the peace in the State of New York.

I suggested to him that he should put me in command of the military district comprising the States of New York and New Jersey, as he had command of the whole department, but he expressed a disinclination so to do, and I, after a conference, yielded and said I would report to the Secretary of War for orders, but that I hoped it would not be necessary. I asked him how many regulars could be spared from the garrison on Governor's Island. He said he thought he could let me have five hundred men. I told him they might as well remain in the garrison as anywhere.

I had been expressly cautioned by the Secretary of War against the machinations of Gen. John A. Green.

Monday my headquarters boat came up with my guard, one hundred Pennsylvanians. They were landed at the battery, and put into barracks there.

That day Major-General Sanford, commanding the division of State militia in the city of New York, called upon me and said that he proposed on the day of election to call out his division of militia to preserve the peace. I told him that that could not be done without his reporting to me as his superior officer; that being assigned to the command of the troops in the city of New York by the President, I of necessity became his commander; and, further, that the Articles of War required that I should be his commander. Of course a militia officer could not agree to that. I then told him that I did not need his division, and that I did not think it would be advisable to have the militia called out; that if they were called out they would be under arms, and in case of difficulty it was not quite certain which way all of them would shoot; and besides, it might cause a claim of interference with the election to have troops called out and hold positions while the election was going on, and thus might vitiate the election.

He was very obstinate about it, and said he should call out the militia.

"Then," said I, "here is an order that you do not. You have no power to call out the militia except in a case of disturbance." Still he did not yield.

"Well," I said, "if there are to be armed forces here that do not report to me, and are not under my orders, I shall have to treat them as enemies. In case of disturbance they may suffer, for I cannot stop to select whom to shoot at of the armed troops which I find in New York not under my orders; but I certainly shall most efficiently take care of those who put them in arms."

He told me he should apply to the governor of the State for orders.

"Your governor is a very high militia officer," said I, "but I shall not recognize his authority here as against the authority of the United States any more than that of any militia officer of lower grade. And from the reported doings of Governor Seymour in the centre of the State in organizing new companies of militia, which I believe to be a rebellious organization, I may find it necessary to act promptly in arresting all those whom I know are proposing to disturb the peace here on election day."

He retired in disgust, and I have never seen the clever old gentleman since. It is sufficient to say that I at once took measures to ascertain where all the arms in the city were, and in whose possession they were.[1] I immediately reported the matter to the Secretary of War,[2] and asked permission to issue a general order on the subject, and to have a territorial jurisdiction given me. The Secretary of War afterwards advised me that I had better not issue a general order, because my right to do that would be the subject of "abstract discussion." But I wanted territorial jurisdiction, not so much for that as for another reason which will appear.

Meanwhile my troops had not arrived. They were not embarked at Fortress Monroe — such were the unaccountable delays — until Friday and Saturday. I then issued my General Order No 1,[1] in which I made it plain that there were several thousand secessionists in New York. They were there in such numbers as to impede the Union men getting lodgings and boarding-house accommodations, the landlords saying that they could let all the room they had to Southerners at their own prices. I took care that the Southerners should understand that means would be taken for their identification, and that whoever of them should vote would be dealt with in such a manner as to make them uncomfortable. That was sufficient, and substantially no Southerners voted at the polls on election day.

[1] See Appendix No. 87.   [2] See Appendix No. 88.   [3] See Appendix No. 89.

Here another question troubled me. Although it had been thought best to have a pretty large force, say five thousand, yet I did not get thirty-five hundred. Much the larger portion of them were New Yorkers who had voted in the field. I consulted with Gen. Daniel Butterfield, who was in New York on leave for some purpose, and he loyally gave me very valuable advice and assistance, for which service I here express my high and grateful appreciation.

The question was, how to have troops in readiness to put down a riot in the city on election day, and yet not have them actually there, lest the votes which they had previously cast in the field should not be counted, — for the law was that troops might vote in the field, but if they were in the State on election day their votes should not be counted.

Examining into the difficulties of this problem, I found that there were nine ferry slips on one side of the city of New York and ten on the other. Into these the largest ferry-boats could be brought to land their passengers. The ferry-boats could each comfortably accommodate more than a regiment of infantry in the saloons, and in the drive-ways as many as four pieces of artillery with their equipment. I determined thereupon to take possession of four of the larger ferry-boats, and place two on the North River and two on the east side of the city. It was arranged to have on each side of the city four swift tugs always with steam up and under the command of my officers. From my headquarters I could communicate with them by the telegraph lines, so that in case of a gathering of rioters in any part of the city I could throw four regiments there, if need be, in less time than I could march them from any place of encampment in the city. That is, the troops being on the ferry-boats and the artillery being all harnessed, I could direct the boat to any slip where the force was needed, and the infantry could immediately land and march double quick across the island to the point where it was needed, the artillery preceding or following, as the case might be. These ferry-boats, while not in action, were to be anchored in Jersey waters.

I made an arrangement with the manager of the Western Union Telegraph Company to bring into a room at my headquarters adjoining my office telegraph lines from more than sixty points. There was one line from High Bridge, where a gunboat was stationed, lest somebody should attempt to break the aqueduct which brought water into the city. There was another line from a gunboat anchored opposite Mackerelville, which was supposed to contain the worst population in New York; and still another from a gunboat anchored so as to cover the Sub-Treasury Building and the Custom House on Wall Street and the United States Arsenal. There was a line from some point near each polling-place in the city.

At the several polling-places I had an officer in plain clothes, in command of my scouts and detective officers who were around the

FORT BRADY, BATTERY COMMANDING JAMES RIVER.

polls. On this officer, in case of any disturbance, the police — who were under the command of Superintendent John A. Kennedy, a very loyal, able, and executive officer,— might call for assistance. Any disturbance was to be immediately communicated to me by telegraph.

On the day of election the officers and men for the polls were to be on duty an hour before the polls opened. Each telegraphic station was numbered, and the officer was to report to my headquarters hourly the state of quiet at the polls.

The remainder of my troops were held on board of transports, ready to land when the point at which they were wanted was indicated by the tug. Steam was kept up and the cables were in readiness to be slipped when the transports were required to move.

At the request of General Dix, instead of bringing my headquarters guard up for my protection, I sent them to guard the United States Arsenal, under command of Captain Crispin, the commandant of the arsenal.

It is but just to say that the number of my troops lying around in transports and ferry-boats was enormously over-estimated as usual; they were understood to be fifteen thousand.

On Thursday evening, it having been generally circulated in the city that General Butler had shut himself up in his headquarters and dared not show himself lest he should be assassinated, I sent an officer of my staff to take a stage-box for us at the opera, having got a new uniform so that I could go in full feather. We appeared there, and were received with some applause, which I acknowledged. I sat out the entertainment. Between the acts Captain DeKay of my staff, who was a society man in New York, left the box to visit one wherein he saw his aunt, and found therein Mr. August Belmont. Mr. Belmont made a statement publicly in his hearing that he would bet a thousand dollars that the election would go for McClellan, and another thousand that gold would go up to 300 by the morning of election. This being reported to me, I told Captain DeKay to say to Mr. Belmont that those bets would be taken; but Mr. Belmont declined.

Friday morning, having a little leisure while waiting for my troops, at the invitation of a gentleman in New York I concluded to take a ride with my staff in Central Park. I said to my staff: "We must go in our camp rig." They remonstrated, because our horses, upon which were still their rawhide saddles, had been very badly bruised on their hips and thighs, and their tails had been badly defaced, in the voyage on the boat, she having met bad weather at sea.

We were a most *outré* looking set. No such equipped cavalcade ever rode along those beautifully ornamented paths before. If it had not been for our well-blacked cavalry boots, and our wicked-looking sabres clanking against the spur and stirrup, and the neatly cased revolvers fast to the belt on the left side, I think we might have been stopped by the police. As it was, we were the observed of all observers, and it shone out in their eyes: "Is this the pomp and circumstance of glorious war?" We were met by the Park Commissioners, the chairman of whom cordially addressed me with the inquiry: "Are you riding in the park for exercise?"

"Oh, no, Mr. Commissioner; on business. I was looking to see where would be the best place in the park to encamp my troops when I am ready to bring them on shore."

"Oh, you would not encamp your troops here, General?"

"Why, Mr. Commissioner," said I, pointing over one of the beautiful lawns, "I have never seen a better camping-ground. What is the objection to it? Plenty of water, isn't there?"

"Well, General," said he, "we must submit, I suppose; but I hope you won't need to."

"Oh, well, I assure you I shall not if I don't need to. I should be happy to see you, gentlemen, at my headquarters at the Hoffman House. Good-morning."

The next afternoon another sphere of duty quite foreign to my professional studies and military experiences was put upon me. I received a message from Mr. John A. Stewart, United States Assistant Treasurer in New York, asking for an interview.[1] I immediately appointed an interview at my headquarters at the Hoffman House that evening. Mr. Stewart called upon me and said: —

"General, I have just returned from Washington, where I have been on very important public matters. I have had an interview with the President and Cabinet and asked them what I could do under the circumstances, if anything, and what they could do in the alarming prospect of affairs. I stated to them, in substance, that I was well informed that a conspiracy was going on among certain brokers and bankers, whose names I gave them, together with the amount of gold transactions of each accompanied by actual deliveries, which were quite enormous. I stated that these men had conspired together with some others, whom I did not know, to raise the price of gold to 300 on election day certainly, and perhaps on Monday. I also told the President and Cabinet that I was powerless to prevent the rise in the price of gold, for I had sold a good deal of gold in order to keep the price down, and in that manner had reduced the amount I held so low that I feared the conspirators had an amount of gold securities due on demand sufficient to swallow up

---

[1] See Appendix No. 90.

more than all the gold I would have left if I should sell any more for the purpose of keeping the premium down. Should I do so, and should they make such large demands, it would bankrupt my treasury, and would of itself throw the price of gold no one knows how high. A long consultation was had upon these subjects, and nobody could suggest anything that could be done, or give me any direction or authority how to act. At last the President said: 'The only thing I see that you can do is this: General Butler is in New York in command. I don't see exactly what he can do, but if anything can be done, he is the only man to do it, and I wish he would do anything that he believes will be for the benefit of the country. Say this from me to him.'"

I said to him: "Mr. Treasurer, what can I do? I have got no gold with which to 'bear' the market. It would be a very dangerous experiment to arrest all these men, even if I had the power, and it might give cause for an *emeute* at election time, which might not otherwise occur. This is rather a ticklish business. It is evident that the large amount of gold that has been thrown upon the market is Confederate gold. Do you know where any of it came from?"

"Yes," he said, "there has been a good deal sent from Canada."

"That may be English gold," I said.

"I cannot say whether it is or not."

"Is it sent to one man or many men?"

"It has all been sent," he replied, "from Montreal to the firm of Lyons & Company."

"Well, Mr. Treasurer, it is evident that the Confederates have got an agent here; have you any idea who he may be?"

"I have not," he replied, "unless it is Lyons, for he has bought within a fortnight an amount exceeding twelve million dollars actual gold, and has received it all and sent it out of the country."

I reflected a moment, and said: "Lyons — Lyons of Montreal; I rather guess I know who he is, and if he is the man I think he is, I know he is a Confederate agent. What do you suggest to me to do?"

"Well, General, I cannot suggest anything to be done; I don't know what you can do. It is a condition of difficulties beyond my comprehension of any remedy."

"Well, Mr. Treasurer, if I send to you for any information, please furnish what I want as early as possible. It is evident that I must undertake a new class of study, with not too much time for learning, either. Do these people know the situation of the treasury?"

"I don't think they know it exactly, for if they did I think they would demand their gold securities to be paid, and if they should demand their payment, and if I should let go enough to pay them, that would tend to increase the price of gold."

I said: "I know Belmont has offered to bet that gold will go up to 300 on election day, and he is a pretty cautious man in such matters."

"Well, General," said Stewart, rising, "if you think of anything I can do, let me know, whatever may be the day or hour."

It will easily be supposed that during that night and the next day, Sunday, I gave my most earnest thought to this class of subjects. I came to a conclusion as to what I would try to do. I sent Lieutenant DeKay early in the morning with my carriage to Lyons' house so as to be sure to get hold of him before he should go down town, with directions to give my compliments to Mr. Lyons and ask him to ride with him to my headquarters to see me. I thought he would come, but in case he should not do so willingly I gave Lieutenant DeKay instructions to bring him.

In a few minutes Mr. Lyons was introduced.

"Mr. Lyons," said I, "there are circumstances connected with your being in New York which render it imperative for me to know your history. I suppose I need not say to you that answers to my questions must be truthfully given, because with me when I am examining any person the sin against the Holy Ghost is untruthfulness."

"I will try to answer you as you wish, General," he replied.

"Well, then," I said, "I think there will be no trouble between us. Before the war where did you live, and what was your business?"

"I lived in Louisville, Kentucky, and my business was that of dealing in finance, — a broker, perhaps."

"Had you any connection with the Peoples' Bank of Kentucky?"

"I did business with that bank, and sometimes for it."

"When did you leave Kentucky?"

"I cannot give the date, General, but it was when Governor Morehead was arrested."

"Where did you move yourself and business?"

"To Nashville, Tennessee."

"Did you continue business there?"

"For a little while."

"When and where did you go then?"

"To New Orleans."

"At what time?"

"When Governor Isham left the State and the Union troops occupied Nashville."

"When did you leave New Orleans?"

"When you took possession of the city."

"Were you in the same business there?"

"Yes, sir."

"Were you connected with any banking firm or financial association?"

"Yes, sir; the Citizens' Bank."

"Where did you go then?"

"To Liverpool, England."

"Ho, ho, Mr. Lyons, then I guess we are business acquaintances. Are you the H. J. Lyons who made claim on the Citizens' Bank of New Orleans from Liverpool for a large amount of money?"

"Yes, General."

"And you claimed to have left this money there as a neutral British subject, didn't you?"

Smilingly he replied: "Yes, General."

"And as I remember, you did not get it?"

"No; it was stopped by your order."

"Did you do business for any time in Liverpool?"

"No, sir."

"Where did you go then?"

"I went to Montreal."

"And went into business there?"

"Yes, sir."

"Was not your business there largely with your Confederate friends, — getting their money into Canada?"

"Yes, sir."

"Did you renew, if you had ever broken it off, your connection with the Peoples' Bank in Kentucky?"

"Yes, sir."

"How long did you remain in Montreal?"

"I came here from there in December, last."

"Did you set up your business here in your present firm name?"

"Yes, sir."

"Who came with you?"

"My brother, younger than myself."

"Who are your partners?"

"My brother and Jesse D. Bright, the president of the Jeffersonville Railroad, Indiana."

"How much capital did you have?"

"Eighty thousand dollars in greenbacks."

"Who put it in?"

"My brother and myself put in one half, and Bright put in the other. I put in thirty thousand dollars and my brother ten thousand dollars."

"This has been your place of business ever since?"

"Yes, sir."

"And what is the exact form of your business, that is, what kind of broker's business do you do?"

"General speculating in gold."

"Your business has been very profitable, hasn't it?"

"Quite profitable; yes, sir."

"And have you had any capital furnished you to speculate with besides your own?"

"Oh, yes; my friends and correspondents have sent me very considerable amounts."

"Well, Mr. Lyons, I have been informed," — reading from a paper which I held in my hand, and which the assistant treasurer had given me — "that in the course of the last fourteen days you have bought and paid for and sent out of the country upwards of twelve million dollars in gold, and have now in your actual possession in your vaults, rising three million dollars in gold. Is that so?"

"I cannot give the actual amount from memory," was his answer, "but you are substantially correct."

"Well," I said, "if you have sent away so much gold you must have received a large portion of it from outside. Your eighty thousand dollars in greenbacks would not have gone a great ways in buying gold at 240. Upon your own statement, and I believe it, you, a young secessionist, left Kentucky after secession to get away from the Union army; and left Tennessee when the other secessionists left there; went to New Orleans and left there as soon as the Union troops arrived; went to Liverpool, and there undertook, as a British neutral subject, to get a large quantity of gold for the use of the Confederates, certainly upon the representation that you had left it there at your own bank, as a neutral British subject. You then came to Montreal, substantially stripped of all your means, and in connection with your brother, and the bitterest Copperhead I know, set up this business of speculating in New York, acting all the time with the Peoples' Bank of Kentucky, which is a financial agent of Jeff Davis. It is difficult to see why, finding you here acting with other conspirators in endeavoring to put up the price of gold in order to interfere with the government, I should not take you and take care of you and punish you under the law for what you are doing and what you have done. How long do you think the clemency of the government will shield you?"

"Then," said he, "I suppose I am to be arrested, General?"

"No, Mr. Lyons; where a man can give as bail three million dollars in gold, — because your gold will never go away until I get through with it and you, — there is no occasion to arrest him. I don't threaten you with arrest; I only say I am going to retain certain gold which I suppose belongs to the Confederacy until I can fully examine into that question. To punish you is not my business now, provided you will aid me in preventing the success of this conspiracy to raise the price of gold to 300. You can do it, and if you will keep gold down until Wednesday morning to not more than 250, — because I am willing you should sell your gold at a little profit, — then I will give you my honor that you shall go where you please and take your gold with you. You will pardon me if I believe that even your clients, the Confederates, won't get much of it, and if the election is determined in favor of Lincoln it is of no consequence where the gold goes afterwards; the country will take care of that. And if he is not elected I have not much interest where it goes, you see where I stand. I make no threats, but I do tell you if gold goes to 300 on election morning I shall know it, and I shall know also where both you and your gold are."

"General," said he, "have you talked with any of these other men as you have with me?"

"When I have talked with them," said I, "they will put the same question to me, and I shall not answer it in their case. What you want to know of me is whether you can go on and deal with your gold in selling it without their knowing what you know. I think you had better sell your gold. There is no reason why it should go up, because to-morrow will be almost a holiday, and there will be no gold wanted for shipment until Saturday, so that you have an opportunity to take care of yourself if you choose to, or to throw yourself in my face and in that of the government if you choose to. I hope, sir, you will determine this matter wisely for yourself, because your interests and mine lie together."

"I think, General," said he, "I will sell all my gold right off."

"I think that would be wisdom, and I will approve of it; but I would advise you to sell it to be delivered day after to-morrow."

We shook hands and parted, and although I have seen the gentleman since I have never spoken to him on this subject.

I made my report of the condition of affairs to the Secretary of War on the afternoon of the 7th.[1]

Gold did not go higher to any appreciable extent on the morning of election. The price increased toward night and it went for a spurt on Wednesday morning, after it was known that Lincoln was elected, to 260, but immediately receded and never went so high again.

On Monday, the 7th, I received a letter from Hon. Simon Cameron from Pennsylvania, asking what time I could see him, and where we could meet. The only intimation of his business was the statement contained in his letter that Stanton, the Secretary of War, was going on the march, and that I should flank him.[2]

I replied the next day that I would be in New York City certainly until Wednesday, and would be glad to see him at my headquarters.[3]

[1] See Appendix No. 88.　　　[2] See Appendix No. 91.　　　[3] See Appendix No. 92.

I afterwards received a letter from him dated the 11th of November, stating that he would be in New York on the following Saturday,[1] and I had the honor of a call from him at the time indicated.

He tendered me his congratulations upon our success in keeping the peace on election day, and then informed me that he had means, which I could understand, of knowing that I could be Secretary of War if I would accept the office. He said that there had been so much stress in the campaign put upon Stanton's severity of action toward the rebels that it might be necessary for the pacification of the country to make a change.

I replied to him in substance that I had no reason to change the determination which I had given him in the spring, namely, that I should hold no office except an active command in the army until the war had terminated. I said that the great encomiums I had received had not turned my head or changed my views as to my loyal duty to my country or to myself; that Stanton had loyally stood by me in everything, and that in ordinary gratitude I could not think of taking his place, in any event, until it was certain that he would leave it whether I took it or not; that in that case it was more than doubtful, in view of the opposition of the officers of the regular army under which I was suffering, whether I could do as well as Stanton had done, he having partially overcome a like opposition to himself; that the only change in regard to the treatment of the rebels which the President would get from me would be that I should act more promptly in punishing rebel offenders.

Mr. Cameron said he had had a personal conversation with the President upon this subject, and that he was very sure that he would regret my determination.

I replied to him that when I saw the President I believed that I could convince him that what I was doing was the best for himself and the best for his cause.

Cameron answered: "Well, General, you stick to your text like an old rusty weathercock."

We discussed for a considerable time the political situation and also the condition of the war. I expressed to him my opinion,

[1] See Appendix No. 93.

which I have heretofore given, and in which he then concurred, that the rebel authorities would now see the hopelessness of their carrying the war further, and would soon treat for peace, which they did.

We parted, as always, the best of friends, and he said he would see the President. Soon after this, public rumor, and some of the newspapers, were very active in discussing this topic, and I myself received many letters about it. To none of these did I return a reply, but threw them all aside, save one. My friend, Col. Edward W. Serrell, of New York, wrote me very intelligently upon the matter, expressing the strongest belief that, notwithstanding the opposition of the regular army, I should receive the appointment if it was known in Washington that I would accept it.[1]

Early in the morning of the 8th of November, election day, I despatched trusty officers to each point where dispositions had been made, to keep the peace and to meet violence, if necessary. I remained at my office to receive reports of the occurrences. The remainder of the day, until the polls closed, was monotonously quiet. The sixty lines of wire brought into the room adjoining my office such messages as these, repeated every hour without variation: " All quiet in No. 10; " "All quiet in No. 25," and so on, as the case might be.

The only special matter reported to me was that Mr. Auguste Belmont lost his vote, which was challenged on the ground that he had made a bet on the result of the election, and under that challenge he declined to vote.

It was also reported to me that very few of the Southerners in the city presented themselves at the polls.

That evening until a late hour was hilariously spent in listening to the good news of the election returns, and I went to bed with the reflection that loyalty to law and order had prevailed.

General Grant, expecting a movement at the front, telegraphed the War Department, urging the early return of the troops sent to New York,[2] and they were returned as fast as possible; but in view of the gold conspiracy Stanton desired me personally to remain some days longer.[3]

---

[1] See Appendix No 94.   [2] See Appendix No. 95.   [3] See Appendix No. 96.

November 10, General Grant telegraphed a very high compliment to Stanton, at the quiet way in which the elections in New York passed off, as follows: —

The elections have passed off quietly; no bloodshed or riot throughout the land; is a victory worth more to the country than a battle won. Rebeldom and Europe will construe it so.[1]

On Monday, the 14th, under the direction of a committee of the most distinguished citizens of New York, a reception was given me at the Fifth Avenue Hotel. The scene was brilliant beyond any possible conception of mine, and the reception ended with a banquet at which I was called upon to make a speech, giving to the assembly my opinion as to what should be done in the future, upon which topic, after properly acknowledging my grateful thanks for the reception, among other things I spoke as follows: —

What is the duty of the government in the present future? War cannot last always; the history of nations shows — the experience of war demonstrates — that war must come to an end. But how? In what way? And war such as this, prosecuted for the purpose of breaking down the power of those opposed to the government and bringing them under the supremacy of its laws, must be terminated either by a reconciliation or by subjugation. In view, therefore, of the unanimity of the American people, in view of the strength, the majesty, the right of the nation, may it not be suggested that now is the time to hold out to the deluded people of the South the olive branch of peace and say to them: "Come back, come back, and leave off feeding on husks, and share with us the fat of the land, and bygones shall be bygones." If bygones are bygones, in one country and under one law we will live in peace hereafter. Are we not able to offer them this now? Are we not strong enough? Do we not stand firmly with unanimity of sentiment enough to offer peace to all if all will submit to the laws? There might have been some complaint, I think, among a proud and chivalrous people that they would not desert their leaders by taking advantage of the unanimous proclamation of President Lincoln. But now when we come to them and say come back, and you shall find the laws the same save so far as they have been altered by the legislative wisdom of the land, both for leaders and followers, can there be any excuse for either if they rebelliously remain in the contempt of the authority of the government? Are

[1] See Appendix No. 95.

we not in a condition now, not taking counsel from our fears or our weakness, but of our strength and magnanimity, again to make such offers of peace and amity in the most beneficent terms and for the last time? By so doing shall we not in the eyes of the world have exhausted all the resources of statesmanship in an offer to restore peace to the country? Who shall hinder their returning, and if they will not come back who shall complain?

Let us not permit the rebel after he has fought as long as he can then, if he chooses, to come back. Let us state some time, perhaps the 8th of January — for the association will be as good as any — for all to lay down their arms and submit to the laws; and when that hour is passed, and every man who shall reject the proffered amity of a great and powerful nation speaking in love, in charity, in kindness, in hope of peace and quiet forever to its rebel sons,— I say then let us meet him or them with sharp, quick, decisive war, which shall bring the Rebellion to an end forever, by the extinguishment of such men wherever they may be found. How is that to be done? Blood and treasure have been poured out without stint or measure, until, taking advantage of the supposed depletion of the treasury, bad men having banded together by speculating in gold, which ought to be the circulating medium, have raised the price of coals upon every poor man's hearth, and the price of bread upon every poor man's table. Let the government take some measure to stop this unholy traffic, and let it be understood that the policy of the government will be, hereafter, to pay no more bounties for the recruitment of soldiers from the taxes of the loyal North. But take counsel from the Roman method of carrying on war and saying to our young men: "Look to the fair fields of the sunny South; they have refused our amity and offers of peace; they have turned away the day of grace; go down there in arms in support of the government, extinguish the rebellion, and you shall have what you conquer in fair division of the lands to each man in pay for his military service. We will open new land offices wherever our army marched, dividing the lands in the rebel States among our soldiers to be theirs and their heirs forever."

A harsh measure, it may be said, but is it not quite as just as to tax ourselves, and thus raise the price of the necessaries of life for the purpose of giving bounty to support the soldier in fighting those rebellious men, whom we have three times over solemnly called to come and enjoy with us the blessings of our liberties and be friends,— saying in 1862, come in June; in 1863, come in December; in 1864, come by the 8th of January, 1865. When the clock strikes the last knell of that parting day, then all hope to those who have not made progress to return should be put off forever and ever. No longer should they be permitted to live on the land or even within the boundaries of the United States. Let them go to Mexico, to the islands of the sea, or some place that I do not care to name,— because I know no land bad enough to be cursed with their presence — but never to live here again.

At the close of my speech the Rev. Henry Ward Beecher was called upon to address the assemblage, which he did in his peculiar way, expressing high consideration for myself, and in the course of his remarks he named me as a possible candidate for the presidency in 1868.

The proceedings were interlarded with toasts, and among others there was one by Gen. Prosper M. Wetmore of my possible candidature.

While all this was sufficiently laudatory, yet to me it was one of the most unhappy and unfortunate occurrences of my life, and it was my own fault that it was so. I only looked upon it as the effervescence of the champagne of the hour, and paid no attention to it as a sober announcement of such possible candidature. Otherwise I cannot account for my not having had wit or wisdom enough to interpose another little speech in which I could have taken the sting all out of it. I should have been wise enough to have said something in substance like this: Gentlemen, you honor me overmuch by your high consideration. The place you name is not due to me. You should have put forward, in my judgment, one whom I should feel honored to support — the lieutenant-general of the army who has carried us through the memorable events of the late campaign with such success and brilliancy and genius of effort — General Grant, who ought to be our next candidate for the presidency when Lincoln retires, and who no doubt will be called by a grateful country to that post.

If I had had brains enough to say that, the sting would have been taken out of the whole affair; nay more, I could have been put in command of the Army of the Potomac if I wished.

CHAPTER XVII.

FORT FISHER.

EARLY in September it was proposed to me by General Grant that I should send down General Weitzel, with Brigadier-General Graham of the naval brigade, to reconnoitre the position of Fort Fisher, and that I should act in conjunction with a fleet which was being prepared by the navy. General Weitzel was accordingly sent down to make that reconnoissance. About the 20th of September, as I remember, he returned and reported the condition of things there.

On the 29th of September, the Army of the James made a march across the river, which resulted in the capture of Battery Harrison and the line that we subsequently occupied on the north bank of the James until the surrender of Richmond in April, 1865. It was from this line that the negro troops under Weitzel marched and took possession of the rebel capital. This movement across the James required all the force I had. General Grant said to me that we could not go on the Wilmington expedition at that time for two reasons. The first of these was the want of disposable forces, although at that time it was not contemplated to send down but about three thousand men, as it was supposed that Fort Fisher could be taken by a surprise. The second and perhaps the more cogent reason was that the fleet had given great notice by its preparation; the ships had gathered at Hampton Roads, and published that they had the largest armament in the world, and were going to take Wilmington. This seemed to cut off all hope of surprise. General Grant then said to me that he would not have anything to do with it, to use his exact phrase, because he could not afford an army for a siege, and he supposed the purpose for which the fleet was getting ready was so far known to everybody that there could be no surprise.

From the 20th of September to the 7th of October the navy gathered a fleet at Hampton Roads, and was practising there. The vessels lay there from that time till the middle of December.

In that time, after hearing of the great destruction for many miles around made by an explosion of gunpowder at Erith, England, I made an examination into the various instances of the explosive effect of large quantities of powder; and I believed that possibly, by bringing within four or five hundred yards of Fort Fisher a large mass of explosives, and firing the whole in every part at the same moment — for it was the essence of the experiment to have the powder all exploded at the same instant — the garrison would at least be so far paralyzed as to enable, by a prompt landing of men, a seizure of the fort.

I went to Fortress Monroe to examine the details of that question among others. While there I received on November 1 a telegram to report at once to Washington, and on reaching there found that I was to be sent to New York to take charge of the city during the election. While at Washington I suggested the powder experiment to the President, to the Assistant Secretary of the Navy, and I think to General Halleck. It was readily embraced by the Secretary of the Navy and with more caution by the President. Further investigation was suggested, and I left the matter in the hands of the navy, and on November 2 went to New York.

When I returned on the 16th of November I found that the idea had received so much favor at Washington that it was determined it should be tried. One consideration which determined the making of the attempt was that if it should prove a success the whole system of offensive warfare by naval procedure would be changed, for no forts near harbors would be safe if a small vessel loaded with gunpowder and run ashore under a fort and exploded would destroy the people in it, and no garrison would ever remain in a fort when such a vessel was seen approaching.

The experiment was well worth trying on another account. The navy had storehouses for more than five thousand barrels of powder in a place, near many of our large cities. Of course, as at Erith, which was one of the English government storehouses, it would only be a question of time when some of those deposits of powder would be exploded either by design, carelessness, or accident. What the effect of such an explosion would be was a question which seemed very necessary to be solved in order to determine the safety of the neighboring cities. The Naval Ordnance Bureau had many reports recommending the removal of the powder so stored lest damage might ensue, but those reports had never been acted upon by Congress. On this account also it was thought best to test the question.[1]

The powder used at Fort Fisher was navy cannon powder, each grain of which is nearly an inch cube, in order that it may burn slowly, so as not to burst the guns.

A commission of naval experts was appointed to examine the subject in behalf of the Navy Department, before whom I was not called. The navy was to furnish a vessel and one hundred and fifty tons of powder. The army at first agreed to furnish one hundred tons of powder and afterwards fifty tons more. A part of this amount was partially damaged powder, all that the army had; and the rest was made up by purchasing blasting powder.

I immediately left Washington, having nothing further to do with this matter, the navy undertaking to see that the powder was properly placed and exploded, and went to my headquarters at the front.

---

[1] No great amount of powder had ever been exploded. The largest known to me at that time was at Erith, where there was only 1,040 barrels of powder, all of which was not exploded, and that was by three distinct explosions Since then, on June 16, 1887, the schooner Parallel, having on board a general cargo, including forty-two tons of giant powder, drifted ashore hard and fast in the Golden Gate below the Cliff House, when, without premonition, there was a terrific explosion, followed a second later by another which seemed to shake the very foundations of the earth. Not a stick of the vessel was to be seen, while debris of the wreck and pieces of iron were scattered about the country for three-quarters of a mile in every direction. The Cliff House, a very large summer hotel, situated on the top of a hill a hundred yards away and a hundred and fifty feet above the sea level, not only was thrown on its side but the wreck was entirely crushed in like card-board. An immense wave, weighing tons, was lifted in the air and carried over the top of the house. Every window and door in the house was shattered into kindling, and the foundations of the building were crushed so as to be unsafe. A two-story cottage of large size, occupied as a private residence, two hundred feet further inland, was blown bodily off its foundations and moved five feet further from the sea. The adjacent stables, two hundred feet long, were utterly demolished, not a single stick being left standing. The shock was felt for many miles.

During the year in which this note was written there was an explosion in Italy of not a very much larger amount of powder than that exploded at Erith, and it caused very widely extended and disastrous damage and loss of life.

Neither of these explosions was instantaneous, but there were consecutive explosions. What would be the effect of an instantaneous explosion of like quantities of powder or dynamite is still left to conjecture.

I write this note with a view to having action taken that no large amounts of powder shall be stored in the vicinity of populous cities, and in order that municipal authorities may have their attention called to the matter. But what is everybody's business is nobody's until a great disaster is realized.

Gilman Marston

Upon my return General Grant left the command to go to Burlington, N. J., to visit his family, leaving me as senior officer in command of both armies until he returned on the 24th of November. I fix the date of his return by the following telegram to the Secretary of War, which was the last telegram I sent while in command of both armies: —

HEADQUARTERS ARMY OF THE JAMES,
Nov. 24, 1864, 11.30 P. M.

HON. E. M. STANTON, SECRETARY OF WAR:

In the absence of Lieutenant-General Grant, I have to report to you that the battery and cavalry horses are suffering for hay, and the government is losing large sums in the depreciation of these horses from this cause. For this there can be no excuse, as there is hay enough in the country. It can only arise from inexcusable remissness somewhere, which needs but to be brought to your attention to be remedied.

BENJ. F. BUTLER,
Major-General Commanding.

During General Grant's absence I was informed that the navy had adopted my plan, and the vessel to contain the powder was being got ready by the navy, which was to furnish one hundred and fifty tons of powder at Fortress Monroe. Later I received in answer to a telegram which I had sent General Dyer, chief of ordnance, a message that the army would also furnish one hundred and fifty tons of powder at Fortress Monroe.[1]

General Grant had then returned. From information received it was supposed that the garrison at Wilmington and all the forces about Wilmington, except a small garrison at Fort Fisher, had been detached to meet General Sherman. Thereupon, after a consultation, General Grant desired me to do two things. One was to send an expedition up the Roanoke River and endeavor to reach the railroad between Weldon and Wilmington, so as to cut off supplies and reinforcements from the enemy going north to Petersburg and Richmond, and also to prevent reinforcements being sent by the Weldon Road to Wilmington in case we moved in that direction. The other was to get a force to be sent down to see if we could not effect a surprise at Wilmington, as it seemed evident that the

---

[1] See Appendix No. 97.

enemy supposed the expedition gotten up early in the fall had been abandoned. This expedition up the Roanoke was to be a link in the chain of operations, and was to be made in conjunction with the navy. I sent a despatch to Admiral Porter about the Roanoke expedition.[1] On the same day, the 30th of November, I received a telegram from General Grant urging the importance of Weitzel's getting off at once with the expedition.[2]

I had gone to Fortress Monroe and had a personal consultation with the admiral upon the Roanoke expedition after my consultation with General Grant. I answered his telegram by repairing to City Point in person to get further instructions from General Grant. They were that we should move as soon as the navy was ready.

Matters remained in that condition until the 4th of December. On that day I received a telegram from General Grant urging me to hurry off the expedition either with or without the powder-boat.[3] On the same day I telegraphed to Admiral Porter to hasten operations, as news which I had received made time of great importance.[4]

On the same day, also, I received word from Admiral Porter that the navy was ready for the one hundred and fifty tons of powder, and asking me to have it packed ready for them.[5] On the 5th of December I telegraphed to Captain Edson, ordnance officer, to have the powder ready at once,[6] and on the same day I received word[7] from Admiral Porter that he was all ready and would call on the ordnance officer for the material, which he got. On the 6th of December, hearing nothing further, I telegraphed to Admiral Porter asking him when he could be ready,[8] and received an answer informing me that he had got most of his ammunition, meaning the powder with which to fill the powder-boat, and would commence loading the next day, when he could tell me within an hour when he would be ready to start.[9]

It will thus be seen that Admiral Porter promised to notify me on the morning of the 7th of December. I had to make all my arrangements by verbal instructions and orders. On the 6th of December I issued, through my chief of staff, Brigadier-General Turner, the instructions intended for the expedition as follows: —

---

[1] See Appendix No. 98. [2] See Appendix No. 99. [3] See Appendix No. 100.
[4] See Appendix No. 101. [5] See Appendix No. 102. [6] See Appendix No. 103.
[7] See Appendix No. 104. [8] See Appendix No. 105. [9] See Appendix No. 106.

HEADQUARTERS DEPARTMENT OF VIRGINIA AND
NORTH CAROLINA, ARMY OF THE JAMES,
IN THE FIELD, Dec. 6, 1864.

MAJ.-GEN. G. WEITZEL COMMANDING :

General :—The major-general commanding has entrusted you with the command of the expedition about to embark for the North Carolina coast. It will consist of about sixty-five hundred infantry, two batteries of artillery, and fifty cavalry. The effective men of General Ames' division of the Twenty-Fourth Corps will furnish the infantry force. General Paine is under your orders, and General Ames will be ordered to report to you in person immediately.

You will confer with these officers and arrange details ;· instruct them to select their best men, making your force about sixty-five hundred men. The chief of artillery in conference with you will designate the artillery to be taken. The horses of the batteries, except one horse for each officer and chief of piece, will be left. Take one set of wheel harness. Fifty men of the Massachusetts cavalry will be ordered to report to you. Forty ambulances (two horse), with the necessary medical stores, have been selected for the expedition, which will be distributed on at least two boats. Take sixty rounds of ammunition for the men, one hundred rounds in boxes, to be distributed through the fleet. If your division trains do not furnish the necessary amount, the balance required will be furnished by the chief of ordnance at the point of embarkation. Three hundred rounds of artillery ammunition per gun will be taken. So much of it as is not contained in limber boxes and caissons will be loaded in boxes at the point of embarkation. Let each regiment draw and take with it on transport five days' rations, three days' cooked meats; twenty days' additional will be taken in at Fortress Monroe, distributing it through the fleet. Field rations only will be taken. Two pack-mules for division and brigade headquarters will be allowed. Mounted officers will take but one horse for personal use.

The chief quartermaster has been instructed to furnish one hundred and fifty mule harnesses. It is expected to obtain the animals from the enemy's country. The chief quartermaster will also furnish a party of wharf builders and a small amount of material for landing, etc. Thirty launches will be taken on board at Fortress Monroe. The chief signal officer has been instructed to order signal officers and men to report to you. Lieutenant Parson, with a company of engineer soldiers, will report to you. Five hundred shovels, two hundred and fifty axes, and one hundred picks have been prepared. It is expected that the necessary transportation will be ready to-morrow at Deep Bottom.

You will report in person to the major-general commanding for further instructions.

I am, very respectfully, your obedient servant,

JOHN W. TURNER,
Brigadier-General and Chief of Staff

[Indorsement.]

Respectfully forwarded to Lieutenant-General Grant for his information, and with the earnest request that he will make any suggestion that may occur to him in aid of the enterprise.

BENJ. F. BUTLER,
Major-General Commanding.

On the same day I received the first written instructions from General Grant as follows: —

HEADQUARTERS ARMIES OF THE UNITED STATES,
CITY POINT, Dec. 6, 1864.

BENJ. F. BUTLER, MAJOR-GENERAL COMMANDING:

General:—The first object of the expedition under General Weitzel is to close to the enemy the port of Wilmington. If successful in this, the second will be the capture of Wilmington itself. There are reasonable grounds to hope for success if advantage can be taken of the absence of a great part of the enemy's forces now looking after Sherman in Georgia. The directions you have given for the number and equipment of the expedition are all right, except in the unimportant one of where they embark and the amount of intrenching tools to be taken. The object of the expedition will be gained on effecting a landing on the mainland between Cape Fear River and the Atlantic, north of the north entrance to the river. Should such landing be effected, whether the enemy hold Fort Fisher or the batteries guarding the entrance to the river there, the troops should intrench themselves, and by co-operation with the navy effect the reduction and capture of those places. These in our hands, the navy could enter the harbor, and the port of Wilmington would be sealed. Should Fort Fisher and the point of land on which it is built fall into the hands of our troops immediately on landing, it will be worth the attempt to capture Wilmington by a forced march and surprise.

If time is consumed in gaining the first object of the expedition, the second will become a matter of after consideration. The details for the execution are intrusted *to you* and the officers immediately in command of the troops. Should the troops under General Weitzel fail to effect a landing at or near Fort Fisher, they will be returned to the army operating against Richmond without delay.

U. S. GRANT,

Lieutenant-General.

By personal arrangement with Grant at City Point at his headquarters, as I went down the river on my way to Fortress Monroe to make final preparations for the expedition, I was to go in its command for a reason which was agreed upon between us in the consultation. The reason was this, that General Weitzel, while a very able general, was quite a young man, and I was very anxious to see this powder expedition go on and succeed, for it was a very grave one.

"I think," said I, "I had better go with the expedition so as to take the responsibility off General Weitzel, as I am an older officer."

To this General Grant assented.

"We shall want," I continued, "an intelligent report of the work around Wilmington, and of the effect of this expedition. Give me your best engineer officer for that purpose. Give me Comstock."

"Certainly, General," he replied, "and any other of my staff that you think will aid you, for we are not doing anything here."

General Grant immediately ordered Colonel Comstock to report to me, and in obedience to that order Comstock went down to Fortress Monroe with me on my boat that evening (the 8th). He was with me all the time, and made a report upon the action of the experiment.

It was further understood that *I was to stay until General Weitzel successfully effected a landing;* and then I was to determine whether there should be a dash made on Wilmington, and go as far as that if necessary, and then come back to my command of the Army of the James. In consequence of this arrangement I took almost my whole staff with me, and also my horses and other means of moving across the country. I went to Fortress Monroe on the evening of the 8th of December. The transportation for the expedition was to be furnished by General Ingalls, General Grant's chief quartermaster.

On the 6th I had moved the troops for this expedition out of the trenches, and got them ready to embark. I fix the date by a telegram from General Terry to General Turner, my chief of staff.[1]

---

[1] See Appendix No. 107.

On the same day I received a telegram requiring me to mass the troops that I had gathered for the expedition, and to stand ready to aid General Grant in a movement that he proposed to make, and to blow out Dutch Gap Canal[1]. I answered at once that orders had been given to carry out these instructions.

On the 7th of December my chief of staff received a telegram from my quartermaster, Colonel Dodge, that he could furnish certain meagre transportation.[2] This showed me that the transportation furnished by General Grant's quartermaster was deficient, for four of the largest boats were behind on that date, and it will also show who, if anybody in the army, was delaying the expedition at that time. My troops were ready on the 6th.

On the 7th, also, I received the following from General Grant in relation to the instructions I had issued, a copy of which had been forwarded to him for his approval: —

HEADQUARTERS ARMIES OF THE U. S.,
CITY POINT, VA., Dec. 7, 1864.

MAJOR-GENERAL B. F. BUTLER,
    COMMANDING ARMY OF THE JAMES :

I had sent you a cipher despatch before receiving your instructions to General Weitzel. I think it advisable that all embarkation should take place at Bermuda. The number of intrenching tools I think should be increased three or four times.

U. S. GRANT,
Lieutenant-General.

The number of intrenching tools was increased. To get additional transportation I sent word to Colonel Dodge that the Baltic was at Annapolis, and could be had.[3] That fact I knew because the Baltic had reported to me at Annapolis with released prisoners. Receiving information from Colonel Dodge in the evening of December 7, that he was now fully prepared to ship the troops, I telegraphed General Grant that General Weitzel's command was encamped at Signal Tower awaiting orders, and that Porter would be ready the next day.[4] On the same day I received a despatch from General Grant instructing me to let Weitzel get off as soon as possible, and stating that he did not want the navy to wait an hour.[5] I trans-

---

[1] See Appendix No. 108.   [2] See Appendix No. 109.   [3] See Appendix No. 110.
[4] See Appendix No. 111.   [5] See Appendix No. 112.

mitted that order to General Weitzel on the date of its receipt,[1] and
on the 8th of December at 9.15 A. M. I received a telegram from
him stating that he was at Bermuda embarking his troops.[2] We
took out one steamer at Fortress Monroe to make out our complement
of transportation.

On the night of the 8th of December, I took Lieutenant-Colonel
Comstock on board my boat, shook hands with General Grant, and
said: "Now, we will get off as soon as we can." I went down the
river and met Admiral Porter on the morning of the 9th, stating
that we were ready to proceed. He said that the powder vessel was
not quite ready, but it would be ready directly; and he said that at
any rate it would not be advisable to go to sea in the state of the
weather then.

On Saturday afternoon, December 10, I asked Colonel Comstock and
General Weitzel to go with me to Norfolk to see Admiral Porter on
board his flag-ship. The conversation with Porter related mostly to
the powder-boat and the time when it would be ready. Both Comstock and myself told Porter that haste was necessary, and that
probably it would be better to dispense with the powder vessels
rather than to delay and give the enemy a chance to send down reinforcements; that the enemy, having made a reconnoissance of my
position that morning, might have discovered that some of our troops
had been withdrawn, and knowing that the expedition had been
contemplated would probably guess its destination. The admiral
said he was hurrying up the putting of the powder on board as much
as he could. We then discussed the weather, which looked un-
favorable, and I telegraphed General Grant that the army was ready,
and was waiting for the navy.[3]

On the next Monday evening the fleet not having yet sailed, I
ordered nearly all the transports to move up Chesapeake Bay to
the Potomac River and Matthias Point, and then if they could, to
return in the night-time and anchor off Cape Henry. They were
started at 3 o'clock on the morning of Tuesday the 13th. We knew
the enemy continually kept scouts in Northumberland County, Va.,
at the mouth of the Potomac, to report every transport that passed up
and down the bay, in fact, everything that occurred there. We had
frequently seen their reports in the Richmond papers. I ordered the

[1] See Appendix No. 113.   [2] See Appendix No. 114.   [3] See Appendix No. 115.

fleet to go up the bay that they might be reported to the enemy as going up the Potomac. Then, after dark, they were to come down the bay again with all lights put out, and thus deceive the enemy as to our movements.

Early on the morning of Wednesday, the 14th, a steamer came in from the Department of the South and reported the sea to be very smooth outside. We at once started the transports already anchored off Cape Henry, and put out to sea. There was no vessel of Admiral Porter's in Hampton Roads when we left.[1] It was arranged that we should meet the naval fleet twenty-five miles off New Inlet.[2] But in order not to arouse any suspicion in regard to Wilmington, and in order that, if it became necessary, we might land at Masonboro' Inlet, which is eighteen miles above Fort Fisher, my fleet was ordered to rendezvous and did rendezvous off Masonboro' Inlet, but far out at sea that they might not be seen. Admiral Porter was notified of this, so that he understood it.

My transport fleet arrived off Masonboro' Inlet the night of Thursday, the 15th of December. The time of sailing had been so arranged that the vessels should sail only so fast, in order that all might get there together, and should not get there in daylight. This was so that it would not be possible for them to be seen by any blockade runner or fishing vessel that might be out there. My own ship being faster than the rest, I went forward eighteen miles down the coast, and twenty-five miles off the land, in order to meet Admiral Porter, who, I supposed, was with his fleet. He had said to me that it would take twelve hours for him to go into Beaufort and get ammunition for his monitors and other vessels, but having had some experience in the delays of naval operations, I allowed him to have thirty-six hours' start.

I reached the blockading fleet off Fort Fisher between six and seven o'clock on the evening of the 15th (Thursday). I inquired if

---

[1] Testimony of General Weitzel before the Committee on the Conduct of the War on the Fort Fisher expedition, pp. 68, 69, 70 : —

"On Wednesday morning early, a steamer came in from the Department of the South and reported the sea as very smooth outside. We at once started, found the transports already anchored off Cape Henry, and started them at once to sea. When we left the harbor, I did not see there a single vessel that belonged to Admiral Porter's fleet.

" I think all the difference between General Butler and Admiral Porter as to the time we sailed is at that one point. Admiral Porter did not know that our transports went up the bay, but supposed they went right out to sea. Thence he says that General Butler started before he did. That, I think, is the cause of difference between them on that point."

[2] See Appendix No. 116.

Admiral Porter had been seen, and was told that he had not. I consulted a few minutes with the officer in charge, and then stood twenty-five miles out to sea, and found the Minnesota and some of the large vessels out there. I spoke them and inquired if they knew where Admiral Porter was. They said they did not, but supposed he was at Beaufort; that they could not get in the harbor of Beaufort, and therefore had come along. Expecting him momentarily, I did not come to anchor, but steamed under what steamboat men call "one bell," — steamed slowly around all that night.

On the evening of the 16th, not seeing Admiral Porter, I stood in towards land with the blockading fleet, my transport fleet still remaining at Masonboro' Inlet, with the exception of my own vessel and a little boat for a tender. I waited that day, which was very fine, and waited also the next day. The sea was so smooth that I lowered my gig and took a row for pleasure. There was not wind enough to fill the sail of a yawl boat that was let down.

I sent General Weitzel and Colonel Comstock on the Chamberlain to make a reconnoissance of the fort, and they ran in so as to draw the fire.

We waited there Friday, Saturday, and Sunday. On Sunday morning (the 18th) I received a letter from Admiral Porter dated the 16th of December, in which he said that he expected to leave for the rendezvous on the 17th, and that if the weather permitted he expected to blow up the powder vessel on the night of the 18th. He also informed me that it had been suggested to him by some of the naval engineers that even at twenty-five miles the explosion might affect the boilers of the steamers and make them explode if heavy steam was carried, and advised that before the explosion took place the fires be drawn and the steam allowed to run down as low as possible.[1]

We waited until Sunday night before Admiral Porter made his appearance. I ran out to meet him and was informed by him that the powder vessel Louisiana, which he said was "as complete as human ingenuity could make her,"[2] having on board two hundred and thirty-five tons of powder,[3] all he could get, had gone to attempt the explosion, and that he proposed to stand in the

---

[1] See Appendix No. 117.   [2] See Appendix No. 118.

[3] The testimony before the Committee on the Conduct of the War shows that only two hundred and fifteen tons were ever got on board. The navy got one hundred and fifty tons of that from the army, and supplied only sixty-five tons instead of one hundred and fifty tons as agreed.

POWDER-BOAT "LOUISIANA" AT FORT FISHER.

moment of the explosion, and open fire to prevent the enemy repairing damages.

Upon the receipt of the letter from Admiral Porter containing that information, it being then eight o'clock at night, and he having said that he would send the powder-boat in with orders to have it exploded, I immediately sent General Weitzel and Colonel Comstock on board the Malvern to represent to the admiral that there would be no use in exploding the powder-boat if the troops could not land.[1] For whatever damage that explosion might do the enemy would have time to repair, and, as we could not land, the advantage of the powder vessel would be lost entirely. As all of us would have to stand off during the northeasterly gale which he foresaw, it would clearly be best not to explode the powder-boat at that time.[2]

When Comstock and Weitzel returned they reported to me that the admiral had agreed with me, and had sent his fast sailing tug to countermand the orders to

[1] See Appendix No. 119.
[2] See Appendix No. 120.

the powder vessels. My officers reported that they had great difficulty in getting on board the admiral's vessel on account of the sea being so rough.

We remained there the night of Sunday. On Monday morning (the 19th) Admiral Porter signalled to me that as it was rough we could not land, and he proposed to exercise his fleet. He got his fleet in line of battle by divisions, and sailed all about, I with my ship following the flag-ship. We all sailed within sight of Fort Fisher. That I believed was the first intimation the enemy had that we were off the coast. I am confirmed in my opinion because Lieutenant R. T Chapman, commanding the rebel battery Buchanan, which was the mound battery just below Fort Fisher, begins his report to the Confederate authorities on the 29th of December, 1864, in these words: "I reported to you on the 20th inst. that the enemy had arrived off this place." When we were exercising the fleet it did go within sight of the mound battery, and it was remarked on the squadron that if we could see them they of course could see us.

On the evening of Monday the 19th, the wind hauled round to the northeast, and it was very evident that there could be no landing of troops at that time. I had taken coal for ten days on the transport vessels, all they could carry. As my flag-ship was running light I could put a hundred tons of coal as ballast in her hold. I had taken ten days' water. Most of the vessels, however, had water condensers with which we could supply ourselves in case of necessity. Having waited in readiness from the 9th of December to the 20th, my ten days' supplies were getting rather short. By Admiral Porter's direction we were to rendezvous under Cape Lookout or in Beaufort Harbor, as many of our vessels as the depth of water would permit to go in.

As I saw that we could do nothing for three or four days, I sent my tender to the fleet at Masonboro' Inlet with a message that all that could do so should go into Beaufort Harbor, which was between sixty and seventy miles from Fort Fisher, and renew their coal and water. I proceeded to Beaufort to superintend that matter because the water was to be brought from a distance of some fifteen miles, which involved great loss of labor and time, not having any railroad facilities.

Admiral Porter says in his report that I had a bad class of transports.[1] If it was so they were such as were furnished me by General
Grant's quartermaster.   But that statement is not true.   They were
transports of an excellent class, as is shown by the fact that they
rode out, without the loss of a man, one of the most considerable
gales that ever occurred on the coast.

On the 20th of December, while lying off Beaufort, I sent to
General Grant a report detailing the movements and operations up
to that time.[2]

I intended to go out of port the afternoon I sent off that report,
but it blew very strongly and continued to blow very hard until
Tuesday night, when it held up a little.

I then sent Capt. H. C. Clarke of my staff to Admiral Porter,
who was lying under Cape Lookout, to say to him that I would
be finished coaling the vessels and be down there Saturday night
ready to commence the attack on Sunday morning, when I hoped
the sea would be smooth.   Captain Clarke went down, but could
not return until the next day, when he reported to me that he
had arrived off Beaufort on his return during the night before, but
that it was so rough as to be impossible for him to get his boat in,
although it was a very good light-draft steamer.

He had seen Admiral Porter, who had told him to say to me that
he would explode the powder vessels at one o'clock that Thursday
night.   Captain Clarke said to him that it would be impossible for
me to get there with the land force because the vessels were not
coaled, although they were doing the best they could, but that he
would go right back and inform me.   He left Admiral Porter at one
o'clock on the afternoon of Friday to come back but did not reach
me until the next morning for the reasons aforesaid.

Having this information that the powder-boat was to have been
exploded at one o'clock the night before,— *and at the time I received
the information it had been exploded,*— I started immediately for Fort
Fisher, ordering the transport fleet to follow me, each vessel as fast
as it got coaled.   Most of them got off directly.

I got down near Fort Fisher between four and five o'clock, and
found the fleet engaging the enemy and bombarding the fort.   I
remained there in sight until the signal was made to cease firing,

---

[1] See Appendix No. 121.   [2] See Appendix No. 122.

when the admiral's ship ran out some four or five miles and came to anchor. I ran alongside of her and anchored, and sent Lieutenant DeKay of my staff on board to say that General Weitzel would be on board that night to arrange a plan of attack the next morning, if the admiral thought it advisable to attack. Admiral Porter sent back word that he was very tired that night, but if I would send General Weitzel and Colonel Comstock on board in the morning he would see them at as early an hour as I chose to send them. I sent General Weitzel as he was to command the troops on shore, and I proposed that all the minor details, corresponding signals and all that, should be arranged between Admiral Porter and Weitzel so that there should be no mistake. And, besides, I supposed that Colonel Comstock would go with me to suggest anything that might occur to him, he being a member of General Grant's staff.

At half past six on the morning of Sunday, General Weitzel repaired on board the Malvern, the flag-ship, and there he had a conversation with Admiral Porter.

I sent Admiral Porter a letter in answer to that conversation in which I suggested that we should go in as early as eight o'clock in the morning.

It was arranged that the naval fleet should silence the Flag Pond Hill and Half Moon batteries, and that we should then land near them.

I directed General Weitzel and Colonel Comstock to urge upon Admiral Porter to run by the fort into Cape Fear River, but Porter said he could not do it because there was not enough water. Now, we had four vessels, blockade runners, which had been caught while trying to run out of the port of Wilmington. They had been captured and turned into gunboats, and it might be supposed that they could get into a place where there was sufficient water to permit them to come out. Yet Porter reported that the navy could not run in there because they had no light draft vessels.

The vessels of the navy lay in a semi-circle around Fort Fisher. Twelve vessels lay up above trying to silence the batteries at Pond Hill and Half Moon, which they did not do except temporarily. These same batteries fired at me afterwards while I lay within six hundred yards superintending the landing of troops.

I ask the reader to take into consideration the difference between a silent fort and a silenced one.   Fortress Monroe is silent to-day, but it is far from being silenced.   From Fort Fisher and the batteries the enemy fired occasional shots all the forenoon.   It is fair to say that when the Brooklyn was in near the Flag Pond Hill battery she did some splendid shooting and the enemy concluded not to fire a great deal.

We stood in, the transport fleet lying each side of me.   I lay within eight hundred yards of the shore when we commenced debarking the troops.   The moment we got on shore skirmishers were to advance and take possession of some woods.   This they did, and then the small party moved down upon Flag Pond Hill battery.   The enemy held out a white flag as our skirmishers came up, and the navy sent in boats and took the prisoners off.[1]   Among them were sixty-five prisoners from the Seventeenth North Carolina, a regiment which lay before my line when I left before Richmond.   Porter reports that no land reinforcements got there, and yet we captured and brought back with us sixty-five men of a rebel regiment which I left at Richmond.

When we landed, the fort was entirely silent, with the exception of a gun fired now and then at some small navy boats which were apparently dragging for torpedoes or taking soundings.

My plan was: First to land five hundred men and reconnoitre, and if it was found that they could hold the landing for the others, then to land force enough to assault the place, and then, if it was possible, to land the rest of the men and what material I had, and intrench.   The first five hundred men were easily landed, and then the boats were sent back and more put on shore as fast as possible.[2]

As soon as the landing was in good progress, I ran down to a point within five hundred yards of Fort Fisher, in General Graham's army boat, "Chamberlain," and at the right of where the monitors lay that were firing upon the fort.   I could run in nearer than they could because my vessel was of lighter draft.   I there met General Weitzel returning from a reconnoissance.   He stated to me that he had been out to the front line, and had seen Fort Fisher,

---

[1] The lieutenant in charge of the boats reports that the navy captured Flag Pond Hill battery and the prisoners.

[2] See Appendix No. 123.

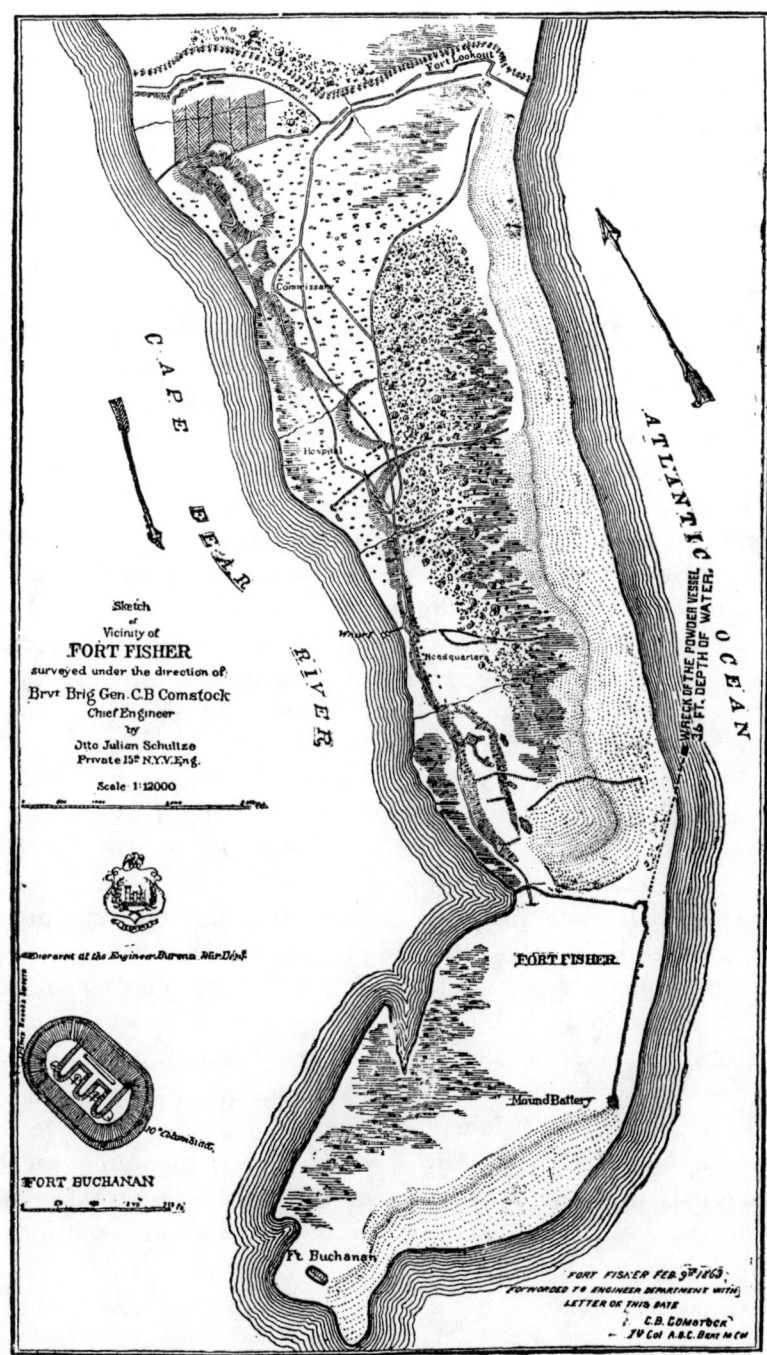

MAP OF FORT FISHER.

and that one of his best officers had been out on the picket line. As a defensive work the fort was uninjured. Its guns were all mounted on the land face, and they had seventeen guns mounted up the beach. "His picket line," he said, "was crouched under the counterscarp of a ditch, which was so high that it covered them." General Weitzel's report to me has since received confirmation from the report of Major-General Whiting, of the rebel service,[1] who reported that "during the day the enemy landed a large land force, and at half past four advanced a line of skirmishers to the left flank of the sand curtain." That is, our men advanced up and crouched under the sand bank which formed the counterscarp of the ditch, which was high enough to protect them from the fire of the fort. There they could lie exposed only to the fire of the navy which was enfilading them, — and we lost ten of our men by that fire from our gunboats.

General Weitzel further stated that he thought it was impossible to assault the fort successfully, and that it would be murder to make such attack upon the fort, and gave his reasons, which were entirely satisfactory to me. But being unwilling to abandon the enterprise without trying, and seeing, from the state of the weather, that it must be an assault or nothing, I said to Colonel Comstock, who was on board with me: "Jump into a boat with General Weitzel, pull ashore and examine with him and report to me if an assault is feasible; to me it does not look so, but I am unwilling to give up." [2]

They went on shore. The surf had begun to rise so that they got very wet in landing.

At the same time Brigadier-General Graham, reporting to me, said: "General, you have either to provide for those troops to-night on shore in some way, or get them off, because it is getting so rough that we cannot land much longer."

General Graham had been a naval officer for many years, but was then in the service of the army commanding the naval brigade. I reflected a moment before determining the course of action. A storm was coming on; the surf was rolling in; the barometer had fallen a half an inch. If we got the men on shore, it might be, and probably would be, a week before we could send any provisions to them.

In the meantime a deserter from the Sixty-Second North Carolina, whom I had captured once before at Hatteras in 1861, having received good treatment from me, came in. He said that they had marched down from Richmond, and that Kirkland's brigade and one other were already down there; and that Hoke was on his way with large reinforcements and had arrived by land the night before at Wilmington, which was about twenty-one or twenty-two miles off.

At that time our skirmishers advanced upon a small body of men who were between Flag Pond Hill battery and the pond. They could not get away because it was a marsh towards the river; and they could not go by the pond and up the beach because there was an opening from the pond into the sea. They could not get down to the fort because we were between them and the fort. Therefore Major Reece, their commander, five officers, and two hundred and eighteen men surrendered. Major Reece was brought to me, and from him I learned that he had marched from Bellville near the Weldon road, where General Warren of Grant's army had made his attack, after they had heard we were at Wilmington. He said that that morning as many of his regiment had been put into the bomb-proofs as they would hold, in addition to the garrison which was there before. As the bomb-proofs were not capable of accommodating his other two hundred and eighteen men, they had marched up the beach out of the way of the fire of the navy. I also learned from him that he had been in the fort that morning, and that it had lost but two men killed from the bombardment, and that there was but one gun on the land face dismounted. Reece seemed to be very communicative, and willing to tell us all he knew.

I then inquired of him where he was the night before last. He said he was lying two miles and a half up the beach. I asked him if he had heard the powder vessel explode. He said he did not know what it was, but supposed a boat had blown up; that it jumped him and his men who were lying on the ground about like pop-corn in a popper, to use his expression.

I then determined upon my course of action, bearing in mind the fact that a storm was coming on, and knowing that, if it became necessary to effect a landing again, we could do it any day, in a smooth sea, in two hours without the loss of a man. I thought it a greatly less risk waiting with the men on board the transports than to attempt to get them on shore and have them intrench there during the night in the coming storm.

I knew very well, for I had studied them very carefully, that my instructions said that we were to blockade Cape Fear River by landing and intrenching there. But finding that the channel of the river was a mile and a half from any spot of ground where I could possibly plant a gun, I was not very hopeful of preventing, with my field guns, blockaders running by. I had obtained information which satisfied me that Hoke's division was there, and when they were all there with the garrisons and reserves that had been thrown in, there would be at least twice as many as I had on shore. Hoke's division alone was about six thousand men, and I had between twenty-one hundred and twenty-three hundred men landed. I had under my command sixty-five hundred men in all. It was evidently impossible to do anything further at that time in the way of landing. But troops can be got off when it is not possible to land them and their supplies. Orders were, therefore, given to get the troops off, and everything was done that could be done to get them away. General Weitzel and Colonel Comstock agreed with me.[1]

Before starting upon this reconnoissance Admiral Porter had sailed by my boat in his flag-ship, and with his speaking trumpet hailed me in these words: —

"How do you do, General?"

"Very well, I thank you," I answered.

"How many troops are you going to land?"

"All I can," said I, — for the navy had agreed to furnish me with the means of landing.

"There is not a rebel within five miles of the fort," said the admiral. "You have nothing to do but to land and take possession of it."

I had a different opinion, and avowed it. I said to those around me: "I think there is a man on shore by the name of Weitzel who will find out if it is so."

That was the first personal communication I had with Admiral Porter after leaving Hampton Roads.

The words were hardly out of Admiral Porter's mouth, and his vessel had not got many lengths from me, when the rebel skirmishers

[1] See Appendix No. 125.

opened on ours, and before an hour's time we had captured the two hundred and eighteen men who had not time to march one mile, and who denied having marched at all within that time, — the over-plus men that could not be put in the bomb-proofs of the fort.

I ran out to the Malvern, for the fleet had come to anchor, and asked Admiral Porter what could be done. He informed me that he had exhausted his ammunition, and that he must go to Beaufort to replenish. As it took him four days to put in his ammunition at a time when I supposed his vessels were already nearly full, I thought it would take him quite as long to fill them when they were quite empty. Now Beaufort was some seventy miles off, and as it would take him at least four days to go there and back, he would be absent certainly a week.

The gale was increasing, and by ten o'clock the sea got so high that I could get off no more men that night with my utmost efforts. In the morning my vessel was rolling so that no man not a sailor could stand on deck, and it was impossible for the navy to come in or open fire upon the fort even if they had had ammunition, — and it will be seen by looking at the report and letter that many of his vessels were actually out of the larger kinds of ammunition. The fleet could do nothing so long as the wind remained as it was then, which was nearly southwest, and if it should shift to the easterly or northeasterly they would be driven on shore. Consequently they must get an offing or be driven on shore. For if they waited there, rolling as the sea was rolling my ship, the fire of the fleet would have amounted to nothing, for under such circumstances their shot would not, with any certainty, have hit a county. But when the fleet retired my men would have no heavy guns to protect them, and would be exposed to attack by large numbers on the peninsula. They might possibly intrench against these, but they would also be exposed to the fire of the heavy guns of the fort, of which there were still sixteen uninjured and bearing directly up the beach. The beach at that point was not more than a third of a mile wide, and the wind of the storm would not affect the accuracy of the enemy's fire from the fort Besides, the drenching rains of the storm would cause suffering and sickness among the unprotected men, as their tents had not been and could not be got on shore, and not even their medical stores had been landed. The fact that as

soon as the fire from our vessels ceased there were plenty of men
with which to repel an attack on the fort, is confirmed by the following
sentence which I take from General Whiting's report above referred
to: "The garrison, however, at the proper moment when the fire of
the navy slackened to allow the approach of the enemy's land force,
drove them off with artillery fire and musketry."

General Whiting shows exactly what my report[1] shows, and what
the report of General Weitzel shows, that our troops were met with
grape and musketry the moment the fire of the navy slackened.
General Whiting also says: "A heavy storm set in and the garrisons
were much exposed, as they were under arms all night."

At eleven o'clock the next day I informed Admiral Porter that in
my judgment there was nothing to be done but to go to Fortress
Monroe, and I went there. Before I got away from the coast of
North Carolina I passed all the heavier vessels of the squadron, such
as the Wabash, the Colorado, and the Ironsides, going up to Beaufort to get ammunition.

Upon my arrival at Fortress Monroe I telegraphed[2] to General
Grant a report of what had been done.

The considerations that determined my mind against remaining
on the beach near Fort Fisher were these: I was by no means
unmindful of the instructions of the lieutenant-general. He had
directed me that if I had fully got my men ashore, not if I had
gotten only a portion of them, I was to remain. But a landing
requires something more than to have twenty-five hundred men out
of sixty-five hundred on a beach with nothing but forty rounds of
ammunition in the cartridge boxes, and with all their supplies
driven off in the storm. I did not think that that was "landing"
within my instructions, and, therefore, I deemed it much better for
the country that I should withdraw as I did; it was much less risk,
and much better for the future. Porter had informed me that he
could not get up the river inside because there was but six feet of
water. But the rebels could come down in that depth of water and
thence operate against Fort Fisher; and they could come prepared to
remain there if I withdrew my forces — and the fact that the fleet
had returned to Beaufort to stay a week to replenish would have
shown the enemy that the expedition had been abandoned. If I

remained there they would keep the forces concentrated at that point; and if I was driven away by the storm coming up, then I should lose the men I had landed.

The failure of the expedition was owing to the delay of the navy in Beaufort; the exploding of the powder-boat before the troops got there to take advantage of the effect of it, whatever it was; the refusal of Admiral Po.ter to run by the fort, and the failure of the bombardment to silence the fire of the fort on the land front.

Porter had been told to run by the forts with a portion of his fleet and go into the river. Then we were to supply him across the strip of land upon which some of our men were landed, and we could have done this marsh or no marsh between us and the river. With the navy in the river, we could have remained on the beach, because we should have had somebody to aid us when the sea was so rough that the fleet could not aid us from the outside. The part of the fleet lying in the river, if he had run by the fort, could have aided us, notwithstanding the weather. The enemy had gunboats in the river, and without having any part of the fleet inside we were more liable to be shelled by them in smooth water, if they retained control of the river, than we were to be protected by the navy from the front in rough water.

One reason given by the admiral for not running by was that he would lose his gunboats by torpedoes. I never heard that there were torpedoes in the channel of the river, nor could I conceive how there could be with blockaders going to and coming from Wilmington, drawing all the water there was in the channel without their running against them.

There was never any excuse given for his delay at Beaufort. That delay gave time for the enemy to meet our whole expedition.

Porter's performance in exploding the powder-boat before two o'clock in the night, when he and his fleet were so far away that they could not get back until twelve o'clock the next day, was also fatal to anything like a surprise.

I think it is my duty to myself and to the country to detail the facts in regard to the powder-boat. They are few and simple. I have stated before that I had learned the particulars of several explosions which showed that large masses of powder, when exploded, produced an effect upon the surrounding earth, atmos-

phere, and buildings of all sorts, in kind with an explosion of a
cannon, in degree according to the mass exploded, and to the
instantaneousness of the ignition of the explosive.

I had never supposed, and I do not now suppose, that the explosion of any mass of a size that could be conveyed there to be
exploded within two or three hundred yards of Fort Fisher, would
blow down its bastions, many feet thick of earth, or blow down its
bomb-proofs, some of them ten or twelve feet of earth, or be likely
to dismantle any of its cannon *en barbette.* Nor did I believe that
the proper explosion could be got from that powder from a vessel
anchored in thirty-six feet of water, because the explosion of the
first ton would stave the vessel all to pieces, or at least blow all the
rest of the powder out of it into the sea to be lost. My proposition
to the Navy Department contemplated using but one hundred tons
of powder. But they immediately suggested more to the amount of
three hundred tons, to make it certain, although I believe, properly
exploded, one hundred tons would have done all that was required.
My plan was that this one hundred tons of powder should be put
into a light-draught steamer, and arranged and packed in such a way
that either by electrical or other apparatus fire could be communicated all through the vessel into every part of the mass of powder at
one and nearly the same instant; that that vessel should be run
ashore; that time fuses or other means of calculating the time
necessary for the explosion should be put in operation, and that with
the vessel hard and fast on shore so that none of the powder substantially could go down into the water until it had time to take fire,
the whole mass should explode. The effect that I expected from that
was that the gases from the burning powder would so disturb the air
as to render it impossible for men to breathe within two hundred
yards; that the magazines of the fort would be burst in and possibly
the magazines themselves be exploded; that by the enormous missiles
that would be set in motion, and by the concussion, many men
would be killed, and if the explosion were to be followed immediately by an attack of even a small number of effective men, the fort
could be captured.

If this experiment had been carried out with anything of the
intelligence with which the plans of it were devised, — for it was
turned over to the experts and ordnance officers of the navy — there

would have been no doubt of its success. If it had been only partially successful, it would have had this effect, namely, that no garrison could be kept in a fort where a small naval vessel in the darkness of the night could be run up under it and explode. It would be less expensive to operate on forts in this way than with expeditions for bombardments which might cost millions.

I knew of and acknowledge one great difficulty which those who actually took charge of the preparation of the powder-boat did not seem to appreciate as I did, — that it is very difficult to explode a large mass of army or navy cannon powder without a considerable delay. But if time enough can be had in which the powder may become fully ignited, then it has rapid but not instantaneous explosive force.

Now, I suppose it is not known to many that the cannon powder in the large guns of the army and navy is in the form of square blocks, each from three-quarters of an inch to an inch every way; and that, before any explosive force can be had from it, there must be time given for the blocks to burn. The powder supply for the powder-boat was of that character, and some that was used was admitted to have been damaged powder. But that was all well enough if it had been given time enough to burn. The problem was so to arrange matters that first every portion of the powder in mass should be set fire to at the same instant, and, secondly, after the vessel was run ashore time should be given before the match was applied to the powder to allow the crew having the vessel in charge to get off in their boats.

At a meeting of naval experts at Fortress Monroe at which I was present it was arranged to use a line of fuse known as the Gomez fuse, of which we had samples. This particular kind of fuse is nothing more than an India rubber tube or case of any required shape filled inside with fulminating powder, like in its properties to that used in percussion caps, which burns with great quickness and force, and after once being ignited cannot be extinguished until the mass has been burned out. So quickly does the fire travel through the tube or case that it will go a mile in four seconds. The experiment was tried, a small Gomez fuse one hundred feet long being coiled up in a tub of water, and its two ends brought over the side. An accurate stop watch could not indicate any lapse of time between the moment when the fire was communicated to one end of the tube, and the rush of the fire out of the other end, after having passed through the whole length of the fuse   The explosion of the fulminate in the tube bursts it at every point along its whole length as it passes through.

It was, therefore, arranged and ordered that the powder should be stored in the boat on the decks above the hold, and the higher the better, and that small boxes full of fine powder should be put in the top of each barrel or bag through the whole mass of the powder, and that from the cabin, where it was to be set on fire, Gomez fuses should be run through all these boxes of fine powder so placed. By this means every box of powder would be exploded at substantially the same instant of time. It was also arranged that all the fuses should start from the cabin where the ends were to be placed in a receptacle filled with powder. When this powder in the receptacle should be fired, it would instantly set fire to the whole mass. The Gomez fuse to be used for this purpose was bought and furnished.

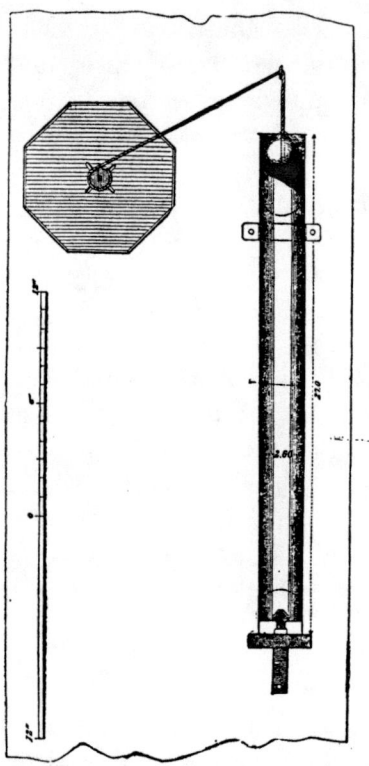

CLOCKWORK DEVISED AND ORDERED TO BE USED TO EXPLODE THE POWDER-BOAT LOUISIANA, BUT NOT USED FOR THAT PURPOSE.

To permit time for the crew to escape an ingenious gentleman devised an apparatus from each of three marine clocks. These were to be set running, in communication with devices, a drawing of which is given, which would drop through a tube, at any time to which the clock should be adjusted, a two-pound shot upon a percussion cap fixed to a nipple at the lower end of the tube. By the fall of the shot the cap would be exploded and fire communicated to the powder in the aforementioned receptacle where the ends of the several fuses were gathered together. A number of experiments were made with this clockwork device, and they worked perfectly. Three sets of apparatus were to be taken lest some disorder of the machinery of one might hinder the proper discharge of the powder. In case they all should fail from any unforeseen contingency, then, in order to prevent this quantity of powder from falling into the hands of the enemy, a fire was to be built on the forecastle· of the vessel, which, by its burning, should at last reach and destroy the powder. But this was to be done, not with any expectation that it would cause a proper explosion, but only as a means of the destruction of the powder without beneficial results.[1]

It was vitally necessary to any success of the explosion that the boat should be in substantial contact with the earth in order to give the explosion effect. It is well known that when a torpedo is exploded in the water with a few feet of water as a cushion between it and the vessel to be destroyed, the effect will be to take from the explosion substantially all its destructive force, and the vessel by that means will escape uninjured.

I have stated with care what was to be done to render this explosion a success. Now, what was done and what left undone?

First, there were but two hundred and fifteen tons of powder put aboard instead of three hundred tons, the amount relied upon.

Second, the illustration given will show the storage of powder as it was ordered to be made, and as it was not made. The hold was to be left empty. The whole of the deck-house was to be filled, and the fuses laid and connected with candles which were to burn a certain time, of which six were prepared. The whole of the powder was to be put as high up as practicable, so as to be as far from the water as possible.

Third, the Gomez fuses were not used at all, but were left hanging up in coils in the cabin at the time of the explosion.

Fourth, the clockwork devices for exploding the powder were not used.

Fifth, the fire was not even built on the forecastle or the forward part of the deck, as it was proposed to be and ought to have been built, but was built in the stern under the cabin of the vessel.

Sixth, the vessel was not run on shore at all, so that it could not sink by the explosion in the water, and the powder drowned out,

[1] See Appendix No. 128.

because of course if the vessel was floating when the explosion took place it would be instantly sunk down into the water. The vessel was not put opposite to the fort, but quite three quarters of a mile [1] above the upper bastion, so that the direct force of the explosion was not felt on the face of the fort.

No accurate survey was made of the distance from the angle of the fort to the powder-boat.

Maj. Thomas Lincoln Casey, of the engineer corps, made a report concerning the powder-boat, but he does not give its distance from the fort. Captain King, in his report on torpedoes, only copies Casey.

General Whiting and Colonel Lamb agree about the distance of the powder-boat from the fort. The fact that some light wooden buildings near the corner of the fort were not destroyed by the explosion shows either that a very small amount of powder exploded, or that the boat was too far distant to do any damage.

As I have said, the clockwork was not started, the fuse was not ignited, and the fire was not lighted in the forecastle, as was directed to be done. On the contrary, it was built under the cabin, and the men and officers left in the yawl and rowed to the Wilderness which was waiting them. They got on board the Wilderness at precisely twelve o'clock. She immediately started at full speed and went some twelve miles out to sea. There they waited for the explosion to take place, which happened at 1.45 A. M. If, as Rhind says, the clockwork was set and the fuses lighted and timed at one hour and a half, the vessel would have exploded at that moment, but it is agreed that it did not explode until twenty-two minutes later. But the explosion did not occur until the after part of the vessel was enveloped in flames.

To do him justice I append so much of Captain Rhind's report as relates to this part of the matter.[2] In his letter, called for by the Ordnance Department of the Navy, he says that the Gomez fuse had not been put into that part of the powder which had been held at Craney Island, Fortress Monroe; that he was ordered to put fuse in, but did not because it could not be done without breaking out the cargo which he did not do.[3] He says he put the fuses in the part which he loaded at Beaufort — a small portion only, — but it could

---

[1] See Testimony of Gen. H. C. Whiting (Appendix 124, Q. 7): "Twelve (12) and fifteen (15) hundred yards, and not nearer."

[2] See Appendix No. 129.   [3] See Appendix No. 130.

not have been done. And even if it were done and the fuses connected with the clocks, they were not the means of exploding the
powder, for he admits that the clocks did not set off the powder.

The failure to start the fire on the forecastle, as he was ordered to
do, and the building it under the cabin, where the flames bursting out
in the after part of the vessel show it was built, made a very great
difference in the result. By looking at the diagram of the vessel
and observing the manner in which the powder was loaded, it will
be seen that between the after part of the vessel and the powder was
the furnace and machinery. This was in a room which, of course,
was made fire-proof, and the fire from the cabin had to burn through
this before it could reach the powder, which the diagram shows was

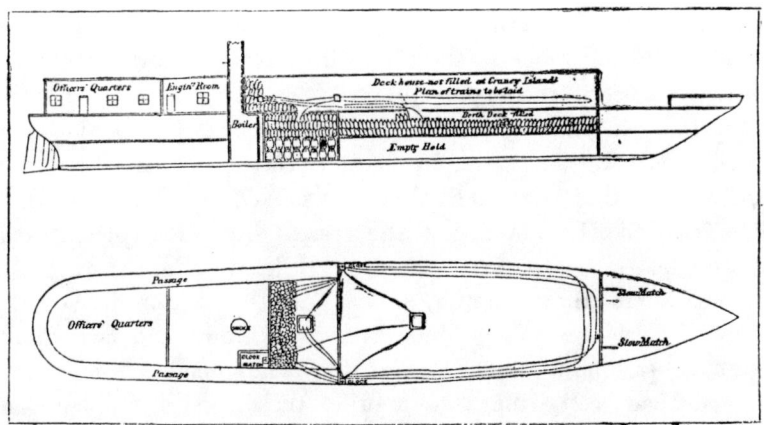

DIAGRAM OF THE POWDER-BOAT LOUISIANA.

protected from the side of the fire-room. There was no protection
between the woodwork of the fore part of the vessel and the powder.
She was anchored head towards the shore, and fastened in that
position by an anchor over the stern at short scope. He did not take
even the only means of exploding her which was to be used in the
last resource, namely, by a fire on her forecastle. He should, while
the vessel was under steam, have turned her and anchored her with
her head from the wind, in order to prevent the fire in the forecastle
being blown too early along the deck into the powder. The reason
of his not having lighted the fire in the forecastle is obvious: he
was afraid that if it were lighted there it would burn too fast to

let him get away far enough to be safe, Porter having told him that the fleet would not be safe short of twenty-five miles at sea, where he had taken the rest of the fleet. So the powder-boat waited until the fire lighted in the stern had burned over the fire-proof enclosure of the engine-room, and struck the powder between decks. This, as soon as it was ignited, exploded and blew all the rest of the powder directly into the sea as if blown from a cannon, because the powder vessel was an iron one, and the berth deck had been entirely cleared out in order to hold powder. It is as safe to say that not nearly one tenth of the powder on board the boat ever exploded, because the moment the explosion took place all the powder in the hold was driven down into the water, and the little powder above the berth-deck was immediately blown into the air. This powder was in bags, and some of the witnesses say they saw a succession of explosions taking place in the air as if of bags of powder which had been thrown up by the explosion.[1]

Rhind admits in his letter to the Ordnance Department — just as Jeffers, who had the matter in charge, testified, — that he was told that the last resort was to explode the powder by building a fire on the forecastle. The fact that the vessel did not explode with all that powder on board until the fire "lighted under her cabin" had been burning nearly two hours, so that the after part of the vessel was enveloped in flames,[2] so as to be seen by Rhind when twelve miles off out at sea, shows that none of the arrangements for exploding the vessel had been either put in order or availed of. Therefore, it is plain that the experiment of the powder-boat never has been tried. The whole performance of the navy as carried out was simply an abortion of the weakest kind. Rhind admits that he purposely steered away from the fort lest he might be discovered and the scheme frustrated. How could the enemy have frustrated it if they had seen the boat?

But the fatal defect, setting aside all others, was that the vessel was not run on shore so as to put the powder where it could burn.

The testimony of Colonel Lamb, who was in command of the fort, upon this subject, shows clearly that the vessel was not observed, and if it had been would probably have been taken for a blockade runner. His testimony shows that the explosion was of no conse-

---

[1] See Appendix No. 131.　　　　　　　　　　[2] See Appendix No. 129.

quence.   He did little more than wake up.   He supposed that some
boat had burst her boiler, but he did not even rise from his bed.
He says also that nothing in the fort, animate or inanimate, was
injured by the explosion.

Porter's admission that he was so afraid that it would explode
the boilers of his steamers twenty-five miles away unless their steam
was run down,[1] shows him as ridiculous in his cowardice as he was
false in his statements.

Let me close this matter of the powder-boat by saying that here
was another of my enterprises to do a service for the country rendered fruitless because the preparation of it was intrusted to the
navy who, through some of its officers, failed utterly to carry it out
properly.   I was blamed and ridiculed for the powder-boat all
over the country, and those who ridiculed me knew no more of
the subject than they knew of the events of an unknown world.
Thus it will be seen that this experiment was another of Butler's
failures through the inefficiency of some of the officers of the
navy, as we have already seen was Dutch Gap Canal by the cowardice of another officer of the navy who was afterwards convicted
therefor.   Yet the experiment was approved to be made by a board
of officers detailed as experts by the President and the Secretary of the
Navy.   They arranged and carried it out.   This board was approved
by Porter and Grant, and over it I did not and could not exercise the
slightest control, even as to indicating the time for the explosion.

By the gallantry of General Terry and his brave troops another
expedition which was afterwards sent down was successful in
assaulting the fort, I admit most willingly, but this throws no light
on the question, and by and by I may consider the motives for sending it down.   Sherman with his army had at that time nearly or
quite enveloped North Carolina or was proceeding in his victorious
march to do so.   In less than thirty days he would be behind
Wilmington which must of course fall as did Savannah.   That
would stop the blockade running into Wilmington as effectually
as it was done by the expenditure of a large amount of money and
the loss of some thousand lives.   When I have made this remark
before I have been answered: "You set the numbers high; Terry
lost only seven hundred killed and wounded in the assault."

---

[1] See Appendix No. 117.

That is true, but he lost a good many by sickness and by explosions within the fort after it was captured, the exact number of which I do not find reported. And Porter, also, in a joint unsuccessful assault, lost some hundreds of sailors and marines who were, in the language of General Weitzel, "simply murdered."

The fact is, that on the first attack after the failure of the powder-boat, Porter did not intend that the attack of the army should succeed.

I know that he says he did, but every act shows he did not, as I propose by a series of quotations from his own reports to demonstrate, and to show that his statements are not at any time to be relied upon.

In regard to the powder-boat, Porter in his report to the Navy Department when the investigation took place, stated that the fire was built on the forecastle,[1] where it should have been made; but in his first report, of the 26th of December, he said, as was the fact, that the fire was set under the cabin[2] [in the stern].

When that department investigated the matter through Chief of Ordnance Wise, both Jeffers and Rodman stated that Porter's report of circumstances for the purpose of that investigation was that the fire was set on the forecastle, as the instructions for its explosion required should be done. Nobody but Porter says so, and he contradicts himself, as we have seen; and the action of the fire, as we have also seen, shows that it could not have been so done. The order of Wise shows that this investigation and all the reports should be "*confidential.*"[3] Why so, unless it was intended that the facts should be kept from me? And they were so kept until I managed to have them developed before the Committee on the Conduct of the War.

Porter was over-anxious that a second attack should be made and therefore he kept up a series of letters and reports to Welles, the Secretary of the Navy, some of which were confidential, begging him to keep the fleet there until more troops could be sent down. To induce the secretary to yield to his desire, he reported the fort as being undefended and incapable of defence, and he threw aspersions upon me for not making the attack, when to do so and to capture the fort was "entirely feasible."

---

[1] See Appendix No. 132.   [2] See Appendix No. 133.   [3] See Appendix No. 134.

Let us see Porter's description of the fort, and its capabilities of defence at the first attack. He says: —[1]

There never was a fort that invited soldiers to walk in and take possession more plainly than Fort Fisher. . . . We silenced the guns in one hour and fifteen minutes' time without the loss of a man [that I have heard of] except by the bursting of our own guns, in the entire fleet. We have shown the weakness of this fort. It can be taken at any moment in one hour's time if the right man is sent with the troops.

Again he says: —[2]

General Bragg must have been very agreeably disappointed when he saw our troops going away without firing a shot, and to see an expedition *costing millions of dollars* given up *when the hollowness of the rebel shell was about to be exposed.*

Again: —[3]

And now, sir, I beg that you will allow me to work this thing out, and leave nothing undone to take the place. Could I depend on the sailors for landing I would ask no army force; but a large portion of the crews are new in the service, having little or no knowledge of the musket or drill, and I intend to make no mistakes if I can avoid it. A repulse is always demoralizing, and sailors cannot stand the concentrated fire of the regular troops.

And yet sixteen days afterwards on the second attack, he landed fourteen hundred of these poor fellows and four hundred marines, and ordered them to assault the fort, and quite one fourth of the whole force were murdered or disabled.[4]

Well, sir, it could have been taken on Christmas with five hundred men without losing a soldier. There were not twenty men in the fort, and those were poor, miserable, panic-stricken people, cowering there with fear, while one or two desperate men in one of the upper casemates some distance above Fort Fisher [mound battery] managed to fire one gun that seldom hit anyone. . . .

---

[1] Porter's Official Report, December 27, 1864.
[2] Porter's Report, December 31, 1864. (See Appendix No. 139.)
[3] Confidential letter to Secretary Welles, December 29, 1864.
[4] See Appendix No. 135.

Both Whiting and Lamb, who were in command of the fort, say that on the first day they fired from the fort — not from mound battery — "six hundred and seventy-two shells by count," firing slowly and deliberately.[1]

Colonel Lamb says they fired on the two days six hundred shells, exclusive of grape and canister. (See page 816.) What becomes of Porter's statement that only one gun was fired by one or two desperate men, and that from the mound battery?

General Weitzel went on shore, determined what the report of the defences would be, for General Butler had made an opinion for him.[2] . . .

If this temporary failure succeeds in sending General Butler into private life it is not to be regretted, for it cost only a certain amount of shells, which I would expend in a month's target practice anyhow.

Again he says : —

The firing this day [the 25th] was slow, only sufficient to amuse the enemy while the army landed.[3]

In his plan of the first attack accompanying his report, and by his general order, the new ironsides and monitors were to lie in not less than three and one half fathoms of water, which he says would place them about three quarters of a mile from the fort. The plan itself shows that the ironsides ranged in a line from a little over three quarters of a mile to a mile from the fort. The next division of vessels lay at a distance of a mile from the fort, and the rest of the fleet, with the exception of the reserves, ranged from about a mile and an eighth to a mile and a half distant from the fort, the reserves being between a mile and a quarter and a mile and a half away. If the plan is a true one, and had been followed, full too long range, as will be seen, was given for the fire on the fort. But it was not followed, as it appears that some of the vessels did not go up within those lines, so that they had to be placed nearer the fort on the attack on the 25th in order that they might be able to throw their shells onto the land, "as they had fallen into the water on the day before," more than a hundred yards short of the fort.[4]

---

[1] See Appendix No. 124.
[2] Confidential letter to Welles, Dec. 29, 1864. (See Appendix No. 138.)
[3] Porter's Report, Dec. 26, 1864. (See Appendix No. 141.)
[4] See Appendix No. 141.

His vessels were short of ammunition : —

As the ammunition gave out the vessels retired from action. . . .
I have ordered the largest vessels to proceed to Beaufort to fill up with ammunition. . . .
In one hour and fifteen minutes after the first shot was fired not a shot came from the fort. . . . Finding that the batteries were silenced completely, I directed the ships to keep up a moderate fire in hopes of attracting the attention of the transports bringing them in.

In his letter of Jan. 9, 1865, to the Secretary of the Navy, attacking me for not making preparation for a more lengthy stay at Fort Fisher because I relied upon the powder-boat, he has the effrontery to say : —

I thought a good deal would be done by the explosion, but still I laid in a double allowance of shell and shot, and did not depend on a doubtful experiment.

Yet after a few hours of not rapid firing upon the fort by his vessels some had to withdraw from the attack, being short of ammunition, and he sent the larger vessels the next day to Beaufort to replenish their supply, the fleet having expended no more shot and shell than he would use in a " month's target practice."[1]
How do these facts comport with his reckless statement that he put in a double allowance of ammunition?
What was Fort Fisher and its condition at the time of the two several attacks upon it?
We have shown what Porter thought of the capabilities of Fort Fisher as a fortification. Now this fort had been constructed at great labor by the Confederacy, and by its ablest and most experienced engineers. It was built to hold one of its most important points, which had become its chief depot for supplies from abroad of arms, clothing, and ammunition. But he says of it, " There never was a fort that invited soldiers to walk in and take possession more plainly than Fort Fisher."[2] This was his opinion after the first attack, and upon it he based all his abuse of me for not accepting the " invitation."

---

[1] See Appendix No. 138.
[2] Report of the Committee on the Conduct of the War, Vol. II., p. 165.

To show what Fort Fisher really was as a military work I will call Porter as my first witness. After it had been taken he thus describes it to the Secretary of the Navy in his official report, dated Jan. 26, 1864 : —

These works are tremendous. I was in Fort Malakoff a few days after it surrendered to the French and English ; the combined armies of the two nations were many months capturing that stronghold, and it won't compare, either in size or strength, to Fort Fisher.[1]

How about its having been devised to "invite" soldiers to come in and take possession of it?

Again in his detailed report to the Secretary of the Navy, dated Jan. 17, 1864, he uses this language : —

I have since visited Fort Fisher and the adjoining works, and find their strength greatly beyond what I had conceived. An engineer might be excusable in saying they could not be captured except by regular siege. I wonder even now how it was done. The work, as I said before is really stronger than the Malakoff tower, which defied so long the combined power of France and England.

I might rest upon this testimony as to the strength of Fort Fisher, but I will not, as my misfortune is that my witness has shown himself to be a reckless, consciousless, and impudent liar, while on the stand, and I must proceed further by better witnesses to show the condition of Fort Fisher at the time of the two attacks. I therefore call Col. William Lamb, of the Confederate Army, who was in command of the fort on the occasion of both attacks, and who largely superintended the construction of the fort, on which he was engaged for years. He had been in command of Fort Fisher since the 4th of July, 1862, and with the aid of General Whiting, who was a very accomplished engineer when he left our army to join the Confederacy, had constructed the work at enormous labor and expense for the purpose of enabling it to sustain a very heavy artillery fire.

The works were of sand. Todleben, the Russian engineer who built the Malakoff at the Crimea, first taught military engineers

---

[1] Report of the Committee on the Conduct of the War, Vol. II., p. 184.
[2] Report of the Committee on the Conduct of the War, Vol. II., p. 190.

that sand was the best material of which to construct a fort to resist a heavy artillery fire, and Whiting, having plenty of that material at hand, used it in the construction of Fort Fisher. Colonel Lamb describes the fort as follows in the "Century War Books" : —

The outer slopes were twenty feet high from the bearme to the top of the parapet, at an angle of forty-five degrees, and were sodded with marsh grass which grew luxuriantly. The parapet was not less than twenty-five feet thick with an inclination of one foot. The revertment was five feet nine inches high from the floor of the gun chambers and these were some twelve feet or more from the interior plane. There were heavy traverses exceeding in size any known to engineers, from enfilading fire. They extended some twelve feet on the parapet and were twelve feet or more in height above the parapet, running back thirty feet or more. In each traverse was an alternate magazine or bomb-proof, the latter ventilated by an air chamber. Passages were constructed through the traverses in the interior to a work forming additional bomb-proofs for the reliefs for the guns.[1]

The land front was about one half mile wide, and over it an assault by troops must be made unless they landed from boats on the sea front of the work. It was very strongly defended. First, there were three lines of subterranean torpedoes extending from the river back to the seashore, the torpedoes being five or six hundred feet up the land face of the work, and so arranged that each line could be exploded without destroying the other. They were placed near together so as to blow up any assaulting column coming down the beach to attack the fort. These were to be exploded by means of underground wires attached to electrical batteries placed in a bomb-proof where they could not be destroyed by any artillery fire. These batteries did survive in working order both attacks on the fort. Next was a line of palisades made of heavy timber sharpened at the top, and nine feet high, pierced with apertures through which the garrison could sweep the plain with musketry.

It was the strongest earthwork built by the Confederacy. It was defended by forty-four heavy guns, twenty of which and four Napoleons had their range up the beach, seventeen of them being on the land front, and three upon the bastions at either end of the land face of the fort.

---

[1] Meaning a place to which the soldiers could retreat for rest, while a new detachment relieved them.

At the time of the proposed attack of Weitzel but one out of the twenty heavy guns had been disturbed by the fire of the navy; the torpedoes and palisades were all in order and the Napoleons ready for use. The fort was not silenced, but was only reserving its scant supply of shot and shell. The single long range gun with which the iron-clad could be reached to do any damage was an English one hundred and fifty-pounder Armstrong gun, and for this there were but thirteen shells, and no other ammunition could be used in it. For the forty-four heavy guns and three mortars the fort had not over thirty-six hundred shot and shell.[1]

The following extract from a letter of Colonel Lamb will show the condition of the fort as regards its capabilities for defence on the occasion of the first attack, December 24 and 25 : —

To the Editor of the Globe : —

Among the papers which were saved and returned to me after the war, was my original MS. report of the first battle of Fort Fisher, December 24 and 25, 1864, and my journal from October 24, 1864, to the afternoon of January 14, 1865, giving details of all important events, and I therefore have not to recall from memory the occurrences of a quarter of a century ago, but have contemporaneous entries made from personal observation and official reports. My New England friends must not, therefore, feel annoyed at my corrections, which I make in the interest of the truth of history.

. . . .

The hand to hand fight in the fort was a prolonged and terrible one.

. . . .

Lastly, upon the authority of some of my men, who were captured, one of your informants says that General Butler could easily have taken the fort on Christmas night. These men did not know what they were talking about, and while General Butler is fully able to take care of himself, it is due to Major-General Weitzel, the accomplished officer upon whose report General Butler withdrew his forces from the attempt to capture Fort Fisher, Christmas night, to say that he acted wisely; that if he had made the attempt, his small force would have been almost annihilated before they reached the works proper, if any could be gotten so far, and it is a shame that Bragg allowed them to re-embark without capture.

---

[1] See Appendix No. 136.

To the average reader the subsequent capture of Fort Fisher seems sufficient to substantiate the charge against General Butler, but in reality the facts connected with the final capture prove that his forces could not have successfully assaulted the work. When Weitzel's skirmish line approached on Christmas afternoon, and the fire of the fleet ceased, I purposely withheld the full fire of the infantry and artillery until an attack should be made in force. Only one gun commanding the land approach had been permanently disabled, and I could have opened a terrific fire of grape and canister from twenty heavy guns and four Napoleons on a narrow beach.

If the troops could have faced this with a knowledge that in their rear was an army equally as large to attack them under cover of darkness when the fight began, I had three lines of subterranean torpedoes in perfect order, which could have blown up consecutively three advancing columns. If, by any possibility, these could have been passed by any portion of an assaulting column, I had an almost perfect line of palisades, behind which I had thrown more than half the garrison. I had that night nine hundred veterans, sixty C. S. N. sailors and marines and four hundred and fifty junior reserves between sixteen and eighteen years of age.

.   .   .   .

Our friends are mistaken in saying that the guns of Fort Fisher were silenced in the first attack, and in this connection I will repeat what I wrote for the " Century War Book " : —

The guns of Fort Fisher were not silenced. On account of a limited supply of ammunition I gave orders to fire each gun not more than once in thirty minutes, except by special order, unless an attempt should be made to run by the fort, when discretion was given each gun commander to use his piece effectively. There were forty-four guns. On December 24, 672 shots were expended ; a detailed report was received from each battery. Only three guns were rendered unserviceable, and these by the fire of the fleet disabling the carriages. On December 25, six hundred shots were expended, exclusive of grape and canister. Detailed reports were made. Five guns were disabled by the fleet, making eight in all. Besides two seven-inch Brooke guns exploded, leaving thirty-four heavy guns on Christmas night. The last guns on the 24th and 25th were fired by Fort Fisher on the retiring fleet. In the first fight the total casualties were sixty-one.

.   .   .   .

I had no fear of an assault, and because during a bombardment which rendered an assault impossible, I covered my men and a few struggling skirmishers, too few to attract attention, got near the fort, and some gallant officers thought they could have carried the work, it does not follow that they would not have paid dearly for their temerity if they had made the attempt.

In the second attack, when my torpedoes were destroyed, my palisades so torn up and cut down that they furnished a protection rather than an impediment to the assailants, when all the heavy guns, save one, bearing on the land approach had been disabled, and the killed and wounded had reduced my available force to about my strength on Christmas night, it took more than three times the number which General Weitzel had, of the very flower of the army and navy, five hours to capture the fort; and so desperate was the resistance of those same men who were with me Christmas night and so doubtful the result in the work, that I have heard that General Terry, naturally fearing an attack from Bragg in the rear, sent word to General Ames to make one more effort, and if he failed, to stop and intrench. Reinforced by additional troops the effort was made, and resistance became less effective until with thin ranks and ammunition exhausted the garrison surrendered.

WILLIAM LAMB.

NORFOLK, VA., Jan. 20, 1890.

Let us now see how the fort appeared to General Weitzel at the time he reconnoitred it from a knoll a short distance from the fort. In his testimony before the Committee on the Conduct of the War,[1] he says : —

I pushed a skirmish line too, I think, within about one hundred and fifty yards of the work. I had about three hundred men left in the main body, about eight hundred yards from the work. There was a knoll that had evidently been built for a magazine, an artificial knoll on which I stood, and which gave me a full view of the work and the ground in front of it. I saw that the work, as a defensive work, was not injured at all, except that one gun about midway of the land face was dismounted. I counted sixteen guns all in proper position, which made it evident to me that they had not been injured ; because when a gun is injured, you can generally see it from the way in which it stands. The grass slopes of the traverses and of the parapets did not appear broken in the least. The regular shapes of the slopes of the traverses and slopes of the parapets were not disturbed. I did not see a single opening in the row of palisades that was in front of the ditch, it seemed to me perfectly intact.

From all the information which I gained on my first visit to New Inlet, as from what I saw on this reconnoissance, together with the information that I had obtained from naval officers who had been on the

---

[1] Report before the Committee on the Conduct of the War, Fort Fisher, pp. 72, 73.

blockade there ior over two years, I was convinced that Fort Fisher was a regular bastioned work ; the relief was very high. I had been told by deserters from it that the ditch was about twenty feet wide and six feet deep, and that it was crossed by a bridge. I saw the traverses between each pair of guns, and was perfectly certain within my own mind that they were bomb-proofs ; they ought to have been and they were. It was a stronger work than I had ever seen or heard of being assailed during this war. I have commanded in person three assaulting columns in this war. I have been twice assailed in this war by assaulting columns of the enemy, when I have had my men intrenched. Neither in the first three cases where I assailed the enemy's works, nor in the two cases where I was myself assailed, were the works, in an engineering point of view, one eighth as strong as that work was. Both times when I was assaulted by the enemy, the intrenchments behind which my men fought were constructed in one night, and in each case after the men had had two or three days of very hard work. I have been repulsed in every attempt I have made to carry an enemy's work although I have had as good troops as any in the United States army, and their record shows it. The troops that I had under my command in the first two assaults have been with General Sheridan in the whole of his last campaign — the first division of the Nineteenth Army Corps — and they fought as well under me as they have under him. The third time that I assailed a position was on the Williamsburg road. I had two of the best brigades of the Eighteenth Army Corps. It was a weakly defended line, and not a very strong one. Still, I lost a great many men, and was repulsed. In the two instances where the enemy assaulted my position they were repulsed with heavy loss.

After that experience, with the information I had obtained from reading and study — for before this war I was an instructor at the Military Academy for three years under Professor Mahan, on these very subjects — remembering well the remark of the lieutenant-general commanding, that it was his intention I should command that expedition, because another officer selected by the War Department had once shown timidity, and in face of the fact that I had been appointed a major-general only twenty days before, and needed confirmation ; notwithstanding all that I went back to General Butler, and told him I considered it would be murder to order an attack on that work with that force. I understood Colonel Comstock to agree with me perfectly, although I did not ask him, and General Butler has since said that he did.

Upon my report General Butler himself reconnoitred the work; ran up close with the Chamberlain, and took some time to look at it. He then said that he agreed with me, and directed the re-embarkation of the troops.

It will be observed that Porter says, when he speaks of the fort as being stronger than Malakoff Tower, "an engineer officer might be excusable in saying that it could not be captured except by regular siege," and that he even wonders how it was captured.[1] So then General Weitzel was excusable in his view of the fort, and he saw the land face, where the assault must be made, was uninjured. But how can the statements of Porter be excused when he says that it "might have been taken on 'Christmas Day by five hundred men without losing a soldier; there were not twenty men in the fort, and those were poor, miserable, panic-stricken people, cowering with fear."[2] Colonel Lamb says he had fourteen hundred and fifty men in the fort on Christmas Day. Had Porter seen any of them go away? How could he suppose that the Confederates had built such a work there and left only twenty men to defend it? In the same report Porter says that only "one or two desperate men managed to fire one gun which seldom hit anyone," during the bombardment. Colonel Lamb says he expended six hundred shot and shell besides grape and canister on that day, and that he had expended six hundred more on the 24th. How shall Porter be excused with such a work before him, its strength visible to every eye, for saying that it was only a "rebel shell"?[3] These reports were only downright falsehoods, made for the purpose of getting Welles to allow him to make another attempt.

Porter's performances at the first attack were not intended to demolish the fort; he did not mean that they should take the fort. He says that his order was that the firing should not be rapid; that only one division of guns should fire at a time from each vessel.[4] His fleet being anchored around the fort, the battery of one broadside of the ships only should be brought to bear. Ship's guns are divided into two divisions at least for each broadside, so that only one quarter of his guns were, according to his orders, used at a time at most, and some of his vessels, he says, did not fire a single shot. He further says that during the day while the troops were being landed, which was most of the day of the 25th, he only fired to amuse the enemy.[5] He further says that all the shell that he expended in both days were not more than what he would expend in target practice in a month anyhow.[6]

---

[1] See Appendix No. 137.   [2] See Appendix No. 138.   [3] See Appendix No. 139.
[4] See Appendix No. 140.   [5] See Appendix No. 141.   [6] See Appendix No. 138.

Had he any motive for doing this? He says the expense was "well incurred as it retires General Butler to private life,"[1] although he admits that the expense amounts to millions.[2]

I had criticised his foolish performances in bombarding for eight pays Forts St. Philip and Jackson, leaving the latter, upon which he expended most of his work, as defensible as before. Weitzel had so reported it, and therefore Porter did not like him, and me he hated as the devil hates holy water, and he did not show me the ordinary courtesy of conferring with me.

He says on the first day (December 24th) Fort Fisher was silenced in an hour and a half.[3] He says substantially the same of it on the 25th. I knew that it was not silenced and that earthworks of that description which he saw before him could not be so silenced.

I had seen him with twenty-one mortars bombarding Fort Jackson on the Mississippi, a little further off, for seven days throwing in thirteen-inch shells, and he did not effectually demolish but one gun. Weitzel had seen the same thing, and he knew that fort was not disabled.

Colonel Lamb, then commander of Fort Fisher, says there was but one gun out of twenty on the land face demolished, and out of his forty-four barbette guns, — that is, guns mounted on top of the works, — but three had been demolished, and two of them, Brooke's guns, had been exploded. He also says that at the first attack the fire of the fleet was desultory, and did but little harm, a large portion of the shells going clear over the fort into the water of the river.

How was it at the second attack? Porter says he made a new plan. The fire was very fast, and from all the broadsides of his vessels which could be brought to bear.[4] His plan shows that he arranged the iron-clads and heavier vessels, some eighteen of them, so as to bear directly on a quarter to a half a mile nearer range than at the first attack (some of them seven hundred to one thousand yards from the land face of the fort), and he reports that the fort was reduced to a pulp.[5]

He doesn't claim any such damage done to the fort or its approaches on the first attack, and in that attack he claims to have expended only as much shot and shell as he would have expended

---

[1] See Appendix No. 138.   [2] See Appendix No. 139.   [3] See Appendix No. 142.
[4] See Appendix No. 143.   [5] See Appendix No. 135.

for target practice in a month anyhow, and he says he expended fifty thousand shells on the fort, and had supplied himself with as many more.

Porter says over and over again that in the second attack he had the most cordial co-operation of General Terry, whom he denominates his beau-ideal of a soldier, and that they had consultation on board his ship, and elsewhere, as to the manner of making the attack, and that he aided Terry with two thousand of his sailors and marines in making the land attack, which Colonel Lamb says he thought was to be the principal assault of the fort.

Upon this whole subject of the condition of Fort Fisher at the time of both attacks of the defences, and of the probable results of an assault, taking the circumstances in view, I call a witness for whose statements I claim the utmost credence.

When the expedition to Fort Fisher was under investigation by the Committee on the Conduct of the War, I sent, by a gentleman of my staff, certain questions to be answered by Maj.-Gen. W. H. C. Whiting of the Confederate army, under whose supervision as an engineer during two years Fort Fisher was built. I did not take his deposition in form, because he was lying a prisoner of war in one of our hospitals on his dying bed, from wounds received in the second attack on Fort Fisher. He died immediately after his communication with me. I apologized to him, saying that I would not add to his sufferings by having a formal deposition taken, but I wished that he would answer as he would under the sanction of an oath, and he gave me his dying declarations, which are received in law in cases of murder as effective as testimony given on the stand.[1] General Whiting desired that the questions might be put, and that he might answer them separately in his own way, which, of course, he was permitted to do, and every one of his answers directly contradicts Porter where they speak of the same matter. I submit the testimony with great confidence to the judgment of the reader.[2]

The Committee on the Conduct of the War investigated this subject in February, 1865, calling all the witnesses who they deemed could give material testimony in regard to it, and having all the papers furnished to them. That testimony was taken under oath. General

[1] General Whiting's statement was received as testimony by the Committttee on the Conduct of the War.
[2] See Appendix No. 124.

Grant, General Weitzel, and Admiral Porter were fully examined by the committee. There were upon the committee members of both political parties, and the result of the investigation was a unanimous report through their chairman, Hon. Ben F. Wade, which closed with the following words: —

In conclusion, your committee would say, from all the testimony before them, that the determination of General Butler not to assault the fort seems to have been fully justified by all the facts and circumstances then known or afterwards ascertained.

Respectfully submitted,

B. F. WADE, *Chairman.*

I had hoped that this report would justify my action in saving the lives of my men without any detriment to the public service, but, unfortunately, so far as I know, it was never published in any of the newspapers which tried me before the country; and whenever any malicious scoundrel wants to make a fling at me and my military conduct, he always says: "How about Fort Fisher?" I will here answer him: —

I believe my withdrawal from Fort Fisher to face the calumny which has rolled its waves over me, and which I calmly looked in the face when I made my decision to withdraw my troops, was the best and bravest act of my life. I feared it would destroy my friend Weitzel, and so I took pains to put before the committee the acts which were done as if they had been done by my command. There was but one subject in regard to which General Weitzel and I disagreed. As a junior officer in the regular army he has said, and I have no doubt he would have done so although against his own judgment, that he would have held on to his position. Indeed, I believe his words were those of a junior officer. "As a junior officer I should not obey the command of my superior, leaving him to bear the blame and responsibility of the event." I believe that if General Grant had been there he would have been of opinion with me, that the troops should have been withdrawn, under the circumstances, and that his order, although in the letter directing differently, would have been reversed by him. Whether it would or not, at any rate I thought it my duty not to be so controlled, nor to throw away the lives and liberties of my brave officers and soldiers by a useless adherence to forms. And though I have suffered more from thus acting on my judgment than from any other act of my life, I rejoice — I trust modestly — with exceeding joy that I had sufficient firmness to do as I did do. Weitzel had no profession but arms, and his disobedience of orders would have ruined him in that profession. That we foresaw the result when we acted, and that I endeavored to repair for Weitzel as much as I could the consequences of his act, will appear from the letters between us : —

WILLARD'S, Jan. 23, 1865.

MAJ.-GEN. G. WEITZEL:

My Dear Weitzel: — I am afraid you have been annoyed lest I might possibly think that your advice at Fort Fisher was not such as I ought to have acted upon. Let me assure you that I have never in any moment, amid the delightful stream of obloquy which is pouring upon me, doubted the military sagacity of the advice you gave, or the propriety of my action under it. Indeed, my friend, I am glad I was there to act as a shield to a young officer in a moment of fearful responsibility, from the consequences of a proper act which might have injured him in his profession, but which cannot harm me, who have a different one. The judgment of cool reason hereafter will applaud it, but hot passion might have harmed you, as it has done me, for the hour. Indeed, it was in view of this very event that I went at all. With the invocation of every blessing upon you and yours,

I am, your friend,

BENJ. F. BUTLER,
Major-General.

CINCINNATI, Jan. 26, 1865.

My Dear General: — I was so delighted this morning to receive your note from Willard's. As the truth became developed I saw I had not made a mistake. At first, I was terribly frightened.

Many of my friends and fellow-citizens here, too, at first, made long faces, and only one paper, our oldest and most respectable, the *Gazette*, stood out for you boldly as against "marking Pot Porter" as they called him.

In one of his best despatches, however, Porter is compelled to acknowledge the correctness of our judgment. . . .

Yours truly,

G. WEITZEL,
Major-General.

Farragut, who had been offered the command of the expedition against Fort Fisher, but was — unhappily for me — too sick to take it, after he learned that the expedition was to go with my army, wrote me a confidential letter in which he strongly advised me not to go with the navy under the command of Porter, because he would not co-operate with me. If I had got the letter in season, — as it expressed my own thought, — I doubt whether I should have gone even for the reasons which urged me to go; but, alas for me! it came too late.

After the affair at Fort Fisher Grant treated Porter very kindly; and Porter was enthusiastic in his praise of Grant, and almost adulatory in his conduct toward him. They were apparently the best possible friends. During this time Porter wrote a confidential letter to Gideon Welles, the Secretary of the Navy. The close friendship of Grant and Porter remained until Farragut died, when Porter was appointed admiral in his place.

Grant appointed Borie, a respectable sugar merchant of Philadelphia, his Secretary of the Navy. Porter immediately claimed that as admiral it was his duty to carry on all matters appertaining to the *personnel* of the navy and its ships, and that Borie should look after what I may call the civil administration of the navy. Porter placed himself in the office of the secretary and attempted to carry on all the business of that office as admiral. Borie's incumbency of his office was short, and Grant appointed Hon. George M. Robeson his successor as Secretary of the Navy. When he entered upon the duties of his office he undertook to be Secretary of the Navy, and finding Porter in his way and interfering with him too much, advised him to remove his office elsewhere, which was done, and Robeson assumed the full administration of the duties of secretary. This mortally offended Porter and he and one of Grant's staff entered into a cabal to get Robeson removed and to lessen his influence with Grant, Porter claiming to Grant that he had been his *fidus achates.* While that was going on one of the clerks in the Navy Department, in examining the correspondence on file, discovered and brought to the attention of Mr. Robeson the confidential letter of Porter to Welles, and that was so abusive of Grant and made such accusation against him that the secretary thought it his duty to bring it to the President's attention. Grant read it with great astonishment and chagrin;

sent for Porter, handed him the letter, and asked him if he wrote it. Porter at first began to deny it but the evidence was too strong and he admitted the writing but attempted to excuse it. Grant said to him that the contents of that letter were such that thereafterwards Porter's relations with him as President should be simply official, and they continued to be official, merely, through Grant's term of office, and Robeson was no longer annoyed with Porter.

I put this letter[1] of Porter's in the appendix as a literary curiosity. It is a photographic illustration of every bad trait in Porter's character, and I think the letter could not have been written by any man in the world but Porter. But of that the reader can judge for himself, bearing in mind the intimate relations existing between Porter and Grant at the time it was written.

[1] See Appendix No. 144.

LIEUT.-GEN. U. S. GRANT.

CHAPTER XVIII.

WHY I WAS RELIEVED FROM COMMAND.

RETURNED to my command on the 16th of November, and there found an order from General Grant which put me in command of the Armies of the Potomac and James, as it informed me of his absence and enclosed an order to General Meade.[1]

General Grant had for a considerable time been impressed with the belief — in which I did not share — that Lee intended to abandon Petersburg with his main army and go down to join Johnston against Sherman; and he feared very much that Sherman might be overwhelmed if Lee was not instantly pursued by the Army of the Potomac, leaving the Army of the James to take care of Petersburg. But no such event happened.

Everything of the official correspondence in relation to the current movements of the Army of the James went on without any intimation to me of any change of our official relations, and without any information as to any comment by Grant upon my report of the operations against Fort Fisher. I noticed nothing, except, perhaps, a want of cordiality in his manner. But on the 8th of January, about noon, I received, through the hands of Colonel Babcock, a crony of W. F. Smith, and a member of Grant's staff, who I had always known was bitterly opposed to me, a sealed envelope containing the following orders: —

WAR DEPARTMENT, ADJUTANT-GENERAL'S OFFICE,
WASHINGTON, Jan. 7, 1865.

General Order No. 1.

I. By direction of the President of the United States, Maj.-Gen. Benjamin F. Butler is relieved from the command of the Department of North Carolina and Virginia. Lieutenant-General Grant will designate an officer to take this command temporarily.

---

[1] See Appendix No. 145.

II. Major-General Butler on being relieved will repair to Lowell, Mass., and report by letter to the adjutant-general of the army.

By order of the Secretary of War:

W. A. NICHOLS,
Assistant Adjutant-General.

HEADQUARTERS ARMIES OF THE UNITED STATES,
CITY POINT, VA., Jan. 7, 1865.

To MAJ.-GEN. E. O. C. ORD,
    Through Maj.-Gen. B. F. Butler.

Special Order No. 5.

I. In pursuance of General Order No. 1., War Department, Adjutant-General's office, Washington, D. C., Jan. 7, 1865, Maj.-Gen. E. O. C. Ord will relieve Maj.-Gen. B. F. Butler in the command of the Department of Virginia and North Carolina temporarily.

II. Maj.-Gen. B. F. Butler will turn over to Maj.-Gen. E. O. C. Ord the records and orders of the department, and all public money in his possession, or subject to his order, collected by virtue of rules and regulations which he may have established.

III. The department staff will report to Major-General Ord for duty.

By command of Lieutenant-General Grant:

T. S. BOWERS,
Assistant Adjutant-General.

I immediately repaired to Fortress Monroe in company with General Ord, and there had a very pleasant interview with him. I exhibited to him all the books of record of the department, especially those relating to any financial transactions; and had the officers who had such matters in charge report in person and explain to him the books, the manner of transacting the business, and the sources from which any moneys in the civil fund of the department had been received during my administration, and exhibit the balances as shown by those books.

I turned over to him $258,000 in money, of which $66,000 was from one fund, $104,000 from another fund, $20,000 from another, $38,000 from another, and other sums from minor sources of revenue amounting to $30,000. I also accounted for the expenditure of an additional sum of more than quarter of a million dollars. The accounts for these expenditures were afterwards forwarded to the War Department and settled, and no item has been questioned to this day.

After I had proceeded in the same manner with the accounts of all the public property, and had recommended to his kind consideration the gentlemen of my staff who were ordered to report to him, he returned to City Point and reported to General Grant. That he was satisfied with the accounts I have an indirect means of knowing, for a gentleman on the staff of General Grant, who happened to be present when the report was made, informed me that Ord said, "Whatever they may say of General Butler, one thing is certain, he is no rogue." And that was Ord's opinion I know, for I had his cordial friendship for years afterwards until his death.

Meanwhile I had received from Washington, through the kindness of an official friend, a copy of the documents which Grant had sent to Washington to get leave to make the order. They showed me that Stanton had nothing to do with it, as he was absent, and that I was indebted to my virulent foe, General Halleck, for the influence which prevented my having any information of the alleged causes.

General Grant's letter to the Secretary of War and his telegram to the President are as follows: —

CITY POINT, VIRGINIA, Jan. 4, 1865.

HON. E. M. STANTON, SECRETARY OF WAR:

I am constrained to request the removal of Maj.-Gen. B. F. Butler from the command of the Department of Virginia and North Carolina. I do this with reluctance, but the good of the service requires it. In my absence General Butler necessarily commands, and there is a lack of confidence felt in his military ability, making him an unsafe commander for a large army. His administration of the affairs of his department is also objectionable.

U. S. GRANT,
Lieutenant-General.

CITY POINT, VIRGINIA, Jan. 6, 1865.

PRESIDENT A. LINCOLN, WASHINGTON:

I wrote a letter to the Secretary of War, which was mailed yesterday, asking to have General Butler removed from command. Learning that the Secretary left Washington yesterday, I telegraph you, asking that prompt action may be taken in the matter.

U. S. GRANT,
Lieutenant-General.

I immediately telegraphed to the President for leave to publish my official report, and the following is his answer: —

[*Telegram.*]

WASHINGTON, 12 M., Jan. 10, 1865.

MAJOR-GENERAL BUTLER:

No principal report of yours on the Wilmington expedition has ever reached the War Department as I am informed there. A preliminary report did reach here but was returned to General Grant at his request. Of course, leave to publish cannot be given without inspection of the paper, and not then, if it should be deemed to be detrimental to the public.

A. LINCOLN.

From this it will be seen that I had no right to publish my report without the permission of my superior; so that while the newspapers of the country were filled with extracts from Porter's reports and abusive criticisms of my conduct, I could not say one word as to what that conduct had been. It will be observed how promptly and kindly the President replied to me.

Soon afterwards I learned that the report which had been sent to Washington had upon it a sufficiently severe endorsement, especially as it contained the baldest misstatement that my report stated that one reason for my return was that I had no intrenching tools, which was untrue, as the report shows.[1]

My report, with the endorsement thereon, which had been sent to Washington, was recalled by General Grant, and the endorsement, which was not in the hand-writing of the lieutenant-general, was changed by somebody who erased in a rather bungling way two or more lines by scratching them out with a knife. General Grant's signature to it, however, was allowed to remain.

I knew then, as I know now, that that endorsement was not written by Grant, but by one of his staff officers. And when the staff officer learned of the misstatement contained in the endorsement, the report was sent for, such parts as he saw fit were scratched out, and the paper was returned to the files. This belief is confirmed by the fact that Grant makes no allusion to my conduct at

---

[1] It is a singular fact that this misstatement originated with Porter, who put it in his report of December 31. The fact was I had ordered that Weitzel should take quite a large quantity of intrenching tools, and as Grant thought the number should be increased three or four times, the whole were taken with us.

Fort Fisher as a reason for relieving me. One reason he gives is that when he was absent I was in command of the whole army, and the corps commanders had not confidence in me, as he had expressed it before, I not having had a technical military education. I had three times been in command of all the armies as the senior major-general, in Grant's absence, and having not too much confidence in some of his major-generals, who generally failed to be on time when an order was given and some of whom were boys at West Point when I was a major-general in command of armies, I never attempted to make any movement during his absence. This I omitted to do because I knew that they would no more obey my command implicitly and promptly than they did Meade's during those last disastrous days, the 16th, 17th, and 18th of June, when Meade was attempting to retake Petersburg, which the colored troops of Smith's corps had once taken, and which he had let go.

It appears by Meade's circular of orders to make the attack on those days, that he did not instruct each corps to attack in exact time and conjunction with the others, so that his superiority of numbers, fifty thousand to ten thousand, would tell in his favor, obliging the smaller number of the enemy to keep their whole line of intrenchments fully manned all the time. On the contrary, he said in substance: "As I find it impossible to have the corps commanders attack simultaneously, each corps commander is ordered to attack as soon as he can get ready." The result of such an uncombined and miscellaneous attack was that the Confederates could mass large bodies of their troops at each point upon which an attack was made, and, after repulsing it, could put them in that portion of the intrenchments next attacked, when some corps commander got ready to make one, after their "interminable reconnoissances," from which Assistant Secretary of War Dana said Meade had suffered so much. The end of it all was that we lost Petersburg and some seventeen thousand killed, wounded and captured; and then, laying down the musket, we took up the spade in a nine months' endeavor to recapture that city, which was at last effected through the starvation of Lee's army.

While the command of the Armies of the James and Potomac devolved upon me as the senior major-general in Grant's absence, the only action that I took while so commanding was to send a telegram to the Secretary of War, communicating the fact that I had

ascertained that through an omission of duty of the quartermaster
of the Department of the Army of the Potomac the horses of that
army were without sufficient forage and means of sustenance,
and asking that the matter might be attended to, which was done.

What there was in that to demonstrate any unfitness to command
a large army, I leave the reader to judge.   My criticism upon the
want of proper action of Ingalls, Grant's quartermaster-general,
who lived with him at City Point, infuriated him, and he joined the
other staff officers with his great influence over Grant, which certainly he had, however obtained.

The thing alleged against me was not my want of success at Fort
Fisher, — for that would not do, as the second expedition had just
sailed and might not succeed, — but that the other generals, when
he was absent, were unwilling to be commanded by me.   That was
a fact that he had always known from the beginning of the campaign, and yet the command of all the troops in Virginia had been
devolved upon me by Grant three times as the senior major-general
in the army.

He adds another reason which is, that the administration of the
affairs of my department was objectionable.   That is answered by
the fact that he had never hinted to me any cause of dissatisfaction,
and in June Halleck had sent down General Meigs, quartermaster-
general of all the armies, and General Barnard, chief engineer of
the Army of the Potomac, to examine into my acts in the command
of the Army of the James, and into my administration of the affairs
of my department, and they had reported to Halleck that I had "*shown
rare and great ability in the administrative duties of the department.*"

On the 11th of January, being then at Fortress Monroe, I telegraphed to General Grant as follows: —

I have asked the President's permission to publish my report of the
Wilmington affair.   He answered that no report had been received at the
department.   You told me you had forwarded it.   Has it been lost
again?   If so, I have a copy.

To that Grant answered, after I had quit the department, that he
had sent to Washington for it, and had it brought back, and that he
was going to send it up by special messenger, and it would get there
on a certain Friday night.

My telegram shows the fact that when I called for it from General Grant in person, it had been lost. It will be seen how this was, because Grant had sent it to the President before the time of my removal; and the sharp criticism upon my action, in not telling the truth about it, had had its effect upon the President's mind. It was not true that the report had been lost, but when I told Grant that I had the copy he did not say that I might publish that copy.

Again I saw the hand of the staff officer.

Grant was called before the Committee on the Conduct of the War after I had testified before the committee and this question had been put to me by Mr. Odell: —

Q. —You have noticed in the communication to which you have reference that one of the alleged causes for your removal was your arbitrary arrests. Has General Grant ever spoken to you upon that subject?

A. — General Grant never spoke to me but once of arbitrary arrest, and with your leave I will state what that one was; and if I am removed for that I am well pleased to meet the issue.

(I will condense my further answer:) Previous to the 26th of May, 1864, a very decided attack upon my action at Drury's Bluff, saying that I had not intrenched as I should have done, was published in the New York *Evening Post.* I sent to General Gillmore on the night of the 26th of May, and asked him if he had authorized the statement in any form. He said he had not. I then went to work to find out who had written that communication, as it evidently came from General Gillmore's headquarters. About a month afterwards I ascertained that it was written by one Chaplain Hudson of the First New York Volunteer Engineers, who was a sort of actor-chaplain. He could not be found. I ascertained that he went away on the morning of the 27th of May, and that was the morning after I sent to General Gillmore.

The 6th of July I sent Chaplain Hudson a peremptory order to return. It was duly served upon him, but he did not come back. About the 1st of September I was in New York on private business, and I hunted him up with a detective. I then sent an order to his colonel, Serrell, to bring him back or put him on his parole if he would promise to come back. Between the 15th and 25th of September, Chaplain Hudson reported to me, and the following conversation, which was taken down in shorthand in his presence, took place : —

"Where have you been, Chaplain Hudson, absent for nearly four months?"

"In New York and Massachusetts."

"What have you been doing there?"

"I left under orders."

"Whose orders?"

"From Major-General Gillmore."

"Produce them."

He produced an order which was, substantially, in these words:—
"Chaplain Hudson will go north on business for the commanding general."

I said: "The general had no right to order you out of my department. On what business did you go on the 28th of May?"

"I went to New York to superintend the printing of a book which Van Nostrand & Co. are printing for General Gillmore."

"What book?"

"A history of the siege of Charleston."

"That is private business," said I, "a private enterprise. Do you mean to say that you, a minister of the religion of Jesus Christ, having charge of all the souls of your regiment, left them, in the face of the enemy, to go off on a private enterprise in this way, remaining away four months, while you are drawing pay from the United States?"

He did not reply to that.

I then said : "You heard of General Gillmore being relieved from command here; you then had no further business with him. Why did you not come back then?"

"General," said he, "I am a bereaved man; I have been watching by the bedside of my dying child."

"No lies to me, Parson Hudson," said I; "your child died on the third day of June; you left on the 28th of May; you have not watched much since. Why did you not come back before the 20th of September? Did you not get my order of the 25th of July?"

"Yes, sir."

"Why did you not return, in obedience to that order?"

"I saw my colonel, and he advised me that I need not come back."

I sent for Colonel Serrell, and asked him about it, and he said he had told the chaplain no such thing. I said to the chaplain : —

"On or about the 27th of May I wrote to General Gillmore, and asked him if he assumed a certain publication, or knew anything about it; he wrote me that he did not. Now, Chaplain Hudson, did you not write the letter which was published in the New York *Evening Post?*"

"Well, yes, I did."

"Did you show it to General Gillmore before you sent it off?"

"I did."

"Did he know you sent it?"

"He did."

"Do you not know that I made the inquiry of him on the night of the 27th of May, and you were sent off on the morning of the 28th so that I should not get at you, and that you have stayed away since because you wrote that letter and were in conspiracy with General Gillmore? Do you not know he sent you away for that reason?"

"I do not know it."

"Do you not believe so?"

"Well, I do."

"Well," said I, "if I were not personally mixed up in this matter, if I were not personally aggrieved, I should know how to punish such a lying, cheating, defaulting chaplain as you are. But I do not think any man should be the judge of his own case; therefore I cannot sit in judgment upon you. I must put you in close arrest, because you would not come back to your regiment when ordered."

And he was put in a tent close to my headquarters. He sent to me, and said he wanted his clothing. I had his trunk hunted up; it took two days to find it, because it had strayed off somewhere. His colonel came to me and asked if Chaplain Hudson should have a bed and bedding. "Certainly," I said, "let him have everything that is necessary."

When I got to New York I met a number of my fellow-churchmen of the Episcopal Church, who said to me: "What have you been doing to Chaplain Hudson?"

I told them.

"He says you have shut him up, and starved him, and all manner of things."

"I beg your pardon, gentlemen," said I, "we will settle that in two minutes."

I sent for Colonel Serrell, and asked him about it. He said: "He has been more comfortably situated and better taken care of since he has been in confinement than I have."

I turned to these gentlemen and said: "Now, gentlemen, I should not alter my treatment of Chaplain Hudson but for this: I am here, and God knows when I may get away. Chaplain Hudson has been kept in confinement without a trial a considerable longer time than he should have been. I will order his close arrest to cease, and order him to stay with his regiment, and I will try him when I get the opportunity;" and I sent an order accordingly.

Two or three days after I had returned from the Wilmington expedition, General Grant told me that Chaplain Hudson had written him a letter, and he had sent for him, and seen him. I gave General Grant the facts that I have now given here, and he appeared to be satisfied. That is the only arbitrary arrest that General Grant ever spoke to me about.

If that was what I was removed for, I can only say that I would do the same again in like circumstances.

There was another thing alleged against me, which I heard of afterwards. It was said that I punished officers wrongfully. I will say here that I will agree to suffer any punishment if it can be shown that I ever punished a good officer; but I was not very chary when I got hold of a bad one.

On one occasion it was reported to me that an officer had tendered his resignation for frivolous reasons. This having been done in the face of the enemy, the regulation required his dismissal. His colonel called the man up to him, and told him that the reasons were frivolous, and that he better not send forward that resignation. The man said he would be d—— if he would not get out of the service either honorably or dishonorably. The colonel did not send forward the man's resignation. A few days afterwards the colonel gave the man some order; he threw his sword down, with a flourish, before his men, and said he would be G—— d——— if he ever did

GEN. BUTLER'S SPEECH FOR HORACE GREELEY IN NEW YORK, 1872, CITY HALL SQUARE.

another day's duty in that regiment. This was mutiny and had to be stopped. What was I to do?

It was just before the election. There were a great many officers at that time in the expectation that if they could be dismissed from the service, and thus be made martyrs of by the Lincoln government, and could go home and participate in the canvass for President, they would be canonized by the McClellan government, which they expected would come in, and they rather sought martyrdom. I issued an order, therefore, the first paragraph of which dismissed this mutinous officer from service for the act of which he had been guilty, and the next paragraph sentenced him to work at hard labor. That man did not go home to electioneer for anybody, that I ever heard of. I do not remember his name; I had no personal knowledge of him; he was, to me, the x, y, or z of an algebraic equation, an unknown quantity to be wrought out for the good of the service.

Again, I withdrew General Curtis' command from the trenches before Petersburg, because it was very much reduced by sickness, and needed rest and "setting up." He issued an order that his officers should always be present at roll-call, and also that they should wear their coats when they came to headquarters. Thereupon five of his officers sent in their resignations, written upon the same day, and upon similar pieces of paper, and nearly all in the same hand-writing, saying that they resigned because they were incompetent to carry out that order. Some of them had been in service for two years. It was said amongst them that they supposed "Old Butler" would dismiss them. Now that was exactly what they wanted; they wanted to get out of the service. All of the intermediate commanders reported that they ought to be dismissed. I said: "What good will that do? That is what they want; they want to go home and go into the election." I did dismiss them in the first paragraph of an order; and in the next paragraph I directed them to be set to work on the fortifications to take the places of better soldiers. That stopped that epidemic. I had no more trouble in that way.

"How could you do that?" might be asked. In this way: If I found civilians within my lines with nothing to do and no right there, I could put them anywhere. After they were dismissed they were civilians, and had no business there. "Yes, but had they not a right to have a reasonable time to go away?" Has a man who does wrong any right from his wrongs? They did this to get out of the service. An army is governed by martial law. It is not a town meeting; it is not civil law that controls it. The Duke of Wellington defines martial law to be the will of the commanding general exercised according to principles of natural equity and justice. Was not this act perfectly just to these conspirators and mutineers? Upon that definition of the law I am willing to have every act of mine examined. Do as nearly justice as you can. In regard to his officers, the commanding general can have no temptation to do anything but right. These officers I never saw,— I only knew their acts.

I kept them at work only a few days; I doubt whether they even worked. They were not very bad, only very foolish. Their friends wrote to General Grant, and he wrote to me, and I said: " Let them out." I only wanted to stop the practice spreading. Because if that practice had been allowed to prevail, it would have demoralized the army in a very little time.

There is another thing about which I would like to say a word. It has been said that offenders should be tried by a commission. It seems to be supposed that there is some peculiar virtue in a military commission. Now, what is a military commission? It is this: The commanding general selects three or more officers to advise him after hearing the evidence, what to do in a given case; and that is all there is to a commission. If he chooses to sit himself, hear the testimony,— and I think I ought to have been quite as competent to do that as any of my officers,— if he will take time for it, work late enough at night and get up early enough in the morning to so do, all the power is in him that there is in a military commission. He must revise and approve all they do or it is null. Why should not the judgment of the commanding general be as likely to be right as that of his subordinates? In no other case is he obliged to call a council of war to advise him what to do, and the commission is only a council of war. He can and ought to act on his own responsibility when the lives of thousands are in the balance; why not in punishing a rascal who has crept into the army?

This matter is not well understood. In the acts of Congress military commissions and courts-martial are associated, and no discrimination is made as to their powers and duties. André is supposed by some historians to have been hung by order of a court-martial. That is erroneous. He was tried by a military commission, upon which was Lafayette. The commission recommended to Washington that he should be hanged, and Washington issued the order to that effect. The commission only ascertained the facts for Washington to act upon. I did not trouble military commissions much, except where there were many controverted facts.

I have said I accounted for and turned over, when I gave up my department, five hundred thousand dollars. No dollar of it ever came out of the treasury of the United States, but it was collected in various ways under my command. I do not know that anybody has objected to my action in this behalf. I will state some of the principal sources of this revenue : —

I found men in the department who were carrying on a speculative trade. I taxed them one per cent. on that trade for the benefit of the United States. That, I believe, brought in about $178,000. They said I had no right to collect that tax of them. I said : " Certainly not ; but then the law requires that before you can do any trade here you shall have a certificate signed by the military commander. Now, there is no law to make me sign the certificate. Your trade is a permissive one only, and if you don't pay this excise I will not sign, and no harm will be done to either. If you don't want to trade under my rules and regulations, then don't, for no one can compel you to."[1]

Again, Congress passed a law allowing the recruiting of soldiers for the loyal States in my department. The result was that a herd of recruiting agents came down there to take away all my able-bodied blacks, to be credited as soldiers to their States, leaving the women and children to be taken care of by the United States. Now, when

---

[1] The ports of the Department of Virginia were all under blockade, and according to the rules and regulations, nothing was permitted to be landed there coming from any place foreign or from the North, but such goods as the commanding general would certify were not contraband of war, and were proper to be imported. All invoices of goods, before they were landed, were required to be sent to my office for my examination. That required a large number of intelligent clerks. When I took command, I found these examinations made by soldiers taken from the ranks to do it, so that their services were lost to the army. I sent back the soldiers and employed civilians as clerks to examine these invoices, for they were legion, and put a charge of one per cent. to pay the clerks and other necessary expenses, such as providing for sick soldiers, and spent $6,000 of the fund to buy vaccinating matter for our soldiers in rebel prisons, and matters of like kind. Norfolk, Hampden, and Yorktown were the points at which the importations and examinations were made.

recruiting was done in the several States, care was taken of the families of the soldiers by providing State aid, or in some other way. I therefore issued an order that no recruiting agent should take a negro out of my department until he paid over one third of the bounty money for the support of the wives and children of the blacks. In that way I collected $68,000, which I turned over to my successor. I should have collected more but for a rascal who was appointed major and sent to recruiting in North Carolina, where he enlisted men on behalf of the United States, sold them out and stole the money.

Congress passed a law to the effect that one fourth of the value of all the cotton brought in from the Confederacy should be paid into the treasury of the United States. It took the Treasury Department some considerable time to devise proper rules and regulations for the government of trade under that law. In the meantime, before these regulations were prepared and the law took effect, the speculators were running out all the cotton they could in order to save the twenty-five per cent. I appointed a cotton agent, put the law into his hands and told him to see that all the cotton which was being brought out of the rebel States paid twenty-five per cent. toll. This he did. After he had been at work a while the Treasury Department sent down to see about appointing an agent under the law for my department. They examined the books of the man whom I had appointed to take charge of the matter and were so well satisfied with what he had done that they continued him as their agent. Before he got his appointment from the department he had collected and turned over $26,000 to the treasury of the United States.

I found stores and shops of all sorts around Fortress Monroe on government land. Some of them had been there for thirty years without having paid a cent of rent. One man had made a quarter of a million of dollars there during the war. I ordered a commission to assess a fair ground rent upon all these store and shop keepers. I took one of the stores, where the owner had previously been convicted of fraud, and sold the ground rent at auction, and made that the basis of the rent for the rest; and I collected from that time so long as I remained in command, at the rate of three thousand dollars a month for such rent.

I found that flag of truce officers received an immense quantity of letters with money accompanying them to pay their postage to their

DISMAL SWAMP CANAL. From Photographs.

1. Deep Creek Lock.　2. West Weir at Deep Creek.　3. Village of Deep Creek.　4. Canal;

destination within the Confederate lines. I saw an opportunity to pay the expenses of the office by collecting these stamps and exchanging our money and stamps for Confederate money or stamps with which to pay Confederate postage to our prisoners. I employed three clerks, paid them out of that fund, and in addition to that I turned over three thousand dollars extra postage, saved by the difference between our postage currency and Confederate currency.

Now what did I do with the money thus gained, — not one cent of which came out of the treasury of the United States? I paid largely the expenses of digging Dutch Gap Canal; I built a hospital at Point of Rocks and furnished it with gas and water, and with cows for milk, and I expended a portion of it in sinking an artesian well, and built barracks for the soldiers at Fortress Monroe.

I found convicts, deserters, and others imprisoned at Fort Norfolk, doing nothing but eating their rations. I got a live Yankee and put him in charge as superintendent, and sent to Massachusetts and got prison uniforms, half black and half gray, and scarlet caps, with which to clothe these convicts, so that they could not easily escape when at work. I gave the superintendent charge of these men and told him to put them to work on the streets of Norfolk. I said to the men: "If you will work well and behave yourselves you shall have so many days deducted from your sentence according to your merits." In consequence they labored well and did an exceedingly large amount of work. The result of this was that permanent work was done which was charged to the city of Norfolk, for paving, etc., and on the Dismal Swamp Canal to which the United States paid large rents, to the amount of about $38,000, while my whole prison labor cost less than $9,000. Besides this, from the 15th of April to the 15th of June there was taken a thousand loads of filth per week from Norfolk, and by this means the yellow fever was kept out.

The act of Congress had provided for a contraband ration. I found that in the way this had been managed there had been great waste.[1] The system of supplying the negroes was re-adjusted, and the saving of some $84,000 in my district, in the rations issued to contrabands, was made.

---

[1] The rations furnished were so many for each contraband, and if a man had a wife and three children he drew five full rations, one half of which would easily support them. By imposing restrictions this other half was saved.

Again, I found that the poor of Norfolk were cared for in this way : Every commissioned officer could give a certificate to any one, that he or she was an indigent citizen, and when this certificate was taken to the commissary's office, rations might be drawn upon it. The result of this was that there were a great many poor young women in Norfolk drawing rations from the government, the number being in proportion to the number of commissioned officers. I broke up that practice. I established a commission to examine and decide who really needed assistance, and thereafterwards rations were issued to those only who were deserving, numbering something like five thousand white people daily,— for the negroes took care of themselves, — and the expense of this assistance to the needy of Norfolk, under the regulations adopted under my administration, averaged for each ration eight or nine cents a day.

From the sources mentioned I was enabled to collect, as I have already stated, something over half a million dollars, over a quarter of a million of which I turned over to my successor. Some of the advantages of having this money at my disposal will be appreciated when I say that in July, 1864, the treasury being very empty so that we could not get money with which to pay our sick and wounded soldiers in the hospital so that they could go home, I loaned $49,000 to the paymaster to pay them so that they might go, and he paid the money back to me when he got his money from the treasury. In the November following, the quartermaster's department was short of money ; the laborers struck for their pay and wages, because they could not live if they were not paid with regularity. I then loaned the quartermaster $53,000 to pay them up and keep the quartermaster's department going until funds could be received from Washington. This civil fund was a handy thing to have in the house.

General Grant said that he learned after I was removed that there had been other arbitrary arrests. That was true, because my arrests were all arbitrary and they were always entered on the guard book as " by order of General Butler." It was not for the good of the service or for the good of the country that the reasons should be set out. His staff officer found some such cases and reported that the persons ought to be discharged because no charges had been made against them. That was true also, and yet it was for the good of the service. I was not asked why I made the arbitrary arrests and confined parties to close imprisonment, treating them very well in some cases, and I now state I would do so again under the same circumstances and submit my action to the judgment of good people.

There was, at Nassau, a gathering of pilots who knew the harbors of Mobile, Savannah, Charleston, and Wilmington. These harbors could only be entered by vessels in the charge of pilots who were expert enough to run in in dark nights only, in order to get by our blockading fleet. The pilots, in the darkest night, could take large blockade runners in through the narrow channel where Porter with all his officers and sixty vessels, four of which had been blockade runners captured there, could not get in in two days in the daylight, even after he had "silenced" the forts that defended the entrance to the harbor. There were not many such skilled pilots to be found, so I asked Admiral Lee if he would not, when any were captured by the blockade squadron on the Atlantic coast, send them to me. When I got them I put them in a comfortable place of confinement and shut them up, and if I could have got all those pilots we would have as effectually stopped blockade running as the capture of Fort Fisher itself did.

Now, these pilots were principally Englishmen, and as soon as they could write to Lord Lyons, the British Minister, then he would call upon Seward, and Seward would of course order them to be delivered up when they could be found. If I had put on the guard house book or prison register: "confined by order of Major-General Butler as a blockade runner," or had had some other identifying description placed thereon, I should have had them all taken away from me, and therefore I did not go into their history or description; but great care was taken that their whereabouts should not be known.

I deemed this action justifiable under martial law, which is the will of the commanding general exercised for the best interests of his country in war. I doubt if I could have convicted one of them if I had tried them in a court of law, because being foreigners and not having committed any offence in my country, although captured while on their way to commit an offence, the charges would hardly have passed judicial action.

There were many other questions in regard to my action examined into by the Committee on the Conduct of the War on the occasion referred to, but as my explanations can be found at any time in the official reports of my evidence, there seems to be no necessity for further referring to them here, especially as they form no part of the reasons for which I was removed.

That I had refused the vice-presidency, and that I had refused the secretaryship of war was known to General Grant.

The fact that at a meeting at the Fifth Avenue Hotel which was represented to him as having been gotten up by my friends for that very purpose, I had been nominated for the presidency, was impressed upon General Grant's mind by officers of his staff, as showing that I was thereafterwards a positive rival. Nothing could have been farther from the truth. But still it had an effect upon his mind, and from that hour until after he was President no kindly word of friendship ever passed from his lips to my ear.

Lest I should do something to my credit, he did not mean that I should go with the expedition to Fort Fisher, and when, not knowing how his mind lay, I persuaded him to let me go, he was glad to take advantage of the fact that that expedition, although not under my charge, was not a success, for the foundation of my removal from command, which he requested within a few days after my return from that expedition.

I know the pressure that was brought upon him to induce his action, and the people who made it I do not forget or forgive. But I do forgive him, because he was misled and deceived. As it was, he alleged against me, as his reason for my removal, nothing except what I had done or left undone as a commander of the army or department. After my removal, to justify Grant's action, his advisers caused to be instituted a very searching and cruelly conducted investigation into the acts of my subordinate officers in the department, especially into those of General Shepley, — afterwards Mr. Justice Shepley of the United States Circuit Court, First Circuit, a most honest and high-minded gentleman, who had the administration of affairs in Norfolk, and afterwards those of the military district, including the vicinage around Norfolk, Fortress Monroe, and Yorktown, which were claimed to have been very improperly administered, — and into the action of my provost marshal of the department, Col. John Cassels. Against neither of these gentlemen could a single fact be found or a suspicion or ground for suspicion against the administration of their offices in any particular, for they had acted in the most honest and high-minded manner, and with a single eye to the performance of their whole duty as gentlemen of probity.

Certainly the commander of a department was never removed before, without any notice, for want of proper administration, when a commission of high officers sent to examine that administration

COL. JOHN CASSELS.

reported only that he had shown in his administrative duties rare and great ability. And as I was in the field subsequent to that time there had been no special administration of duties of that department excepting to let it go on in the line in which it had been conducted and directed. But this was done without the slightest intimation to me, and with no faulty action specifically alleged in either capacity. I have too much respect for the memory of General Grant to believe that he would have done this great wrong unless he had been deceived and also moved by a feeling of political jealousy, which I know was impressed upon him by members of his staff, especially by one whom Grant, when President, put in a high position.   Here he betrayed his chief by acts implicating him in the whiskey frauds upon the government, which caused him to be removed from his position and indicted upon accusation from the Treasury Department.   He is dead now, and I forbear to mention his name.

Upon the representations set forth, Grant obtained my removal from command.   With what regret, nay, grief, the blow was received can be better judged than described.

I never sought to be returned to my command or to be given another military place, and have never until now related fully the story of General Grant's injustice.

I did not entertain great harshness of feeling toward Grant on account of my removal by him, because I did not believe that it was really the act of his own mind.   I was certain that it was not when he assigned as the only cause, except that the corps commanders of the Army of the Potomac did not like to serve under my command, that he thought the administration of the affairs of my department objectionable, and, as he has elsewhere said, on account of my harshness.   Now, as I have once before said, I had no personal administration of my department substantially after I had gone into the field, the 4th of May ; and, in addition to my being reported upon favorably by the commissioner, Grant himself officially stated in a paper to go before the President that :

" *As an administrative officer General Butler has no superior.   In taking charge of a department where there are no great battles to be fought, but a dissatisfied element to control, no one could manage it better than he.*"

I knew very well where the pressure came from, and also whence it got its vitality in the mind of Grant.   The pressure came from his West Point staff officers, who were trying in every way to have me vilified and abused.   Grant had not, theretofore, permitted that to be done, and yielded only under that pressure of ambition for the highest office which has caused so many next in position to murder their chief to attain his place.   Such effects of overweening ambition are strung along as guide-posts through the whole history of the governments of the world.

That this condition of my feeling toward Grant is no afterthought of mine, and that I understood the circumstances of my removal as fully then as now, is shown by a letter written by me on the 13th of January, 1865, to Gen. John A. Rawlins, chief of General Grant's staff, who was not a West Point officer, but above them all, and afterwards became Secretary of War.[1]

I never spoke with General Grant upon these matters until shortly after his inauguration as President, when a mutual friend, Geo. Wilkes, Esq., spoke to him of the occurrence and told him of my feelings and views in regard to it. Grant said to him: " I would like to see General Butler; will he come to see me?"

" No," replied my friend, " not unless you send to him and express a wish to have him come."

Grant said: " Tell General Butler to come and see me, and say to him that I wish to have a conference with him."

" When shall I say he may come?"

" To-morrow evening, at which time I shall be at home."

I received from Mr. Wilkes the following letter on this subject: —

WASHINGTON, D. C.

HON. B. F. BUTLER.

Dear General: — In a recent interview with General Grant, I took the liberty of expressing the regret that any misunderstandings should continue to exist between himself and you, and particularly now, that public events required both of you to co-operate to the extent of your abilities in a common cause.

I suggested that these events and the responsibilities which they involve seemed, of themselves, to propose a reconciliation; and that I had ventured, therefore (without consulting you), to ascertain from him, if possible, whether the matters in dispute were not susceptible of explanation and adjustment.

General Grant did not at first seem desirous of conversing on the subject, but I went on to say that I knew of but two points of difficulty in the premises, the first of which was the remark in his report about your military position at Bermuda Hundred, and the other the matters growing out of the invitation to his family soiree; and here I ventured to remark, that while I was quite sure that General Butler believed himself to be entirely justified in the interpretation he had given to these incidents, I was equally certain he was under a misapprehension in relation to them both.

---

[1] See Appendix No. 146.

General Grant thereupon assured me I was quite correct in this last opinion. He said that the phrase in his report which had given so much offence had not been originated by him, and had not been adopted in the way of disrespect. It had been used first by General Barnard, chief of engineers, by way of illustration merely, during a consultation with him about a new disposition of the forces before Richmond. That in a few days thereafter, being himself required to make his report, he used Barnard's illustration because it was apt and on his mind, but without the slightest intention of reflecting upon General Butler.

In relation to the soiree or "reception," General Grant said that he had entrusted the matter of the invitations, as usual, to one of the members of his staff; that the officer alluded to had for his guide the cards which had been left at his (Grant's) house, the names of members of Congress, and other persons of distinction who were known to be in town. That General Butler, at the date of the party, was *not* a member of Congress; and, as his card had not been left at his house, the officer had no direct means of knowing that he was in town. For these reasons, no invitation had been sent to General Butler at the time when the other invitations were issued; but his (Grant's) attention having been called by Mrs. Grant, on the afternoon of the reception day, to the fact that General and Mrs. Butler were in Washington, he at once directed invitations to be sent to them — certainly not with the intention of showing disrespect, but with a directly opposite purpose.

I beg leave, therefore, to call your attention to the fact that General Grant has thus frankly disclaimed to me, as a declared friend of yours, any, nay, the slightest intention of reflecting upon you in the first instance, or of showing you other than entire respect in the second.

These facts are submitted to you simply as matters of fact; and they are referred, without suggestion, to your judgment by one who has complete confidence therein, and who has the honor to remain,

Very truly yours,

GEO. WILKES.

This being communicated to me, I said: "Very well; I will go and see General Grant and have a talk with him."

I called at the White House and was very cordially received. We sat down together and went over our whole past relations. I soon learned what had been impressed upon his mind as to my feelings toward him by those around him, some of whom he had discovered not to be the honorable and unselfish men he had believed them. He asked if our former kindly relations might not be restored. I said to him that under his explanations I certainly felt greatly relieved, and I hoped that that might be the case, and would be glad that it should be so. I had had an opportunity to do a service for him, which he appreciated highly.

I was in Congress during his administration as President, in which I gave him my hearty support; and from that time until the day of his death no word of unkind difference passed between us; and I can say without fear of contradiction, that few men possessed a greater share of his confidence, or had more personal influence with General Grant upon public questions than I had.

Grant in his report of the operations of the armies of the United States, dated July 22, 1865, was thoughtless enough to use a phrase — I say "thoughtless" because his explanation which I shall set out will show that it was so done — which was used more to my prejudice with the people of the country than anything else he could have said. The following is an extract from that report: —

On the 16th (of May) the enemy attacked General Butler in his position in front of Drury's Bluff. He was forced back or drew back into his intrenchments in the forks between the James and Appomattox Rivers. The enemy intrenched strongly in his front which cut him off from his railroads, the city, and all that was valuable to him. His army, therefore, though in a position of great security, was as completely shut off from further operations directly against Richmond as if it had been in a bottle strongly corked.[1]

General Grant makes his amendment and corrections of the whole matter in his " Personal Memoirs," [2] as follows : —

The position which General Butler had chosen between the two rivers, the James and Appomattox, was one of great natural strength, one where a large area of ground might be thoroughly enclosed by means of a single intrenched line, and that a very short one in comparison with the extent of the territory which it thoroughly protected. His right was protected by the James River, his left by the Appomattox, and his rear by their junction — the two streams uniting near by. The bends of the two streams shortened the line that had been chosen for intrenchments, while it increased the area which the line enclosed.

---

[1] War Record, Series 1, Vol. XXXVI., Part I., page 20.
[2] Personal Memoirs of U. S. Grant, Vol. II., pp. 151-153.

Previous to ordering any troops from Butler, I sent my chief engineer, General Barnard, from the Army of the Potomac to that of the James to inspect Butler's position and ascertain whether I could again safely make an order for General Butler's movement in co-operation with mine, now that I was getting so near Richmond; or, if I could not, whether his position was strong enough to justify me in withdrawing some of his troops and having them brought round by water to White House to join me, and reinforce the Army of the Potomac. General Barnard reported the position very strong for defensive purposes, and that I could do the latter with great security; but that General Butler could not move from where he was, in co-operation, to produce any effect. He said that the general occupied a place between the James and Appomattox Rivers which was of great strength, and where with an inferior force he could hold it for an indefinite length of time against a superior; but that he could do nothing offensively. I then asked him why Butler could not move out from his lines and push across the Richmond and Petersburg Railroad to the rear and on the south side of Richmond. He replied that it was impracticable, because the enemy had substantially the same line across the neck of land that General Butler had. He then took out his pencil and drew a sketch of the locality, remarking that the position was like a bottle and that Butler's line of intrenchments across the neck represented the cork; that the enemy had built an equally strong line immediately in front of him across the neck; and it was therefore as if Butler was in a bottle. He was perfectly safe against an attack; but, as Barnard expressed it, the enemy had corked the bottle and with a small force could hold the cork in its place. This struck me as being very expressive of his position, particularly when I saw the hasty sketch which General Barnard [1] had drawn; and in making my subsequent report I used that expression without adding quotation marks, never thinking that anything had been said that would attract attention — as this did, very much to the annoyance, no doubt, of General Butler, and, I know, very much to my own. I found afterwards that this was mentioned in the notes of General Badeau's

---

[1] It will be remembered that Barnard was the engineer sent down by Halleck on the 21st of May, 1864, to examine my defences and report whether I could move my army for offensive operations. He reported to Grant on the 24th of May recommending that "for offensive operations" twenty thousand of my troops be sent out of the bottle to reinforce and rescue Grant at Cold Harbor, which was done. And it also appears that Barnard in attempting to describe my fortifications by a picture, used this phrase, which Grant remembered and put in a report to Halleck.

It is a just criticism to say, how could the engineer officer, seeing more than twenty miles of smooth rivers to be crossed by pontoon bridges everywhere, protected by the navy, a fine harbor with quays and landings for the embarkation of troops at City Point and Bermuda Hundred, report to his general that my army was corked up as if in a bottle so that it could not be moved at all for offensive operations?

Here is another instance of an engineer picture-drawer who did me great harm, and it is the only act of his done during the campaign of 1864 that has any chance of going down in history.

book, which, when they were shown to me, I asked to have stricken out; yet it was retained there, though against my wishes.

I make this statement here because, although I have often made it before, it has never been in my power until now to place it where it will correct history ; and I desire to rectify all injustice that I may have done to individuals, particularly to officers who were gallantly serving their country during the trying period of the war for the preservation of the Union. General Butler certainly gave his very earnest support to the war ; and he gave his own best efforts personally to the suppression of the Rebellion.

May I ask the reader to go back with me for a few moments and look at the map of Bermuda Hundred where the exact configuration, topography, and situation of the peninsula of the Bermuda Hundred is accurately shown.[1] If he will then examine pages 627 and 628 of Chapter XIV., he will find that I met General Grant on the 1st of April, 1864, and with a map of Bermuda Hundred before him explained to him its relation to Petersburg, Richmond, and their vicinage on the James and Appomattox Rivers, showing him that by the possession of the two rivers, at a point between the Point of Rocks on the Appomattox and Osborn on the James, where the rivers were about three miles apart, a line of intrenchments could be thrown over that distance so as to make that peninsula, some thirty square miles, an intrenched camp as impregnable as Fortress Monroe. I described all its advantages and explained how his army could have a base of supplies there when it came to operate on the south side of the James. It would make a stronghold, within eight miles of the defences of Richmond by land, where his army could be encamped with safety, be defended by a small force, and operate thence by the rivers over all sides towards the North and South. This plan General Grant approved against the objections of Gen. William F. Smith.

Looking a little further on, the reader will find the order of General Grant directing me to seize City Point and fortify the peninsula so that it might be held (as was ever afterwards done) as an impregnable base of supplies and army occupation in case of disaster certainly so long as our navy could hold the river. Those intrenchments across the neck of the peninsula were made so strong that although even attacked by the enemy they were always held during the war. I was

[1] See pp. 659-662.

to put the stopper in the bottle,— that is, I was to construct the impregnable line of intrenchments.

Was that bottle Butler's or Grant's?

He thought the cork was in so strongly that afterwards he advised me that I could hold it against the army of Lee by one man to every six feet of its line. If it should be said that the enemy put a line of intrenchments in front of my line equally strong, I answer that if that had been done it would have been of no consequence. I should have been glad if they had put a Chinese wall across there without an opening in it. I had determined that they should not come in there, and I had no call to go out because I had a line of more than twenty miles on its shores guarded by our navy where troops could be embarked and where expeditions could be sent across the rivers by pontoon bridges.

I had three pontoon bridges, one across the Appomattox, during the whole time of my occupation, and two across the James, one at Deep Bottom, and one at Varina. Over these, between the 14th of June and the 25th of December, 1864, Grant ordered the following expeditions, composed of a corps or more, sometimes from both armies, to move in attack upon Richmond and elsewhere: —

May 28, Smith's corps to Cold Harbor; returned June 14.

June 9, Gillmore crossed the Appomattox and attacked Petersburg.

June 11, I sent Gillmore to attack Petersburg.

June 15, the Eighteenth Corps under Smith was sent to attack Petersburg by order of Grant.

June 16, the Sixth Corps under Wright; afterwards sent thence to Washington.

June 21, expedition to Deep Bottom, crossing the pontoon bridge to the south side of the James River.

July 14, the Eighteenth Corps, Kautz's Cavalry, attacked Petersburg, crossing the Appomattox by the pontoon bridge.

July 17, Birney's Corps crossed the pontoon bridge over the James to meet Hancock, and attacked the enemy's works on the north bank, and returned.

August 19, part of the Second and Tenth Corps crossed the pontoon bridge to attack the defences on the north side of the river around Richmond.

In August my Eighteenth Corps held Grant's lines around Petersburg while his army attacked the enemy through the mine.

September 29, the whole Army of the James, save the garrison, attacked Richmond directly, carrying Fort Harrison and the outer line of works around Richmond, which were ever afterwards held.

October 3, my Nineteenth Corps sent to defend Washington under the orders of Grant.

This does not include several minor expeditions of small bodies of troops which were from time to time sent from my intrenched camp. And added to all this is the fact that from the 15th of June, 1863, until the surrender of the army of Lee, April 12, 1865, General Grant had during the whole time his headquarters always in the " bottle," guarded by troops of the Army of the James which garrisoned the " bottle." How did he get out, as he never went through the nozzle, which was tightly corked.

I am convinced that it was Badeau who wrote the report wherein this phrase was used so much to my detriment, because Grant, who was an honest and truthful man, so far as I know, never could have written it with the knowledge he had ; and I am the more thoroughly so persuaded because in the " Military History of General Grant," written by Badeau, and in the " Personal Memoirs of General Grant," of which Badeau claims the substantial authorship, the same identical words, " corked as in a bottle," are used upon the subject.

Grant, who had seen the mischief that the untruthful criticism had done me, says : —

I found afterwards that this was mentioned in the notes of General Badeau's book [Military History of General Grant] which, when they were shown to me, I asked to have stricken out ; yet it was retained there, though against my wishes.[1]

I make this statement here because, although I have often made it before, it has never been in my power until now to place it where it will correct history.[2]

---

[1] This is conclusive evidence that Badeau did not write " Grant's History " or any other book according to Grant's wishes, but put in matters which Grant did not wish should be in the books, against Grant's wishes and direction, to gratify his own malice and spleen.

[2] Personal Memoirs of U. S. Grant, Vol II., page 152

In Badeau's Military History of Grant there is a long and untruthful narrative showing his animus towards me, twisting and distorting every fact. All this Grant omits in his "Memoirs." [1]

I believe the reader will come to the conclusion that the "bottle" was made exactly according to the orders of Grant and according to his understanding of the situation on April 1; and also that it was

---

[1] I should feel it my duty to follow the criticisms of Badeau — which I take to be the French for "dirty water" — at length, but he has destroyed himself, and I do not see how any honorable man, knowing his character from his own exposure of it, could believe a word he says, or meet him except to avoid him. Badeau found himself in the army a lieutenant of infantry, unassigned, serving as aid of Brigadier-General Sherman [not William T.]. He seems to have attached himself to Grant as a sort of military secretary. His name does not appear, even "mentioned" in the War Records of the campaign around Richmond. He availed himself of his intimacy to publish a history of Grant to his own great profit. Grant appointed him Secretary of Legation and afterwards Consul-General at London, one of the most profitable offices in the gift of the President. He remained there nine years. Hayes removed him and appointed him Consul-General at Havana, another very lucrative office, where he remained until his conduct was such as to require his resignation. In the meantime for his great services to the Union in suppressing the Rebellion he was retired as an officer of the army of rank with large pay and emolument.

He then claimed that he was employed by Grant to assist him in revising the composition of his "Memoirs," which Grant, having become entirely wrecked in fortune by the failure of the Marine Bank, in a dying condition, was trying to compose on his sick-bed, assisted by his son as amanuensis, so that the sale of the book might leave something for the support of his amiable wife in her widowhood. Grant's book, written with such heroic effort and for such a purpose, was not the book it would have been if he had had the health and strength to write it himself; but yet, as it was written under such circumstances, it was looked upon by almost every citizen to be a duty to buy a copy, and its sale fortunately was productive of quite large profit.

Badeau had received through Grant benefit and money enough that he should have gratefully written for him his whole life. But as soon as his great benefactor lay silent in the tomb, Badeau came upon his widow and family with an exorbitant claim for his services for a short time in aiding the general in revising his "Memoirs." The family resisted this demand of ten thousand dollars upon the grounds that he claimed the authorship of the book. Thereupon Badeau brought a suit for a large sum, flew into the newspapers to try his case, and in his correspondence attempted to raise such a scandal upon Grant, his family, and his "Memoirs," that the Hon. Charles A. Dana offered to pay from his own pocket the sum claimed by Badeau if he would "shut up," as Dana had grateful remembrances of his friendly relations with Grant as Assistant Secretary of War during the campaign from the Rapidan to the James.

Colonel Grant, to justify the family in their refusal to pay that large sum for Badeau's work, produced a letter composed by General Grant on his death-bed and signed by him, in which he says to Badeau: "I have voluntarily stipulated for a small compensation for the various services rendered to me; I thought and you thought the compensation large at the time." It seems Badeau had made claim on his dying benefactor, the result of which was, as Badeau says, that for two months before his death, Grant and himself had no friendly communication, and his letter seems to be the last communication between them. I do not know who in fact paid the money, but Badeau took the ten thousand dollars and did "shut up," as he would have taken anything else, I doubt not, that did not belong to him.

His next exploit was to attempt to make the government pay him a salary as a retired army officer while he drew a very large salary as Consul-General at Havana, a part of which the treasury refused to pay, and as he had in fact drawn double salary during the largest part of all these years, they sued Badeau for the money taken by him without law, so he in turn sued the United States. But the Supreme Court sat down on that performance, saying that the law forbade it but there was no law by which the same could be recovered back. [See Badeau vs. U. S. Sup. Court Reports, Oct. Term, 1888.]

I have no objection to being slandered by such a man, and therefore allow the criticisms of this unassigned lieutenant upon me to remain unanswered except by showing what sort of a creature made them.

intended by me to be exactly what it was, admittedly an intrenched camp that could not be taken by the rebels so long as the navy held the river, as it never was taken ; and that General Grant regretted very much the statements made by Badeau in his report and elsewhere concerning it, so far as they reflected upon me, especially as they actually reflected upon Grant himself.

It will also have appeared that Bermuda Hundred, including City Point, was a strategic point where there could be an intrenched base

CAPT. GEORGE A. KENSEL.

in which the supplies for Grant's army could always be safe, to which he could resort, and, leaving a small garrison there, demonstrate upon Petersburg to the southerly and against Richmond northerly, as he many times did do.

After he had demonstrated at Cold Harbor that he could not drive Lee's army into Richmond, his losses being so severe, he determined to take the other alternative of the plan agreed upon April 1, which Smith himself admits was my plan of the campaign, to

make his further attacks upon Richmond and Petersourg, the capture
of the latter being in effect the capture of Richmond as is now
agreed.　He had at that time exhausted all hope of present reinforcements, by calling upon three fourths of my effective men to be sent
to Cold Harbor, where the last fight with Lee's army in the field
was made.

　Let us see now what in his cool judgment, after he had received
all the information that the whole history of the campaign could
give him, and after he knew exactly all that I had done, for I do
not know that he complains of anything that I had left undone
which I was ordered to do, surely never having met with any
disaster in my movements,— let us see, I say, what were Grant's
opinions of me and what his view of my military acts in his cool
judgment when written through another pen than that of Badeau.
In his voyage to the East, he was accompanied by Mr. John Russell
Young, afterwards United States Minister to China, as his personal
and valued friend.　Mr. Young made minutes of his conversations,
which with Grant's permission were afterwards published.　In one
of these Grant said : —

　I have always regretted the censure that unwittingly came upon
Butler in that campaign, and my report was the cause.　I said that
General Butler was " bottled up," and used the phrase without meaning
to annoy the General or give his enemies a weapon.　I liked Butler and
have always found him not only, as all the world knows, a man of great
ability, but a patriotic man, and a man of courage, honor, and sincere
convictions.　Butler lacked the technical experience of a military education, and it is very possible to be a man of high parts and not be a great
general.　Butler as a general was full of enterprise and resources, and
a brave man.　If I had given him two corps commanders like Adelbert
Ames, Mackenzie, Weitzel, or Terry, or a dozen I could mention, he
would have made a fine campaign on the James and helped materially in
my plans.　I have always been sorry that I did not do so.　Butler is a
man it is a fashion to abuse, but he is a man who has done to the country
great service and who is worthy of its gratitude. [1]

　General Grant, in an interview with John Russell Young, in
New York *Herald*, 1878, said : —

---

[1] John Russell Young's "Around the World with General Grant," Vol. II., p. 304.

As it was, I confronted Lee, and held him and all his hosts far from Richmond and the James; while I sent, the same day of my advance across the Rapidan, a force by the James River sufficient, as I thought, to have captured all south of Richmond to Petersburg, and hold it. I believe now that if General Butler had had two corps commanders such as I might have selected, had I known the material of the entire army as well as I did afterwards, he would have done so, and would have threatened Richmond itself so as materially to have aided me farther north.

With this most thorough and full indorsement of General Grant, I might close what I have to say on this subject with satisfaction to my readers, but not with satisfaction to myself.

During my whole service in the army it was always thrown in my face by the regular officers that I had no technical military education. That meant that I had not been to West Point. Now a West Pointer if he graduated very high never was employed in the army in managing troops until our war. He was simply assigned to public works, generally of a civil description, until he was fifty years old at least. If he graduated in the next grade he was to command a battery of artillery until he was about the same age, except a few of them who served in the Mexican war. If he graduated in the next grade he was to command an infantry company, and they were so few and scattered that he got near fifty before he ever commanded a company of them as a rule, and very few of them got to be captains before they were fifty years old, and except against the Indians they never acquired any experience in the field. The lowest rank was to be a lieutenant of cavalry. So, with the exception of the Mexican veterans, there were no West Pointers at the breaking out of the war who had had any experience in the field. But during the Rebellion all was changed. It was assumed that West Point officers knew the whole art of war and were ready-made generals. McDowell was only a major in the regular army when he fought the first battle of Bull Run, and had had no experience with troops. A few — but not too many — of those officers read military books. It is wonderful how soon this claim of theirs burst out after the war commenced, and even then how little ambition for fighting these men had.

I was sent as major-general commanding to Fortress Monroe on the 22d of May, 1861, and I was told by General Scott that I was fortunate in having there some sixteen young officers who would aid

me in organizing troops. Now, of those sixteen young men, ten had
had relations with General Taylor, who was commissary general of
the army, and they at once got detailed to positions in the commissary
department where they could buy pork and beans for the army, which
was thought to be a very soft place. Four of the others got detailed
into the quartermaster-general's department, where they could buy
mules and hire steamboats. Two more of them got into the adjutant-
general's department, where they sat at desks. There were three
or four older officers, — one of whom was the lamented General
Williams, of whom I have already spoken, — who had been in the
Mexican War, who retained their commands in the line and took
their chances in battle. Now, I am not saying one word against
those young men, but I am only showing to what — for some of them
afterwards were on my staff and served well — an education at West
Point brought the ambition of its pupils. It was not the fault of the
men, but of the system.

The claim to that superiority, because they had a regular education,
broke out not always in the most polite manner. Sometimes it was
discussed before me how superior all West Pointers were to volunteer officers.

I thought I would put a stop to that, so I invited some of the
officers to a dinner party at my headquarters with some of my per·
sonal staff who were volunteers. I believed that at that dinner party
such discussions might be renewed, so I called Captain Haggerty of
my staff, a very bright young lawyer, and told him to go to the library
and read the descriptions of one or two of Napoleon's famous battles,
naming Marengo, and to ascertain the pivotal point or movement upon
which the battles turned, so as to be able clearly to tell me what it
was when I asked him. We all came to dinner in a very pleasant
mood, but between one or two of the officers, regulars, and volunteers,
the discussion broke out and became quite animated, and I feared it
would go so far that it might become necessary for the general to
take notice of it. The claim was very loudly made that nobody could
be fit to command troops who had not been to West Point. I never
had been there except to examine the institution, as a member of the
board of visitors, having been appointed in 1857 by Jefferson Davis
while Secretary of War, for my supposed military knowledge as a
civilian. I at that time held the title of brigadier-general, and was

met there by General Scott, who reminded me that he was the oldest, as I was the youngest, general in the United States.

I knew the young gentlemen at the table meant no harm, but I thought it was well enough to give them a little lesson.

I said : " You gentlemen of the regulars can doubtless give me, a volunteer general, some information by answering a question. Can any of you tell me the movement of Napoleon at the battle of Marengo which was the one upon which he wholly relied for his success in that famous battle ? "

They looked one to the other and the other to the one, but nobody replied. I then turned to Captain Haggerty, who sat well down the table, and said : " Captain, can you answer that question ? "

" Yes, General, I think I can."

" Then explain to us what that battle was."

Haggerty gave a very exact account of it, and I said : " I am very much obliged to you, Captain. You see, gentlemen, it will be convenient during this war to have some volunteer officers along with us, so that if we get into a like predicament with Napoleon we shall have somebody who knows what was done under like circumstances."[1]

The conversation was not renewed. In due time we separated, and the question of the military superiority of West Pointers was never discussed in my hearing by that set of officers afterwards.

Now, what sort of education does the student get at West Point which enables him to perform the greatest acts of generalship quite independently of his natural abilities of which Grant has kindly given me the credit of having some ? I suppose I am at liberty to take as a sample of the education acquired at West Point, that which enabled one West Pointer to outstrip all volunteer officers, and all West Pointers, engineers, picture drawers, captains of artillery, and captains of cavalry, and stand forth the greatest general of his country and perhaps of the world. Of course it will be seen that I must refer to General Grant, whom I cheerfully acknowledge to be a great general in very many respects. How much of his·supremacy as a

---

[1] The point of this question may not be recognized by an unprofessional reader. The victory of Marengo which produced greater results to Napoleon than any in his career, was confessedly fought in the utmost confusion without any plan or order of battle, nearly lost by a series of blunders, and won by an accident of which, and over which, Bonaparte had neither knowledge nor control. Jomini calls it an affray, refusing to dignify it by the name of battle, and Matthieu Dumas says Marengo was an enclosed field in which one of two armies must perish. It is distinguished in history above all others by having nothing of the art of war in it.

war general did he get from West Point? Lest I may be accused of not making a fair presentation of the case in my statement, I give it in his own words as set down in his " Personal Memoirs " : —

A military life had no charms for me, and I had not the faintest idea of staying in the army even if I should be graduated, which I did not expect. The encampment which preceded the commencement of academic studies was very wearisome and uninteresting, When the 28th of August came — the date for breaking up camp and going into barracks — I felt as though I had been at West Point always, and that if I stayed to graduation, I would have to remain always. I did not take hold of my studies with avidity, in fact I rarely ever read over a lesson the second time during my entire cadetship. I could not sit in my room doing nothing. There is a fine library connected with the Academy from which cadets can get books to read in their quarters. I devoted more time to these than to books relating to the course of studies. Much of the time, I am sorry to say, was devoted to novels, but not those of a trashy sort. I read all of Bulwer's then published, Cooper's, Marryat's, Scott's, Washington Irving's works, Lever's, and many others that I do not now remember. Mathematics was very easy to me, so that when January came, I passed the examination, taking a good standing in that branch. In French, the only other study at that time, in the first year's course, my standing was very low; in fact, if the class had been turned the other end foremost, I should have been near the head. I never succeeded in getting squarely at either end of my class, in any one study, during the four years. I came near it in French, artillery, infantry, and cavalry tactics, and conduct.

Early in the session of the Congress which met in December, 1839, a bill was discussed abolishing the Military Academy. I saw in this an honorable way to obtain a discharge, and read the debates with much interest, but with impatience at the delay in taking action, for I was selfish enough to favor the bill. It never passed, and a year later, although the time hung drearily with me, I would have been sorry to have seen it succeed![1]

We have now seen General Grant's description of his literary education in the art of war that he obtained at West Point. How was it in regard to tactics, the school of the soldier, of the company, and of the battalion? The cadets at West Point are formed in battalions commanded, in all offices of the line, by the men best versed in military tactics, in the use of the musket, in the formation of a

---

[1] Personal Memoirs of U. S. Grant, Vol. I., p. 38.

company, and in the movements of these companies in the battalion, the superintendent or one of his staff being commandant of the battalion.

The first promotion for a man who is a well-drilled soldier is to the rank of corporal; then if he shows capacity, to that of sergeant and then to that of lieutenant.

These officers, therefore, in accordance with their grade during the four years of their cadetship, are supposed to be the best-drilled men, and those who have made the most improvement in the art of being soldiers. The least proficient remain privates.

Let Grant tell his own story of how he rose in efficiency in the ranks : —

I had not been " called out " as a corporal, but when I returned from furlough I found myself the last but one,— about my standing in all the tactics — of eighteen sergeants. The promotion was too much for me. That year my standing in the class, as shown by the number of demerits of the year, was about the same as it was among the sergeants, and I was dropped and served the fourth year as a private.[1]

Assuming the perfect accuracy of this, which I do not doubt in the least, I take leave to state the conclusion to which it irresistibly leads my mind :—

Grant evidently did not get enough of West Point into him to hurt him any ; he was less like a West Point man than any officer I ever knew. The reader sees how much of a military education I lost in not having gone to West Point to get a military education like that of Grant. The less of West Point a man has the more successful he will be. We see how little Grant had. All of the very successful generals of our war stood near the lower end of their classes at West Point. As examples, take Grant, Sheridan, and Sherman. All the graduates in the higher ranks in their classes never came to anything as leaders of armies in the war. The whole thing puts me in mind of an advertisement I saw in a newspaper in my youth. It contained a recipe for making graham bread out of coarse unbolted flour mixed with sawdust. The recipe ended as follows: " N. B.— The less sawdust the better."

Notice how little the young student was interested at West Point, in those studies which pertained to the art of war, and in particular

---

[1] Personal Memoirs of U. S. Grant, Vol. 1, p 41.

to the handling of troops, called tactics. No grand tactics can be or is taught at that institution. Tactics is moving troops in sight of the enemy. Grand tactics is moving them at a distance and out of sight of the enemy.

It will be observed that while he was reading some very fine novels, his mind did not turn to military novels, of which there were many in the library. He does not speak of ever having read a single work describing the carrying on of war from Alexander down to Napoleon, or even the battles of the Revolution and our war with Great Britain. He got to be a second lieutenant in a company in the Mexican War, and soon after resigned his command and took employment as clerk in the office of Captain Craig, a quartermaster in the army. I am not saying one word of this in any disparagement of General Grant. I am only attempting to show what military education a man may get passing through a course of study at West Point and graduating with such military accomplishments as will entitle him to a command in the regular army, and which, when war occurs, may be the impelling motives of governors of States in appointing such persons as colonels of their finest regiments of volunteer troops.

Now I suppose I may say without offence that I had read before I was twenty-one, starting with the campaigns of Cæsar, the history of the military operations of all the principal wars of Europe, and before I went into the army had read critically two histories of the Crimean War, and the most detailed lives and military histories of Napoleon that I could get, and had made examinations of all his military movements, and had read the histories of the wars of our own country until they were nearly as familiar to me as the operations of the campaigns of the armies of the Potomac and James were afterwards. As I have said, I had passed my leisure hours in learning the school of the soldier, the company, and the battalion, and the tactics of the division, which Sherman frankly states he had never studied until after he was a brigadier-general and was drilling his brigade before Washington in 1862. Having a taste for the military art, I made this reading my principal study outside of the demands of my profession.

I had an opinion, but not founded on sufficient evidence, that I owed my removal from my command largely to Halleck. Since then, I have come in possession of part of the documentary evidence tend-

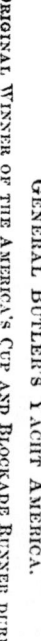

GENERAL BUTLER'S YACHT AMERICA.

ORIGINAL WINNER OF THE AMERICA'S CUP AND BLOCKADE RUNNER DURING THE WAR.

ing to sustain me in that opinion, but, I regret, not all of it, because the correspondence between the higher officers of the army has not been published down to a later date than July, 1864, and I was relieved on the 8th of January, 1865. By good fortune I got from a private source a letter [1] written by Halleck, which led me to the opinion above mentioned. This letter was written at the time that Halleck's friend Smith, of whom he speaks so highly, made his first attempt to get me removed and himself put in my place. It states a good many untruths. For instance, I had not quarrelled with anybody, even with Gillmore; I only took care to make the proper orders in due course of military usage when I found that he had not obeyed orders and lost his expedition. I had made no " demands for reinforcements " up to the time that letter was written, I had only suggested that those which had been promised me might be sent — as I have before stated. I did not ask to be sent anywhere or to do anything that Grant did not ask to have me do at that time. Halleck had received a report that I was doing my duty faithfully and well. The only thing that he ever complained of was, that there was some irregularity in the command of troops in Fortress Monroe while I was in the field. As there were no troops there to be commanded, and the fort was a depot of supplies, and as I had a very competent man there as quartermaster, a captain in the regular army, I thought that a quartermaster might be left in command, as we had absolutely no soldiers there. That was the irregularity to which he called my attention, and I promptly remedied it by removing Brigadier-General Shepley from Norfolk to Fortress Monroe to take charge of that district. I had never written Halleck an unkind letter, and had, until I saw the letter referred to, never had any unkind thoughts of him. Indeed, I knew nothing of him. I have since learned his character, which, as I always speak plainly, I find to be that of a lying, treacherous, hypocritical scoundrel with no moral sense.

Hard words, you say, General Butler. Yes; I use them when they are the only ones which ought to be used, and I only give them as expressing my opinions when the facts will justify me. These facts I will briefly set out here.

I call Secretary Stanton as a witness. He speaks of Halleck from his knowledge of him before the war. General McClellan says:—[2]

---

[1] See Appendix No. 82.   [2] McClellan's Own Story, p. 137.

Speaking of Halleck a day or two before he arrived in Washington, Stanton came to caution me against trusting Halleck, who was, he said, probably the greatest scoundrel and most barefaced villain in America. He said that he was totally destitute of principle, and that in the Almaden quicksilver case he had convicted Halleck of perjury in open court.

Again the editor of "McClellan's Own Story" gives testimony as to Halleck's untruthfulness. Halleck had testified against McClellan before the Committee on the Conduct of the War. The editor says in calling attention to Halleck's testimony:—[1]

That this testimony of General Halleck was distinctly false is now demonstrated beyond any dispute by the publication of his own correspondence with McClellan during the period August 26 to August 31, and by other proofs.

Again McClellan accuses him to Grant of falsehood, hypocrisy, and betrayal, and more than intimates to General Grant, who did not learn of Halleck's perfidy for some years, that he stole despatches from the office of the general-in-chief in order that Grant might not see them when he came to Washington to take that office. McClellan says:—[2]

On the morning of Sunday, March 2, 1862, desiring to give orders for the further movements of Buell's and Halleck's commands, I went to the military telegraph office — then in the headquarters of the Army of the Potomac at the corner of Pennsylvania Avenue and Jackson Square — and caused communication to be cut off from all wires except those leading to Halleck's headquarters at St. Louis and Buell's at Nashville. I then called Buell and Halleck to their respective offices, and asked for a full report of the condition of affairs, number, position, and condition of their troops, that of the enemy, etc. Buell promptly gave me the information needed. Halleck replied the same day:—

. . . I have had no communication with General Grant for more than a week. He left his command without my authority and went to Nashville. His army seems to be as much demoralized by the victory of Fort Donelson as was that of the Potomac by the defeat of Bull Run. It is hard to censure a successful general immediately after a victory, but I think he richly deserves it. I can get no returns, no reports, no information of any kind from him. Satisfied with his victory, he sits down and enjoys

[1] McClellan's Own Story, p. 539.   [2] McClellan's Own Story, p. 216, *et seq.*

it without any regard to the future. I am worn out and tired with this *neglect and inefficiency.* C. F. Smith is almost the only officer equal to the emergency.

To this I replied : —

Your despatch of last evening received. The success of our cause demands that proceedings such as Grant's should be at once checked. Generals must observe discipline as well as private soldiers. Do not hesitate to *arrest him at once*, if the good of the service requires it, and place C. F. Smith in command. You are at liberty to regard this as a positive order, if it will smooth your way. I appreciate the difficulties you have to encounter, and will be glad to relieve you from trouble as far as possible.

On the 4th Halleck telegraphed me : —

A rumor has just reached me that since the taking of Fort Donelson Grant has resumed his former bad habits. If so, it will account for his repeated neglect of my often-repeated orders. I do not deem it advisable to arrest him at present, but have placed General Smith in command of the expedition up the Tennessee. I think Smith will restore order and discipline. . . .

On the 6th Halleck telegraphed to Grant : —

General McClellan directs that you report to me daily the number and position of the forces under your command. Your neglect of repeated orders to report the strength of your command has created great dissatisfaction and seriously interfered with military plans. Your going to Nashville without authority, and when your presence with your troops was of the greatest importance, was a matter of serious complaint *at Washington*, so much so that I was *advised* to arrest you on your return.

On the 31st of March Halleck informed Grant : —

General McClellan directed me to place General Smith in command of the expedition until you were ordered to join it.

On the 10th of March the adjutant-general of the army, by direction of the President, required from Halleck a report as to Grant's unauthorized visit to Nashville and as to his general conduct. On the 15th, Halleck replied that Grant had gone to Nashville to communicate with Buell, that his motives were proper, and advised that no further proceedings be had in the case.

Now to the story which prompts me to insert these despatches. More than a year after the events in question, Franklin wrote to me that on meeting Grant at Memphis, or some such point on the Mississippi, Grant asked what had made me hostile to him. Franklin replied that he knew that I was not hostile but very friendly to him. Grant then said that that could not be so, for, without any reason, I had ordered Halleck to relieve him from command and arrest him soon after Fort Donelson, and that Halleck had interfered to save him. I took no steps to undeceive Grant, trusting to time to elucidate the question.

In the latter part of 1866, while I was in Europe, General Grant, through one of his staff, communicated with General Marcy in regard to papers missing from the files of the office of general-in-chief during my tenure of the place.

In searching my papers, General Marcy[1] found my retained copy of the despatch of March 2 from Halleck in which he reports Grant's unauthorized absence, etc. This he forwarded to General Grant, who was thus for the first time informed of the truth. This despatch and my reply had, with many others, *disappeared* from the files in the office. So with regard to my correspondence as general-in-chief.

The military-telegraph office was first established by me, and was located, as already stated, in the headquarters of the Army of the Potomac. . . .

Some one abstracted the telegrams above alluded to. As to Halleck's conduct with regard to Grant, no comment by me is necessary. The facts speak for themselves.

Let me give General Grant's side of this transaction. He seems not to have known of it until 1866 when McClellan was in Europe and Grant applied to him to know what these disappeared despatches were, and got from him the copies, as they have been hereinbefore set out. Grant gives his version of the matter in his "Memoirs" as follows : —[2]

On the 2d of March [1862] I received orders [from Halleck] dated March 1 to move my command back to Fort Henry, leaving only a small garrison at Donelson. From Fort Henry expeditions were to be sent against Eastport, Mississippi, and Paris, Tennessee. We started from Donelson on the 4th, and the same day I was back on the Tennessee River. On March 4, I also received the following despatch from General Halleck : —

Maj.-Gen. U. S. Grant, Fort Henry :

You will place Maj.-Gen. C. F. Smith in command of expedition, and remain yourself at Fort Henry. Why do you not obey my orders to report strength and positions of your command ?

H. W. Halleck,
Major-General.

---

[1] General Marcy was McClellan's chief-of-staff and also his father-in-law.
[2] Personal Memoirs of U. S. Grant, Vol. I. p. 325.

I was surprised. This was the first intimation I had received that General Halleck had called for information as to the strength of my command. On the 6th he wrote to me again : " Your going to Nashville without authority, and when your presence with your troops was of the utmost importance, was a matter of very serious complaint at Washington, so much so that I was advised to arrest you on your return." This was the first I knew of his objecting to my going to Nashville. That place was not beyond the limits of my command, which, it had been expressly declared in orders, were " not defined." Nashville is west of the Cumberland River, and I had sent troops that had reported to me for duty to occupy the place. I turned over the command as directed and then replied to General Halleck courteously, but asked to be relieved from further duty under him.

Later I learned that General Halleck had been calling lustily for more troops, promising that he would do something important if he could only be sufficiently reinforced.[1] McClellan asked him what force he then had. Halleck telegraphed me to supply the information so far as my command was concerned, but I received none of his despatches. At last Halleck reported to Washington that he had repeatedly ordered me to give the strength of my force, but could get nothing out of me ; that I had gone to Nashville, beyond the limits of my command, without his authority, and that my army was more demoralized by victory than the army at Bull Run had been by defeat. General McClellan, on this information, ordered that I should be relieved from duty and that an investigation should be made into any charges against me. He even authorized my arrest. . . .

On the 13th of March I was restored to command, and on the 17th Halleck sent me a copy of an order from the War Department which stated that accounts of my misbehavior had reached Washington and directed him to investigate and report the facts. He forwarded also a copy of a detailed despatch from himself to Washington entirely exonerating me ; but *he did not inform me that it was his own reports* that had created all the trouble. On the contrary, he wrote to me : " Instead of relieving you, I wish you, as soon as your new army is in the field, to assume immediate command, *and lead it to new victories.*" In consequence I felt very grateful to him, and supposed it was his interposition that had set me right with the government. I never knew the truth until General Badeau unearthed the facts in his researches for his history of my campaigns.

[1] Halleck's complaint of me, as shown in his letter to Grant, was that I was demanding reinforcements. He evidently mistook himself for me.

Grant never forgave Halleck for his treatment of him to the day of his death.   By reading Halleck's fawning despatches to Grant during the campaigns of 1864 another illustration of his character will be observed.

Let us see how he treated General Sherman, with whom he had been apparently on kindly relations. When at Raleigh, North Carolina, in April, 1865, Sherman entered into a negotiation with Johnston for the surrender of his army, and according to military usage he agreed with Johnston on a truce and the cessation of all hostilities between the United States forces and Johnston's army until the negotiation should be finished.   The two generals met and entered into a convention under which Johnston should surrender his army.   It was agreed to by Johnston and signed provisionally by Sherman and forwarded to Washington for acceptance.

The wisdom of that convention is a matter not here and now to be discussed ; but President Johnson strongly objected to it and it was returned to Sherman through General Grant with instructions that Johnston should be held to surrender on the same terms as Lee had done, which he afterwards did.

Before Grant went down to Raleigh with those instructions, he had ordered Meade to march the armies of the Potomac and James to Burksville, a convenient point from which those armies could move on Johnston and join Sherman in case the negotiations failed.

Meanwhile Halleck had got himself appointed to the command of the armies of the Potomac and James, apparently without Grant's knowledge. He immediately went into Virginia, and ordered Meade's armies to move on Johnston, notwithstanding the existence of the truce.   Sherman was exceedingly indignant, as he well might have been, and reported to Grant that he would, with his army, maintain the truce he had agreed to at all hazards of loss of life, and that while he would obey his orders and the orders of the President, he would not obey any order from Halleck.   Grant advised Sherman to withdraw his report and amend it.   Sherman said he would not amend it, but would let the record stand as it was written.   Thereupon Halleck, being in Virginia, issued an order to Sherman's troops not to obey him, and published the order.   Afterwards finding that Johnston's army had been surrendered, and being about to march his troops into Virginia, Halleck invited Sherman to Richmond to become his guest.   Sherman declined, writing back that he had seen his order and was going to march his troops into Virginia, and that Halleck had better keep out of the way because he would not be answerable for what might happen to him at the hands of some rash men in his command. And Sherman and Halleck remained the bitterest enemies until the last.

It will be seen in Halleck's letter to Grant, to which I have re_ferred, that he says I quarrelled with everybody. If there can be found any such quarrels on my part with anybody as those of Halleck with all the generals with whom he came in contact, I will agree that I am a more quarrelsome man than Halleck suggested me to be. Witness his quarrel with Banks about the expedition up Red River. Halleck repeatedly suggested an order to be made, against the better judgment of Banks, who over and over again reported to Halleck his objections to making it. Halleck afterwards made the most slanderous reports to Grant against Banks for doing what he himself had suggested, so that Banks was removed with contumely. Halleck does not intimate in his letter that in my quarrels I lied or cheated and betrayed all my friends and even my enemies, but he did recommend that I should be sent into Rosecrans' department to have a quarrel with him, with whom also Halleck was then in a quarrel.

Before I made a movement in the campaign of 1864, as will be seen by reading the despatches to Grant, and before I could be accused of having made any failure in the field, Halleck commenced a series of despatches, which he kept up to the last, advising Grant to have me removed from the army. At last he succeeded, but only after Grant's mind had become soured by false representations of political rivalry and enmity on my part.

But, I may be asked, what was the motive of Halleck in all this? What had you done to him?

Nothing in the world. There were two vacancies in the rank of major-general in the regular army,—which I never thought of or desired,—and Grant had recommended one of his own favorites for appointment. Thereupon Halleck wrote the following letter to Grant:—

HEADQUARTERS OF THE ARMY, WASHINGTON, May 23, 1864.
LIEUTENANT-GENERAL GRANT:

What you say in your note of the 20th about the major-generals is correct. There are two vacancies. The law allows five. You filled an original vacancy, and I last year urged Sherman's name for Wool's place, but could not get him appointed. Your promotion makes a second vacancy, and I have urged the names of Meade and Sherman, and Hancock for Meade's place as brigadier. There is some obstacle in the way and I can't remove it. I am not certain what it is, but can guess. Perhaps you will be enlightened a little by knowing what are some of the outside influences. I understand the names of Butler and Sickles have been strongly urged by politicians, in order, they say, to break down "West Point influence." It will not be difficult to draw conclusions. This is *entre nous.*

Yours truly,

H. W. HALLECK.

The motive becomes clearer when he accuses with me Major-General Sickles, the hero of Gettysburg, without whose movements that great Union-saving battle never would have been fought, and who lost a limb on the field, or the battle would have been followed up, I doubt not. Sickles' friends were pressing him for a promotion thus well earned (I had none to press me), because he was a volunteer general, one of the civilian generals. But West Point must have the possession of the regular army.

This called to mind my own unfortunate condition, which was like Sickles' in this one respect. We were both prominent Democrats. War was not our *trade.* We had left our professions, where we were receiving lucrative employment very far beyond the piled-up emolument of the generals of the regular army, to give our services in doing what we could toward saving the country. That left us both without any influence of politicians, because Democratic politicians had no influence, and because we were the objects of the jealousy of the Republican politicians of our respective States.

All the generals in the army who were Republicans had members of Congress and senators of their own States to take care of their interests and advance them by every sort of Congressional action and influence upon the department. Although I served during the war and did some things which caused members of Congress of other States to bring my name before Congress, so that I received a vote of thanks in one House for my administration in New Orleans, yet any motion in my behalf, brought forward by either senator or representative from Massachusetts where all were Republicans, yet remains to be made. The nearest approach to it was this: President Lincoln recommended that one of the Twiggs swords of the three given him by Congress before his treason, and captured by me after it, should be by that body voted to me for patriotic services. This recommendation was made by the President without any application on my part to him. It was referred by the Senate to its military committee, at the head of which was Henry Wilson of Massachusetts. He presented the bill, had it referred to his committee, and put it in one of his pigeon-holes, where it has ever since slept the sleep that knows no waking.

We enjoyed one set-off to the clannishness of West Point, and its opposition to every high officer that was not a graduate, and to the intrigues of each to pull the other down and set up himself. This was that the Confederate army enjoyed identically the same sort of setbacks from West Point, and I am inclined to think, in a degree quite as great, if not greater. There was the same opposition to volunteer officers of the higher grades, so that but one or two achieved any distinction or had opportunity so to do except, perhaps, because of political standing or as partisan leaders.

On the Confederate side, Braxton Bragg was at the ear of Davis, and was constantly maligning all the generals, especially Beauregard. Bragg was the counterpart of Halleck on our side who had the same position with Lincoln, and did his duty in the same way with great zeal, energy, and success. Longstreet and Lee were quite continually at variance, and at the close of the war, Mahone was almost the only volunteer general left in high position. His celebrated brigade was the only fighting organization left near Lee at the time he was forced to surrender at Appomattox, some of the other generals having virtually allowed their divisions to disband before the surrender; for while Lee had thirty thousand men when he abandoned the intrenchments of Petersburg on the eighth day of April, he actually surrendered, on the ninth day of April, only eight thousand of his army who gave the parole, the balance having either deserted or been abandoned.

Mahone was a railroad engineer, and held only the rank of brigadier-general, having refused several times promotion as major-general. How much his merit for leadership was recognized by Lee will presently appear. After the retreat from Gettysburg, when his army had reached Virginia, Lee manfully acknowledged that the loss of the campaign was due to his own mistaken strategy of Gettysburg, and fearing that he might have lost the confidence of his army and his people, tendered his resignation of command of the Army of Northern Virginia to Davis, in a private note, recommending that some younger man than himself should be appointed in his stead to be the leader of that army. While Davis undoubtedly — because his views of conducting the army in the field frequently varied from Lee's — would have been glad to accept that resignation, yet he declined to do it.

Lee's social position in Virginia, his family connections, and the love and respect of the people, were all so strong that Davis felt that Lee's resignation accepted would be nearly a death-blow to the Confederacy. Accordingly he returned for answer that the loss of Gettysburg was only one of the accidents of war ; that he saw no occasion for reproach of General Lee, and he begged him to withdraw his resignation. This Lee did, and continued his leadership.

In September, 1863, however, Davis desired Lee to take command of the Western army, and said in effect that his command there would be better than reinforcements by a corps. But Lee was by no means willing to be buried in the West, and Davis, in order to make Lee's position agreeable in the Army of Northern Virginia, sent Longstreet and his corps there instead.

Lee's resignation and what depended thereon was kept a profound secret. It was hardly known to any one, certainly not until long afterwards. When it did come out, however, that Lee had tendered his resignation, recommending a younger officer for the command of the Army of Northern Virginia in his place, there was great curiosity and inquiry as to who that general was.

Of the fact that some younger general was recommended by Lee at the time of the resignation, I have undoubted authority, and if anybody questions it I can make that authority known at any time.

It has come out, however, that Gen. William Mahone was the man recommended by Lee, and the statement is from Lee's own mouth. Since Mahone's change of politics in Virginia it has been most stoutly contradicted. It is but just to Mahone to say that at the time, he was ignorant both of Lee's resignation and of his recommendation.

I present here a fac-simile letter of a gentleman of the highest standing in Virginia which tells the story in such words and with such directness that nobody will have any doubt of the fact. But it

HOTEL CHAMBERLIN.
M°PHERSON SQUARE.

Washington, D.C. March 11ᵗᵏ 1889

My Dear General

It gives me great
pleasures to hand to you a written
statement of a conversation at the
table of General R E Lee which
years ago I stated to your wife
yourself and some twenty gentleman
at your table The occasion
was the first commencement
of washington and Lee University. Gen¹ Wade Hampton
delivered the Address before
the Litterary societies and I
the Address before the Allumni
Gen¹ Lee gave a sort of

HOTEL CHAMBERLIN
McPHERSON SQUARE.

Washington, D.C.   188

state dinners. Thirty gentlemen.
"I think I was the only officer
at the table below the rank of
Colonel. And the honor was accor-
-ded to me because I was the Orator
of the day. After the cloth was
drawn, and the wine began to
circulate some gentleman a
Brigadier from Georgia (I think
it was Gen'l Jackson. from the
lower end of the table asked
Gen'l Lee if he did not think
that Gordon of Georgia had
developed the highest qualities
for command Gen'l with his

HOTEL CHAMBERLIN
McPHERSON SQUARE.

Washington, D.C 188

habitual quiet dignity replied,
where all did so well certainly
it would be invidious and
improper for me to particalourize
Genl Gordon was a brave and
efficient soldier. Then rising
he said gentlemen fill up your
glasses, Etiquette demanded that
this official dinner should be
made in accordance with rank,
gentlemen I propose a toast
which all will drink with
pleasure to the privates of the
Army of Northern Virginia
who I still sometimes think

HOTEL CHAMBERLIN.
McPHERSON SQUARE.

Washington, D.C.   188

came near winning immortal
fame for us. The toast was drunk
standing. After this the conver-
-sation became general and some
one down the table seemed to
be telling a good story. Genl
Hampton sat on the right and
I as orator of day on left of
Lee. Turning to Hampton Genl
Lee said something in a low
tone, I leaned back as I thought
it was possible it might be
something confidential. Laying
his hand upon my knee he said
lean over Major I only wish

HOTEL CHAMBERLIN.
McPHERSON SQUARE.

Washington, D.C. ___188

Hampton and yourself to hear.
Then. "Genl Hampton, in the dark
days which preceded the fall of the
Confederacy. For a good while I
was almost hopeless. and you
know I did not share this poor
life. for I thought it became
me to fall on one of those fields
of glory My artillery was handled
there the Cavalry was in the very
hands, after the death of Stuart
that I preferred to any other.
But I often thought if a stray ball
should carry me off who could
best command the "incomparable

HOTEL CHAMBERLIN,
McPHERSON SQUARE

Washington, D C   188

Infantry of the Army of Northern
Virginia. Of Course I could not
nominate a successor That whole
matter was with in the hands of the
President. But among the younger
men, I thought William Mahone
had developed the highest qualities
for Organization and Command. "

The words were written
down by me that evening and
are in my desk at Ellwood.
I write them now hastily in a
public room But I know they
are accurate. We drifted so
far apart politically and

HOTEL CHAMBERLIN.
ON LAFAYETTE SQUARE

Washington, D.C.   18

I so entirely condemned your policy and methods that I would not give them to The World. Now I cheerfully write them and, as far as I am concerned this may be an open letter, to the World.

Very truly yours

J. Horace Lacy

To General William Mahone.

is so galling to West Point on the rebel side of the house that it has been vehemently denied but never, so far as I can discover, with any evidence to support that denial.

I may not refer further to General Halleck, as he has gone to his own place.

On the 11th of January, 1865, I left my command of the Army of the James, making to my comrades an address which I beg leave here to reproduce : —

HEADQUARTERS DEPARTMENT VIRGINIA AND NORTH CAROLINA,
ARMY OF THE JAMES, Jan. 8, 1865.

SOLDIERS OF THE ARMY OF THE JAMES :

Your commander, relieved by the order of the President, takes leave of you.

Your conduct in the field has extorted praises from the unwilling.

You have endured the privations of the camp and the march without a murmur.

You have never failed in attack when ordered.

You have stormed and carried works deemed impregnable by the enemy.

You have shown the positions to be so by holding them against the fiercest assaults in the attempt to retake them.

Those skilled in war have marvelled at the obstacles overcome by your valor.

Your line of works have excited the wonder of officers of other nations who have come to learn defensive warfare from the monuments of your skilled labor.

Your deeds have rendered your name illustrious.

In after times your general's proudest memory will be to say with you : " I, too, was of the Army of the James."

To share such companionship is pleasure.

To participate in such acts is honor.

To have commanded such an army is GLORY.

No one could yield it without regret.

Knowing your willing obedience to orders, witnessing your ready devotion of your blood in your country's cause, I have been chary of the precious charge confided to me.

I have refused to order the useless sacrifice to the lives of such soldiers, and I am relieved from your command.

The wasted blood of my men does not stain my garments.

For my action I am responsible to God and my country.

To the colored troops of the Army of the James:

In this army you have been treated not as laborers but as soldiers.

You have shown yourselves worthy of the uniform you wear.

The best officers of the Union seek to command you.

Your bravery has won the admiration even of those who would be your masters.

Your patriotism, fidelity, and courage have illustrated the best qualities of manhood.

With the bayonet you have unlocked the iron-barred gates of prejudice, opening new fields of freedom, liberty, and equality of right to yourselves and your race forever.

Comrades of the Army of the James, I bid you farewell! farewell!

BENJ. F. BUTLER,

Major-General Commanding.

H. C. CLARKE, *Captain and A. D. C.*

CHAPTER XIX.

OBSERVATIONS UPON MATTERS CONNECTED WITH THE WAR.

I THINK it is due that some word should be said in particular, before closing this account of my military life, of certain gentlemen of my staff and officers who contributed so largely to any success achieved by me. I think I have sufficiently dealt with those who got in my way.

Gentlemen holding staff positions in the army, and especially at Washington in time of peace, who have been educated at West Point, in the language of General Sherman, "too commonly construe themselves into the *élite*, as made of better clay than the common soldier." I had a few of such detailed to me, but they never stayed long, and I will not trouble myself to speak of them.

My personal staff, that is, my aides-de-camp, I selected from civil life. For my field staff who should have charge of the technical matters of military campaigning, such as chief quartermaster, chief commissary, chief of artillery, chief of ordnance, engineers, surgeons, and inspectors, I took the most experienced and best officers I could get. Gallantly, well, and faithfully did they serve, evincing great ability and entire loyalty to their chief, and there were no better officers or men. But as such staff officers, they had no opportunity to distinguish themselves in their line of duty so as to come into much notice in the course of the history of military campaign, although their services were invaluable.

When I led the First Brigade of Massachusetts troops into Washington in April, 1861, I had but three staff officers. Two of these served only until the 16th of May, and when I was commissioned major-general they left. One of them, Major Haggerty, served with me until I was relieved at New Orleans. I have had occasion to speak of him before, and now have only to add that he was a very able man, and good soldier, sometimes serving as judge advocate general.

When I took command of the Department of New England, I had as assistant adjutant-general and chief of ordnance, Maj. George C. Strong. I have said of him all I could say of any man, during the progress of this work. While I was at home unemployed in 1863, Major Strong's love of battle and hope of glory impelled him not to wait until I could have another appointment, and having been promoted he was sent to Charleston to report to General Gillmore. He was put in command of a brigade and ordered to assault Fort Wagner, where he lost his life by a wound that caused him a lingering and painful illness. Upon my recommendation the President appointed him a major-general, and his commission reached him on his dying bed.

Col. George A. Kensel was my chief of artillery and inspector-general. He was a Kentuckian, having been appointed to West Point by General Breckinridge, but was loyal to the cause. He was one of the young artillery officers who, when I went to Fortress Monroe in 1861, had accepted an appointment made through the kindness of a friend as quartermaster instead of lieutenant of artillery, which was his lineal rank.

Disgusted with his employment in substantially civil affairs, while his comrades were in the field, he applied to me for an appointment on my staff. He went with me to New Orleans, was detailed as chief of ordnance, and served with me through that campaign. He accompanied me to the Army of the James, and served there through the war. A braver or more loyal officer was not in the army. I can give no better illustration of his courage than by a short anecdote. In the movement on Drury's Bluff, which I have hereinbefore described, I had occasion to send an order in writing in great haste by a route which lay between the lines of the two armies where fighting was going on between the Tenth Corps and the enemy. Kensel was sitting beside me as I wrote the order and gave it to one of my staff, saying: "You must ride between the two lines, because that distance will be scarcely a mile. If you go the other road you will be stopped by Proctor's Creek, and have to go around to the ford, and that will take you quite two hours." That aid was Captain Martin, who was a volunteer. I turned to Kensel and said: "My personal staff are all absent as you see. It is very important that that order shall reach Gillmore at once. The chances are very great that Martin will be killed." Tearing the written duplicate from my despatch book, I continued: "Will you please take this order, and follow Martin?" He took it without a word except to say, "Good by, General," and was soon lost to my sight in the fog. Fortunately both orders got through. Kensel died in command of a military post as a major of artillery several years after the war.

My quartermaster was a volunteer, Capt. Paul R. George, of whom I can say no more words of commendation than I have already said. He died in 1864.

My commissary was my brother, of whom I see no occasion to speak further.

My surgeon in this department was my neighbor and family physician, Dr. Gilman Kimball, one of the ablest and most skilful surgeons of our State.

While I was at Annapolis, I found it necessary to establish hospitals, meaning to make an extensive depot hospital for the sick soldiers who would be forwarded to Washington through Annapolis. I called upon the surgeon-general to furnish me a surgeon for that purpose, and was told that none could be spared, and that I must furnish myself. I called upon Doctor Kimball, who put aside his most lucrative practice, and came down there to serve his country. When I left the Department of Annapolis he accompanied me to Fortress Monroe to see to it that my hospitals were properly organized. The army hospitals there, being only for two or at most three companies of regular troops, would not answer for the sick from the ranks of fifteen thousand men. As soon as his work in organizing the hospital service there was fully performed, he returned home to his practice. When I came back to Lowell in command of the Department of New England, as it was known that I should leave that department in the course of a few months, he accepted service again temporarily in order to aid the cause. His services were invaluable to me because he taught me what a hospital should be, and the necessity of my giving active and personal attention to the inspection of my hospitals, and I followed his suggestions in that regard during my whole term of service.

Of my personal staff, Maj. Joseph Bell left his large practice as a lawyer to go with me to the South with the New England division. If I knew any words that I could add to what I have said of him I would say them.

Capt. R. S. Davis, of Boston, was upon my staff, holding the position of assistant adjutant-general of the Department of New England, and went with me to New Orleans. He served through that campaign, joined me in the Department of Virginia and North Carolina, and served until he was relieved late in the summer of 1864 for sickness. He died in China, where he went on a mercantile enterprise.

Another of my volunteer aids who left the law books he was writing to join the service with me, was J. Burnham Kinsman, afterwards brevet major-general. He volunteered without pay and without anything but an acting appointment. He served me as long as I was in the service, and distinguished himself very greatly for gallant conduct. He was appointed by the President as lieutenant-colonel in the regular army, and attached to the staff of General Wool, and by the President's request Wool assigned him to serve on my staff. He was afterwards employed by the Secretary of War, serving him directly upon important matters where great prudence, courage, and discretion were required. For his meritorious services he was promoted to brevet major-general, when Mr. Rawlins, who knew him in the Army of the James, was Secretary of War. It was well deserved, but was not recommended by me, because I had at one time previous to his appointment an idea that my recommendation might do him more harm than good. I have already spoken of his services as I think they deserve to be spoken of.

Another volunteer aid was Lieut. Haswell C. Clarke, of Boston, quite a young man, hardly arrived at his majority. He served with me faithfully and well in the Department of New England, in the Department of the Gulf, and in the Army of the James. A brave and gallant young officer, he did his duty thoroughly and acceptably wherever he was called.

At my request and by the designation of General McClellan,

there was added to my staff at New Orleans as engineer, Gen. Godfrey Weitzel, in commendation of whom as an officer and a loyal friend I can say no more than has been said of him in previous chapters. He also died while serving as brigadier-general in the regular army.

While at New Orleans, Col. J. W. Shaffer, a personal friend of Mr. Lincoln, was detailed to me as chief quartermaster, in which capacity he served upon my staff. He also went with me to the Army of the James, and was there promoted to be chief of my staff. He served as such until he went home in the summer of 1864 suffering with a disease which afterwards caused his death, having been appointed governor of Utah Territory. His services, although not of a character that makes men so distinguished in a campaign as to find a place in history, were of the greatest value in whatever position he found himself.

With Colonel Shaffer there was sent to me Brig.-Gen. J. W. Turner. He had graduated at West Point. He was my chief commissary, and afforded me very great and efficient aid in seeing to the provisioning not only of the army, but of a large portion of the people of New Orleans, including a very great number of dependent negroes. His services were such in his department that personally I had no occasion for thought of any danger that my commissariat would not be ready for any emergency. When Colonel Shaffer left, he acted as my chief of staff. His services were so valuable in the field while serving in the Army of the James that he was promoted to brigadier-general. He afterwards became major-general commanding a division in the Eighteenth Army Corps, and distinguished himself in action on several occasions. He was detailed from Bermuda Hundred to go over with his division to hold the lines while Grant's troops left them to attack the enemy on the occasion of the explosion of the mine. Finding that there was no movement of the enemy toward the point occupied by his troops, he went over and entered the mine after the explosion, when the cavity was filled as if with a swarm of bees by the colored soldiers, and there was no general of division or brigade or field officer in that mine but himself, and he had no business to be there. He was an intelligent and capable military officer, and possessed a further qualification — he was a good business man. After the war was over he went to

Chicago, and established himself in business there. Later he was called to St. Louis, where he was put at the head of public works of that city, and where he now lives with his family deserving many years.

I had another volunteer aid in New Orleans, Capt. John Clark, who acted as assistant commissary. He had been editor, and I think proprietor, of the Boston *Courier*, and when I seized the *Delta* newspaper he and Lieutenant-Colonel Brown, of the Eighth Vermont, volunteered to keep up the publication as a Union journal. They did it with exceeding ability and success, and I have a lively and strong remembrance of the aid they gave me through that newspaper in writing truly the state of things in New Orleans. Captain Clark died soon after the war.

When I got to New Orleans I had not with me a single surgeon who had ever treated a case of yellow fever. I made an appeal to the surgeon-general to send me an army surgeon if he had one who was able to deal with what I looked upon as the most dangerous foe to my army. Through the necessary detentions and delays of official correspondence, it was many weeks before I received a reply, so that I had to make all my dispositions against that enemy before I got any assistance of professional skill. But when it did come it brought Dr. Charles MacCormick. He was a man very considerably advanced in years, who had been a surgeon in the United States Army for quite a long period, and had been stationed at New Orleans during the great epidemic of yellow fever which more than decimated the city in 1853, of which I have spoken. Doctor MacCormick deserves that a book should be written upon his services, for they deserve much more than the brief notice my limits will permit me here to give. He was exceedingly efficient in organizing the hospitals for which I had taken possession of some of the largest buildings in the city, notably the St. Louis Hotel. He gave me great confidence because he entirely approved of what I had done, and relieved me from the load of care and anxiety which was added my labors. He went with me to the Army of the James, and such were his exertions that we had an army in better health than any other army in the field. He continued to serve with me until his own health failed. He died in the city of New York several years after the war. He was one of the truest friends I ever had.

Lieut.-Col. Jonas H. French was also upon my staff for a short time in New Orleans after he had been deprived of his command of the Thirty-First Massachusetts Volunteers by Governor Andrew. When General Shepley was designated by the President as Governor of Louisiana, Lieut.-Col. French was promoted from acting provost marshal on my staff to the post of provost marshal general of the State of Louisiana, and remained in that office when I left New Orleans. To his energy and ability the quiet and good order of the populace of New Orleans may be largely ascribed.

Col. S. H. Stafford, of a New York Regiment, who had been acting as assistant provost marshal, took Colonel French's place on my staff when he was promoted, and showed himself to be a brave, determined, and thorough executive officer who fully executed the duty devolved upon him by all orders. Afterwards he commanded a brigade in Hinks' division of colored troops in the Army of the James. He is not now living.

I had detailed upon my staff Lieut. J. W. Cushing, of the Thirty-First Massachusetts Volunteers, as acting chief quartermaster, and Lieut. James E. Esterbrook, of Worcester, of the Thirtieth Massachusetts, as acting chief commissary, who served until the detail from Washington of Shaffer and Turner.

When I was sent to New Orleans I had three brigadier-generals assigned to me: Gen. J. W. Phelps, Gen. Thomas Williams, and General Sherman. The latter died from heart failure very soon after he joined me.

I had no better soldier or officer, none in whose care I felt any more safe to leave everything in possession, than General Phelps. I had got him his promotion in 1861, and asked to have him transferred to the Army of the Gulf. He had but one fault: he was an anti-slavery man to a degree that utterly unbalanced his judgment. While in command of a portion of the troops on Ship Island in the Gulf of Mexico near the State of Mississippi, he, in the winter of 1861–62, upon his own motion, issued a proclamation of emancipation of the slaves. No notice was taken of it, as it was simply a dead letter. He disciplined his troops very admirably, and upon my arrival in New Orleans, I put him in command of the forces stationed above the city at Carrolton. The history of that command I have already stated. Differing with me on the slavery questions because I held that nothing could be done about freeing the slave, except through the President, he resigned his command and reported to Washington to argue the question with the President, so that I lost him. He is now deceased.

Of General Williams and his services I said all that ever can be said in my general order of notice of his untimely death.

Gen. George F. Shepley was promoted to be brigadier-general and at the same time was appointed Governor of Louisiana.

I would that space permitted me to speak in detail of other officers, regimental commanders, etc. But they made their own mark, especially in the histories of their several regiments, and as I cannot speak of all as I would do, it would seem invidious to mention any.

In November, 1863, when I relieved General Foster in the command of the Department of Virginia and North Carolina, he took his personal staff with him, and the departmental staff reported to me.

Most of my staff at New Orleans whom I have already noticed were assigned to duty, and need not be further mentioned.

Maj. J. L. Stackpole, the judge advocate-general of the Department of Virginia and North Carolina, who had been acting as provost judge, I replaced with Major Bell, and remitted Major Stackpole to his duties as judge advocate-general, in the performance of which I found him one of the most competent officers that I have ever seen filling that position. He was faithful, diligent, and a good lawyer, and he retained his position during my command. He now pursues his profession in the city of Boston, with the esteem of all who know him.

I also found upon the departmental staff Lieut.-Col. Herman Biggs, chief quartermaster, a thoroughly able and efficient officer. I shall never cease to remember with gratitude his great aid in enabling me to make the expedition, of which I have heretofore spoken, up the river with the Army of the James to City Point.

I found Lieut.-Col. John Cassels as provost marshal of the department. I did not reappoint him when I made up my staff.

There are no more arduous duties in the administration of a military department than those devolving upon the provost marshal. He is charged with the arrest of all citizens whose doings make such action necessary, and also to put in close confinement the officers or soldiers whose detention may be ordered. He is charged with the duty of breaking up all irregular places in which any infractions of the law either military or civil are carried on. In short, he is the chief of police of the department, and he is also charged with the prosecution of all civil offences before the provost court. If he is an honest and efficient man that makes him exceedingly obnoxious, so that my experience was that if no complaints were made against a provost marshal he clearly was not doing his duty.

I had scarcely taken possession of my office before the traders, sutlers, liquor dealers, and citizens who had been dealt with before the provost court came flocking in with complaints against Colonel Cassels. He, of course, was an utter stranger to me, and if I put him in charge of the office, it would result in his having in his possession very considerable amounts of money to be accounted for, and I knew bribes would be offered to induce him to wink at all sorts of transgressions. I thought it my duty, therefore, to investigate fully without saying anything to him and even without letting him know that I was investigating him, until I should come to something on which I could base a serious charge. I therefore announced an officer of the Twenty-Seventh Massachusetts as provost marshal, and that sent Colonel Cassels back to his regiment, the Eleventh Pennsylvania Cavalry.

I had brought with me some secret service men on whom I could rely, but who were not announced to be on my staff, or even to be known to me by sight. I had one there before I came, for the purpose of investigating certain matters in regard to the recruitment of negro troops. I investigated every complaint made regarding Cassels that was not utterly frivolous, and I came to the conclusion that these complaints were beyond all question the ebullitions of spleen or hatred. Among other things Cassels was charged with having taken a sum of money from one man, another sum from another, and so on, always for his own use; but by an examination of the records of his office, which had been placed in the hands of the acting provost marshal, I found that in every instance the sums were not only admitted to have been taken, but that he had charged himself with those sums on the books to be turned over on the settlement of his accounts. I finished my examination about 11 o'clock

P. M., on the 8th of December, and sent an orderly to Colonel Cassels' tent with directions that he should report to me forthwith. He immediately reported to me, and I said to him: "You are appointed lieutenant-colonel and aide-de-camp on my staff, and detailed as provost marshal of the department. You will proceed to duty to-morrow morning. I have examined all the complaints against you, and I believe they are all unfounded, and that you are an honest man."

He held that office, and fulfilled its duties to my entire satisfaction so long as I was in command. When I was relieved his accounts and conduct were investigated at great length in the most vindictive manner, but nothing was developed to his discredit.

I ought not to forget the unwearying pains taken to serve me and the faithful endeavor of my two assistant quartermasters, Capt. William H. James at Fortress Monroe, and Capt. George S. Dodge, who was assistant quartermaster during the campaign at Bermuda Hundred. Captain Dodge is deceased. Captain James is an honored business man in Philadelphia.

Lieut. Frederick Martin was a volunteer lieutenant on my staff. For gallantry of conduct as well in New Orleans as in the Army of the James, I promoted him to be aide-de-camp with the rank of captain and had him assigned as commissary of musters, the duties of which he performed to my entire acceptance. I have spoken of Colonel Kensel as having carried a second order through a line of fire on May 16, 1864; Captain Martin was my aid who took the first one.

In the early part of the campaign two very young men came to me with high recommendations. One was Sidney B. DeKay, of New York, whom I accepted as an aid although he had not reached his majority. His services were so energetic and faithful that he remained on my personal staff until the last. After the war was over, a war broke out between Turkey and Greece, and he went to Athens and took a position in the Greek army, serving with great distinction until he received an accidental wound from the falling of a carbine which disabled him from further service. Later he served as assistant district-attorney of the United States of the city of New York, and remained one of my most valued friends until his death, a short time ago.

The other was Mr. John I. Davenport, of Brooklyn, New York, who
came to me as a stenographer.　I soon employed him in ascertaining
the strength of Lee's army, and put him at the head of my Bureau of
Information with the rank of lieutenant, and made him my military
secretary.　His capacity, which he has shown since for many years,
so that he has made a proud name for himself in the service of the
government as chief supervisor of elections in the city of New York
for many years, coupled with his great energy, enabled him to render

JOHN I. DAVENPORT.

almost invaluable service to the country.　I showed his reports of the
condition of Lee's army in our front to General Grant, and after
examining them and comparing them with the information received
from his own source, Grant said : " This is a more accurate roster of the
strength of Lee's army than I believe Lee himself has."　Our strong,
personal friendship, only increasing in strength, remains to this day.
　I have no occasion to remark here upon the good conduct of my
several commanders of corps, divisions, brigades, and regiments of

the Army of the James. I cannot give space to speak of them all as I would wish to do, but that is not necessary, for they made history for themselves wherein their great services appear; and I have mentioned many of them in this, my own history, as it progressed. If I had only had as corps commanders at first, men like those who were my corps commanders at last, and almost without exception their subordinates, the Army of the James would have had a more brilliant story told of the results of their bravery, conduct, and efforts in the service of their country.

By the middle of January, 1865, to Grant and to all who knew the condition of the Confederate army and the impossibility of their recruiting more soldiers, it was evident that Lee must abandon Petersburg and Richmond and take a position further south, coming, if possible, in conjunction with Johnston. It was also apparent that as soon as he began that retreat and could no longer fight behind intrenchments, he would be easily defeated, by reason of the increased morale of our army derived from following him, and by reason of his great want of supplies. As the winter had been a very rainy one, the roads he would have to go over would be almost impassable early in the season; consequently he must wait until milder weather and the drying up of the mud before he could make the move. So confident was Grant of this that early in March he recalled Sheridan with his ten thousand cavalry. Sheridan had been operating in the Shenandoah Valley, and came down toward the north side of the James River so as to join Grant at once with his whole force. As soon as Sheridan's horses had been rested and his army had been refitted, Grant, fearing all the time that Lee would escape him, commenced a series of operations on Lee's right flank to drive him into Richmond and hold all communication on the south side. Hence the battle of Five Forks, which was successful. Lee made a counter attack on Grant's right wing, which was at first quite successful, his lines being broken through the day so that Meade was cut off from his headquarters; but that disaster was soon repaired. From that moment Grant had no further doubt of the end and was very much concerned lest Lee should vacate Petersburg in the night and escape him, of course abandoning Richmond. Grant was being all the time reinforced by troops from the North and other sources, while Lee could get no more reinforcements. This impossibility of obtaining reinforcements led Lee to make a proposition to the Confederate government to arm the slaves as a last resort, but this was rejected.

I had anticipated this condition of want of reinforcements of the Confederacy, and in a conversation with General Grant many months before, I stated to him that Lee could get no more reinforcements unless they should arm the slaves. I had long previously told him that by their conscription they had already robbed the cradle and the grave to get troops, which phrase Grant says in his Memoirs he copied from me.[1]

Although I had no command in the army assigned me and had not asked for any, I retained the full confidence of the President, and from time to time when I happened to be in Washington, where indeed I was much of the time, he talked with me very freely. In those conversations I assured him that it was only a matter of months, if not of weeks, when the question would be before him on what terms a peace could be concluded. He said he cared for but two things : That the power of the United States over its territory should be acknowledged by the several Confederate States, and thus the Union be preserved ; and that his emancipation proclamation should be agreed by the rebels to be the law of the whole land. Beyond these two things, but one question disturbed him, and that would not arise until peace was established. He told me that he had met, in the last of January, the Confederate commissioners who came to Hampton Roads to treat of peace, and that he informed them very distinctly of these terms, and that he stated to them he would substantially leave to them all other terms upon which they could come into the Union and consent to live with us as a part thereof. [2]

---

[1] Personal Memoirs of U. S. Grant, Vol. II., p. 435.

[2] His proposition made to the rebel commissioners at Hampton Roads, as Grant reports it, (Personal Memoirs of U. S. Grant, Vol. II., pp. 422, 423), was that "there would be no use in entering into any negotiations unless they would recognize, first, that the Union on a whole must be forever preserved, and, second, that slavery must be abolished. If they were willing to concede these two points, then he was ready to enter into negotiations, and was almost willing to hand them a blank sheet of paper with his signature attached, for them to fill in the terms upon which they were willing to live with us in the Union and be one people."

These terms got into the newspapers in a more or less exaggerated form, and caused a great deal of excitement in the North. They were looked upon as being a giving up of the war in this, that these men who had fought us for four years, and whom we had conquered, should then say upon what terms they would come and live with us as one people (i.e., the terms upon which they would permit us to live with them as one people), so that many, many harsh things were said against Lincoln in the press of the country, and among the people, especially the radical portion who were now in majority, which pained him very much.

A conversation was held between us after the negotiations had failed at Hampton Roads, and in the course of the conversation he said to me : —

"But what shall we do with the negroes after they are free ? I can hardly believe that the South and North can live in peace, unless we can get rid of the negroes. Certainly they cannot if we don't get rid of the negroes whom we have armed and disciplined and who have fought with us, to the amount, I believe, of some one hundred and fifty thousand men. I believe that it would be better to export them all to some fertile country with a good climate, which they could have to themselves.

"You have been a stanch friend of the race from the time you first advised me to enlist them at New Orleans. You have had a good deal of experience in moving bodies of men by water,— your movement up the James was a magnificent one. Now, we shall have no use for our very large navy ; what, then, are our difficulties in sending all the blacks away ?

"If these black soldiers of ours go back to the South I am afraid that they will be but little better off with their masters than they were before, and yet they will be free men. I fear a race war, and it will be at least a guerilla war because we have taught these men how to fight. All the arms of the South are now in the hands of their troops, and when we capture them we of course will take their arms. There are plenty of men in the North who will furnish the negroes with arms if there is any oppression of them by their late masters.

"I wish you would carefully examine the question and give me your views upon it and go into the figures, as you did before in some degree, so as to show whether the negroes can be exported. I wish also you would give me any views that you have as to how to deal with the negro troops after the war. Some people think that we shall have trouble with our white troops after they are disbanded, but I don't anticipate anything of that sort, for all the intelligent men among them were good citizens or they would not have been good soldiers. But the question of the colored troops troubles me exceedingly. I wish you would do this as soon as you can, because I am to go down to City Point shortly and may meet negotiators for peace there, and I may want to talk this matter over with General Grant if he isn't too busy."

I said: "I will go over this matter with all diligence and tell you my conclusions as soon as I can."

The second day after that, I called early in the morning and said: "Mr. President, I have gone very carefully over my calculations as to the power of the country to export the negroes of the South, and I assure you that using all your naval vessels and all the merchant marine fit to cross the seas with safety, it will be impossible for you to transport them to the nearest place that can be found fit for them,— and that is the Island of San Domingo,— half as fast as negro children will be born here."

"I am afraid you are right, General," was his answer; "but have you thought what we shall do with the negro soldiers?"

I said: "I have formulated a scheme which I will suggest to you, Mr. President. We have now enlisted one hundred and fifty thousand negro troops, more or less, infantry, cavalry, and artillery. They were enlisted for three years or for the war. We did not commence enlisting them in any numbers until the latter part of 1863 and in 1864. I assume that they have a year at least on an average to serve, and some of them two to three years. We have arms, equipment, clothing, and military material and everything necessary for three hundred thousand troops for five years. Until the war is declared ended by official proclamation, which cannot be done for some very considerable time, they can be ordered to serve wherever the commander-in-chief may direct.

"Now I have had some experience in digging canals. The reason why my canal, which was well dug, did not succeed you know. My experience during the war has shown me that the army organization is one of the very best for digging. Indeed, many of the troops have spent a large portion of their time in digging in forts and intrenchments, and especially the negroes, for they were always put into the work when possible. The United States wants a ship canal across the Isthmus of Darien at some proper and convenient point. Now, I know of a concession made by the United States of Colombia of a strip thirty miles wide across the Isthmus for that purpose. I have the confidence of the negroes. If you will put me in command of them, I will take them down there and dig the canal. It will cost the United States nothing but their pay, the clothing that they wear will be otherwise eaten by the moths, the arms are of no worth, as we have

EMANCIPATION PROCLAMATION.

so many of them in excess ; the wagons and equipments will otherwise rust out. I should set one third of them to digging. I should
set another third to building the proper buildings for shelter and the
rest to planting the ground and raising food. They will hardly need
supplies from the government beyond the first season, having vege-
table supplies which they will raise and which will be best for their
health. After we get ourselves established we will petition Congress
under your recommendation to send down to us our wives and children. You need not send down anybody to guard us, because if
fifty thousand well-equipped men cannot take care of ourselves
against anybody who would attack us in that neighborhood, we are
not fit to go there. We shall thus form a colony there which will
protect the canal and the interests of the United States against the
world, and at least we shall protect the country from the guerilla warfare of the negro troops until the danger from it is over."

He reflected a while, having given the matter his serious attention,
and then spoke up, using his favorite phrase : " There is meat in
that, General Butler ; there is meat in that. But how will it affect
our foreign relations ? I want you to go and talk it over with Mr.
Seward and get his objections, if he has any, and see how you can
answer them. There is no special hurry about that, however. I
will think it over, but nothing had better be said upon it which will
get outside."

" Well, then, Mr. President," I said, " I will take time to elaborate
my proposition carefully in writing before I present it to Mr. Seward."

I bowed and retired, and that was the last interview I ever had
with Abraham Lincoln.

Some days afterwards I called at Mr. Seward's office, reaching it,
as near as I can remember, about two o'clock in the afternoon. He
promptly and graciously received me, and I stated to him that I came
to see him at the request of the President, to place before him a plan
that I had given to the President for disposing of the negro troops.

" Ah," he said, " General, I should be very glad to hear it. I
know Mr. Lincoln's anxiety upon that question, for he has expressed
it to me often, and I see no answer to his trouble. But you must
excuse me this afternoon ; it is mail day, as we say in the department, and I have got some important letters to write so that they
may reach New York to-morrow morning. Come and take an early

dinner with me at six o'clock, and after dinner we will discuss the matter at our cigars."

Shortly before six o'clock, however, as he was returning from his drive, he was thrown from his carriage by his horses becoming frightened and running away, and was so seriously injured that his life was despaired of. He lay on his sick-bed until the 14th of April, when Lincoln was assassinated, and he himself was so brutally assaulted that he was detained in bed for many weeks afterwards.

Meantime, Mr. Lincoln had gone to City Point and remained absent several days, returning only to meet the assassin's pistol.

On the night of the 14th of April, I took the train at Washington for New York, and in the morning met in the train the newspapers announcing the assassination. On the night of April 16 I returned to Washington in order to be present to give any assistance in this crisis of the country.

I remained in Washington for some time in conference with Mr. Stanton, who was the moving spirit of that day, and with President Johnson. Previous to this time I had had no special relation with Johnson, but the fact that his oft-repeated declarations upon taking the presidential office, that the Rebellion must be subjugated, and the traitors must take back seats, were in the line of my own thought, brought me into conference with him. I believed those were his true views of the situation and that he thought the Rebellion ought to end, as it should have, in subjugation, so that all the Confederate State governments should be wiped out as well as the Confederate government. The governments of those States were part and parcel of the Confederacy and should, in my view, have been entirely obliterated. I thought enough of the army should be retained to provide a stable military government for the South until the white men should be taught what loyalty to the Union was, and I believed that the negroes should be taught what their position as citizens was before the right of suffrage should be accorded to them. I advised and so urged that the States in rebellion should be divided into territories held under military control for a sufficient length of time to teach them that the lost cause and the lost Confederation was utterly obliterated and to be forgotten. I advised that those territories should be given specific names. For instance, Virginia should be the territory of Potomac; North Carolina, the territory of Cape

Fear; South Carolina, Georgia, and Florida, the territory of Jackson; Louisiana, the territory of Jefferson; Texas, the territory of Houston, and Arkansas, the territory of Lincoln. I believed that the lines of those territories should be so drawn as to cut up the boundaries of the original States so that there should be nothing of State pride left. By their proceedings the people of these States had forfeited all honorable mention, and when they should be fit to come back into the Union,— which they would have been at an early day,— they should come in with the boundaries and names given, and that would have blotted out forever all brotherhood of Confederation against the United States.

I would have confiscated the real estate of all those who had voluntarily taken an active part in the Rebellion. I would have permitted all to run away who desired to and expatriate themselves as they had tried to do by bloody war,— and some of them by so going away justified the propriety of my suggestion. Their lands so forfeited I would have divided among the private soldiers of the army, to be theirs at the end of five years of occupation.

The terms of surrender of Johnston's army agreed to by Sherman[1] I would have revoked, as President Johnson did with the advice of his Cabinet, but I should not have advised that Halleck be sent down to violate a truce, as was done, because that was breaking faith. But there was a justification for the action of Johnson and his Cabinet in going so far as they did. I know the information upon which they acted. They were informed of the fact that Johnston called to his assistance the cabinet of Jeff Davis to draw those terms of surrender, and they were drawn by Mr. Reagan, one of the members of Davis' cabinet. As evidence, fac-simile of them is produced on the next three pages by courtesy of Brev. Brig.-Gen. H. V. Boynton.

It is true Sherman does not copy Reagan's words exactly, but he copies his paper so far as the substance is concerned, wording it differently so as to make it his own, or, as Johnston says, to make it fuller, and he adds that Sherman wrote his copy with Reagan's before him. These terms had been submitted to Davis and his cabinet, and they were of the unanimous opinion that such terms would restore State governments to power and give the Confederacy a chance for existence. Especially would they save slavery, because when the

[1] See Appendix No. 147.

[Fac-simile of the original draft of Sherman's terms with Johnston, as drawn by John H. Reagan, the Confederate Postmaster-General.]

As the avowed motive of the government of the United States for the prosecution of the existing war with the Confederate States, is to secure a re-union of all the States under one common ~~government~~, and as ~~both~~ ~~our~~ wisdom and sound policy alike require that a common government should rest on the consent and be supported by the affections of all the people who compose it, now in order to ascertain whether it be practicable to put an end to the existing war and to the consequent distruction of life and property, having in view the correspondence and conversation which has recently taken place between

Major General W. T. Sherman
and myself, I propose the
following points as a basis
of pacification.—

1st The disbanding of the Military
forces of the Confederacy; and

2nd The recognition of the constitution and authority of
the government of the United
States, on the following conditions

3rd The preservation and continuance of the existing State
governments.

4th The preservation to the people
of all the political rights and
rights of person and property
secured to them by the constitution of the United States and
of their several States.

5th Freedom from future pros
ecution or penalties for their
participation in the present
war

6th Agreement to a general suspension of hostilities pending these negociations.

General Johnston will see that the accompanying memorandum omits all reference to details, and to the necessary action of the States & the preliminary reference of the proposition to General Grant for his consent to the suspension of hostilities, and to the government of the United States for its action. He will also see that I have modified the 1st article, according to his suggestion, by omitting the reference to the consent of the President of the Confederate States, and to his employing his good offices to secure the acquiescence of the several States to this scheme of adjustment and pacification. This may be done at a proper subsequent time. –

John H. Reagan

April 17th /65.

Confederate State governments were once restored to power then they could establish slavery in their several States, and under the Constitution, as it then stood, the United States could not abolish it.

President Johnson and his Cabinet understood that there was some agreement expressed or implied among the leading officers of Sherman's army whom he had called together in conference, that the army should sustain these terms. They also knew that a paper had been circulated among the commanders making a closer union upon that subject. They further knew the obstinacy of Sherman in sustaining his opinions, and they feared this. Indeed, they looked upon it as almost treasonable in intent, which I did not. They knew also what is disclosed in the agreement, namely, that Sherman proposed to his leading officers, and they agreed to it, that a ship should be provided at Charleston for the escape from the country of Davis and such of his cabinet and others as chose to go with him.

Now Davis was intent upon getting to Texas and there making new headway against the United States, and he was so far committed to the plan that after the surrender of the army he made his flight in order to get to a vessel on the Florida coast and sail for Texas, and there, west of the Mississippi, to continue to prosecute the war.

They also felt it important to take away the command of his army from Sherman, and they were justified in coming to that conclusion, certainly, because Sherman had written that if the government should undertake to break the truce with Johnston that he had declared, he would resist it. That was in his official report to Grant, and when Grant asked him to change it, saying that he thought that language was unnecessary, Sherman said: "He [Halleck] knew I was bound in honor to defend and maintain my own truce and pledge of faith *even at the cost of many lives.*"

I insert here the reasons given by the authorities at Washington for rejecting the convention of Sherman and Johnston which, as I have said, was unanimously accepted by the rebel cabinet, and the rejection by one cabinet and the acceptance by the other arrived at Raleigh on the same day, and before they had heard of the assassination of Lincoln :—

First. It was an exercise of authority not vested in General Sherman, and on its face shows that both he and Johnston knew that General Sherman had no authority to enter into any such arrangement.

Second. It was an acknowledgment of the rebel government.

Third. It is understood to re-establish rebel State governments that had been overthrown at the sacrifice of many thousands of loyal lives and immense treasure, and placed arms and munitions of war in the hands of rebels at their respective capitals, which might be used as soon as the armies of the United States were disbanded, and used to conquer and subdue loyal States.

Fourth. By the restoration of the rebel authority in their respective States, they would be enabled to re-establish slavery.

Fifth. It might furnish a ground of responsibility by the Federal Government to pay the rebel debt, and certainly subjects loyal citizens of the rebel States to debts contracted by rebels in the name of the States.

Sixth. It put in dispute the existence of loyal State governments, and the new State of West Virginia, which had been recognized by every department of the United States Government.

Seventh. It practically abolished the confiscation laws, and relieved rebels of every degree who had slaughtered our people, from all pains and penalties for their crimes.

Eighth. It gave terms that had been deliberately, repeatedly, and solemnly rejected by President Lincoln, and better terms than the rebels had ever asked in their most prosperous condition.

Ninth. It formed no basis of true and lasting peace, but relieved the rebels from the pressure of our victories, and left them in condition to renew their effort to overthrow the United States Government and subdue the loyal States, whenever their strength was recruited, and any opportunity should offer.

Sherman believed that the terms would be accepted as those of a military convention which could not well be disregarded; and in his letter to Johnston of April 21, 1864, he says:—

Although strictly speaking, this is no subject of a military convention, yet I am honestly convinced that our simple declaration of a result will be accepted as good as law everywhere. Of course, I have not a single word from Washington on this or any other point of our agreement, but I know the effect of such a step by us will be universally accepted.

I have put forward these facts because I think they justify the President and Secretary of War in their action, and in some degree excuse General Sherman by taking away implications of bad motives. I do this under some little pressure of conviction against him, because, as has been seen, my terms of acceptance and capitulation would have been very different from his. And although subsequent events have shown me that the States have got together again never to be disunited, yet I think we should have much sooner come together and without the harshness of feeling which has existed so long between the North and the South, and without the horrible butcheries of the negroes that have taken place. For the two races of the South have not got together, and I feel that there is great danger they will not do so save by another conflict of arms.

After the capture of Jefferson Davis *en route* across the Mississippi to carry on the war, he was held in close confinement for almost two years in Fortress Monroe and a part of the time in irons. Although an "outlaw," I have always regretted this, for the chains were not necessary for his safe keeping, and I have a horror of punishing men before they are convicted either by imprisonment or by the enormous bail imposed by some foolish judges of the lower order, not as a means of restraining the prisoner, but by way of expressing their horror of the crime with which he is charged. I do not know how far I should have been stirred in the direction of putting Davis in chains had I stood beside the death-bed of Mr. Lincoln as did Stanton, who fully believed for months that Davis incited the crime, which beyond all controversy now was not the fact.

While President Johnson held to the opinions originally expressed that traitors must take back seats and be punished, and while he had Davis in custody and the general impression of the people of the North was that Davis was implicated immediately or remotely in the fact of Lincoln's death, the President was much embarrassed as to what he should do with Davis and in what manner he should be tried. His acts of treason had all been committed in the Southern States and by the Constitution he must be tried, if tried by a civil court, by a jury of the vicinage of those acts. There certainly could not be a jury got in those States fairly impanelled, some of whom would not have been of his political faith, and interference with the selection of the jury by the prosecutor or otherwise was of all things the most to be condemned.

Mr. Johnson, on the recommendation of Senator Wade, who at the first of his administration was his warmest supporter, but when Johnson changed became one of his bitterest foes, sent for me as a lawyer to consult with him on this question. We talked over the difficulties of this position and the effect. As it would not do to try Mr. Davis by a negro jury in Virginia, and as such a trial, continuing perhaps at great length and occupying the public mind, might cause great bitterness of feeling especially in the South, he asked me if I could devise a way in which it might be best legally brought to trial so as to give him a fair trial, and requested that I should give some attention to that subject.

After reflection and examination of the subject, I suggested to him that this might be done: Davis, while making his escape, was captured as a prisoner of war. He was confined in Fortress Monroe, a garrisoned fort of the United States in the military district of Virginia, where his criminal acts, if any, had been perpetrated, then and ever afterwards under martial law. As the war still existed, the President as commander-in-chief might call a military commission in due form to advise him what should be done in regard to the offences of Mr. Davis against the Constitution and laws both civil and military. That commission should be composed of five, seven, or nine, of the major-generals in the army, to be selected by the President, to pass upon the facts and give him advice as to what he should do. This is all that a military commission can do, and is what was done in the case of Major André, a captured prisoner of war in the Revolution, the commission in his case being headed by General Lafayette. And as to the conduct of such a commission on the trial, I supposed that the fact of my being the senior major-general of the army might put me at the head of it. If so, I should conduct it substantially in this way: Charges should be preferred against Mr. Davis, of committing treason in carrying on war against the United States in the district of Virginia, and the overt acts alleged against him should be his reviewing of troops in arms against the United States and giving orders to them in person as the commander in that district. The proof of those facts would be easy and certain even if they were denied. The other fact necessary for a conviction would be his oath of office as Secretary of War of the United States wherein he had sworn to bear true faith and allegiance to the Constitution of the United States.

I assumed that when Mr. Davis was brought before that commission duly convened under proper orders, and allowed counsel of his own selection, the first thing that would be set up would be the objections to the jurisdiction of the military tribunal.

To that the tribunal should answer that being ordered there by the President of the United States to do what they were doing, they were not at liberty to disobey the orders of the commander-in-chief.

That the next thing that would be set up would be the legal existence of the Confederate government, and the rights of the State to secede, and his acting in conformity with the directions of his own State after secession.

To that it should be answered : " All of us sitting here have fought four years to decide those questions in the negative, and therefore it would be useless to have them argued here.

" In answer to the charges preferred against you, do you wish to deny the facts to be true as set out therein ? If you do you are at liberty to call for proofs."

I assumed that he would not deny any of the facts. If he did they could be established in an hour's time.

Then he should be asked : " Have you any further facts to set up in justification of your action thus proved? If so, let your witnesses be called." His witnesses having been heard, the commission would order him to proceed with his defence.

After the hearing the commission would order the prisoner to be remanded and would enter into consultation. I assumed that the result would be, that we should come to the conclusion to advise the President that he was guilty of the acts alleged against him, and that he would then be called before the commission and informed of the conclusions of the commission substantially in the following form : " After considering your case the commission will advise the President and Commander-in-Chief that you are guilty of the treasonable acts alleged against you in the manner and form in which they are set forth, and will advise that he should proceed with your execution by hanging on a day to be by him fixed. But the commission is not insensible that you have raised some very important questions of law, and we wish to do everything we can to give you the advantage of them by a decision of the highest tribunal. We therefore notify you that we shall advise the executive to give time in which all that has been done here can be brought before the Supreme Court of the United States in some proper manner, of which there are several, concerning which your learned counsel will instruct you. And if that Court shall decide any one of the questions that you have raised here in your favor, or that in anything this commission has over-stepped its power in doing any act or omitting to do anything which it should have done according to its powers and duty, so that your trial has not been a fair and just one according to military law and usage, the President will be advised in any such case that you be discharged and go of these accusations without day, and if he deem it expedient that he grant you executive clemency."

I said : " If that is done in due order, Mr. President, no man will say that Davis has not had a fair trial, and you will have referred the question of his guilt to the highest court of the country and will be at liberty to act at your discretion under the best guides you have. At any rate you will have lifted the burden of this case from yourself to the courts."

The President said that he thought well of this plan and would take it into consideration.

Soon after this he began to waver in his determination that treason should be punished and traitors take back seats, and the commission was never called together. I understood that Mr. Secretary Welles alone of the Cabinet objected to my plan and said the trial must be by jury under the Constitution.

CHAPTER XX.

CONGRESSMAN AND GOVERNOR.

IN 1863 I provided myself with a piece of land on Cape Ann, on the northeast coast of Massachusetts, for a summer home for myself and family. I pitched my tent on the southerly side of it next to Ipswich Bay, a beautiful and picturesque piece of water, where the sunsets are equal to those of the Bay of Naples. With my two boys and their tutor I established myself in this tent on the beach as a seashore home. We all neglected that residence somewhat in 1864, but then we were occupying a tent with the Army of the James in Virginia. In the summer of 1865 we were on Cape Ann again, where we spent a very delightful season in sailing and fishing, and the full enjoyment of a free life. This residence was about forty miles from my home at Lowell, and outside of the congressional district in which that city is situated. When autumn came we struck the tent, and afterwards I spent the winter at Washington before the courts there. In 1866 we returned to our tent, and in fishing and fowling spent another summer delightfully. That fall came the election for representatives to Congress.

I had no wish or desire to antagonize the sitting member from the Lowell district, the Hon. George S. Boutwell, in his re-election. But the Hon. John B. Alley, who then represented the district where my tent was, familiarly known in Massachusetts as the Essex district, informed me that he did not desire to be a candidate again, and asked me if I would like to succeed him. Reflecting upon the matter, and feeling a little curiosity to know whether I could be elected in a district where I was only a carpet-bagger, I said I would try it.

The convention was called, and without any special effort I was nominated. There was a large Republican majority in that district, so that, in spite of the carpet-bagism, I was elected to Congress while I lived in the tent on the beach. Appeal was made to the executive that the certificate of my election should be withheld because I was not a resident of that district. That, I answered, was nobody's business but the electors', and upon that question nobody could decide but the House of Representatives. More than that, there was no constitutional inhibition upon any citizen of the State being elected to Congress to represent any part of the State. So I got my certificate in due form, and entered Congress in 1867.

The Hon. Schuyler Colfax was elected speaker oı the House. I was put upon the committee on appropriations, and devoted myself to the duties of that committee with great diligence during the Congress. I also gave attention to the current business of the House, receiving perhaps more attention from the House than is usually accorded to a new member.

My attention was very early called to two great matters: First, whether the bonds of the United States should be paid in gold and silver in preference to the other debts of the United States. Second, what were the legal tender notes of the United States; were they constitutional currency, money, or were they only promises to pay?

I early took the proposition that there was no difference between the legal tender notes of the United States and gold and silver as money. The proposition of the bondholders that their debts against the United States were more sacred than any other, and that they should be paid in specie while the pensions and other just debts of the United States were not to be so paid, I combatted and resisted. But there were more bondholders in Congress than a majority of each House, and they naturally had their way.

I urged that the greenbacks were constitutional currency of the United States, and therefore the lawful money of the United States. Upon this question controversy arose, and it was discussed in Congress and the newspapers in the bitterest manner. The legal tender notes were called "rag-baby currency"; it was said that no honest man could stand by it as money; that they were forced loans, broken promises to pay; and that banknotes should be substituted for them, in other words, that the promise of a national bank to pay a given sum was better than the promise of the United States, when all that made a national banknote worth a dollar was, that it was endorsed by the United States to be redeemed in legal tender notes. It was claimed that the only authority for issuing such notes was the war power under the Constitution, and that all that were issued during times of peace were simply valueless and would be so held by the Supreme Court. The contest about the currency lasted during my whole congressional life.

Immediately there came a division in my congressional district upon these questions. I proclaimed myself there and everywhere a greenbacker, and that term was applied to me everywhere as the last term of ignominy. The banking interests organized a split in the Republican party. The Democrats had quite a following there, and it was thought better to have a Democrat elected by withdrawing the Republican votes from myself than to have so pestilent a greenbacker represent that solid old Republican district in Congress.

Therefore, Mr. Richard H. Dana, Jr., a gentleman of very respectable talents indeed and of considerable learning, and one who prided himself on his ancestry, was procured to run against me. He was supplied with money for the purposes of an electioneering campaign, and used it with great liberality. We canvassed the district, but not together, but we answered each other's speeches on alternate nights to different audiences. The people gathered around me; the bondholders gathered around him. It was evident that if he could not get the people away from me his votes would be scarce. He himself claimed to be of the aristocratic class in Massachusetts, and he attempted in his speeches to put himself on a level with the common people for the purpose of getting their votes, and his efforts afforded me infinite amusement as I replied to him.

He went among the workingmen of Lynn, who are almost all shoemakers, and showed how well he knew the manner in which people liked to be approached by those who seek their votes. He undertook to answer a charge made against him of being an aristocrat and wearing white gloves and holding himself apart and above the people. He laid himself out in the speech in which he did this, and it was the most amusing one I ever read. He said in substance: —

Fellow-citizens, I am accused of being an aristocrat. It is said that I wear white gloves. Well, I shall have to plead guilty to that last charge. I do wear white gloves for the purposes of society. You are told that I go about dressed in a very expensive, cleanly manner. I assure you, fellow-citizens, that when I was a young man, and was a sailor before the mast on the coast of California, it became a part of my labors to carry raw-hides down the banks to the sea, and wash them, and put them on board the vessel, and I had to put them in a pit to do so, and when I was washing them and stamping out the filth, I assure you, fellow-citizens, I was as dirty as any of you. But how does my opponent live? If you will come down to my cottage at Manchester-by-the-Sea and visit me, I will take you in my one-horse wagon and drive you around the town and show you our beaches, which are a very pleasant sight, my friends; but as we are riding along over our seashore roads we will hear a noise behind us and turning around see a carriage with two or four horses driven at full speed and with perhaps out-riders on horseback, and it will come dashing by us covering us with dust, and in that carriage will be my opponent.

The next evening, before another audience, it came my turn. I said something like this: —

My neighbors and friends! My opponent last night in defending himself from the accusation of being an aristocrat, admitted to you among other things that he wore gloves for the purposes of society. Now, I want to say to you that I wear gloves as well as my opponent, but I wear them to keep my hands warm, and I advise you to do the same. As to the averment that it is necessary to be dirty in order to get to be your equal, I assure you I shall not have to get into a manure pit to be fit to associate with you, but simply be a respectable, well-clad, decent American citizen, who knows that one man who behaves well and does his duty to his country and his family is as good as another. As to horses, fellow-citizens, when I came down here into this district from Lowell, where I used to live, I brought my horses with me, and I thought I had a good span; but when I got among you I found that my constituents had better horses, and I proposed to get as good a pair as I could, and I have got a good pair, and if you will come down and ride with me I assure you we won't take anybody's dust.

I instance this as some of the amenities of the stump speaking of the campaign.

Mr. Dana was beaten out of sight. When the next elections came I supposed the contest would be given up. At least, I was so assured by the Republican State Committee, and as the Republican National Committee wanted my services in Indiana, and promised to

VIEWS AT GENERAL BUTLER'S HOME AT LOWELL. LIBRARY.

take care of my district, I spent many weeks in the Western States. I spoke on the platform there and made a great many personal friends whether I made any Republican votes or not. But I returned only to find that in the meantime my district had been stolen away from me. This was in the year 1874, the off congressional year. It was the year of the first congressional election after the inauguration of the President, and according to the almost universal law the administration was beaten, and there was an opposition majority in the House, many of the congressional districts having changed from the Republican to the Democratic party.

My friends were very much more chagrined than myself. They gathered around me and said they would see that I was nominated and elected from that district the next time beyond all dispute. "No, gentlemen," said I, "I am very much obliged to you for all you have done for me, but I would not represent this district again if I could have every vote cast in my favor. I have made your district of some consequence in the Congress of the United States, and I now propose to let it take care of itself. But I am going to be a candidate for the next Congress from the district where I have always lived, man and boy, to see whether they will take me after my apparent desertion here."

At the proper time the canvass was opened, and I was regularly nominated in the Republican convention by a fairly counted majority of votes. Whereupon up started the Hon. Ebenezer Rockwood Hoar, who had been an office-holder nearly all his life, and wanted to be the rest of his life by getting Grant to appoint him as associate justice of the Supreme Court of the United States, while he was attorney-general, but whose confirmation for reasons affected by public policy and private wishes I had caused to be rejected by the Senate. Mr. Hoar thought this election would be a good time to revenge himself upon me. There was a very popular Democratic friend of mine running against me, who had every element to draw to him the strength of his party. So Mr. Hoar called together some of his friends in a Boston hotel and had himself nominated as the bolting candidate of the Republican party. He had before been elected to Congress in that district or perhaps he might have succeeded in beating me. But my constituents knew him too well, as they had had enough of him.

He announced himself in a speech which was very bitter and derisive towards me. Of course it was published and circulated. In answer to it I sat down and wrote him a letter which I regret I cannot spare the space to reproduce here as an exhibit of what can be done to a political opponent when a man of any resources sets himself earnestly at work to do it.

Harvard College was called upon to do missionary work in my district to push Mr. Hoar, who was one of its fellows. Money was forthcoming, as it usually is when that class of people undertakes to influence and control the elective franchise.

I had substantially none of the Republican orators of the day with me because they were all busy trying to elect Mr. Hayes as President. The result followed that while Mr. Hayes got a very large vote, Mr. Tarbox as my congressional Democratic opponent got also a very large vote. But my self-constituted opponent, Mr. Hoar, got hardly enough votes in the district where he lived to count for mile-stones.

With that term ended my congressional career, and I thought, as I had given ten years to the country in Congress, I had done all that should be required of me.

But to return to my position in Congress. In 1867 the question of the impeachment of Andrew Johnson began to be discussed. Indeed, its discussion was in large part rendered possible by his performances in a western tour in advocacy of his own re-election. They disgusted everybody. Meanwhile Johnson undertook to quarrel with Stanton and depose him as Secretary of War. Congress resisted that, and Stanton stuck to his office. His efforts to remove Stanton caused a resolution for Johnson's impeachment to pass through the House of Representatives by a large majority. The ablest men of the house, barring myself, were elected on the board of managers to present and advocate articles of impeachment to the Senate.

I did not quite agree to the articles presented or to the doctrines which were the guides by which they were presented. A great many men in and out of Congress, especially college professors, who always claim to know more about free trade and government than any practical man in the country, held that "high crimes and misdemeanors" named in the Constitution must be some crimes that were known in the catalogue of offences punishable by imprisonment or penalties, and that the President could not be impeached unless it could be shown that he had done something for which he might be brought before a court and indicted and sentenced to pay a fine at least.

Let me illustrate: The President in their view could be impeached for stealing a chicken, because there is a penalty attached to that by the law; but if he broke his constitutional obligations to his country in any form however gross, an offence not punishable by law, he could not be impeached. Many articles were written to establish this doctrine.

I held entirely different opinions. I believed that the framers of the Constitution, knowing full well the parliamentary and common law of England, which permitted the impeachment of any high officer for any misdemeanor in office or any act detrimental to the crown or country, had with that same view put the words "high crimes and misdemeanors" into our fundamental law wholly regardless of technicalities, so long as these offences were such as would affect the dignity and purity of conduct in office. When the board of managers met, Thaddeus Stevens, of Pennsylvania, the "great commoner," as he was styled, wished to be chosen chairman of the board as he had drawn up one of the principal articles of impeachment. While he was a very great man he was very erratic, and the majority of the board was in favor of the appointment of the Hon. Geo. S. Boutwell, of Massachusetts, afterwards Secretary of the Treasury, or of the Hon. John A. Bingham, of Ohio. And I suppose it is no harm to state at this day that considerable acrimony arose between the managers on the subject. I took no part in this because I was desirous of having my own place in the first presentation of the case to the Senate. This would insure my putting the evidence before the Senate in the trial.

The House insisted upon immediate prosecution. We had but three days then in which to get our case ready and prepare the opening arguments for its presentation before the highest court of justice in the land. We spent most of the morning over the question of selecting the chief manager, in selecting the Hon. Thaddeus Stevens chairman of the board, who was to make the closing argument in behalf of the House. That having been settled, I said: "But who is to make the opening argument, and put the case in form for presentation in the

Senate. There are less than three days in which to prepare it. Who is anxious for that place?" There were not many candidates for that labor and I said: "Very well; I suppose as usual the opening of the case will fall upon the youngest counsel, and that is myself." The members of the board unanimously said: "Will you undertake it?" "Yes, if the board desires it, and no one else will take it, I will." It was agreed upon that I should prepare the case and make the opening argument, and I thought that it would not be of much consequence after that was done who did the rest. And thus I became the leading figure of the impeachment, for better or worse.

The three days devoted to the preparation of this case were three of the hardest labor of my life. Of those three days I used only nine hours to sleep, and I was working under many disadvantages. But I had a corps of faithful stenographers around me, and, fortunately, the Hon. William Lawrence, of Ohio, a man of a good deal of learning and industry, assisted me in getting together all the legal authorities bearing upon the subject. I was so sure when I came away from home that there would be an impeachment during that session that I took to Washington with me my copy of the English state trials so as to have them handy, and they were of great service to me.

No member of the board of managers called upon me to offer any aid, although Governor Boutwell did call in towards the night of the third day to inquire how I was getting along in the work, and whether it would be necessary to move the Senate for a postponement. "By no means," said I, "you will remember that we promised the Senate we would be ready without any delay, when we were discussing the fixing of the time for the trial."

Another great difficulty was the crowd of newspaper men who were trying to get at me and at my speech which was to be printed at the government printing-office before its delivery. Hundreds of dollars were offered to get a copy of it. But with the aid of my private secretary we devised means by which it could be kept away from everybody except those who worked on it and put it together. It was put in type in disconnected parts, no one part being complete in itself or having anything to do apparently with the others, there being no connection between them. But the key to the connection was held by us, so that at last when the proofs were completed they were pasted together in their proper and consecutive order. While it was being printed, one of my friends was standing beside the matter in the printing-office from the time it was put on the press until every copy printed had been delivered to him and the type had been distributed.

I was ready at the appointed hour. When I entered the Senate chamber from the vice-president's room the scene was almost appalling to one who had to address such an audience. The floor of the · Senate chamber was filled because the House attended in committee of the whole ; the galleries were also crowded with those interested in the case, and the ladies' gallery shone resplendent with bright, beautiful women in the most gorgeous apparel. I came as near running away then as I ever did on any occasion in my life. But summoning up such courage as I could, I stuck to my post and addressed the Senate in a speech of two hours' length, of which forty thousand copies were ordered by the House the next day for circulation throughout the country. The board of managers occupied the floor of the Senate chamber at the left of the chief justice. On the right sat Attorney-General Stanbury, Mr. Evarts of New York, Judge B. R. Curtis, of Massachusetts, Judge Nelson, of Tennessee, and other gentlemen, counsel for Andrew Johnson, President of the United States.

I had brought it to the attention of the board of managers that we should have Mr. Johnson brought in and placed at the bar of the Senate to be tried according to the forms of the English law, — or as Judge Chase had been tried when Aaron Burr presided over the Senate, — and required by the presiding officer to stand until the Senate offered him a chair. But our board of managers was too weak in the knees or back to insist upon this, and Mr. Johnson did not attend.

The morning after the opening of the argument, I asked one of the board of managers, a very clever gentleman, to have the kindness to offer a piece of written evidence, but his hand shook so while he was examining the paper that I concluded to relieve him. As to myself, I came to the conclusion to try the case upon the same rules of evidence, and in the same manner as I should try a horse case, and I knew how to do that. I therefore was not in trepidation. When I discussed that question with the managers they seemed to be a good deal cut up. They said: " This is the greatest case of

the times, and it is to be conducted in the highest possible manner."
" Yes," I said, "and that is according to law; that is the only way
I know how to conduct a case." Finding me incorrigible, they left
me to my devices.

There is no occasion for my taking up time or space in giving the
details of the case. They were all printed and can be found in the
congressional reports in any respectable library.

Upon the close of our case, the opening argument for the defence was
presented by Judge Curtis, and it is due to the truth of history to say,
as I once before remarked, that after he had presented the case of his
client, in my judgment nothing *more* was said in his behalf, although
in the five or six closing speeches presented by his other counsel much
else was said.

The trial went on, such evidence as we thought proper being presented. Mr. Stanbury, the attorney-general, presented most of the
evidence for the defence. As to the method of its production, I objected to much of it as I would in any other court, and the report will
show that most of my objections were sustained by the Senate. Then
all the counsel for the defendant, except Mr. Curtis, made closing
arguments in defence of their client ; each of the managers on the part
of the House, save myself, made an argument in closing the prosecution, and the question was submitted to the Senate.

After some deliberation by the Senate a vote was taken resulting in one vote less than a majority of two thirds for conviction.

Johnson had been suspected by many people of being concerned in
the plans of Booth against the life of Lincoln or at least cognizant of
them. A committee — not the board of managers — of which I
was the head, felt it their duty to make a secret investigation of that
matter, and we did our duty in that regard most thoroughly. Speaking for myself I think I ought to say that there was no reliable
evidence at all to convince a prudent and responsible man that there
was any ground for the suspicions entertained against Johnson. On
the day of the assassination Johnson was in Washington, residing at
a hotel known as the Kirkwood House. Booth shot Lincoln at
Ford's Theatre a few blocks away from the Kirkwood House at
ten o'clock at night. At nine o'clock the same night Booth
called at the Kirkwood House and left his card for Mr. Johnson,

who was not in, though it could not be ascertained by the committee where he was. The card was put in the proper box for the delivery of all such matters in Mr. Johnson's room, and he never saw it. This fact was substantially all the evidence which would tend to implicate him.

After the capture of Atzerott and other fellow-conspirators with Booth, it was confessed by some of them that Atzerott was to have attacked Johnson. But as he did not, that should end the belief that there had been previously a conspiracy to abduct Lincoln, and that this scheme to kill him and Seward was substituted for it almost within the day when it was to be carried out. It seems to me that the call of Booth and his leaving a card might have been only for the purpose of finding out whether Johnson was at home. We felt it a duty to the country that nothing should be said or done to give a foundation for any such suspicion against its President — certainly not without the most overwhelming proofs.

In 1867 there was pending before Congress a proposition so to change the law as to pay the issue of five-twenty bonds of the United States to the amount of fifteen thousand millions made by the terms of the act authorizing them payable in twenty years at six per cent. interest, both principal and interest payable in lawful money, and they were sold at a little more than the ten-forty bonds, that is, bonds payable in forty years in gold or silver, principal and interest at five per cent. By this change of law the five-twenty bonds, although sold to the bankers at a discount of sixty and seventy per cent., more or less, were to be paid in gold and silver, which made the interest, in fact, nearly treble. I looked upon the proposition to be an enormous robbery of the people for the benefit of the bankers, without justice or reason. I made an impromptu argument in my first term in Congress upon that question and the currency in reply to Mr. Blaine of Maine. There were a majority of bondholders in both houses of Congress. I take leave to append extracts of the principal portions of that speech.

MR. CHAIRMAN: Having been so pointedly and directly called upon by the gentleman from Maine [Mr. Blaine] to reply in some small degree as I may to his criticisms upon what he has been pleased to term my financial scheme, I may have to ask the House,— as I have neither a speech written nor printed, and speak, therefore, with great slowness, because one cannot speak glibly on the grave subjects of finance, unless he speaks from a written or printed paper — to thus hear me.

The gentleman from Maine seeks in the first place to meet this great question of the finances of the nation, more important than any question we have settled except the question of slavery, by an argument to the prejudice of the House, knowing full well that the gentleman from Ohio [Mr. Pendleton] may have some theories on this question and political opinions in general which are distasteful to this House. He has sought to prejudice the argument at this point by coupling the views expressed by me with those expressed by the gentleman from Ohio. Now, why should he do that if he has a good case? My argument, sir, will be neither better nor worse, my views are neither more nor less correct, because they are agreed to by a gentleman from the West with whom on other questions I disagree. It is because the gentleman from Maine attempts to meet this question, I respectfully submit to the House, not by argument, but by prejudice.

The views entertained by Mr. Pendleton and the views which I have put forth differ in this: so far as I understand him — and if I do him wrong it is because I have not seen any authoritative exposition of his position — he would issue legal-tender notes to an amount sufficient to take up all the national interest-bearing bonds that may become due; he would by the fiat of the government issue promises to pay without interest, to be used as currency in excess, it may be, of the wants of the country, to cancel the interest-bearing debt. The only proposition which I hold in common with Mr. Pendleton is that by the law of the land and by the legal interpretation of the words of the contract five-twenty bonds are payable, not in coin, but in lawful money of the United States.

Now, there are three grounds upon which the gentleman from Maine [Mr. Blaine] insists that the five-twenties are not payable in the lawful money of the United States. He says first, by the letter of the law the five-twenties are payable in coin. Let us carefully examine that proposition. And in order to understand precisely how the law applies, take it with you that up to the time of the issuing of the five-twenties no loan of the United States had ever been issued payable in anything else than coin. The gentleman says no loan had ever been issued in which anything was said as to what was the currency in which it was payable. Why? Because up to that time there was never any currency known to the Government of the United States other than coin. Therefore the seven-thirties of 1861 and the six-twenties payable in 1881, with all the debt prior to the war, were, in letter and in spirit, payable in coin. Because Congress in issuing them was dealing with a condition of things and a currency then existing, and therefore the 1881 sixes are payable, according to the fair spirit of the contract, in coin. Therefore I enunciate, as my first proposition, and one that I shall endeavor to enforce on the House and the country, that every dollar of indebtment of the United States which is contracted by the acts of Congress making it payable in coin shall be paid in coin although it takes the last dollar to pay it; but every debt contracted not payable in coin shall be paid in the lawful money of the United States, such as you paid your soldiers with and such as you furnish to your citizens; such as alone is now used as money of the government, and upon which alone you impress the image and superscription of the government as a guarantee that it shall hereafter be made good.

Now, then, when the argument is pressed upon me that in the loan bills passed previously to the five-twenty loan nothing was said as to the currency in which the bonds should be paid, I reply that there was but one currency at the time they were passed in which they could be contracted or payable. But that state of things changed on the 25th of February, 1862. The Congress of the United States had to provide means for carrying on the war; accordingly it passed a law, the first section of which provided for $150,000,000 of legal-tender notes, the language of which, as to their validity and effect, is in these words : —

" And such notes, herein authorized, shall be receivable in payment of all taxes, internal duties, excises, debts, and demands of every kind, due to the United States, except duties on imports, and for all claims and demands against the United States of every kind whatsoever " —

Except what?

" except for interest upon bonds and notes, which shall be paid in coin; and shall also be lawful money and a legal tender in payment of all debts, public and private, within the United States, except duties on imports and interests as aforesaid."

These are the provisions of the first section of the act, thus creating " a lawful money," payable and receivable for every debt, public or private, known to the law or known in the United States, except what? Except interest on the bonds and notes of the United States.

Now, what does the second section provide ? It authorized $500,000,000 of bonds registered or coupon, payable at the option of the United States in five years, and in twenty years at all events. Payable how ? Let me read again, so that I may not be mistaken : —

" to an amount not exceeding $500,000,000, payable in twenty years from date, and bearing a rate of six per cent., payable semi-annually."

Not a word is here said as to the money in which these bonds shall be paid, either as to principal or interest. And why? Because the very section preceding had provided that the interest of all notes or bonds of the United States should be paid in coin, and had further enacted another lawful money which should be receivable in payment of all indebtment of the United States whatsoever, except duties on imports, and interest on the public debt. Is not the principal of the debt an indebtment other than interest?

There is the plain letter of the law. I need not discuss this point further. If there is any lawyer who, reading this law without taking into consideration anything except what stands on the statute-book, will tell me that this law enacts that the principal of the five-twenties is payable in coin, then " for him have I offended," and either he is or I am so stupid as not to be worthy of an argument.

But the gentleman does not leave his proposition upon this only. The next ground he puts it on is, what this or that congressman said or omitted to say in his speech as to the currency in which this loan should be paid. And the first evidence of the contract he puts forward is that the honorable member from Pennsylvania [Mr. Stevens] — not now in his seat — did not say, at the time the act was passed, that the principal was payable in currency. Well, the gentleman from Pennsylvania sets forth in a letter recently written by him as a reason why he did not say it was payable in currency, that he did not think anybody but a fool would think it was not. That is not my language ; it is his ; that is the ground he puts it on ; and when he comes in he and the gentleman from Maine can fight the battle out. I am quite certain that the old man sarcastic will take care of himself when he does get here without any aid from me ; and therefore I pass from further consideration of this topic.

But it is said that various speeches were made on the one side and the other, which are cited to interpret this contract. I had supposed that there is no better settled rule of interpretation of either public or municipal law, or of the law of nations, than that nobody is bound by any portion of the negotiations or any portion of the declarations made either in regard to a treaty or a law prior to the enactment of the law or conclusion of the treaty, because the enactment settles the terms of the whole obligation, and you cannot go to the speech of this member or that member, in case of legislation, to find out what the legislation means, nor can you go to the protocols and negotiations prior to a treaty to find out what the treaty means. You must take it upon the letter, and I have never yet found any man bold enough — until my friend from Maine exhibited a degree of courage much superior to any bravery required to face Minie bullets in the field — bold enough to insist that the letter of the law did not authorize payment of the principal of the five-twenty bonds in lawful money of the United States.

The next class of arguments that the gentleman from Maine puts forward on this question is the proposals in the advertisements of those he terms the authorized agents of the United States who disposed of the loan. Allow me here to say that for contracting a national debt I know no other authorized agent of the nation but the Congress of the United States; I know no broker, whether he is in the treasury office or out of it, that has a right to fix the terms of the national debt for the United States. No man is authorized to pay a dollar of money unless appropriated by the Congress of the United States, and therefore no man can contract a dollar's debt unless authorized directly and distinctly by an act of the Congress of the United States. I agree that Mr. Jay Cooke advertised, after some sort, when endeavoring to sell it, that the principal of this loan was payable in coin; but in the same newspaper you find another of his advertisements, intended also to sell the loan, that "a national debt is a national blessing." Are we bound by contract to that? If, as the gentleman claims, we are bound by advertisements in the one case, we are bound as well in the other; and does my friend insist that Mr. Jay Cooke has bound the country to the proposition that a national debt is a national blessing to anybody except bankers? With that amendment I might agree to the declaration. When I called the attention of the country to this some little time ago, Mr. Jay Cooke, for whom I have very high respect, wrote me that I was mistaken; that what he did advertise was that a national debt rightly managed was a national blessing. I am at issue with him upon that. I insist that a national debt managed any how, by anybody — the Angel Gabriel or Jay Cooke or any other body — is not a national blessing. [Laughter.] No management of a national debt can make it a national blessing. And yet, if we are bound by brokers' advertisements, we are bound to the doctrine that it is a national blessing which we must enjoy and bequeath to our posterity forever!

The next evidence which the gentleman from Maine presents in support of his contract to pay the five-twenties in gold is the declarations of Secretaries of the Treasury. Now, no Secretary of the Treasury had a right to make any declarations on this subject which can be binding on the country. The gentleman does not claim that he had; he only says that Congress stood by and saw the secretary make declarations and did not interfere. Once for all, I protest against Congress being bound by what secretaries do or do not do that Congress does not interfere with.

If you once admit that doctrine you will involve Congress in difficulties which it will take a long time and great wisdom to unravel.

But no one of the secretaries ever has said that the contract is that the principal of this loan is payable in coin; and if there has been disingenuousness on this subject it has not been on our part, but on the part of the secretaries in their attempts to interpret this law so as to sell the loan. The first thing said about the probability that this debt would be paid in gold was in the answer of Secretary Chase to a letter sent him from abroad — Frankfort, I believe. It was said in that letter — I do not give the words, but the substance —"It is not understood here in Frankfort that these bonds are payable in gold. If it should be so understood they would bring a much higher price." Why was it not so understood? Because a foreign lawyer reading the act would never think of such a thing for a moment. The bonds were selling — for what? For forty cents on the dollar, and that at a time when the Confederate loan was at a premium in Europe.

Now, I will not think so meanly of this country as to believe it could be supposed these bonds were payable in gold, and then were at this discount even in Europe, which was against us. And I will not think so meanly of this nation as to believe that there could have been any question in the minds of the people of Europe as to our being able to pay more than thirty per cent. of our debt in gold if such had been our plain contract and obligation. No, sir; the bankers in Europe of that day were simply betting as to whether we should pay our paper money in gold; they were betting on that proposition when they were buying our bonds at from sixty to seventy per cent. discount. They knew that every other government that had issued paper money had depreciated it, and the question was whether we, who set out here so differently from other governments, would in the end depreciate our paper money.

This letter was sent over here as a stock-jobbing proposition to Mr. Chase. How did he answer it? Through his assistant secretary. The answer all will remember: "The Government of the United States has always paid all its obligations in gold, and it is to be presumed that it always will." It was an evasive answer — an answer tending to mislead; whether intended so to do I do not know or say.

I have a bone to pick with Mr. Fessenden upon this subject. I am very glad he has been brought in here. Mr. Fessenden, as Secretary of the Treasury, was called upon to say whether the three-year loan treasury notes, issued in 1861, when there was nothing but gold to pay with, and for which gold was paid by the people to the government, was payable in coin or in currency. He decided that these gold-bought and gold-contracted notes were payable in currency; and the whole of that issue, put forth at a time when there was nothing but gold as currency, for which the faith of the country was pledged, under the decision of Mr. Fessenden, had to be received by the people (who paid for it in gold) in paper, or they were compelled to convert it into such bonds as the government chose to give them.

Mr. BLAINE. Will the gentleman from Massachusetts [Mr. Butler] allow me to read one sentence?

I answered, Certainly.

Mr. BLAINE. The decision in regard to the payment of the first series of seven-thirty notes was made on the 18th of May, 1862, by Salmon P. Chase, Secretary of the Treasury, in these words: —

"The three-year seven-thirty treasury notes are part of the temporary loan, and will be paid in treasury notes, unless the holders prefer to exchange them," etc.

That was three months before Mr. Fessenden went into the treasury. He found the question *res adjudicata.*[1] The gentleman is all wrong in charging this upon Mr. Fessenden. There is not the remotest foundation for his assertion.

I replied: The House will judge whether I was wrong, without the *dictum* of my friend from Maine [Mr. BLAINE]. I did not say that Salmon P. Chase was not guilty of the same thing; I only said that William P. Fessenden was guilty of it; that is the distinction. [Laughter.] If Salmon P. Chase had broken the faith of this government — if he had said that, although the government had received gold in the hour of its necessity, immediately after the first battle of Bull Run, the darkest day the government ever saw, and had pledged gold in return — for then we paid gold to meet all our obligations — if Salmon P. Chase, on the 18th of May, 1864, when called upon to say whether we should pay gold for the gold we had received, broke the faith of the government, if he was one of those repudiators and scoundrels and knaves we hear of so glibly when we attempt to discuss this question of finance, why did not and why should not Secretary Fessenden overrule him when he became Secretary of the Treasury? If so great a wrong was *res adjudicata*, it was *res* very badly *adjudicata*, and should have been forthwith set right.

My friend does not pretend that Mr. Fessenden altered this; and when we, who believe in maintaining the faith of the nation, but not in oppressing the people with taxation, are attacked on all hands by hard words and strong inferences, and when, to get us down, we are yoked up with everybody who happens to have bad political sentiments, I would

---

[1] *Res adjudicata.* A thing adjudicated or determined.

ask who was the first repudiator? The gentleman chooses to cite Mr. Chase as the promisor of this bad note. Be it so; I am dealing only with the indorser, William Pitt Fessenden. He indorsed it and acted upon it. By his decision the seven-thirty notes of 1861, issued when there was no other currency, were caused to be paid in greenbacks, and the gold-paying public creditor was obliged, for his gold paid to the government, either to take his pay in greenbacks or convert his government notes into bonds; and that whole loan was thus redeemed. And on what ground was this so great a wrong on the public creditors perpetrated? It was said by the secretary that this three-year seven-thirty gold loan was a temporary loan only. Oh, then, it is right to cheat the temporary credit-ors of the government; the hand-to-mouth men, who loan their hard coin for a few days to save the government; but the long-bond creditors of the government you must not cheat; you must let them cheat you. Is not that the proposition? Is there any escape from it? Is not that the Maine doctrine of finance, if you please? [Laughter.] My friend here from Maine [Mr. BLAINE], following in the footsteps of the Secretary of the Treasury from Maine, holds it to be in the last degree wrong if we do not pay principal and interest of our debt in gold. He invokes us, in the name of national honor, national faith, and everything else that is sacred, to save the long-bond creditor, who bought our bonds for currency, while the short creditor, who paid for his notes in coin, has lost his gold by the action of the Secretary of the Treasury from Maine. We have had many things good from Maine — among others a "Maine law" — and now we have got Maine finance. I repudiate the last, and I am afraid my State has repudiated the other. [Laughter.]

The next authority adduced by the gentleman in support of his contract to pay gold for the five-twenties bonds is Secretary McCulloch. Well, if this House proposes to be bound by the financial theories of Secretary McCulloch I should hardly wish to argue this question further. But even Secretary McCulloch does not undertake to say that there is a contract to pay gold for these bonds. When asked by a foreign banker, "What is the contract as to the payment of the principal of the five-twenties?" what does the secretary reply? Does he say that the contract is to pay in gold? Oh, no; he says that all the government obligations that have fallen due have been paid in gold (he forgot that temporary loan), and that it is the policy of the government to pay all its obligations in gold. I agree with him; such is the policy of the government. But that is not the question. The question is, what has the government contracted to do, and what is it able to do? I wish that we could pay this enormous debt in gold, or in anything else, so that we could relieve the people from taxation. You will find running all through this letter of Secretary McCulloch an evasion of this question. What is the contract by law?

When the $900,000,000 loan, commonly known as the ten-forty loan, was issued, what did the Secretary of the Treasury do? Of the six per cent. five-twenty loan (which the gentleman from Maine contends was payable in gold) he says only some $25,000,000 of the $500,000,000 authorized had been issued; yet he makes the Secretary of the Treasury guilty of the absurdity of attempting to put on the market $900,000,000 of the five per cent. ten-forty loan as a competing loan, expecting to get that taken up, when he could not get his five-twenty six per cent. gold-payable loan in principal and interest taken up. Why did he do this? If both loans were payable in gold, he must have been entirely demented. But no; the ten-forty five per cent. loan was payable, principal and interest, in gold by its terms; and this same Secretary of the Treasury, through his brokers, advertised this ten-forty loan as the only one the principal and interest of which were payable in gold. And nobody objected in this House. I was not here then; but where was the eloquent voice of my friend from Maine protesting against selling this five per cent. loan upon an advertisement that it was the only loan payable principal and interest, in gold? Why did he allow the public creditors to think that the only loan payable in gold was the five per cent. loan; that the six per cent. loan was not payable in gold? This only illustrates the fact that, in interpreting public law, we must not deal with what members of Congress do individually, but we must be bound by the statute.

Mr. BLAINE. Does the gentleman mean to say that the government agents advertised that the ten-forty loan was the only loan payable in gold?

I replied : Yes, sir; I do. Certain government agents, called the New York *Tribune*, the New York *Times*, or the New York *Evening Post*, contained that advertisement, and if the gentleman will go there he will find it.

Mr. BLAINE. Authorized by whom?

I answered : Authorized by the Secretary of the Treasury, so headed. It was a little difficult at that time to find out who the negotiators were. That was the advertisement. You can find it. If I had known this question was to arise at this time I would have had the advertisement to present to the House.

Mr. BLAINE. I gave the gentleman notice some days ago that I should speak on this subject.

I said : True. But while I presumed the gentleman would speak on this subject, it never entered my conception that he would make such a speech as he has. [Laughter.]

If the gentleman will tell me why it is that we are to construe this law differently from any other law I will be obliged to him. If he will inform this House why the people of this country should tax themselves to the amount of many millions ($400,000,000 is the difference this day and this hour), whether these five-twenties are payable in gold, as gold stood yesterday, or in greenbacks.

The only answer suggested is, why agitate this now? These loans are not payable now, and therefore we may wait until the twenty years are out, when we all believe greenbacks and gold will be correlative terms. I believe so, too, in twenty years; but in the meantime the interest on these five-twenties is sinking this country, the labor, the manufacture, and the commerce of this country, to a degree that even its vitality and its strength will hardly be able to meet it.

What is the rate of interest on the five-twenties? Six per cent. in gold, payable semi-annually, gold being at 140 to 145, equal to 150 and upward. That makes nine per cent.; they are exempt from State and municipal taxation, which makes from two to three per cent. more. So on these almost two thousand million of interest bonds the people of this country are paying at this day, and at this hour, either by remission of taxes or otherwise, in the currency of the country, from eleven to twelve per cent. What is the consequence? They could stagger under this burden of taxes if needed to pay the soldiers; they could deal with this burden of taxes if it even were to be thrown into the sea; but the difficulty is that paying this high rate of interest on these five-twenties of from eleven to twelve per cent. causes capitalists to withdraw from legitimate business and keep their money in these bonds. See how it operates. I have my money in five-twenty bonds at eleven per cent., and I am told that I am to have gold at the end of the twenty years for the principal besides. You cannot tempt me then to go into any enterprise which shall not promise me more than eleven to twelve per cent. I must have much more before I will take my money out of government securities and put it at the risk of business. And it is this high rate of government interest which is crushing the life out of the industrial pursuits of the people. There can be no mistake about this. Look at the market reports of Cincinnati, one of the great marts of the West. No money can be got there for less than fifteen to eighteen per cent. Why? Because our capitalists get from eleven to twelve per cent. on five-twenties, and they are encouraged to hold on to their bonds and keep their money out of the business of the country; because the gentleman from Maine tells them that the government will pay the principal in gold, although they paid but forty cents on the dollar for them when they bought them. This is the reason why this five-twenty loan is crushing our people, and why we must get rid of it at all hazards consistent with national honor and national faith, and no man asks that to be broken.

But I am told if we undertake to pay any portion of this debt in greenbacks we shall depreciate greenbacks so that they will be worthless; that there will be an inflation of prices. The gentleman from Maine riots in imagination over the picture of the payment of $200 for a pair of boots if we issue any more legal-tender notes, that is to say, notes not bearing interest.

Speaking of greenbacks, I am reminded of one thing to which I meant to have adverted, on the question: of the nation's being bound by the advertisements by which its bonds were sold. My friend says we did not notify capitalists that we would claim the right to pay these five-twenty bonds in any other way than in coin. Why, we put it upon $150,000,000 of United States notes, and thus advertised everybody we did not mean to pay them in gold. This notice was put on the back of every greenback. Let me read from one : —

" This note is a legal-tender for all debts, public or private, except duties on imports and interest on the public debt."

There is " *inclusio unius exclusio alterius* " [1] for the gentleman.

The common idea is that there will be inflation when you issue paper money. It is drawn from the old idea of bank circulation. A bank issued its notes without any basis except the gold basis. That gold basis was sometimes one to four. Let me illustrate : suppose there were four hundred millions of bank paper in circulation on one hundred millions of gold as a basis, then I agree it would be an inflation to issue another one hundred millions, making the relation of the paper dollar to the gold dollar as one to five. But what is a greenback? Have gentlemen considered? A dollar greenback as it stands to-day is one twenty-five hundred millionth part of the debt of the United States, secured by a mortgage upon every dollar of public or private property in the United States. Is it not that, under my theory or anybody else's theory of finance? Now, suppose we issue five hundred millions of greenbacks, and pay up five hundred millions of the interest-bearing debt of the United States, what is a greenback then? Why, it is still one twenty-five hundred millionth part of the national debt of the United States,

---

[1] In a contract, *inclusio unius exclusio alterius*, " the inclusion of one thing is the exclusion of the other."

appreciated, and not depreciated, by the amount of interest which we have saved by buying up five hundred millions of the interest-bearing debt. The way to test it would be this: suppose we could issue the whole amount and pay all interest-bearing debt at once, then the one hundred and fifty millions of customs which we have to pay for interest without getting ahead in payment of our debt at all could be directed to redeeming the greenbacks. There is a limitation on this power of issuing greenbacks, and only one, and that limitation my friend does not seem to understand. It is this: these greenbacks are non-interest-bearing notes, and therefore they can only be issued in such quantities without depreciation in fact, as will be absorbed by the community to the degree that they are required for business purposes. They may be issued to the degree they will be absorbed as currency. I think that the country can bear to-day some two hundred millions more of them, not issued primarily and arbitrarily for the purpose of paying off the interest-bearing debt, but issued for the purpose of providing a currency for the country which should not be so contracted as to bring ruin, as now, upon the business interests of the country. When you have issued two hundred millions more of these greenbacks and paid your interest-bearing debt with them, have you altered their relation to property, to each other, or to gold? Are they appreciated or depreciated? Appreciated, in fact, because you save the interest on the two hundred millions which you have paid off with them; depreciated if you issue more than will be absorbed as currency, because business men do not want non-interest-bearing notes on hand; and if they are not needed as currency they will sell them at a discount for some property that will pay interest.

Now, then, sir, let me state, for the benefit of my friend, my proposition of finance, and the House can contrast it with any other that may be better, and there will be found better I doubt not. There are now some two thousand five hundred millions of debt. Some two thousand millions of it stand in the shape of interest-bearing debt. There are nineteen different kinds of that description of debt bearing different rates of interest and times of payment. There are some five hundred millions, more or less, in various forms of non-interest-bearing debt, gold certificates, legal-tender notes, and others. Now, my proposition is that, in the first place, we should substitute greenbacks for the national bank currency, releasing to the banks the bonds which we hold as security for that national bank currency. It can be done without shock to the business of the country.

I agree, sir, that any proposition of legislation is vicious which tends in any considerable degree to interfere with the industrial pursuits of the people, but I propose we should enact in some proper form that the Secretary of the Treasury should each month retain in the treasury all the national bank bills which have been collected by the collectors of the internal revenue, or which have come through other means into the Treasury of the United States, and at the same time should issue to the banks, if they desire to receive them, or to issue in payment of the interest-bearing notes which are payable in currency an equal amount of legal tenders. In a very few months, four or five, the national bank notes would be drawn from circulation and their place supplied with greenbacks without any shock to the business of the country; and, *pari passu*,[1] the bonds of the banks held as security for these notes could be restored to them. This proposition, sir, if carried out would put into circulation some three hundred million dollars more of national legal-tender notes without increasing that circulation, and release the country from the payment of between twenty and thirty million dollars in currency which is now paid to the national banks on these bonds, and the place of their bills would be taken by the non-interest-bearing notes of the United States without any shock to the business of the country.

What objections are urged to this proposition? The first is that it would be a breach of faith with the banks. I would like some gentleman to put his finger upon any act of Congress by which we pledged ourselves for a single day longer than good pleasure and discretion of the Congress of the United States thought best to allow this bank currency to exist. What effect would it have upon the banks? Those dependent wholly upon their circulation, which are not in fact banks of loans and deposits, would wind up, and their managers would seek some other and equally honest employment. Banks that are needed would still be banks of loan and discount, but not of circulation.

It is said that the banks furnish now the best currency this country ever saw, because it is the same in New Orleans, Boston, New York, and Chicago. But what is the currency? It is the notes of the bank. What makes them equal all over this country? It is the indorsement of the United States. So that we have come into this very remarkable position, that when a bank breaks its currency is better than when it was solvent, and sells at a slight premium.[2] Therefore, as the United States is primarily

---

[1] *Pari Passu*, with equal step.

[2] At the time of this speech, the amount of bank currency was limited, so that no new bank could be formed until an old bank broke and its bills became redeemable. Then the capitalists who wanted to start a new bank (and this was very profitable) would buy up the bills of the broken bank, and when they got enough would apply for a bank charter and get it. Therefore bills of a broken bank would sell for three or four per cent. premium to be used for that purpose.

responsible for all the circulation, we ought to supply the currency to the people and receive the profit of doing it.

But it is said that the banks really cost the United States nothing. One of the ablest bankers of them all, Mr. Jay Cooke, has undertaken to tell us that the banks pay in taxes a large amount, and therefore in equity we ought not to disturb them.   Sir, if Mr. Jay Cooke or any one else will tell me of any business in this country that is not taxed and does not pay a large amount of taxes, then I will agree that the banks are not favored. Take, for example, a manufacturer.   Take a single case, only two years ago, in the State of Massachusetts, of a manufacturing corporation of $750,000 capital and of $1,500,000 annual product of manufactured goods. It exactly divided profits with the United States.   Its stockholders received two dividends of five per cent. each on $750,000, and it paid five per cent. tax on the entire amount of production, $1,500,000 ; so that they in fact took the United States into partnership, only the United States got all the profits, but the stockholders bore all the loss.   Now, if there is any greater or more onerous burden of taxes on the banks than that, I have yet to learn where it is.

Again, it is said that this banking system is a better one than we ever had. For some purposes so it is. And it is said, further, that if we do not encourage it we shall go back to the old State bank system. No, Mr. Chairman, never, never! The day of State banks has gone by. They were always, in my poor judgment, unconstitutional; but they got themselves fastened on to the country, and there was never power enough, until the necessities of the country required a new system of finance, to break off their hold. We have rid the country of them, and the Congress of the United States, ay, and the good judgment of the people, will never permit that system again to be imposed upon the country.

What is the next proposition? Why, it is said we must not interfere with the national banks because they patriotically helped us during the war. Upon that I take issue with each and every advocate of the banks.   On the contrary, they helped themselves, not us.   It is said they loaned money to the government.   How did they do it?   Let me state the way a national bank got itself into existence in New England during the war, when gold was 200, and five-twenties were at par, in currency, or nearly that.   A company of men got together $300,000 in national bank bills, and went to the Register of the Treasury with gold at 200 and bought United States five-twenty bonds at par.   They stepped into the office of the Comptroller of the Currency and asked to be established as a national bank, and received from him $270,000 in currency, with interest, upon pledging these bonds of the United States they had just bought with their $300,000 of the same kind of money. Now, let us balance the books, and how does the account stand ? Why, the United States Government receives $30,000 in national bank bills more from the banks than it gave them in bills; in other words, it borrowed of the bank $30,000 in currency, for which, in fact, it paid $18,000 a year in gold interest, equal to $36,000 in currency, for the use of this $30,000. Let me repeat. The difference between what the United States received and paid out was only $30,000, and for the use of that the government pay on the bonds deposited by the company, bought with the same kind of money, $18,000 a year interest in gold, equal to $36,000 in currency.

But the thing did not stop there. The gentlemen were shrewd financiers; their bank was a good one; they went to the Secretary of the Treasury and said: " Let our bank be made a public depository." Very well; it was a good bank; the managers were good men; there was no objection to the bank. It was made a public depository, and thereupon the commissaries, the quartermasters, the medical director and purveyor, and the paymasters were all directed to deposit their public funds in this bank. Very soon the bank found that they had a line of steady deposits belonging to the government of about a million dollars, and that the $270,000 they had received from the Comptroller of the Currency would substantially carry on their daily business, and as the government gives three days on all its drafts, if the bank was pressed it was easy enough to go on the street if they had good security. They took the million of government money so deposited with them and loaned it to the government for the government's own bonds, and received therefor $60,000 more interest in gold for the loan to the government of its own money, which in currency was equal to $120,000. So that when we come finally to balance the books the government is paying $156,000 a year for the loan of $30,000. And this is the system which is to be fastened forever on the country as a means of furnishing a circulating medium!

This, only using round numbers for the purpose of illustration, is an actual and not a feigned occurrence. You will see it was a perfectly safe operation for the banks, though not a very profitable one for the government, because they held ample security for the government deposits in its own bonds. But the difficulty is the government was paying interest all the while on its own deposits; and this state of facts is only rendered possible by this system of supplying the banks with circulation by the government without interest.

The next reason advanced why we should not interfere with these banks, if I understand it, is that we are told by very high authority this system will become the banking system of the world ; having inaugurated it, we are so much in love with it that all the nations will pattern after it. Let the rest of the world try it for a few years when we have done with it, and then, if the rest of the nations adopt it, we can return to it, we can return it, but not till then.

Sir, am I slandering these institutions ? Are they not making money at a rate which is beyond all precedent? Let me state another case, which might be an actual case, and perhaps I could call the name of the man. A very shrewd man takes his $100,000 and goes to the treasury and obtains bonds; he then gets a banking charter, and receives his bills amounting to $90,000 ; then he buys with those same bills $90,000 worth of bonds, and comes home and sits in his office, and that is his bank, and his money is all in circulation. Says he: why should I trouble myself to lend my money to the farmers around me on sixty-day notes when I can lend it at from ten to twelve per cent. on long twenty-year government bonds, and Mr. Blaine says I am to be paid in gold for them; that is as good banking as I want to do; the bills never come home ; they are going all over the West and South, and I am getting $22,800 interest on my original $100,000 ; what do I want more ? I am comfortable and happy ; I think this " banking system is the wisest one the world ever saw, and that it ought to be adopted all the world over."

But let us take the banks' own exhibit of themselves. I hold in my hand the abstract of reports of national banking associations for the first of October last. Let us see their condition. They have $419,000,000 of capital stock paid in ; they have been in operation on an average of less than four years; they have divided from twelve to twenty per cent., about twelve in New England and from fifteen to twenty per cent. where money is scarcer and the rate of interest rules higher. In addition to these, dividends take their own statement: " surplus fund, $66,000,000 ; undivided profits, $33,000,000 ; " showing that they have got, after all these dividends, nearly twenty-five per cent. surplus of that capital stock laid away. What other business, taxed or untaxed, if any untaxed business can be found in this country, will allow a yearly dividend of from fifteen to twenty-five per cent. and a surplus accumulation in four years of twenty-five per cent. on the capital ? And from whom and from where do these profits come? They come ultimately from where all taxation, all profits, all productions must come, the laborer of the country and nowhere else ; and we are asked here to perpetuate a system which takes these immense profits from the labor of the country and puts them into the hands of capitalists without a pretence of adequate benefit received by the people.

Why, sir, it is an axiom in finance, if there are any axioms in finance, that any business which is safe should have small profits, and business that is hazardous should have large profits; but here the state of things is reversed; the banking business, which, if well conducted, is the safest business on earth, and which heretofore has always been content with small profits, is now the most profitable of all businesses, and has the largest returns without any risks.

Every member of this House can argue these propositions for himself better than I can argue them for him. It is my part only to suggest the topics upon the question of currency. I insist, as my first proposition, that there should be this change in bank circulation, and by that means we would diminish our interest-bearing debt $300,000,000 by redeeming it with the greenbacks we should thus issue.

We have to-day in circulation in various forms in round numbers $759,000,000. A portion of it, I agree, is locked up in banks; fifteen per cent. in the country, and twenty-five per cent. in the city banks as their currency for the redemption of their bills; a procedure the wisdom of which I have yet to be taught, because the United States is the final indorser and payer of all their bills. I do not see how it makes it any safer to lock up fifteen or twenty-five per cent. of the indorser's notes for their redemption; and I desire some of the able bankers in this House to explain to me what good result is hoped for from this smothering of a portion of the national currency, which the banks take care, however, shall be interest-bearing to them.

I will suggest a reason why that requirement was placed in the statute book. There was a lingering idea in law of the old specie basis, and of getting an equivalent in its place. Legislators seem to have forgotten that we had wandered away from the specie basis; that they were putting in its place but the notes of the United States to redeem notes of the United States. If we can release, therefore, the whole circulation of about $700,000,000, perhaps that will relieve the present contraction in the currency.

We are told that we must preserve the national banks, because if we do not there will be nobody to circulate our money. Let us examine that a moment. If money will not circulate it is because nobody wants money. My anxiety is to provide the people with money that they do want and will circulate, not with money they do not want. I have never yet seen any man who has refused the notes of the United States when the government has paid them out. When I find such a man, I will agree to charter a bank for the purpose of forcing them upon him, and not until then.

The truth is, that at the present hour the country is suffering from the want of those very notes. We have nominally some seven hundred and fifty millions of currency, but actually only about five hundred and fifty millions in circulation. I wish I could stop to explain to the House how this can be, but it can easily be seen by examining the bank returns. We find the fact to be that we have not circulation enough. Compare it with what was the circulation before the war. Mr. Chase reported the circulation of this country before the war, including gold, to be about $477,000,-000, and upon examination I can see no reason to find fault with that estimate. Now we have only $550,000,000 in actual circulation, though we are doing more than three times the business calling for the use of cash that we were doing before the war. During the ten years from 1847 to 1857 the deposits and circulation of the banks averaged about thirteen dollars per capita. Now, on account of our doing so much more of our business for cash, the deposits and circulation of the banks are about twenty-four dollars per man. And if you take into consideration the currency furnished by the United States, the $300,000,000 of greenbacks, or about that sum, you will find that it is about thirty-four dollars per capita, reckoning thirty-six million people in the United States. This shows that we require in our business three times, or certainly two and a half times, as much cash as before the war. Everybody knows this to be a fact.

How was it before the war with the eastern manufacturer? He sent to New Orleans and bought his cotton, giving drafts for six or eight months. The merchant in New Orleans came East and bought the manufactured goods, giving his notes for from six months to a year; and all the cash that was wanted was enough to settle up the balances.

And now, when we send out for cotton we must send out greenbacks, because of the change in the mode of doing business: and we have a currency that stands at par there, and for what they want from us they must send the greenbacks. Every one knows that the business of this country is done twice or thrice as much in cash as it was before the war; and therefore I think this country will bear from eight hundred to a thousand million dollars of circulation without redundancy as soon as business revives, and that will make it revive. But my friends say " that may be too much." Perhaps it may be ; but it is very easy, it seems to me, for us to have that amount of circulation without redundancy ; and as each legal-tender note is, as we have seen, a part of the debt secured by mortgage of the whole property of the United States, without depreciation.

Our debt now is $2,500,000,000, about $2,200,000,000 of it interest-bearing. Suppose we issue our legal-tender greenbacks, as I will call them for convenience, and buy up or redeem our interest-bearing debt that is due to the amount of $1,000,000,000. Then our debt stands,

James F. Wilson, Iowa.   Geo. S. Boutwell, Mass.   John A. Logan, Ill.
Benj. F. Butler, Mass.   Thaddeus Stevens, Penn.   Thos. Williams, Penn.   Jno. A. Bingham, Ohio.
MANAGERS OF THE HOUSE OF REPRESENTATIVES OF THE IMPEACHMENT TRIAL OF ANDREW JOHNSON.

$1,000,000,000 of non-interest-bearing debt, and $1,500,000,000 of interest-bearing debt. Now, if that $1,000,000,000 of circulation is too much, i. e., more than is needed for currency, I agree with the gentleman from Maine that it will be depreciated. But what is too much? Too much is more than will be absorbed as currency in the business of the country. That is to say, if because of an over-issue by the government there is an accumulation of non-interest-bearing notes, greenbacks, in the hands of any man, they are not productive, and he will dispose of them at a discount, if he can do no better, for something that is productive. The only question as to redundancy, therefore, is whether the notes in his hands are worth more for use in his business as currency than they would be to him if invested in a loan to the government. Now, then, I propose that for $300,000,000 of this non-interest-bearing debt we shall issue an interest-bearing loan at once which shall be that exact loan which my friend from Maine yesterday thought would be so absurd — a loan bearing a low rate of interest and convertible and reconvertible into greenbacks at the pleasure of the holder at any day and any hour.

Let us see how such a loan would operate. A man has more money than he wants to use. He with such a loan can go to a public depository, leave his money and take his bond. Then when he wants his money again he goes to the depository, leaves his bond and takes his money for his bond, principal and interest; that is to say, when the non-interest-bearing notes of the United States are worth less to a business man than this bond he will exchange it for this bond; when the notes as currency are worth more to him to use in business or speculation than the investment he will return the bond and take the currency. Thus, without any banks to push out the circulation just when it is not wanted or draw it back just when it is wanted, as the practice now is, we shall have an automatic financial system, self-regulating, or rather regulated by the great law of supply and demand, the best of all regulators. When money is wanted by the business community up to the amount of notes issued by the United States, it will be at once got; when it is not wanted, it will be returned to the government, which being a borrower for a long series of years to come will be glad to take it. There can be no redundancy, because every man will know exactly where to place these non-interest-bearing notes when he has got through with them as money. When money is wanted at the West to move your crops in the fall you take it from the treasury and move the crops; when you get through with the money you take it back to the treasury and get the bonds, in the same manner as when you have got through with your wagons you put them back in your barns for use next year. Thus the whole monetary system of the country will go on without redundancy and without shock and without inflation.

More than that, sir, as I believe I have demonstrated, it will be impossible to have inflation, because this currency being convertible and reconvertible from time to time, and being always an integral part of the public debt, it will never change its relative value to the property of the people of the United States. Why, sir, what is the measure of the value of your house? If it is worth $10,000 it is ten thousand twenty-five hundred millionth parts of the public debt; and it will remain so until a portion of that debt is paid, when it will be appreciated, or until the public debt is expanded, when it will be depreciated. It will remain of exactly the same relative value, however much the form of the public debt be changed, but will always be more valuable as the public debt grows more valuable, i. e., as it diminishes.

My hour is nearly exhausted and I am warned that I must spend no more time in elaborating the details of this proposition; but I ask gentlemen to apply to this question their own acute judgments and tell me, if *they can, where is the fault in the reasoning; because the only valuable purpose that can be served by this discussion is to elicit what we all desire to arrive at — the best system of finance, to do what? To lessen the burden of taxation and to relieve the loyal, true-hearted, but over-burdened people from this so great weight of taxation.*

Now, sir, if I am right, and if the country will bear this thousand millions of non-interest-bearing notes as currency — and if it will not, the good judgment of the Ways and Means Committee, and the Committee on Banking and Currency will settle that for us on full examination, so that I certainly may use that sum for illustration in so far as it will bear it — so far will it diminish the interest-bearing debt. You will, therefore, bring the interest-bearing debt down to $1,500,000,000, where it can easily be managed. It is said you must not pay these five-twenties in greenbacks? Why, sir, you will never need to pay them in greenbacks.

What shall you do, then? You should issue a loan on long time, at a low rate of interest, thirty or fifty years, with the proceeds of which to redeem them or to be exchanged for them. For, sir, I am not for this generation paying all this debt. I think we had done our share when we contracted it. [Laughter.] We ought to leave it to our children to do theirs by paying it.[1] I see gentlemen smile. But, sir, in all solemnity, when we contracted this we contracted it with the loss of the best blood of the nation and the loss of the best lives we had; in suffering, in sorrow, in labor, in woe, amid horrors unnumbered,

---

[1] This has been done and is now being done nearly a quarter of a century afterwards.

to save this great experiment of government, republican in form, and freedom for all, for them and for our posterity forever, and they owe us some debt of gratitude for that so great boon; and should we who bore all the suffering and agony bear also all the taxation consequent upon this great work?

But I do not desire that the greenback currency should be made to serve the country as it has done, vilified, insulted, depreciated by the act of the government itself; being refused not only to be received for all debts due the government, but not even paid for all demands due from the government.

The "American system of finance," which will obtain in the near future, — and I hope at once, — which I desire is:

First. A dollar that shall have at all times a certain fixed and stable value below which it cannot go.

Second. I demand that that dollar shall be issued by the government alone, in the exercise of its high prerogative and constitutional power, and that that power shall not be delegated to any corporation or individual, any more than Charles the Second ought to have delegated his prerogative of stamping gold coin for the benefit of his paramours, as a monopoly.

Third. I want that dollar stamped upon some convenient and cheap material of the least possible intrinsic value, so that neither its wear nor its destruction will be any loss to the government issuing it.

Fourth. I also desire the dollar to be made of such material for the purpose that it shall never be exported or desirable to carry out of the country. Framing an American system of finance I do not propose to adapt it to the wants of any other nation and especially the Chinese, who are nearly one quarter of the world.

Fifth. I desire that the dollar so issued shall never be redeemed. I see no more reason why the unit of measure of value should be redeemed or redeemable, than that the yard-stick with which I measure my cloth or the quart with which I measure my milk should be redeemed.

Sixth. For convenience only, I propose that the dollar so issued shall be quite equal to or a little better than the present value of the average gold dollar of the world, not to be changed or changeable, if the gold dollar grows lower in value, or grows higher, or to be obliged to conform itself in value in any regard to the dollars of any other nation of the world, keeping itself always stable and fixed so that when all the property of the country adjusts itself to it as a measure of value it shall remain a fixed standard forever. But if it is ever changed, it shall change equally and alike for the creditor and the debtor; not as the dollar based upon supposed gold whose changes always have given the creditor the advantage.

To give the greenback currency thus described a fixed and stable value, I would make it fundable at all times, and at a sufficient number of places convenient to the people, in coupon or registered bonds of $50 and the multiples thereof up to $10,000, bearing interest at 3.65 per cent., payable semi-annually, which bonds should be reconvertible into currency at the pleasure of the holder at every public depository.

Thus I would have a currency better than a gold currency ; unalterable in value because founded upon the wealth, power, and property together with all the gold and silver of the country ; held by all the people, whose interest it would be to keep it a steady measure of value to which all property would soon accommodate itself, and ultimately the whole national debt would be brought home from abroad and funded into this national bond.

The war as to the currency still went on. In my last term I made a speech upon the question of the greenback being the constitutional money of the United States, whether issued under act of Congress in war or in peace.

The following is an extract : —

Therefore, Mr. Speaker, I am ready to say with the preacher (Ecclesiastes, v. 10): " He that loveth silver shall not be satisfied with silver." We want the greenback for our currency and mean to have it. Of that currency I said on this floor nine years ago and repeat now with all the confidence gained by experience : —

I stand here, therefore, for inconvertible paper money, the greenback, which has fought our battles and saved our country ; which has been held by us as a just equivalent for the blood of our soldiers, the lives of our sons, the widowhood of our daughters, and the orphanage of their children.

I stand here for a currency by which the business transactions of forty million people are safely and successfully done, which, founded on the faith, the wealth, and property of the nation, is at once the exemplar and engine of its industry and power ; that money which saved the country in war, and which has given it prosperity and happiness in peace. To it four million men owe their emancipation from slavery ; to it labor is indebted for elevation from that thrall of degradation in which it has been enveloped for ages. I stand for that money, therefore, which is by far the better agent and instrument of exchange of an enlightened and free people than gold and silver, the money alike of the BARBARIAN and the DESPOT.

Mr. Chittenden, a member from Brooklyn, N. Y., who was an honest opponent of my doctrine, came to me after I had finished my speech, and said : " You evidently believe in the legal correctness of your opinion ? "

" Certainly."

" Can this question be brought before the Supreme Court ? "

" Certainly."

" If it can, will you present the matter from your standpoint ? "

" I will."

" How can it be done ? " he asked.

" Let an amount of merchandise," said I, " be bought by A payable, according to the custom of the trade, in thirty days. The transaction must exceed in value five thousand dollars to go to the Supreme Court for jurisdiction. Let A when the debt is due procure greenbacks issued from the treasury since the war under act of Congress, so as to get rid of the question whether issuing of greenbacks is constitutional as a war measure, because if it is constitutional in time of peace, it certainly would be in time of war. Let him make a tender legal in form of such notes, in payment of the just claim of B. Let B refuse the tender as not legal, not being made in constitutional money, and bring a suit against A in the circuit court of the United States for the amount of his claim. Let A answer his tender of greenbacks as his sole defence in the suit of B. Let B demur to to that answer, and that will raise the question, and the single question."

" And will you defend the suit ? "

I said : " It is better that I should not. I certainly shall not in the circuit court, but I will see that it is properly defended in the Supreme Court without charge to anyone, and you had better gather the best talent you can to argue your side of the question in the Supreme Court."

" Whom would you suggest ? "

" I would suggest that you get Senator Edmunds, if you can."

The suit was brought, and the steps which I suggested were taken in it. The judge of the circuit court overruled the demurrer. The suit was taken to the Supreme Court of the United States. I assisted in preparing the brief upon which it was presented, but 'I did not argue the case before the court for I desired to divest the case of all political complexion.

It was a long time before it could be argued before that court, for it was a very great constitutional question, and the bench did not desire to pass upon it so long as there was a vacancy in that court. At last, the vacancy being filled, the case was fully heard and very well argued on both sides.

After deliberation the court decided, eight to one, that greenbacks were the constitutional money of the United States, Mr. Justice Field alone dissenting ; this decision will never hereafter be questioned. Since then the legal tender money of the United States has been at all times at a par with gold, and under some circumstances at a premium over it.

The bonds of the United States bearing five and six per cent. interest payable in gold, immediately rose to a high premium. The treasury had a surplus with which they had been redeeming these bonds as fast as they became due, sometimes buying them at a premium when it appeared necessary, in time of a panic or great stringency, to relieve the money market.

Investing capital in United States bonds which were worth a premium, was a great promoter of stringency and when that condition of the market took place, the bonds were an almost insuperable obstacle to a speedy relief. The reason for this state of things is this : In a tight money market the premium on the bonds went up because capitalists having their money invested in such bonds, their favorite investment, would not sell them and put the money in circulation. For example : Money is tight ; A, who is perfectly good and is known to be, but short of money of the circulating medium for his business, goes to his friend B for a loan. B says : "My money is in United States bonds ; I cannot loan any without selling my bonds, and if I do sell them and you take the money, say for six months, I don't know what premium I shall have to pay for the bonds when I want to reinvest my money in them ; it may be once or twice as much as any extra interest you could afford to pay me for the loan of the money."

I had introduced a proposition in the House for an interchangeable bond, that is, a bond which the treasury should issue at par payable in greenbacks, bearing 3.65 per cent. interest annually, the holder of the bond being privileged at any time to bring it back to the treasury and receive for it its amount and accrued interest. The rate of interest at that time was certain to be changed by the issue of bonds at a lower rate of interest without the interchange-able feature. Therefore whoever invested in the interchangeable bonds would be willing to loan them wherever he could get perfect security and a slightly advanced interest, because he would always reinvest his money in the same character of bond he loaned, at the treasury at any time at par. The party borrowing a bond could deliver it to his creditor, and if the creditor wanted to dispose of it he could also deliver it as money, the money for it being in the United States Treasury to be had for the asking. So that the very bond would become an extension of the currency, being used in business interchangeably with currency.

This proposition, which was intended for relief both of the United States from high rates of interest, and of the people from stringen-cies of the money market, met the utmost opposition of the treasury and the bankers, and a stream of derision was poured upon the plan as from the outlet of a fire engine. But it neither annoyed nor dis-turbed me, and I have lived to see the same proposition recommended by the treasury some years afterwards and favored in the Senate. But it did not suit the bankers.

I brought before the Treasury Department and endeavored to have adopted another system of financial action intended to utilize the national debt and also the financial machinery of the government, in lowering the rate of interest and establishing a system by which certain classes of people might invest their money in perfect safety for their support and comfort, and in which the investment would inure to the payment of the public debt. This was an adaptation of the system of " terminal annuities " resorted to in England when the government was under pressure to borrow money. But from their laws regarding the accumulation of property, it is not resorted to except in cases of necessity.

In this country our laws provide, somewhat, but do not go far enough, for the distribution of great estates among the people, upon the termination of the lives of those who own them. We abolished the laws of primogeniture by which such estates could be held together. Great Britain still retains that system, and great estates can thereby be held together from generation to generation. We have something which is worse in our system — corporations and trusteeships which keep moneys together in separate estates for several generations, and preserve great accumulations of it. More than this, it enables the estates to conspire together, to vitiate the purity of our elections, and, as is asserted and believed, the possessors of such estates have the power to buy their seats in the highest councils of the nation.

There is a necessity for some means of permanent investment for the benefit of those not able to take care of their property and themselves, which shall perfectly secure them the comforts and necessaries of life that their money would bring to them if they could spend it all while they lived. Further, it must be so secure as to leave them in no possible want during life. There was no such means in the country then and there is not now.

I am putting forth this matter here in the hope that it may attract the attention of the people, and that hereafter a system may be devised for carrying it out. Let me give an illustration or two so that every one may understand it.

I have a sister who is incapable of earning money or investing the money she has so that it will be absolutely safe. She has ten thousand dollars. If I can invest that so that she can spend the whole of that ten thousand dollars during her life, she can live in perfect comfort.

Oh, but it will be said, buy an annuity for her with her money in some annuity company.

True, but the annuity people want to make great profit out of that. She will get the least possible sum, and who shall say the annuity company will not fail in a series of years?

Now, let me take that ten thousand dollars and go to the government and say: "Calculating by the life tables, how much will you pay quarterly to my sister upon this deposit of ten thousand dollars, payment to stop when she dies and the deposit to revert to the United States?"

There can be no risk in that to the United States, because if my sister's health is not strong she may not live a great while; the rate depending on the average of lives, if she dies sooner than the average, the government will stop paying sooner and make so much money by it. Now, the income of ten thousand dollars, deducting the taxes and the risk of the investment, is only a very moderate sum to live upon. But if she can have in instalments the whole amount of her money, the principal and interest, to spend during her life, she can live in great comfort. Further, the money that the government receives as deposit may be invested at the highest rate of interest in payment of the national debt, and as the annuitants die out the debt will be paid. Let that annuity be non-assignable and not attachable, and let the checks for it go only to the annuitant personally and quarterly, or if she becomes insane, to her legal guardian.

As it is now I know of no place where such an investment can be made with perfect safety and certainty without its being very costly, heavy charges being collected to pay the profits of some company.

Let me take another case of which, unfortunately, there are so many unhappy ones existing which cannot now be provided for. A man who has worked the earlier part of his life and accumulated a large property, wishes to retire from business, or he would be glad to put his business into the hands of his children to be carried on for their benefit if he could safely do so. Under the terminal annuity system let him take one hundred thousand dollars of his money, or any other sum, and put it into the hands of the government, and receive back from them such portion of it every three months during his lifetime as such a sum will afford. Then he is certain, whatever happens to his business or whatever happens to his children, that he will have a lifelong support of comfortable size, or even better than that during his old age. And when he dies so much of the national debt will have been paid, because that one hundred thousand dollars has already been invested in the payment of the national debt and will not have to be paid over again.

I have said that the system of terminal annuities is an excellent way to borrow money, and in England the government issues annuities when it must have money. But as a rule the English system is that a man shall accumulate all he can to go to his son or according as he may will it. The English plan tends to keep accumulating property in the family, and is opposed to a man's spending all he has upon himself during his lifetime, and thus distributing his estate.

I laid this before two secretaries of the treasury, and the only objection ever made to it was that the government could not do any financial business. With such men as we have often had for

Secretary of the Treasury that is true. The Secretary of the Treasury has no time to attend to any such thing. He has an immense department wherein all the money received and all the money paid out by the United States must be taken care of by one man. It might be possible for him to do that, but still I think there ought to be two secretaries of the treasury, one to take care that the government gets all the money that it ought to get and to take care that it is paid into the treasury, and the other to take care of all the money that is paid out and to see that the government does not pay out anything it ought not to. But the difficulty with a single Secretary of the Treasury is that he has an immense collection of officers under him, and has the virtual appointment of them all; and there is not an honest Secretary of the Treasury that will not say that more of his time is taken up in discussion about offices, in signing commissions, and examinations into their action and in removing them, especially when there is any change in administration, than in all the rest of the business of the treasury.

Such a system of terminal annuities could be carried on very simply, without any complications whatever, and with no opportunity of loss to the government, and with immense gain to our people. It is not half as complicated or exposed to danger and loss as is the money-order system of the post-office department, and yet a few years ago it was thought impossible for that to be done by the government. Here and now is no place to argue these propositions, but simply to state the facts of the advantages of the system, so that, attention being called to them, it may help to work its way to being established.

The other great question which occupied my attention was that of reconstruction. With the radical Republicans of my party I held the proposition that I had before enunciated, namely, that the rebel States should be held as Territories under military government until all possibility of a race war or race dissensions between white and black should be obliterated, and that then those Territories might be admitted into the Union as States when the negro had learned how to be a citizen, and the white man had learned how to be a loyal one.

Slavery had been abolished by the thirteenth article of amendment to the Constitution. Although I finally agreed to this amendment, yet I differed somewhat from the radical men of my party in that I disbelieved in giving the negro a vote at once. For he was not yet quite taught how to use it, and was about as unfit to as the white man of the Southern States. The white man had misused it grievously and in a manner dangerous to the country, and might so do again ; and subsequent events have shown that he has in the matter of State government.

There were gentlemen of the Republican party in the House with political aspirations and hopes of the presidency, which I had not. These gentlemen were running a race to see how soon the Southern States could be admitted so as to take part in the election, and they were very bitterly opposed to my ideas. It is needless to say that the Democratic minority were equally opposed,— I am sorry I cannot with truth say more than " equally." The reason was that the Republican side desired the advantage of the negro vote and the other side wished to take advantage of the white vote.

Meanwhile some States were admitted, and, the ballot having been by constitutional amendment granted to the colored men, the white citizens of those States undertook to control the negro in the use of that ballot by a series of outrages and murders never equalled in a civilized country. There were numerous large bands of organized marauders called the Ku Klux, who were dressed in fantastic uniforms, and who rode at night and inflicted unnumbered and horrible outrages upon the negro so that he should not dare to come to the polls. Indeed, the men of the South seemed to think themselves excused in those outrages because they wanted to insure a white man's government in their States.

I desired that Congress should pass laws, which, with their punishments and modes of execution, would be sufficiently severe under the circumstances to prevent those outrages entirely, or at least to punish them. What those laws should be was the subject of most bitter controversy. Many of the Republicans in the House were more bitter in their opposition to stringent laws than were gentlemen on the other side who had served in the Confederate armies. The result was that a bill was taken away from the committee on the revision of laws of which I was the chairman, and given to a special committee. I am desirous of letting bygones be bygones, and I do not write this book for the purpose of reviving old controversies and quarrels but simply to justify myself in my course, and I mention no names and I do not go into particulars. But if any of my colleagues in Congress, at that time, especially from my own State choose to criticise this part of my work, I shall be very happy hereafter to meet them upon this proposition with an answer in which, if it becomes necessary, I shall declare the *whole* truth and nothing but the truth.

A bill was reported by that special committee. By the bill this murdering of negroes by Ku Klux riders at night was to be deemed conspiracy, and punished by fine and imprisonment. But the prisoner would first have to be convicted by a Southern jury, and upon these juries other members of the Ku Klux could serve if their own cases were not on trial. That bill was passed, and the government made great show of enforcing it. The chief justice of the Supreme Court of the United States even went down to give dignity to the trials and to expound the law; but nobody was convicted, with some few exceptions where the charges were made against some unlucky and unpopular white man of the South. After trying cases a few weeks, the chief justice gave up in despair, and the riders at night went on with their outrages until the good sense of the respectable people of the South put their condemnation upon it and then they stopped. But the outrages did not stop, and murders of white men and colored men on political inducements in some parts of the South have continued to this day. I take leave reverently to thank God that no drop of that blood sprinkles even the hem of my garments.

Early in the administration of President Johnson, under Mr. Seward, Secretary of State, attempts were made to negotiate with England for reparation for the acts — injurious to us — committed by her during the war. These subsequently became known as the Alabama claims, after the captures by the rebel cruiser Alabama and her consorts of our vessels during the war, which drove our commerce substantially from the seas. When the war broke out, America's commerce was the second largest in the world, and not far behind that of Great Britain. When the war closed, our flag had been substantially driven from the ocean. The ports of Great Britain and its colonies had been made depots from which arms, ammunition, and every manner of supplies were shipped to the Confederates. Not to any considerable extent was this the case with the ports of other nations, save, perhaps, of Cuba. It compelled us to establish,

WENDELL PHILLIPS.

at an enormous cost, and maintain for four years, blockading fleets whose business was simply to prevent the running in and out of Confederate ports of vessels loaded with arms, ammunition, provisions, and every class of smuggled goods. As I have stated before, Southern cotton had advanced from ten cents a pound at the beginning of the war to a dollar a pound. It must be had in England or the laborers of her cotton manufactories would starve. The steamship builders of Scotland and England supplied large numbers of blockade runners of the finest construction, and of the greatest speed, so as to elude and escape our slower, old-fashioned naval vessels.

All these smuggled supplies substantially were paid for in cotton, and one half of all the cotton shipped abroad was by the act of the Confederate Congress to be devoted to the purchase of Confederate governmental supplies.

There is a curious fact that I desire to state in regard to blockade running and the capture of blockade runners: An examination of the captures will show a much larger number of the higher class blockade runners captured when coming out again from blockaded ports than when running in. A Scotch runner could be loaded up with supplies of various sorts and run in, we will say at Wilmington, eluding our blockaders by its swiftness. Because of the necessities of the South the cargo of supplies was sold to them at enormous prices and paid for in cotton at ten or fifteen cents a pound, with which the vessel was then loaded to its utmost capacity. That cotton if brought to Europe or a Northern port would bring a dollar a pound, so that the cargo was exceedingly valuable — very much more valuable than the cargo brought in. Every ton would be worth say $2,000, or a hundred tons $200,000, and proportionally more for larger vessels, and that would be the worth of the capture in proportion if the blockade runner was caught coming out and sent as prize to New York. Now one half of the proceeds was always paid to the capturing crew and fleet. But vessels captured when they were running in with an ordinary cargo on board, and sent to New York, would pay not much more, when sold at auction, than the legal costs and expenses of the transaction. Thus our system of prize money was in fact a bribe to every one of our blockading vessels of many, many dollars to let all blockade runners in with their supplies and catch them when they came out with their cargo of cotton.

Yet our Secretary of the Navy never waked up during the four years of the war to that condition under which he put his blockading fleets.

The Dominion of Canada was made a headquarters for the concoction and carrying out of all sorts of incursions upon our territory, robbing banks, setting fire to our cities, sending garments charged with infectious disease to be distributed among our people, and affording a path for supplies of British gold by which our currency was debased by speculators in gold, by raising large premiums upon gold supplied through English sources. These, with the encouragement given by England from the very beginning of the war that if the South could make sufficient headway to justify the British government in declaring the independence of the Confederacy it would so do,— all these formed an aggregate of national wrongs and injuries that could not be compensated for by money. Through the greed of the influence thus moving upon President Johnson, a treaty was concluded which made a settlement of the Alabama claims for the actual destruction of some property. This treaty was submitted to the Senate and rejected, but was again renewed in the commencement of the administration of President Grant. A commission from England was sent to Washington to negotiate it. A treaty was negotiated called the Treaty of Washington, which I then believed, and still believe, to be exceedingly adverse to American interests.

I advised President Grant against it in every possible form, and against any treaty. I said our claims as a nation against England are simply incalculable, and the only negotiation should be to see what recompense other than money we should receive from her. I suggested that in the most diplomatic language possible and with all the amenities of statecraft, we should say in substance to England: " You have done more against our country than you can ever repay. To settle those injuries we want you to remove yourself as far as possible from being our neighbor, and give up the province of Canada. You have been an exceedingly bad neighbor from the beginning, and we want you near us no more. Cede Canada to us and we will settle all difficulties and give you a clean release of all claims."

Grant was impressed with my idea, but the bondholders changed his determination. They claimed that if we had any trouble with England our bonds would be depreciated. To that I answered: "What harm in that depreciation? We shall pay the interest on them to the last dollar, and some day we shall be able to pay the principal, and whether they are quoted on the stock exchange as worth more or less they will finally be as valuable in fact as if we were in a state of perfect peace."

But nothing that I could do or say would bring him to the point of asking proper reparation from England. We had allowed to us by the Geneva tribunal the sum of $15,000,000, reckoning interest, one third of which we had to pay back because our fishermen fished in Canadian waters, and this one third was claimed to be the value of the fish swimming in the sea we might have caught. That is all that the government ever got for national injuries. All that we did get has been paid out to private claimants, so as a nation we took nothing.

I took no part in the proceedings of the Republican party in seating Hayes, and had nothing to do with what I believed then and still believe was a wrong to the country in debasing the elective franchise.

With the exception of my services in Congress, I had but one other call to public duty on the part of the United States. At the close of the war we had a large number of soldiers wounded and disabled in the line of duty, who had no homes in which they could be properly cared for and no places of refuge at all competent for their condition, save the almshouses of the cities, counties, and States. In 1866 Congress established a national asylum for the relief of the disabled volunteer officers and men, and appointed a Board of Managers to take charge of the same. Of this board I was president and executive officer, which position I continued to hold for some fourteen years.

In 1871 I had a desire to know two things: First, whether having been a consistent Republican and acting with that party, the opposition towards me evinced in all my campaigns for Congress had ceased; and secondly, whether I had not a right to aspire to be governor of my State. Therefore I offered myself to the Republican party as a candidate for the nomination for that office. Upon the contest before the election I was not unfairly beaten by the Hon. William B. Washburn, who was nominated by a small majority over me, and whose election I supported as I ought.

In 1872, supposing that I had gauged the strength of the opposition, I presented myself again as a candidate for the nomination against Governor Washburn. He had some advantage over me in the fact that he had been governor one year. At the primary meetings for the election of delegates to the convention more than a majority of the delegates elected were in my favor. The State Central Committee, who were bitterly opposed to me, organized the convention against me. They got up contesting delegations and kept the contest going on over those delegates until midnight. By this hour the delegates from the country, who were my friends, had largely gone home. Then the committee were enabled, through fraud and deception, by substituting their own friends for these absent delegates and by putting tickets of admission to the floor into the hands of those who were not elected delegates, to cast a larger number of ballots at midnight than rightfully constituted the convention, and thus they defeated my nomination.

They then declared that I never should be governor of Massachusetts. I answered that declaration of war by saying that I would be governor of Massachusetts. I then came to the conclusion that I could not be governor in the Republican party. I allowed myself to be put in nomination as an independent candidate for governor in 1878, and as such reduced the Republican majority largely. I also had the nomination of the Democratic party; but the same class of men in that party that had always opposed me in the Republican party made a bolt from the convention and ran a candidate against me, so that I was not elected, although I received a very large number of votes. In 1879, I was again candidate for governor, having the nomination of the Democratic party. The Hunker Democrats ran a bolting candidate, and I was again defeated, but held substantially the same vote that I had received the year before.

In 1880 I supported the nomination of General Hancock for President, the first Democratic candidate I had supported for President since the war began.

In 1882 I came to the conclusion to try the question of my being governor of Massachusetts directly and fully against the Republican party, although they had the prestige of just electing a president and had the administration. The hunkers of the Democratic party, having found their utter inability to carry any votes worth counting, did not run a bolting candidate, and I received my nomination from the party with great unanimity. I canvassed the State again and was elected governor by a plurality of nearly 14,000, the total vote of the State being in the neighborhood of a quarter of a million.

I took my seat and gave the legislature an address in which I advocated many democratic measures. Many of them have since been adopted by the Republican party in their attempts to hold their power.

As this book may be read by people not living in Massachusetts, I may say that the governor of Massachusetts has less administrative power than the governor of any other State. The legislature was in large majority against me. Of his own motion the governor can nominate officers, but these officers cannot serve until the appointments are agreed to by an executive council of nine. In my council every member but one was opposed to me. The governor cannot even pardon an innocent man out of the State prison except by the advice and consent of the council. There was but one thing that I could do, and that was to attempt to reform the eleemosynary institutions of the State. I found that the State almshouse at Tewksbury, where there were some seven or eight hundred State paupers, more or less, had been carried on with such extent of peculation, that even the corpses of the paupers that died there were sold as a matter of traffic, and were delivered at Harvard College for use there; and that sometimes the bodies were skinned and the skins tanned. I attempted an investigation of that lazar house. The Republican party employed counsel to sustain the officer of the institution at great expense, and did everything it could to embarrass me and hinder the investigation. But I managed to have officers appointed to the institution that would do their duty, and for awhile since it has been properly carried on so far as I know and as a private citizen have means of being informed.

This investigation was productive of great good because it called the attention of the whole people of the country in the several States to the condition of things in institutions, and investigations of like character into their affairs in the succeeding year were quite general and caused great reforms.

I forgot to mention that there is one other thing that the governor of Massachusetts by long custom and law can do, and that is to issue a proclamation appointing in the spring a day of fasting and prayer, and in the autumn after the harvest a day of thanksgiving. Thanksgiving is usually the last Thursday of November, and the day of fasting and prayer is the first Thursday of April.

To state the fact exactly, I had forgotten my duty as to the fasting proclamation. A few days before the time, the Secretary of State came into the executive office, and said: "Governor, have you got your Fast Day proclamation ready?"

"No, I have not," said I.

"Well, you ought to get it ready, because the Friday preceding Fast Day I am to put copies of the proclamation into the hands of the sheriffs of all the counties and to clergymen, who on the next Sunday are to give notice of the fast and read the proclamation from their pulpits. I have but little more than time to do it now, and therefore I want to have the proclamation in the hands of the printer at the earliest possible moment."

"You shall have it, sir," I said," "and I am obliged to you for calling it to my attention." I then reflected. I had written something about almost everything, but my composition had not usually been in the line of Fast Day proclamations. I had heard some read from the pulpit and they were generally pretty lengthy and verbose compositions filled with religious and pious sayings and recommendations. My utter inability to do that sort of thing well, even if I had ever so much time, weighed upon me. But I managed by the second morning afterwards to put into the hands of the Secretary of State a proclamation that was quite satisfactory to me—indeed I thought it a very good one. He took it and distributed it, and on the Friday before Fast Day it was published in the newspapers—that is, in some of the few that would publish anything of mine. I insert here a copy of the proclamation:—

COMMONWEALTH OF MASSACHUSETTS.

By His Excellency Benjamin F. Butler, Governor and Commander-In-Chief.

A PROCLAMATION

FOR A DAY OF HUMILIATION, FASTING, AND PRAYER.

In conformity with the invariable uses of this Commonwealth and with a sense of our absolute dependence upon the beneficent parent of mankind, and of our numerous and aggravated offences against His holy will and commandments, I have thought fit to appoint, and by and with the advice and consent of the Council, I do appoint THURSDAY, the 5th day of April next, as a day of public humiliation, fasting, and prayer in this Commonwealth. And I request the ministers and people of every religious denomination throughout the same to assemble on that day in their several places of worship that we may unitedly humble ourselves in the presence of Almighty God, and acknowledge, with deep contrition, our manifold sins and transgressions ; that we may devotedly deprecate His judgments and implore His merciful forgiveness through the merits of our blessed Lord and Redeemer.

While we thus bow in humble adoration before the Most High, let us render Him our unfeigned thanks for the numerous instances of His continual bounty toward us and our fathers, whom He planted in this fruitful soil, and, in an especial manner, that He endowed them with wisdom to render this a land of piety, freedom, and order. And, inasmuch as we have disregarded their example and neglected those principles by which they obtained and transmitted to us the inestimable blessings of the Christian religion, of law and of liberty, let us earnestly beseech Him to heal our backslidings and restore us to that temper and conduct by which alone we can hope to be happy in this world and in that which is to come.

At the same time that we look with all humility to His grace for the remission of our sins, let us, with one mind and one voice, supplicate His blessings for us and our beloved country, that He would alike preserve us from the pestilence that walketh in darkness and the destruction that wasteth noonday ; that he would graciously smile on the labors of the husbandmen, and cause the earth to bring forth her increase in due season ; that He would relieve our commerce from the embarrassments with which it is burdened, and grant that prosperity may again distinguish our navigation and fisheries, so that they who "go down to the sea in ships" and do business in great waters, may have abundant reason to praise His holy name.

That He would afford success to our manufactures and prosper all the works of our hands.

That He would graciously condescend to direct the Government of the United States, and give them wisdom to discern and firmness to pursue the true interests of the country ; that He would preserve us from war and from all connections that lead to dishonor and adversity ; that He would dispel the clouds that encompass us about, and continue to us the enjoyments of peace, liberty, and religion ; that He would influence the governors of the several States to do everything within their respective spheres to preserve the Union, order, tranquility, and independence of the United States; that He would protect us from the assaults of open enemies, and from the snares of insidious friends; that He would suffer no weapon formed against us to prosper, but would set as naught the councils of those who devise mischief against us.

That He would vouchsafe His blessings on our university, our colleges and seminaries of learning; that He would bless all means used for propagating true religion, and promote the pious purposes of those who endeavor to disseminate a knowledge of the Holy Scriptures that all may learn His will and obey His commandments.

And it is recommended that all unnecessary labor and recreation be suspended on that day; *and I do specially exhort the ministers of the gospel on that day to feed their flocks the divine word, and not discourse upon political and other secular topics which divert the serious thoughts of the people from the humble worship of the Father.*

Given at the council chamber in Boston this 11th day of February, in the year of our Lord 1883, and in the 107th year of the independence of the United States of America.

BENJAMIN F. BUTLER.

By his Excellency the Governor, with the advice and consent of the Council.

HENRY B. PEIRCE, *Secretary.*

GOD SAVE THE COMMONWEALTH OF MASSACHUSETTS.

Now, be it known that the good and pious gentlemen who occupied many of the pulpits in Massachusetts were quite active politicians, and it was very common for them to preach political sermons on Fast and Thanksgiving Days. Just as the professors of colleges know all about political economy, and therefore nearly all of them teach free trade, so these clergymen believed they knew all about finance, when the only financial operation which most of them had, except drawing their salaries, was to count the money in the contribution-boxes. I learned on the Monday before Fast Day that a great many of the clergymen had refused to read such a blasphemous proclamation as mine to their congregations; and that some had read it and commented upon it as they read, and that some after reading it carefully emphasized the customary closing phrase, " God save the Commonwealth of Massachusetts " with great fervor, as if under the present governor there was great necessity for such intervention in **that** direction. Some of the newspapers criticised it severely. On Fast Day many of the clergymen preached upon it, and expounded its extreme obnoxiousness to everything that was decent and proper.

I bore all this with a patient shrug, " for sufferance is the badge of all our tribe." I even waited until my good friends, the parsons, could have another lick at the proclamation on the next Sunday. Then I thought this matter had gone far enough, and I was put in mind of it by receiving a call from a short-hand reporter representing one of the leading journals of Boston, who came to me and asked me if I had read any of the criticisms of my Fast Day proclamation in the papers or any of the Fast Day sermons that had been published, and whether I would be willing to say anything about them for publication. I told him that my attention being called to the matter of the preparation of the proclamation I sat down to the task and as I was very busy and pressed for time, I bethought myself that possibly some one of my venerable predecessors in office might have issued a proclamation which would suit my case, and I sent for some of the earlier proclamations, and after examining them found one that just suited me. It was the proclamation of Governor Christopher Gore in 1810. I knew something of his history. He was a very learned and pious man, a graduate of Harvard College, for whom one of their principal halls had been named as a memorial. His proclamation calling for prayers for our fishing, navigation, and manufacturing interests seemed appropriate to my condition, and its tone was admirable. It covered every point except one, and that I inserted. Governor Gore asked the people to abstain from all secular labors, but went no further because the clergymen of that day did not usually preach upon secular topics. I added the necessary exhortation against that in the following words :

" I do specially exhort the ministers of the gospel on that day to feed their flocks with the divine word and not discourse upon political and other secular topics which may direct the serious thoughts of the people from the humble worship of the Father."

So that all the criticism except upon that one sentence, for the rest was verbatim, was directed against that learned and pious man and not against me. I was glad that I made the selection of the proclamation of Governor Gore, because I could throw all the blame for want of piety or proper religious sentiment that might appear in that document upon him, and I claim no credit about the matter except for the selection of the proclamation of Governor Gore, which seemed to me to be the best of those I examined.

I heard that after the publication of my statement in the newspapers pretty much the whole Commonwealth enjoyed themselves in laughing at the ministers' mistakes.

It is needless to mention that the good clergymen of the Commonwealth have subsequently preached against me, although I earnestly hope they all now pray for me.

During my term of office I appointed a few executive officers and some judicial ones to which my council would not consent. I appointed some other officers to whom they were obliged "to advise and consent."

Massachusetts, as it may be remembered, was a strong anti-slavery State. That very humane but rather aggressive doctrine absolutely flamed over the State for years, but no governor had ever appointed a negro to any prominent office.

In the judiciary district of Charlestown, a portion of Boston, the office of judge became vacant, and as we had as a member of the bar in Boston a very reputable and well-read lawyer who was a negro, a Democrat, and formerly a member of the legislature, Edwin G. Walker, Esq., I nominated him for the position, but my Republican council would not advise and consent he should have his commission. I then looked around for another reputable negro lawyer who should be a Republican in politics, and finding one, George L. Ruffin, Esq., nominated him, and the council dared not take the responsibility of his rejection. This judge held his office during his life and to the entire acceptance of the community.

The State prison being in a condition of revolt when I took possession of the executive office I appointed a fellow-soldier, Col. Roland G. Usher, an independent Republican, to be its warden. It had been the custom of former wardens to go around through the prison armed from head to foot. Indeed, years before one warden had been killed by the prisoners. The new warden carried no weapons, and had no guard, and the prisoners treated him as their friend and benefactor. He retained his office through several administrations that succeeded mine, and was asked still further to retain it but resigned to attend to his private business affairs.

No Irish Catholic had ever been appointed to a judicial office in Massachusetts, and a vacancy occurring on the bench in the judicial district of Boston, I appointed an able friend of mine, of that nationality and religious belief, the Hon. M. J. McCafferty, who held the office until his death, with high encomiums from all.

The office of insurance commissioner is one of the most important in Massachusetts. It covers fire and life insurance and a very large number of associations doing business in the State in creating funds by assessments to relieve the necessities of future want, accident, disease, and, in most cases to provide insurance on lives. There had been great complaint of the administration of that office, and the insurance commissioner who had held it for many years resigned. I at first appointed one of my ablest friends, N. A. Plympton, Esq., to that office. But as he had been one of my ardent political friends and, as such, had done what he could to aid me in my canvass, his appointment was of course not consented to by the council. I then appointed my opponent for election to Congress in my last election, Hon. John K. Tarbox, a warm personal friend. His commission issued and he held the office until his death some years afterwards. He inaugurated a system of reforms and put the business of the department on such a basis and brought it up to such a standing that he was re-appointed by those who succeeded me as Republican governors. And, indeed, I may say here that substantially all the officers appointed by me were allowed to serve for years afterwards, so long as health permitted and they chose so to do.

Another amusing incident occurred, the history of which had better be preserved. From the beginning of the government under our Constitution, Harvard College, which was a State institution and was adopted as such by our fathers in the Constitution, had always been visited by the governor in such state as he saw fit upon the occasion of its annual commencement, and it had been the regular custom of the board of overseers of that institution to issue a diploma for the honorary degree of Doctor of Laws to every governor, whether his former life had been that of a shoemaker, a paper maker or a woollen manufacturer, neither of whom made any pretence of a knowledge of the law more than would be required by any intelligent business man. But the government of the institution was composed in a large majority of my political adversaries, and the president of the board was Mr. Ebenezer Rockwood Hoar, the bolting candidate who ran against me for Congress in 1876, and whom I destroyed utterly by a kindly open letter to him describing his political acts and character, as I have before set forth. Another matter, of which I have already given an account, which might have influenced that board against me, was the investigation of the Tewksbury almshouse. I had brought to light the manner in which the college was unlawfully supplied with many bodies of paupers for dissection.

I now learned that for the first time this rule of conferring a degree upon the governor was to be broken, and that it had been voted that the degree of LL. D. should not be conferred upon me. It was also rumored that if the governor attended the commencement he would not be treated by the students with the respect due to his office.

I was not particularly troubled about the degree of LL. D., for that had been conferred on me several years before by the rival of Harvard college in Massachusetts, Williams College; and I now hold that degree in colleges in three New England States, and I can read my diploma in the Latin tongue, as perhaps one half my predecessors in the executive office who got the degree could not do.

The treatment of the students I did not fear, and upon the whole I thought it would be more proper and dignified conduct on my part to attend the commencement with all the state and escort with which any governor had ever attended, especially as I received the customary invitation so to do from the high-minded and learned president of the college, Mr. Eliot. Almost as a matter of course, therefore, I was received with very proper courtesy and treatment upon my visit, which was really a very enjoyable occasion.

One result of this visit was that I broke the mould; the college has not since conferred at its commencement the degree of LL. D. upon all the governors irrespective of their merits to that literary distinction, and they felt themselves obliged to refuse it to my successor, Gov. Geo. D. Robinson, although he was an eminent lawyer, and as such was entitled to that honor.[1]

---

[1] The college had also been accustomed for many years to give that degree to the President who should visit Massachusetts during his term of office, and it was given to every one without question until it became a matter of discussion in the case of President Andrew Jackson; and while the degree was conferred upon him in due form, one of the students in the senior class addressed the President in behalf of the class in Latin, of which of course he understood not a word. The opposition made much of this and among the jokes, Major Jack Downing, the

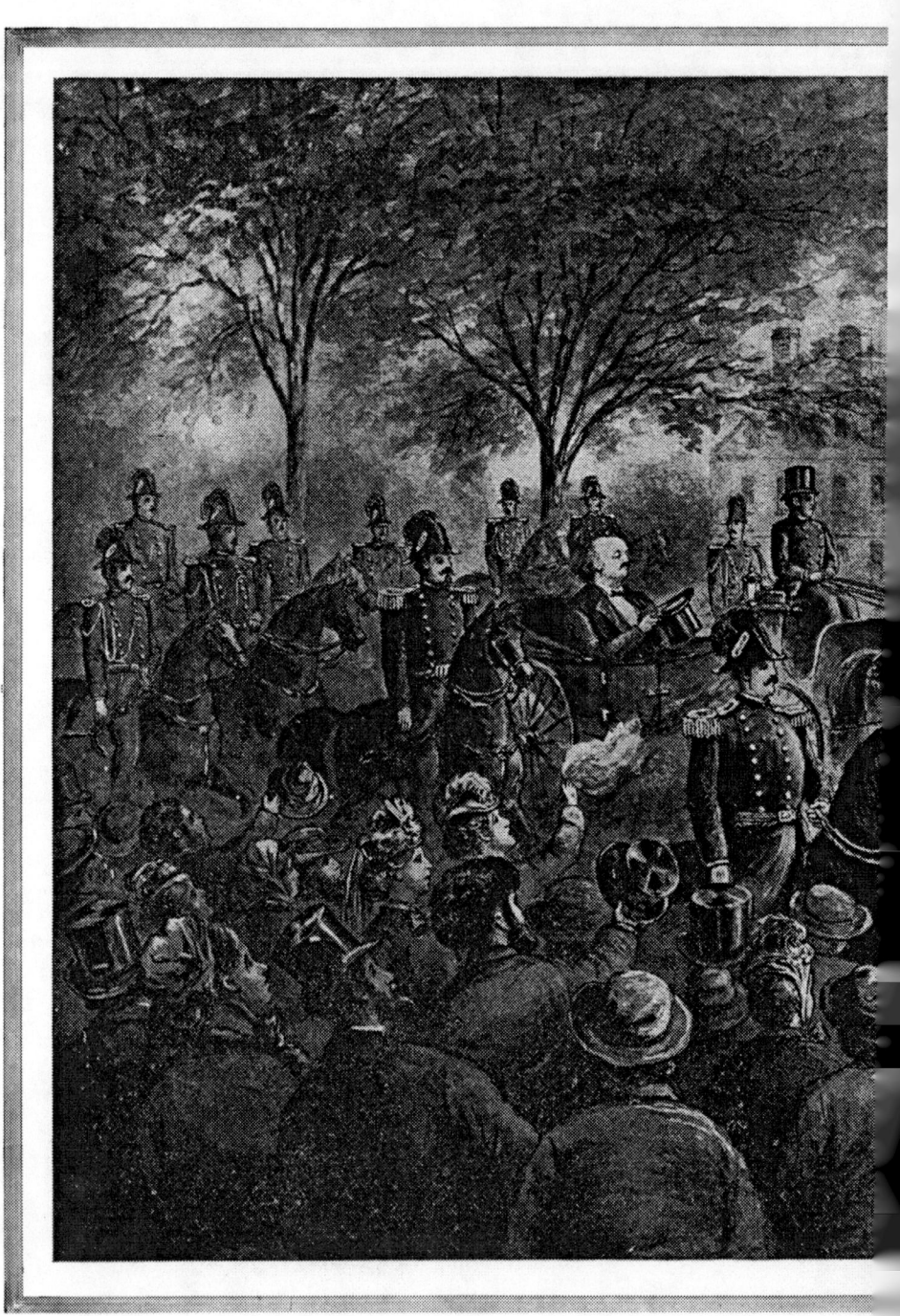

GOV. BENJ. F. BUTLER AND ESCORT ON THE

TO UNIVERSITY EXERCISES AT HARVARD, 1883.

When the necessity for the proclamation of Thanksgiving came I took time to write my own proclamation and it passed muster without a word of adverse criticism, but that was perhaps because it was issued after my defeat at the November election.

At the wishes of my friends I entered into the canvass for a re-election and a very bitter and fatiguing one it was. The Republican party, knowing that if I was re-elected it had lost the State, possibly for all time, put forth every energy to beat me. It may be well for my readers outside the State to know that every man was then required to pay a poll tax before he could vote. The expenditure of money in the State for the payment of poll taxes would very largely increase the vote, and I may say every means was used by my opponents for that purpose. My defeat was wholly due to the opposition headed by the rum element of the Democratic party in Boston, for I carried a majority of the votes in the other portions of the State. This element had been induced, by what means I know not, except that I had done nothing in my administration to favor their traffic, to use their combined efforts in behalf of my opponent. I was informed and believe that the inducement for their so doing was the payment of money by the Republican party to that end. One thing happened: the press in Boston upon which were being printed my ballots the night before election fortunately for them broke down, so that there was a great scarcity of my ballots at the polling-places.

Although I received in excess of 150,000 votes, and the balance of my State ticket received an average of over 146,000, I was defeated by some 9,000 in a total vote largely exceeding that cast in any preceding election.

Having redeemed my promise to my enemies that I would be governor of Massachusetts I have never put myself in the way of being voted for for that place since.

In 1884, I was elected by the Democratic State Convention of Massachusetts one of the delegates at large to attend the National

---

humorous letter writer who accompanied Jackson, describing the scene, asserts that at Downingville where the President was received and made a speech, some one called out: " You must give us some Latin, Doctor," whereupon the President off with his hat again and said: " Fellow-citizens, *e pluribus unum, sina qua non.*"

The college still continues its habit of conferring this degree upon the President. The whole performance is a cheap, convenient mode of advertising the college, and in some cases withholding the degree offers a better means of extensive advertising than would have been obtained by conferring it.

Convention at Chicago. I was very kindly received by the multitude attending that convention and was put upon a committee to report a platform for the party. There were very able men in that committee and men of very decided and somewhat discordant opinions.

We found no difficulty in coming together on most questions, but we divided nearly in the middle upon the question of the tariff. As I have stated before I had the strongest belief in the necessity for the protection of American labor, and I have always remained of that conviction. In the then state of the country I thought all other questions were subordinate to this one. On this question the committee remained in conference three days, and I may as well say nights. I could not agree that the Democratic party, which I supposed would be in the ascendant, could stand upon anything but the Jackson doctrine of a "*judicious tariff,*" a tariff to raise sufficient revenue for the wants of the country and to give American industry incidental protection against foreign labor. I was overruled and some mongrel resolution was adopted which meant anything or nothing as one chose to construe it.

The committee reported its resolution, and I made a report of the labor convention and received not so large a support as I could wish, but a very generous one. I said I could not support the nominee whoever he might be who stood upon such a platform as had been reported. I thought the nominee should be a western man, a man from a State where large American industries, beside agriculture, were carried on, and I hoped very much that Hendricks of Indiana would be the man Upon a conference with him I said I would support him if nominated notwithstanding the platform, because I knew how a man from a State like Indiana would construe it. But the delegation of the State of New York carried the nomination of Mr. Cleveland by insisting upon voting as a unit, by voting a majority, which States had not unfrequently done in the Democratic conventions before the war. I remember an instance of Virginia voting a great many times in the Baltimore convention which nominated Pierce in favor of Buchanan, although they stood eight to seven as between Buchanan and Douglas.

The nomination of Mr. Cleveland I looked upon as a victory of the free traders of New York City. The convention adjourned and we went home. I had several strong inducements offered me by my friends, purporting to come from the highest authorities, that in case I would support Mr. Cleveland I should receive the highest consideration in his administration. I replied to that, that I wanted for myself nothing of office; my own law office was better pecuniarily and every other way for me than any office I could have under an administration, and I did not care very much to go further into politics. It is of no special consequence that the three propositions which were adopted by him and that wholly related to public affairs should be set down here and now; they are past.

Looking at the men who were gathered around Mr. Cleveland and at the doctrines they entertained, I thought I foresaw great danger to the country in his election. If the Republican party won, the preservation of the tariff was assured. I thought I would see, by a fusion of the greenback party and the Democrats in the Western States and in New Jersey and New York, if enough votes could not be procured to prevent the election of Mr. Cleveland by getting enough electoral votes for the fusion ticket.

I labored assiduously throughout the campaign to this end. It was supposed that a fusion could be made in Michigan, Indiana, West Virginia, and New Jersey; the fusion was made in Michigan, and we voted a generous ticket with the understanding that the electors should represent the respective parties to the fusion in the proportion of the votes cast by each—that is, if the Democrats cast one half the vote they were to have one half the electors, and the greenbackers were to have the other half, or whatever the relative vote of the two parties was to the electors, they were to be divided in the same proportion.

In Indiana the fusion failed, those having charge of the fusion party in that State, for some reason never explained to me, having given way. In West Virginia and in New Jersey the fusion also failed. The only hope was then in my drawing enough votes from the Democratic party from the State of New York to prevent its throwing its vote for Cleveland. I was supported by the strongest man, the one of the greatest influence that I knew in the State of New York, Mr. John Kelly, who represented the opposition to Mr. Cleveland.

Election day came, and there were votes enough thrown for me several times over to have prevented Mr. Cleveland's election, but in many of the polling-places they were counted not for me, but for Cleveland, and so the electoral ticket for the State of New York was counted for him by a few hundred votes only.

At first I intended to have an investigation made to prove the facts I have stated, as could have been done ; but Mr. Kelly was taken sick almost immediately after the election and could not attend to business. With him to aid me I could have proven the case ; without him I could not bring in the witnesses against the great influence of a successful administration and would fail of proof, and therefore the investigation was not instituted. But I felt certain then, as I do now, that there were votes to the number of several thousand that were wrongly counted in that election.

Since that time I have taken no part in politics, save that in the campaign of 1888 I made a single speech in Boston in behalf of the tariff, and I repeated that speech at Detroit, at the request of President Harrison. Michigan was regarded as a doubtful State, as another attempt was being made to have a fusion between the Democrats and greenbackers in that campaign, such as was carried out in the previous one, and I used all the influence I could to prevent its being done.

CHAPTER XXI.

PRACTICE OF THE LAW.

THE beginning of Chapter II. of this book having brought the events of my life down to my preparation for my profession and my admission to the bar, I thought it best to postpone a narration of the events of my professional career until I had set forth in due order the circumstances and opinions which brought me into the war and politics and until I had given the history of what I did or omitted to do in those great contests. Since that has been done, imperfectly as it may be, I propose to deal in the following pages, so far as the limits of my undertaking may allow, with the history of my pursuit of my profession. One event which controlled me in this regard was that declining years made it uncertain how long my health and strength would permit me to undergo the great labor of studying and writing a history of the war so far as it concerned myself. Therefore I was induced to do that first, so as to be sure that the narrative of all I had done in the war should be set forth by my own hand, — for nobody could make it complete but myself; and it was due to my own reputation and my children and friends that that should be done at all hazards, if life lasted so long. With this thought I had made provision with my publishers that if health and strength failed me, the rest of my history might be written by an editor who could present that part of my life-work better than I could do it myself, and we had agreed that that editor should be my friend, Mr. James Parton, the historian, who promised, if called upon, to undertake the work. But it has so happened that while writing this book I have been obliged to bow my head with sorrowing anguish beside his coffin.

I began the practice of the law September 3, 1840, being between twenty-one and twenty-two years of age, illy prepared, I admit. I was not obliged, before entering the courts, to pass through the novitiate that delays most young men. My teacher, Wm. Smith, Esq., had some cases in court which he placed in my charge, he never afterwards himself trying a case in court, to my knowledge, and this brought me early before courts and juries.

During my studies I became enamored with the rules of pleading, and especially with the rules of criminal pleading which seemed to me almost an exact science, requiring accuracy of statement, clearness and earnestness of thought, and exactness in logic, for if the pleader tripped in any one part he failed in all. The statement of civil cases, which at one time was as exact, had so been relaxed by the statutes of jeofails and amendment, that if a lawyer failed to state his case correctly he has an opportunity of trying again by amendment. This was very convenient, but it tended to raise up a class of very poor lawyers, who instead of carefully studying their cases at first, and thinking them out so as to put them in order with exactness, slovenly trusted to regain their lost ground by amending their statements. As the rules of pleading in regard to many petty offences were quite as strict as in higher and more important cases, my attention was turned to the defence of criminals. Not so with civil cases, for of those of importance the young lawyer gets very few.

I tried my cases critically, catching at every point in the faults of my opponents, and of course was immediately called "sharp" by the attorneys conducting criminal causes, who frequently begged of me to overlook their blunders which might enable me to save my clients. But upon these matters I was inexorable; I held that a good point of law in his favor was as much the property of my client as was a good point of fact, and that I had no more right to waive one than to give up the other.

I was quite successful in my defences of criminals, and very early, while it was expected of me that I should speak to the court only with bated "breath and whispering humbleness," I ran against an elderly judge, quite a good lawyer, who believed that young men should take back seats and keep them. I may be permitted to give the incident: —

Peter Moore was indicted for adultery with one Mary Stuart, she being then a married woman, and having a husband alive. Now adultery in Massachusetts was punishable by confinement of three years in the State Prison, whereas the laws of some States leave that crime as if it were almost an accomplishment.

When Moore was called to plead guilty or not guilty, I took the objection that no offence was stated against him because it was not alleged in the indictment that Mary Stuart was not Moore's wife. The prosecuting attorney, a lawyer advanced in years, stated that that form of indictment was taken from Davis' Precedents, Davis having a great many years before been solicitor-general of the State, and that a great many persons had been convicted upon such an indictment, and the objection had never been taken before. To that I replied that this was a question of pleading, and however long the fault existed it was clear that it did not aver the offence. The court having heard the argument stated that the point was a "sharp" one, and although he might be wrong in his ruling, yet he preferred to err with the ancients, rather than be right with the new notions which were being pressed upon the court. Somewhat to his surprise and disgust I remarked to him that I proposed to show that he had "erred with the ancients," and to do so I should bring a writ of error to the Supreme Court. The case was taken to that court, and after argument the point was decided in my favor. When I got a copy of that decision of the court, I enclosed it to my friend, the presiding justice at the trial, saying that I hoped he would read the decision and have the pleasure of knowing that he had "erred with the ancients." I afterwards tried many cases before him, but he never repeated that phrase to me.

Perhaps the reader will permit another illustration: Elijah Record, who was a burglar by trade, got short of false door-keys and went down to supply himself one morning through one of the principal streets of Lowell. Whenever he saw a key left in the door lock, and the owner of the shop not in sight, he would take it out of the lock and put it in his pocket, for a little filing would make of it a skeleton key which would open several locks. He had got one or more keys and then, coming to a shop, the door of which stood open, being unable to see anybody, he proceeded to take the key from the door and put it in his pocket. But the owner of the store was sitting directly behind the door reading a newspaper. He heard the noise made by turning the key, and saw the key taken out of the door. He sprang after Record, who, unfortunately for himself, fell into the arms of a police officer within a few feet, and was arrested, having dropped the abstracted key on the sidewalk, which the owner picked up. It was marked, and Record was taken to the lock-up.

Now Record was known to the district attorney, as he had escaped him once or twice, and he was very glad to get a clear case against him. The city marshal, the prosecuting officer, was so assured of the prosecution of the case, that when he learned that I had been retained by Record's wife for his defence, he said to me : —

"Are you going to defend Record?"

"Yes."

"Well, if you get him off, I will throw up my commission."

"Mr. Adams," I said, "I did not expect so large fees for trying this case, but for it I will do my best."

Record was indicted for stealing from a building, and we went to trial. The fact that he took a key out of a door lock and ran away with it was proven beyond all question. While I was cross-examining a witness, — the man that lost the key, — an elderly member of our bar and friendly to me, said : —

"Butler, why do you take such cases, when you know you are sure to be beaten?"

"It's a custom I have," I said.

When the witness stepped down the district attorney said to the court: "The government rests its case here."

I said: "Mr. Attorney, you don't intend to ask for a verdict of the jury in a case like this, do you ? "

"I should like to know why not," said he.

"Well," I answered, "I will tell the court. Larceny is the taking of personal property furtively and devoting it to one's own use. Here it is proven that the prisoner took a key out of a door and ran away with it. Now, if your Honor please, when a key is in its proper place in the door it cannot be stolen, because then it is real estate. When a man dies, his personal estate goes to his executor, his real estate goes to his heirs. Here is the decision that keys in a house pass to the executor. The evidence is that the prisoner at the bar took the key out of its proper place in the door, and that is taking real estate, and taking real estate is not larceny. I move the court to direct a verdict of acquittal."

"What answer have you to make to this, Mr. District Attorney?" said the judge.

He hadn't any, and my client was acquitted.

"Have you anything further against Record, Mr. District Attorney?" continued the judge. "If not, let him be discharged."

"Will your Honor please stop a moment," said I. "I don't want Record discharged. I have not got all my fees yet."

"I thought," the judge laughingly said, "that you were too well instructed a lawyer not to know that it is best to get your fees before you try such cases?'

"I usually do, your Honor," said I; "but in this case, I was promised by the city marshal who sits there that if I got Record clear he would throw up his commission. If he declines to do it, I move your Honor to enforce his promise."

"Well," said the judge laughing, "if I attend to that, I cannot at this time, Mr. Butler."

"I hardly supposed you could," I said, "and Record may go."

The legislature at its next session passed an act which made severing portions of real estate for a felonious intent larceny,—so that now one may be indicted for stealing apples from trees, which before could not be done. I do not mean it should be understood that I won in all the sharp points I took; far from it, but I took them all the same and not infrequently won.

On the 19th of August, 1841, Congress passed an act establishing a system of bankruptcy. There had been no bankrupt law since that of 1800, and I saw that I should, by studying it, know as much about the new law as anybody, and more, if I examined the decisions under the old system and under the English bankrupt laws with more diligence than anybody else. I also reasoned that there would be a large number of private cases arising under that law. I therefore gave it most painstaking and exhaustive study, devoting to it all the time I had and what I could rob from sleep, in order to prepare myself in this branch of professional work. This was noised about in the profession, and I was applied to at once by some of my seniors at the bar, and I also had some cases of my own under that law. Thus it came about that in 1842 I tried the first two bankrupt cases to a jury. One was before Judge Story in the Circuit Court in the District of Massachusetts, and the other before Judge Harvey in the Circuit

Court of New Hampshire. I won them both, and I believe this was the first instance where a lawyer two years at the bar tried cases of such importance to a jury in the Circuit Court of the United States. I trust I may not appear boastful in making this narrative, because I had nothing to boast of save a devotion to my profession. I do not believe in genius carrying a man along in the practice of the law, and I want here to record for the benefit of the young men who come after me in the profession, that diligence, hard study, and careful thought are the only roads to success in any branch of the law except that possibly a turn for oratory may help the advocate. But the mere advocate, however brilliant, will lose the most cases although he may win the most verdicts.

A legal friend said to me: "I wish, Brother Butler, that in your book you would tell the profession those habits of life and conduct which led you to success as a lawyer." I can do that in a few words: —

The closest application to the study of the law applicable to any case in hand, and careful thought of what the law ought to be as applied to the case, and then the most careful study of the books to see how it has been applied in like instances. I thought out my cases and thought out the law as applied to them, and then verified or corrected my thought by the opinions of the courts. The highest legal authority has declared the common law to be the perfection of common sense, so that any man who thoughtfully applies his common sense ought to know what the common law is. The only need he has of the cases in the books is not so much to guide himself as to use them to direct the minds of the judges to adopt his common sense as the law of the case, resulting from precedents. Therefore I want to repeat, find out the law of the case yourself first, and then by comparison of the cases pertaining to it decide it; perfect your sense as to what the law is. I by no means advise a young man to make himself simply what is known as a "case lawyer," because lawyers of that class endeavor to remember and find a case like their own which has been decided and they rest there in their minds without other diligence or study to see how far that decision sustained the case.

There is a curious fact which has occurred in my own practice, and which I suspect has occurred in the practice of any experienced lawyer. I won more cases which I tried in behalf of the plaintiff in the younger years of my profession than I win now of the same class in proportion to the number tried after fifty years of professional labor. This would seem to be almost a paradox but an easily explained one. As a young man I took my cases as they came to me, and prepared them for trial substantially before I brought them. Thus, unless I met with some surprise in the state of facts upon which I proceeded, — and I generally took care to know the facts in my cases on both sides before I began, which was the best time to find them out, — it was my fault if I did not sufficiently prepare myself to learn the law in my case. But in later years it is supposed the client does not as a rule apply to the lawyers of years' standing in the profession to have his case begun. This, I take it, is through fear of being put to the expense of large fees. In later years I have been applied to most frequently to take charge of cases that have been substantially lost by proceedings had in them before they came to me, cases that in many instances could have been won if they had been properly taken in hand earlier. In other words I am called in largely in desperate cases. But I have made it the rule of my life never to refuse to assist in trying cases, however desperate, if I believe there is any chance to win. That there should be no mistake of my mention upon this topic I think I may state a case, in a narrative form, so as not to be too tedious : —

Some years ago I was sitting in my office in Washington when a gentleman came in, having under his arm a thick pamphlet with that dirty red paper cover which designated the record of the Supreme Court of the United States. Producing a letter of introduction from a valued friend, giving him a very high character for probity and standing, he said to me : —

"We have a case in the Supreme Court of which this is the record. It has been decided against us. I want you to examine the record carefully and see if there is any way we can save ourselves. What will you charge to do that thoroughly and give us a written opinion ? "

Looking ruefully at that thick record I said : "I should not like to state a price without knowing something about the case. Perhaps I shall not choose to give an opinion at all. You appear to be a gentleman of intelligence; please state your case so that I may see what it is."

"I am acting," said he, "in behalf of the American Emigrant Aid Society of Connecticut. Our business has been procuring lands in the western country, generally those denominated swamp lands, and settling emigrants upon them. We got a large quantity of such swamp lands of Adams County, Iowa, after considerable negotiation. They gave our trustee a full deed of them, and we paid them by building a court-house for them, which they received as payment on account, and by paying the balance in money at the price agreed. Afterwards there was a political change in the county officers, and a young lawyer became a member of the board of county authorities. The county under his advice brought a suit against us in the State Court to set aside our deed on the ground that in our negotiations with the county we stated that the lands were worth much less per acre than they were actually worth, and got them at too low a price on that misrepresentation."

BENJ. F. BUTLER IN 1856.

From a Photograph.

"Were the lands part of the county?"

"Yes."

"Is that the only complaint they make against you?"

"Yes; they claim to recover back the money as obtained by false pretences."

"That is impossible; that is against the Scripture: 'It is naught, it is naught, saith the buyer, but when he has gone his way then he boasteth.' Well, what was done with your case?"

"It was brought in the Supreme Court of the State, and being Yankees we took it to the Circuit Court of the United States, and it was tried there and we were beaten. Then we appealed to the Supreme Court, and it has lain there three or four years. We were heard fully, and the Supreme Court has decided against us."

"You must have left out something in your statement of your case," I said. "The county lived on and owned the lands and knew as much about them as you did. The claim of false pretences cannot be sustained for a moment."

"I have told you the case exactly as it is," said he.

"Very well; has anything else happened?"

"Yes; we moved for a rehearing in the Supreme Court, and that has been decided against us."

"Has anything else happened to your case?"

"Yes; they moved to have a mandate upon which the money was to be accounted for sent down in advance of the usual time. We had a hearing upon that, and that was also decided against us last Monday."

"Now, then," I said, "the patient being dead and buried, and the sexton having gone home to supper, you come to me for resurrection. I must say that I see no earthly opportunity; the rule of the Supreme Court is that it will have but one rehearing in a case."

"But," said he, "it is much to us; we have got seventeen more just such cases with other counties in Iowa or elsewhere, and they will all bring suits."

"Well," said I, "when they bring another suit I will endeavor to do something for you if I can, but it is no use for me to look into this record, this case is a by-gone."

"Well, all the same I want you to look into the record of this case and tell me what is your charge?"

"I ought not to charge anything, for it will do you no good. But I do not read such records for fun; but if you insist upon it, after what I have told you, I will examine it, and give you my opinion, and charge you $500 for so doing."

He wrote his check for the amount, threw his record down on the table, and said: "Whenever you want to see me, send for me, but spare no expense to put this right."

I took the record with me to my house. The next morning, after having finished my New England Sunday breakfast of baked beans and fish-balls, being curious, I opened the record and read it carefully through in all its particulars, and I found my client to be exactly right in all his statements of the case. The case as he stated it was all that was set forth in the pleadings, and all to which the evidence applied. I had not the copy of the decision nor the brief of either side so as to know upon what ground the decision was put, and I was exceedingly puzzled, so much so that I read the record once more with great care, and still found myself utterly at a loss. The next morning I sent to the clerk's office for a copy of the decision of the court, and after reading that carefully I was still more puzzled how any such a decision could have been reached. For the court had decided at first that there was nothing in the claim of the county for a right to recover back the money for the lands because of any representations of the buyer that he believed them to be worth less than they were, and I could find nothing else in the record on which a decision could be made against the buyer. During the week I examined all the papers in the case and prepared a motion for another rehearing.

On the following Monday morning I went before the court and with my best bow asked leave to file a motion for a rehearing in the case of the American Emigrant Aid Society, Plaintiff in Error, against the County of Adams. The chief justice looked at me with a little surprise.

"Are you aware, Mr. Butler," said he, "that there has been one motion for a rehearing heard and denied, and that this was the unanimous opinion of the court?"

"Mr. Chief Justice," I replied, "I should not have prepared myself as I ought to have done in the case if I had not learned those facts. I find no fault with the opinion of the court in denying a rehearing, but the whole matter has proceeded upon a very vital mistake."

"How many rehearings," said the chief justice, "do you think ought to be permitted by the court in a given case?"

"I am aware of the rule, your Honor," said I, "but I should say in answer to that question, in the abstract, as many hearings as are necessary to establish the truth and justice of the case; in the concrete, as many as any gentleman fit to practice at your bar will peril his reputation by moving for. And I take leave to assure the court with all due solemnity that a great error has been unfortunately committed in this case, which the court, if you will grant me a rehearing, will thank me for having brought it to their attention."

Judge Clifford, who sat at the right of the chief justice, and Judge Swayne, who sat at the left, observing my earnestness, leaned forward and conversed with him a moment, and then the chief justice said: "Very well, you may file your motion. You are aware that it is to be argued in writing only?"

"Yes, may it please your Honor; I have some slight acquaintance with the rules of this court. My argument will be on your Honor's consultation table by Saturday, if that will do."

He bowed and I left. During that week I prepared an argument, in the heroic vein, I am bound to say, and had it laid before the court. They held it under consideration about three weeks, and then Judge Bradley, who had delivered the opinion of the court at first, said that he was instructed by the court that the mandate should be withdrawn, the decree reversed, and the case stand for argument on the first day of the next term.

At that term I was present and argued my case, although I was exceedingly busy in my candidature for the governorship. The court took the case under advisement and three or four weeks later Judge Bradley delivered an opinion reversing the former decree and ordering the plaintiff's bill to be dismissed, and that the appellant recover his costs. And afterwards Judge Swayne in a friendly conversation recalled to me what I had said in making my motion for a rehearing, and stated that he personally did thank me for bringing that case again before the court, as a mistake had been made which ought not to have occurred, and which was only accounted for by the haste with which the court had to do its work. I believe this is the only case which has ever been reheard by the court on the second rehearing, except the legal tender cases, and I happened to be concerned with them also.

It is naturally distasteful to me to recall matters wherein I may seem to be making a boast of my own qualities, and as the reader may be led to think that he is not getting an impartial history, I have concluded to set out here what one of the ablest lawyers of Massachusetts, John Quincy Adams Griffin, Esq., and others have said of me as a practitioner at the bar, without my knowledge, rather than to have so much of such details written by myself: —

General Butler has the power, possessed by but few men, of attending to several important mental operations at the same time. An incident will show you my meaning: —

In a trial of quite an important matter, in the year 1860, I was counsel on the same side with General Butler. It was a busy season of the year for lawyers like him, who always had an overflowing docket. The trial began just after his return from the nomination of Breckinridge. He was to make a report of his doings to his constituents at Lowell. The meeting was called to be held at night. Dissatisfaction existed in the party, and the General must, therefore, speak with care and consideration. He determined to write what he was to say. But the court began early and sat late. He took his seat in court, and while the adverse party examined their witnesses in chief, he wrote out his speech, apparently absorbed therein. But he cross-examined each witness at great length, with wonderful thoroughness and acuteness, evincing a perfect knowledge, not only of what the witness had said in substance, but when needful, of the phrases in which he had uttered it. At noon, over our dinner, he read over what he had written and made such corrections as were needful, which were quite as few, I thought, as would have been found if the speech had been written in the quiet of his study. In the afternoon he went through the same routine, and at night made his speech. This is but an instance. Amid confusion of transactions, where other men became indecisive, he always saw his way clear. Whatever his occupations, however intently his mind was employed, it was always safe to interrupt him by suggestions or inquiries about the matter in hand, or anything else, for he could answer on the instant, clearly and without the slightest confusion or distraction of his purpose.

Unexampled success attended his professional efforts, so characterized by zeal and shrewdness. When the war summoned him from these toils, he had a larger practice than any other man in the State. I have no doubt that he tried four times more causes, at least, than any other lawyer, during the ten years preceding the war. The same qualities which made him efficient in the war, made him efficient as a lawyer: Fertile in resources and strategem, earnest and zealous to an extraordinary degree, certain of the integrity of his client's cause, and not inclined to criticise and inquire whether it was strictly constitutional or not, but defending the whole line with a boldness and energy that generally carried court and jury alike. His ingenuity is exhaustless. If he makes a mistake in speech or action, it has no sinister effect, for the reason that he will himself discover and correct the error before any " barren spectator " has seized upon it.

He is faithful and tenacious to the last degree. There is no possibility of treachery in his conduct. "He would not betray the devil to his fellow." Every other prominent Massachusetts Democrat, when it became profitable to do so, condemned a previous coalition that had been entered into between them and the Free Soilers after they had taken and consumed its fruits. General Butler's political interests strongly urged him to the same dishonor. But he never hesitated an instant, and uniformly justified the coalition, and openly defended it in every presence and to the most unwilling ears. In his personal relations the same traits are observable. He is quite too ready, I have sometimes thought, to forgive (he never forgets) injuries, but his memory never fails as to his friends.

"The basis of Napoleon's character," says Gourgand, "was a pleasant humor." "And a man who jests," continues Victor Hugo, "at important junctures, is on familiar terms with events."

A pleasant humor and a lively wit, and their constant exercise, are the possession and the habit of General Butler. Everybody has his anecdote of him. Let me refer to one anecdote of him in this respect, and that shall suffice for the hundreds that I might recall.

The General was a member of our House of Representatives one year when his party was in a hopeless and impotent minority, except on such occasions as he contrived to make it efficient by tactics and strategems of a technical, parliamentary character. The speaker was a Whig, and a thorough partisan. The Whigs were well drilled and had a leader on the floor of very great capacity, Mr. Lord, of Salem. During one angry debate, General Butler attempted to strangle an obnoxious proposal of the majority by tactics. Accordingly he precipitated upon the chair divers questions of order and regularity of proceeding, one after the other. These were debated by Mr. Lord and himself, and then decided by the speaker uniformly according to the notions advanced by Mr. Lord. The General bore this for some time without special complaint, contenting himself with raising new questions. At length, however, he called special attention to the fact that he had been overruled so many times by the chair, within such a space of time, and that, as often, not only had the speaker adopted the result of Mr. Lord's suggestions, but generally had accepted the same words in which to announce it; and, said he: "Mr. Speaker, I cannot complain of these rulings. They doubtless seem to the speaker to be just. I perceive an anxiety on your part to be just to the minority and to me, by whom at this moment they are represented, but you feel as did Saul in his trance on the road to Damascus, 'Lord, what wilt thou have me to do?'"

No man in America can remember facts, important and unimportant, like General Butler. Whatever enters his mind remains there forever. And his knowledge, as I have said, is available the instant it is needed, without confusion or tumult of thought. The testimony delivered through days of dreary trials, without minutes or memoranda of any kind, he could recall in fresher and more accurate phrases, remembering always the substance, and generally all the important expressions, with far more precision than the other counsel and the court could gather it from their " writing books," wherein they had endeavored to record it. Practice for a long series of years had so disciplined his mind in this respect that I think it quite impossible for him to forget.[1] And as he has mingled constantly with every business and interest of humanity since he was admitted to the bar, he has become possessed of a marvellous extent and variety of knowledge respecting the affairs of mankind.

Here are also some comments of other of my associates, and narratives of my cases and conduct, which I prefer to have told in their own words : —

One example of what a writer styles General Butler's legerdemain. A man in Boston, of respectable connections and some wealth, being afflicted with a mania for stealing, was, at length, brought to trial on four indictments; and a host of lawyers were assembled, engaged in the case, expecting a long and sharp contest. It was hot summer weather; the judge was old and indolent; the officers of the court were weary of the session, and anxious to adjourn. General Butler was counsel for the prisoner. It is a law in Massachusetts that the repetition of that crime by the same offender, within a certain period, shall entail a severer punishment than the first offence. A third repetition involves more severity, and a fourth still more. According to this law, the prisoner, if convicted on all four indictments, would be liable to imprisonment in the penitentiary for the term of sixty years. As the court was assembling, General Butler remonstrated with the counsel for the prosecution upon the rigor of their proposed proceedings. Surely one indictment would answer the ends of justice; why condemn the man to imprisonment for life for what was, evidently, more a disease than a crime ? They agreed, at length, to quash three of the indictments, on condition that the prisoner should plead guilty to the one which charged the theft of the greatest amount. The prisoner was arraigned.

---

[1] Very early in my practice I adopted as a maxim, that if the jury were obliged to remember all testimony without memoranda, so as to decide the case upon it, the lawyer should be able to remember it as accurately as they, to state it to them exactly in the argument. So I learned to try all cases without taking any minutes.

" Are you guilty or not guilty ? "

" Say ' guilty,' sir," said General Butler, from his place in the bar, in his most commanding tone.

The man cast a helpless, worried look at his counsel, and said nothing.

" Say ' guilty,' sir," repeated the General, looking into the prisoner's eyes.

The man, without a will, was compelled to obey, by every constitution of his infirm mind.

" Guilty," he faltered, and sunk down into his seat, crushed with a sense of shame.

" Now, gentlemen," said the counsel for the prisoner, " have I, or have I not, performed my part of the compact ? "

" You have."

" Then perform yours."

This was done. A *nol pros.* was duly entered upon the three indictments. The counsel for the prosecution immediately moved for sentence on the fourth, to which the prisoner had pleaded guilty.

General Butler then rose, with that indictment in his hand, and pointed out a flaw in it, manifest and fatal. The error was in designating the place where the crime was committed.

" Your honor perceives," said the General, " that this court has no jurisdiction in the matter. I move that the prisoner be discharged from custody."

Ten minutes from that time, the astounded man was walking out of the court-room free.

The flaw in the indictment, General Butler discovered the moment after the compact was made. If he had gone to the prisoner, and spent five minutes in inducing him to consent to the arrangement, the sharp opposing counsel, long accustomed to his tactics, would have suspected a ruse and eagerly scanned the indictment. He relied, therefore, solely on the power which a man with a will has over a man who has none, and so merely commanded the plea of guilty. The court, it is said, not unwilling to escape a long trial, laughed at the manœuvre, and complimented the successful lawyer upon the excellent " discipline " which he maintained among his clients.

His audacity and quickness stood him in good stead. One of his first cases being called in court, he said in the usual way : " Let notice be given ! "

" In what paper ? " asked the aged clerk of the court, a strenuous Whig.

" In the Lowell *Advertiser*," was the reply. Now, the *Advertiser*, being a Jackson paper, was never mentioned in a Middlesex court ; and of its mere existence few there present would confess a knowledge.

"The Lowell *Advertiser?*" said the clerk, with disdainful nonchalance, "I don't know such a paper."

"Pray, Mr. Clerk," said the lawyer, "do not interrupt the proceedings of the court; for if you begin to tell us what you don't know, there will be no time for anything else."

He was always prompt with a retort of this kind. So, at a later day, when he was cross-questioning a witness in not the most respectful manner, and the counsel interposing, reminding him that the witness was a professor in Harvard College, he instantly replied: "I am aware of it, your honor; we hung one of them the other day."

I tried causes frequently in the States of New Hampshire, Maine, and Massachusetts, and in quite all the circuit courts of all the districts of the latter State. My docket contained causes of every description of practice and in regard to all possible business, so that from necessity preparing myself to examine and cross-examine experts in every class of business, I became more or less an expert in all myself. I suppose I may mention a few of the more important cases, especially where great principles were decided, in all of which I was engaged as leading counsel.

In 1853 the legislature passed an act annexing the city of Charlestown to the city of Boston, provided both cities, by ballot in the majority, should decide to accept the annexation, such acceptance to be certified to the Secretary of State by a certificate of the popular vote by a majority of the mayor and aldermen of each city. The vote of Boston was strongly in favor of annexation. There was a very strong feeling against it in Charlestown. Public meetings were held; all sorts of printed publications made, in fact a regular canvass. The vote in both cities was held on the same day. The Boston majority for the annexation was duly certified at once to the Secretary of State, and by him published. The fact that Charlestown had, by a small majority, voted in the affirmative duly appeared in the journals, but four out of seven aldermen were opposed to annexation, and determined to prevent it if they could. As they had nothing to do but certify the vote, apparently, it would be held that they would be obliged by a mandamus from the court to do that. Boston rejoiced greatly, and without waiting for the action of its sister city, Charlestown, proceeded to take possession of Charlestown, divided it into wards, laid out streets and did everything as if the matter was settled. The aldermen who had determined to obstruct the annexation proceedings applied to me and Mr. Griffin and declared that if they could escape the penalties of the law they would not certify the vote if that would do any good. We examined the question carefully and gave an opinion that under the statute, annexation could not take place until the popular vote in favor of it was duly certified to the Secretary of State by a majority of the mayor and aldermen of the city of Charlestown. And if a majority of that board would not certify it, they might be compelled to do so upon a petition of the attorney-general to the Supreme Court for a mandamus. The aldermen exhorted us to do everything we could to prevent annexation. We thereupon notified the attorney-general that my clients peremptorily refused to certify to the vote on the ground that the act requiring them to do it was unconstitutional and void, and not within the legislative power.

The leader of the other side in Charlestown moved upon the attorney-general for a petition for mandamus to be brought. All the facts were agreed, and the questions arose as they would under bill and answer in equity. The case was argued before five justices, at the head of whom was the most learned and the ablest judge of this State, Lemuel Shaw, Esq.

I was no favorite of his in my earlier days. He was a man of somewhat forbidding exterior and manners, but of the finest qualities of head and heart. Liking or disliking a man did not interfere with his doing him full justice on the bench. He had a brusque sort of humor which all who knew him enjoyed very much.

On one occasion there had been sent me a lot of very fine black otter skins by a member of the Hudson Bay Company. These I had made into a very nice coat, which in the inclement weather covered me from the cold and wet. One morning I went into the consultation room of the Supreme Court to meet Judge Shaw on a mere formal matter like signing an order. He greeted me very pleasantly and kindly. We sat a moment after what the judge had to do was done, and he admired my coat exceedingly, looking it over and praising it highly. At last looking up with a quizzical smile he said: " How is it, Mr. Butler? what are those lines in Pope? Aren't they something like this : —

The fur that warmed a monarch warms a bear.

I said: " I think you are a little mixed in your tenses this morning, Mr. Chief Justice."

" Not as to the last fact," said he.

I said he was brusque in his manner, especially on the bench. One day shortly before my Charlestown case came up I was going down in the cars from Lowell to Boston, and at the request of a merchant friend of mine, whose watch dog had been poisoned, I was taking down my own to leave with him. My dog was an immense mastiff, with a black muzzle, very quiet but very powerful. The smoking-car was always a sort of exchange as we went down. It was used by the passengers for playing cards and for familiar chat. I had no sooner entered the car with the dog behind me than I was saluted with: " Halloa, halloa, Butler, where are you going this morning ? "

" Down to the Supreme Court, gentlemen."

" Is that your dog ? "

" Yes."

" What are you taking him down to court for ? "

" Oh," I said, " I thought I would show him the chief justice so as to teach him to growl."

Shortly afterward, the Charlestown case was tried and decided upon every point in my behalf, the chief justice delivering the opinion, and it was so conclusive that it put off the annexation of Charlestown to Boston for twenty years.

Shortly after this I called in the course of business into the consultation room where sat the chief justice alone, and after the usual salutation he began: " Well, Mr. Butler, you won your Charlestown case ? "

" Oh," I said, " thanks, Mr. Chief Justice; I am exceedingly obliged to you for giving me that case."

" Well, then, Mr. Butler, I take it you have no fault to find with that last growl of the chief justice."

My last act toward him was after he resigned at the end of thirty years' service as chief justice. I was chairman of the committee of the bar to make a proper address on that occasion in their behalf. Our committee went to his house on Mt. Vernon Street, as he was not able to come out in the inclement weather. I took great pains with that address, feeling every appreciative word in it from my very heart. The chief justice attempted to reply to it, but his feelings

GENERAL BUTLER ARGUING AGAINST THE ANNEXATION OF CHARLESTOWN TO BOSTON.

overcame him.   He broke down in his expressions, but came forward to me, and pressing my hand, said : "And this, too, to come from your lips and inspired by your kindness."

I never saw him again because in the following spring I left for the war and he died during that year.

My connection with the Charlestown case was of very great advantage to me because it brought me prominently and successfully forward as an advocate in the higher branches of constitutional law.

In 1845 I was admitted to the Supreme Court of the United States, upon the motion of the Hon. Levi Woodbury, Jackson's Secretary of the Navy and Secretary of the Treasury.   It was at the same term in which Seward and Lincoln were admitted, and I believe I am now the oldest living practitioner in that court by date of commission.   I was then in my 27th year, and among the youngest, if not the youngest, ever admitted to that court, for in the olden time only the elder members of the bar got to Washington to be admitted.   But I had the fortune to have drawn the specification for the patent of Elias Howe, a native of Massachusetts, for his invention of the sewing machine. This brought me there to argue a motion in that court, but I did not do so as the case was settled.

The first important case that I argued in the Supreme Court was in 1857.   It was Sutter *vs.* the United States.   Sutter had been fortunate enough to find gold in the raceway of his sawmill near Sacramento in 1849.   The case involved the effect of the laws and action of the provincial governors of Mexico in granting titles to very extended parcels of lands.   The rules which should govern the distribution of that land and the validity of titles to such land under our treaty of Guadalupe Hidalgo were under discussion in that case. It was a leading case upon those questions and affected the title of real property to the value of many millions.   The case brought me somewhat before the people of the Western country, and I have had occasion to argue quite a number of cases since involving questions of Mexican law.   This, I believe, has not happened to any other New England lawyer, certainly not to the extent it has to me.

I was employed by Mr. Speed, the Attorney-General of the United States, to assist Mr. Stansbury in the argument of the case of Milligan vs. the United States.   This case involved questions of new and untried law in this country, and which had not been distinctly settled anywhere else. The case was this: —

There was a body of quasi-secessionists in Indiana and the adjoining States known as the Knights of the Golden Circle. Milligan was a member of that body and there was an accusation made against him of being a party to a conspiracy to release the Confederate prisoners of war from Johnson's Island and send them back to the assistance of the enemy.[1]

Milligan was tried by a military commission, duly convened. The commission heard the case in due form and advised his punishment. Being held in prison to await the result of that proceeding, a writ of *habeas corpus* was brought in his favor to have him released, and in due course of the law it came before the Supreme Court of the United States.

It was alleged in the charges that Indiana was, at the time of the acts set forth, the theatre of war in time of war and that the State was held by military forces of the United States which were guarding it against these transactions, and had military control of the State. It was further alleged that Milligan was not a soldier of the United States and was, therefore, within the jurisdiction of these military forces and amenable for his military offences to the action of the military commission.

This was the first time that the action of a military commission had come directly before the Supreme Court. Every step in the proceedings was contested by the learned counsel who appeared for Milligan, the Hon. Jere S. Black, the Hon. David W. Field, and General Garfield, the latter of whom was brought into the case to give it some tinge of loyalty, and other counsel. The cause of the United States was sustained by the court in every point but one, and that was, as the Circuit Court of the United States was open in Indiana, that therefore, Milligan had a right to be tried before the circuit court. There was no allegation in the pleadings that the circuit court was open. But the court said that it would take judicial notice of that, and that in consequence of its being open the case was not within the jurisdiction of the military authorities for trial. While, of course,

---

[1] This conspiracy has been most ably treated by Gen. John A. Logan in his work, "The Great Conspiracy," showing its vast extent and importance. He was one of the ablest and most successful volunteer generals, and a most loyal Democrat, and he afterwards entered the United States Senate — as a Republican.

bowing to the decision, I have always thought, with all deference, that it was a pusillanimous one. The opinion was sustained by a majority of only one, the chief justice being a dissenter.

My argument on that point was this: The record alleged that the acts were done while Indiana was the theatre of war; that was admitted. All acts to rescue prisoners of war and afford aid and comfort to the enemy and turn the prisoners loose upon their guards, are warlike acts. I held that this was in time of war, and while Indiana was under military jurisdiction. If the courts were open, they were open only by military permission. They were not open for the purpose of trying cases which were within military jurisdiction, but for proceedings between party and party and with the ordinary business arising in those courts in the time of peace, and such as had no effect upon the Government of the United States. I called the attention of the court to the fact that the courts of the District of Columbia were open, when the sounds of the rebel General Early's cannon were ringing in the ears of the judges of the courts, and everybody else was under the full jurisdiction of the military. Could it be said, then, that the men of Early who were captured were to be tried by civil law by the courts of the district which were utterly powerless to give any force and effect to their decrees? I argued that the court could not take judicial notice of the fact that the courts of Indiana was open; all they could have notice of was that the court ought to have been open, as peace ought to have reigned in Indiana, but it did not.

I take the liberty to remark here, that during the whole War of the Rebellion the government was rarely ever aided by the decisions of the Supreme Court, but usually was impeded and disturbed by them. After I left Baltimore Chief Justice Taney issued a *habeas corpus* to release a secessionist who had been captured and was held by the orders of the President of the United States. So that the President was obliged to suspend the writ of *habeas corpus* in order to relieve himself from the rulings of that chief justice who delivered the opinion substantially that the negro had no rights that a white man was bound to respect.

While I remained in Washington, I was trying cases before the supreme court of the district and the Supreme Court of the United States. There was one case which I tried before both courts which was very important, not only for the amount involved, but as establishing a precedent which had not then been established in England or in this country.

In April, 1862, when Farragut made his wonderful passage with his fleet to New Orleans, he took possession of a large amount of water-borne property, especially coal afloat, and many vessels, a considerable number of which originally belonged to Northern owners who had sent them down there before the war broke out. Among them were several valuable river steamers.

When I occupied the city with my troops, many of these vessels became necessary as a means of transportation, and were turned over by the navy to the army by appraisement. So also was the coal and other property captured afloat, for it was the prize of war.

The Prize Act makes it the duty of the Secretary of the Navy, upon the capture of property, to see that it is brought before a prize court within three months, or the captor may bring suit in prize in any court after that time.

The whole value of the property captured amounted to nearly two million dollars. Farragut was by far too busy fighting during the war to go around with a marking pot, — as Porter did, stencil-marking bales of cotton on shore in the Red River campaign: "Captured by the U. S. Navy. D. D. Porter," — and, there being no district court in New Orleans, this property captured by Farragut could not by him be brought before a prize court there.

After the close of the war, nothing having been done, Vice-Admiral Theodorus Bailey, second in command, called upon me and asked me to get the vessels and other property captured by himself and Farragut condemned as prizes. Accordingly, I filed libels in prize against the property in the supreme court of the district. The Secretary of the Navy employed counsel to represent that department in the matter. We had a hearing before the circuit court of the district sitting in admiralty, which made the decision that the libels should be sustained, and that a prize commissioner should be appointed to take testimony. This decision was made by a single judge, and no appeal was taken from this decision. While the testimony was being gathered up and taken before the prize commissioner, I went home to Massachusetts. In my absence a meddling attorney, by the name of Corwine, went to the Secretary of the Treasury and told him that the Farragut cases would take a large sum of money out of the treasury, and that if he could be employed he could stop the proceeding.

Now, these cases were no more the business of the Secretary of the Treasury, than was the question what the Emperor of China should have for breakfast the next morning. Two departments, the Law Department and the Navy Department, were already engaged in the case to look after the interests of the United States. But Corwine got his employment, and then proceeded, without any notice to anybody engaged in the case on any side of it, to make a motion before a single judge of the supreme court of the district. This judge, without giving a hearing and without notice to anybody, ordered the libels to be dismissed. How that could be done I never could understand or account for, except that there was a story that this judge sometimes drank more of something besides water than was good for him. However that may be, I did not get any notice of that most disreputable proceeding for months, and then I found it out only by looking at the docket of the court to see at what time I could give notice to go on with the taking of the testimony. I then took an appeal from that proceeding to the whole court sitting in banc, and without any difficulty got my case reinstated.

Utterly disgusted with being obliged to try a case involving more than a million in money where such unheard-of proceedings could take place, and desiring nothing but the best adjudication of the case, I appealed to the Attorney-General, the Secretary of the Navy, and the Secretary of the Treasury, as he had got into it, for an agreement that the case should be referred by the rule of the court to three arbitrators, — two of them men of the highest standing as lawyers, the Hon. Henry W. Paine, of Massachusetts, and the Hon. Thos. J. Durant, of Louisiana, and the third, the Hon. Gustavus V. Fox, late assistant Secretary of the Navy, — who would have a knowledge of the course· involved in the proceedings, with the right to appeal from the judgment of the admiralty court to the Supreme Court.

When I presented this agreement to the Attorney-General, he said : " Who ever heard of a question of prize being submitted to arbitration ? Have you got any precedent for it ? "

" No, Mr. Attorney-General, I have not, but I do not see why you should object. If we go on and try under arbitration and it is not proper jurisdiction you can set it all aside if you want to. It gives you one more chance against me; but I am willing to take that risk rather than to try the case before the admiralty court, some of the judges of which are at all times a *full* court."

The agreement for the rule of arbitration, being signed by the Attorney-General, the Secretary of the Navy, and the Secretary of the Treasury, was presented to the court. The rule was made absolute and the referees were appointed. The case was heard at length before the arbitrators and an award found in favor of Farragut for substantially all the items claimed. The award was confirmed by the Court of Appeals. A bill was taken in the United States Supreme Court, the United States wanting to have a full hearing. The judgment in our favor, carrying more than one million dollars, was sustained. The precedent decided that any controversy between party and party, under the rule of the court, might be sent to a board of referees or arbitrators to be tried.

By the rules of prize cases, as all the costs are to come out of the prize money, including fees of counsel, there must be judgment by the court for those fees. When that question was brought up I happened not to be in Washington, so that I could not appear in my own favor. The court awarded me seventy-five thousand dollars,— little enough, because the case was one of great labor and had been before the several courts a number of years. I only mention the question of fees now because when I was before the people of the State of Massachusetts in the campaign for the governorship, the Republican party and Republican speakers attacked me very virulently regarding the enormous charges that I had demanded and received from the United States, insisting that nothing but some false and underhanded agreement could account for it.

A lawyer in full practice who carefully prepares his cases must study almost every variety of business and many of the sciences. Thus of necessity he is taught many things by his professional labors, which would not be taught to a man in any other pursuit of life. In almost all important cases, especially those relating to personal injuries of any sort,— including of course death by murder,— and those relating to the action of machines and machinery in pressing patent cases, if a lawyer hopes for success he should make himself fully acquainted with everything of science or fact that pertains to the case in hand.

In quite all important cases more or less expert testimony is introduced before the court,—that is, testimony of men thoroughly acquainted with the matters of the subject. The lawyer must be prepared to cope with such testimony on the one side for himself, and to cross-examine the witnesses of his opponent whenever produced. An expert's testimony, for which large sums are generally paid, is usually a sworn argument for the benefit of the party who calls him. It is, therefore, of the greatest importance that the opposing counsel should be expert enough on the matter in question to be able to cross-examine and detect the weak points in the expert argument against him.

I have defended scores of cases where the question of sanity was the main one in the case, and I have brought many suits against physicians for malpractice as to many parts of the human frame. So that, in preparing myself in that class of cases, I have been obliged to make full studies in regard to the operation of the mind and also studies of the separate parts of the body, and the character of their ailments and the treatment thereof, so as to be able in some degree to cope with the hundreds of surgeons

JEREMIAH MASON

Engraved from a Life-size Bust in General Butler's Library.

and physicians who have come upon the stand to testify as experts to save their brothers.

So in accident cases upon railroads : I have spent days in examining all parts of engines and trains and especially the capabilities to start and stop a train. I have ridden many hundred miles upon the engine upon different roads and learned enough so as to run an engine myself, a knowledge which did me good service at one time in Louisiana.

I have spent days in machine shops upon the same and kindred questions. In one very important case I spent a week in the repair shop of a railroad and a part of the time with my coat off, with a hammer in my hands, ascertaining the capabilities of iron to resist pressure, and studying the probable result of the breakage of an axle under the tender of an engine. On these points my case turned ; and I may say that my instruction so acquired saved the case.

In fine, a lawyer who sits in his office and prepares his cases only by the statements of those who are brought to him will be very likely to be beaten.

When I was quite a young man I was called upon to defend a man for homicide. He and his associate had been engaged in a quarrel which proceeded to blows and at last to stones. My client with a sharp stone struck the deceased in the head on that part usually called the temple. The man went and sat down on a curbstone, the blood streaming from his face, and shortly afterwards fell over dead.

The theory of the government was that he died from the wound in the temporal artery. My theory was that the man died of apoplexy, and that if he had bled more from the temporal artery he might have been saved, — a wide enough difference in the theories of the cause of death.

Of course to be enabled to carry out my proposition I must know all about the temporal artery, its location, its functions, its capabilities to allow the blood to pass through it, and in how short a time a man could bleed to death through the temporal artery ; also, how far excitement in a body stirred almost to frenzy in an embittered conflict and largely under the influence of liquor on a hot day, would tend to produce apoplexy. I was relieved on these two points in my case because the government did not come prepared to deal with that subject, but relied wholly upon the testimony of a surgeon that the man bled to death from the cut on the temporal artery from a stone in the hand of my client. That surgeon was one of those who we sometimes see on the stand who think that what they don't know on the subject of their profession is not worth knowing. He testified positively and distinctly that there was and could be no other cause for death except the bleeding from the temporal artery, and he described the action of the bleeding and the amount of blood discharged.

Upon all these questions I had thoroughly prepared myself. On cross-examination, I said: "Doctor, you have talked a great deal about the temporal artery; now will you please describe it and its functions? I suppose the temporal artery is so called because it supplies the flesh on the outside of the skull, especially that part we call the temples, with blood."

" Yes; that is so," he answered.

" Very well. Where does the temporal artery take its rise in the system? Is it at the heart?"

"No," he said, " the aorta is the only artery leaving the heart which carries blood toward the head. Branches from it carry the blood up through the opening into the skull at the neck, and the temporal artery branches from one of these."

" Doctor, where does it branch off from it? on the inside or the outside of the skull?"

" On the inside."

" Does it have anything to do inside with supplying the brain?"

" No."

" Well, Doctor, how does it get outside to supply the head and temples?"

" Oh," he said, " it passes out through its appropriate opening in the skull."

" Is that through the eyes?"

" No."

" The ears?"

" No."

" It would be inconvenient to go through the mouth, would it not, Doctor?"

Here I produced from my green bag a skull. " I cannot find any opening on this skull which I think is appropriate to the temporal artery. Will you please point out the appropriate opening through which the temporal artery passes from the inside to the outside of the skull?"

He was utterly unable so to do.

I said: " Doctor, I don't think I will trouble you any further; you can step down." He did so, and my client's life was saved on that point.

The temporal artery doesn't go inside the skull at all.

Perhaps I may state another case illustrative of the necessity for the lawyer in trying his cases to have some knowledge of the human system and the causes of its disturbances.

I had a young client who was on a railroad car when it was derailed by a broken switch. The car ran at considerable speed over the cross-ties for some distance, and my client was thrown up and down with great violence on his seat. After the accident, when he recovered from the bruising, it was found that his nervous system had been wholly shattered, and that he could not control his nerves in the slightest degree by any act of his will. When the case came to trial, the production of the pin by which the position of the switch was controlled, two thirds worn away and broken off, settled the liability of the road for any damages that occurred from that cause, and the case resolved itself into a question of the amount of damages only. My claim was that my client's condition was an incurable one, arising from the injury to the spinal cord. The claim put forward on behalf of the railroad was that it was simply nervousness, which probably would disappear in a short time. The surgeon who appeared for the road claimed the privilege of examining my client personally before he should testify. I did not care to object to that, and the doctor who was my witness and the railroad surgeon went into the consultation-room together and had a full examination in which I took no part, having looked into that matter before.

After some substantially immaterial matters on the part of the defence the surgeon was called and was qualified as a witness. He testified that he was a man of great position in his profession. Of course, in that I was not interested, for I knew he could qualify himself as an expert. In his direct examination he spent a good deal of the time in giving a very learned and somewhat technical description of the condition of my client. He admitted that my client's nervous system was very much shattered, but he also stated that it would probably be only temporary. Of all this I took little notice; for to tell the truth I had been up quite late the night before and in the warm court-room felt a little sleepy. But the counsel for the road put this question to him : —

" Doctor, to what do you attribute this condition of the plaintiff which you describe ? "

" Hysteria, sir ; he is hysterical."

That waked me up. I said : " Doctor, did I understand — I was not paying proper attention — to what did you attribute this nervous condition of my client ? "

" Hysteria, sir."

I subsided, and the examination went on until it came my turn to cross-examine.

" Do I understand," I said, " that you think this condition of my client wholly hysterical ? "

" Yes, sir; undoubtedly."

" And therefore won't last long? "

" No, sir; not likely to."

" Well," said I, " Doctor, let us see; is not the disease called hysteria and its effects hysterics ; and isn't it true that hysteria, hysterics, hysterical, all come from the Greek word ὑστέρα ? "

" It may be."

" Don't say it may, Doctor; isn't it? Isn't an exact translation of the Greek word ὑστέρα, the English word 'womb'? "

" You are right, sir."

" Well, Doctor, this morning when you examined this young man here," pointing to my client, " did you find that he had a womb? I was not aware of it before, but I will have him examined over again and see if I can find it. That is all, Doctor; you may step down."

I may be permitted perhaps to give one more case in which I was engaged, not very long before I went into the army, which illustrates the instruction which full law practice brings to a lawyer. It was this : —

The son of a very warm friend had been on board the ship Storm King at Hong Kong in China. The Storm King had prepared for a race from Hong Kong to London with another clipper ship, so she was obliged to start as nearly as might be when her rival did. My client was third mate, but owing to some claimed misunderstanding between him and the captain he was dismated and sent forward to live with the crew in the forecastle. There was no time in which to furnish the ship with fresh meat and vegetables for the voyage, such as would prevent the breaking out of the scurvy, or at least it was not done. Indeed, all the fresh meat on board consisted of a small pig, and that was disposed of on the cabin table. The vessel made a direct course to London, beating her competitor, I believe. A part of the crew were Chinamen, and by the time they got past the Cape of Good Hope the whole crew were affected with the scurvy. To such an extent did this prevail that when the vessel anchored in London, out of her crew of twenty-six men, as I remember the numbers, all but seven had to be hoisted over the side because it was impossible for them to help themselves. Among them was my client.

After examining the question I brought suit against the captain of the ship, alleging that my client had had the scurvy because the vessel had not taken any sufficient supplies of fresh provisions and vegetables for a long voyage, and because the captain did not stop anywhere to get any. The suit was brought in the County of Middlesex, of course, where my client lived. The owner of the vessel, who stood at the head of the East India trade, took the suit in great dudgeon. He said he did not want any country lawyer — meaning me — to control the method of fitting out ships for the East India trade; that it was as good as it could be; that everything for their comfort and convenience was given to the crew, and that the case should be fought as far as he could go. He employed a lawyer, afterwards most famous as an advocate, G. A. Somerby,

RUFUS CHOATE

Engraved from a Life-size Bust in General Butler's Library.

Esq., and also the Hon. Rufus Choate, who was the first advocate of New England if not of the United States. I had with me a young gentleman who did not practise much in the courts in the trial of cases,— a relative of the plaintiff and quite capable. As I had been notified, every possible defence was to be taken. In the first place they were to claim that the ship was entirely properly fitted out as regards provisions; second, that there was no place in which the ship could stop to get even fresh potatoes; and, third, that my client hadn't the scurvy at all but a disease which bore no relation to it.

The whole East India trade and a large portion of the Boston merchants came as witnesses for the defence. I said to Mr. Choate that that defence would cost his client, I was certain, a good deal more than we had claimed for damages, and that perhaps his client would like to make some settlement, for I confess that I was a little alarmed and scurvy hadn't been much in my line. I knew that Captain Cook had buried the members of his crew who had the scurvy in the earth at the Sandwich Islands to cure them, and that is all I knew, and I saw very extended and onerous study would be necessary in many parts of the case. Mr. Choate told me it was no use to speak of compromise. The East India trade was determined to make an example of this case so that its trade should never be interfered with again. " Very well, then," I said, " let her go ; we will have an example for somebody."

The trial of the case was commenced, and it lasted nineteen working days. It was tried from nine o'clock in the morning to four o'clock in the evening in the court, and the rest of the time I was occupied in preparing it. The whole of sanitary science and the whole of sanitary law, the narratives of navigators and the usages of navies, reports of parliamentary commissions and diaries of philanthropical investigators, ancient log-books and new treatises of maritime law, the testimony of mariners and the opinions of physicians, all were made tributary to the case. I exhibited to the jury a large map of the world, and taking the log of the ship in my hand, read its daily entries, and as I did so, I marked on the map the ship's course, showing plainly to the eyes of the jury that on four different occasions, while the crew were rotting with the scurvy, the ship passed within a few hours' sail of islands, renowned in all those seas for the abundance, the excellence, and the cheapness of their vegetables.

Mr. Choate contested every point with all his skill and eloquence. As I have said, the end of the daily session was only the beginning of my day's work; for there were new points to be investigated, other facts to be discovered, more witnesses to be hunted up. I rummaged libraries, pored over encyclopædias and gazetteers, ferreted out old sailors, and went into court every morning with a mass of new material, and followed by a train of old doctors or old sailors to support a position shaken the day before. In the course of the trial, I had on the witness-stand nearly every eminent physician in Boston, and nearly every sea-captain and ship-owner. I studied five treatises on scurvy, one very old German one printed in Latin. 1 mention that because it contained an authority that I could find nowhere else, and when I brought it to the attention of one of the defendant's physicians on the cross-examination he admitted that he had never heard of it before, and more than that I had to read it to him as he could not read its language.

The case was submitted to the jury on a very able and impartial charge of the presiding justice, and we obtained a verdict of three thousand dollars, which was paid with interest and a very large amount of costs.

The education of this case was of immense value to me and I think to the country during the war. Three occasions presented themselves where I found the men under my command affected with scurvy. Not one of the doctors of their regiment had reported it to me, and I found out the fact myself only because I inspected my own hospitals and knew what I was looking for.

I have mentioned above that in preparing cases I have had to spend days in a machine shop, and I will state a case in which that happened, as an encouragement and an instruction to my young friends of the bar as to how I think a case should be prepared.

In November of the year 1852, it will be remembered, General Franklin Pierce of New Hampshire was elected President. In the December following, himself, his wife, and only son, a lad about ten years old, got on board the cars at Boston to go to their home at Concord, New Hampshire. When about twenty-four or twenty-five miles from Boston, and between two and three miles from the town of Andover, the train was derailed by the breaking of the forward axle of the tender on the left side. The train happened to be on a slight curve and along a high embankment built up largely of rubble-stone. By the shock the cars were thrown from the track, and some of them went down the embankment. The President and his wife were substantially unhurt, but the son, who was standing up looking out of the window, was instantly killed. Some half dozen others were killed and many were wounded.

By the law of Massachusetts the administrator of a passenger killed by negligence or malfeasance of a railroad corporation in running a train could recover by indictment five thousand dollars penalty for the death. In the year following the accident, a son who was the administrator of his father, whose name I do not now remember, had an indictment found against the railroad for the death of the father upon the train. The negligence relied on in the case was that the axle, which broke at the journal,— that is, at the line inside of the box in which the axle runs, and between it and the wheel,— had been cracked for a very long time. The crack had opened clear around the axle, which was two and one half inches in diameter, and the wheel had been wabbling backward and forward on that crack until the faces of the iron in the axle had all been worn and pointed, yet not absolutely smooth. A portion a little less than an inch in diameter in the centre of the axle alone held it at the moment when it broke.

The condition in which the axle was found was the fact relied upon by the prosecution to show that the crack had been there a very long time; and at first sight without careful thought it would seem almost conclusive. If the crack had been there for the time supposed to be necessary to give the axle that appearance on the broken end, it seemed clearly negligence on the part of the railroad not to have discovered it by some means or tests.

I had nothing to do with the case, pro or con, but one morning I received a note from President Pierce, who was in Washington, saying that he wished that I would take part in the case and defend the road. He did not himself believe that the road was in any way to blame, but believed it was a pure accident, and he did not desire to have any measures taken against the road in behalf of his son's estate. More than that, Mrs. Pierce believed it was a pure accident, and wanted to have it shown as such, because she believed that it was a visitation of special Providence to take away from the President his son that he might better be prepared to devote himself wholly to the duties of his great office.

I had known General Pierce from my youth up; I had tried cases with him and I had tried cases against him, and I felt highly complimented at his selection of me to go into the case. I reverenced the deep piety of Mrs. Pierce, who was one of the most devout women I ever knew, although I did not quite concur with her logic, because I could not see why Divine Providence might not as well work through the means of a drunken brakeman, which would be negligence of the corporation, as from a pure accident.

I replied to the President that if he wished it I would take hold and do what I could to demonstrate that it was a pure accident, but there was a difficulty in the way. I had brought and tried a great many more suits against that corporation than I had defended, and I did not see how I was to get retained in the case.

He wrote me back thanking me and saying that he would attend to that. The next thing that happened was that the president of the corporation called at my office, saying that he wanted to retain me in the case, and wanted me to take every pains to defend the corporation. Meantime I had looked in the report of the legal examiner whose duty it was to examine into such questions, and I had thought out a little my course of defence.

" Then, Mr. President," I said, " I shall want in the preparation of your defence to have access to your repair shop, and to have everything done there that I desire."

" Certainly," said he, and wrote an order to that effect.

As soon as I had opportunity I went up to the repair shop and took a look at the broken axle. I saw that it was of fine iron or it would not have held as long as it did. I examined particularly the man detailed to inspect axles by tapping them with a hammer, that I might learn whether he knew that he tapped it that day before the train went out, and whether he detected anything, by the sound, of the presence of a crack. He assured me with great positiveness that he had struck the axle twice, but found no signs of a crack. I did not believe much in that, because, in the first place, I doubted if it would show by the sound whether it was cracked, and I also thought that he would say what he did say whether he had heard it or not.

I then caused an axle of the same size and of the same iron to be broken square off by hydraulic pressure, the ends showing the same grain of iron as was shown in the centre of the one broken in the accident. I had a piece of this newly broken axle put solidly in a vise. I then asked a skilled mechanic to take a fourteen-pound hammer used for riveting large rivets, and with such blows as he would use in heading a rivet, keeping an account of them accurately, to make the broken end of this axle as nearly an exact fac-simile as possible of the one broken under the tender. I stood over him while he did it, keeping the account myself of the number of blows.

Next, I interviewed the engineer and fireman of the train, and asked them if anything to attract their attention had happened to the train after it left Boston. They said there had not until they got to Andover, but passing the street at Andover they struck a very severe blow on a frog, which afterwards was found to have been misplaced, and although they slowed up the speed of the train they could see no evil effects from this, and therefore went on until the time of the accident, when suddenly the axle broke and the train was derailed.

They said on the next morning they went down to this spot where they felt the shock and found that the frog was very much bruised by something having struck it, and upon inquiry they had learned that a heavy load of stone had passed over the upper portion of the frog and displaced it so as to push the end of it away from the line of the track on which the train was running at the time of the accident.

I had a very careful measurement made of the distance between the frog and the place of the derailment of the train. The fireman said that he was on the tender shovelling coal at the time of the blow, and that apparently it was very much heavier on the tender than it was to the engine. Assuming that the axle was cracked back there at the frog, and that the crack opened and closed at least once with every revolution of the wheel, by taking the circumference of the wheel I was able to calculate that the crack would open and close more times in running the distance than it took blows of the hammer to smooth the end of the axle experimented upon, provided the weight of the tender was as effective only as the blow of the hammer.

The prosecution evidently had not reflected upon these circumstances, if they knew of them.

They put on the stand a very honest, reliable and competent railroad machinist, from the Providence Railroad repair shop, I think. They showed him the axle and asked him to explain to the jury how it broke. He said in substance that a crack had been started around the axle in the line made by the tool in turning out the journal; that after it was cracked, as the wheel revolved, the pressure was brought upon every part of that crack as the surfaces separated by the crack were brought together; and that pressure would tend to wear the surface of the iron in the crack until it was given the appearance shown in the axle ; and that the crack went on opening and closing and operating as a hammer would operate until it got so far enough down in the axle that the iron that was left was not strong enough to sustain the weight of the tender on the axle. He supposed that it broke at the moment that it did because of some shock given in turning the curve.

He was asked how far the wheel would have to run in order to have the broken face worn down as much as it was. He said he had never seen any experiment from which to judge, but as it must have started at first very slowly, he should think it must have taken a very great number of revolutions of the wheel. He thought that it might have run for three months to make the axle look as it was ; how much more he could not say, and it might be considerably less, but he thought not much.

Upon cross-examination I presented him my fac-simile of the axle and asked him what difference, if any, he could see between it and the one broken in the accident. He looked at them very carefully and said that he saw no special difference. I asked him if my fac-simile could be made by ordinary blows with a riveting hammer of fourteen pounds weight. He said he thought it might.

" Well," said I, " would the weight of the tender, as the wheel revolved, make an impact as heavy as an ordinary blow of such a hammer ? "

" When the crack first started," he said, " it might not, but subsequently and especially toward the last it would be very much heavier, because the crack then would have got so far open as to give an actual blow when it closed."

" Here," I said, " is another piece of axle broken short off. Will you, if I will pay you for your time and trouble as I ought to, after you leave the stand take this to a neighboring machine shop and put it in a vise, and see how long it will take you to make this last piece of axle resemble as nearly as possible the broken one of the tender ? "

" Yes, if it won't take me too long," said he, very good-naturedly.

" I hope it won't keep you too long," I said, " but I want you to keep an account of the blows that you strike, and also keep an account of the time, and in the morning I will finish your cross-examination."

When he came in in the morning he brought in his work and he had made rather a better fac-simile than mine. I asked him the number of blows used, which he gave me, and which I now forget.

" Now," said I, " suppose that by some sudden jar this crack had been started in the axle under the tender and had gone on until it broke, would not the broken end look exactly as it does now and as the one you have made with the hammer ? "

He said he did not see why it would not.

" First the circumference of the wheel we know as so much," I continued. " Now, the cracked surface of the axle would receive a blow at least every time the wheel revolved in running the distance of two and one half miles. Won't you take your pencil and calculate and tell us whether it would not receive more blows in going that distance than it took you to smooth down the end of the axle which I gave you?"

He started back after he got through his calculation, saying: " I never thought of this before ; I shall have to take back my answer about how long it would take to put the axle in this condition

Engraved from a Life-size Bust in General Butler's Library.

after the crack commenced, and saying I don't know anything about it."

I then put on my own testimony upon the matter and showed that some quarter less blows were used in preparing the end of the other axle than the broken axle received in going the distance from the frog in Andover to where the derailment took place. I then put on the testimony of my engineer and fireman, who gave their evidence in a very straightforward, honest manner. I also put on my man who said he tapped the wheels, but after he left the stand I told the jury I was bound to call him but I didn't place any special reliance on his testimony, because he was under great temptation to tell the story as he did to save himself from harm, although I believe he honestly thought so. It went to the jury, who gave us a verdict.

There were no other cases drawn out of this derailment tried to my knowledge. I am happy to say that the verdict of the jury entirely confirmed Mrs. Pierce in her belief, and as she thanked me more than once for my exertion in ferreting out the matter I certainly did not enter into any discussion as to her faith.

I have spoken of defending men when on trial for their lives. It is never a profitable thing to do, and always an unpleasant thing, because involving great responsibility. One sometimes does not get as payment even the gratitude of his client when he is successful. I have a curious incident of that :

A man of about twenty-six or twenty-seven years of age broke into a small way station or depot of the Fitchburg railroad in Waltham, Mass., but did not find anything there which he chose to take away. He was seen in the act of departing on the train and went up the road a few miles to Lincoln. A telegram was sent after him with directions for the depot master, who was also a constable, to arrest him for breaking into a railroad depot. The constable identified him, and when the train started took him out of the train which went on, leaving at the depot only the constable and two boys of eight or nine years of age and the prisoner. The constable was about closing up his depot and said to the man, whose name was Carey: "I have got to take you back to Waltham, but it is dinner-time, and if you will go into the house with me,"— which was a little distance from the depot —" we will have some dinner before we go."

He had hardly uttered the words when Carey jumped through the window on the opposite side of the door and ran away. The constable immediately ran after him, followed by the boys. Carey, not knowing the ground, ran for the woods, and ran directly into a *cul de sac* made by the Stony Brook River in its meanderings there. It was too wide for him to cross readily, and Carey was brought to bay. He turned upon the constable and produced a revolver, saying: "If you come near me I will shoot you."

No braver man ever lived than that constable Heywood. He jumped for his prisoner, and Carey fired and shot him directly through the heart, and he fell dead. The boys immediately ran away and gave the alarm, and Carey disappeared in the bushes. The hue and cry was raised, and the culprit, having gone quite a distance through the woods, came out where there were three or four of his pursuers, who immediately laid hold of him. A thing that showed the steadiness of his nerve was that he then had in his hand a gray squirrel which he had shot with his pistol while he was being pursued. The evidence of the boys was plenary, and he was committed to jail for murder.

Lincoln is about six miles from Concord. I was at Concord attending the court. The constable was a Democratic friend of mine who always used to go to the convention as a delegate, and I always sent him the political documents of the campaign to be distributed. Hearing of his death, and not being engaged on the day of the funeral, I took my horse and rode over to Lincoln to attend his funeral, with as much grief as I would attend the funeral of any dear friend.

In the February term Carey was indicted for murder, and in the April term of the Supreme Court at Lowell he was arraigned and pleaded not guilty.

Now, there is a custom which has become a law that where a prisoner who is to be tried for his life has no counsel the court must appoint someone to defend the case. I had never seen the prisoner, and knew nothing about him, but when the chief justice asked him: "Carey, have you any counsel?" he said: "I should like to have Mr. Butler."

The horror of defending the murderer of my friend quite overcame me. I said: —

"I would like to ask your Honor to appoint other counsel. Your Honor knows I have been engaged to defend quite a number of men on trial for their lives and it is a thankless and profitless task."

My using the word "profitless" was very unfortunate, because the chief justice thought that I was making the question a matter of fees, and he replied with some severity: —

"Mr. Butler, this is a duty which, when the court assigns a member of the bar, he cannot very well decline. Whom shall I appoint to assist you?" I saw that I was in for it and asked for a member of the bar to aid me. He was duly assigned. I think it was the

Hon. Benjamin Dean, of Boston, but I may be mistaken. We examined our client's apparently desperate case. I don't know whether I or Mr. Dean first suggested the point, but we came to the conclusion that we would raise the following question : —

Our statutes for burglary, breaking and entering, include almost every description of building save a depot or railroad station house, and the evidence was that he broke into a depot in Waltham. If that was not within the statute, it was a breaking and entering not a felony, for which the constable could not arrest him without a warrant, and therefore the constable's proceedings were wholly illegal. The resisting of illegal arrest, and the defending of himself against it even with a pistol, and with death ensuing, was not murder, and the man must be convicted of manslaughter only.

Murder trials were before at least three justices of the Supreme Court at that time, and on the trial we took the above-mentioned point. The law perhaps was clear enough on the question of what the building was. The question was argued with great ability for the prosecution by the attorney-general, and I replied with a great deal of earnestness in defence of my point of law. The court took it into consideration and spent three hours in consultation, and at last gave an opinion two to one sustaining my point. Thereupon Carey was convicted of manslaughter and sentenced to twenty years in the State prison, the longest term for which the law allowed him to be sentenced. After he was sentenced I stepped back to the dock and said: "Carey, you have had a narrow escape; I think you may feel obliged for that point of law."

"No; I wish I had been sentenced to be hanged."

"I wish you had let me know your preference a few hours ago," I said, "and I would have accommodated you." And that was all the fee I got for trying this case except $2.50 which the law paid to me.

That was not all. Cambridge is perhaps twelve miles distant from Lincoln, which is a nice little town, at that time not having a doctor, a pauper, or a lawyer in it. The constable, I believe, had also been tax collector and held several other local offices, for he was one of the most popular of their townsmen. The people of the town had many of them turned out to see his murderer convicted, and their disgust was infinite when they saw his fast friend of years, and a man who had attended his funeral, earnestly and zealously defending his murderer's life, and at last saving it. They came to the determination that a lawyer so utterly lost to every sense of decency and proper conduct, hardly deserving to live, should never have a vote in that town if he ever ran for office; and they with vigor carried out that determination at the next election.

That was a favorite method in Massachusetts of dealing with a lawyer who did not carry on his business to suit a community, and this I will illustrate by another case: —

The town of Malden, a very excellent town in which very fine people lived, and in which I was reasonably popular, got its first fire engine. Then they had a fire and the engine squirted. The boys had never seen an engine squirt. Then they had cakes and coffee, which were distributed freely to the firemen and boys. Soon afterwards they had another fire in which rather a worthless barn was burned, and the engine turned out again and squirted some more, and more cakes and coffee were distributed. Then shortly after another barn took fire, and there were more cakes and coffee. By that time the good farmers of Malden came to the conclusion that there was a "fire bug" in their midst who was going to burn down everything, and the town offered $300 or $500 reward to anybody who would catch the "fire bug."

One of the constables of the town had observed that three of the finest boys in the town were always together at the fires, and he came to the conclusion that they had something to do with the fires, or knew something about them. So he went to them separately and told each one of them that the other two had confessed to him that they had started the fires, and that if the one present then did not confess he would be sent to prison, but if he would confess he should have a part of the reward. And when he had got that confession he proceeded to have the boys arrested for arson in the night-time, and had such large bail fixed that it would be very difficult to get. And then he went before the grand jury and told his story of what they said to him. The boys were in prison, and of course there were three weeping fathers and mothers in my office the next day.

I heard them and told the fathers to go down to the jail and tell their boys not to speak a word to anybody about what they had done, no matter what was said or done by anyone; that I was their counsel, and if they wanted to speak to any person they could speak to me. In a day from that time I saw them.

In the course of a few weeks they were brought to Lowell for trial, and pretty much all Malden came up to see the "fire bugs" dealt with. I moved for separate trials and got them. I had learned exactly all that the constable had told the boys. They had told me truly and the only danger was that the constable would deny telling what he did tell them.

The constable was put on the stand and he glorified himself slightly in describing his efforts to arrest the boys. Then he was asked what the boy on trial said to him.

"Stop a moment, Mr. Constable," said I; "may it please your Honor, I want to find out first what he said to the boys, because perhaps it won't be of any consequence what they said to him. Now," said I, "Mr. Constable, I want you to tell exactly what you said to the boys. I know from them, and you must tell the truth about it, because there are three of them to one. Didn't you tell the boys each that the others had confessed in these words?" — giving the words.

"Yes, sir."

"And didn't you tell my client at the bar that if he would confess he should have a part of the $500, and wasn't that before he confessed anything?"

"Yes, sir."

"Well," I said, "may it please your Honor, I think we won't hear anything from this man of what the boys said to him, because any confession obtained by an officer by an inducement cannot be heard in a court of justice. Mr. District Attorney, you had better call your next witness."

The court sustained my point. The attorney hadn't any next witness, and that boy went free, and there was no other testimony against the other two boys, and they all went home that evening, and so did the rest of the inhabitants of Malden. But that night they hanged the poor lawyer in effigy.

I am glad to say that Malden was not in my district then, so that it didn't alter the votes. The next time I was a candidate, and afterwards when I was running for office, Malden was largely on my side. I am certain the three boys voted for me every time, whatever the constable may have done.

So that it will be seen that a lawyer's life is not free from thorns, and that sharp points of law even in favor of the greatest criminals are not to be despised or disregarded.

I think I ought to set out here the facts of a story which has been in circulation in the newspapers for quite fifty years, and about the only one that was always told in my favor that was so circulated. I do this in order to show that there is not one word of truth in it. I

VIEWS AT GENERAL BUTLER'S HOME AT LOWELL. SLEEPING APARTMENT.

have not felt it my duty to expose it before because I thought there were so many lies told against me that I had a sort of proprietary right to the only one told in my favor. Very many of my readers will recognize it when I say it is the story about my attaching the water-wheel of a mill to get a girl's wages. The exact facts are these: —

We had a rule in our mills in Lowell, and a very proper one, among the eight or ten incorporated manufactories, that wages should be paid the last Saturday in every month. This rule was religiously kept until the law interfered, requiring payments weekly.

Another rule was that whenever a person was discharged from the service by the authority of the corporation he was to be paid. A third was that operatives discharging themselves were not to be paid until the pay-day next following. The rule, although it appears harsh at first, was quite reasonable because it prevented the necessity of keeping a quantity of money exposed to loss or fire. Very many of the operatives left work and were refused their pay. They went to a lawyer to have a suit brought for it, the writ to be returnable a fortnight later. But by that time the pay-day would probably come round, and it was not always quite certain whether any recovery could be had.

With the officers of some of the mills I was quite intimate and on friendly terms. Others thought it their political duty to be on unfriendly terms. I had an arrangement with some of the mills by which, when I was applied to in such cases, I was to send a note up to the paymaster to ascertain what was due and he would send the information, and I would pay the amount over to my client, and send to the paymaster for the amount at pay-day. The only loss to anybody was the diminution of my bank account for fifteen or twenty days for such sums, but I would much rather endure that than be bothered with the bringing of suits.

One morning a snappy-eyed old maid from Vermont came into my office and sat herself down and said: " Are you Lawyer Butler?"

"Yes, madam."

"I have been to work in the ———— corporation for five years, and I wanted to go home, and so I told my overseer that I was going home, and asked for my pay. He said I must work out my notice [which was a regulation for two weeks' work] or wait until pay-day. I said I would not do either. I know exactly what my pay is because I work by the piece. Now, I want you to sue the corporation for my pay for I want to go home to-morrow."

"Well, my good woman," said I, "I could not by suit get it by to-morrow, but I will see what I can do for you." I turned to my desk, wrote a little note to the paymaster, handed it to my boy, and he went out.

She resumed the conversation saying: "Yes, you can get it if you will attach the great wheel and stop the mill."

Now that was a proceeding that I had never heard of. I said laughingly:—

"That would be a great thing to do for so little, don't you think so?"

"Well," said she, "they ought to pay me, and I will have my pay."

"Well," I said, "you come back here in the course of an hour, and I will see what I can do for you."

Meanwhile the boy had returned with information of the amount that was due her, and that they would reserve it for me. Then, when my black-eyed friend came in, I said: "Well, I have got your money and made a receipt for it, and here it is."

She said: "I knew you would if you would attach the great wheel. How much am I to pay you?"

"Oh," I said, "nothing. I will look for my pay to the other side. You can go to Vermont to-morrow morning, if you wish to."

She did go, and frequently told the story that I did attach the great wheel, which was a thing that could not be done by any legal legerdemain whatever, because the great wheel is a part of the real estate, and real estate can only be attached in Massachusetts by filing a paper in the county clerk's office. But the story has been going the rounds ever since.

I purposely omit all professional matters at present pending or lately decided, because I think it my duty not to use this means of dealing with professional subjects to the annoyance of living men or to the prejudice of matters now in the course of decision. It will be time enough to deal with such subjects when they are in a condition to be a matter of history.

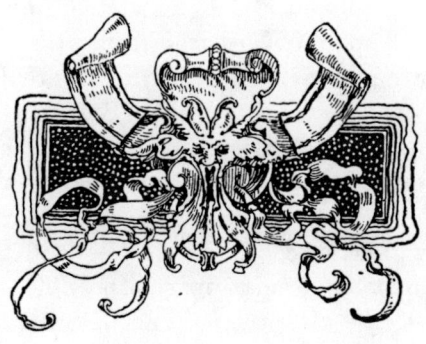

L'ENVOI

TO THE READER.

SUMMARY.

MUCH has been said and written as to my failure to do anything in my military capacity for the country, or to be of any service to it in any form. I hope I may be pardoned in bringing together for the purpose of recalling to memory, several things which are proven in this narrative to whomsoever shall carefully read it, which have been done by me, although I am supposed to have needed a "technical military education."

With foresight and persistent effort I caused the Massachusetts Volunteer Militia to be so made ready that they were the first organized armed force marched into Washington for its defence.

I seized Annapolis, one capital of Maryland, and held it, and thus opened and held open a way for the transportation of Northern troops to the capital, which insured its safety.

I occupied and fortified the heights at the Relay House, and so prevented an assault upon Washington from Harper's Ferry, which the rebels had captured and were occupying for that purpose.

From thence I made a descent upon Baltimore and established it a Union city, which it always remained. These movements prevented the secession of Maryland, and held her loyal during the war.

At Fort Monroe I first declared the legal principles by which, under military law, slaves could be set free, and thereby made the President's proclamation of emancipation possible.

Within forty-five days after the fall of Sumter, without orders from anybody having a "technical military education," of my own motion,

I seized and strongly fortified the important strategic point of New-port News, at the mouth of the James River, which was held during the war, thus keeping open a water-way for the transportation of troops and supplies to the intrenchments around Richmond, and by which the Army of the Potomac under McClellan escaped from Harrison's Landing.

In co-operation with the navy I captured Fort Hatteras and Fort Clark, thus making the holding of the sounds of Virginia and North and South Carolina practicable.

I raised a division of more than six thousand men for the United States without payment of bounties or impressment. With the division thus raised, aided by an equal number of troops added to that force, co-operating with the fleet of the immortal Farragut to his entire satisfaction, we opened the Mississippi River, captured New Orleans, subdued Louisiana, and held all of it that was ever afterwards permanently held as a part of the United States. I enforced respect there to the nation's flag, its laws and power.

By proper sanitary regulations I rescued New Orleans, the commercial port of the Gulf of Mexico, from its most potent danger, the yellow fever, from the ravages of which in no year had it ever escaped, a foe which the enemies of my country surely relied upon to destroy my army, as it would have done if uncontrolled.

I enlisted there the first colored troops ever legally mustered into the army of the United States, thus inaugurating the policy of arming the colored race before Congress or the President had adopted it, by so doing, pointing the way to the recruitment of the armies of the United States by the enlistment of colored men to the number of one hundred and fifty thousand, and establishing the negro soldier as a component part of the military resources of the country forever.

In the spring of 1864 I devised, organized, and perfected the strategy for a campaign against Richmond by having an impregnable intrenched camp containing thirty square miles of territory within its boundaries, which could be held by ten thousand men against the whole rebel forces forever, within eight miles of the rebel capital, like a hand upon its throat never to be unclenched, as it never was. I fortified it as a refuge to which the Army of the Potomac could repair in safety as a base of supplies, as it did when it failed to drive Lee's army in retreat to the defences of Richmond. I took possession of this camp to be intrenched by a march wholly of my planning and execution, by moving more than thirty thousand men, with their artillery supplies and munitions of war, by water seventy-five miles through the enemy's country in a single day without the loss of a man, and without any knowledge on the part of the rebels of my presence until I was in camp.

From that intrenched camp at Bermuda Hundred, on the 15th of July, I captured Petersburg, but lost it through the sloth or incompetency of a corps commander who had a "technical military education."

With the Army of the James on the 29th of September, I captured Fort Harrison and a line of intrenched works, a strong part of the defences of Richmond, which were held by my colored troops until Richmond was evacuated.

I planned, carried out, and constructed the great strategic work, Dutch Gap Canal, which was prevented from being made entirely efficient only by a naval officer, who was afterward convicted for cowardice in that matter, and which remains to this day a most valuable public work, worth more as a commercial avenue in time of peace than all it cost as a military undertaking.

By firmness of purpose which subsequent events have shown to have been the best military judgment, as I knew it was then, I prevented my major-general of division from making an assault on Fort Fisher by which very many of the troops of the expedition would have been slaughtered in a useless attack.

In all military movements I never met with disaster, nor uselessly sacrificed the lives of my men.

In all I did and in all I left undone I never had over twenty-five thousand effective troops under my command for offensive operations, but usually commanded much smaller forces.

If any of my readers doubt upon any one of these propositions, let them examine carefully the verified record in my narrative. I write in no boastful spirit, claiming only justice and fair play. If any general officer with the same means did more in the war for the life of the nation, I congratulate him most heartily, but I would like to see his list.

In my congressional career my proudest boast is that through my advocacy and efforts, the legal tender greenback was made the constitutional money of the United States, to be issued in peace or in war, during the existence of the nation; and I believe soon it will be the only money of the United States, gold and silver taking their appropriate places as products of the mineral resources of the country.

In closing I apologize most humbly for the many omissions and imperfections of my work, and I claim for it but one merit: it has been earnestly and fairly done.

> " What is writ, is writ, —
> Would it were worthier ! but I am not now
> That which I have been, and my visions flit
> Less palpably before me, — and the glow
> Which in my spirit dwelt, is fluttering, faint and low."

APPENDIX.

APPENDIX.

[**No. 1.** *See page* 585.]

To MAJOR-GENERAL BUTLER: WASHINGTON, Nov. 13, 1863.

There is an urgent necessity to provide in your department a suitable depot for rebel prisoners of war, without any delay. I beg to recall the subject to your attention and ask you to take immediate measures to establish a depot at such point as you may deem suitable in your department, and inform me how soon you will be ready to receive prisoners of war, and in what numbers.

EDWIN M. STANTON,
Secretary of War.

To MAJOR-GENERAL BUTLER: WASHINGTON, Nov. 16, 1863.

Your report in regard to place for confinement of rebel prisoners has been received, and on consultation with the general-in-chief, it is believed to be inexpedient to select either Sewall's Front or Hatteras for the present. Therefore, all action in the matter is suspended.

EDWIN M. STANTON,
Secretary of War.

[**No. 2.** *See page* 586.]

HEADQUARTERS DEPARTMENT OF VIRGINIA AND NORTH CAROLINA,
FORTRESS MONROE, Nov. 18, 1863.

HON. E. M. STANTON, SECRETARY OF WAR:

Sir :— In the limits of a telegram, and for the public eye, it was impossible to explain my full thought on the subject of exchange of prisoners. I believed there was some misunderstanding upon the questions involved when I telegraphed, and your answer, with the sentiments of which in every word I concur, convince me that I was right in my belief.

No one will go farther in exerting every power of the government in protecting the colored troops and their officers, than myself. And if that is the question which prevents exchange, and we stand before the country upon that question, I have not a word further to urge. But I fear that is not the point, or at least it is not now understood by the country, that it is upon the pledge of the country's honor that all men, white or black, who fight for us, shall be protected, that we now feel obliged to let our fellow-soldiers starve, if such shall be the inhumanity of the rebels.

I ought to premise, perhaps, why I interfere where it is not specially within my command. Believing that I could do something for the good

3

of the service, I take the liberty of making the application, and with your leave shall continue to make suggestions wherever and whenever I think the government may be aided by so doing, although not strictly called upon so to do, to complete my routine of duty.

I am informed and believe that the rebel authorities will exchange every officer and soldier they now hold in custody, whether colored or not, upon receiving an equivalent number in rank from us.

Indeed, I can put no other interpretation upon the letter of Robert Ould, Esq., agent of exchange in Richmond, of October 20, referring to a letter of a previous date, in which he says : — "More than a month ago I asked your acquiescence in a proposition that all officers and soldiers, on both sides, should be released in conformity with the provisions of the cartel. In order to obviate the difficulties between us, I suggested that all officers and men, on both sides, should be released, unless they were subject to charges, in which event the opposite government should have the right of holding one or more hostages if the retention was not justified. You stated to me, in conversation, that this proposition was very fair, and that you would ask the consent of your government to it. As usual, you have as yet made no response. I tell you frankly, I do not expect any. Perhaps you may disappoint me, and tell me that you reject or accept the proposition. I write this letter for the purpose of bringing to your recollection my proposition, and of dissipating the idea that seems to have been purposely encouraged by your public papers, that the Confederate government has refused or objected to a system of exchange.

"In order to avoid any mistake in that direction, I now propose that all officers and men, on both sides, be released in conformity with the provisions of the cartel, the excess on one side or the other to be on parole. Will you accept this? I have no expectation of an answer, but perhaps you may give one. If it does come, I hope it will be soon."

I have forwarded copies of all the correspondence, so that you can refer to it. If there is any interpretation to the contrary, it is not made apparent to the country; and the government, for all that appears from the correspondence between the two commissioners, is now suffering our soldiers to be starved to death upon the proposition of inequality in the computation and value of paroles. If you will examine the correspondence, it will be seen that the whole question turns upon that point; not a suggestion is made that color, caste, or condition has anything to do with the dispute. It would seem that the discussion had grown sufficiently acrimonious to have lost sight of the point of dispute, as we know many discussions do.

I do not mean to impute blame to any party, because I am not sufficiently informed, nor have I the authority so to do, but simply to suggest a remedy. I assume that we have, in actual custody, some twenty-six thousand prisoners, against thirteen thousand that the rebels have. Now, then, why may not Ould's proposition be accepted, and we exchange man for man, officer for officer, until the rebels stop? If then every prisoner they hold has been exchanged, then the question of color does not arise, and our men will have been relieved from starvation up to that number. But, if the colored prisoners and their officers shall not be produced by the rebels for exchange, we shall have ten thousand of their men upon whom to work both retaliation and reprisal to the fullest extent, to wring from the rebels justice to the colored soldiers. It is not necessary to argue this point; its statement is the argument. This action — not offers and correspondence — will place the government right before the country, and if then the negro prisoners, whether civilians or soldiers, or their officers, are kept in prison or maltreated, the world will justify us in reprisal and retaliation to any extent.

I believe that this exchange will be made by the rebels from information derived from various sources, and specially from J. W. Monfort, agent of the State of Indiana, who has gone to Washington, and from whom you can learn the facts that lead to my belief.

Without suggesting any blame upon the part of the agent of exchange, would it not, in fact, seem to be that such a state of feeling has grown up between himself and the rebel agent that, without doing anything which would impute wrong, or detract from the appreciation ot the efforts of General Meredith, this might be done as if outside of either agent.

This is submitted for consideration with a single desire, to relieve the soldiers now in a condition to enlist all our sympathies.

I can make these suggestions all the more freely, as I leave this evening to arrange the affairs of this department in North Carolina, and can have probably no personal part in the matter.

I have the honor to be,
Very respectfully, your obedient servant,
BENJ. F. BUTLER,
Major-General Commanding.

[**No. 3.** *See page 587.*]
WAR DEPARTMENT,
WASHINGTON CITY, Dec. 8, 1863.

General: — I am directed by the Secretary of War to inform you that your action in regard to supplying vaccine matter for the use of the Union prisoners at Richmond is approved by this department.
Very respectfully, your obedient servant,
JAS. A. HARDIE,
Assistant Adjutant-General.

MAJ.-GEN. B. F. BUTLER, *Commanding, etc.*
Fortress Monroe, Va.

[**No. 4.** *See page 596.*]
WASHINGTON, 11 P. M., April 14, 1864.

TO MAJOR-GENERAL BUTLER:

Your report respecting negotiations with Commissioner Ould for the exchange of prisoners of war has been referred to me for my orders.

Until examined by me, and my orders therein are received by you, decline all further negotiations.
U. S. GRANT,
Lieutenant-General.

[**No. 5.**　*See page 596.*]

HEADQUARTERS ARMIES OF THE UNITED STATES,
In FIELD, CULPEPPER COURT-HOUSE,
VIRGINIA, April 17, 1864.

MAJ.-GEN. B. F. BUTLER,
　　COMMANDING DEPARTMENT OF VIRGINIA AND NORTH CAROLINA,
　　FORTRESS MONROE, VA. :

General : — Your report of negotiations with Mr. Ould, Confederate States agent, touching the exchange of prisoners, has been referred to me by the Secretary of War, with directions to furnish you such instructions on the subject as I may deem proper.

After a careful examination of your report, the only points on which I deem instructions necessary, are : —

1st. Touching the validity of the paroles of the prisoners captured at Vicksburg and Port Hudson.

2d. The status of colored prisoners.

As to the first. No arrangement for the exchange of prisoners will be acceded to that does not fully. recognize the validity of these paroles, and provide for the release to us of a sufficient number of prisoners now held by the Confederate authorities to cancel any balance that may be in our favor by virtue of these paroles. Until there is released to us an equal number of officers and men as were captured and paroled at Vicksburg and Port Hudson, not another Confederate prisoner of war will be paroled or exchanged.

As to the second. No distinction whatever will be made in the exchange between white and colored prisoners; the only question being, were they, at the time of their capture, in the military service of the United States. If they were, the same terms as to treatment while prisoners and conditions of release and exchange must be exacted and had, in the case of colored soldiers as in the case of white soldiers.

Non-acquiescence by the Confederate authorities in both or either of these propositions, will be regarded as a refusal on their part to agree to the further exchange of prisoners, and will be so treated by us.

　　I am, General, very respectfully, your obedient servant,

　　　　　　　　　　　　　　U. S. GRANT.
　　　　　　　　　　　　　　Lieutenant-General.

[**No. 6.**　*See page 605.*]

　　　　　　　　　　　　CITY POINT, Oct. 12, 1864.

To MAJOR-GENERAL BUTLER :

Your correspondence with Judge Ould on the subject of exchange, and also the affidavits upon which you rely for proof of the unwarrantable conduct of the enemy in employing prisoners of war at work on fortifications, and your letter informing Mr. Ould of the steps taken to retaliate are received and the whole approved. I will forward the whole to the Secretary of War with my approval.

　　　　　　　　　　　　　　U. S. GRANT,
　　　　　　　　　　　　　　Lieutenant-General.

[**No. 7.** *See page* 605.]

Major-General Butler: City Point, Oct. 15, 1864, 4.20 p. m.

I think it probably advisable, whilst Major Mulford is here, to get the naval prisoners on hand put through the lines. Points of difference may serve a good purpose hereafter.

U. S. Grant,
Lieutenant-General.

[**No. 8.** *See page* 608.]

Headquarters Department of Virginia and North Carolina,
Army of the James.
In the Field, Va., Oct. 20, 1864.

General Order No. 134.

It having been officially certified by General Lee, commanding Confederate forces, that the prisoners of war of this army put to work in the trenches near Fort Gilmer have been withdrawn, to be treated as prisoners of war, it is ordered, that the prisoners of war of the Confederate forces put to work in the canal at Dutch Gap, in retaliation, shall be at once withdrawn and sent to Point Lookout, to be held and treated hereafter as prisoners of war.

Numbers of these prisoners having certified in writing to the commanding general their desire to take the oath of allegiance, because of the inhumanity of the Confederate authorities towards them, which application was declined lest it should be said that these prisoners took the oath of allegiance to the United States under duress, it is now ordered, that so many of them as choose, after this order is read to them, be permitted to take the oath of allegiance and be sent north, to be there found employment by the government, as other prisoners of war have been who have returned to their loyalty to the United States.

By command of
Major-General Butler.

[*Official.*]
Ed. W. Smith, *Assistant Adjutant-General.*

[**No. 9.** *See page* 608.]

Office Assistant Agent for Exchange of Prisoners,
Fortress Monroe, Va., Nov. 6, 1864.

Major-General Butler, Commissioner for Exchange, etc.:

General: — I have the honor to inform you that I am still here awaiting transportation for the sick prisoners now on board steamers Atlantic and Baltic and more particularly our own men whom I am to receive in return. It would be worse than barbarous, General, for me to undertake, in the ships now at my disposal, the transportation of those feeble and dying men, now anxiously awaiting my arrival at Savannah and whose sufferings are protracted and aggravated and whose mortality is fearfully increased by this needless delay. My fleet as organized by yourself was indeed a noble one, for a noble purpose; one that would reflect honor upon our government and carry joy and gladness to many thousand anguished hearts. Of that portion still left me, no fault can be found, but the most essential part of this expedition is withheld. I am, by an order from Washington, to Colonel Webster, chief quartermaster of this department, deprived the use of the only hospital ships in the fleet, and knowing so well as I do, for what a wretched freight I am to provide on my return trip, I feel assured you will approve my course in insisting upon some proper provisions being made for the sick before I sail.

I have now here loaded the steamers Atlantic, Baltic, Northern Light, H. Livingston, and New York, in all some three thousand men; have lost over fifty since their arrival at this place. One other vessel, the Crescent, is loaded with stores, clothing, etc.

I have turned over to the quartermaster, five of the large vessels for transportation of troops. The balance of the fleet are still here. Quartermaster-general informed Colonel Webster he had ordered vessels from New York to relieve the Atlantic and Baltic. They have not arrived yet, nor have we farther advice of them. Please direct me what to do, and believe me,

Very respectfully, your obedient servant,
JOHN E. MULFORD,
Lieutenant-Colonel and Assistant Agent of Exchange.

[**No. 10.** *See page* 608.]

NEW YORK, Nov. 8, '64.
COLONEL J. E. MULFORD,
ASSISTANT AGENT OF EXCHANGE, FORTRESS MONROE, VA.:
Start immediately with the Atlantic and Baltic.
It is by order of the Secretary of War.
Do not yield the point to anything but armed force and let General Shepley have sufficient force to meet even that.

B. F. BUTLER,
Major-General Commanding.

[**No. 11.** *See page* 609.]

OFFICE ASSISTANT AGENT FOR EXCHANGE OF PRISONERS,
FLAG OF TRUCE STEAMER NEW YORK,
SAVANNAH RIVER, Nov. 21, 1864.
MAJOR-GENERAL BUTLER, COMMISSIONER FOR EXCHANGE:
General: — I have the honor to inform you that I have up to the present time received over three thousand of our men. Their physical condition is rather better than I expected, but their personal is worse than anything I have ever seen — filth and rags. It is a great labor to cleanse and clothe them, but I am fairly at work and will progress as rapidly as possible. I have much to say, but have little time for writing now. I have got off two vessels to-day and will try and get off two to-morrow, and so on. Matters have been rather queerly managed here in the mode of conducting truce business. I have nothing whatever to do with the old matters, or the business of this department. Enclosed I send you latest papers and have the honor to be,

Very respectfully, your obedient servant,
JOHN E. MULFORD,
Lieutenant-Colonel and United States Agent for Exchange of Prisoners.

[**No. 12.** *See page* 609.]

OFFICE OF THE COMMISSARY-GENERAL OF PRISONERS,
WASHINGTON, D. C., Dec. 16, 1864.

General Order No. 3.

Arrangements having been made between the United States Government and the rebel authorities by which each is to supply its own prisoners of war with necessary supplies, and Brig.-Gen. H. E. Paine, on the part of the Federal Government, and Brig.-Gen. Wm. W. R. Beale, on the part of the rebel authorities, having been appointed agents to carry out these arrangements, every necessary and proper facility for the purpose will be given by the commanding officers of the various military prisoners when request is made or properly authorized by Brigadier-General Paine.

By Order,

H. W. WESSELS,

Brig.-Gen. U. S. V., Inspt. and Comy. Gen. of Prisoners.

[**No. 13.** *See page* 611.]

HEADQUARTERS, ETC., NEAR BOTTOM'S BRIDGE, June 12, 1864.

ADJUTANT-GENERAL,

HEADQUARTERS ARMIES OF THE CONFEDERATE STATES:

Sir: — Will you please bring to the immediate attention of General Bragg a cause which is producing great discontent among the troops of my command. It appears that to the troops of the Army of Northern Virginia, the ration issued is very much larger than the same given to my troops, although they are doing the same duty. For instance, Kirkland's brigade, Army of Northern Virginia, is guarding the York River Railroad bridge over Chickahominy, and the local troops are performing the same service at Bottom's Bridge; the former receive a half pound of meat, flour bread (at least, in part), rice, pease, sugar, coffee, and vegetables; the local troops get but one-fifth pound of meat, and corn bread. If they receive sugar and coffee (only six pounds of one and three of the other to 100 rations) the meat is stopped. The same exists as to all my command. It very naturally and justly produces discontent. If the rations can be increased for the whole of the Army of Northern Virginia, it seems to me it ought to be done for the troops who are on exactly the same service in this department. I wrote to Colonel Northrop, and he replied that all would be reduced to the same; but nearly a week has passed and the same distinction is made. I trust the general commanding will have proper orders given in the matter.

Very respectfully, your obedient servant,

R. RANSOM, JR.,
Major-General.

(First Indorsement.)

June 13, 1864.

Respectfully referred to the Honorable Secretary of War.
Such discrimination must produce discontent and should be corrected.

BRAXTON BRAGG,
General.

[**No. 14.** *See page* 619.]

HEADQUARTERS 18TH ARMY CORPS,
DEPARTMENT OF VIRGINIA AND NORTH CAROLINA,
FORTRESS MONROE, April 14, 1864.

LIEUT.-GEN. U. S. GRANT, COMMANDING U. S. ARMIES:

General: — I have the honor to enclose official copies of the correspondence between General Pickett, commanding Confederate forces, District of North Carolina, and General Peck, commanding United States forces in said district, relative to the execution of certain prisoners belonging to the Second North Carolina Regiment. Many of these men were conscripted by the rebels. All of them were citizens of the United States, who owed their allegiance to our government; if misguided, they forfeited their allegiance, repented, and returned to it again. They have only done their duty, and, in my judgment, are to be protected in so doing. I do not recognize any right in the rebels to execute a United States soldier because either by force or fraud, or by voluntary enlistment even, he has been once brought into their ranks and has escaped therefrom. I suppose all the rights they can claim as belligerents is to execute one of the deserters from their army while he holds simply the character of a deserter during the time he has renounced his allegiance, and before he has again claimed that protection and it has been accorded to him. Therefore by no law of nations, and by no belligerent rights, have the rebels any power over him other than to treat him as a prisoner of war if captured.

I would suggest that the Confederate authorities be called upon to say whether they adopt this act, and that upon their answer such action may be taken as will sustain the dignity of the government, and give a promise to afford protection to its citizens.

I have the honor to be, General, very respectfully, your obedient servant,

BENJ. F. BUTLER,
Major-General Commanding.

[Inclosure No 1.]

HEADQUARTERS ARMY AND DISTRICT OF NORTH CAROLINA,
NEW BERNE, N. C., Feb. 11, 1864.

MAJOR-GENERAL PICKETT, DEPARTMENT OF VIRGINIA AND NORTH CAROLINA, CONFEDERATE ARMY, PETERSBURG:

General: — I have the honor to enclose a slip cut from the Richmond *Examiner* of Feb. 8, 1864. It is styled " The Advance on New Berne," and appears to have been extracted from the Petersburg *Register*, a paper published in the city where your headquarters are located.

Your attention is particularly invited to that paragraph which states " that Colonel Shaw was shot dead by a negro soldier from the other side of the river which he was spanning with a pontoon bridge, and that the negro was watched and followed, taken, and hanged after the action at Thomasville."

The Petersburg *Register* gives the following additional particulars of the advance on New Berne : —

Our army, according to the report of passengers arriving from Weldon, has fallen back to a point sixteen miles west of New Berne. The reason assigned for this retrograde movement was that New Berne could not be taken by us without a loss on our part which would find no equivalent in its capture, as the place was stronger than we anticipated. Yet in spite of all this, we are sure the expedition will result in good to our cause. Our forces are now in a situation to get large supplies from a country still abundant; to prevent raids on points westward, and keep tories in check and hang them when caught.

From a private, who was one of the guard that brought the batch of prisoners through, we learn that Colonel Shaw was shot dead by a negro soldier from the other side of the river which he was spanning with a pontoon bridge. The negro was watched, followed, taken, and hanged after the action at Thomasville. It is stated that when our troops entered Thomasville a number of the enemy took shelter in the houses and fired upon them. The Yankees were ordered to surrender but refused, whereupon our men set fire to the houses, and their occupants got bodily a taste in this world of the flames eternal.

The Government of the United States has wisely seen fit to enlist many thousand colored soldiers to aid in putting down the revolution, and has placed them on the same footing in all respects to our white troops. The orders of the President on that subject are so just, full, and clear, that I inclose a copy for your information : —

Executive Mansion,
Washington, D. C., July 30, 1863.

It is the duty of every government to give protection to its citizens of whatever class, color, or condition, and especially to those who are duly organized as soldiers in the public service. The law of nations and the usages and customs of war, as carried on by civilized powers, permit no distinction as to color in the treatment of prisoners of war as public enemies. To sell or enslave any captured person on account of his color, and for no offence against the laws of war, is a relapse into barbarism and a crime against the civilization of the age.

The Government of the United States will give the same protection to all its soldiers ; and if the enemy shall sell or enslave anyone because of his color, the offence shall be punished by retaliation upon the enemy's prisoners in our possession.

It is therefore ordered, that for every soldier of the United States killed in violation of the laws of war, a rebel soldier shall be executed ; and for every one enslaved by the enemy, or sold into slavery, a rebel soldier shall be placed at hard labor on the public works and continued at such labor until the other shall be released and receive the treatment due to a prisoner of war.

Abraham Lincoln.

Believing that this atrocity has been perpetrated without your knowledge, and that you will take prompt steps to disavow this violation of the usages of war, and to bring the offenders to justice, I shall refrain from executing a rebel soldier until I learn your action in the premises.

I am, very respectfully, your obedient servant,

John J. Peck,
Major-General.

[Inclosure No. 2.]

HEADQUARTERS ARMY AND DISTRICT OF NORTH CAROLINA,
NEW BERNE, N. C., Feb. 13, 1864.

MAJOR-GENERAL PICKETT, DEPARTMENT OF VIRGINIA AND NORTH
CAROLINA, CONFEDERATE ARMY :

General:— I have the honor to enclose a list of fifty-three soldiers of the U. S. Government who are supposed to have fallen into your hands on your late hasty retreat from before New Berne. They are loyal and true North Carolinians, and duly enlisted in the Second North Carolina Infantry. I ask for them the same treatment in all respects as you will mete out to other prisoners of war.

I am, very respectfully, your obedient servant,

JOHN J. PECK,
Major-General.

[Inclosure No. 3.]

HEADQUARTERS DEPARTMENT OF NORTH CAROLINA,
PETERSBURG, VA., Feb. 16, 1864.

MAJ.-GEN. JOHN J. PECK, U. S. ARMY, COMMANDING AT NEW BERNE :

General:—Your communication of the 11th of February is received. I have the honor to state in reply that the paragraph from a newspaper enclosed therein is not only without foundation in fact, but so ridiculous that I should scarcely have supposed it worthy of consideration ; but I would respectfully inform you that *had I caught any negro* who had killed officer, soldier, or citizen of the Confederate States, I should have caused him to be immediately executed.

To your threat expressed in the following extract from your communication, viz.: "Believing that this atrocity has been perpetrated without your knowledge, and that you will take prompt steps to disavow this violation of the usages of war and to bring the offenders to justice, I shall refrain from executing a rebel soldier until I learn your action in the premises," I have merely to say that I have in my hands and subject to my orders, captured in the recent operations in this department, some 450 officers and men of the U. S. Army, and for every man you hang I will hang ten of the U. S. Army.

I am, General, very respectfully, your obedient servant,

G. E. PICKETT,
Major-General Commanding.

[**No. 15.** *See page* 619.]

YORKTOWN, Feb. 4, 1864.

General : — Accept my grateful and sincere thanks for your letter of to-day, just arrived by despatch boat, and for all your manifold kindness and consideration ever since I happily came a second time under your command. . . .

At 2 A. M. on the 7th, we make the attempt to surprise Bottom's Bridge, with the hope of striking Richmond at 5 A. M. following.

If the principal cavalry officers are *brave*, the thing must succeed.

With renewed and heartfelt thanks for your uniform kindness, and not the least of them — this opportunity given me — permit me to call myself,

Your sincere and attached friend,

I. J. WISTAR.

P. S. — On Sunday morning, at five o'clock, pray for our country and for me. I. J. W.

[**No. 16.** *See page* 619.]

GENERAL WISTAR'S REPORT OF OPERATION.

YORKTOWN, Feb. 9, 1864.

Major: — I have the honor to report the following operations of the forces under my command, undertaken with a view to the surprise and capture of Richmond, and incidental results :

All the infantry and cavalry placed at my disposal by the general commanding, being about four thousand of the former and two thousand two hundred of the latter, were suddenly concentrated behind my lines at Williamsburg after dark on the evening of the 5th instant, together with Hunt's and Belger's light batteries.

The infantry, consisting of three white regiments, brigaded under Col. R. M. West, First Pennsylvania Light Artillery, and three colored regiments under Colonel Duncan, Fourth U. S. Colored Troops, moved thence at 9 A. M. on the 6th, carrying on the person six days' rations in the knapsack and seventy rounds of cartridges — forty in the boxes and thirty in the knapsack.

The cavalry, being detachments of five regiments under Col. S. P. Spear, Eleventh Pennsylvania Cavalry, moved two hours later. Colonel Spear was directed to arrive at Bottom's Bridge, twelve miles this side of Richmond, by 3 A. M. of the 7th, surprise it, and move on rapidly to Richmond. A picked company under Captain Hill, First New York Mounted Rifles, with selected horses, was placed in advance to ride down the three pickets — at New Kent, Baltimore Cross-Roads, and at the bridge. Arrangements had been previously made to have the telegraph wire between Meadow Station and Richmond cut between dark and midnight of the 6th. By these means it was hoped to surprise the enemy's Battery No. 2, on the Bottom's Bridge road near Richmond, and occupy Capitol Square in that city for at least two or three hours ; detachments previously detailed and carefully instructed breaking successively from the main column, on entering, for various specific purposes. Of course the success of the enterprise was based upon the sudden and noiseless surprise of the strong picket at Bottom's Bridge, without which it would be impossible for cavalry alone to pass Battery No. 2. Colonel Spear reached Bottom's Bridge, a distance of fifty-one miles, ten minutes before the time designated, but found the enemy there in strong force, with infantry, cavalry, and artillery. They had received notice some sixteen hours previously, and had during that time been vigorously making preparations. The bridge planks had been taken up, the fords both above and below effectually obstructed, extensive earthworks and rifle-pits constructed, and a strong force of troops brought down by the York River Railroad, by which large accessions were still arriving.

The darkness prevented an attack till morning, when a detachment of the New York Mounted Rifles, under Major Wheelan, made a gallant but unsuccessful charge on the bridge by the only approach — a long causeway flanked on either hand by an impassable marsh. The enemy opened with canister, first checking and then repulsing the charge, with a loss to us of nine killed and wounded and ten horses killed. All our men were subsequently brought off, as well as the saddles and equipments. The river was reconnoitred both above and below for some miles, but at every possible crossing the enemy was found in force with newly placed obstructions.

Our infantry had marched, on the 6th, thirty-three miles, arriving at New Kent Court-House at 2 A. M. on the 7th.

It is the obvious fact that a small force in this vicinity, actively handled, can and should hold a much superior force of the enemy in the immediate vicinity of Richmond inactive except for its defence.

I have the honor to be, Major, with great respect, your obedient servant,

ISAAC J. WISTAR,
Brigadier-General Commanding.

MAJ. R. S. DAVIS, *Assistant Adjutant-General.*

HEADQUARTERS DEPARTMENT OF VIRGINIA AND NORTH CAROLINA,
FORTRESS MONROE, Feb. 12, 1864.

Report approved.

The operation was skilfully and brilliantly done. It gives the commanding general renewed confidence in General Wistar as a commander of a division.

BENJ. F. BUTLER,
Major-General Commanding.

[**No. 17.** *See page 636.*]
CULPEPPER COURT-HOUSE, VA.,
April 8, 1864–8.30 P. M. (Received 9.30 P. M.)

MAJOR-GENERAL HALLECK:

It is the intention to operate up the James River as far as City Point, and all the co-operation the navy can give, we want. Two of the ironclads are wanted as soon as they can be got. . . .

U. S. GRANT,
Lieutenant-General Commanding.[1]

CULPEPPER COURT-HOUSE, VA., April 9, 1864.

MAJ.-GEN. G. G. MEADE,
COMMANDING ARMY OF THE POTOMAC:

Gillmore will join Butler with about ten thousand men from South Carolina. Butler can reduce his garrison so as to take twenty-three thousand men into the field directly to his front. The force will be commanded by Maj.-Gen. W. F. Smith. With Smith and Gillmore, Butler will seize

---

[1] War Records, Vol. XXXIII., p. 821.

City Point and operate against Richmond from the south side of the river. His movement will be simultaneous with yours.

Lee's army will be your objective point. Wherever Lee goes, there you will go also. The only point upon which I am now in doubt is whether it will be better to cross the Rapidan above or below him. Each plan presents great advantages over the other, with corresponding objections. By crossing above, Lee is cut off from all chance of ignoring Richmond and going north on a raid; but if we take this route all we do must be done while the rations we start with hold out; we separate from Butler, so that he cannot be directed how to co-operate. By the other route, Brandy Station can be used as a base of supplies until another is secured on the York or James Rivers. . . .

Should by Lee's right flank be our route, you will want to make arrangements for having supplies of all sorts promptly forwarded to White House, on the Pamunkey. Your estimates for this contingency should be made at once. If not wanted there, there is every probability they will be wanted on the James River or elsewhere.

If Lee's left is turned, large provision will have to be made for ordnance stores. I would say not much short of five hundred rounds of infantry ammunition would do. By the other, half the amount would be sufficient.

U. S. GRANT,
Lieutenant-General.[1]

[**No. 18.** *See page* 637.]

HEADQUARTERS 18TH ARMY CORPS,
DEPT. OF VIRGINIA AND NORTH CAROLINA.
FORTRESS MONROE, April 15, 1864.

[*Unofficial.*]

My Dear General: — You dealt so kindly with the suggestions as to the movements which I desired should be made from Fortress Monroe up the James and upon Richmond, and showed so much consideration for the views I ventured to express, that it has occurred to me possibly you might, in some slight degree, have bent your plan of campaign to meet those views and wishes, although, perhaps the inclination of your more matured judgment would lead you to prefer a movement through North Carolina, of which you at first spoke to me.

Specially has this thought pressed itself upon my mind since I have been called upon to furnish transportation for two millions and a half of rations to North Carolina, which inclines me to believe that a movement is intended in that direction.

If this be so, as I have a very strong opinion that but one co-operative movement with the Army of the Potomac should be made on the south of the James, and fearing lest a desire to oblige me might possibly in some degree have swayed your judgment, I take leave to say to you that any disposition of the troops under my command will be most agreeable to me, which shall, in your opinion, subserve the public service. So that, if you think it best to have my troops for the North Carolina movement,

---

[1] War Records, No. L., p. 827.

do not regard in the least degree my supposed wishes or position, as I shall be most happy to co-operate most heartily in any of your movements.

I pray you, General, to take this note in the exact spirit in which it is meant. I believe fully that but one movement (and that the one I indicated) south of the James with all the concentrated forces that can be spared, able to fight Lee in the field if we can get men enough, or if not, as near it as we can, is feasible, and so believing, I do not for a moment desire that any thought of myself or of its effect upon the extent of my command should stand in the way of such concentration wherever it shall be thought best. This, besides being a duty, is at least but a just return for the kind consideration you have shown me.

I have possessed General Smith with my views as well upon the subject of the movement as upon the number of troops which can be spared from my lines for the purpose, and beg to refer you to him for any explanation you may desire. Believe me truly yours,

BENJ. F. BUTLER.

To LIEUT.-GEN. U. S. GRANT, *Com'd'g.,* etc., etc.

[**No. 19.** *See page* 637.]

[*Confidential.*]　　　　　　HEADQUARTERS ARMIES IN THE FIELD.
CULPEPPER COURT-HOUSE, VA., April 16, 1864.

MAJOR-GENERAL BUTLER, COMMANDING DEPARTMENT OF
　　　VIRGINIA AND NORTH CAROLINA:

General:—I have just this moment received your letter of the 15th of April, brought by the hands of Maj.-Gen. W. F. Smith.

You are entirely right in saying there should be but one movement made south of James River. At no time has more been intended.

I went to Fortress Monroe for the express purpose of seeing you, and telling you that it was my plan to have the force under you act directly in concert with the Army of the Potomac, and as far as possible towards the same point. My mind was entirely made up what instructions to give, and I was very much pleased to find that your previously conceived views exactly coincided.

All the forces that can be taken from the coast have been ordered to report to you at Fortress Monroe by the 18th inst., or as soon thereafter as possible. What I ask is that with them and all you can concentrate from your own command, you seize upon City Point and act from there, looking upon Richmond as your objective point. If you can send cavalry to Hicksford and cut the railroad connection at that point, it is a good thing to do. I do not pretend to say how your work is to be done, but simply lay down what, and trust to you, and those under you, for doing it well.

Keep what vessels may be necessary for your operations. No supplies are going to North Carolina except such as may be necessary for the troops there. I presume the call for vessels is in consequence of the preparations ordered for supplying our armies after a new base is established.[1] The Q. M. did not know where they were to go, but that he was

---

[1] *i. e.* At Bermuda Hundred. Called City Point in General Grant's and General Halleck's despatches.

to have supplies afloat, and supposed they were for North Carolina. I hope this delusion will be kept up both North and South until we do move.

If it should prove possible for you to reach Richmond so as to invest all on the south side of the river and fortify yourself there, I shall have but little fear of the result.

The rains have now continued so long that it will be impossible to move earlier than the 25th, so I will set that date for making your concentration. All men afloat could then be sent up York River as you proposed, to conceal our real design, if you were not then ready to move.

I am, General, very truly, your obedient servant,

U. S. GRANT,
Lieutenant-General.

[**No. 20.** *See page* 637.]

HEADQUARTERS ARMIES IN THE FIELD.
CULPEPPER COURT-HOUSE, VA., April 19, 1864.

MAJ.-GEN. B. F. BUTLER, COMMANDING DEPARTMENT OF
NORTH CAROLINA AND VIRGINIA:

General: — I send Lieutenant-Colonel Dent, of my staff, with this, not with the view of changing any instructions heretofore given, but more particularly to secure full co-operation between your command and that of General Meade. I will, as you understand, expect you to move from Fortress Monroe the same day General Meade starts from here. The exact time I will telegraph as soon as it can be fixed. At present the roads are in such a condition that the time could not be fixed earlier than the 27th inst. You can understand, therefore, you have fully to that date to make your preparations. You also understand, that with the forces here I shall aim to fight Lee between here and Richmond, if he will stand. Should Lee, however, fall back into Richmond, I will follow up, and make a junction with your army on the James River. Could I be certain that you will be able to invest Richmond on the south side, so as to have your left resting on the James above the city, I would form the junction there. Circumstances may make this course advisable anyhow. I would say, therefore, use every exertion to secure footing as far up the south side of the river as you can, and as soon as possible. If you hear of our advancing from that direction, or have reason to judge, from the action of the enemy, that they are looking for danger to that side, attack vigorously, and if you cannot carry the city, at least detain as large a force there as possible.

You will want all the co-operation from the navy that can be got. Confer freely with Admiral Lee upon your plans, that he may make as much preparation as possible.

If it is possible to communicate with you after determining my exact line of march, I will do so. If you can possibly get scouts through to me, do it.

Inform me by return of Colonel Dent your present situation and state of readiness for moving.

Very truly, your obedient servant,

U. S. GRANT,
Lieutenant-General.

MEMORANDUM OF INSTRUCTIONS.

Instruct the commanding officer at Plymouth to hold the place at all hazards, unless it is of no importance to hold. Have transports there ready to carry off such troops as it was intended to bring off, and place aboard of them all baggage to be removed with the troops. Instruct the officer in command, the moment the enemy abandon their siege, to put the force previously designed to draw from there aboard, and start with them. If the enemy will continue to hold a force to threaten the place, we can well afford to keep enough to resist them, and make by the bargain. The enemy will unquestionably, however, bring everything to Richmond the moment we begin to move.

When I telegraph we will start, rain or shine we will start, and hope that from all points there will be a responsive move. I have made preparations, or am making them, for a full siege equipment to use if the enemy should fall within the intrenchments at Richmond. Nothing of this kind need be looked after by General Butler further than he expects to require such auxiliaries whilst acting separately. Every effort is being made to draw troops from the Northern States to Washington, so as to have reserves ready if they should be required at any point.

Speak to General Butler particularly about the possibility, and for what I now see, probability, of my making my appearance on the south side of the river.

[No. 21.   *See page* 638.]

HEADQUARTERS DEPARTMENT OF VIRGINIA AND NORTH CAROLINA,
[*Confidential.*]   FORTRESS MONROE, April 15, 1864.
REAR-ADMIRAL S. P. LEE, COMMANDING, ETC.:

Admiral: — As I had the honor to suggest to you in a personal interview in which we had the pleasure of interchanging views upon the subject, — it is intended to land at City Point and above, on the south side of the James River, below a point called Osborn, a force of from thirty to thirty-five thousand men, with the necessary supplies, artillery, and trains. To this purpose it is proposed to use the Appomattox as far up as Port Walthall, as a convenient rendezvous for transports. To move this force will take a fleet of about fifty transports, besides some thirty schooners and barges for landing and other purposes. From this position it is contemplated to move along the south side of the James upon Richmond, in co-operation with General Meade's army.

To effect this landing and keep this position, it is expected that the navy will hold the James from above Farrar's Island, and the Appomattox from above Port Walthall, free from all attacks by rebel water craft, at all hazards, as upon this depends the success, and, indeed, the safety of the expedition. In order to prevent annoyance by the enemy, as well of the transports as the naval vessels, it is proposed to seize and hold Fort Powhatan and Wilson's Wharf, nearly opposite each other on the James, which are supposed to be the only bluffs, or high points below City Point, from which we can be substantially annoyed by the enemy's light artillery or sharpshooters.

It is proposed to start a flying column on board transports, with means of effecting a landing, and seize Wilson's Wharf and Fort Powhatan, and leave an adequate force there to intrench the same; thence proceeding upwards to seize City Point, and commence landing on both sides of the Appomattox, while the navy take and hold Osborn, as indicated above.

The navy will be expected to cover the landings at each of the places indicated, by its guns, and to aid, by a flanking fire, the army in holding its positions until intrenched. As this movement is to be in the nature of a surprise, it will be necessary for the naval vessels to go up with the leading column of army transports with the utmost celerity, so that the several positions indicated may be taken both by the land and naval forces before the enemy can concentrate opposition. The commanding general offers the use of the armed boats of the army, being of very light draft, to precede the naval force, and drag the river for torpedoes or obstructions, as their loss (if so unfortunate) would not be so serious as a loss of more valuable naval vessels with their armament,— to be, if desired, under your orders.

It is required by the commanding general of the army that the joint expedition be ready for this movement at a date not later than the 30th instant.

After the landing is effected, in the ulterior operations as well as before, the army will expect to render all the aid and co-operation in its power to the navy, to enable it to clear the river of water craft and obstructions, and to receive that hearty and genial co-operation from the navy which the commanding general has always had the good fortune to receive from the navy — such as protecting his water transportation and covering his flanks when lying on the rivers,— so that the great objective point, the capture of Richmond, may be the joint enterprise of the united services of the army and navy.

I believe, Admiral, I have answered each of the propositions contained in your note of to-day with as much particularity and distinctness as the subject-matter will admit, and upon which, and every point and part of which I would desire to interchange views with you in person, and to do so will hold myself in readiness to meet you when and where you will honor me with an appointment for that purpose.

I desire specially to call your attention to the question whether you can hold the point at Osborn as against the rebel water craft, as that is vital; or whether I shall make provision to aid you by sinking obstructions in the channel, or such other devices as engineering skill shall suggest.

I have the honor to be, very respectfully, your obedient servant,

BENJ. F. BUTLER,
Major-General Commanding.

[*Confidential.*]   FLAG-SHIP MINNESOTA,
NEWPORT NEWS, VA., April 25, 1864.

General: — I will thank you to inform me of the extent and character of the joint expedition which you propose to make, showing the exact service which you expect the navy to render, the time when and the points to which the different military and naval movements are to be made, and the assistance which the army will give the navy in taking and holding the different positions deemed necessary (which should be named), the number and kind of transports requiring convoy and protection, where to and when. In a word, to give me such full and perfect information in writing as will enable the Navy Department fully to understand the nature of the service to be performed, to ascertain its ability to furnish the means needed, and to enable me to make timely professional dispositions.

I send this by Fleet-Captain Barnes, my chief of staff, and solicit an early reply.

I have the honor to be, General, respectfully yours,

S. P. LEE,

Acting Rear-Admiral, Com'g N. A. Blo'g Squadron.

To MAJ.-GEN. B. F. BUTLER, *Commanding Dept. of Virginia and North Carolina, Fortress Monroe.*

[No. 22. *See page 638.*]

[*Confidential.*]

FLAG-SHIP NORTH ATLANTIC BLOCKADING SQUADRON.

HAMPTON ROADS, VA., April 27, 1864.

Received 8 P. M.

General : — I received, late on the night of its date, your confidential communication of the 25th inst., referring to our previous interview, and giving me more fully your views respecting the movement you contemplate, and including the Appomattox to Port Walthall as part of the base of your operations. This plan was, in our interview yesterday with the Assistant Secretary of the Navy, modified in this — that you abandoned the idea of landing troops, or sending your transports, above City Point, on James River.

I have the Onondaga, and I expect also three Monitor iron-clads, and with these I shall be able to co-operate with you as far up James River as their draft and the depth of water will allow them to go; viz: to Trent's Reach, in which there are but eight and one half feet of water. Our iron-clads cannot enter or operate in the Appomattox, but I can co-operate with you in small wooden vessels to Broadway, and, perhaps, as high as Point Rocks, if there are no obstructions in the river, or rifle-pits on the banks to drive the men from their guns on these open deck vessels, or batteries with which such vessels cannot contend. The iron-clads can, barring accidents, average five knots an hour to Harrison's Bar, which is fifty miles above Newport News. They require high water by day to cross that bar. The river at Harrison's Bar, before City Point, in the Appomattox, and from City Point to Farrar's Island, requires to be examined for torpedoes, and if we meet with no resistance, this can be done by day, and in part of a day.

I thankfully accept the offer of your light-drafts to act under my orders in the performance of this important duty. The engineering device of defense by obstructions (the means of making which you kindly propose to provide) above the iron-clads in James River, would materially aid in preventing the success of attempts to blow them up, and of surprise by torpedo vessels and fire-rafts. The confusion and loss which would inevitably ensue among your numerous transports, crowded in the river, in the event of such an alarm, would be very serious.

I would suggest Trent's Reach, or Dutch Gap, as a good location for such obstructions.

I do not see clearly how such a movement can be made a surprise, as the enemy has a signal corps in operation along James River.

I would respectfully suggest that the occupation of Dutch Gap, which is high and narrow, could be a great advantage to us, and that a body of skirmishers, to land, clear, and picket the bluffs on the left bank, between Eppes' Island and Farrar's Island, would be a very desirable protection to the gunboats against sharpshooters and torpedo operators.

The wooden gunboat force expected is not as large as I have desired; it will, however, I hope, be sufficient to give the convoy required, and assist the iron-clads in covering the landings contemplated.

Be assured, General, that intelligent and hearty co-operation is the first wish of myself, and will be the effort of the officers and men of my command.

I have the honor to be, General,

Very respectfully, your obedient servant,

S. P. LEE,
Acting Rear-Admiral,
Com'd'g North Atlantic Blockading Squadron.

To MAJ.-GEN. BENJ. F. BUTLER, *Com'd'g Dept. Virginia and North Carolina, Fortress Monroe.*

[**No. 23.** *See page* 639.]

HEADQUARTERS ARMIES OF THE UNITED STATES,
CULPEPPER COURT-HOUSE, VA., April 28, 1864.

MAJOR-GENERAL BUTLER, COMMANDING DEPARTMENT OF VIRGINIA AND NORTH CAROLINA:

General: — If no unforeseen accident prevents, I will move from here on Wednesday, the 4th of May. Start your forces the night of the 4th, so as to be as far up James River as you can get by daylight on the morning of the 5th, and push from that time with all your might for the accomplishment of the object before you. Should anything transpire to delay my movement, I will telegraph you.

Acknowledge the receipt of this by telegraph. Everything possible is now being done to accumulate a force in Washington from the Northern States, ready to reinforce any weak point. I will instruct General Halleck to send them to you should the enemy fall behind his fortifications in Richmond. You will therefore keep the headquarters in Washington advised of every move of the enemy, so far as you know them.

I am, General, very respectfully, your obedient servant,

U. S. GRANT,
Lieutenant-General.

[**No. 24.** *See page* 639.]

HEADQUARTERS DEPARTMENT OF VIRGINIA AND NORTH CAROLINA,
FORTRESS MONROE, April 20, 1864.

LIEUT.-GEN. U. S. GRANT, COM'D'G ARMIES OF THE U. S.:

General : — On Monday evening I received a note from General Gillmore, by hand of General Vogdes, who arrived here with two regiments of troops from Hilton Head. The letter contained the following extracts, which are all that are specially material as to the time when General Gillmore will probably be here : —

"Brigadier-General Vogdes bears this letter, and is directed to report to you to take command of the Tenth Corps as it arrives from time to time. Brigadier-General Terry will follow in a day or two, and will then command the corps until my arrival. General Turner will remain a few days longer still, while I do not propose to leave here, or turn over my command of this department, until all my troops are in motion, and the last regiment ready to embark. Great delay has occurred here in concentrating my scattered forces, but it could not be avoided."

From the tone of his letter and my conversation with General Vogdes, I am of opinion that he will not be able to be here, or to even get his troops here, until at least ten days from to-day. I have directed those troops to assemble at Gloucester Point, opposite Yorktown, under the immediate command of General Vogdes, assigning General Smith to the Camp of Instruction at Yorktown, and the command of the troops on both sides of the river.

I have information upon which I most implicitly rely, that the enemy have three iron-clads done near Richmond. One, I am informed, but of that I am not certain, is up the Appomattox River. I shall take measures to make certain that fact. Neither of the iron-clads to be furnished by the navy have yet reported, nor do I believe they will be here for some time. I have some two thousand of my cavalry dismounted for want of horses, although the requisitions have been in a long time, and I have forwarded my officers for the purpose of inspecting them. General Halleck telegraphs me that you will decide whether I shall be filled up, or the other armies, and as you know my needs, I am very well content to abide by your decision. I have no further news from Plymouth in addition to my telegram, save the report of Captain Flusser, the naval commander there, to Admiral Lee, "that he needed no reinforcements, but was confident of success against" the rebel ram.

I have the honor to be, very respectfully, your obedient servant,
BENJ. F. BUTLER,
Major-General Commanding.

[*Cipher.*] [**No. 25.** *See page* 639.]

By Telegraph from CULPEPPER COURT-HOUSE, 10 A. M., May 1, 1864.

MAJOR-GENERAL BUTLER, COMMANDING :

Have any more iron-clads reached you? Has General Gillmore arrived?
U. S. GRANT,
Lieutenant-General.

[*Cipher.*] Fortress Monroe, Sunday. 12 m., May 1, 1864.
Lieut.-Gen. U. S. Grant :
  One iron-clad has arrived ; two more due. Four gunboats due besides.
General Gillmore not yet arrived.

Benj. F. Butler,
Major-General Commanding.

[*Cipher.*] *By Telegraph from* Culpepper, 10 p. m., May 2, 1864.
Major-General Butler :
  Start on the date given in my letter. There will be no delay with this
army. Answer, that I may know this is received, and understood as regards date.

U. S. Grant,
Lieutenant-General.

Fortress Monroe, Va., May 3, 1864.

Lieutenant-General Grant, Commanding Armies U. S. :
  Your telegram is received this morning. General Gillmore has just
arrived, but has not yet landed. We understand the order to be on
Wednesday, the 4th, at 8 o'clock p. m., and it will be obeyed.

Benj. F. Butler,
Major-General Commanding.

[No. 26. *See page* 639.]

By Telegraph from Yorktown, Midnight, May 4, 1864.

Major-General Butler :
  Two divisions have started. The miserable conveniences for embarking
troops have been a cause of great delay. No greater speed could have
been made under the circumstances.

Q. A. Gillmore,
Major-General.

[No. 27. *See page* 642.]

Fortress Monroe, Va., May 4, 1864.

Major-General Gillmore, Gloucester Point :
  Having waited for your army corps from Port Royal. I am not a little
surprised at waiting for you here.
  Push everything forward.

Benj. F. Butler,
Major-General Commanding.

[No. 28. *See page* 642.]

Off City Point, Thursday Eve., May 5, 9 o'clock.

Lieutenant-General Grant, Commanding, etc., Washington :
  We have seized Wilson's Wharf, landing a brigade of Wild's colored
troops there ; Fort Powhatan, landing two regiments of same brigade.
Have landed at City Point Hincks' division of colored troops, remaining
brigades and battery.
  Remainder of both Eighteenth and Tenth Army Corps are now being
landed at Bermuda Hundred, above the Appomattox. No opposition
thus far,— apparently a complete surprise. Both army corps left York-

town during last night. Monitors all over the bar at Harrison's Landing and above City Point. The operations of the fleet have been conducted to-day with energy and success.

Generals Smith and Gillmore are pushing the landing of their men.

General Graham, with the army gunboats, led the advance during the night, capturing the signal stations of the rebels. Colonel West, with eighteen hundred cavalry, made demonstration from Williamsburg yesterday morning. General Kautz left Suffolk this morning with three thousand cavalry for the service indicated in conference with the lieutenant-general.[1] The "New York" flag of truce boat was found lying at the wharf, with four hundred rebel prisoners which she had not time to deliver. She went up yesterday morning. We are landing the troops during the night; a hazardous service in face of the enemy.

BENJ. F. BUTLER,
Major-General Commanding.

HEADQUARTERS DEPT. OF VIRGINIA AND NORTH CAROLINA,
NEAR CITY POINT, VA., May 6, 1864.

LIEUTENANT-GENERAL GRANT, COMMANDING ARMIES U. S. :

In continuation of my telegram of yesterday, I have to report that we have not been disturbed during the night; that all our troops are landed; that we have taken the positions which were indicated to the commanding general at our last conference, and are carrying out that plan.

BENJ. F. BUTLER,
Major-General Commanding.

[**No. 29.**   *See page* 643.]

By Telegraph from WASHINGTON, D. C., May 7, 1864.

MAJOR-GENERAL BUTLER:

No communication from General Grant has been received since the date of my telegram last night, nor any reliable information, except that a severe engagement took place yesterday without any decisive result. Various conflicting reports are in circulation of success and disaster on both sides, but they are mere conjectures or inventions.

EDWIN M. STANTON.

HEADQUARTERS, BERMUDA LANDING, May 7, 1864.

MAJOR-GENERAL GILLMORE, COMMANDING TENTH ARMY CORPS:

General: — I send you a copy of despatch just received. It will be necessary to put your line in posture of defence at once. Your rations will be along in time. I took your teams for the purpose of sending along your shovels. Work first, eat afterwards.

I presume the reasons for not making the demonstration ordered were perfectly satisfactory to you. I trust they will be to me when I see them.[2]

The navy have been shelling out some pickets on the other side of the river.

BENJ. F. BUTLER,
Major-General Commanding.

---

[1] Cutting the railroad at Hicksford and destroying the bridges.
[2] Those reasons were never communicated to me.

HEADQUARTERS BERMUDA LANDING, May 7, 1864.
MAJOR-GENERAL SMITH, COMMANDING EIGHTEENTH ARMY CORPS:

General: — I send you a copy of a despatch just received from Washington. No bad news there. But hurry up your defences anyhow. Let there be every diligence in putting your line in posture of defence.

. . . .

BENJ. F. BUTLER,
Major-General Commanding.

[**No. 30.** *See page* 643.]

HEADQUARTERS, May 7, 1864.
MAJOR-GENERAL SMITH, COMMANDING EIGHTEENTH ARMY CORPS:

I have ordered one brigade from each division of General Gillmore's command to report to you at eight o'clock this morning, for the purpose of cutting the enemy's line of communication between Richmond and Petersburg.

You will cause a like force to be detailed from your command on the line, and under such division commanders as you choose, cause attack to be made.

BENJ. F. BUTLER,
Major-General Commanding.

HEADQUARTERS, May 7, 1864.
MAJOR-GENERAL GILLMORE, COMMANDING TENTH ARMY CORPS:

You will cause one brigade of each division of your command to report to General Smith at eight o'clock this morning, for the purposes of an attack upon the line of railroad.

The detail should be of your best troops, and under your best brigade commanders. Answer hour of execution of this order.

BENJ. F. BUTLER,
Major-General Commanding.

[**No. 31.** *See page* 643.]

HEADQUARTERS BERMUDA LANDING, May 7, 1864.
Maj.-Gen. W. F. Smith, commanding Eighteenth Army Corps, is directed to take command of the detached forces from the Tenth and Eighteenth Army Corps, now operating towards Petersburg and Richmond, on the railroad.

BENJ. F. BUTLER,
Major-General Commanding.

[**No. 32.** *See page* 643.]
[*Telegram.— Cipher.*]

HEADQUARTERS BERMUDA LANDING, May 7, 1864.
HON. E. M. STANTON, SECRETARY OF WAR:

We have made demonstrations to-day on the railroad between Petersburg and Richmond, and have succeeded in destroying a portion of it, so as to break the connection. We have had pretty severe fighting to do, but have succeeded. We hear, from a rebel deserter, and a citizen, that

Lee is dangerously wounded; Pickett also; Jones and Jenkins killed. We have no news from General Grant. If he has been in any degree successful there, can we not have here ten thousand of the reserves? They can be here in three days after the lieutenant-general gives the order. Transportation is at Annapolis for them. If the Army of the Potomac is unsuccessful, then we want them here for the safety of the country. Please send them forward. Beauregard is in command in person. In three days our line will be perfect. We have to strongly garrison the point on the river to save our transportation, which weakens us a good deal for a movable column. All is submitted to your judgment.

BENJ. F. BUTLER,
Major-General Commanding.

[*Cipher.*]　　　　　　*By Telegraph from* WASHINGTON, May 8, 4.30.
MAJOR-GENERAL BUTLER :

Your despatch of the 7th has just reached me. We have, as yet, no official reports from Grant. Nothing is known of his condition except from newspaper reports, which represent two days' hard fighting on Thursday and Friday; from six to eight thousand wounded are sent back, and Ingalls telegraphs yesterday at noon to General Meigs that "It is said the enemy are retiring." In respect to the reserves mentioned in your telegram, there are none now at the disposal of the department. General Grant has with him all the troops, and you will have to depend only upon such as may have been provided in your programme with him. Your despatch will be forwarded to him, to apprise him of your condition and for his instructions. Your success thus far is extremely gratifying to the President and this department, and we hope your skill and good luck may accomplish all your wishes.

E. M. STANTON,
Secretary of War.

[**No. 33.**　*See page* 644.]

[*Confidential.*]　　　HEADQUARTERS BERMUDA LANDING, May 7, 1864.
HON. HENRY WILSON :

My Dear Sir : — I must take the responsibility of asking you to bring before the Senate at once the name of General Gillmore, and have his name rejected by your body. General Gillmore may be a very good engineer officer, but he is wholly useless in the movement of troops. He has been behind in every movement. He has lost twenty-four hours here in putting his line in a state of defence ; but, above all, he has refused to move when ordered. I directed him to co-operate with General Smith when he went to make demonstrations on the Petersburg Railroad, and he failed to do so, and then sent me word that he did not obey the order for reasons that seemed good to himself, and has not deigned to give me the reasons, although he has sent me a report of his operations, or rather want of operations. I have known General Gillmore only since he came here, but I find many of his troops are desirous of getting away from him. I have a good corps commander here in his place. I write only for the good of the service. We have made demonstrations to-day on the railroad, cut it, and are about to destroy it permanently. If we can hold on here we can drive Lee out of Virginia. His great line of supplies and operations is gone. We have been eminently successful thus far. If you desire to know exactly where we are, take a map, look up Point of Rocks on the Appomattox, then look across to Farrar's Island on the James. That is our line, directly on the rebel communications. We are intrenching here; will then advance from this base. Telegraph your action; time is important.

BENJ. F. BUTLER.

[**No. 34.** *See page* 645.]

HEADQUARTERS IN THE FIELD, May 9, 6.35 P. M.

GENERAL HINCKS:

Upon consultation, it is thought best that you should not advance beyond your picket line before 7 o'clock, so that all the force may be drawn to the advance of General Smith. When you hear his guns and have word from him, engage the enemy and push on.

BENJ. F. BUTLER,
Major-General Commanding.

[**No. 35.** *See page* 646.]

WAR DEPARTMENT, 3.20 P. M., 9th May.

MAJOR-GENERAL BUTLER:

A bearer of despatches from General Meade has just reached here by way of Fredericksburg.

States that on Friday night Lee's army were in full retreat for Richmond, Grant pursuing with his army. Hancock passed Spottsylvania C. H., before daylight yesterday morning. Meade's headquarters were yesterday at Ladd's Tavern. We occupy Fredericksburg. Twenty-Second New York occupied it about 8 o'clock last night.

EDWIN M. STANTON,
Secretary of War.

[**No. 36.** *See page* 646.]

[*Telegram.—Cipher.*]   WASHINGTON, D. C., May 9, 4 P. M.

MAJOR-GENERAL BUTLER:

A despatch from Grant has just been received. He is on the march with his whole force; army to form a junction with you, *but had not determined his route.* Another despatch from him is being translated.

E. M. STANTON,
Secretary of War.

[**No. 37.** *See page* 646.]

By Telegraph from WASHINGTON, D. C., May 9, 1864.

MAJOR-GENERAL BUTLER:

Advices from the front give reason to believe that General Grant's operations will prove a great success and complete victory.

On Saturday night the enemy had been driven at all points, and Hancock was pushing forward rapidly to Spottsylvania Court-House, where heavy firing was heard yesterday. It was reported yesterday by a deserter, that the enemy's only hope was in heavy reinforcements from Beauregard.

EDWIN M. STANTON,
Secretary of War.

[**No. 38.** *See page* 646.]

HEADQUARTERS NEAR BERMUDA LANDING, May 9, 1864.
HON. E. M. STANTON, SECRETARY OF WAR:

Our operations may be summed up in a few words. With seventeen hundred cavalry we have advanced up the peninsula, forced the Chickahominy, and have safely brought them to our present position. These were colored cavalry, and are now holding our advance pickets toward Richmond.

General Kautz, with three thousand cavalry from Suffolk, on the same day with our movement up James River, forced the Blackwater, burned the railroad bridge at Stony Creek, below Petersburg, cutting in two Beauregard's force at that point.

We have landed here, intrenched ourselves, destroyed many miles of railroad, and got a position which, with proper supplies, we can hold out against the whole of Lee's army. I have ordered up the supplies.

Beauregard, with a large portion of his force, was left South by the cutting of the railroads by Kautz. That portion which reached Petersburg, under Hill, we have whipped to-day, killing and wounding many, and taking many prisoners, after a severe and well-contested fight.

General Grant will not be troubled with any further reinforcements to Lee from Beauregard's force.

BENJ. F. BUTLER,
Major-General.

[**No. 39.** *See page* 647.]

By Telegram from FORTRESS MONROE, May 9, 1864.
MAJOR R. S. DAVIS, A. A. G., BERMUDA HUNDRED:

Attack on New Berne. After two days' fighting the enemy retired. Captain Smith, U. S. N., attacked the ram, and drove her up Roanoke River. Was unable to sink her or roll her over.

HENRY T. SCHROEDER,
Lieut. and A. A. A. G.

[**No. 40.** *See page* 647.]

SWIFT CREEK, 7 P. M., May 9, 1864.
MAJ.-GEN. B. F. BUTLER, COMMANDING DEPARTMENT OF
VIRGINIA AND NORTH CAROLINA:

General: — We have conferred together upon the problem before us, and respectfully suggest for your consideration, whether it would not be better, and secure to us greater advantages, to withdraw to our lines to-night, destroying all that part of the road this side of Chester Station which we left to-day, and then cross the Appomattox on a pontoon bridge, that can be thrown across below General Smith's headquarters, and cut all the roads which come into Petersburg on that side. Such a bridge can readily be constructed in one night, and all the work of cutting the road, and, perhaps, capturing the city, can be accomplished in one day, without involving us in heavy losses. If we should remain here and be successful to-morrow, the roads coming into Petersburg on that side will remain intact, with the Appomattox between us and them, and we may even then be forced to adopt the plan we now suggest.

Very respectfully, your obedient servants,

Q. A. GILLMORE,
Maj.-Gen. Com'd'g Tenth Army Corps.

W. F. SMITH,
Maj.-Gen. Com'd'g Eighteenth Army Corps.

[**No. 41.** *See page* 648.]

HEADQUARTERS DEPARTMENT OF VIRGINIA AND NORTH CAROLINA.
BERMUDA HUNDRED, May 9, 1864.

MAJOR-GENERALS W. F. SMITH AND Q. A. GILLMORE,
COMMANDING EIGHTEENTH AND TENTH ARMY CORPS:

Generals : — While I regret an infirmity of purpose which did not permit you to state to me, when I was personally present, the suggestion which you made in your written note, but left me to go to my headquarters under the impression that another and far different purpose was advised by you, I shall not yield to the written suggestions, which imply a change of plan made within thirty minutes after I left you. Military affairs cannot be carried on, in my judgment, with this sort of vacillation.

The information I have received from the Army of the Potomac convinces me that our demonstration should be toward Richmond, and I shall in no way order a crossing of the Appomattox for the purpose suggested in your note. If, as I believe, General Kautz has been successful, the communications of the enemy have been cut so far below Petersburg as to render the Lynchburg and Petersburg Railroad useless as a means of communication with the South, and if the Danville road is to be cut at all, it had better be cut near Richmond on the south side, in conformity with the plan agreed upon between the lieutenant-general and myself. Therefore, as early as possible, consistently with safety, you will withdraw your forces from Swift Creek, attempting, in the first place, to destroy the railroad bridge, and then complete a thorough destruction of the railroad as we return to our position, with the intention of making a subsequent early demonstration up the James from the right of our position. I have written you this note jointly because you have agreed in a joint note to me.

I have the honor to remain, very respectfully, your obedient servant,

BENJ. F. BUTLER,
Major-General Commanding.

[**No. 42.**　*See page* 648.]

HEADQUARTERS, 9.30 P. M., May 9, 1864.

BRIGADIER-GENERAL HINCKS, COMMANDING, ETC., ETC.:

We have very good news from the Army of the Potomac. This involves change of plan. You will therefore not move on Petersburg. Labor diligently to make all safe at City Point, and go yourself at once to Fort Powhatan to give personal supervision to the work neglected by Colonel Stafford.

BENJ. F. BUTLER,
Major-General Commanding.

[**No. 43.**　*See page* 648.]

HEADQUARTERS EIGHTEENTH ARMY CORPS, May 10, 1864.

MAJOR-GENERAL BUTLER, COMMANDING DEPARTMENT:

General :—I have the honor to state that yesterday evening I requested Major-General Gillmore to relieve General Heckman's brigade, which has been fighting three days out of the four that we have been here, by a brigade of General Turner's division, stating at the time that I had no troops not actually in the presence of the enemy, and that I was anxious to give General Heckman a chance to make some coffee for his men, which they could not do on the front. This request was denied. Later in the evening, upon being informed by General Gillmore that our rear was threatened by infantry and cavalry, I requested General Gillmore to give me one regiment to guard the roads leading to the rear of my lines, stating at the time that I had no regiment that I could safely withdraw from my front, on this duty. Still later in the night, at a time when I thought General Burnham was being driven back, and knowing that the safety of our command depended, in a great measure, upon that position being held, to save time I sent directly to General Turner, asking him to give me two regiments to aid General Brooks to maintain that position. I have therefore, now, respectfully to request, that in accordance with the usages of military service, that General Heckman's brigade be relieved by troops that have not been to the front, at once.

Very respectfully,
WM. F. SMITH,
Major-General.

HEADQUARTERS TENTH ARMY CORPS,
NEAR SWIFT CREEK, May 10, 1864.

MAJ.-GEN. B. F. BUTLER, COMMANDING DEPARTMENT OF
VIRGINIA AND NORTH CAROLINA:

General :—I have received your despatch in reply to the note signed by General Smith and myself. That note contained simple suggestions, nothing more. It could not have contained any recommendation from me to change plans, as I did not know what the plan of operation was, further than to cut the Petersburg and Richmond Railroad. Presuming that it was desirable to cut all the railroads leading out of Petersburg, I could see no better way to do it than the one proposed. *I had had no opportunity to confer with General Smith until I met him in your presence, and did not converse with him upon the nature of his instructions, or the objects aimed at, until after you had left.* My orders from you were to destroy the railroad, and afterwards, verbally, to support General Smith's movement on Swift's Creek. Further orders from you, regulating the movements of the two corps, seem necessary. At Brandon Bridge the enemy have infantry and cavalry this side of the creek, and the approaches are open and covered by artillery on the other side. No practicable ford has been found yet. I am destroying the railroad near the junction.

Very respectfully, your obedient servant,

Q. A. GILLMORE,
Major-General Commanding.

[No. 44. See page 648.]

May 10, 1864.

MAJOR-GENERAL BUTLER, COMMANDING DEPARTMENT OF
VIRGINIA AND NORTH CAROLINA:

General: — I have the honor to acknowledge receipt of your letter directed to General Gillmore and myself, and to reply to it only so far as myself am personally concerned.

Just *after* you had left yesterday *General Gillmore proposed this plan,* and it seemed to me to be one worthy of your consideration, as having a tendency to save waste of life to a certain extent, and to more effectually cut the enemy's communications, than any infantry force on this side the river could do. I understood you yesterday positively to say that Colonel Kautz was going south on the railroad, which he had already cut. This was, in my mind, a leading idea in giving to this plan the weight which I did. The objections to it were, first, that it would have the semblance of a repulse here; and, secondly, that if we could force our way across the creek, we would gain valuable time over the other plan. These considerations, which I know would occur to you, were, therefore, unnecessary to mention. The suggestions were made, so far as I was concerned, merely to call your attention to a plan which seemed to me to possess merit. I am happy to state that General Gillmore's idea received the sanction of General Weitzel and Colonel Dutton. I have made this long explanation for peculiar and private reasons, and can only say in conclusion, that as I have never before been accused of infirmity of purpose, I shall not take the charge as one seriously affecting my military reputation. I had forgotten to mention that the letter was not drawn up or signed by me as a formal protest, but only in a semi-informal manner and in the quickest time of conveying to you the ideas which had been discussed by General Gillmore and myself. Pure consideration for the troops here and the cause in which we are engaged, it becomes my duty to you to express the opinion that the withdrawal from this point must be made in accordance with some well-regulated plan published from head-quarters of the army, and not according to the separate wishes and interests of corps commanders.

Very respectfully, your obedient servant,

WM. F. SMITH,
Major-General.

[**No. 45.** *See page* 649.]

CITY POINT, May 10, 1864, 9 A. M.

MAJOR-GENERAL BUTLER:

I have arrived here with my entire command. Have burned the Stony Creek Bridge, the Nottoway Bridge, and Jarratt's Station. I have about one hundred and thirty prisoners. Loss in my command about thirty killed and wounded. I want rations and forage as soon as I can get them.

A. V. KAUTZ,
Brigadier-General.

[**No. 46.** *See page* 651.]

IN THE FIELD, NEAR DRURY'S BLUFF, May 13, 1864, 9 A. M.

REAR-ADMIRAL LEE, COMMANDING, ETC.:

Would it not be possible for you to bring up the gunboats, monitors, opposite Dr. Howlett's, so as to cover our flank on the river, and relieve a considerable body of my troops? Both sides of the river there are low and flat, and it is an excellent point for the gunboats to lie.

BENJ. F. BUTLER,
Major-General.

May 13, 1864.

REAR-ADMIRAL S. P. LEE:

I think it would be of great public service if you can put your boats so as to cover my landing for supplies at Howlett's House.

BENJ. F. BUTLER,
Major-General Commanding.

U. S. STEAMSHIP AGAWAM, TRENT'S REACH,
JAMES RIVER, May 15, 1864, 3.30 P. M.

MAJ.-GEN. B. F. BUTLER:

Your despatch answered by signal corps. Enemy vigorously intrenching on the heights at Howlett's, under a destructive fire from gunboats. They will doubtless mount guns to-night to command Trent's Reach. Only a land attack can dislodge them. River falling. Careful soundings to-day show [that we] cannot cross this bar.

S. P. LEE,
Actg. Rear-Admiral, Comdg. North Atlantic Block. Squad.

P. S. 4 P. M. The rebel artillery has appeared on the heights at Dutch Gap.

S. P. LEE,
Acting Rear-Admiral.

[**No. 47.** *See page* 651.]

WASHINGTON, D. C., May 13, 1864, 6 A. M.

MAJOR-GENERAL BUTLER, IN THE FIELD (VIA FORTRESS MONROE):

Your despatch of yesterday 3.30 has been forwarded to General Grant. A despatch just received from the battle-field reports a general attack by Grant at 6 A. M., in which great success was achieved. Hancock had captured Maj.-Gen. Edward Johnson's division, taken him and Early and forty cannon, and the prisoners were counted by thousands. Nothing has been heard for two days from General Sherman. The lines are broken by a heavy storm.

EDWIN M. STANTON.

[No. 48. *See page 652.*]

WAR DEPARTMENT, WASHINGTON, May 13, 1864, 6.40 P. M.
MAJOR-GENERAL BUTLER, IN THE FIELD:

Lee abandoned his works last night and retreated. Grant is pursuing. There has been thirty-six hours' hard rain, and the roads are heavy. At last account Hancock had come up to his [Lee's] rear guard.

EDWIN M. STANTON,
Secretary of War.

[No. 49. *See page 652.*]

May 13, 1864, 7 P. M.

GENERAL AMES:

General Gillmore has carried the enemy's works on their right. We are before them on the left. Glorious news from Grant inclosed. Can you hold your own without help? Guard against surprise and night attack. Report to me frequently, near Half-Way House (Dr. Cheatham's).

B. F. BUTLER,
Major-General Commanding.

[No. 50. *See page 653.*]

HEADQUARTERS IN THE FIELD, May 14, 1864, 7 P. M.
LIEUTENANT-COLONEL FULLER:

Your despatch received. My compliments to General Sheridan. Say to him I think he had better not come over with his forces, but should be happy to receive him. Give him all the forage and rations he needs. Tell him I have reliable information from a deserter and a prisoner that to-night there are but two hundred men at Chaffin's farm, thirteen miles only from where he is, and opposite where I am now fighting. All the rest have been hurrried over to fight me. They have no bridge. Can he not take Chaffin's farm?

BENJ. F. BUTLER,
Major-General Commanding.

[No. 51. *See page 653.*]

IN THE FIELD, May 14, 1864, 9. P. M.

GENERAL SHERIDAN:

Since I wrote a hurried note to Lieutenant-Colonel Fuller, I have thought best to request you to join me with your command. You can aid us very much in our operations here, and, as we shall soon be joined by Lieutenant-General Grant, you will be able best here to report to him. I wish you might be able to capture Chaffin's farm as I suggested in my note to Colonel Fuller. At any rate, I wish you would do this service to the navy. They are much annoyed by torpedoes. These torpedoes are exploded by means of galvanic batteries on the shore. The person who brings the note will have with him a negro who can give you all information in regard to torpedoes. Please send up a force along the north bank of the James as far as Chaffin's farm, and make diligent search for torpedoes and the wires. Burn any house where such machines are harbored. Capture and bring to me all persons that have anything to do with them. I shall be most happy to see you personally at the earliest possible moment.

Respectfully,

Benj. F. Butler,

Major-General Commanding.

[**No. 52.** *See page* 653.]

May 15, 1864, 3 p. m.

General Sheridan :

You will bring your command at once across the river to Bermuda Landing, then march it on to the ground near Howlett's house, and between that and the railroad, encamp it there, and give your horses rest. No more duty on horseback will be required of you than to picket your own position and the approaches leading thereto. The utmost despatch in getting to your position is desired. Quartermaster will supply transportation and forage.

Benj. F. Butler,

Major-General Commanding.

[**No. 53.** *See page* 653.]

Headquarters, May 15, 1864, 3 p. m.

General Sheridan :

You will turn over all your disabled and unserviceable horses to the quartermaster at Bermuda Landing, by him to be turned out to graze in the neighborhood there for the purpose of recruitment. You will at once make all the necessary requisitions upon the quartermaster, commissary, and ordnance officer, to the end that we may send to Fortress Monroe for supplies.

B. F. Butler,

Major-General Commanding.

[**No. 54.** *See page* 655.]

May 16, 1864, 6 a. m.

General Gillmore:

The enemy has advanced from his works on our right and made a vigorous demonstration there. A rapid movement on the left would, I think, carry his lines in your front. Make it at once.

B. F. Butler,

Major-General Commanding.

[**No. 55.** *See page* 655.]

May 16, 1864, 7.07 A. M.

MAJOR-GENERAL BUTLER:

Since my despatch of 6.40 the enemy have made two assaults on General Terry's front in force, and have been repulsed. No troops have been taken from my front.

Q. A. GILLMORE,
Major-General.

[**No. 56.** *See page* 657.]

HDQRS. DEPT. OF NORTH CAROLINA AND SOUTHERN VIRGINIA,
DRURY'S BLUFF, VA., May 14, 1864.

GEN. B. BRAGG, COMMANDING C. S. ARMIES, RICHMOND, VA.:

General: — Considering the vital importance of the issue involved, and resting upon the success of the plan I suggested to you this morning, I have deemed it advisable and appropriate that their substance should be briefly communicated in writing. General Lee's army, at Guiney's Station, and my command, at this place, are on nearly a right line passing through Richmond. Grant's army is on the left flank, and Butler's on the right. Our lines are thus interior. Butler's aim is unquestionably to invest and turn Drury's Bluff, threatening and holding the Petersburg and Danville railroads, opening the obstructions in the river at Fort Drury for the passage of war vessels, and necessitating the return of General Lee to the lines about Richmond. With the railroads held by the enemy, Grant in front and Butler in rear of the works around Richmond, the capital would be practically invested, and the issue may well be dreaded.

The plan submitted is: That General Lee should fall back to the defensive lines of the Chickahominy, even to the intermediate lines of Richmond, sending temporarily to this place fifteen thousand men of his troops. Immediately upon that accession to my present force, I would take the offensive, and attack Butler vigorously. Such a move would throw me directly upon Butler's communications, and, as he now stands, with his right flank well turned toward his rear, General Whiting should also move simultaneously, and Butler must necessarily be crushed or captured, and all the stores of that army would then fall into our hands; an amount, probably, that would make an interruption of our communications for a period of a few days a matter of no serious inconvenience. The proposed attack should be accomplished in two days at furthest after receiving my reinforcements. This done, I would move with ten thousand more men to the assistance of General Lee than I drew from him, and Grant's fate could not long remain doubtful. The destruction of Grant's forces would open the way for the recovery of most of our lost territory, as already submitted to you in general terms.

Respectfully, your obedient servant,

G. T. BEAUREGARD,
General Commanding.[1]

---

[1] War Records, Chapter XLVIII., Part II., p. 1024.

PLAN OF CAMPAIGN.

HDQRS. DEPT. OF NORTH CAROLINA AND SOUTHERN VIRGINIA,
HANCOCK'S HOUSE, 2 1-2 MILES NORTH OF WALTHALL JUNCTION, VA.,
May 18, 1864, 9 P. M.

The crisis demands prompt and decisive action. The two armies are now too far apart to secure success, unless we consent to give up Petersburg, and thus place the capital in jeopardy. If General Lee will fall back behind the Chickahominy, engaging the enemy so as to draw him on, General Beauregard can bring up fifteen thousand men to unite with Breckinridge, and fall upon the enemy's flank with over twenty thousand effectives, thus rendering Grant's defeat certain and decisive in time to enable General Beauregard to return with reinforcements from General Lee to drive Butler from before Petersburg, and from his present position in advance of Bermuda Hundred. Petersburg and Richmond could be held three days, or four at most, by the forces left there for that purpose. Without such concentration nothing decisive can be effected, and the picture presented is one of ultimate starvation. Without concentration General Lee must eventually fall back before Grant's heavy reinforcements, whereas the plan presented merely anticipates this movement for offensive purposes. Meantime, it is impossible to effectually protect our lines of communication with North Carolina, and impossible to hold our present line in front of Butler with a much more reduced line. At present, three thousand men can be spared from there with safety; day after to-morrow perhaps two thousand more, for our lines will probably be stronger if, as we expect, our advanced line can be occupied to-morrow.

G. T. BEAUREGARD.

[**No. 57.** *See page 664.*]

IN THE FIELD, May 20, 1864, 11.20.

Brigadier-General Weitzel will make a tour of inspection of the lines of intrenchments, and his orders and suggestions in regard to working parties and supports will be implicitly carried out by corps, division, and brigade commanders.

BENJ. F. BUTLER,
Major-General Commanding.

[*Circular.*]   HEADQUARTERS, May 20, 1864, 1 P. M.

General Weitzel is serving as chief engineer in absence, by sickness, of Captain Farquhar, and his orders will be mine and will be given in my name.

BENJ. F. BUTLER,
Major-General Commanding.

HEADQUARTERS DEPARTMENT OF VIRGINIA AND NORTH CAROLINA,
IN THE FIELD, VA., May 20, 1864.

General Order No. 65.

1. Brig.-Gen. Godfrey Weitzel is hereby announced as chief engineer of this department and army, and will be obeyed and respected accordingly. . . .

By command of Major-General Butler :

R. S. DAVIS,
Major and Assistant Adjutant-General.

[**No. 58.** *See page 666.*]

GENERAL BRAGG :   May 18, 1864.

I have about nineteen thousand infantry, two thousand cavalry, and four battalions artillery this side Swift Creek; beyond Swift Creek Walker's brigade and two regiments (Dearing's brigade) cavalry.

G. T. BEAUREGARD,
General Commanding.[1]

[**No. 59.** *See page 666.*]

GENERAL BUTLER'S HEADQUARTERS, May 20, 1864, 10 P. M.
(Received 7.40 A. M., 21st.)

HON. EDWIN M. STANTON, SECRETARY OF WAR :

Have been fighting all day. Enemy are endeavoring to close in on our lines. We shall hold on. Have captured rebel General Walker, of Texas troops. General Sheridan is at White House, and has sent for a pontoon bridge, which I have forwarded him. Have also sent one of my army gunboats with launches up the Rappahannock, as requested.

B. F. BUTLER,
Major-General.

[**No. 60.** *See page 669.*]

NEAR CHESTER, May 30, 1864, 10 P. M.

GEN. R. E. LEE, AT LEE'S STATION :

Hoke's division and Read's battalion of artillery have been ordered to report to you forthwith. I will follow with Johnson's as soon as enemy's movements here will permit.

G. T. BEAUREGARD.

[**No. 61.** *See page 670.*]

HEADQUARTERS DEPARTMENT OF VIRGINIA AND NORTH CAROLINA,
HALF-WAY HOUSE, May 14, 1864.

General:— You are authorized to make the change in the troops indicated. Fort Powhatan is a very important position. Require from my ordnance officer what heavy guns you may need for Fort Powhatan, but get them here soon. I cannot at present spare the colored cavalry, but will as soon as Kautz gets through.

By command of Major-General Butler:

H. C. CLARKE,
Capt. & A. D. C.

BRIGADIER-GENERAL E. W. HINKS, *Commanding, etc.*

[**No. 62.** *See page 671.*]

WASHINGTON, May 24, 7.30 P. M.

MAJOR-GENERAL BUTLER :

General Grant directed that you have twenty thousand men, exclusive of artillery and cavalry, which are not wanted, ready to be moved as may be ordered. Your position at City Point will be prepared for defence by a small force. General Grant crossed the North Anna near railroad bridge on the 22d, and on the 23d was moving on the South Anna.

HALLECK,
Major-General.

---

[1]War Records, Chapter XLVIII, Part II, p. 1025.

[**No. 63.** *See page* 671.]

HEADQUARTERS IN THE FIELD, May 28, 1864, 7.15 P. M.

HON. E. M. STANTON, SECRETARY OF WAR.

As I informed General Halleck in my despatch of 8.30 of May 26, I had already got my best troops into a movable column for the purpose of offensive operations. My defensive line is in such position as to be safe to leave it with the dismounted cavalry, the invalids, and a few good troops. I found that the rebels had uncovered Petersburg, and its importance as a depot to them cannot be overrated. I had proposed to attack the place to-morrow morning, with every prospect of success, but the imperative orders transmitted through General Halleck, and the arrival of the transportation, although not sufficient, in my judgment, but yet sufficient to begin with, rendered necessary a change of order. General Smith embarks to-night. I have now left here one division and two regiments of infantry, invalids, dismounted cavalry, and artillery. Much of the light artillery I shall send away as soon as my transports return. I regret exceedingly the loss of this opportunity upon Petersburg.

BENJ. F. BUTLER,
Major-General.

[**No. 64.** *See page* 677.]

During the latter part of September last, General Grant sent for me to come to his headquarters. He told me that an expedition was being prepared to close the mouth of Cape Fear River, near Wilmington. . . .
He said that the War Department had selected an officer to command the land forces of the expedition, but he did not wish that officer to command them, as he had once shown timidity.

. . . .

Q. Who was that officer selected by the War Department to whom General Grant objected?
A. General Gillmore.[1]

[**No. 65.** *See page* 687.]

NEAR BETHESDA CHURCH, June 1, 1864, 5 P.M.
(Received 6.10 P. M., 2d.)

As I reported in my despatch of 10 A. M., Warren was ordered to attack a column of the rebel infantry which was passing toward Cold Harbor, but instead of falling upon it in force he opened with artillery, and at 3 P. M., reported that the intrenchments of the enemy were exceedingly strong, and that his own lines were so long that he had no mass of troops to attack with. It seems that Wright blundered in the execution of his order to march to Cold Harbor. Instead of having his advance there at 9 A. M., as was General Grant's and Meade's design that his whole corps should be on the ground at daylight, when a rapid attack in mass would certainly have routed the rebel force which a little later assaulted Sheridan, and an advantage might easily have been gained which, followed up by

---

[1]Testimony of Major-General Weitzel before the Committee on the Conduct of the War, Fort Fisher Expedition. Report Part II., pp. 67-73].

Sheridan's two divisions of cavalry, might have led to the dispersal of Lee's army. Both Generals Grant and Meade are intensely disgusted with these failures of Wright and Warren.

Meade says a radical change must be made, no matter how unpleasant it may be to make it; but I doubt whether he will really attempt to apply so extreme a remedy. Meanwhile the two corps have been ordered to withdraw from the lines before the enemy, and take up a position in reserve behind Sheridan. This will give us a heavy movable column for attack or defence under a general who obeys orders without excessive reconnoitring. . . .

C. A. DANA.

HON. EDWIN M. STANTON, *Secretary of War.*[1]

[**No. 66.** *See page* 687.]

June 15, 1864, 7.20 P. M.

GENERAL SMITH:

I grieve for the delays. Time is the essence of this movement. I doubt not the delays were necessary, but now push and get the Appomattox between you and me. Nothing has passed down the railroad to harm you yet.

BENJAMIN F. BUTLER,
Major-General Commanding.

[**No. 67.** *See page* 690.]

NEW YORK, Dec. 7, 1891.

MAJ.-GEN. BENJ. F. BUTLER, LOWELL, MASS:

My Dear General: — In response to your request that I should put in writing a statement as to my action as one of your staff officers on the 15th of June, 1864, in connection with the movement upon Petersburg by a portion of the Army of the James upon that day, I have the honor to say: —

Gen. Wm. T. Smith ("Baldy" Smith), commanding the Eighteenth Army Corps of the Army of the James, was ordered by you, as the major-general commanding that army, to move upon Petersburg early on that day. His action and that of his forces under his command were most anxiously waited for by you, during the long hours of the forenoon and well into the afternoon.

Becoming impatient at not hearing that he had assaulted the works of the enemy before that city, you directed me, about three o'clock in the afternoon, to ride to General Smith, to ascertain why nothing had been heard from him, and why he had not made the assault. I was also directed to say to General Smith that it was your order that an immediate assault should be made upon the intrenched lines before Petersburg.

In compliance with these instructions I made the ride from the Bermuda Hundred front to Smith's forces, whom I found were before the enemy's intrenchments. Inquiring for General Smith at his head-

---

[1] War Records, Vol. XXXI., Part I., p. 85.

quarters, I was informed that he was personally engaged in a reconnoissance of the enemy's position. I at once started in the direction which I was told he had taken, and finally found him on, or a trifle beyond his picket line.

I there delivered to him your messages of surprise at his non-action, your desire to be informed of the causes, and your order for an assault. General Smith replied that the delay had been first occasioned by reason of the engagement he had with the enemy in the morning some miles from his then position, and since his arrival before Petersburg he had been engaged in a personal reconnoissance of the enemy's position ; that his reconnoissance was then completed, and that he should shortly direct the assault ordered.

I reported back to you about 7 P. M., stating in detail what I had seen and done, and General Smith's replies to your inquiries and order, all which are here set forth in condensed form only. I further reported that I had carefully observed the enemy's line with an eye to the forces which were probably confronting us, and that everything seen and unseen indicated that the information in your possession as to their strength — about two thousand men — was correct. I further reported that on my return ride from General Smith to you, I had run into and passed a portion of General Hancock's corps of General Meade's army (I believed it to be Birney's division) at about half-past five, some four miles from General Smith's position, and that they were marching to join him.

About 8.30 P. M. an aid to General Smith reported to you that at half-past seven Smith's forces had carried the line of defence near Jordan's, and were moving toward the Appomattox. Soon after this you sent for me and expressing your anxiety lest General Smith should allow nightfall to close his operations for the day, you directed me to again visit Smith, and convey to him your command that there should be no cessation of his movements, but a continued renewal of his assaults ; that Petersburg could be taken that night, and should be, and he must put himself and his troops south of the Appomattox.

Returning to General Smith I found him in conversation with General Hancock near the latter's headquarters. Seeing me ride up and dismount, General Smith drew aside, and I delivered to him your commands. He replied that he had " determined to make no further attack that night." I expressed to him my regret at receiving such a reply; said to him that you knew there had been no reinforcements received by General Beauregard from Lee's army; that while the enemy's strength might have been added to somewhat, it could only have been increased either from being drawn from the Bermuda front, or from the forces then on the north side of the James — the lines before Richmond; that with his own and Hancock's command, two divisions of which, he informed me, were up, he must have all of thirty thousand men ; that I knew both General Grant and yourself expected Petersburg to be taken that night, and urged him to change his determination not to continue the movement, and to at once comply with your command.

His only response was "General Hancock's arrival has left me the junior officer." With this remark he turned away. General Hancock had left when General Smith turned to walk with me. I started to return to you, but Smith's manner and tone had been such as to leave upon my mind the most unpleasant reflections. The inference I drew from his remark was, that General Hancock, whom I did not then personally know, but whom I had always regarded as a most brave and loyal officer, had asserted his superior rank and sought to command the combined forces in any subsequent movement. I therefore turned back and went to General Hancock's headquarters for the purpose of ascertaining the facts with respect to that matter. I did not find Hancock there, but from his staff I learned that General Hancock had promptly, upon arriving on the field, waived his rank, placed himself and his command at the service of Smith, and that his (Hancock's) troops were then preparing to relieve Smith's men in the front.

All this I reported to you between eleven and twelve that night, and I can never forget your surprise, your sorrow, or your disgust when you learned of Smith's refusal to obey orders and the evident intent upon his part to place upon General Hancock the responsibility for no further movements that night. After a few moments' reflection you turned to me and asked if I would make a third ride to Smith, saying, that while I had had a hard day's work, my knowledge of the roads, of the position of the army, and of the situation in front of Petersburg was such as to make it almost necessary that I, rather than any other officer of your staff, should go. To that I responded that I would cheerfully go.

You then directed me to see General Smith personally and to say to him that you peremptorily ordered him, *upon the receipt of your command sent by me*, to cause an immediate attack to be made upon the defences of Petersburg by all the forces then present.

I arrived at the front upon this mission between one and two o'clock on the morning of June 16. I found General Smith's headquarters camp and rode directly to the tents thereof. Inquiring of the sentries as to which was General Smith's tent, no one seemed to know and they stated that they had not seen him. I then made inquiry of some of his staff as to his whereabouts and was informed that they were unknown; that he had gone earlier in the night to General Hancock's headquarters and had not returned to camp.

Smith's camp was pitched on the right of the road in a piece of woods, and after thorough inquiry there, which was answered each time with a denial of all knowledge of· the general's whereabouts, I proceeded to General Hancock's headquarters and to those of the division commanders of Smith's command. At none of these places could I obtain any knowledge or information as to him. Returning to the neighborhood of his headquarters camp I endeavored to reach it from another side than that on which I had originally entered it, and found that the bushes, trees, and undergrowth prevented this, and after looking the ground over became satisfied that the path I had originally taken to it from the main road was practically the only approach to it which had been beaten down and used. It was then between two and three o'clock in the morning, and throwing my bridle over one arm I placed my rubber blanket on the ground and lay down across the path leading from the main road to Smith's camp, well knowing that no one could pass over me or around my mare without awakening me. I then dozed off, getting something over an hour's broken sleep.

Upon awakening I left my horse and started through the camp, opening the flies of several of the tents and looking in at the occupants. I proceeded in this way through that portion of the camp occupied by the officers without obtaining a sight of General Smith. Passing then to the rear where the tents of the orderlies and servants were pitched, I saw a tent some distance from those occupied by Smith's staff, and close to those the orderlies' quarters. Opening the fly of this tent I came face to face with General Smith who had evidently just arisen. He manifested great surprise at seeing me. I proceeded at once to state to him the efforts I had made to find him, at the same time expressing my surprise at his locating himself so far from that portion of his camp occupied by his staff as to have precluded them from any knowledge of his whereabouts. His reply was that " I was very tired and came here for the purpose of securing rest, and being where I would not be likely to be disturbed." I then delivered to General Smith your positive command for an immediate assault upon the receipt of the order, stating that your order was equally as good at that hour as it would have been had it been delivered at an earlier one. He responded that " he would look his position over and prepare to attack the enemy."

These facts I reported to you upon my return to headquarters between 6 and 7 A. M. on June 16.

I desire to call your attention to the fact that the night of the 15th of June was one of the most favorable nights which an army had ever presented for a night assault. The moon was substantially full, and the night as clear and bright as any I ever saw.

One other matter should be noticed. You will find that in one of your telegrams to General Grant on the night of the 15th, you speak of Hancock's troops having been passed by one of your staff about half past *nine* P. M. some four miles from Petersburg.

The hour they met was half past *five* P. M. The error was a clerical one due to haste in writing, and while such mistakes were not frequent in the army when the number of hastily written telegrams is considered, they did occur many times. A most notable instance is in one of General Hancock's despatches in which he says his force joined that of General Smith at *five* P. M. Gen. Francis A. Walker, chief of staff to General Hancock, in his history of Hancock's corps says the hour intended to be stated was *eight* P. M. This accords with the now well-established facts, as the assault made by General Smith's command was over at 7.20 P. M., and the Second Corps arrived shortly thereafter.

The facts as here stated of your orders, and my delivery of the same, are indelibly impressed upon my memory, and have been frequently told by me to personal friends and brother officers, during the nearly thirty years which have elapsed since their occurrence.

In view of them is it to be wondered at that, during that entire time General Smith has, so far as any public utterances of his are known, never by word or by pen, answered the severe and adverse criticisms upon his failure to capture Petersburg on the 15th of June, although, with hardly an exception, every speaker and writer upon the subject on either side has maintained that nothing but his inaction prevented it from being taken?

Had he obeyed his orders Petersburg would have been ours that night, our forces would have been south of the Appomattox, thereby putting that between us and Lee, the fall of Richmond would have immediately ensued, and no one now doubts that at least fifty thousand wounded men and dead would have been spared from suffering and death.

Very sincerely yours,

JOHN I. DAVENPORT,
Late Lieut. (Brevet-Captain) and A. D. C.,
Ass't. Provost-Marshal Army of the James.

[**No. 68.** *See page* 691.]

CLAY'S HOUSE, 3.30 P. M., June 17, 1864.

MAJ.- GEN. W. H. F. LEE :

Push after the enemy and endeavor to ascertain what has become of Grant's army. Inform General Hill.

R. E. LEE.

[**No. 69.** *See page* 691.]

CLAY'S HOUSE, 3.40 P. M., June 17, 1864.

GEN. G. T. BEAUREGARD, PETERSBURG, VIRGINIA :

Have no information about Grant's crossing James River, but upon your report have ordered troops up to Chaffin's Bluff.

R. E. LEE.

[**No. 70.** *See page* 691.]

June 11, 1864.

GENERAL BEAUREGARD, COMMANDING :

General:—I am so much disturbed about our condition, but especially about our relations to Petersburg, that you must excuse me for a suggestion. It seems to me that there is but one way to save the country and bring the authorities to their senses, and that is to say: "I cannot guard Bermuda Hundred and Petersburg both, with my present forces. I have decided that Petersburg is the important point and will withdraw my whole command to that place to-night." It is arrant nonsense for Lee to say that Grant can't make a night march without his knowing it. Has not Grant slipped around him four times already? Did not Burnside retire from Fredericksburg, and Hooker from the Wilderness without his knowing it? Grant can get ten thousand or twenty thousand men to Westover and Lee know nothing of it. What, then, is to become of Petersburg? Its loss surely involves that of Richmond,— perhaps of the Confederacy. An earnest appeal is called for now, else a terrible disaster may, and I think will, befall us.

Very respectfully,

D. H. HILL,
Major-General and Aide-de-Camp.

[**No. 71.** *See page* 692.]

JACKSON, N. H., July 8, 1891.

GEN. B. F. BUTLER:

Dear Sir : — Your letter of the 25th ultimo addressed to me at Cambridge has followed me to this place where I am invalided for the summer, my physicians having advised me that I must seek recuperation in a change of climate, as my health was so much shattered that they could do nothing to help me but to recommend such a change. I have no records or reports available here to which to refer, and therefore can only reply to the suggestions contained in Mr. Campbell's communication, herewith returned, from memory.

It seems to me to have been of little consequence where the Ninth Corps might have been on the 16th of June, 1864, as far as the operations against Petersburg were concerned, if it could not have been in front of the defences of that place before night on the 15th.

The Second Corps, I believe, crossed the pontoon bridge on the 14th of June, and was on the march towards Petersburg on the 15th, arriving within a mile of the portion of the works already captured by my division at about sunset, and at about ten o'clock at night, perhaps later, occupied the captured works, my division being withdrawn about one hundred yards to its rear.

About sunrise on the morning of the 16th a vigorous attempt was made to dislodge the Second Corps and recover possession of the works by Confederate troops, not militia men, but understood at the time to be veterans of Beauregard's old command, who had begun to enter Petersburg about nine o'clock the night before. The attack was continued for several hours with heavy casualties on both sides, and terminated without loss or gain of position to either side. My division remained in support of the Second Corps until the attack was repulsed, when it was withdrawn towards the right.

Concerning the failure of the Eighteenth Corps to capture Petersburg on the 15th of June, I can only state from memory that the corps marched from the vicinity of Broadway on the Appomattox at 7 o'clock A. M. or later; I had expected that the movement would begin at a much earlier hour, as I had recommended in a plan of operations previously submitted by myself, and my division had been in readiness to move at any moment after 1 o'clock A. M. On the march Kautz's brigade of cavalry was at the head of the column, my command next in order, and the divisions of Martindale and Brooks followed. When a portion of the column had passed the City Point Railroad, and the cavalry was opposite Cedar level near Baylor's farm, the enemy's guns opened fire from the open field on the opposite side of Cedar level; this was somewhat of a surprise to me, as a few days before I had, with an escort, ridden over Baylor's farm, finding no signs of the enemy except a picket-post in the woods on the side towards Petersburg of the open field in which the guns were evidently now planted; and when discovered the men, a dozen or so in number, discharged their muskets full in the faces of myself and staff at short range, hitting nothing, and fled through the woods towards Petersburg. I, therefore, now told General Smith that I did not believe it possible that the enemy occupied the position in any considerable strength, and he (General Smith) at once directed General Kautz to charge with his cavalry through the open road across the level, and dislodge the force obstructing our way. Kautz started off briskly, and hardly had the rear of his brigade disappeared from sight in the circuitous road when the head of it reappeared coming as briskly to the rear, his column having been repulsed, doubled up and thrown into considerable disorder; he reported to General Smith, as I understood, that the enemy was in considerable force directly in front of the road, and could not be dislodged by any direct movement through that road. General Smith then said he would send the division of Brooks around the right of Cedar Level Swamp, and dislodge the enemy by a flank movement. I suggested that this would involve a long countermarch and much delay, and that I believed a line could be pushed through the swamp in our front; he thought the swamp was entirely impractical for any troops, but said I might try it if I chose, and rode away to give directions to General Brooks. First placing my batteries in position to cover the movement, I directed several regiments to deploy and enter the swamp on either side of the road, and to push on with the utmost vigor; this movement was promptly executed, several men being killed, and a number of officers and men wounded in the swamp; but as soon as our men appeared in the opposite side of the swamp the enemy fled, leaving behind one field-piece covered with *chevaux-de-frise*, but escaping with the limber.

My division was now on either side of the swamp, which Martindale's division had not passed, and Brooks' division had been diverted from its route; therefore, considerable time was taken to re-form the column, it being past noon, I think, when the march was resumed from Baylor's farm towards the Jordan Point road. I should here state that during the affair at Baylor's farm, my horse failed in an attempt to leap the railroad ditch, and in his fall I was caught and pressed between his shoulder and the bank, causing severe internal injuries and pain which greatly interfered with my activity and usefulness during the day.

It was considerably past noon, as I remember, when my division reached Jordan Point road; the divisions of Martindale and Brooks having been directed by General Smith to move from Baylor's farm towards Petersburg by approaches to the right of the Jordan Point road and Kautz's cavalry being ordered to move to the left of that road. Of the movements of these commands during the remainder of the afternoon of the 15th and on the forenoon of the 16th I saw nothing and have no personal knowledge.

On reaching the Jordan Point road my division moved by it towards Petersburg, General Smith accompanying me; and on the head of my column debouching from the woods in front of the Confederate works, the enemy's artillery along the whole line of redoubts opened fire with deliberation and precision. General Smith, after examining the position, thought that the only practical method of successful assault was to send forward successive lines of skirmishers to within easy musket range of the works until a cloud of skirmishers had secured such a lodgment, and then after picking off some of the gunners to charge into the works with the whole line. Having directed me to execute these preliminary details, but not to assault the works until his return, General Smith rode towards the right. After an hour or two he returned and personally inspected every part of my advanced line, and expressed himself as satisfied that everything was in readiness on my line for a successful assault; he then directed me to await a signal from the right, and on receiving it to push forward with my whole command. It was 6 o'clock P. M. or after when the signal was received and the troops were immediately in motion,—dashing forward at a run — the centre was momentarily repulsed, but was promptly rallied by its field officers and mounted the works with a shout of triumph. Having gained the works in their front, the regiments of the Second Brigade swung to the left and successfully assailed the redoubts in flank and rear, the enemy making a brief stand in each and then retiring to the next on the left until we had captured five or six redoubts and their intervening defences, and twelve additional field-pieces, all thoroughly equipped and in excellent condition.

General Smith rejoined me a little before sunset, if I remember correctly, and extending his hand his first exclamation was: " Why, Hinks, this is a stronger position than Missionary Ridge." He then cautioned me to hold my troops well in hand, and on my asking him if he proposed to move forward he replied: " Oh, no; if we attempt to capture more we may lose all we have gained," or words to that effect. I then asked if any further movement should be made towards the left and he replied in substance, rather emphatically : " Not at all. We have already captured as much as we can securely hold; " and then directed me to set my command at work, reversing the captured works as rapidly as possible. He then again rode towards the right, and about half an hour later while I was engaged in stationing my command and in giving instructions for reversing the works, a staff officer approached and informed me that the commander of the Second Corps wished to see me on the Jordan Point road some distance to the rear. I at once rode to near the intersection of the roadway from Baylor's farm with the Jordan Point road, and there found General Birney (or was it General Gibbons) in command of the Second Corps (General Hancock having, for some reason, remained behind) ; he said to me that he had been ordered to march the corps to the support of the troops that were operating against Petersburg, and I explained to him as briefly as I could what had been accomplished and the existing situation, and suggested that he move directly forward to the rear of my division, then deploy to the left in the open field and continue the occupation of the enemy's works in that direction, as I thought he would meet with but slight resistance, if any at all ; this he objected to, saying that he would not move his troops at night in presence of the enemy upon grounds with which he was not familiar. I then suggested that he move his command forward towards my division and await instructions from General Smith who was in command, and I had no authority to give any instructions. To this he made no definite response, and as I felt that my presence at the front was important, I hastened back to my command, and at once sent information to General Smith of the proximity of the Second

Corps. At about ten o'clock at night the corps moved into the works already captured by my division, General Smith being then upon the ground, and by his orders my division was withdrawn to the rear some seventy-five or one hundred yards, as stated in the beginning of this narrative.

What the cavalry brigade of Kautz or the infantry division of Martindale and Brooks were doing in the afternoon while my division was capturing guns and defences, I have never learned; but a day or two afterwards while conversing with General Martindale, he generously said that in his judgment whatever credit was won by the troops on the 15th was mainly due to the movements of my division, for which he heartily congratulated me.

I am, General, very truly yours,

EDWARD W. HINKS.

[No. 72. See page 694.]

June 21, 1864, 9 A. M.

MAJOR-GENERAL SMITH :

To so meritorious and able officer as yourself, and to one toward whom the sincerest personal friendship and the highest respect concur in my mind, I am and shall ever be unwilling to utter a word of complaint; yet I think duty requires that I should call your attention to the fact that your column which was ordered to move at *daylight* in the cool of the morning is now just passing my headquarters in the heat of the day for a ten-mile march.

The great fault of all our movements is *dilatoriness*, and if this is the fault of your division commanders let them be very severely reproved therefor.

I have found it necessary to relieve one general for this among other causes, where it took place in a movement of vital importance, and in justice to him you will hardly expect me to pass in silence like fault when of less moment. The delay of Grouchy for three hours lost to Napoleon Waterloo and an empire, and we all remember the bitterness with which the Emperor exclaimed, as he waited for his tardy general, " *Il s'amuse a Gembloux.*"

Respectfully,

B. F. BUTLER,
Major-General Commanding.

[No. 73. See page 694.]

HEADQUARTERS EIGHTEENTH ARMY CORPS,
3.40 P. M., June 21, 1864.

General: — I have the honor to acknowledge the receipt of your extraordinary note of 9 A. M. In giving to your rank and position all the respect which is their due, I must call your attention to the fact that a reprimand can only come from the sentence of a court-martial and I shall accept nothing as such. You will also pardon me for observing that I have some years been engaged in marching troops, and I think in experience of that kind, at least, I am your superior. Your accusation of dilatoriness on my part this morning or at any other time since I have been under your orders is not founded on fact, and your threat of relieving me does not frighten me in the least.

Your obedient servant,

WM. F. SMITH,
Major- General.

[No. 74. See page 694.]

June 21, 1864, 5.30 P. M.

GENERAL SMITH:

When a friend writes you a note is it not best to read it twice before you answer unkindly? If you will look at my note you will find that it contains no threat; on the contrary there are some words interlined, lest upon reading it over it might be possibly be so.

Please read the note again and see if you cannot wish the reply was not sent. Pardon me for saying in all sincerity that I never thought you in fault as to the movement, as I understood your orders to be as mine were.

Truly your friend,

B. F. BUTLER.

[No. 75. See page 695.]

HEADQUARTERS EIGHTEENTH ARMY CORPS,
IN THE FIELD, VA., June 21, 1864.

BRIGADIER-GENERAL RAWLINS:

General: — I have the honor to forward to you copies to correspondence to General Butler. I have no comments to make, but would respectfully request that I may be relieved from duty in the Department of Virginia and North Carolina.

Very respectfully your obedient servant,

WM. F. SMITH,
Major- General.

[No. 76. See page 695.]

CITY POINT, July 8, 1864.

MAJ.-GEN. W. F. SMITH,
COMMANDING EIGHTEENTH ARMY CORPS:

There will probably be no movements for a week or ten days, and you have permission to use this time to visit New York. Communicate this to General Butler with whom the lieutenant-general has spoken.

By command of Lieutenant-General Grant:

JOHN A. RAWLINS,
Brigadier- General and Chief of Staff.

[**No. 77.** *See page* 69ŏ.]

HEADQUARTERS ARMIES OF THE UNITED STATES,
In the Field, May 21, 1864, 7 A. M.
(Received 10.35 A. M.)

MAJ.-GEN. H. W. HALLECK, CHIEF OF STAFF:

I fear there is some difficulty with the forces at City Point which prevents their effective use. The fault may be with the commander, and it may be with his subordinates. *General Smith, whilst a very able officer, is obstinate, and is likely to condemn whatever is not suggested by himself.* Either those forces should be so occupied as to detain a force nearly equal to their own, or the garrison and the intrenchments at City Point should be reduced to a minimum and the remainder ordered here. I wish you would send a competent officer there to inspect and report by telegram what is being done, and what in his judgment it is advisable to do.

U. S. GRANT,
Lieutenant-General.

[**No. 78.** *See page* 696.]

CITY POINT, VA., July 10, 1864, 1.30 P. M.
(Received 8.40 P. M.)

MAJ.-GEN. H. W. HALLECK, CHIEF OF STAFF:

General Orders No. 225 of July 7, 1864, would take the Eighteenth Corps from the Department of Virginia and North Carolina,and leave it a separate command, thus giving a third army in the field. As the Tenth Corps is also serving here, I would not desire this change made, but simply want General Smith assigned to the command of the Eighteenth Corps, and if there is no objection to a brigadier-general holding such a position, Gen. Wm. T. H. Brooks to the command of the Tenth Corps, leaving both these corps in the department as before, the headquarters of which is at Fortress Monroe. When the Nineteenth Corps arrives, I will add it to the same department. I will take the liberty of suspending this order until I hear again. I will ask to have General Franklin assigned to the active command in the field under General Butler's orders as soon as he is fit for duty.

U. S. GRANT,
Lieutenant-General.

[**No. 79.** *See page* 696.]

HEADQUARTERS ARMY OF THE UNITED STATES,
CITY POINT, July 19, 1864.
Special Orders No. 62.

. . . .

III. All troops of the Nineteenth Army Corps arriving at this point will report to Maj.-Gen. B. F. Butler, commanding Department of Virginia and North Carolina at Bermuda Hundred for orders.

IV. Subject to the approval of the President, Maj.-Gen. W. F. Smith is relieved from the command of the Eighteenth Army Corps, and will pro-

ceed to New York City and await further orders. His personal staff wil
accompany him. The corps staff of the Eighteenth Army Corps will
report to Brig.-Gen. J. H. Martindale, temporarily commanding, for duty.[1]

[**No. 80.**   *See page 696.*]

[*Copy.*]
College Point, L. I., July 30, 1864.

Hon. S. Foot :

Dear Senator : — I am extremely anxious that my friends in my native
State should not think that the reasons of General Grant relieving me
from duty was brought about by any misconduct of mine, and, therefore,
I write to put you in possession of such facts in the case as I am aware of,
and think will throw light upon the subject.

About the very last of June or the first of July, Generals Grant and
Butler came to my headquarters and shortly after their arrival, General
Grant turned to General Butler, and said: "That drink of whiskey I took
has done me good," and then directly afterwards asked me for a drink.
My servant opened a bottle for him and he drank of it, when the bottle
was corked up and put away. I was aware at this time that General
Grant had within six months pledged himself to drink nothing intoxicating,
but did not feel it would better matters to decline to give it upon his
request in General Butler's presence.

After the lapse of an hour or less the general asked me for another
drink, which he took. Shortly after his voice showed plainly that the
liquor had affected him and after a little time he left. I went to see him
upon his horse, and as I returned to my tent, I said to a staff officer of
mine, who had witnessed his departure: "General Grant has gone away
drunk; General Butler has seen it and will never fail to use the weapon
which has been put into his hands." Two or three days after that I
applied for a leave of absence for the benefit of my health, and General
Grant sent word to me not to go, if it were possible to stay, and I replied,
in a private note, warranted by our former relations, a copy of which
note I will send you in a few days. The next day the Assistant Secretary
of War (Mr. Dana) came to tell me that he had been sent by General
Grant to say what it becomes necessary to repeat in view of subsequent
events, to wit: That he, General G., had written a letter the day before
to ask that General Butler might be relieved from that department July
2, and I placed in command of it, giving as a reason that he could not
trust General Butler with the command of troops in the movements
about to be made, and saying also that next to General Sherman he had
more confidence in my ability than in that of any general in the field.
The order from Washington dated July 7, sent General B. to Fortress
Monroe, and placed me in command of the troops, then under him, and
General Grant said he would make the changes necessary to give me the
troops in the field belonging to that department. I had only asked that
I should not be commanded in battle by a man that could nct give an
order on the field, and I had recommended General Franklin or General

---

[1]This order was approved by the President in General Order No. 36, adjutant-general's office,
July 28, 1864.

Wright for the command of the department. I was at the headquarters of General Grant on Sunday, July 10, and there saw General B., but had no conversation with him. After General B. had left, I had a confidential conversation with General Grant about changes he was going to make. In this connection it is proper to state that our personal relations were of the most friendly character. He had listened to and acted upon suggestions made by me upon more than one important occasion. I then thought and still think (whatever General Butler's letter writers may say to the contrary) that he knew that any suggestion I might make for his consideration would be dictated solely by an intense desire to put down this Rebellion, and not from any personal considerations personal to myself, and that no personal friendships had stood in the way of what I considered my duty with regard to military management, a course not likely to be pursued by a man ambitious of advancement. In this confidential conversation with General Grant, I tried to show him the blunders of the late campaign of the Army of the Potomac and the terrible waste of life that had resulted from what I considered a want of generalship in its present commander. Among other instances I referred to the fearful slaughter at Cold Harbor, on the 3d of June. General Grant went into the discussion defending General Meade stoutly, but finally acknowledged, to use his own words, "that there had been a butchery at Cold Harbor, but that he had said nothing about it because it could do no good." Not a word was said as to my right to criticise General Meade then, and I left without a suspicion that General Grant had taken it in any other way than it was meant, and I do not think he did misunderstand me.

On my return from a short leave of absence on the 19th of July, General Grant sent for me, to report to him, and then told me that he "could not relieve General Butler," and that as I had so severely criticised General Meade he had determined to relieve me from the command of the Eighteenth Corps and order me to New York City to await orders. The next morning the general gave some other reason, such as an article in the *Tribune* reflecting on General Hancock, which I had nothing in the world to do with, and two letters which I had written before the campaign began to two of General Grant's most devoted friends, urging upon them to try and prevent him from making the campaign he had just made. These letters, sent to General Grant's nearest friends, and intended for his eye, necessarily sprang from an earnest desire to serve the man upon whom the country had been depending, and these warnings ought to have been my highest justification in his opinion and, indeed, would have been, but that it had become necessary to make out a case against me. All these matters, moreover, were known to the general before he asked that I might be put in command of the Department of Virginia and North Carolina, and, therefore, they formed no excuse for relieving me from the command I held. I also submit to you that if it had been proven to him that I was unfitted for the command I then held, that that in no wise changed the case with reference to General Butler and his incompetency, and did not furnish a reason why he should not go where the President had ordered him at the request of General Grant, and that as General

Grant did immediately after an interview with General Butler suspend the order and announce his intention of relieving me from duty there, other reasons must be sought, different from any assigned, for this sudden change of views and action. Since I have been in New York, I have heard from two different sources (one being from General Grant's headquarters and one a staff officer of a general on intimate official relations with General Butler) that General Butler went to General Grant and threatened to expose his intoxication if the order was not revoked. I also learned that General Butler had threatened to make public something that would prevent the President's re-election. General Grant told me (when I asked him about General Butler's threat of crushing me) that he had heard that General Butler had made some threat with reference to the Chicago convention, which he (Butler) said "he had in his breeches pocket," but General Grant was not clear in expressing what the threat was. I refer to this simply because I feel convinced that the change was not made for any of the reasons that have been assigned, and whether General Butler has threatened General Grant with his opposition to Mr. Lincoln at the coming election, or has appealed to any political aspirations which General Grant may entertain, I do not know, but one thing is certain, I was not guilty of any acts of insubordination between my appointment and my suspension, for I was absent all those days on leave of absence from General Grant. I only hope this long story will not tire you, and that it will convince you that I have done nothing to deserve a loss of the confidence which was reposed in me.

Yours very truly,

Wm. F. Smith,
Major-General.

P. S. I have not referred to the state of things existing at headquarters when I left, and to the fact that General Grant was then in the habit of getting liquor in a surreptitious manner, because it was not relevant to my case; but if you think at any time the matter may be of importance to the country I will give it to you. Should you wish to write to me, please address care of S. E. Lyon, Jauncy Court, 39 Wall Street, N. Y.

Wm. F. S.

[**No. 81.** *See page* 705.]

History of the Second Army Corps by Francis A. Walker, pp. 555, 556.

DEEP BOTTOM.

The terrible experiences of May and June in assaults on intrenched positions; assaults made, often, not at a carefully selected point, but "all along the line"; assaults made as if it were a good thing to assault, and not a dire necessity; assaults made without an adequate concentration of troops, often without time for careful preparation, sometimes even without examination of the ground — these bitter experiences had naturally brought about a reaction, by which efforts to outflank the enemy were to become the order of the day, so that the months of July and August were largely to be occupied in rapid movements, now to the right and now to the left of a line thirty to forty miles in length, in the hope of somewhere, at some time, getting upon the flank of the unprepared enemy — the sentiment of headquarters, and perhaps the orders, being adverse to assaults. Unfortunately this change of purpose did not take place until the numbers and *morale* of the troops had been so far reduced that the flanking movements became, in the main, ineffectual from the want of vigor in attack, at the critical moments, when a little of the fire which had been exhibited in the great assaults of May would have sufficed to crown a well-conceived enterprise with a glorious victory. But that fire had for the time burned itself out; and on more than one occasion during the months of July and August, 1864, the troops of the Army of the Potomac, after an all-day or all-night march which had placed them in a position of advantage, failed to show a trace of that enthusiasm and *élan* which characterized the earlier days of the campaign. This result was not due to moral causes only. Physically the troops were dead-beat, from the exertions and privations of the preceding two months.

[**No. 82.** *See page* 715.]

[*Private.*]

HEADQUARTERS OF THE ARMY, WASHINGTON, July 3, 1864.
LIEUT.-GEN. U. S. GRANT, CITY POINT, VA.:

General : — Your note of the 1st instant in relation to General Butler is just received. I will, as you propose, await further advices from you before I submit the matter officially to the Secretary of War and the President. It was foreseen from the first that you would eventually find it necessary to relieve General B. on account of his total unfitness to command in the field, and his generally quarrelsome character. What shall be done with him, has therefore, already been, as I am informed, a matter of consultation. To send him to Kentucky would probably cause an insurrection in that State and an immediate call for large reinforcements. Moreover, he would probably greatly embarrass Sherman, if he did not attempt to supersede him by using against him all his talent at political intrigues and his facilities for newspaper abuse. If you send him to Missouri nearly the same thing will occur there. Although it might not be objectionable to have a free fight between him and Rosecrans, the government would be seriously embarrassed by the local difficulties and calls for reinforcements likely to follow. Inveterate as is Rosecrans' habit of continually calling for more troops, Butler differs only in demanding instead of calling. As things now stand in the West, I think we can keep the peace; but if Butler be thrown in as a disturbing element, I anticipate very serious results.

Why not leave General Butler in the local command of his department, including North Carolina, Norfolk, Fortress Monroe, Yorktown, etc., and make a new army corps of the part of the Eighteenth under Smith? This would leave B. under your immediate control, and at the same time would relieve you of his presence in the field. Moreover, it would save the necessity of organizing a new department. If he must be relieved entirely, I think it would be best to make a new department for him in New England.

I make these remarks merely as suggestions. Whatever you may finally determine on I will try to have done. As General B. claims to rank me, I shall give him no orders wherever he may go, without the special direction of yourself or the Secretary of War.

Yours truly,

H. W. HALLECK,
Major-General.

[**No. 83.** *See page* 715.]

HEADQUARTERS, Aug. 13, 1864.

MAJOR-GENERAL BIRNEY,
COMMANDING TENTH ARMY CORPS:

In accordance with verbal instructions heretofore given you upon consultation, you will take all the men that can, in your judgment, be spared from the lines between the Appomattox and the James, march across the pontoon bridge at Deep Bottom at such time as will enable you to strike the enemy in front of Brigadier-General Foster in the most feasible form, on the morning of the 14th. You will take such portion of General Foster's command and add it to your own as you think will be prudent. As you are to advance, leaving Deep Bottom behind you, in my judgment a small force will be necessary. You will turn over the command of the line of defences to Brigadier-General Turner, instructing him what troops you have left for that purpose. I shall be able to add from the dismounted cavalry, and from Graham, possibly, eight hundred men. You may order such portion of the garrison of Fort Converse as you think can be spared at present,— perhaps you can draw largely. I forbear giving instructions in writing because the details have already been arranged between us personally.

You will report to Major-General Hancock, who will be at Deep Bottom in the course of the night. Any other instructions that you may desire from me will be promptly met by telegraph.

Very respectfully,

BENJ. F. BUTLER,
Major-General Commanding.

[**No. 84.** *See page* 753.]

[*Cipher.*]

CITY POINT, VA., Nov. 1, 1864, 3.30 P. M.

MAJOR-GENERAL BUTLER, FORTRESS MONROE:

I am just in receipt of despatch from Secretary of War, asking me to send more troops to the city of New York, and if possible, to let you go there until after the election. I wish you would start for Washington immediately and be guided by orders from there in the matter.

U. S. GRANT,
Lieutenant-General.

[**No. 85.** *See page* 754.]

WAR DEPARTMENT, WASHINGTON CITY, Nov. 2, 1864.
MAJOR-GENERAL BUTLER:

General:—You will please proceed immediately to New York and report to Major-General Dix for temporary duty in the Department of the East, and for assignment to the command of the troops in the harbor and city of New York that may be forwarded by General Grant's orders.

By order of the Secretary of War:

E. D. TOWNSEND,
Assistant Adjutant-General.

[**No. 86.** *See pages* 755 *and* 768.]

WASHINGTON, D. C., Nov. 2, 1864 [Received 1 P. M.].
LIEUTENANT-GENERAL U. S. GRANT, CITY POINT, VA.:

I am here in obedience to your order. Am ordered to report in New York to General Dix. From the state of things, as I can learn them, we should have at least five thousand good troops, and at least two batteries of Napoleons. There is necessity for haste in getting them off. They can easily be spared from the Tenth and Eighteenth corps. A show of force may prevent trouble. I have directed the quartermaster at Fortress Monroe to have ready all transportation there, making use of that provided for Colonel Mulford except the Atlantic and Baltic. I would desire that the particular brigades or regiments to be sent should be left to the selection of Generals Terry and Weitzel. They will have ample enough to hold their lines after reliable troops are sent to me. Shall leave to-night for New York, Fifth Avenue Hotel.

BENJ. F. BUTLER,
Major-General.

[*Cipher.*]

CITY POINT, VA., Nov. 2, 1864, 5 P. M.
MAJOR-GENERAL TERRY:

Send a good large brigade of infantry with two batteries of Napoleon guns to report to General Butler at New York at once. If you have Western troops, they will be preferable. Answer what troops you send.

U. S. GRANT,
Lieutenant-General.

[*Cipher.*]

WASHINGTON, D. C., Nov. 2, 1864 [Received 1 P. M.].
MAJOR-GENERAL TERRY,
HEADQUARTERS TENTH ARMY CORPS, NEAR VARINA, VA.,
IN THE FIELD NEAR RICHMOND:

You will be ordered to send troops to me at New York. Select those which are reliable. Confer with Weitzel. It may become necessary to make composite brigades. Great activity in getting them off will be required. They are to be going to Wilmington.

BENJ. F. BUTLER,
Major-General Commanding.

[**No. 87.** *See page* 758.]

NEW YORK, Nov. 8, 1864.

MAJOR-GENERAL BUTLER, COMMANDING CITY OF NEW YORK:

Sir: — By one of my detectives, corroborated by a member of the staff of Major-General Sandford, I learn that no arms or ammunition have been sent from the State arsenal in 7th Avenue, into the interior of the State, since July last, when a large quantity of both were transferred to the custody of Gen. John C. Greene.

I also learn, by same authority, that there are now in the arsenal, four twelve-pound howitzers, and about eighteen hundred stand of arms, with but a small quantity of ammunition.

The arms enumerated include those just deposited by the Seventy-Seventh Regiment National Guard, who have been on duty at Elmira for one hundred days, but are not regarded as very reliable.

There are no packages of any kind in the arsenal to denote an intention to remove anything more.

I also learn that the Seventh National Guards have six four-pound howitzers with about one thousand stand of arms at their armory, Tompkins' Market.

That the Twenty-Second N. G. have two twelve-pound howitzers, one thousand Enfield rifles (their private property), and ten thousand ball cartridges at their armory, Palace Garden, 14th Street.

Very respectfully,
JOHN A. KENNEDY,
Superintendent.

[**No. 88.** *See page* 758.]

HEADQUARTERS, CITY OF NEW YORK, Nov. 7, 1864.

HON. E. M. STANTON, SECRETARY OF WAR:

Sir: — I beg leave to report that the troops detailed for duty here have all arrived and dispositions made which will insure quiet.

I enclose a copy of my order and I trust it will meet your approbation. I have done all I could to prevent the secessionists from voting and think have had some effect.

I think I may be able to punish some of the rascals for their crimes after election.

All will be quiet here. The State authorities are sending from the arsenal in New York arms and ammunition to Mr. John A. Green, brigadier-general at Buffalo, and I am powerless to prevent it.

This is what I mean by wanting "territorial jurisdiction." I am in command of troops solely. It is none of my business to prevent arms and ammunition being sent to Buffalo.

This is one of the dozen cases wherein I cannot act without colliding with General Dix and the State authorities both.

I have not landed any of my men save those I have sent to Buffalo, which are two (2) regiments of regulars and one hundred (100) men at Watervliet for Albany. Now these regiments report to General Peck, but Peck does not report to me. He has some regulars besides those arriving and to arrive.

That is another instance of what is meant by wanting " territorial juris-diction."

I have three (3) batteries on ferry-boats all harnessed up ready to land at a moment's notice at any slip on North or East River; gunboats cov-ering Wall Street and the worst streets in the city, and a brigade of infantry ready to land on the battery, and the other troops placed where they can be landed at once in spite of barricades or opposition. A reve-nue cutter is guarding the cable over the North River and a gunboat covers High Bridge on Harlem River which is the Croton aqueduct.

I have given you these details so that you may understand the nature of my preparations, and perhaps the details may be interesting and of use at some other time.

I propose, unless ordered to the contrary by you, to land all my troops on the morning of election in the city. I apprehend that, if at all, there will be trouble then. I have information of several organizations that are being got ready under General Porter, Duryea, and Hubert Ward, disaf-fected officers, and others who are intending, if the elections are close, to try the question of inaugurating McClellan, and will attempt it, if at all, by trying how much of an *emeute* can be raised in New York City for that purpose. They propose to raise the price of gold so as to affect the neces-saries of life and raise discontent and disturbance during the winter, declare then that they are cheated in the election by military interference and fraudulent ballots, and then inaugurate McClellan.

Now, that there is more or less truth in this information I have no doubt. One thing is certain, that the gold business is in the hands of a half dozen firms who are all foreigners or secessionists, and whose names and descrip-tions I will give you.

You are probably aware that the government has sold ten (10) or twelve millions (12,000,000) of gold within the past twenty days. The Secretary of the Treasury will tell you how much, it is none of my business to know; but one firm, H. J. Lyons & Co., have bought and actu-ally received in coin, by confession to me, more than ten millions (10,000,000) within the past fortnight, and his firm is now carrying some three millions (3,000,000) of gold. I felt bound to look up the case of Gentlemen H. J. Lyons & Co. I sent for Lyons, although I suppose I had no right to do so, wanting territorial jurisdiction, set him down before me, and examined him. His story is, as I made him correct it by appealing to my own investigations, as follows: His firm consists of himself, his brother, and the president of the Jeffersonville Railroad, Indiana. He is from Louisville ; left there when Governor Morehead was arrested; went to Nashville ; left there just before the city was taken by the Union troops; went to New Orleans; left there just before the city was taken ; went to Liverpool; left there; went to Montreal and went into business; stayed in Montreal until last December; came here with his brother younger than himself, and set up the broker's business. He claims to have had a capital in greenbacks of eighty thousand (80,000) dollars, thirty thousand (30,000) put in by himself, ten thousand (10,000) by his brother, and forty thou-sand (40,000) by the other partner. This in greenbacks equal now at two forty-five (2-45) to about thirty thousand (30,000) dollars in gold. On this capital he was enabled to buy and pay for, not as balances, but actually in currency, almost twelve millions (12,000,000) of dollars in gold within the last fortnight, and now is carrying about three millions (3,000,000). This shows that there is something behind him.

He confessed that he left Louisville afraid of being arrested for his political offences. During the cross-examination, he confessed he was agent for the People's Bank of Kentucky, a secession concern which is doubtless an agent for Jeff Davis. Having no territorial jurisdiction, all I could do was to set before him the enormity of his crime, the danger he stood, having forfeited his life by rebellion to the government, and to say to him that I should be sorry if gold went up any to-day, because, as he was so large an operator, I should have cause to believe that he was operating for some political purpose, but that this was a free country and I had no right to control him. Does the Secretary of War suppose that, if I had an actual and not an emasculated command in the city of New York, such a rascal would have left my office without my knowing where to find him? He said, indeed, when he went out, that he thought he should not buy gold any more, and sell to-day all he has. It has got noised around a little that we are looking after the gold speculators, and gold has not risen any to-day up to five (5) o'clock, the time at which I am now writing, although Mr. Belmont's bet is that it would be at three hundred (300) before election, and the treasury is not selling.

Now, what I desire is to spend about a week in which I will straighten the following firms, which are all the men that are actually buying gold:

H. J. Lyons & Co., before spoken of; Vickers & Co., of Liverpool, an English house; H. G. Fant, of Washington; H. T. Suit, Washington house; Hallgarten & Heryfield, a Baltimore house of German Jews; and also to see if some of the rebels that are here cannot be punished. Substantially, none of them registered under General Dix's order.

I have stated all the reasons why I desire to be here. It is respectfully submitted to the Secretary of War, if I am desired to do anything at all, to telegraph me what I shall do, and it shall be done, or please let me return in the front. I have the honor to be, very respectfully,

Your obedient servant,

BENJ. F. BUTLER,

Major-General.

WAR DEPARTMENT, WASHINGTON CITY, NOV. 9, 1864.

MAJOR-GENERAL BUTLER:

General:—Your communication of day before yesterday has been submitted to the President who has directed the Secretary of the Treasury to be conferred with on that part which relates to the gold conspirators. Your views have been explained to the Secretary of the Treasury and when his opinion is received instructions will be sent to you by telegraph.

Your obedient servant,

EDWIN M. STANTON,

Secretary of War.

[**No. 89.**   *See page* 758.]

HEADQUARTERS, CITY OF NEW YORK, Nov. 5, 1864.

General Order No. 1.

In obedience to the orders of the President and by the assignment of Major-General Dix commanding Department of the East, Major-General Butler assumes command of the troops arriving and about to arrive, detailed for duty in the State of New York to meet existing emergencies.

To correct misapprehension ; to soothe the fears of the weak and timid ; to allay the nervousness of the ill-advised ; to silence all false rumors circulated by bad men for wicked purposes, and to contradict once and for all false statements adapted to injure the government in the respect and confidence of the people—the commanding general takes occasion to declare that troops have been detailed for duty in this district sufficient to preserve the peace of the United States ; to protect public property ; to prevent and punish incursions into our borders, and to insure calm and quiet.

If it were not within the information of the government, that raids like in quality and object to that made at St. Albans were in contemplation, there could have been no necessity for precautionary preparations.

The commanding general has been pained to see publications by some not too well informed persons, that the presence of the troops of the United States might by possibility have an effect upon the free exercise of the duty of voting at the ensuing election.   Nothing could be further from the truth.

The soldiers of the United States are specially to see to it that there is no interference with the election of anybody unless the civil authorities are overcome with force by bad men.

The armies of the United States are "ministers of good and not of evil."   They are safeguards of constitutional liberty which is *freedom to do right, not wrong.*   They can be a terror to evil-doers only, and those who fear them are accused by their own consciences.

Let every citizen having a right to vote, do according to the inspiration of his own judgment freely.   He will be protected in that right by the whole power of the government if it shall become necessary.

At the polls it is not possible exactly to separate the illegal from the legal vote —" the tares from the wheat " ; but it is possible to detect and punish the fraudulent voter after the election is over.

Fraudulent voting in pre-election of United States officers is an offence against the peace and dignity of the United States.

Every man knows whether he is a duly qualified voter, and he who votes, not being qualified, does a grievous wrong against light and knowledge.

Specially is fraudulent voting a deadly sin and heinous crime deserving condign punishment in those who having rebelliously seceded from and repudiated their allegiance to this government when at their homes in the South, now having fled here for asylum, abuse the hospitality of the State and clemency of the government by interfering in the election of our rulers.   It will not be well for them to do so.

Such men pile rebellion upon treason, breach of faith upon perjury, and forfeit the amnesty accorded them.

There can be no military organization in any State, known to the laws, save the militia united and armies of the United States.

The President is the constitutional commander-in-chief of the militia and army of the United States; therefore, where in any portion of the United States an officer of superior rank is detailed to command, all other military officers in that district must.

BENJ. F. BUTLER,
Major-General Commanding.

[**No. 90.** *See page* 762.]

UNITED STATES TREASURY, NEW YORK, Nov. 5, 1864.

My Dear General : — I want to see you at your earliest convenience, in relation to a matter affecting the best interests of the government, and in regard to which I can better confer with you here than elsewhere. Please let me know by bearer if you can grant me an interview.

With great respect, yours, etc.,
JOHN A. STEWART,
Assistant Treasurer United States.

MAJOR-GENERAL BUTLER.

[**No. 91.** *See page* 768.]

HARRISBURG, Nov. 7, 1864.

How long, my dear General, will you remain in New York? Will you stop in Philadelphia, or what would be better, can't you come this way? It is quite as near from New York to Washington.

I go to Philadelphia Thursday and if I cannot see you there or here I will go to you.

It is my private opinion that Stanton is to go on the march, and you should take his flank.

We will carry the State handsomely. Will telegraph you Wednesday morning.

Your friend,
SIMON CAMERON.

MAJOR-GENERAL BUTLER.

[**No. 92.** *See page* 768.]

Nov. 8, 1864.

HON. SIMON CAMERON:

My Dear Sir :—I may be here some days, certainly till after Wednesday. If you could come here then and come to the Hoffman House (my headquarters), I could make you very comfortable, and would be glad to see you. All is quiet here. The only thing we have to watch after election will be the gold operators who intend to run up the price till they can so affect the price of food and necessaries as to raise discontent amongst the laboring classes.

Yours truly,
BENJ. F. BUTLER.

[**No. 93.** *See page* 769.]

PHILADELPHIA, Nov. 11, 1864.

Dear General:— I will be in New York Saturday noon at the Astor. Will you please call there or drop me a note, and say where I shall call on you.

SIMON CAMERON.

GENERAL BUTLER.

[**No. 94.** *See page* 770.]

No. 57 WEST WASHINGTON PLACE,
NEW YORK, Nov. 19, 1864.

General:—Supposing it possible that it may be of interest to you and the public service to know that the quite considerable interest here who are unfriendly to your further advancement, are circulating most industriously a rumor that you do not want to be Secretary of War, that your ambition lies in some other direction, etc., I tell you that such is the case.

Gen. P. M. Wetmore came to me yesterday to ask if you would accept if appointed, saying he knew it would receive the support of every newspaper worth having, in New York, and that it was rumored you did not wish the appointment.

An army influence here (regulars) is industriously circulating the rumor that you would not accept, and they say you could have the appointment if it was known at Washington you wanted it; but it is said to be the opinion there that you would not accept.

Your obedient servant,

EDWARD W. SERRELL.

MAJOR-GENERAL BUTLER.

[**No. 95.** *See page* 770.]

CITY POINT, VA., Nov. 10, 1864, 10.30 P. M.

HON. EDWIN M. STANTON, SECRETARY OF WAR:

Enough now seems to be known to say who is to hold the reins of government for the next four years. Congratulate the President for me for the double victory. The election having passed off quietly, no bloodshed or riot throughout the land, is a victory worth more to the country than a battle won. Rebeldom and Europe will so construe it.

U. S. GRANT,
Lieutenant-General.

WASHINGTON, Nov. 10, 1864, 2 P. M.
(Received City Point, Nov. 10, 1864, 2.45 P. M.)

LIEUTENANT-GENERAL GRANT:

Orders have been made requesting the immediate return of all troops to the field, and the utmost diligence of the department will be directed to that object. General Dix reports that all of Butler's troops except five hundred regulars can return. A copy of his despatch is given. Before ordering Butler back, I will wait a day until the New York election be more definitely ascertained.

E. M. STANTON,
Secretary of War.

[Inclosure.]

Hon. E. M. Stanton, Secretary of War:

The triumph and election of the President, and the indications of a quiet acquiescence in the result, renders unnecessary to detain here the troops under the command of General Butler, with the exception of about five hundred regulars now in the interior of New York, under General Peck. These I should like to detain about a week. As no exigency exists in this department requiring the rest to be kept longer away from the Army of the Potomac, I deem it my duty to advise you promptly that the necessary orders may be given for their return.

Jno. A. Dix,

Major-General.

[**No. 96.** *See page* 770.]

[*Cipher.*]

Hoffman House, New York, Nov. 11, 4.05.

Colonel Townsend, A. General, Washington:

Telegram received. The troops shall be embarked as soon as transportation can be had. Have sent for the regulars who are on the borders. Your telegram gives me no orders. I have some private business which will detain me till Monday. Will the secretary allow my stay?

Benjamin F. Butler,

Major-General Commanding.

By Telegram from Washington, Nov. 11, 1864.

Major-General Butler:

Your telegram of this date to General Townsend has just been brought to my house.

General Grant is urgent for the return of your troops quickly.

The order contemplated your return with them, and if not specified on the official telegraph was omitted by the inadvertence of the adjutant-general.

You have leave to remain till Monday if you desire to do so.

(Signed)   E. M. Stanton,

Secretary of War.

[**No. 97.** *See page* 779.]

Washington, Dec. 1, 1864.

Major-General Butler:

Telegram received. One hundred tons mining powder was sent from New York and Boston between the 24th and last of November to Captain Edson at Fortress Monroe, who is ordered to hold the same subject to your order; fifty tons will leave New York in a day or two.

A. B. Dyer,

Chief of Ordnance.

[**No. 98.** *See page* 780.]

HEADQUARTERS ARMY OF THE JAMES,
IN THE FIELD, NOV. 30, 1864.

ADMIRAL PORTER:

Brigadier-General Wild will hand you this note, and brings also orders to General Palmer about the matter of which we were speaking. Please give him an order, to be transmitted through him to the commander of your naval forces in the sound, to co-operate in the fullest extent with General Palmer, and to move with all promptness and celerity.

General Wild will show you the orders, which are unsealed for that purpose, which he takes to General Palmer.

If anything occurs to you which I have not covered in my instructions, please telegraph me, and I will reach General Wild by telegraph before he reaches Fortress Monroe.

I have the honor to be, very respectfully, your obedient servant,

BENJAMIN F. BUTLER,
Major-General Commanding.

[**No. 99.** *See page* 780.]

HEADQUARTERS ARMIES OF THE UNITED STATES,
CITY POINT, NOV. 30, 1864.

MAJOR-GENERAL BUTLER:

I have files of Savannah and Augusta papers by Colonel Mulford, from which I gather that Bragg has gone to Georgia, taking with him, I judge, most of the forces from about Wilmington. *It is, therefore, important that Weitzel should get off during his absence ;* and if successful in effecting a landing he may, by a bold dash, succeed in capturing Wilmington. Make all the arrangements for his departure so that the navy may not be detained one moment for the army. Did you order Palmer to make the move proposed yesterday? It is important that he should do so without delay.

U. S. GRANT,
Lieutenant-General.

[**No. 100.** *See page* 780.]

HEADQUARTERS ARMIES OF THE UNITED STATES,
CITY POINT, VA., Dec. 4, 1864.

MAJOR-GENERAL BUTLER:

I feel great anxiety to see the Wilmington expedition off, both on account of the present fine weather, which we can expect no great continuance of, and because Sherman may now be expected to strike the sea coast at any day, leaving Bragg free to return. I think it advisable for you to notify Admiral Porter, and get off without delay, with or without your powder-boat.

U. S. GRANT,
Lieutenant-General.

[No. 101. *See page* 780.]

[*Cipher.*]

DEPARTMENT OF VIRGINIA AND NORTH CAROLINA,
Dec. 4, 1864.

ADMIRAL PORTER:

When can you be ready with our little expedition? Captain Edson, ordnance officer at Fortress Monroe, will put ordnance stores at your disposal. Time is valuable from the news we get.

BENJAMIN F. BUTLER,
Major-General Commanding.

[No. 102. *See page* 780.]

NORFOLK, Dec. 4, 1864.

MAJOR-GENERAL BUTLER:

We are ready for the one hundred and fifty (150) tons of powder. Will you give directions to have it bagged ready to go on board?

D. D. PORTER,
Rear-Admiral.

[No. 103. *See page* 780.]

[*Cipher.*]

Dec. 5, 1864, 11.20 A. M.

CAPTAIN EDSON:

Please have at once all the powder of which I spoke to you put in sand bags or flour sacks ready for shipment. You will see Admiral Porter on the subject, and will get the bags of the engineer department at Fortress Monroe. If not, notify me by telegram.

BENJAMIN F. BUTLER,
Major-General Commanding.

[No. 104. *See page* 780.]

FORTRESS MONROE, Dec. 5, 1864, 4 P. M.

MAJOR-GENERAL BUTLER:

I am all ready, and shall call on the ordnance officer at Fortress Monroe for material.

D. D. PORTER,
Rear-Admiral.

[No. 105. *See page* 780.]

[*Cipher.*]

Dec. 6, 1864.

ADMIRAL PORTER:

What day can we start for the fort? I wish not to keep troops on board transports a day longer than possible, as it will take some days to reach " Savannah "[1] any way. Is there anything I can aid you in?

BENJAMIN F. BUTLER,
Major-General Commanding.

---

[1] The word Savannah was used in place of Wilmington, lest the telegram should fall in wrong hands.

[*Cipher.*]

[**No. 106.** *See page* 780.]

FORTRESS MONROE, Dec. 6, 1864, 9.30 P. M.

MAJOR-GENERAL BUTLER :

Your telegram is received. The vessels to carry the ammunition will be ready in the morning completely filled. The ordnance officer here at Fortress Monroe is doing everything he can to expedite matters. Most of our ammunition is here, and will commence loading up to-morrow. I will report perhaps to-morrow evening so that you can make your calculation when to embark. I think I can by to-morrow tell you within an hour when we can be ready. We are ready in every other respect.

D. D. PORTER,
Rear Admiral.

[**No. 107.** *See page* 783.]

Dec. 6, 1864.

GENERAL TURNER :

When will Ames' corps be moved out of here? Will there be any others to supply their place, or shall I fill the gap by extending the first division to the left and the third to the right?

A. F. TERRY,
Brevet Major-General.

[**No. 108.** *See page* 784.]

CITY POINT, Dec. 6, 1864.

MAJOR-GENERAL BUTLER :

A movement will commence on the left to-morrow morning. Make immediate preparations so that your forces can be used north of the river if the enemy withdraw, or south if they should be required. Let all your men have two (2) days' cooked rations in haversacks. During to-morrow night withdraw to the left of your line at Bermuda the force you propose sending south, unless otherwise ordered. It will be well to get ready as soon as you can to blow out the end of the canal.

U. S. GRANT,
Lieutenant-General.

[**No. 109.** *See page* 784.]

Dec. 7, 1864, 11.05 P. M.

GENERAL TURNER, CHIEF OF STAFF :

We have here now the following boats [giving the name of vessels that had been furnished him]. These boats will carry seven thousand men, leaving space for ambulances, etc.

GEORGE S. DODGE,
Colonel, etc.

[**No. 110.** *See page* 784.]

Dec. 7, 1864.

COLONEL DODGE :

The Baltic is at Annapolis. Get her ; we shall need her.

BENJ. F. BUTLER,
Major-General Commanding.

[**No. 111.**   *See page* 784.]

. [*Cipher.*] .

Dec. 7, 1864.

LIEUTENANT-GENERAL GRANT :

General Weitzel's command is encamped at Signal Tower near Point of Rocks, and awaits orders. Admiral Porter telegraphs that he will be ready by to-morrow.

BENJ. F. BUTLER,
Major-General Commanding.

[**No. 112.**   *See page* 784.]

HEADQUARTERS ARMIES OF THE UNITED STATES,
CITY POINT, VA., Dec. 7, 1864.

MAJOR-GENERAL BUTLER :

Let General Weitzel get off as soon as possible. I don't want the navy to wait an hour.

U. S. GRANT,
Lieutenant-General.

[**No. 113.**   *See page* 785.]

' Dec. 7, 1864, 9 P. M.

MAJOR-GENERAL WEITZEL :

You will embark your command and get off to Fortress Monroe as soon as possible after daylight to-morrow morning.

BENJ. F. BUTLER,
Major-General Commanding.

[**No. 114.**   *See page* 785.]

BERMUDA, Dec. 8, 1864, 9.15 A. M.

MAJOR-GENERAL BUTLER :

I am here embarking the troops in case you should have anything to communicate.

GODFREY WEITZEL,
Major-General.

[**No. 115.**   *See page* 785.]

FORTRESS MONROE, Dec. 10, 1864, 11.45 A.M.

LIEUTENANT-GENERAL U. S. GRANT, CITY POINT :

Has been blowing a gale ever since we arrived. Is clearing up a little. We are all ready waiting for the navy.

Any news from Warren or Sherman?

BENJ. F. BUTLER,
Major-General.

[**No. 116.**   *See page* 786.]

NORTH ATLANTIC SQUADRON, UNITED STATES FLAG-SHIP MALVERN,
HAMPTON ROADS, Dec. 13, 1864.

MAJ.-GEN. B. F. BUTLER :

General: — The rest of the fleet will leave here in three hours, and will proceed to the rendezvous twenty-five miles east of Cape Fear River.

The powder vessel will go to Beaufort and take ninety tons of powder I had there. I shall follow and communicate with you after she leaves

Beaufort for her destination. I think the Louisiana will carry the three hundred tons. She has now two hundred on board, and room for two hundred more, though that would sink her too deep. She has delayed us a little, and our movements had to depend on her.

Very respectfully, your obedient servant,

DAVID D. PORTER,
Rear-Admiral.

[**No. 117.** *See pages* 787 *and* 807.]

NORTH ATLANTIC SQUADRON, U. S. FLAG-SHIP MALVERN,
OFF BEAUFORT, N. C., Dec. 16, 1864.

MAJ.-GEN. B. F. BUTLER,

COMMANDING DEPARTMENT VIRGINIA AND NORTH CAROLINA:

General:—I take advantage of the tug Du Pont, going out, to write you a few lines.

I think all the vessels will leave here to-morrow morning for the rendezvous, and if the weather permits, I think we will be able to blow up the vessel by the next night. In talking with engineers, some of them suggested that even at twenty-five miles the explosion might affect the boilers of steamers, and make them explode if heavy steam was carried; and I would advise that before the explosion takes place, of which you will be duly notified, the steam be run down as low as possible, and the fires drawn.

I hear the rebels have only a small garrison at the forts at New Inlet. I don't know how true it is.

Very respectfully, your obedient servant,

DAVID D. PORTER,
Rear-Admiral.[1]

[**No. 118.** *See page* 787.]

NORTH ATLANTIC SQUADRON, U. S. FLAG-SHIP MALVERN,
AT SEA, Dec. 18, 1864.

MAJ.-GEN. B. F. BUTLER:

General:—The powder vessel Louisiana has gone in to attempt the explosion. The weather looks threatening; the wind may haul to the west, but it is not likely. The barometer is high yet, though the weather does not please me.

. . . .

The powder vessel is as complete as human ingenuity can make her — has two hundred and thirty-five tons of powder, all I could get, though she would not have carried much more.

I propose standing in, the moment the explosion takes place, and open fire with some of the vessels at night, to prevent the enemy repairing damages, if he has any.

. . . .

Very respectfully, your obedient servant,

DAVID D. PORTER,
Rear-Admiral.

---

[1] Report of the Committee on the Conduct of the War, Fort Fisher Expedition, p. 18.

[**No. 119.** *See page* 788.]

TESTIMONY OF MAJ.-GEN. GODFREY WEITZEL.[1]

When Captain Breese came on board he stated to General Butler that the powder-boat would be exploded at twenty minutes after nine o'clock that night, and that the fleet would stand in at daylight. General Butler at once objected to that, saying that if the powder vessel was exploded so early in the night, all the advantage got would be lost entirely. If it had any effect either in injuring the works or the guns, or stunning the garrison, there would be ample time, before the proposed attack of the navy, for the enemy to recover from it. This was my opinion, and also the opinion of Colonel Comstock, of General Grant's staff, very forcibly expressed.

[**No. 120.** *See page* 788.]

TESTIMONY OF BREV. BRIG.-GEN. C. D. COMSTOCK.[2]

After we had spent those three days of good weather off New Inlet in perfect readiness to make the attack if the navy had been ready, in the afternoon of the third day Admiral Porter arrived. He ordered the powder-boat to be taken in and exploded that night. But the wind blew so in the afternoon that it seemed to us impossible to land the troops, and General Weitzel and myself went to Admiral Porter and requested that he should postpone sending in the powder-boat until the water should be smooth enough to enable us to go in and land the troops. He, therefore, sent in discretionary orders to the officer in charge of the powder-boat not to explode it until we could land. The next day the wind blew strongly; our transports had got short of coal and water, and we were forced to go into Beaufort. I was informed by a naval officer remaining there, that while we were gone there was no time when a landing of troops could have been effected, it was so rough; that it was one steady severe gale.

On the 23d of December General Butler sent an officer of his staff to Admiral Porter to inform him that we should be ready to start the next morning. This officer saw Admiral Porter and returned, not getting back until the morning of the 24th. He brought a message from Admiral Porter that the powder-boat would be exploded at one o'clock that morning.

[**No. 121.** *See page* 790.]

NORTH ATLANTIC SQUADRON, U. S. FLAG-SHIP MALVERN, BEAUFORT, N. C., Jan. 9, 1865.

HON. GIDEON WELLES, SECRETARY OF THE NAVY,
 WASHINGTON, D. C.:

Sir:— . . . The military part of the expedition was got up in a most unmilitary manner; the troops were placed in inferior transports that could not condense water, and had a short allowance only on hand; the troops had four days' cooked rations (which were eaten up while lying in the storm at Hampton Roads) and ten days' other rations; there were

---

[1] Report of the Committee on the Conduct of the War, No. 5, p. 70.
[2] Report of the Committee on the Conduct of the War, Fort Fisher Expedition, p. 83.

no intrenching tools of any kind, no siege guns; the whole proceeding indicated that the general depended on the navy silencing the works, and he walking in and taking possession. . . .

I am, sir, very respectfully, your obedient servant,

DAVID D. PORTER,
Rear-Admiral.[1]

[**No. 122.** *See page* 790.]

OFF BEAUFORT, N. C., Dec. 20, 1864, 10.30 A.M.

LIEUT.-GEN. U. S. GRANT:

General: — I have the honor to report that the troops under the command of Major-General Weitzel left Fortress Monroe, as I informed you, on Wednesday, the 14th, and got off Cape Henry at 4 P. M., and arrived the next afternoon at the place of rendezvous designated by Rear-Admiral Porter. Admiral Porter left with the naval squadron the day previous, and as soon as possible after the storm.

We were exceedingly fortunate in our weather, and lay off New Inlet on Friday, Saturday, and Sunday in very smooth water and pleasant weather. The admiral arrived on Sunday evening from Beaufort, having been detained there from Wednesday night for reasons presumed to be satisfactory.

Sunday night the wind freshened, so that it would be impossible to land troops on the outside near Fort Fisher.

The admiral was desirous to explode the torpedo vessel that night at 10 o'clock, and attack the next morning with the fleet, although we might not be able to land. I sent General Weitzel with Colonel Comstock, who agreed with me in opinion, that as the navy did not propose to run by the fort into the river, whatever might be the effect of the explosion, it would be useless unless the troops could be landed to seize the point, and it would specially be inexpedient to explode the torpedo at that hour, giving eight hours for the enemy to repair damages, before the attack even by the fleet was made.

The admiral, upon these representations, countermanded his orders which had been given for the explosion, and we have waited until now for a smooth sea. Last evening I received a telegram from the admiral by signal, saying that the sea was so rough that it would not be possible to land this morning, whereupon I steamed to this port, where I am coaling my ship, and shall return this afternoon.

Very respectfully yours,

BENJ. F. BUTLER,
Major-General.

[**No. 123.** *See page* 792.]

TESTIMONY OF BREV. BRIG.-GEN. C. D. COMSTOCK.[2]

Question. — Did you find any difficulty when you attempted to land the troops?

Answer. — It was easy enough when we commenced to land them. But in the afternoon the wind rose, and by eight o'clock that night it was diffi-

---

[1] Report of the Committee on the Conduct of the War, No. 5, p. 177.
[2] Report of the Committee on the Conduct of the War, Fort Fisher Expedition, p. 84.

cult to land the troops, and by ten or twelve o'clock that night it was impossible to land troops there.

Q. You did not land all your troops?

A. No, sir.

Q. About what portion did you land?

A. I have nothing official in regard to that, but my opinion is that there were about twenty-three hundred landed.

Q. How many troops altogether were with the expedition?

A. About sixty-five hundred.

[No. 124. *See pages* 794 *and* 810.]
Statement of H C. Whiting.[1]

. . . .

Q. 7. How near did the powder-boat which exploded come to the fort?

A. Between twelve (12) and fifteen hundred (1,500) yards, not nearer.

Q. 8. Were you in the fort at that time?

A. I was not.

Q. 9. Was the powder-boat observed; and if so, what, if any, was the effect of the explosion?

A. Powder-boat was observed and reported at midnight aground and set on fire. Explosion reported at 12.45 A. M. No effect at all on the fort. Explosion heard plainly in Wilmington. When I telegraphed Colonel Lamb to know what it was, he replied, " Enemy's gunboat blown up."

. . . .

Q. 11, 12, 13. What was the effect of the naval fire of the first day upon the fort?

How many and what guns did it dismount or disable?

Please state whether any part, and if so, how much of the damage done to the fort by the fire of the navy was repaired during the night?

A. Casualties first day: Killed, none; wounded, one (1) mortally, three (3) severely, and nineteen (19) slightly; total, 23. Five (5) gun-carriages disabled.

Second day: Killed, three (3); wounded, nine (9) mortally, six (6) severely, and twenty-eight (28) slightly; total, 46. Damage but very slight; one (1) 10-inch, two (2) 32-pounder, and one (1) 8-inch carriages disabled, and one (1) 10-inch gun disabled. Damage repaired at night. Enemy's fire formidable and sustained, but diffuse, unconcentrated. Apparent design of the fleet to silence the channel batteries, in order to force an entrance with his vessels, and not to attack by land. The garrison was in no instance driven from its guns, and fired in return, according to orders, slowly and deliberately, six hundred and sixty-two (662) shot and shells.

Q. 14. By reason of the cessation of the bombardment at night, were you not able to rest and recruit your garrison?

A. We were able to do both. . . .

---

[1] Report of the Committee on the Conduct of the War, Fort Fisher Expedition, p. 106.

Q. 17. At the time our skirmish line was deployed before the fort, what was the condition of the guns and defences upon the land side, as to efficiency for a defensive purpose?

A. The guns and defences on the land front were in perfect order at the time referred to, except two (2) disabled guns on the left; nineteen guns in position: palisade in perfect order, and the mines the same, the wires not having been cut.

Q. 18. In view of the condition of the fort and its garrison, would it have been possible, with either three (3) or six (6) thousand men, to have taken the work by assault? (Note. In answering this question, please give as many of the details for the reason you may give as possible.)

A. Possible, yes. Probable, no. The work was very strong, the garrison in good spirits and ready; and the fire on the approaches (the assaulting column having no cover) would have been extraordinarily heavy. In addition to the heavy guns, I had a battery of Napoleons, on which I placed great reliance. The palisade alone would have been a most formidable obstacle.

Q. 19. Please state whether with a force holding the beach, from the nature of the ground and from the configuration of the channel of Cape Fear River, it would have been possible for the Confederates to have reinforced or provisioned the fort to any extent?

A. No difficulty at all by the river. . . .

Q. 21. In view of the condition of the weather immediately following the demonstration of the 25th of December, and in view of the force that might have concentrated upon the peninsula, as well above as below the place of landing, would it, in your judgment, have been possible for six thousand (6,000) men, without artillery, to have held out there, without being captured or overwhelmed, from the 26th of December to the 15th of January?

A. No; and it is a matter of grave charge against General Bragg, that the whole force was not captured on the 26th of December. He had the force and the position.

Q. 22. Please state, as specifically as you may be able, the differences in the condition of the fort from the fire of the navy at the time of the first and second attack. Please state the effect of the fire.

A. There was great difference in the position of the ships in the two attacks, and in the nature and effect of the fire. The first was a general bombardment, not calculated to effect particular damage. The second firing had for definite object the destruction of the land defences, and the ships were placed accordingly, to destroy them by enfilade and direct fire. On that front and the northeast salient the whole enormous fire was poured without intermission, until the slope of the northeast salient was practicable for assault. Not a gun remained in position on the approaches, the whole palisade swept away, communication with the mines cut off, rendering them useless, and the men unable to stand to the parapets during the fire. *There was all the difference in the world.*

Q. 23. Please state whether or not the fire of the navy, at the time of the second attack, was, unlike the time of the first attack, continuous; and if so, for how long, and what number of guns were dismounted by it?

Also, whether the garrison at the time of the second attack had any time to rest or recruit, or even to repair damages?

A. In the second attack the fire was continuous during the night. Not so heavy at night, but enough to prevent repairs, and to keep the garrison from rest and food. The land guns all disabled; field-pieces only left to depend on.

Q. 24. Would you have deemed it the part of wisdom on the part of the commander of the Federal forces to have exposed his troops in the situation referred in question twenty-one?

A. I do not. Neither attack was practicable in the presence of the supporting force, provided that they had been under a competent officer. The first landing ought assuredly to have been captured entirely; and as for the second, although deriving much greater advantages from the different mode of attack by the fleet, and though pressed with greater vigor, it is due to the supineness of the Confederate general that it was not destroyed in the act of assault. . . .

W. H. C. WHITING,

Major-General P. A. C. S., Prisoner of War.

[**No. 125.** *See pages* 794 *and* 796.]

TESTIMONY OF MAJOR-GENERAL WEITZEL.[1]

I pushed a skirmish line to, I think, within about one hundred and fifty yards of the work. I had about three hundred men left in the main body, about eight hundred yards from the work. There was a knoll that had evidently been built for a magazine, an artificial knoll on which I stood, and which gave me a full view of the work and the ground in front of it. I saw that the work, as a defensive work, was not injured at all, except that one gun about midway of the land face was dismounted. I counted sixteen guns all in proper position, which made it evident to me that they had not been injured; because when a gun is injured, you can generally see it from the way in which it stands. The grass slopes of the traverses and of the parapet did not appear broken in the least. The regular shapes of the slopes of the traverses and slopes of the parapets were not disturbed. I did not see a single opening in the row of palisades that was in front of the ditch; it seemed to me perfectly intact.

From all the information which I gained on my first visit to New Inlet, from what I saw on this reconnoissance, together with the information that I had obtained from naval officers who had been on the blockade there for over two years, I was convinced that Fort Fisher was a regular bastioned work; the relief was very high. I had been told by deserters from it that the ditch was about twenty feet wide and six feet deep, and that it was crossed by a bridge. I saw the traverses between each pair of guns, and was perfectly certain within my own mind that they were bomb-proofs; they ought to have been, and they were. It was a stronger work than I had ever seen or heard of being assailed during this war. I have commanded in person three assaulting columns in this war. I have been twice assailed by assaulting columns of the enemy, when I have had my men intrenched. Neither in the first three cases where I assailed the

---

[1] Report of the Committee on the Conduct of the War, Fort Fisher Expedition, p. 72.

enemy's works, nor in the two cases where I was myself assailed, were the works, in an engineering point of view, one eighth as strong as that work was. Both times when I was assaulted by the enemy, the intrenchments behind which my men fought were constructed in one night, and in each case after the men had had two or three days of very hard work. I have been repulsed in every attempt I have made to carry an enemy's work, although I have had as good troops as any in the United States army, and their record shows it. The troops that I had under my command in the first two assaults have been with General Sheridan in the whole of his last campaign — the first division of the Nineteenth Army Corps — and they fought as well under me as they have under him. The third time that I assailed a position was on the Williamsburg road. I had two of the best brigades of the Eighteenth Army Corps. It was a weakly defended line, and not a very strong one. Still I lost a great many men, and was repulsed. In the two instances where the enemy assaulted my position they were repulsed with heavy loss.

After that experience, with the information I had obtained from reading and study—for before this war I was an instructor at the Military Academy for three years under Professor Mahan, on these very subjects — remembering well the remark of the lieutenant-general commanding, that it was his intention I should command that expedition, because another officer selected by the War Department had once shown timidity, and in face of the fact that I had been appointed a major-general only twenty days before, and needed confirmation ; notwithstanding all that, I went back to General Butler, and told him I considered it would be murder to order an attack on that work with that force. I understood Colonel Comstock to agree with me perfectly, although I did not ask him, and General Butler has since said that he did.

Upon my report, General Butler himself reconnoitred the work, ran up close with the Chamberlain, and took some time to look at it. He then said that he agreed with me, and directed the re-embarkation of the troops. The troops were re-embarked, and we came back to Fortress Monroe, to our camp. When we stopped at City Point going up, to permit Colonel Comstock to disembark, General Butler went ashore, as he told me, to see General Grant. Upon his return, I asked him whether the general was satisfied with what we had done. He said, yes, he was perfectly satisfied with it.

Question.—Who was that officer, selected by the War Department, to whom General Grant objected ?

Answer.—General Gillmore.

[No. 126. *See page* 798.]

HEADQUARTERS DEPARTMENT OF VIRGINIA AND NORTH CAROLINA,
ARMY OF THE JAMES, IN THE FIELD, Jan. 3, 1865.

LIEUT.-GEN. U. S. GRANT,

COMMANDING ARMIES OF THE UNITED STATES :

General :— On the 7th of December last, in obedience to your orders, I moved a force of about sixty-five hundred efficient men, consisting of General Ames' division of the Twenty-Fourth Corps, and General Paine's division of the Twenty-Fifth Corps, under command of Major-General Weitzel, to an encampment near Bermuda.

On the 8th the troops embarked for Fortress Monroe.

On the 9th, Friday, I reported to Rear-Admiral Porter that the army portion of the conjoint expedition directed against Wilmington was ready to proceed.

We waited there Saturday the 10th, Sunday the 11th, and Monday the 12th.

On the 12th, Rear-Admiral Porter informed me that the naval fleet would sail on the 13th, but would be obliged to put into Beaufort to take on board ammunition for the monitors.

The expedition having become the subject of remark, fearing lest its destination should get to the enemy, in order to divert from it all attention, on the morning of Tuesday the 13th, at three o'clock, I ordered the transport fleet to proceed up the Potomac during the day to Matthias Point, so as to be plainly visible to the scouts and signal men of the enemy on the northern neck, and to retrace their course at night and anchor under the lee of Cape Charles.

Having given the navy thirty-six hours' start, at 12 o'clock noon of the 14th, Wednesday, I joined the transport fleet off Cape Henry, and put to sea, arriving at the place of rendezvous off New Inlet, near Fort Fisher, on the evening of the 15th, Thursday.

We there waited for the navy Friday, the 16th, Saturday, the 17th, and Sunday, the 18th, during which days we had the finest possible weather and the smoothest sea.

On the evening of the 18th, Admiral Porter came from Beaufort to the place of rendezvous. That evening the sea became rough, and on Monday, the 19th, the wind sprang up freshly, so that it was impossible to land troops; and by the advice of Admiral Porter, communicated to me by letter, I directed the transport fleet to rendezvous at Beaufort. This was a matter of necessity, because the transport fleet, being coaled and watered for ten days, had already waited that time, to wit: from the 9th, the day on which we were ready to sail, to the 19th.

On the 20th, Tuesday, 21st, Wednesday, 22d, Thursday, and 23d, Friday, it blew a gale. I was occupied in coaling and watering the transport fleet at Beaufort.

The Baltic, having a large supply of coal, was enabled to remain at the place of rendezvous, with a brigade on board of twelve hundred men, and General Ames reported to Admiral Porter that he would co-operate with him.

On the 23d, I sent Captain Clarke, of my staff, from Beaufort, on the fast-sailing armed steamer Chamberlain, to Admiral Porter, to inform him that on the evening of the 24th I would again be at the rendezvous with the transport fleet, for the purpose of commencing the attack, the weather permitting.

At four o'clock, on the evening of the 24th, I came in sight of Fort Fisher, and found the naval fleet engaged in bombarding, the powder vessel having been exploded on the morning previous about one o'clock.

Through General Weitzel, I arranged with Admiral Porter to commence the landing under the cover of the gunboats as early as eight o'clock the next morning, if possible, as soon as the fire of the Half-Moon and Flag-Pond Hill batteries had been silenced. These are up the shore some two or three miles above Fort Fisher.

Admiral Porter was quite sanguine that he had silenced the guns of Fort Fisher. He was then urged, if that were so, to run by the fort into Cape Fear River, and then the troops could land and hold the beach without liability of being shelled by the enemy's gunboats (or the Tallahassee being seen in the river).

It is to be remarked that Admiral Farragut, even, had never taken a fort except by running by and cutting it off from all prospect of reinforcements, as at Fort Jackson and Fort Morgan, and that no casemated fort had been silenced by naval fire during the war. That if the admiral would put his ships in the river the army could supply him across the beach, as we had proposed to do Farragut at Fort St. Philip. That at least the blockade of Wilmington would be thus effectual, even if we did not capture the fort. To that the admiral replied that he should probably lose a boat by torpedoes if he attempted to run by.

He was reminded that the army might lose five hundred men by the assault, and that his boat would not weigh in the balance, even in a money point of view, for a moment, with the lives of the men. The admiral declined going by, and the expedition was deprived of that essential element of success.

At 12 o'clock noon of the 25th, Sunday, Captain Glisson, commanding the covering divisions of the fleet, reported the batteries silenced and his vessels in position to cover our landing.

The transport fleet, following my flag-ship, stood in within eight hundred yards of the beach, and at once commenced debarking. The landing was successfully effected. Finding that the reconnoitring party just landed could hold the shore, I determined to land a force with which an assault might be attempted.

Brevet Brigadier-General Curtis, who deserves well for his gallantry and conduct, immediately pushed up his brigade within a few hundred yards of Fort Fisher, capturing the Half-Moon battery and its men, who were taken off by the boats of the navy.

This skirmish line advanced to within seventy-five yards of the fort, protected by the glacis which had been thrown up in such form as to give cover, the garrison being completely kept in their bomb-proofs by the fire of the navy, which was very rapid and continuous, their shells bursting over the work with very considerable accuracy. At this time we lost ten men, wounded on the skirmish line by the shells from the fleet.

Quitting my flag-ship I went on board the Chamberlain and ran in within a few hundred yards of the fort, so that it was plainly visible.

It appeared to be a square bastioned work of very high relief, say fifteen feet, surrounded by a wet ditch some fifteen feet wide. I was protected from being enveloped by an assaulting force by a stockade which extended from the fort to the sea on the one side, and from the marshes of Cape Fear River to the salient on the other.

No material damage to the fort as a defensive work had been done.

Seventeen heavy guns bore up the beach, protected from the fire of the navy by traverses eight or ten feet high, which were undoubtedly bomb-proof shelters for the garrison.

With the garrison kept within their bomb-proofs it was easy to maintain this position; but the shells of the navy, which kept the enemy in their bomb-proofs, would keep my troops out. When those ceased falling the parapet was fully manned.

Lieutenant Walling, of the One Hundred and Forty-Second New York, pressed up to the edge of the ditch, and captured a flag which had been cut down by a shell from the navy. It is a mistake, as was at first reported to me, that any soldier entered the fort. An orderly was killed about a third of a mile from the fort, and his horse taken.

In the meantime the remainder of Ames' division had captured two hundred and eighteen men and ten commissioned officers of the North Carolina reserves, and other prisoners. From them I learned that Kirkland's and Hagood's brigades of Hoke's division had left the front of the Army of the James, near Richmond, and were then within two miles of the rear of my forces, and their skirmishers were then actually engaged, and that the remainder of Hoke's division had come the night before to Wilmington, and were then on the march, if they had not already arrived.

I learned, also, that these troops had left Richmond on Tuesday, the 20th.

Knowing the strength of Hoke's division, I found a force opposed to me outside of the works larger than my own.

In the meantime the weather assumed a threatening aspect. The surf began to roll in so that the landing became difficult. At this time General Weitzel reported to me that to assault the work, in his judgment, and in that of the experienced officers of his command who had been on the skirmish line, with any prospect of success, was impossible.

This opinion coincided with my own, and much as I regretted the necessity of abandoning the attempt, yet the path of duty was plain. Not so strong a work as Fort Fisher had been taken by assault during the war, and I had to guide me the experience of Port Hudson, with its slaughtered thousands in the repulsed assault, and the double assault of Fort Wagner, where thousands were sacrificed in an attempt to take a work less strong than Fisher, after it had been subjected to a more continued and fully as severe fire. And in neither of the instances I have mentioned had the assaulting force in its rear, as I had, an army of the enemy larger than itself.

I therefore ordered that no assault should be made, and that the troops should re-embark.

While superintending the preparations for this, the fire of the navy ceased. Instantly the guns of the fort were fully manned, and a sharp fire of musketry, grape, and canister swept the plain over which the column must have advanced, and the skirmish line was returning.

Working with what diligence we could, it was impossible to get the troops again on board before the sea ran so high as to render further re-embarkation, or even the sending of supplies ashore, impossible. I lay by the shore until eleven o'clock the next day, Monday, the 26th, when, having made all proper dispositions for getting the troops on board, I gave orders to the transport fleet, as fast as they were ready, to sail for Fortress Monroe, in obedience to my instructions from the lieutenant-general.

I learned, from deserters and prisoners captured, that the supposition upon which the lieutenant-general directed the expedition, that Wilmington had been denuded of troops to oppose General Sherman, was correct. That at the time when the army arrived off Wilmington, there were less than four hundred men in the garrison of Fort Fisher, and less than a thousand within twenty miles.

But the delay of three days of good weather, the 16th, 17th, and 18th, waiting for the arrival of the navy, and the further delay from the terrible storm of the 21st, 22d, and 23d, gave time for troops to be brought from Richmond, three divisions of which were either there or on the road.

The instructions of the lieutenant-general to me did not contemplate a siege; I had neither siege trains nor supplies for such a contingency.

The exigency of possible delay, for which the foresight of the commander of the armies had provided, had arisen, to wit: the larger reinforcement of the garrison. This, together with the fact that the navy had exhausted their supply of ammunition in the bombardment, left me with no alternative but to return with my troops to the Army of the James.

The loss of the opportunity of Friday, Saturday, and Sunday, the 16th, 17th, and 18th, was the immediate cause of the failure of the expedition.

It is not my province even to suggest blame to the navy for their delay of four days at Beaufort. I know none of the reasons which do or do not justify it. It is to be presumed they are sufficient.

I am happy to bring to the attention of the lieutenant-general the excellent behavior of the troops, both officers and men, which was all that could be desired.

I am under special obligations to Captain Glisson, of the Santiago de Cuba, for the able and efficient manner in which he covered our landing; to Captain Alden, of the Brooklyn, for his prompt assistance and the excellent gunnery with which the Brooklyn cleared the shores of all opposers at the moment of debarkation. Lieutenant Farquhar, of the navy, having in charge the navy boats which assisted in the landing, deserves great credit for the energy and skill with which he managed the boats through the rolling surf. Especial commendation is due to Brigadier-General Graham and the officers and men of his naval brigade, for the organization of his boats and crews for landing, and the untiring energy and industry with which they all labored in re-embarking the troops during the stormy night of the 25th and the days following. For this and other meritorious services during the campaign since the first of May, which have heretofore been brought to the notice of the lieutenant-general in my official reports, I would respectfully but earnestly recommend General Graham for promotion.

The number of prisoners captured by us was three hundred, including twelve officers, two heavy rifled guns, two light guns, and six caissons.

The loss of the army was one man drowned, two men killed, one officer captured, who accidentally wandered through our pickets, and ten men wounded, while upon the picket line, by the shells of the navy.

Always chary of mentioning with commendation the acts of my own personal staff, yet I think the troops who saw it will agree to the cool courage and daring of Lieut. Sidney B. DeKay, aide-de-camp, in landing on the night of the 25th, and remaining aiding in re-embarkation on the 27th.

For the details of the landing and the operations, I beg leave to refer you to the reports of Major-General Weitzel, commanding the division landed, which are hereto appended.

Trusting my action will meet with the approval of the lieutenant-general, this report is respectfully submitted.

Benjamin F. Butler,
Major-General.

[*Official copy.*]

E. D. Townsend, *Assistant Adjutant-General.*

Adjutant-General's Office, Nov. 18, 1865.[1]

[No. 127. See page 798.]

Headquarters Department Virginia and North Carolina,[2]
Fortress Monroe, Dec. 27, 1864, 8 p. m.

Lieut.-Gen. U. S. Grant, City Point, Virginia :

I have just returned from the expedition. We had a storm from Monday until Friday, which was the earliest hour I could get out of Beaufort, where I had put in for coal, most of the transport fleet having got out of coal and water. Without waiting for my return Admiral Porter exploded the torpedo at one (1) o'clock on Friday morning and commenced his attack at twelve fifty-five (12.55) in the afternoon, twelve hours afterwards. He continued the bombardment of the fort until night. I arrived in the evening and commenced landing on the beach the next morning; got a portion on shore about two (2) o'clock. Weitzel moved down upon the works, capturing three hundred (300) men and ten (10) commissioned officers. He brought his picket line within fifty (50) yards of the work, when he was opened upon by canister and musketry. He found seventeen (17) guns bearing upon the beach, which was only wide enough for an assault of a thousand men in line, the guns protected by traverses, and but one (1) dismounted, notwithstanding the fire of the fleet had been opened upon them for five (5) hours. In the meanwhile the surf had so arisen as to render further landing nearly impracticable. After a thorough reconnoissance of the work, finding it utterly impracticable for a land assault, and that at least two (2) brigades of Hoke's division from before Richmond had arrived there, and that the rest was on the road, I withdrew the forces and ordered a re-embarkment, and had got on board all of the troops, with the exception of about six

---

[1] Report of the Committee on the Conduct of the War, Fort Fisher, p. 35.
[2] Report before the Committee on the Conduct of the War, Fort Fisher, p. 26.

hundred (600), when the surf was so high as to prevent either getting on or off the shore. I lay by until morning and took measures for their relief as soon as the sea might go down. They were under cover of the gunboats, and I have no doubt they are all safely off.

Our loss when I left was but twelve (12) wounded, ten (10) of whom were by the shells of the navy on our picket line near the fort. I will be up in the morning.

Benj. F. Butler,
Major-General Commanding.

[No. 128. See page 803.]

Extract from Report of Commodore W. N. Jeffers.[1]

The remainder of the powder put on board at Norfolk, making in all one hundred and eighty-five (185) tons, was stowed against the after bulkhead of the deck-house, and filled the space over the boiler, extending as far as the hatch to the after hold or coal-bunker, leaving about four fifths of the space in the deck-house empty. . . .

When the probable effects of the explosion were under discussion, it was the unanimous opinion of the experts in ordnance that, to produce the maximum effect, the fire should be communicated, and the explosion take place in many points simultaneously, all the accounts of accidental explosions of large quantities of powder agreeing that large quantities of unconsumed powder were blown away from the focus of ignition, causing a great reduction of effect.

Electricity was proposed as offering the most probable means of securing this result; but as this agent is known to be very unreliable in action, it was determined to use several clockwork arrangements, a slow match, and finally to set the vessel on fire to insure an ultimate explosion, and not bestow so large a quantity of material on the enemy in the event of a failure of one or more of the modes of exploding it.

The arrangement of the clockwork being confided to me, I made a very simple one. Removing the face and hands of an ordinary marine clock, I secured to the arbor of the minute-hand a small cylinder with four pins set into the circumference, and equidistant — that is, fifteen (15) minutes of time apart. Three clocks were thus arranged. These clocks were secured to a board; by the side of the clock a copper tube was secured, in the bottom of which was brazed a mass of metal with a common musket cone screwed into it, to be capped with a percussion cap.

An eight-inch grape shot, weight two pounds, diameter 2.5 inches, was attached to one end of a piece of catgut which was led through an eyebolt at the top of the tube, and hooked by a loop in the other end, over one of the pins on the clock cylinder. It is easy to see that by the revolution of the cylinder the loop would slip off, the grape shot drop, and the explosion of the cap take place in 15′, 30′, 45′, or 60′, as desired; this it never failed to do in many trials. I frequently set the three clocks going, and the explosion occurred within two minutes of each other at the end of an hour. To determine the time of explosion it was only neces-

---

[1] Report before the Committee on the Conduct of the War, No. 5, p. 249.

sary to put the loop over the proper pin, remove a stop, and set the apparatus in motion.

Major Rodman arranged with great care, and after numerous experiments, to insure safety and certainty, the slow matches, six in number, which were to be distributed in as many places.

In the event of the electricity failing the clocks were to be the next dependence; it was, therefore, necessary to so distribute them that in case the vessel was boarded from the shore they could not be conveniently reached; and also to lead the flame rapidly to many points.

This it was proposed to accomplish by the aid of the "Gomez fuse train," which is incomparably quicker in its action than the flame of gunpowder, approximating electricity.

From each clock and each slow-match this train was to be laid through the exterior layers of bags in the deck-house and into each hatch; and, in order to secure this simultaneous ignition in many places, the fuse train from each of the clocks was to be grafted into the other fuse train from each of the other clocks at all points of crossing.

By the report of Admiral Porter it would appear that the powder was finally exploded from the effects of a fire kindled in the forecastle; no results of value were to be expected from this mode. It was proposed only as a final resort in order to prevent the vessel in any contingency from falling into the hands of the enemy. It was certain that the greater portion of the powder would be blown away if ignited in a single point, and the effect very much diminished.

The three explosions spoken of are readily accounted for, the deck-house, the after hold, and the berth-deck would take fire in succession if ignited at one point.

I cannot in any way account for the failure of the clocks, if set to the proper time, except on the supposition that possibly the turn on the cylinder may have been taken the wrong way, and instead of unwinding they wound up the balls!

I am not aware that any attempt was made to use the electric wire; but it was not favorably considered by those charged with the execution of the plan. Mr. Beardslee, who was to undertake this matter, came to Norfolk, made himself acquainted with the requirements and returned to New York to obtain the necessary means, but had not reached Norfolk when the vessel sailed.

A part of the programme required that the vessel should be grounded, which appears not to have been the case. No very sanguine expectations were entertained of a successful result unless the vessel could be placed within three hundred yards, and then only after all the precautions had been taken to insure a maximum effect.

[**No. 129.** *See pages 804 and 806.*]

TESTIMONY OF COMMANDER A. C. RHIND, U. S. N.[1]

The fuses were set by the clocks to one hour and a half, but the explosion did not occur till twenty-two minutes after that time had elapsed, the after part of the vessel being then enveloped in flames.

---

[1] Report before the Committee on the Conduct of the War, Fort Fisher, p. 131.

[**No. 130.** *See page* 804.]
UNITED STATES STEAMER AGAWAN,
NAVY YARD, NORFOLK, Feb. 2, 1865.
REAR-ADMIRAL D. D. PORTER, COMMANDING N. A. B. SQUADRON:

Admiral : — . . . No part of the fuse used was circulated through the parts of the vessel already stowed (marked N. and E.), and it was impossible to place it there without breaking out the cargo. On the arrival of the vessel at Beaufort, about thirty tons more powder was put in her, making in all about 215 tons, as much as the vessel would carry without being too deep in the water. . . .

As to my " impression of the results and the effect produced," I stated in my report to you of December 26, that, owing to the want of confinement and insufficient fusing of the mass, that much of the powder was blown away before ignition, and its effects lost. . . .

Respectfully, your obedient servant,
A. C. RHIND,
Commander.[1]

[**No. 131.** *See page* 806.]

. . . The death of the gallant Preston, who fell in the subsequent assault upon Fort Fisher, deprives the record of his written testimony; but in an interview with Commander Wise, while in Washington as a bearer of despatches, he stated that he heard two distinct explosions; others said that they heard three; but this was not his opinion. He could see, however, repeated explosions in the air, evidently those of the ignited powder bags which had been thrown up by the explosion of the lower strata of powder. . . .

[**No. 132.** *See page* 808.]
REPORT OF T. J. RODMAN, MAJOR OF ORDNANCE AND MEMBER OF
THE COMMISSION THAT DEVISED THE CLOCKWORK.[2]

By report of Admiral Porter it would appear that the powder was finally exploded from the effects of a fire kindled in the forecastle. No results of value were to be expected from this mode. It was proposed only as a final resort, in order to prevent the vessel in any contingency from falling into the hands of the enemy. It was certain that the greater portion of the powder would be blown away if ignited in a single point, and the effect very much diminished. The three explosions spoken of are readily accounted for — the deck-house, the after-hold, and the berth-deck would take fire in succession if ignited at one point.

[**No. 133.** *See page* 808.]
REPORT OF D. D. PORTER, DEC. 26, 1864.[3]

The gallant party, after coolly making all their arrangements for the explosion, left the vessel. The last thing that they did was to set her on fire under the cabin. Then taking to their boats, they made their escape

---
[1] Report before the Committee on the Conduct of the War, No. 5, p. 252.
[2] Report before the Committee on the Conduct of the War, Fort Fisher, p. 251.
[3] Report to Secretary of Navy of D. D. Porter, Dec. 26, 1864. Fort Fisher, p. 123.

off to the Wilderness, lying close by. The Wilderness then put off shore with good speed to avoid any ill-effects that might happen from the explosion. At forty-five minutes past one of the morning of the 24th, the explosion took place, and the shock was nothing like so severe as was expected. It shook the vessel some, and broke one or two glasses, but nothing more.

[**No. 134.** *See page* 808.]

BUREAU OF ORDNANCE, NAVY DEPARTMENT, Jan. 10, 1865.

REAR-ADMIRAL D. D. PORTER, U. S. N.,

COMMANDING N. A. B. SQUADRON, OFF WILMINGTON, N. C.:

Sir : — The bureau desires that you will direct the officers who were in charge of the powder-boat, recently exploded near Fort Fisher, to forward to the bureau a full and detailed statement, *but secret and confidential,* of all the circumstances connected with the arrangement of the powder, the fuses, and other appliances intended to secure a uniform and simultaneous explosion, together with the manner in which the plan was executed, and their impressions of the result and the effects produced.

This information is desired as early as practicable.

I am, sir, your obedient servant,

H. A. WISE,
Chief of Bureau.[1]

[**No. 135.** *See pages* 809 *and* 819.]

U. S. FLAG-SHIP MALVERN, OFF FORT FISHER, Jan. 15, 1865.

HON. GIDEON WELLES, SECRETARY OF THE NAVY, WASHINGTON, D. C.:

Sir : — I have the honor to inform you that we have possession of Fort Fisher and the fall of surrounding works will soon follow. As I informed you in my last, we had commenced operations with the iron vessels, which bombarded while we landed the troops. On the 14th, I ordered all vessels carrying eleven-inch guns to bombard, with the Ironsides — the Brooklyn taking the lead. By sunset the fort was reduced to a pulp; every gun was silenced, by being injured or covered up with earth, so that they would not work. . . .

It is a matter of great regret to me to see my gallant officers and men so cut up, but I was unwilling to let the troops undertake the capture of the works without the navy's sharing with them the peril all were anxious to undergo, and we should have had the honor of meeting our brothers in arms in the works had the sailors been properly supported. We have lost about two hundred in killed and wounded, and among them some gallant officers. . . .

I don't suppose there ever was a work subjected to such a terrific bombardment, or where the appearance of a fort was more altered. There is not a spot of earth about the fort that has not been torn up by our shells. . . .

I am, sir, very respectfully, your obedient servant,

DAVID D. PORTER,
Rear-Admiral.[2]

---

[1] Report before the Committee on the Conduct of the War, No. 5, p. 243.
[2] Report before the Committee on the Conduct of the War, No. 5, p. 182.

[**No. 136.** *See page* 814.]

THE DEFENCES OF FORT FISHER.[1]

By its Commander, William Lamb, Colonel, C. S. A.

. . . Lee sent me word that Fort Fisher must be held, or he could not subsist his army. . . .

At the land face of Fort Fisher, five miles from the intrenched camp, the peninsula was about half a mile wide. This face commenced about a hundred feet from the river with a half bastion, and extended with a heavy curtain to a full bastion on the ocean side, where it joined the sea face. The work was built to withstand the heaviest artillery fire. There was no moat with scarp and counterscarp, so essential for defence against storming parties, the shifting sands rendering its construction impossible with the material available. The outer slope was twenty feet high from the berme to the top of the parapet, at an angle of forty-five degrees, and was sodded with marsh grass, which grew luxuriantly. The parapet was not less than twenty-five feet thick, with an inclination of only one foot. The revetment was five feet nine inches high from the floor of the gun-chambers, and these were some twelve feet or more from the interior plane. The guns were all mounted in barbette, on Columbiad carriages; there was not a single casemated gun in the fort. Experience had taught that casemates of timber and sand-bags were a delusion and a snare against heavy projectiles; and there was no iron to construct them with. Between the gun-chambers, containing one or two guns each (there were twenty heavy guns on the land face), there were heavy traverses, exceeding in size any known to engineers, to protect from an enfilading fire. They extended out some twelve feet on the parapet, and were twelve feet or more in height above the parapet, running back thirty feet or more. The gun-chambers were reached from the rear by steps. In each traverse was an alternate magazine or bomb-proof, the latter ventilated by an air-chamber. Passageways penetrated the traverses in the interior of the work, forming additional bomb-proofs for the reliefs of the guns.

The sea face for a hundred yards from the northeast bastion was of the same massive character as the land face. A crescent battery, intended for four guns, joined this. It had been originally built of palmetto logs and tarred sand-bags, and sand-rivetted with sod; but the logs had decayed, and it was converted into a hospital bomb-proof. In its rear a heavy curtain was thrown up to protect the chambers from fragments of shells. From this bomb-proof a series of batteries extended for three quarters of a mile along the sea, connected by an infantry curtain. These batteries had heavy traverses, but were not more than ten or twelve feet high to the top of the parapets, and were built for ricochet firing. On this line was a bomb-proof electric battery, connected with a system of submarine torpedoes. Farther along, where the channel ran close to the beach, inside the bar, a mound battery, sixty feet high, was erected, with two heavy guns, which had a plunging fire on the channel; this was connected with the battery north of it by a light curtain. Following the line of the

---

[1] From the "Century War Books."

works, it was over one mile from the mound to the northeast bastion at the angle of the sea and land faces, and upon this line twenty-four heavy guns were mounted. From the mound to nearly a mile to the end of the point was a level sand plain, scarcely three feet above high tide, and much of it was submerged during gales. At the point was Battery Buchanan, four guns, in the shape of an ellipse, commanding the inlet, its two eleven-inch guns covering the approach by land. It was garrisoned by a detachment from the Confederate States navy. An advanced redoubt with a twenty-four-pounder was added after the attack by the forces under General Butler and Admiral Porter on Christmas, 1864. A wharf for large steamers was in close proximity to these works. Battery Buchanan was a citadel to which an overpowered garrison might retreat, and, with proper transportation, be safely carried off at night, and to which reinforcements could be sent under the cover of darkness. . . .

As a defence against infantry there was a system of sub-terra torpedoes extending across the peninsula, five to six hundred feet from the land face and so disconnected that the explosion of one would not affect the others; inside the torpedoes, about fifty feet from the berme of the work, extending from river-bank to seashore, was a heavy palisade of sharpened logs nine feet high, pierced for musketry, and so laid out as to have an enfilading fire on the centre, where there was a redoubt guarding a sally-port, from which two Napoleons were run out as occasion required. At the river end of the palisade was a deep and muddy slough, across which was a bridge, the entrance on the river road into the fort; commanding this bridge was a Napoleon gun. There were three mortars in rear of the land face.

[**No. 137.** *See page* 818.]

NORTH ATLANTIC SQUADRON, U. S. FLAG-SHIP MALVERN,
OFF FORT FISHER, Jan. 17, 1865.

HON. GIDEON WELLES, SECRETARY OF THE NAVY,
WASHINGTON, D. C.:

Sir: — . . . I have since visited Fort Fisher and the adjoining works, and find their strength greatly beyond what I had conceived. An engineer might be excusable in saying they could not be captured except by regular siege. I wonder even now how it was done. The work, as I said before, is really stronger than the Malakoff tower, which defied so long the combined power of France and England; and yet it is captured by a handful of men under the fire of the guns of the fleet, and in seven hours after the attack commenced in earnest. . . . We expended, in the bombardment, about fifty thousand shells, and have as much more on hand.

I am, sir, very respectfully, your obedient servant,

DAVID D. PORTER,
Rear-Admiral.[1]

---

[1] Conduct of the War, No. 5, p. 187.

[**No. 138.** *See pages* 810, 811, 818, *and* 819.]

NORTH ATLANTIC SQUADRON, UNITED STATES FLAG-SHIP MALVERN,
BEAUFORT, N. C., Dec. 29, 1864.

HON. GIDEON WELLES, SECRETARY OF THE NAVY,
WASHINGTON, D. C.:

Sir: — . . . Well, sir, it could have been taken on Christmas with five hundred men, without losing a soldier; there were not twenty men in the forts, and those were poor, miserable, panic-stricken people, cowering there with fear, while one or two desperate men in one of the upper casemates, some distance above Fort Fisher, managed to fire one gun that seldom hit anyone. . . .

General Weitzel went on shore, determined what the report of the defences would be, for General Butler had made an opinion for him. The department, sir, has no cause to be dissatisfied with the share the navy has taken in this affair; the ships did their work so beautifully that you will hear of but one opinion expressed by lookers-on.

If this temporary failure succeeds in sending General Butler into private life, it is not to be regretted, for it cost only a certain amount of shells, which I would expend in a month's target practice anyhow. . . .

I am, sir, very respectfully, your obedient servant,

DAVID D. PORTER,
Rear-Admiral.[1]

[**No. 139.** *See pages* 809, 818, *and* 819.]

NORTH ATLANTIC SQUADRON, U. S. FLAG-SHIP MALVERN,
BEAUFORT, N. C., Dec. 31, 1864.

HON. GIDEON WELLS, SECRETARY OF THE NAVY,
WASHINGTON, D. C.:

. . . General Bragg must have been very agreeably disappointed when he saw our troops going away without firing a shot, and to see an expedition costing millions of dollars given up when the hollowness of the rebel shell was about to be exposed. . . .

I am, sir, very respectfully, your obedient servant,

DAVID D. PORTER,
Rear-Admiral.[2]

[**No. 140.** *See page* 818.]

PORTER'S REPORT OF DEC. 29 TO HON. GIDEON WELLES, SECRETARY
OF THE NAVY.

At no time did I permit the vessels to open on them with all their batteries, limiting some of them to about two shots a minute, and permitting the large vessels to fight only one division of guns at a time.

---

[1] Conduct of the War, No. 5, p. 169.
[2] Conduct of the War, No. 5, p. 171.

[**No. 141.**   *See pages* 810 *and* 818.]

NORTH ATLANTIC SQUADRON, UNITED STATES FLAG-SHIP MALVERN,
AT SEA, OFF NEW INLET, NORTH CAROLINA, Dec. 26.

HON. GIDEON WELLES, SECRETARY OF THE NAVY:

. . . At daylight, on the 24th, the fleet got under way, and stood in, in line of battle. At 11.30 A. M. the signal was made to engage the forts, the Ironsides leading, and the Monadnock, Canonicus, and Mahopac following. The Ironsides took her position in the most beautiful and seamanlike manner, got her spring out, and opened deliberate fire on the fort, which was firing at her with all its guns, which did not seem numerous in the northeast face, though we counted what appeared to be seventeen guns; but four or five of these were fired from that direction, and they were silenced almost as soon as the Ironsides opened her terrific battery.

The Minnesota then took her position in handsome style, and her guns, after getting the range, were fired with rapidity, while the Mohican, Colorado, and the large vessels marked on the plan, got to their stations, all firing to cover themselves while anchoring. By the time the last of the large vessels anchored and got their batteries into play, but one or two guns of the enemy were fired, this *feu d'enfer* driving them all to their bomb-proofs.

The small gunboats Kansas, Unadilla, Pequot, Seneca, Pontoosuc, Yantic, and Huron took positions to the northward and eastward of the monitors, and enfilading the works.

The Shenandoah, Ticonderoga, Mackinaw, Tacony, and Vanderbilt took effective positions as marked on the chart, and added their fire to that already begun.

The Santiago de Cuba, Fort Jackson, Osceola, Chippewa, Sassacus, Rhode Island, Monticello, Quaker City, and Iosco dropped into position according to order, and the battle became general. In one hour and fifteen minutes after the first shot was fired, not a shot came from the fort. Two magazines had been blown up by our shells, and the fort set on fire in several places; and such a torrent of missiles were falling into and bursting over it that it was impossible for anything human to stand it. Finding that the batteries were silenced completely, I directed the ships to keep up a moderate fire in hopes of attracting the attention of the transports and bringing them in. At sunset General Butler came in, in his flag-ship, with a few transports (the rest not having arrived from Beaufort).

Being too late to do anything more, I signalled the fleet to retire for the night for a safe anchorage, which they did without being molested by the enemy.

There were some mistakes made this day when the vessels went in to take position. My plan of battle being based on accurate calculation, and made from information to be relied on, was placed in the hands of each commander, and it seemed impossible to go astray if it was strictly followed.

I required those vessels that had not followed it closely to get under way and assume their proper positions, which was done promptly and without confusion. The vessels were placed somewhat nearer to the works and were able to throw in their shell which were before falling into the water.

One or two leading vessels having made the mistake of anchoring too far off, caused those coming after them to commit a like error; but when they all got into place, and commenced work in earnest, the shower of shell (115 per minute) was irresistible. So quickly were the enemy's guns silenced that not an officer or man was injured. . . .

At 7 A. M., on the 25th, I made signal to get under way and form in line of battle, which was quickly done. The order to attack was given, and the Ironsides took position in her usual handsome style, the monitors following close after her. All the vessels followed according to order, and took position without a shot being fired at them, excepting a few shots fired at the four last vessels that got into line.

The firing this day was slow, *only sufficient to amuse* the enemy while the army landed, which they were doing five miles to the eastward of the fleet. . . .

In the bombardment of the 25th the men were engaged firing slowly for seven hours. The rebels kept a couple of guns on the upper batteries firing on the vessels, hitting some of them several times without doing much damage. The Wabash and Powhatan being within their range, the object seemed mainly to disable them, but a rapid fire soon closed them up. Everything was coolly and systematically done throughout the day, and I witnessed some beautiful practice. . . .

I am, sir, very respectfully, your obedient servant,

DAVID D. PORTER,

Rear-Admiral.[1]

[**No. 142.** *See page* 819.]

NORTH ATLANTIC SQUADRON, U. S. FLAG-SHIP MALVERN,
OFF WILMINGTON, Dec. 24, 1864.

HON. GIDEON WELLES, SECRETARY OF THE NAVY,
WASHINGTON, D. C.:

Sir: — I have the honor to inform you that I attacked the forts at the mouth of the Cape Fear River this morning at 12.30, and after getting the ships in position, *silenced it in about an hour and a half,* there being no troops here to take possession. I am merely firing at it now to keep up practice. The forts are nearly demolished, and as soon as troops come we can take possession; we have set them on fire, blown some of them up, and all that is wanted now is troops to land to go into them.

I suppose General Butler will be here in the morning. We have had very heavy gales here, which tugs, monitors, and all rode out at their anchors. The transports have gone into Beaufort, North Carolina.

I am, sir, very respectfully, your obedient servant,

DAVID D. PORTER.

[1] Conduct of the War, No. 5, p. 122.

[**No. 143.** *See page* 819.]

NORTH ATLANTIC SQUADRON,
FLAG-SHIP MALVERN, Jan. 2, 1865.

. . . Fire deliberately. Fill the vessels up with every shell they can carry, and fire to dismount the guns, and knock away the traverses. The angle near the ships has heavy casemates; knock it away. Concentrate fire always on one point. With the guns disabled, the fort will soon be ours. . . .

DAVID D. PORTER,
Rear-Admiral, Commanding North Atlantic Squadron.[1]

NORTH ATLANTIC SQUADRON,
FLAG-SHIP MALVERN, Jan. 9, 1865.

. . . If practicable, the New Ironsides and the monitors will be ordered on to bombard the fort and dismount the guns while the troops are getting on shore. This will be done when the signal is made to the New Ironsides to attack, the monitors following her. . . .

DAVID D. PORTER,
Rear Admiral, Commanding North Atlantic Squadron.[2]

[**No. 144.** *See page* 824.]

NORTH ATLANTIC SQUADRON, U. S. FLAG-SHIP MALVERN,
CAPE FEAR RIVER, Jan. 24, 1865.

HON. GIDEON WELLES, SECRETARY OF THE NAVY,
WASHINGTON, D. C.:

My Dear Sir: — I received your kind letter of the 17th inst., and thank you warmly for the confidence you repose in my opinion that this place could be taken.

To the Navy Department alone is the country indebted for the capture of this rebel stronghold, for had it not been for your perseverance in keeping this fleet here, and your constant propositions made to the army, nothing would have been done. As it was, after the proposition had been received and General Grant promised that the troops should be sent, it was not done until General Butler consented to let the matter go on, and where he hoped to reap some little credit from the explosion of the powder-boat. Now, the country gives General Grant the credit of inaugurating the expedition, when on both occasions he permitted it to go imperfectly provided. In the first place, it had neither head nor tail, as far as the army was concerned. In the second place, he (Grant) sent too few men, when he ought to have calculated that the rebels would have more strongly defended the works after seeing what a narrow escape they had. Nothing but the most desperate fighting and determination to win on the part of the army gave us the victory. The gallant band of sailors who fearlessly went into the works, amid a shower of canister and

---

[1] Conduct of the War, No. 5, p. 196.
[2] Conduct of the War, No. 5, p. 198.

bullets, drew the enemy's attention away from the assault on the land side, and enabled the troops to obtain a secure footing. I don't say this to detract from the gallantry of the soldiers, for never did men fight harder or more handsomely than did our troops on that day.

Now that the most important fort on the coast has been gained, as usual you will hear but little of what the navy did, and, no doubt, efforts will be made again to show that the work was "not substantially injured as a defensive work." To General Grant, who is always willing to take the credit when anything is done, and equally ready to lay the blame of the failure on the navy, I feel under no obligations for receiving and allowing a report to be spread from his headquarters that there were three days when the navy might have operated and did not.

He knows as much about it as he did when he wrote to me, saying that the "only way in which the place could be taken was by running the ships past the batteries," showing, evidently, that he had not studied the hydrography of Cape Fear River, and did not know the virtue there was in our wooden walls when they went in for a fair stand-up fight. Any fort in rebeldom can be taken, if we can only get within reach of it.

I have served with the lieutenant-general before, where I never worked so hard in my life to make a man succeed as I did for him. You will scarcely notice in his reports that the navy did give him any service, when, without the help it has given him all the way through, he would never have been lieutenant-general. He wants magnanimity, like most officers of the army, and is so avaricious as regards fame that he will never, if he can help it, do justice to our department. When the rebels write the history of this war, then, and only then, will the country be made to feel what the navy has done.

I do not feel at all kindly toward General Grant for the indifference he displayed in this matter until he found his reputation at stake; then he was glad to throw the elephant overboard that had weighted him down so heavily. He could not help but know that General Butler was going in command of this expedition. The matter was constantly discussed with him. He knew that he had placed himself and all his numerous staff on board the flag-ship Ben de Ford, and everybody spoke of him as commander of the troops.

In a conversation with General Grant I expressly told him that I wanted nothing to do with General Butler, and he promised me faithfully that he should not have any connection with the expedition. Two months I waited, the fleet ready to sail at an hour's notice, and I acquiesced in the lieutenant-general's decision that he could not spare troops for fear of endangering the defences in his front. I said: "Then the expedition will never go until Butler has a finger in the pie;" and, sure enough, when Butler said go, we went. The fear of weakening the defences disappeared on Butler's presenting his plan of blowing the forts down, and an army was shipped so quick (unprepared) on the transports, that they almost sailed in the middle of a heavy gale. General Grant knew that I did not care a fig for the powder-boat, though I was very willing to try it as an experiment, but not disposed to trust to it altogether. I think it was most unhandsome in him to listen for a moment to the idle talk of Butler's staff, and his timid, calculating engineer, Comstock, who wanted some excuse for not doing their duty.

The lieutenant-general and I were together eighteen months before Vicksburg. He never had to wait for me, nor did any of his generals (but I have had to wait for them), and he should have supposed from the past, and my anxiety to go to work, that I had not become any slower in my movements than I was on the Mississippi. His course proves to me that he would sacrifice his best friend rather than let any odium fall upon Lieutenant-General Grant. He will take to himself all the credit of this move now that it is successful, when he deserves all the blame for the first failure to take the place.

All this now is saddled on General Butler, and history will tell nothing of General Grant's share in it. I tell it to you for your own personal satisfaction, that you may know and feel that you are entitled to the entire credit for getting this expedition off, and for its success. I am merely the agent, and only use to advantage the ample means placed at my disposal, which any one else could have done as well as I. I expect you sometimes think I am a little too impolitic in what I say, but that is my nature. I am always ready to fight right away, if any one reflects upon the navy. I know that no country under the sun ever raised a navy as you have done in the same time, and that no navy ever did more. Could the navy operate in James River, Richmond would now be ours. Vicksburg, a stronger place, fell when the navy was brought to bear upon it. Every place has fallen where naval cannon have been brought into play. Our success here has been beyond my most sanguine expectations. I knew that we would have Caswell in less than a month; but I had no idea that the rebels would blow that and other works up so soon and leave us sole possession.

I am uneasy now for fear the enemy may turn all their force this way, and throw forty thousand men into the peninsula. They would retake Fort Fisher, even with the gunboats we have here, and turn the guns of the fort on us. The object is a great one, and if I was general of their forces, I would do it at all hazards. Yet this is not a pet place with the lieutenant-general, and he leaves it with about seven thousand men, and I don't think knows much of the situation. An army man thinks if he has a gunboat at his back he is all safe; but this is one case where, at times, the gunboats are driven off by bad weather, and those inside cannot co-operate effectively. I have given you a long letter, but find an apology for myself in the fact that I know your whole heart is with the navy, and that everything concerning it interests you. Again permit me to thank you kindly for the confidence you have always placed in me and the opportunities you have given me for distinction; and, assuring you that it has been my warmest wish to merit only your approbation, I remain, respectfully and sincerely,

Your obedient servant,

DAVID D. PORTER.

PORTER'S REPORT OF JANUARY 9, 1865.[1]

. . . I thought a good deal would be done by the explosion, but still I laid in a double allowance of shell and shot, and did not depend on a doubtful experiment. Starting as that expedition did, was not the way to make war. . . .

[**No. 145.** *See page* 827.]

CITY POINT, VA., Nov. 15, 1864.

MAJ.-GEN. B. F. BUTLER, COMMANDING ARMY OF THE JAMES:

As I am about leaving City Point to be absent for five or six days, I have just sent instructions to General Meade, of which the enclosed is a copy. These instructions contain all that is necessary for you, if the contingency upon which they are based should arise. All that I would add is that in case it should be necessary for you to withdraw from north of the James, you abandon all of your present lines except at Deep Bottom and Dutch Gap. Just occupy what you did prior to the movement which secured our present position. · Preparatory to this, remove at once within the line to be held all heavy guns that cannot be drawn off readily. Open the rear of all enclosed works so that when we want to retake them they will not be directed against us. General Barnard, chief engineer in the field, by my direction, informed the chief engineer, Army of the James, of the work to be done in this respect.

U. S. GRANT,
Lieutenant-General.

CITY POINT, VA., Nov. 15, 1864.

MAJ.-GEN. G. G. MEADE, COMMANDING ARMY OF THE POTOMAC:

The movements now being made by the army under General Sherman may cause General Lee to detach largely from the force defending Richmond, to meet him. Should this occur, it will become our duty to follow. In such case the Army of the James will be promptly withdrawn from the mouth of the James River and put in the trenches about Petersburg, thus liberating all of your infantry and cavalry and a sufficient amount of artillery. To prepare for such emergency, therefore, I would direct that you hold yourself in readiness to start in the shortest time, with twelve days' rations, six being carried on the person, and forty rounds of ammunition in the wagons. Select from your command the best batteries to accompany you, not exceeding one gun to one thousand men. It is not intended that these preparations shall be made to start at a moment's notice, but that the articles shall be where they can be reached and loaded and all preparations made for starting by the time your troops can be relieved by the troops of General Butler, after such movement on the part of the enemy is discovered. A copy of this will be forwarded to General Butler with instructions to carry out his part promptly, moving night as well as day, if the contingency should arise.

U. S. GRANT,
Lieutenant-General.[2]

---

[1] Report of Secretary of Navy, p. 59.
[2] Personal Memoirs of U. S. Grant, Vol. II., p. 150.

[**No. 146.**   *See page* 853.]

[*Private.*]

FORTRESS MONROE, Jan. 13, 1865.

My Dear Rawlins: — You know that I like to see a thing well done if done at all, and I must say my enemies about your headquarters are very *bungling* in their malice, and will bring the General into remark. Take the article in the *Herald* by Cadwallader, and it will appear to have been dictated at headquarters, where I know the General had nothing to do with it.   It was not telegraphed, and to have reached Tuesday's *Herald* must have left in the mail boat at 10 A. M., when the order for my removal was not served on me till 12 M. of the same day, Sunday.   Unless the orders of the General are disclosed before they are made public, how could the " News of General Butler's removal excite much comment, but as far as I can learn but little or no animadversion."   It could not have been known beyond General Grant's personal staff, and whatever may have been the feelings of some of those gentlemen toward myself, I should not expect much if any animadversion with them.   Again Cadwallader could never have written this sentence : " It has been General Butler's misfortune to appoint too many of (these) selfish and irresponsible persons to official positions of trust and responsibility.   Their indiscretions have cost him dearly, etc."   Now as I appointed Cadwallader myself as a lieutenant in the United States Volunteers, as I supposed and believed at the wish of General Grant, for the selfish reason on Cadwallader's part that he wished to escape the draft which would take him away from general headquarters as a reporter, and as he is wholly " irresponsible " and as not only I, but General Grant is " suffering from his indiscretion," although he had this piece of news in advance of anybody else, I do not believe he would wish to communicate it to the *Herald.*   Now, wasn't the fellow who got up this despatch a bungler?

Again, to put the removal on the ground that I was the last of the " civilian generals " brings an issue between the regulars and volunteers, and I assure you that the person who penned that does not love the General, or else is as stupid as a quartermaster who would let the horses of a whole army starve for want of forage when there is plenty in the country if he had a little energy to get it.   Because the regular army *do not* like the General.   They did not before the war, and his great success since has not increased their love, and his day of trial is coming, and therefore they seek to throw off those of the volunteers who would be his friends.   And it is of no consequence to him whether the injury proceeds from their enmity or incapacity.   Now, my dear Rawlins, look after those stupid fellows a little or they will do mischief to their chief.   They have already circulated a story that General Grant has always been opposed to me, and that I have been thrust upon him for political reasons, so, if possible, to get a personal issue between me and the General.   It will be his fault if that issue comes, not mine.   It will be my misfortune and the work of his subordinates.   The navy waits at Beaufort again, and the army waits for them.

Yours truly,

BENJ. F. BUTLER,
Major-General no longer.

[**No. 147.** *See page 909.*]

Memorandum or basis of agreement, made this 18th day of April, A. D. 1865, near Durham's Station, in the State of North Carolina, by and between General Joseph E. Johnston, commanding the Confederate Army, and Major-General W. T. Sherman, commanding the Army of the United States in North Carolina, both present.

I. (See 6, Reagan's draft.) The contending armies now in the field to maintain the *status quo* until notice is given by the commanding general of any one to his opponent, and reasonable time, say forty-eight hours, allowed.

II. (See 1, Reagan.) The Confederate armies now in existence to be disbanded and conducted to their several State capitals, there to deposit their arms and public property in the State arsenal, and each officer and man to execute and file an agreement to cease from acts of war, and to abide the action of the State and Federal authorities. The number of arms and munitions of war to be reported to the chief of ordnance at Washington City, subject to the future action of the Congress of the United States, and in the meantime to be used solely to maintain peace and order within the borders of the States respectively.

III. (See 3, Reagan.) The recognition by the Executive of the United States of the several State governments, on their officers and legislatures taking the oaths prescribed by the Constitution of the United States, and where conflicting State governments have resulted from the war, the legitimacy of all shall be submitted to the Supreme Court of the United States.

IV. The re-establishment of all Federal courts in the several States, with powers as defined by the Constitution and laws of Congress.

V. (See 4, Reagan.) The people and inhabitants of all States to be guaranteed, so far as the Executive can, their political rights and franchises, as well as their rights of person and property, as defined by the Constitution of the United States and of the States respectively.

VI. (See 5, Reagan.) The executive authority of the Government of the United States not to disturb any of the people by reason of the late war, so long as they live in peace and quiet, abstain from acts of armed hostility, and obey the laws in existence at the place of their residence.

VII. In general terms the war to cease, a general amnesty, so far as the Executive of the United States can command, on condition of the disbandment of the Confederate armies, the distribution of the arms, and the resumption of peaceful pursuits by the officers and men hitherto composing said armies.

Not being fully empowered by our respective principals to fulfil these terms, we individually and officially pledge ourselves to promptly obtain the necessary authority, and to carry out the above programme.

W. T. SHERMAN,
Major-General Commanding Army of the United States in North Carolina.

J. E. JOHNSTON,
General Commanding Confederate States Army in North Carolina.

[**No. 67.**　*See page 690 and Appendix page 41.*]

[This addition to Appendix No. 67, page 41, 24th line (Lieutenant Davenport's letter) was unfortunately omitted to be inserted in the correct place.]

You then directed me to see General Smith personally, and to say to him that you peremptorily ordered him, *upon the receipt of your command sent by me*, to cause an immediate attack to be made upon the defences of Petersburg by all the forces then present; that General Hancock was there under an order from you, who was his (Hancock's) senior, which order was given by you to Hancock by express direction of Lieutenant-General Grant, and that he (Hancock) would co-operate with you most cheerfully.

INDEX.

INDEX.

A

ABBOTT, Judge J. G., 50.
Adams Express Co., 515, 517.
Adams County Iowa Suit, 992-995.
ADAMS, So. Carolina Commissioner of Secession, 156.
Advertiser, Lowell, anecdote of, 999.
ALABAMA claims, 962-967.
ALLEY, Hon. John B., member of Congress, 919; succeeded by Butler, as member of Congress, 919.
ALMADEN, quicksilver case. Halleck convicted of perjury in, 872.
ALLEN, Hon. Stephen M., interviews on conduct of war, 580, 583.
American Emigrant Aid Society, suit against, 992-995.
AMES, Brig.-General, reference to, 651, 690, 816; despatch to, 652; in Roanoke expedition, 781; reference to, 862.
AMES, Adelbert, son-in-law, 81; stationed at Perryville, 211.
AMES, Butler, grandson, 81.
AMES, Seth, studied Latin with, 52.
ANDERSON'S Corps, first to reinforce Petersburg, 703.
ANDERSONVILLE, great loss of life in prison, 609, 610; lack of water at, 611.
ANDOVER, Mass., President Pierce's son killed, 1020.
ANDRE, tried by military commission, 843, 916.
ANDREW, Gov. John A., interview on war, 161-162; action by, to have Massachusetts troops in readiness, 162, 163, 165, 166; details Butler as brigade commander, 171-173; notified of attack on Sixth Regiment, 175; notified of march from Philadelphia, 183, 184; reprimands Butler and is answered, 211, 216, 261; hostility of, expected, 298; pleasant and unpleasant interviews with, 305, 306, 307, 308; "a one idea'd abolitionist," 318; has Butler's appointments rejected, 356; cousin of, in New Orleans, 511, 513; reference to, 896.
ANNAPOLIS, arrival at, 191; occupation of, 195; stay in, 196, 210; departure from, 217; moves troops from, 694; establishes hospitals at, 892.

Army of the James, address to, 888-889.
Army of Northern Virginia, address to, 701-702.
Assistant Secretary of Navy, powder experiment suggested to, 775.
Attack upon; by Brick Pomeroy, regarding spoons, 43; by Massachusetts papers, for advocating ten-hour law, 92, 107-108; by New York Tribune and other papers for voting for Davis, 142; by persons in Lowell for voting for Breckinridge, 148-149; by northern newspapers for seizing Baltimore, 227; by northern newspapers for Big Bethel disaster, 271; by northern newspapers for buying sugar at New Orleans, 384; by various persons for issuing "woman" order, 420-421; by various persons for hanging Mumford, 443; for course at New Orleans, 538, 561, 567-568.
Attorney-General, in Farragut prize case, 1011.
ATZEROTT, fellow-conspirator with Booth, 931.
Australian ballot law criticised, 115.

B

BABCOCK, Colonel, bearer of order relieving Butler of command, 827.
BADEAU, General, in military history of General Grant, 856, 857, 859, 860 ; in Personal Memoirs of U. S. Grant, 859; character and career, 860; references to, 875.
BAILEY, Capt. Theodorus, consulted regarding operations against New Orleans, 359; passes the forts, 365-367; and Lieutenant Perkins first to enter New Orleans, 370; Vice-Admiral suit in prize court, 1010-1012.
BAKER, admonition to, Senator from Oregon afterwards General, 175; Colonel defends Butler in Senate, 275; assigned to Butler's command, 276-277.
Ballot law, secret of 1850, 114; Australian criticised, 115.
BALTIMORE, passage of Sixth Regiment through, 175, 181; occupation of, 225, 237; Butler brings troops to, 694; Convention, 982.

1135

H

Printed in the United States
141184LV00003B/15/A